I0146040

Cooperativism and Democracy

Studies in Critical Social Sciences Book Series

Haymarket Books is proud to be working with Brill Academic Publishers (www.brill.nl) to republish the *Studies in Critical Social Sciences* book series in paperback editions. This peer-reviewed book series offers insights into our current reality by exploring the content and consequences of power relationships under capitalism, and by considering the spaces of opposition and resistance to these changes that have been defining our new age. Our full catalog of *SCSS* volumes can be viewed at https://www.haymarketbooks .org/series_collections/4-studies-in-critical-social-sciences.

Series Editor
David Fasenfest, Wayne State University

Editorial Board
Eduardo Bonilla-Silva (Duke University)
Chris Chase-Dunn (University of California–Riverside)
William Carroll (University of Victoria)
Raewyn Connell (University of Sydney)
Kimberlé W. Crenshaw (University of California–LA, and Columbia University)
Heidi Gottfried (Wayne State University)
Karin Gottschall (University of Bremen)
Alfredo Saad Filho (University of London)
Chizuko Ueno (University of Tokyo)
Sylvia Walby (Lancaster University)
Raju Das (York University)

COOPERATIVISM AND DEMOCRACY

Selected Works of Polish Thinkers

EDITED BY
BARTŁOMIEJ BŁESZNOWSKI

TRANSLATED BY
MICHELLE GRANAS

Haymarket Books
Chicago, IL

First published in 2017 by Brill Academic Publishers, The Netherlands.
© 2017 Koninklijke Brill NV, Leiden, The Netherlands

Published in paperback in 2018 by
Haymarket Books
P.O. Box 180165
Chicago, IL 60618
773-583-7884
www.haymarketbooks.org

ISBN: 978-1-60846-090-8

Trade distribution:
In the U.S. through Consortium Book Sales, www.cbsd.com
In the UK, Turnaround Publisher Services, www.turnaround-uk.com
In Canada, Publishers Group Canada, www.pgcbooks.ca
All other countries, Ingram Publisher Services International, ips_intlsales@ingramcontent.com

Cover design by Jamie Kerry and Ragina Johnson.

This book was published with the generous support of Lannan Foundation and the Wallace Action Fund.

Printed in United States.

10 9 8 7 6 5 4 3 2 1

Library of Congress Cataloging-in-Publication Data is available.

Contents

Acknowledgements

I wish to express my gratitude to all the people whose support contributed to the creation of this book. Special thanks are due to: Eugeniusz Zochniak, curator of the Museum of the History of the Cooperative Movement in Warsaw, who helped me reach some of the pre-war cooperativists' heirs; Róża Sułek, whose support and interest in the project was invaluable; Dr. Adam Duszyk, who put me in contact with Jan Wolski's heirs, and Wanda Trzeciak, Alina Gisin-Trzeciak and Marianne Mayerhöfer-Trzeciak, for their enthusiastic acceptance of the idea of including one of their uncle's articles in this book; Jacek Taylor, heir of Edward Taylor, Grzegorz Grabski, heir of President Stanisław Wojciechowski, and Jerzy Szumski, heir of Maria Dąbrowska, for their openness to the publication of their ancestors' writings; Prof. Zofia Chyra-Rolicz for setting aside time to allow for consultations aimed at finding the heirs of authors whose writings were to be included in the book; Dominika Potkańska, who co-created the "Laboratory of Cooperation" with me (a project popularizing cooperativism in Poland) and Dr. Aleksandra Bilewicz, who collaborated with me on a research project devoted to the history of the Polish cooperative movement—for them "cooperativism" is more than just a beautiful word of the past; and Michelle Granas, the translator of this volume, whose patience and hard work contributed significantly to its publication. Last but not least I would like to thank Michał—my best friend, in whom I trust implicitly, my Father—a man who is always with me, and Ola, whose love is pure energy—it has helped me through many difficult moments.

List of Illustrations

Tables

About the Contributors

Edward Abramowski
(1868–1918) was a socialist, political thinker, social psychologist, theoretician, and popularizer of cooperativism. From his earliest years, he was connected with the workers' movement; he helped create one of the first Polish socialist groupings, "Proletariat II." Living in exile in Geneva, Paris, London, and Zurich, he wrote political and agitprop texts, as well as doing research in psychology and creating the innovative concept of the social self and unconscious. In 1892 he took part in the founding congress of the Polish Socialist Party in Paris. In his political theory, he criticized both state coercion and the free market, creating a model of self-organization and mutual aid based on cooperativism. In 1905 in Warsaw he co-founded the Union of Social Self-Help Societies, which led to the emergence of "Społem," one of the largest Polish cooperatives. He established the independent Institute of Psychology, and in 1915 became head of the department of psychology at the University of Warsaw, where until his death in 1918 he gave lectures on experiential metaphysics, which were the culmination of his "ontology of brotherhood."

Fr. Stanisław Adamski
(1875–1967) was a Catholic priest and one of the leaders of the agricultural cooperative movement in the Greater Poland region. Beginning in 1916 he headed a secret pro-independence organization. He also helped create several other organizations, including the Union of Catholic Societies of Polish Workers and the Society of People's Libraries. He particularly had success in the cooperative movement as patron of the Union of Labor and Farming Cooperatives and chairman of the Union of Cooperative Associations. During the Greater Poland Uprising (1918–1919) he was Chief Commissar of the Main People's Council in Poznań; in the years 1919–1922 he was a deputy to the Polish Legislature, and in the years 1922–1927 he was a senator (belonging to the Christian Democratic Party). After the May Coup in 1926 he withdrew from political life. In 1930 he was consecrated Bishop of Katowice. He was famous in Silesia for his work on behalf of the unemployed and regarding the integration of minorities. Banished by the Nazis to the General Governate he served as a chaplain during the Warsaw Uprising. He wrote several works on the social teachings of the Church, theology, and agricultural cooperativism.

Bartłomiej Błesznowski
(b. 1983)—historian of ideas and sociologist of knowledge, Assistant Professor in the Institute of Applied Social Sciences at the University of Warsaw. In his

work, he deals with issues of power, politics and democracy in contemporary society, combining social science with philosophy. He is a co-editor (with Prof. Marcin Król) of a series of books: "Genealogia współczesności. Historia idei w Polsce 1815–1939" ("Genealogy of Contemporaneity. History of Ideas in Poland 1815–1939"). He is also one of the main creators of research enterprise "Laboratory of Cooperation" and research project "Traditions of Polish Cooperativism." He is an author of a monograph on Michel Foucault *Batalia o człowieka. Genealogia władzy Michela Foucaulta jako próba wyzwolenia podmiotu*, 2009 (*A Battle of a Man. Michel Foucaults Genealogy of Power as an Attempt at Liberation of a Subject*), and editor of the Polish edition of his late writings: Michel Foucault, *Kim Pan jest, Profesorze Foucault? Debaty, rozmowy, polemiki*, 2013 (*Who Are You, Proffesor Foucault? Debates-Discussions-Polemics*). He has also edited a volume on Polish cooperative movement (*Kooperatyzm, spółdzielczość, demokracja*, 2014).

Zygmunt Chmielewski

(1873–1939) was an activist in the cooperative movement and one of the leaders of rural cooperativism. Associated with the Polish Socialist Party from youth, in 1897 he fled from the tsarist police to Galicia, where he encountered Franciszek Stefczyk, the creator of savings and loan banks. He founded a dairy cooperative in Radziszyn near Kraków; this was an organizational experiment that later allowed him to develop the cooperative sector in the Austrian and Russian partitions. From 1908 he directed the Dairy Division of the Central Agricultural Society in Warsaw, while simultaneously being the city's vice-mayor. In 1919, during the government of Ignacy Paderewski, he served as minister of agriculture, after which he returned, in reborn Poland, to developing the cooperative movement. In the years 1924–1928 he directed the Central Bank of Agricultural Cooperatives and worked with the Cooperative Scientific Institute. In 1930–1934 he directed the State School of Agricultural Cooperatism, which had been founded on his initiative, and in 1932–1934 he was chairman of the Union of Agricultural Cooperative Associations of the Republic of Poland. He wrote many works on cooperative theory, including "Psychological Factors in the Cooperative Movement."

Zofia Daszyńska-Golińska

(1866–1934) was an economist, historian, socialist activist, and creator of the foundations of social policy in Poland. In 1883 she entered Poland's socialist movement (the "Solidarity" Workers' Party). She completed studies in political economics and history in Zurich, where she later received a doctorate. She lectured at the "Flying University" and the Adam Mickiewicz People's University, the Polish Socialist Party's school. She was a member of the Polish Social Democratic Party. During the First World War, she was strongly connected to the Piłsudski camp. After Poland acquired independence, she worked in the Ministry of Labor and Social Welfare and continued her academic activities, obtaining the title of professor at the Polish Free University. After the May Coup in 1926 she supported Piłsudski, as part of the leftist wing of the "Sanation" regime. Her most important works are *Przełom w socjalizmie* (*A Turning Point in Socialism*), *Współczesny ruch kobiecy wobec kwestii robotniczej* (*The Contemporary Women's Movement in Regard to the Labor Question*), *Zarys ekonomii społecznej* (*An Outline of the Social Economy*), *Przez kooperatywy do przyszłego ustroju* (*Through Cooperatives to the Future Order*), *Prawo wyborcze kobiet* (*Women's Suffrage*), and *Polityka społeczna (ekonomia społeczna)* (*Social Policy (the Social Economy)*).

Maria Dąbrowska

(1889–1965) was an outstanding Polish writer, a disciple of Edward Abramowski, and an activist and social publicist propagating cooperativism. She published several dozen articles on cooperativism in the cooperativist press and in social and political magazines. She conducted research on the cooperative movement in Poland and abroad for use in her books: *Finlandia—wzorowy kraj kooperacji* (*Finland—A Model Country of Cooperativism*) (1913), *Kooperatyzm we wsi belgijskiej* (*Cooperativism in a Belgian Village*) (1913), *Spółdzielczość zwyciężająca. Dzieje angielskiej hurtowni stowarzyszeń spożywców* (*Cooperativism Triumphing: The History of the Wholesale Enterprise of English Consumer Cooperatives*) (1920), *Sprawa mieszkaniowa a kooperacja* (*The Housing Question and Cooperativism*) (1921) and *Ręce w uścisku* (*Clasped Hands*) (1938). Cooperative issues also appeared in the pages of her literary works: *Noce i dnie* (*Nights and Days*), *Przygody człowieka myślącego* (*Adventures of a Thinking Person*), *Pielgrzymka do Warszawy* (*A Pilgrimage to Warsaw*), and *Gałąź czereśni* (*The Cherry Branch*). After the Second World War, she was critical of the communist regime's nationalization of Polish cooperatives, although she retained her esteem for the ideas of her teacher.

Jan Hempel

(1877–1937) was a Marxist, translator, philosopher, and cooperative activist. He worked on the construction of the Eastern Chinese railway in Manchuria and was later in Brazil, where he edited the journal Polak (The Pole). In 1908 he traveled to Paris, where he became involved with anarcho-syndicalism and joined the Polish Socialist Party–Left Wing. After a brief period in Piłsudski's Legions he went to Lublin, where he began political and educational activities in trade unions and the cooperative movement, founding the Lublin Consumer Cooperative, among other entities. In 1919 he was selected to be secretary of the Union of Labor Cooperative Associations; he also gave courses at the People's University of the Polish Socialist Party. He was removed from power in the Union on account of supporting the communists in the organization. In 1921 he was a co-founder of the Warsaw Housing Cooperative. As a member of the Communist Labor Party of Poland he edited many labor journals, including Aleksandr Wat's *Miesięcznik Literacki* (*Literary Monthly*). In the 1930s, in connection with his communist activities, he was arrested multiple times by the police; he fled to Moscow, where during the Great Purge he was arrested by the NKVD and executed.

Jerzy Kurnatowski

(1874–1934) was a lawyer, economist, publicist, evangelical activist, and freemason. He studied law at the University of Warsaw. In the years 1919–1923 he worked successively for Poland's Ministry of Communications, where he was co-editor of the journal Bandera Polska (Poland's Standard), the Ministry of Public Works, and the Main Statistical Office. In the years 1919–1934 he was a professor at the School of Political Sciences and directed the department of social and economic history. In 1929–1934 he lectured on economic policy and the history of trade and industry, while also being a professor at the Institute of Commercial and Orientalist Studies. He lectured on cooperativism in the Polish Free University. As an expert and translator of French social thought, he propagated a social solidary close to that of Émile Durkheim's school and the cooperativism of the School of Nîmes. He was awarded the Cross of Valor (twice), the Legion of Honor, and the Czechoslovakian Order of the White Lion.

Romuald Mielczarski

(1871–1926) was a leader of the cooperative movement and created the organizational principles of Polish consumer cooperativism. In exile, he was active in the Central Organ of the Union of Polish Socialists Abroad and in Polish Socialist Party structures. He studied at the Commercial Institute in Antwerp, which was then considered to be the best European school of economic sciences. After periods of work in Georgia as a mine director, and in the Ukraine, where he managed wholesale products, he returned to Poland and engaged in consumer cooperative activities as a specialist in trade and management. From 1911 he directed the Warsaw Union of Consumer Associations (later the Union of Polish Consumer Associations, colloquially known as "Społem"). He created numerous educational or publishing initiatives aimed at developing and propagating the principles of cooperativism in independent—since 1918—Poland.

In 1920 he helped draft the Polish act on cooperatives. A year before his death he achieved his main goal—the unification of consumer cooperatives, beyond ideological barriers. The resultant Union of Consumer Cooperatives of the Republic of Poland was the largest commercial enterprise in Poland at the time.

Remigiusz Okraska

(b. 1976) is a sociologist and publicist who has been actively involved in leftist and ecological initiatives for over twenty years. He is editor in chief of the journal *Nowy Obywatel* (*New Citizen*), which appeared as *Obywatel* in 2000–2010, and in 2001–2005 he was also editor in chief of the environmental monthly *Dzikie Życie* (*Wild Life*). He is the originator and creator of the portal Lewicowo.pl, the first and only portal devoted to the history and achievements of Poland's patriotic, democratic, and non-communist leftists. He is one of the creators of the portal Kooperatyzm.pl, which is devoted to remembrance of the achievements and traditions of the socialist movement. He has written over 500 published works and is the editor of around 20 books. He is the initiator, editor, author, or co-author of forwards or epilogues for books and brochures devoted to remembering past achievements in the world of ideas in Poland, including the work of such authors as Edward Abramowski, Jan Gwalbert Pawlikowski, Romuald Mielczarski, Stanisław Thugutt, Ludwik Krzywicki, Andrzej Strug, Maria Dąbrowska, Jan Wolski, and Franciszek Stefczyk. He is the author of a long interview with the legendary Solidarity activists, Joanna and Andrzej Gwiazda.

Maria Orsetti

(1880–1957) was a social activist with a doctorate in social science and economics, an anarchist, and one of the leaders of the cooperative movement. From the time of her studies in Brussels, she was a popularizer of cooperativism, translating a number of works and writing over a dozen brochures and several hundred articles. She was one of the leaders of the Lublin Consumer Cooperative, which was among the most dynamic and leftist of Polish consumer cooperatives. At the turn of the 1920s to 1930s she was editor in chief of the cooperative journal *Społem!* (*Together!*), and then director of the cooperative publishing house Książka. She strove to improve working conditions in cooperatives and was, among other things, editor of the journal *Pracownik Spółdzielczy* (*The Cooperative Worker*), the organ of the Trade Union of Cooperative Workers of the Republic of Poland. In 1935 she was a co-founder of the Cooperative Women's Guild. She was the main popularizer in Poland of the work of Piotr Kropotkin, writing a popular biography of him and translating three of his books.

Adam Próchnik

(1892–1942) was a socialist thinker, a cooperative activist, and a historian of the socialist movement in Poland. In his youth, he was an activist of the Polish Social Democratic Party. During the First World War, he organized the Polish military structures in Lwów and took part in the struggles to defend the city, obtaining the rank of second lieutenant. In independent Poland, he was an activist of the Polish Socialist Party; he worked as a historian-archivist and was harassed by the Sanation authorities. In 1928 he was elected a member of parliament from the Polish Socialist Party list; in the 1930s he was one of the leaders of the Warsaw Housing Cooperative's "Glass Houses" project; and in the years 1934–1939 he was a member of the Supreme Council of the Polish Socialist Party. Initially an advocate of cooperating with the communists, he changed his mind after the Moscow trials. He was the author of *Demokracja kościuszkowska* (*Kościuszko-Type Democracy*), *Bunt łódzki w roku 1892* (*The Łódź Revolt of 1892*), *Ideologia spółdzielczości robotniczej* (*The Ideology of the Labor Cooperative Movement*), and *Idee i ludzie* (*Ideas and People*). After the outbreak of the Second World War he was active in the political underground.

Marian Rapacki

(1884–1944) was an activist and cooperativist theoretician. He left Poland in 1903 to study at the Commercial School of Leipzig, where he completed two semesters. In 1904 he began work in London for the Anglo-Siberian Gold Mining Society, while simultaneously studying at Pitman's Metropolitan School. In 1905 he moved to Gdańsk for an internship in a grain company; a year later he commenced work in the Savings and Loan Association in Piotrków. In April of that year he started work in the Warsaw Agricultural Syndicate. From 1906 he was connected with the savings and loan cooperative movement, and later with agricultural cooperatives. He was an activist of the Union of Polish Youth ("Zet") and afterwards of the National Labor Union. In the interwar period, he was, among other things, chairman of the Union of Consumer Cooperatives of the Republic of Poland ("Społem"), a lecturer at the Higher School of Commerce, and editor in chief of the journal Społem. Toward the end of his life his views approached those of the social left. He perished during the Warsaw Uprising. He was awarded the Cross of Valor.

Franciszek Stefczyk

(1861–1924) was a historian, self-educated economist, and cooperative activist. In 1889, in Czernichów near Kraków, he founded Poland's first savings and loan cooperative, on the German model of Friedrich W. Raiffeisen. In succeeding years, similar savings and loan banks (known as Stefczyk banks) were

enormously successful in the lands of the Austrian partition. At that time Ste-
fczyk was also active in the agricultural cooperative movement, creating the
National Central Bank for Agricultural Companies in 1908. That same year he
was elected to the National Parliament of Galicia as a deputy from the Polish
People's Party, and when the First World War erupted he supported Piłsudski's
Legions. In 1919–1924 he was director of the Cooperative Scientific Institute.
Thanks to his initiative, the savings and loans of Galicia, Cieszyn Silesia, and
Upper Silesia united under the aegis of one organization—the Union of Ag-
ricultural Cooperative Associations. He lectured in the Higher Cooperative
Course at Jagiellonian University, where on June 30, 1924, he defended his ha-
bilitation degree. He died the same day.

Edward Taylor
(1884–1964) was a Polish economist and national activist, the creator of the
"Poznań School of Economics" and organizer of economic studies and tax
law at the Adam Mickiewicz University of Poznań and the Academy of Commerce in Poznań. After 1945 he also lectured in political economy at the University of Łódź. He was an opponent of statism and an advocate of economic
individualism, representing the neoclassical school in economics. In the years
1930–1932 he was a member of the city council of Poznań. In 1918 he was one of
the founders of the Society of Polish Economists and Statisticians, and in 1945
he helped establish the Polish Economics Society. His most important works
were *O istocie współdzielczości* (*On the Essence of Cooperativism*) (1916), *Statyka
i dynamika w teorii ekonomii* (*Statics and Dynamics in Economic Theory*) (1919),
Wstęp do ekonomiki (*Introduction to Economics*) (volumes 1–2, 1936–1938), *Teo-
ria produkcji* (*A Theory of Production*) (1947), *Historia rozwoju ekonomiki* (*A History of Economic Development*) (volumes 1–2, 1957–1958). He also translated the
classics of economics, including J.S. Mill's *Principles of Political Economy*.

Stanisław Thugutt
(1873–1941) was an activist of the people's movement and a popularizer of cooperativism. In 1903 he founded a consumer cooperative in Ćmielów in the
Kielce area. During the First World War, he was politically active (initially in
the National Independence Party, later in the Polish People's Party). He sympathized with the Piłsudski camp, joined the Legions, and took part in heavy
fighting on the front. At the end of the war he became minister of the interior in Ignacy Daszyński's Temporary Government; after its dissolution and
Poland's acquisition of independence he held the same post in the cabinet of
Jędrzej Moraczewski. He was seriously wounded in the Polish-Bolshevik war of
1919–1921 and was awarded the Cross of Valor. After the war, he was the leader

of the Polish People's Party "Liberation," a champion of agricultural reform, and from 1924 deputy prime minister in Władysław Grabski's cabinet. As the deputy prime minister, he was responsible for relations between the national minorities in Poland. He was critical of the Sanation regime and in 1931 became leader of the united peasants' parties. From 1929 he was a member and chairman of the Cooperativists' Society of Społem, chairman of the Cooperative Scientific Institute, editor in chief of the Społem magazine, member of the International Cooperative Institute, and a popularizer of cooperativism in the countryside. His most important book is *Spółdzielczość. Zarys ideologii* (*Cooperativism: Outline of an Ideology*).

Teodor Toeplitz
(1875–1937) was an activist in the cooperative and self-government movement. He was an urban planner and was for many years connected with the Polish Socialist Party. He was a co-founder of the Society of Polish Urbanists; one of the creators of the Warsaw Housing Cooperative's "Glass Houses" project; and a founder and chairman of the Construction Cooperative—the main contractor for the Warsaw Housing Cooperative and other Warsaw cooperatives, as well as cooperatives in Gdynia and Kraków. In 1929 he founded the Polish Society for Housing Reform, which on his initiative organized the first Polish Housing Congress in 1937 (he died a few months before). He helped create the Union of Polish Cities and was vice-chairman of the International Union for Housing Affairs. He was the author of numerous publications devoted to housing cooperativism, social and living conditions in workers' housing, urban planning issues, and so forth. After his death, the Warsaw Housing Cooperative created the Teodor Toeplitz Scholarship Fund.

Stanisław Wojciechowski
(1869–1953) was a politician, an activist in the cooperative movement, and second president of the Republic of Poland. He was originally a member of the nationalist Union of Polish Youth ("Zet"). From 1891 he belonged to the socialist Workers' Association and to the Polish Socialist Party, and later in exile he was in the Union of Polish Socialists Abroad. As a secret agent of the Union he was engaged in education and propaganda in the ranks of the Polish Socialist Party, and also in the smuggling of arms and printing presses to Poland. After his return to the country he was involved in the cooperative movement: he co-created the Union of Consumer Societies. During the First World War, he favored Poland's cooperation with Russia and led the Polish Inter-Party Union in Moscow, but after the Bolshevik revolution he returned to Poland. In the years 1919–1920 he was minister of internal affairs. From 1921 he belonged to

the Polish People's Party "Piast." In the years 1922–1926 he was president of the Republic of Poland. As a result of the May Coup he resigned his position. He then ceased to take an active part in politics, concentrating on cooperative and academic work. He lectured at the Warsaw School of Economics and the Main School of Rural Economics; in the years 1928–1929 he was director of the Cooperative Scientific Institute. He was the author of many scholarly works on the history and theory of cooperativism.

Jan Wolski

(1888–1975) was an activist, theoretician, and organizer of labor cooperatives. From 1909 he belonged to the Polish Socialist Party, and from 1915 he was engaged in secret educational activities for the workers' association "Wiedza." In November 1915, he was arrested by the German police and interned. In 1917 he entered the People's University, where he became acquainted with Edward Abramowski. Under Abramowski's influence he began to work actively in the cooperative movement. During the war in 1920 he served in the Legions, organizing a network of cooperative army canteens at the front. Later he was active in the Union of Labor Cooperative Associations. In 1928 he initiated the establishment of the Section for Labor Cooperativism in the Polish Society for Social Policy, and in 1937 he was one of the participants of the founding meeting of the Democratic Club in Warsaw. From 1945 to 1948 he was director of the Central Educational Center of Labor Cooperativism; from 1956 to 1959 he was a member of the Central Council of the Union of Labor Cooperativism and the Main Cooperative Council. Harassed by the communist authorities, from 1956 he was an opposition activist of the Krzywe Koło Club. To the end of his life he tirelessly proclaimed Abramowski's ideas of brotherhood.

CHAPTER 1

Utopia in the Service of Modernity: On the Sources of Cooperativism

Bartłomiej Błesznowski

Utopianism is the polestar of all planning.

ERNST BLOCH, *"Anticipated Reality"*

The science of society rests on the accord between social reason and social practice. Well, it will be given to our era to admire that science [...], in all its grandeur and sublime harmony!

PIERRE-JOSEPH PROUDHON, *System of Economical Contradictions: or, the Philosophy of Poverty*

∴

The roots of cooperativism, which is a political, social, and partly also historiosophical idea, reach at least to the beginning of the nineteenth century. The first source of the cooperative idea lies much further back though: in the dream, present from the dawn of thought, of creating an ideal society based on cooperation, mutual aid, and equal access to power and goods. With the beginning of modernity and the decline of the old sacral-feudal order this "utopian"—as some might sneer—dream assumed previously unknown dimensions. Strengthened by the Enlightenment ideal of reason and the moral imperative, it acquired many forms and grew continually in the ideological landscape of modern history, sometimes resulting solely in ivory-tower peregrinations and at others leaving a permanent stamp on world events.

One of the indubitably most emblematic figures in the history of cooperativism and simultaneously the most difficult to appraise and classify is Charles Fourier, the self-styled apostle of social renovation, a dreamer, visionary of happy humanity, and author of several dozen works in which serious political criticism is combined with theosophy and mesmerism, and economic theory is dependent on a theory of planetary movement. In placing him in his era, Walter Benjamin noted that

The secret cue for the Fourierist utopia is the advent of machines. The phalanstery is designed to restore human beings to a system of relationships in which morality becomes superfluous. [...] Fourier does not dream of relying on virtue for this; rather, he relies on an efficient functioning of society, whose motive forces are the passions. [...] Fourier harmony is the necessery product of this combinatory play.[1]

With his characteristic penetration, Benjamin listed the basic features of the utopia that was to give rise to the idea of free associations and consequently to begin certain socialist, solidarity, and cooperative movements. First, at the basis of Fourier's utopia—which comes after the initial civilizational development and the industrial revolution—lies the idea that the foremost task of the new egalitarian society is to free humanity from the shackles by which civilization has fettered it. It was not, however, a matter of returning humanity to the state of prehistoric natural communities, leading interdependent lives without complicated machines and tools, undisturbed by greed, but rather of giving power over industrial processes back to the people. The aim, as Marx would later say, was to invalidate the process of alienation, in which goods and money, through their social vehicles—the owners of large capital—rule the greater part of humanity. If the world is full of riches, they are not for the workers, not for their producers, as these are divided from their own products. It's a "topsy-turvy"[2] world, claimed Fourier, in which "penury results from excess itself,"[3] that is, from the concentration of capital, the negative "sympathy" of things. The growth of industrial civilization thus stimulates development of the idea of free associations in a dual, somewhat subversive sense: industrialization and capitalism, while leading to poverty and the exploitation of working people, also furnish them with an opportunity no previous generation enjoyed; in pushing them to the edge of expropriation and economic vegetation, it causes them to begin seeking alternative paths to ensure decent living conditions for themselves and participation in power. Here, however, Fourier's thought encounters its basic weakness: How was the future society to be reached? How were new laws to be effectively decreed? How was a society that could survive within capitalism to be constructed? Later cooperativists would say that the path derives not from above, not from the office of a legislator or visionary

---

1   W. Benjamin, *The Arcades Project*, translated by H. Eiland and K. McLaughlin, Cambridge, Massachusetts, and London, England 1999, The Belknap Press of Harvard University Press p. 16.

2   M. Orsetti, *Karol Fourier. Apostoł pracy radosnej* [*Charles Fourier: The Apostle of Joyous Work*], Warsaw 1927, Wydawnictwo Związku Spółdzielni Spożywców RP, p. 15.

3   F. Armand, R. Maublanc, *Fourier*, translated J. Hochfeld, Warsaw 1949, Książka i Wiedza, p. 210. Translated from the Polish—Tr.

reformer, but from below, from organized labor, in which the same people, as producers, consumers, and citizen-managers build, of their own accord, their own life among their peers.

Second, pre-Marx socialists (whose ideas Marxists differentiated from their own "scientific" doctrines by calling them "utopian") such as Claude Henri de Saint-Simon, Robert Owen, Pierre-Joseph Proudhon, and above all, Charles Fourier, believed in a perfectly arranged world. Even though the task of "arrangement" still lay before humanity, it was not, contrary to appearances, a matter of turning the world upside down and bringing transcendent change to counteract all existing laws. No, Fourier conceived his somewhat fantastical idea of *phalanstères* solely as a completion of industrial society's potential: They were to be perfectly organized communities regulating the life of man from birth to grave; productive establishments of work and consumption, whose social and economic energy would be used for the good of all members; temples of wisdom and culture, which, harnessed with creative work, would be the start of man's new wisdom and new "reason."[4] Although these first socialist thinkers had a very different view of what the final point of this new, better, communist society would be—for Fourier, it was *phalanstères* satisfying all the needs of their members, for Owen something closer to an agricultural commune—the majority combined the principle of self-organization with mutual aid and also the political participation of all members of the society. In this context, Maria Orsetti (an important activist of the Polish cooperative movement and author of popularizing books on Fourier) had an interesting observation: Fourier's fascination with architecture,[5] both as an important element in organizing the new collective system, as well as a metaphor of the cosmic order (this parallel played an important metaphysical role in the Fourier "system") placed him in the line of thinkers whose ideas were close to the classical concept of an enlightened "order" and mathematically arranged reality—its structure, once known, would be the instrument for the harmonious development of the human species. This thought, which is not foreign to various kinds of communism and is explicitly contained in the positivist doctrine, also turns out in this case to be the driving force behind modern political ideas, whose ties to this—scientific—idea are stronger than might at once appear.

---

4 Cf. the passage on the wisdom of the people that will prevail after the introduction of the new social and cosmic order. Ch. Fourier, *O wolnej woli* ["On Free Will"], translated by A. Siemek, in A. Sikora, *Fourier*, Warsaw 1989, Wiedza Powszechna, p. 202. Translated from the Polish—Tr.

5 Cf. M. Orsetti, *Karol Fourier: Apostoł pracy radosnej* [*Charles Fourier: The Apostle of Joyous Work*], op. cit., p. 25.

Third, in connection with the preceding trait, nineteenth-century utopian socialism (and to a lesser degree also Marxism) was based on the conviction that society can be organized by the efficient management of human passions, benefiting from what is good in man and exploiting what is less valuable.

> The associative system [...] absorbs individual greed in the collective interest of the series, in the impulses of uniting, etc.; at the same time it absorbs the collective claims of the series in the individual interests of each participant in the collection of other series.[6]

How could the key to such management be found, though? Where were the principles to be sought? Fourier, like other nineteenth-century thinkers (not only of socialist provenance) was convinced that the chief task of science is the mathematical understanding of the principles ruling the universe. Reality is governed, according to him, by three principles: God (the active principle), matter (the passive principle), and mathematics (just proportion, comprising the relation between God and matter, the essential law by which God appears in matter). "For harmony to be established between the three principles God must be in accord with mathematics as he moves or modifies matter."[7] The greatest discovery of science thus far, Fourier thought, was Newton's law of gravity, but even Newton had not understood its true, metaphysical meaning[8]— this was the principle ruling the movement of these principles, the "universal movement" pervading all spirits and matter, beginning with plants and insects and ending with planets and galaxies. This discovery was Fourier's own. Thus according to Fourier, the same movement at different levels of existence permeates the world of animals, vegetation, planets, and people. As a universal affinity, it rules the cosmic sympathy of things, links them, and sets them to vibrating; it is the motor of their passion, copulation, and reproduction— this concerns both physics and sociology. "Thus the book of nature in its essential truth can only be read by studying the book of the human tribe, as its truth is the truth of the world and all forms of existence," wrote Adam Sikora, commenting on the metaphysical aspect of the French visionary's doctrine.[9] Furthermore, the movement permeating human society constitutes a force that

6   F. Armand, R. Maublanc, *Fourier*, op. cit., p. 246.
7   Ch. Fourier, *Theory of the Four Movements*, translated by I. Patterson, Cambridge 1996, Cambridge University Press, p. 37.
8   A. Sikora, *Fourier*, op. cit., p. 57.
9   Idem, *Fourier, czyli solidarność rzeczy, Archiwum Historii Filozofii i Myśli Społecznej* ["Fourier, or the Solidarity of Things," *Archive of the History of Philosophy and Social Thought*], 1989, vol. 34, p. 264.

can influence the remaining, lower movements; it is a kind of communicating medium of God and nature. Therefore too, "our passions, which have been treated so disparagingly by the philosophers"—claimed Fourier—"actually play the most important part, after God, in the movement of the universe [...] because it was his wish that the whole universe should be organized in the image of the effects they produce in the social movements."[10]

The idea of one principle, whose study was supposed to occupy future science, is one of the most important doctrines of the nineteenth century. Why? Because for all its naivety, it marks the beginning of science understood as a methodical and formalized sphere of cognition, which, at least in theory, is capable not only of understanding the human condition but also of transforming and managing it. This doctrine was elaborated in most areas of philosophy in the nineteenth and early twentieth century, beginning with positivism, through neo-Kantism, and ending with phenomenology. Cooperativists also derived their doctrine from a scientific understanding of social conditions. They considered it to be the practical development and realization of cognitive ideals resulting from the study of history and contemporary social problems—a kind of Comtesque "positive politics."

> Its pride is that it develops its practical activity in accord with the theoretical postulates of sociology and economics. Thus it should properly be called applied sociology.[11]

In spite of all the romanticism of the revolutionaries and social reformers, in ascribing to this cognitive ideal they indubitably belonged to the calm and rational world of the Enlightenment. Was it not Kant who said,

> The problem of organizing a state can be solved, however hard it may seem, even for a race of devils (if only they are intelligent) [...] For such a task does not involve the moral improvement of man, but finding out how the mechanism of nature can be applied to men [...]?[12]

Faith in the possibility of final knowledge of the laws governing both physical and social reality also dictated the search for fundamental solutions for the

---

10   Ch. Fourier, *Theory of the Four Movements*, op. cit., p. 38.

11   E. Milewski, *Sklepy społeczne (Rzecz o kooperacji spożywców)* [*Communal Shops (On Consumer Cooperatives)*], Warsaw 1930, Związek Spółdzielni Spożywców RP, p. 88.

12   I. Kant, *Do wiecznego pokoju* ["Perpetual Peace"], in: idem, *Rozprawy z filozofii historii* [*Essays in the History of Philosophy*], translated by T. Kupiś et al, Kęty 2005, Wydawnictwo Antyk, p. 186 [English translation at http://www.constitution.org/kant/1stsup.htm].

human world, which was after all subject to the same principles as those ruling nature. Although on the one hand the classical idea of *methesis universalis*, the mathematical structure of the universe, was still close to the pre-scientific (occult and theosophical) concepts of the Renaissance, on the other hand, it gave hope that some ontological core of reality exists and that, in connection with the Kantian epistemological revolution (giving primacy to the subject as a transcendental source of knowledge), that core lies in man—man, inextricably connected with the conditions surrounding him, is capable of changing himself and through himself the world.[13] Not so far from the later cooperativists' dreams was Fourier's rather amusing and simultaneously disturbing—for its prophetic-metaphysical tone—prediction that the harmonious development of the human world would bring it closer to the world of plants and animals, and that these would develop in an exclusively beneficial direction for it. In the thirties still, in his famous *Program*, whose importance for the Polish cooperative movement is difficult to overestimate, Marian Rapacki wrote with faith that

> The original systems were to a small degree the work of conscious human will. They emerged under the pressure of natural forces. [...] Man was not then aware of the entirety of socio-economic, or even natural, phenomena. Human knowledge gradually increases, however [...]. And thus this becoming aware of all the social phenomena and developing a program is not only of abstract scientific importance but of practical importance, because on the basis of consciousness the will to change conditions awakens, and when the will awakens, the process, which is natural, based on the immutable laws of social development [...] can be fulfilled.[14]

---

13   The dialectic of man as a knowing subject and the object of knowledge appears to be one of the constituting aporia of modernity, to which this era owes both its cognitive vitality and its unsuccessful attempts to ground a metaphysics of the self-aware subject in the process of knowing, which in consequence leads to denial of the same by the humanist sciences (cf. M. Foucault, *The Order of Things. An Archaeology of the Human Sciences*, London—New York 2002, Routledge, particularly Chapter 9: "Man and his Doubles." The "creative" aspect of this dialectic—an apology for the individual, Nietzchean "overman," freeing himself from the fetters of humanist metaphysics—doubtless inspired Abramowski as a kind of reaction to the neo-Kantism of his day.

14   M. Rapacki, "*Program gospodarczy spółdzielczości spożywców. Referat wygłoszony na Zjeździe delegatow 'Społem' Związku Spółdzielni Spożywcow RP dnia 14 czerwca 1936 roku*" ["Economic Program for Consumer Cooperatives: A Report Given at an Assembly of Delegates of the Społem Union of Consumer Cooperatives of the RP on June 14, 1936"] (pp. 177–178).

Although later, in the formulation of a truly pragmatic program, this strong faith in the possibility of scientific knowledge and grassroots management of social conditions through self-sufficient communities would undergo many changes, it survived as an idea and dream, which, as a kind of political myth, drove a vigorous cooperative movement for several decades, until the disruption of its exuberant growth. In the West, this movement dissipated within the free market, becoming one of several forms of management, akin rather to joint stock companies than to true cooperatives or associations of various members; in the East, however, being centrally controlled and subject to the communist yoke, it became solely a toy in the hands of the rulers and in consequence lost its grassroots and participatory character. One point is nevertheless important: this movement has a permanent place in the history of democratic ideas, even if today, like its protoplasts, it has been somewhat forgotten. As can also be seen, there are great convergences between it and the great dreams of modernity about an ideal society—and not only in the imaginative sphere but in the epistemological field as well. They require that cooperativism be placed within the framework of the great dream of modernity in the Kantian sense, in Enlightenment categories, as "the emergence of mankind from immaturity"— with all the humanist achievements brought by the ideas of this era but also with the utopian baggage, which is the indelible mark of nineteenth-century leftist doctrine (and not solely leftist, obviously).

How are we thus to appraise the earlier socialists and other thinkers on the subject of renewing social life—both the revolutionary ones and those favoring slower, evolutionary social changes—whose ideas so strongly inspired later cooperativism? The first socialists undoubtedly created utopian ideas, which, etymologically speaking, supposedly meant that they dreamed about places that did not exist, about worlds that were not on the map and did not appear in the past tense but were rather postulates, possibilities, ideas. Their potential existence nevertheless had measurable effects in real life. If we consider Saint-Simon with his great *New Encyclopedia* to be the father of Comte's positivist doctrine,[15] and Fourier as one of the most important forerunners of Marxism,[16] then their influence on modern social science is undeniably hard to over appreciate. On the one hand, their doctrines were a reaction to Enlightenment postulates for the creation of a system of knowledge that would embrace all Mankind in the universal sense; on the other, as visions of a new social world,

---

15   J. Szacki, *Historia myśli socjologicznej* [*History of Sociological Thought*], Warsaw 2002, Wydawnictwo Naukowe PWN, p. 162.

16   L. Kołakowski, *Main Currents of Marxism. Its Origins, Growth and Dissolution*, vol 1: *The Founders*, translated by P. S. Falla, Oxford-New York 1982, Oxford University Press, p. 202.

these doctrines called for political work to hasten its coming. Nineteenth-century socialist doctrine was situated thus somewhere between science (sociology), which was still understood fairly idealistically and in terms of postulates, and political utopia—anticipation of the ideal system, a vision of a future classless society. Because they were the first to introduce "a deeper analysis of such ideas as 'association' and 'community,' which were to become the leading concepts of early sociology,"[17] they also became—particularly Owen and Fourier—the initiators of the cooperativist doctrine. The tension in their vision between large capitalist structures and the modern state on the one hand and limited, grassroots, associations of an egalitarian nature on the other constitutes one of the most important distinctions on which cooperativism is based. The first socialists were thus a link between the Enlightenment and future social doctrines (not necessarily of leftist provenance), among which cooperativism was to be found as an element of the cooperative movement.

Mutual Aid and War—The Anarchism of Pyotr Kropotkin

Cooperativism as a political doctrine and a social idea grew in part from the same source as Marxism (in this case, the affinity seems obvious), and in part from the social teachings of the Catholic Church, whose main policy document was the *Rerum Novarum* encyclical of Pope Leo XIII (especially cooperativism's branches connected with the credit cooperativism of Hermann Schulze-Delitzsch and Friedrich Wilhelm Raiffeisen).[18] In the case of its anarchic or socialist branches it also has much in common with positivism, with which it has complicated and varied relations.[19] It could be said that both trends are a kind of return to the above-mentioned Enlightenment idea. Both also belong to the same rank of concepts that see opportunity for freeing mankind from the yoke of poverty, ignorance, and political captivity in the development of manufacturing techniques, scientific knowledge, and education (even Fourier, the spiritual father of cooperativists, who thought industrial civilization took freedom from mankind, noted that only the proper utilization of technology and industry could lead to a truly "natural" social and cosmic order).

---

17   J. Szacki, *Historia myśli socjologicznej* [*History of Sociological Thought*], op. cit., p. 160.

18   Pioneers of nineteenth-century credit cooperatives in Germany.

19   On the subject of Edward Abramowski's interest in positivism, cf. U. Dobrzycka, *Abramowski*, Warsaw 1991, Wiedza Powszechna, pp. 31–32. The closeness of cooperativism and positivism is undeniable; they grew from the same source and are filled with the spirit of the same era.

As offspring of the nineteenth century, positivism, Marxism, and cooperativism all inherited the certitude that man, as the ultimate center of knowledge, is capable of shaping his own existence through science. They had the
Promethean conviction that the moment had come in which the self-aware
human (and social) entity was standing on the path to a progress in knowledge
unknown to previous generations and thereby to the possibility of unlimited
betterment of its own existence. Naturally, the followers of Comte were filled
with this faith, as were, in Poland, enthusiasts of "work at the base" such as
Aleksander Świętochowski or Eliza Orzeszkowa, for instance. One of the main
motifs of Marxism—that social life can be defined and verified through its
likeness to the laws of nature—also rested on it.[20] What distinguished ortho-
dox Marxism and all cooperativist movements, beginning with positivism, is
the basic assumption concerning social development and its relation to the
idea of "mutual aid" and "class struggle" as the principle of social life and transformation. As we will discover later, there was no agreement between cooperativists themselves and Marxism on this question. In trying to analyze the
concept, we will refer to the ideas of an important nineteenth-century thinker
who inspired many leftist-oriented cooperativists (including in Poland[21])—
Pyotr Kropotkin.

According to Kropotkin, the main factors influencing the course of social
change are the survival instinct, which is related to the particular will of the
individual, and the social instinct, which is governed by the rule of mutual assistance. In Thomas Hobbes' view, the first instinct is an inalienable, inherent

---

20   Cf. Information on the subject of enlightenment and determinist ideas in Marxism:
     L. Kołakowski, *Main Currents of Marxism. Its Origins, Growth and Dissolution*, vol 1: *The
     Founders*, op. cit., p. 403–408.

21   The connection between the thinking of Jan Wolski and the anarchist trio of historical
     leaders—Proudhon, Bakunin, and Kropotkin—is underscored by, among others, Adam
     Benon Duszyk in the book *Ostatni niepokorny: Jan Wolski 1888–1975* [*The Last Rebel: Jan
     Wolski 1888–1975*], Kraków-Radom 2008, Radomskie Towarzysto Naukowe, p. 40 et seq.
     In reminiscing about Abramowski and Wolski, Stanisław Szwalbe, member of the Pol-
     ish Socialist Party and an important cooperative activist connected with the Warsaw
     Housing Cooperative and Workers' University Society, described him as "an important
     theoretician of cooperation in the anarcho-syndicalist sense," "a follower of Kropotkin's
     theories" (*Wspomnienia działaczy spółdzielczych* [*Memories of Cooperative Activists*] vol.
     1, Bronisław Krauze (editor in chief), Warsaw 1963, Zakład Wydawniczy CRS, p. 159. Al-
     though these words do not yet place them with complete certainty among the unques-
     tioned representatives of anarchism or anarcho-syndicalism, they testify to how these
     theoreticians were regarded by the cooperativist milieu and about the influence that, at
     least declaratively, these currents had in either case.

right "by all means we can to defend oursleves,"[22] which is responsible for all social behaviors. These, as we know, are caused by fear, according to Hobbes. However, in Kropotkin's theory, the second instinct, which is socialization, is equally important and key to the development of animal organisms as well as humans. The conclusions Kropotkin drew from studying animal "sociability" and the development of communities among humans were

> [...] permanent presence of a double tendency—towards a greater development, on the one side of sociality, and, on the other side, of a consequent increase of the intensity of life, which results in an increase of happiness for the individuals, and in progress,—physical, intellectual, and moral.[23]

These tendencies function side by side, complementing each other. In a developed human society, they are inseparable. They allow a functioning community to be built, where the mutual aid of individuals produces ties and a field for self-realization and—as Kropotkin writes—"self-definition." "the periods when institutions based on the mutual-aid tendency took their greatest development were also the periods of the greatest progress in arts, industry, and science."[24] In these areas the individual very often became key to innovation and the spontaneous, creative development of the social group. Self-definition and cooperation are the instincts and also the developmental tendencies on which humanity depends. Unfortunately, a struggle can arise between these two tendencies; according to Kropotkin, this conflict has been the basis for social conflicts since the dawn of time, as reflected in philosophy, religion, and morality.

Kropotkin firmly denied the ideas of the seventeenth-century political philosophers—Locke, and particularly Hobbes, who claimed that the life of the original human was a continual fight for survival between himself and his peers. These thinkers—who assumed that man's nature is egoistical and

22   T. Hobbes, *Lewiatan czyli Materia, forma i władza państwa kościelnego i świeckiego* [*Leviathan: Or the Matter, Forme, and Power of a Common Wealth Ecclesiastical and Civil*], translated by C. Znamierowski, Warsaw 1954, PWN, p. 114 [English translation at http://socserv2.socsci.mcmaster.ca/econ/ugcm/3ll3/hobbes/Leviathan.pdf].

23   P. Kropotkin, *Etyka, pochodzenie i rozwój moralności* [*Ethics: Origin and Development*], unnamed translator, Łódź 1949, Spółdzielnia Wydawnicza Słowo, p. 27 [English translation at https://theanarchistlibrary.org/library/petr-kropotkin-ethics-origin-and-development].

24   P. Kropotkin, *Pomoc wzajemna jako czynnik rozwoju* [*Mutual Aid: A Factor of Evolution*], unnamed translator, W. Goslar et al (eds.), Poznań. 2006, Oficyna Wydalnicza Bractwa Trojka, p. 142. [English translation at: https://theanarchistlibrary.org/library/petr-kropotkin-mutual-aid-a-factor-of-evolution#toc10].

that development is based on struggle and conflict—imagined an ideal state of nature and a social contract requiring a complicated moral theory (Locke) or social pragmatics (Hobbes) for legitimation. Kropotkin claimed that nature is something more then "a field of slaughter"[25] while not being yet an oasis of peace and harmony, as Rousseau would have it.

For Kropotkin, Hobbes' morbid pessimism and Rousseau's "naïve" optimism are both exaggerations and thus falsifications of the objective side of things. Observing nature and analyzing research into the social behavior of animals, Kropotkin noticed that although a struggle between species and individuals is observable, nevertheless aid and interaction are equally frequent tendencies and have much greater significance for the development of species. Throughout his book *Mutual Aid* he tries to present irrefutable proofs of "social life" among animals, in order to move later to the history of human societies. In this book, his aim is to prove that the paradigm of the struggle for survival, as one of the factors shaping the biological and social development of species, is only a theoretical construct, without relation to reality. Kropotkin gives many examples of "socialization" in the wild and tries thereby to reveal the errors of thinking represented, in particular, by social Darwinists. He also claims, with all his force, that "those species which best know how to combine, and to avoid competition, have the best chances of survival and of a further progressive development. They prosper, while the unsociable species decay"[26] The above idea also explains for him the development and size of the human species, which could survive and resist predatory nature only by uniting in cooperative groups. He says that at every level of humanity's historic development there have been types of communities whose existence expressed the social instinct of man—beginning with the first uncomplicated tribal organizations and ending with modern industrial society, which is guided by global dependencies and the relations of impersonal capitalist forces.

According to Kropotkin, correcting the claims of an overly narrow social evolutionism means objecting to its leading idea: social evolution is the effect of the struggle of opposing social forces, shaped—in exploitation of the Darwinian idea of evolutionism—by the biological law of natural selection. This idea was the basis for many trends of thought at the end of the nineteenth century, foremost of which was Herbert Spencer's idea of "super-organic evolution."[27] Thomas Henry Huxley, a British zoologist, paleontologist, and

---

25   Ibidem, p. 26 [English translation at: https://theanarchistlibrary.org/library/petr-kropot kin-mutual-aid-a-factor-of-evolution#toc10].

26   Ibidem, p. 58 [English translation at: https://theanarchistlibrary.org/library/petr-kropot kin-mutual-aid-a-factor-of-evolution#toc10].

27   Cf. J. Szacki, *Historia myśli socjologicznej* [*History of Sociological Thought*], op. cit., p. 315.

doctor, was one of its main adherents, considering himself a continuer of Darwin's theory of evolution, while simultaneously simplifying the theory to the extreme.

> It happened with Darwin's theory as it always happens with theories having any bearing upon human relations. Instead of widening it according to his own hints, his followers narrowed it still more.[28]

According to Kropotkin, Huxley's basic and compromising error was to over-value "the struggle for existence" by stressing the factor of selection, which allows for the survival only of the strongest individuals, and thereby to under-appreciate contrary, communal tendencies. While not forgetting the significance of the above factors for man's social existence, Kropotkin disagreed with Huxley. According to Kropotkin, although the aspect of conflict is important, it is only one of the evolutionary tendencies—necessary at a certain stage of social development but indubitably not dominant. Basing himself on the theory of the Russian zoologist Karl Kessler, Kropotkin expressed the view that the constructive element of all communities is not rivalry but rather cooperation. In the first chapter of *Mutual Aid* he quotes Kessler's words:

> I obviously do not deny the struggle for existence, but I maintain that the progressive development of the animal kingdom, and especially of mankind, is favoured much more by mutual support than by mutual struggle ...[29]

Kropotkin devoted his own *Ethics* to demonstrating this idea. "Mutual aid" is for him not only a necessary element in the development of humanity, it is the constitutive element. This specific kind of behavior is the instinct that makes a human being a human being—he exists, acts, and lives as an element of the community. It is not so much man who establishes the polis for a certain aim (as adherents of the "social contract" theory proclaim), rather the existence of the polis means that we can speak of a human being at all.

The "prince of anarchists" sees the existence of thinking human beings as inseparably linked with the community. The human being as such does not exist outside of society. "For Kropotkin, the opposition disappears between the pre-social state and society, between 'natural,' primitive man and social

---

28   P. Kropotkin, *Pomoc wzajemna jako czynnik rozwoju* [*Mutual Aid: A Factor in Evolution*], op. cit., p. 25 [English translation at: https://theanarchistlibrary.org/library/petr-kropotkin-mutual-aid-a-factor-of-evolution#toc10].

29   Ibidem, p. 27.

man [...]. Society precedes the individual, the unit,"[30] and exists only on the grounds of intersubjective social communication. "Social life—that is, *we*, not *I*—is the normal form of life. *It is life itself*."[31] Kropotkin underlined the role of the social element in the life of the human being—according to him, what is individual exists only within what is social. It is curious that the author of *Mutual Aid*, like his "Darwinian" adversaries, arrives at a sort of biological extreme. Sociability is for him a category of instinct, a deeply rooted element in the human being, in the bio-psychological existence of the individual, who after all is a "human being" only in relation to his peers. Solely in coexistence with the human environment can he differentiate his "I" from the surrounding chaos of events and thoughts. Thus "The conceptions of 'virtue' and 'wickedness' are zoological, not merely human conceptions,"[32] claims Kropotkin.

Following the example of Kropotkin—to whom, inspired by anarchism, some thinkers of cooperativism in Poland referred, if usually indirectly—we can understand the roles played by the paradigms of conflict (the evolutionary struggle for survival, racial conflict, and class conflict) and mutual aid in the development of the cooperative idea. Classic thinkers of Polish cooperative thought, headed by Edward Abramowski, Edward Milewski, and Stanisław Wojciechowski, rejected the view that conflict and competition constituted the basic factor in economic and social development. This criticism was directed above all at the liberal, free-market economic model and, as in the case of Kropotkin, against the extreme version of social biologism inspired by Darwin's theory. Social Darwinism, as an ideology supporting individualist attitudes and promoting the uncontrolled accumulation of capital within the framework of "free competition," was a particularly dangerous doctrine for promoters of a cooperative economy, because it conferred on itself the prerogatives of "natural law" (both in the sense given to it by philosophers and lawyers of the seventeenth century and in Comtean categories of the fundamental laws of nature)—a law contrary to their ideas on every point.

In 1922, Jerzy Kurnatowski, propagator of solidarism, one of the fundamental branches of "neutral" cooperativism, wrote about it thus:

> At the moment when solidarism arose, the theory of conflict held undivided sway in the world of ideas: the Darwinian struggle for survival,

---

30   W. Rydzewski, *Kropotkin*, Warsaw 1979, Wiedza Powszechna, pp. 118–119.

31   P. Kropotkin, *Etyka, pochodzenie i rozwój moralności* [*Ethics: Origin and Development*] op. cit., p. 66 [English translation at https://theanarchistlibrary.org/library/petr-kropotkin-ethics-origin-and-development].

32   Ibidem, p. 28 [English translation at https://theanarchistlibrary.org/library/petr-kropotkin-ethics-origin-and-development].

which liberal economists transported to the social context and adopted as the basis of their apology for free competition, unhampered by any curb on the part of the state or social organizations; the class struggle of Marx; finally the racial struggle, which was actually formulated by the Frenchman Gobineau but was developed and perfected in Germany in the numerous Gobineau Societies which emerged in that country. In the second half of the past century, ideas of conflict resounded everywhere in the kingdom of thought and prepared the psychological foundations for war, which was soon to pour over humanity in a bloody wave. These ideas explained both the past and the present, and were also supposed to point to the future. We find them in sociology, in political economics, and in international and social policy.[33]

However, cooperativists—very often also those with an anarchic or socialist orientation—did not share the opinion that conflict is the only motor of social change. The majority of them, particularly in Poland, saw opportunities for pushing through a new "social" vision of society rather in the paradigm of general cooperation and in grassroots, participatory labor institutions "unblocking the natural forces" of mutual aid. The source of these institutions should be sought in the human social instinct and—importantly—in a kind of political pragmatism: the weak, by uniting in a group, could not only ensure themselves economic success but could also work out the democratic mechanisms for governance and social coexistence. In this context, the words of Maria Orsetti, for one, are significant:

> ... nature teaches us by a thousand examples that cooperation, mutual aid, is the strength of the weak. The flight of a flock of birds, the wonderful results of the social work of ants, bees, and wasps, and the helplessness of large animals contrasted with the solidary attitude of the small ones, is a speaking testimony. Thanks to this tested path of mutual aid, an economic power could arise from market baskets [...].[34]

Thus in establishing various associations, various consumer unions and labor cooperatives, we are not only caring for our economic interests, but also

33 J. Kurnatowski, *Solidaryzm jako doktryna demokracji* [*Solidarism as a Doctrine of Democracy*] (pp. 112–113).

34 M. Orsetti, "Kobieta, której na imię miliony" (*Rzecz o zadaniach kobiet w ruchu spółdzielczym*) ["Woman, Whose Name is Millions" (*On Women's Tasks in the Cooperative Movement*)] (p. 141).

hastening the arrival of new political conditions. This idea, which perhaps for many is close to Fourier's utopian ideas or at least to slightly utopian thinking, underlay the kind of political paradigm that put its deep impress on Polish interwar cooperativism.

Original Communism and Social Radicalism

As we can see, the identification of biological, economic, psychological, and social ideas to create a kind of scientific superstructure influenced the entire corpus of Polish cooperativist thought. This tendency is particularly visible in the metaphysical, sociological, and psychological investigations of Edward Abramowski—undoubtedly one of the most original thinkers in this field, whose work provides the most developed and cohesive version of cooperativism in Poland both in partition times and in the interwar period. Many excellent articles and books have already been written on the subject of Abramowski's theories; in the present essay I would only like—always in accord with the letter of his writings, if sometimes rather instrumentally—to outline certain themes of his thought. In one of his earliest theoretical works, *Społeczeństwa Rodowe [Clan Societies]* (1890), Abramowski constructed a paradigm of cooperation that later had a strong influence on his other works, both those on social subjects and the philosophical-psychological ones. This work, devoted to the structures, principles, and transformation of "primitive" clan or tribal communities, is strongly rooted in both the Marxist-Engelian logic of social evolution and in the then fashionable ethnological perspective. *Clan Societies* is on the one hand a work of an historical-ethnographic nature, and on the other a political manifesto expressing—not necessarily only implicitly— Abramowski's views on the future changes and social revolution.

The main subject of Abramowski's work is the historical mechanism governing the sequence of social formations and transformations undergone over the centuries by the communist element in the first societies. The entire argument of the text has one leading idea: the mutual aid and common work that marked these societies (according to ethnographic studies and Abramowski's observations). Although *Clan Societies* is not formally of a propagandizing nature, it might be inferred in reading it that the author writes not so much from the position of a researcher-analyst of original communism as from the position of a practitioner, a political activist seeking the archetype of community, the source element of sociability. In seeking "paradise lost," Abramowski withdraws to times when man was functioning still on the borders of nature and not yet fully formed civilization. His descriptions of the original clan

organizations of the Slavs or New World tribes involve a logical (and simultaneously rhetorical) treatment similar to classical schemes of the "state of nature" or the "happy savage," enabling him to contrast contemporary time with
a world which, he wants us to believe, was governed by entirely different laws:
the "real" world in which everything was in its place. He identifies the social
element par excellence with the original cooperation and interdependence of
people facing the forces of nature through the principle of mutual aid. Unfortunately, the development of manufacturing centers, successive specializa-
tions of labor, and the accompanying class divisions led to the deregulation of
the primary autarchic state and in consequence to blurring the original principle of tribal cooperation. "With the emergence of trade, money, and private
property, clan society began to decline: freedom, equality, and fraternity slowly
disappeared."[35]

Through his visitation of the past Abramowski is doubtless trying to draw
attention to a current, or even universal, process. The three main premises of
cooperativism, which he would also develop in his later writings, are: (1) the
principle of mutual aid as the main vector of sociability, and moreover, as an
unconscious factor in the development of individual personalities; (2) capitalism as a social formation that is a historically necessary stage of social development and is simultaneously contrary to human nature; and (3) return to
the free life of social institutions emerging from the very nature of human beings and based on equal participation in every sphere. Abramowski remained
under the strong impact of the idea of grassroots associations, which could
slowly but ineluctably, without revolutionary upheaval, like water wearing
away stone, lead to communism.

Such a "cooperative orientation"[36]—to use the words of Andrzej Mencwel—characterizes not only Abramowski, but also many left-leaning authors
at the turn of the nineteenth century in Poland, including Ludwik Krzywicki,
Stefan Żeromski, Wacław Nałkowski, and above all many of the "cooperativists" in Abramowski's circle—Maria Dąbrowska, Edward Milewski, Stanisław
Wojciechowski, Zygmunt Chmielewski, and Jan Wolski. The Polish intelligentsia of this period was permeated by a fairly radical sociology, expressed in
the conviction that the individual human was a reflection of the social world,

---

35   E. Abramowski, "Społeczeństwa rodowe" ["Clan Societies"], in: idem, Pisma popularnon-
      aukowe i propagandowe. 1890–1895 [Popular Scientific and Propaganda Writings], selected
      and with an introduction by J. Kulas, Warsaw 1979, Książka i Wiedza, p. 45.

36   A. Mencwel, Etos lewicy. Esej o narodzinach kulturalizmu polskiego [The Leftist Ethos: An
      Essay on the Birth of Polish Culturalism], Warsaw 2009, Wydawnictwo Krytyki Politycznej,
      p. 107.

being both its basic atom and the starting point for transforming that world—always in the direction of the community. The needs of individuals are met solely by real participation in socio-economic relations. They are not met in a society alienating labor from its product, the citizen from the government, and changing the consumer into a mindless market object. Abramowski points to this difference between "real" social life—that is, "real" community, based on equal access to governments and the creative process—and "false" social life, which is similar to a Marxist "false consciousness."[37]

This special "social radicalism" refers primarily to the tradition of the Polish intelligentsia—so strongly emphasizing the worth of the individual in the community framework, glorifying the heroic model of the activist fighting at the social base: the quiet hero and ethical reformer who is not ashamed to "go down" to lower levels.[38] As Andrzej Mencwel writes:

> Social radicalism drew from a tradition that grew out of Poland's social history, but it can not be dissected into the old elements; it was an approach as new and as important—in our culture the most important—as the questions it raised and with which it struggled: the sovereignty of the species, that is, man as the creator and lawmaker of his world; national independence; social justice, or the equal rights of human coexistence; personal dignity; and thus the conscious joint contribution to increasing that equality, independence, and sovereignty.[39]

---

37 This aspect of Abramowski's thought remained largely influenced by Marx: as an ineradicable element of social relations, a false consciousness is simultaneously the reflection of class struggle at the cognitive level. It departs from actual social relations and the relations of production, constituting an element of the ideological superstructure defining social epistemology and its hierarchies. The task of the workers' movement is thus to invalidate the division between base and superstructure, to extract "the truth of brotherhood," and thus not merely to build a new society but to enable the evolution of the social element of the human personality. This is what Abramowski considers to be the basic, real element of social ontology.

38 As Zofia Chyra-Rolicz writes, "Cooperative ideas coming from the West reached the group of positivists, found recognition, and were propagated." (*Pod spółdzielczym sztandarem. Z dziejów spółdzielczości polskiej do 1982 roku,* [*Under the Cooperative Standard: Episodes in the History of Polish Cooperativism to 1982*] Warsaw 1985, Wydawnictwo Spółdzielcze, p. 38). The group included the economist Mścisław Trepka, Józef Kirszrot-Prawnicki, who remained under the influence of Hermann Schulze-Delitzsch (one of the pioneers of co-operativism in Germany), and Aleksander Makowiecki (ibid, p. 39).

39 A. Mencwel, *Etos lewicy. Esej o narodzinach kulturalizmu polskiego* [*The Leftist Ethos: An Essay on the Birth of Polish Culturalism*], op. cit., p. 82.

These new questions touched the first generation of Polish leftists at two levels, determining the indefinite but mutually reinforcing conglomerate of issues whose solution was supposed to involve giving new shape to a nation dismembered by the partitioning powers and seeking a new vision of society—one that would permit the nation to avoid the route of unbridled capitalism and protect the dignity of the individual, while formulating an ideal of conscious participation in associations, the state, and the nation. For many so-called co-operativists, the answers to these socio-national questions, with their sources in Polish history, were to be found in the new ideas and methods: in bitter Fourierian criticism of free market liberty as an illusion deceiving the eyes of mankind; in the legend of the Rochdale pioneers, whose work proved the profitability of cooperation;[40] in the Marxist "sociology of knowledge," revealing the mechanisms of alienation; and, not to be forgotten, in the social ideas announced in the *Rerum Novarum* encyclical, which were distanced both from socialism and liberalism. This fairly varied and therefore difficult pedigree gave force to a movement whose dream came to be construction of a new world not through revolution but through "work and the transformation of human consciences."

Criticism of Arithmetical Democracy—Carl Schmitt and the Cooperativists

The critique of liberalism and capitalism that the cooperativists were conducting in the first part of the twentieth century obviously coincides with the tradition of Marxism, which had an enormous impact on cooperative milieus. What is interesting is that it shared many similarities with ideas presented by contemporary thinkers from an entirely different political register. In reading the works of Abramowski or the reports and proclamations of such activists as Marian Rapacki, Stanisław Wojciechowski, or Maria Dąbrowska, we might sometimes have the impression that in some points their vision of a democracy "falsified" by the logic of the market[41] involved what Carl Schmitt considered to be the chief sin of liberal democracy: the process of separating the social and the political sphere—what is private and what is public—which in effect takes any sort of political sovereignty away from the people.

---

40   "The Rochdale pioneers" were a group of weavers from the English town of Rochdale, who in 1863 established the first modern consumer cooperative. Their famous principles became a model for cooperatives all over the world.

41   Dąbrowska even wrote about the "metaphysics of advertising" (M. Dąbrowska, *Ręce w uścisku* [*Clasped Hands*] [p. 104]).

In Carl Schmitt's theory of politicality, political order is defined by the fundamental relation of friend and enemy. This differentiation is ontological in nature and every political relation can properly be reduced to it. As Schmitt writes, "the concept of the state presupposes the concept of the political";[42] nevertheless, it is important that "the equation state = politics becomes erroneous and deceptive at exactly the moment when state and society penetrate each other."[43] Why? Schmitt's answer is simple: each of these elements constitutes a separate order—the political, moral, religious, or economic orders are all different; the forms acquired by those elements and areas in which politicality is realized are also different: associations, the economy, the state. Each of these areas can be (although need not be) political; none, however, is exclusively about politics. The problem appears when one of these areas appropriates the public sphere: for instance, the total state expands the political outside the usual boundaries, or the economy saps politicality understood as sovereign decision, replacing it with decisions of an economic nature. "Heretofore ostensibly neutral domains—religion, culture, education, the economy— then cease to be neutral in the sense that they do notpertain to state and to politics."[44] The state is not thus the source of politicality but is nevertheless a political institution in the strict sense.

A symmetrical operation occurs when society—understood in the spirit of the eighteenth-century Scottish moralists as a place for realizing the particular interests of individuals—begins to dominate the state. Only in appearance are we dealing here with a state typical of democracy, in which individuals through their representatives exert supreme influence on the will of the body politic. Unfortunately, in this case, individuals do not at all exist as a political unit; their will remains separate from any political force. This happens when the political order comes to be dominated by an external mechanism of an entirely different construction, for instance, a legal, moral, or religious one. Liberalism, according to this German lawyer, is precisely such an unhealthy mixture of orders. As such, it constitutes "a policy destroying all politics." With its liking for the free initiative of the individual and demand for minimal influence of state political institutions, liberalism equates social conditions with the market and reduces the people—the political entity—to a disorganized collective of individuals directed by perfectly individualized needs: that is, clients.

In modern liberalism (and particularly "neo-liberalism," or even "neo-conservatism," as the idea is called in its homeland, the United States), the

---

42   C. Schmitt, "The Concept of the Political," translated by G. Schwab, Chicago and London 1996, The University of Chicago Press, p. 19.

43   Ibidem, p. 22.

44   Ibidem.

public sphere (the place for realizing the political interests of the community) and the private sphere (an area for the activities of the particular entity) have become one. A mixing occurred of two logics, whose relations, previously constituting a rather negotiable question, came to be perceived as a common mechanism—a universal law seeing the ontological side of social life in entirely free market competition. The citizen had to cede the field to the consumer; the agonistic language of politics (friend vs. enemy) was dissipated in the discourse of economic liberalism, "an entire system of demilitarized and depoliticized concepts."[45] Thus liberalism is characterized by a special naturalism, that is, it makes the market the sole natural environment for the human being, where not only economic interests are pursued, but the truth of interhuman relations is also produced. By this same fact an equation sign is placed between the market and society (and even humanity). Society, though, is seen within the frame of two "individualist" orders, allowing people to be valued in accordance with categories belonging to the world of individuals: productivity, efficiency, virtues. "Ethical or moral pathos and materialist economic reality combine in every typical liberaql manifestation and give every political concept double face."[46] The unity that Carl Schmitt expected from a nation (understood here rather as a political community and less as a cultural community) subject to the strong control of a sovereign, is dismembered.

> A politically united people becomes, on the one hand, a culturally interested public, and, on the other, partially an industrial concern and its employers, partially a mass of consumers.[47]

Liberal democracy thus means the primacy of the "economistic" paradigm over political reality. The system of parliamentary representation, in accord with Rousseau, takes direct political supremacy away from mankind and thus takes away its essence.

> The idea of the normative character of majorities, however, contains a misunderstanding, and it is possible principally because the methods of liberal individualism, in particular of the secret individual ballet and (since Condorcet) the mathematical orientation toward the mere

---

45   Ibidem, p. 71.
46   Ibidem.
47   Ibidem, p. 72.

tabulation of voting results, which is a purely quantitative, arithmetic idea, has obscured the distinctly political concept of democracy.[48]

The political entity understood in this manner is already exclusively the subject of a special metaphysics within which the private sphere becomes the ontological basis of governing—a place for the realization of the particular interests of individuals, of rational market players. According to Schmitt, the subject of liberal doctrine is a strictly nonpolitical creation; liberal democracy is thus purely discursive in nature; in itself it is already a kind of politics. In the Marxist spirit, cooperativists would doubtless add: class politics.

My intention is not at all to liken the motivations for Schmitt's critique of liberal democracy with those of the participants in the cooperativist movement who were his contemporaries. Schmitt's starting point was the crisis of legitimation consuming parliamentary democracies and above all the inertia of the political powers, which, given over to individualistic liberalism, were changing into political nothingness, a technology of managing the chaos of courts and elections. Although these same reasons underlay the criticism that thinkers of the cooperative movement were directing at the contemporary system, they emphasized primarily that the liberal "siphoning of politicality" consisted in taking political initiative and participation from the people—the fundamental subject of politics. The aim of future politics should thus be a new combination of political subjectivity and political power in a conscious citizenry, which is directly linked with participation in the world of labor and the world of consumption. Labor and consumption are social acts, and thus can produce results that are political par excellence. "Often enough, experience has confirmed that every popular assembly, even one that initially appears nonpolitical, intrinsically contains unexpected political possibilities,"[49] wrote Schmitt in 1928. More than twenty years earlier Edward Abramowski had noted:

> Democracy [...] and freedom are created only when people, instead of demanding reforms from the state, introduce those reforms themselves, by the force of voluntary solidarity, where instead of a person as an "election vote," instead of a pawn in the hands of bureaucracy or party leaders, instead of a person who knows only how to rule or how to listen, a person

---

48   C. Schmitt, "Constitutional Theory," translated by J. Seitzer, Durham 2008, Duke University Press, p. 280.

49   Ibidem, p. 272.

appears who is a free creator of life, knowing how to act in solidarity with others without being forced and to perfect his life.[50]

Thus, the future system whose existence was the ultimate goal of cooperativism was to bring about the recreation of a continuity broken by capitalism and liberal parliamentary democracy. The democracy of the future, taking seed within capitalism by the participation of individuals in the affairs of social, economic, and cultural society through the intermediary of appropriate associations and cooperatives, was to recombine the sphere of individual needs and individual potential (understood by the classic thinkers of liberalism as the private sphere, an area of negative freedom) with the sphere of public activities and governance of the community. For the same reason, labor, social aid, and art were treated here as strictly political activities, with measurable effects in the public sphere. Thus, for Abramowski and other adherents of the cooperative doctrine, regardless of whether they belonged to the right side of politics, inspired by the social teachings of the Church (as, for instance, Fr. Franciszek Adamski or Leopold Caro) or to the left side, closer to socialism or to anarchism, the cooperative system was to constitute an answer to the alienating force of capitalism and take advantage of the primary social instincts slumbering in humanity. All political change has its source in the human subject, thus, as Małgorzata Augustyniak writes: "The process of perfecting individuals leads to perfecting society."[51] This activity has indeed an Aristotelian character, that is, it signifies raising the individual anew to the political community, but in such a manner that that individual—citizen, consumer, producer—does not lose his proper place as the principle subject of political sovereignty.

I would like to point out that the arguments Schmitt presents against liberal democracy (although they lead to entirely different conclusions in so far as regards the functioning of the state authorities) are very close to the criticism that cooperativism directed at the capitalist economy and the associated "arithmetical" liberal democracy. It is not coincidental that Schmitt's theory

50   E. Abramowski, "Znaczenie spółdzielczości dla demokracji" ["The Meaning of Cooperativism for Democracy"], in: idem, *Braterstwo, solidarność, współdziałanie. Pisma spółdzielcze i stowarzyszeniowe* [*Fraternity, Solidarity, Cooperation: Cooperative and Association Writings*], selected and edited by R. Okraska, Łódź–Sopot–Warsaw 2009, Citizen-to-Citizen Association, National Council of Cooperatives, Institute for Civil Affairs, Stefczyk Institute, pp. 19–20.

51   M. Augustyniak, *Myśl społeczno-filozoficzna Edwarda Abramowskiego* [*The Socio-Philosophical Ideas of Edward Abramowski*], Olsztyn 2006, University of Warmia and Mazury Press, p. 97.

was rediscovered in the last decades of the twentieth century thanks to the contemporary intellectual left—mainly due to the agonistic concept of politics of the Belgian philosopher Chantal Mouffe[52]—which indicated those points where liberal political logic contradicts the postulate of the people's direct participation in the process of governing the political body and subordinates the political sphere to the actions of "individuals." This version of politics leads to a technology of governance and increasing productivity. In thus reducing politicality to the properties of a monad—a rational actor (the model propagated by the neoliberal Chicago School)—western democracy basically loses sight of it, no longer posing "political questions," as these are perceived now as questions of managing the choices of millions of consumers.

Liberalism appears thus to cooperativists and sympathizers of various "community" ideas as a kind of "false ontology" consisting in the reduction of all social and political phenomena to the economic sphere. Interestingly, the same critique in this case is made by cooperativists of both the right and the left about vulgar Marxism, whose materialist premises are taken to the extreme in claims about the means of production as the source of all social phenomena. It is worth stressing that "economism," in the liberal as well as the Marxist version, meets with special criticism on the part of solidarism (a doctrine inspired particularly by the social teachings of the Church and the sociological concepts of Émile Durkheim). Leopold Caro, one of the main Catholic adherents and propagators of this idea in Poland, wrote that

> Both liberalism and Marxist socialism slide over the surface of life, deeming economic phenomena to be the most important and essential, and all others, spiritual and moral, as "superstructure." All their failures flow from this erroneous and narrow horizon.[53]

Caro and other followers of Christian solidarism (which is close to the cooperative idea) placed particular emphasis on the fictional, metaphysical nature of the liberal theory of the individual as a market entity and on the theory leading thus to the subordination of all manifestations of individual life—in morality, religion, or art—to the laws of the market and trade. According to Caro, it is only a model, an ideal type, which many—particularly

---

52   Cf. Ch. Mouffe, *On the Political*, New York–London 2005, Routledge.

53   L. Caro, *"Istota solidaryzmu"* ["The Essence of Solidarism"], in: idem, *Zmierzch kapitalizmu* [*The Decline of Capitalism*]. Selected, introduction, footnotes by D. Grzybek, Kraków 2012, Institute of Political Sciences—Department of International and Political Studies, Jagiellonian University, p. 64.

neoliberal—economists take for reality,[54] and furthermore, for reality in the eternal, ontological sense.

The Individual and the Community—Edward Abramowski

We find a similar motif in the writings of Edward Abramowski, author of *Zagadnień socjalizmu* [*Questions of Socialism*]. He refutes the premises of liberalism, concentrating on expropriation and the alienating function of capitalist economy and the extreme individualistic concept of the human individual as a conscious entity making rational decisions within the market framework. His proposed method for revealing the metaphysics of liberalism is, on the one hand, clearly akin to the Marxist analysis of capitalist economy, but on the other rests on the quite dissimilar premises of a personalistic theory of the human individual. Abramowski, who was doubtless the leading ideologist of the cooperative movement in Poland, was one of the heralds of the idea of "mutual aid." For him "true individualism" (that is, the kind that appreciates and develops the creative side of the human individual and sees in it the source of all activity transforming the political status quo) is not at all a value contrary to the premises of the cooperative system. The cooperative system proposed by Abramowski is based on the symbiosis of the individual and society in such a manner that the functional existence of the community is assured while individual needs and initiatives are preserved.

> In the existing capitalist society there are conditions, forces, and forms that enable the creation of a new society based on economic commonality and a democracy of the workers. These are primarily consumer cooperatives [...][55]

For Abramowski, participation in a common endeavor based on collective cooperation, mutual respect, and solidarity—on the cooperative—signified a life with a conscious and quantifiable opportunity to influence the shape of the world, with harmony between mind and action, idea and material, man and society.

It is well known that in Abramowski's view the essence of a social phenomenon was to be sought neither in Durkheim's methodological premises concerning the collective nature of social facts, nor in the extreme psychologism

---

54   Ibidem, p. 79.

55   E. Abramowski, *Idee społeczne kooperatyzmu* [*Social Ideas of Cooperativism*] (pp. 100–101).

of Gabriel Tarde, who claimed that the sole social reality is the statistical individual. The first view leads, in Abramowski's words, to the fetishization of behaviors and institutions of collective life as sui generis reality (it is not a matter here, however, of Durkheim's methodological premises but of the results of this identification in the political sphere, of which we spoke earlier in regard to Schmitt). The latter leads to a kind of methodological artifactization: in proceeding "as if" social facts were beings recognizable by the aid of empirical perception, we thus give them the "appearance" of beings, the illusion of existence. We take the result for the cause, the sign of a being for the being itself. In acting in accord with Tarde's theory, conversely, we reduce all manifestations of collective life to the mode of the individual consciousness of the individual. This view thus makes social reality the psycho-physical reality of the individual person, reducing Tarde's claim to a methodological absurdity: society can be understood exclusively as the sum of individuals, while individuals are knowable in so far as we are able to compare them. Thus—as Durkheim doubtless was also aware—we construct another artifact: "the average person,"[56] a statistical figure, composed of the average qualities of the population, a homunculus at the service of the researcher. From Abramowski's perspective both views are typical of science in the nineteenth-century efflorescence of the positivist search for certainty, that is, of elementary empirical findings on the subject of reality. Abramowski was aware, however, that both the objective view (Durkheim's sociologism) and the subjective view (Tarde's psychologism) on collective life passed over the essential in this—somehow ungraspable—subject: duality, cleavage, the "factual-psychological" nature of a social fact.

> If [...] we take the psychological nature away from a social phenomenon, what remains is either material—the subject of natural history studies—or the formal aspect of organizations, of institutions in the abstract; it is an abstract idea, not to be found in any fact of life, and whose value is thus purely metaphysical. On the other hand, all properties of a social phenomenon, that by which it manifests itself in various specific facts, are found in the coexistence of both these characters.[57]

---

56   Cf. É. Durkheim, *Suicide: A Sociological Study*, translated by J.A. Spaulding and G. Simpson, New York 1977, The Free Press.

57   E. Abramowski, *"Pierwiastki indywidualne w socjologii"* ["Individual Elements in Sociology"], in: idem, *Metafizyka doświadczalna i inne pisma* [*Experiential Metaphysics and Other Writings*], selected, with an introduction and commentary by S. Borzym, Warsaw 1980, PWN, p. 124.

Abramowski's sociological phenomenalism is a subversive doctrine whose task is not only to harmonize the individual element with the community but also to show their mutual conditioning, the self-referentiality of the social in the actions—and moreover in the consciousness—of the individual.

> This was a search for the kind of individualism that would not contain what is generally considered basic for it: the contradiction between the individual and the collective. The introduction of such dual differentiations makes it possible to grasp Abramowski's fundamental but usually unnoticed intention, which is maintained through all his works: to show a perspective in which the affirmation of individualism would mean affirmation of the community and vice versa.[58]

This postulate has a dual significance: a methodological one in that Abramowski uses it to study and describe the social reality of man, and also a political one—it marks an ideal toward which the labor and consumer democracy movement should aim.

If, as Abramowski claims in one of his most important works, *Zagadnienie Socjalizmu* [*Questions of Socialism*], both statements are valid and support each other—the first, that "a person is the sole social reality, which means that the whole of social life plays out solely in his individual consciousness [...]" and the second, that "the only reality is society; the individual is an incidental systematization of phenomena, an illusion deriving from the subconscious sphere"[59]—then the search for true individualism occurs in parallel with the search for true community. This search assumes that human nature has certain immutable basic features, which are easy to falsify or deform through the influence of external factors arising from the action of social forces. If the fundamental value of capitalist reality is property, then, as Oskar Lange writes, commenting on this aspect of Abramowski's thought, "The essence of bourgeois ethics is [...] egoism and competition."[60] This statement is not limited solely to consequences in the moral or economic sphere but has a primarily anthropological dimension: the basic vision of man and the individual

58   S. Borzym, *"Abramowski—filozof epoki modernizmu"* ["Abramowski—a Philosopher of the Modern Era"], in: E. Abramowski, *Metafizyka doświadczalna i inne pisma* [*Experiential Metaphysics and Other Writings*], op. cit., p. XXXVIII.

59   E. Abramowski, *"Zagadnienia socjalizmu"* ["Issues of Socialism"], in: idem, *Filozofia społeczna. Wybór pism* [*Social Philosophy: Selected Writings*], Warsaw 1965, PWN, p. 112.

60   O. Lange, *Socjologja i idee społeczne Edwarda Abramowskiego* [*The Sociology and Social Ideas of Edward Abramowski*], Kraków 1928, Krakowska Spółka Wydawnicza, p. 29.

corresponding to the capitalist model is narrowed to a substantial entity: being a conscious participant in the market play of individuals, whose choices are subject to the final judgment of an authority expressing moral, economic, and political truth—employers (capitalists representing the market) and the political power. In the capitalist system, the relations of individuals with the market and state play out around the ideal of accumulating things, assuring oneself of goods, of work understood exclusively as the production of objects having nothing in common with our existence, counted as money. In writing *Questions of Socialism*, Abramowski drew extensively from the Marxist concept of alienation, placing great stress, however, on the collective possibilities for liberation from the yoke of things—goods and money.

The individual, according to Abramowski, is a carrier of social forces, the basic atom of the community, in which nevertheless—differently than for Tarde—the community expresses its full, true existence. As I wrote above, in seeking the "real social environment" we can observe the existence of these forces exclusively through the existence of individuals. These latter, through individual material-psychological equivalents of social life, communicate with the social exterior, providing the beginning of all socialization and at the same time creating a supra-individual world of collective needs and practices.

> In this manner various degrees and types of association arise from the subjective moments of the soul: they are objectified as the expressions and products of labor, and in a higher degree as laws, faiths, and institutions; the first sign of a social world is speech and purposeful creation, the next is its development—social organization, and various forms of joint action.[61]

Cooperation is the highest form of socialization. Abramowski studied its traces in individual humans and sought forms of activity which through the individual, through respect for individual needs and the exploitation of the creative energy of the entity, would give birth to a higher, more democratic form of communal life—"more democratic" meaning the kind where the particular elements and the collective are as close to one another as possible. This did not mean, however, a return toward collectivism on the pattern familiar to him from, among other places, the writings of many of his contemporary socialist thinkers; it was rather a matter of an original "social individualism," which in fulfilling Fourier's dream pins the individual will to collective sense

---

61   E. Abramowski, *Pierwiastki indywidualne w socjologii* [*Individual Elements in Sociology*], op. cit., p. 127.

and action. Cooperatives, concentrating people around similar needs, values, and activities, are excellent environments for raising new forms of communication and cooperation: in the interaction between the group and its member a true transformation of social reality occurs, a transformation of the social existence. This latter exists as a fact only in the individual consciousness, and in connection with this claim Abramowski also maintains that "the tragedy of the death of a system that has endured and the birth of a new social world is thus a tragedy of social psychology [...]"[62] All political transformations, that is, those that influence the shape and functioning of the community, are thus based in an actual socio-economic environment, but their catalyst is the individual consciousness—the conscience.

> "The human conscience" can thus be compared with a prism from which the simple economic fact emerges split into its coordinates of other social categories; it is the living, feeling point of its transformation into variety, into the whole of collective life.[63]

According to Abramowski, expanding cooperatives would become the start for the transformation of the capitalist state without the need for revolutionary upheaval, a dictatorship of the proletariat, or the rejection and elimination of national tradition.

Immanent Change and Criticism of the State—A Digression on Syndicalism

Abramowski's sociological phenomenalism draws both from contemporary sociological disputes and the Marxist theory of class struggle (treated fairly instrumentally, however); it is also undoubtedly close to collectivist and community forms of anarchism and syndicalism, although his idea should not be identified with any of these.[64] Abramowski is linked to anarchists and

---

62   Ibidem, p. 185.

63   Ibidem, p. 186.

64   Edward Abramowski and Jan Wacław Machajski—anarchists, founders of the workers'
        movement, anti-intelligentsia and anti-state—are described as follows by Rafał Chwe-
        doruk, scholar of Polish syndicalism: "While their importance in terms of the originality
        of Polish socialism's ideological thinking is indubitable, what is rather open to discussion
        is their link to the syndicalist tradition in its various mutations. It should rather be said
        that their ideas are to be located at the crossroads of various socialist currents; in this sense
        they could have played a role in strengthening the influence of syndicalist movements in

syndicalists by a certain conviction about the conservative and oppressive role of the state and by the same ties as several other Polish activists connected with cooperativism, for instance, Maria Orsetti or Jan Wolski.[65] First, there is the conviction of the high "revolutionary" role of grassroots action in "disassembling" the capitalist system through the creation of an alternative political and economic organization within the capitalist state. Second, importantly, *"action directe"* (as it was called by syndicalists on the order of George Sorel or Émile Pouget)[66] was supposed to strike at the very heart of the state organization.

From Marx, anarchists and syndicalists adopted the view of the state as an organization serving to protect the interests of the dominant class, which by controlling the means of production, also controlled the development of the superstructure—the consciousness of the proletariat. Such a state should be destroyed through the armed activities of underground organizations and the political power of trade unions (syndicates), whose basic weapon is the general strike—stopping the political and economic machine of capitalism by one irreversible decision whereby the working class takes the initiative. Syndicalism rests on the premise that overcoming the state begins within it as a result of gradually building the structures of trade organizations and by a later rapid assumption of power. The closeness of cooperativism and syndicalist general action is in their emphasis on the immanent genesis of political change; nevertheless these concepts differ fundamentally on its form and course. French cooperativists belonging to the so-called School of Nîmes, headed by Charles Gide, planned to rebuild the state from inside through the expansion of an organization that would replace all its functions, beginning with the purely economic ones, and ending with joint political decision-making about the further fate of the communities working in cooperatives, which were to adopt the role of local centers of the future republic.

---

the II Republic and later" (R.Chwedoruk, *Ruchy i myśl polityczna syndykalizmu w Polsce* [*Movements and Political Ideas of Syndicalism in Poland*] Warsaw 2011, Elipsa, p. 82).

65   Cf. in particular the reflections on Wolski's anarcho-cooperativism in the book: A.B. Duszyk, *Ostatni niepokorny* [*The Last Rebel: Jan Wolski 1888–1975*], op cit. p. 33.

66   The doctrine of "direct action" (*action directe*) is one of the most important tactical elements of revolutionary syndicalism. As one of its creators, Émile Pouget, wrote: "Direct action is nothing more than the materialization of the principle of liberty, its realization in the masses—not through a veiled and difficult abstract formula but through an open and practical application [...]" (É. Pouget, *"L'action directe"* (1910), in: *Le Syndicalisme Révolutionnaire*, H. Dubief (sel.), Paris 1969, Armand Colin, p. 181, cited after: R. Chwedoruk, *Syndykalizm rewolucyjny—antyliberalna rewolta XX wieku* [*Revolutionary syndicalism— the Anti-Liberal Revolt of the 20th Century*], Warsaw 2013, Elipsa, pp. 33–34).

The difference between these two movements is fundamental: cooperativism rejects the violence and terror proposed by syndicalists as an indispensable tool of class struggle in favor of deliberate, slow action to eliminate capitalist institutions—primarily economic ones (trade and production), and therefore also political ones. In this manner, in some measure from below, it tries to take over the management of succeeding areas of social life. For cooperativism, as for syndicalism, the state is nevertheless a kind of obstacle to overcome on the road to the socialism of the future, the ideal of self-government and solidarity of the working masses. The difference consists in that, according to the syndicalists, the abolishment of the state is a fundamental condition for building the future society; according to the cooperativists, it is sufficient to transform and subordinate the state on the way to a grassroots transformation of ideas and mechanisms based on the "community." Leaving aside the fact that the cooperativism of the School of Nîmes did not have such a strong class character as various other varieties of syndicalism, the aims of the two, at least in their later forms, were fairly convergent while their means entirely different. Abramowski drew from both the above doctrines, although he did not accept either uncritically. From syndicalism he undoubtedly adopted the idea of "direct action," which begins in the very center of the capitalist formation, and from cooperativism the conviction that the force capable of destroying that formation would be the development of social institutions and the spread of the idea of solidarity.

However, Oskar Lange claimed that Abramowski differs from the School of Nîmes in two regards. First, cooperativism in Abramowski's view is a movement with a proletarian, a class nature; the School of Nîmes considered cooperativism to be neutral, classless. Second, the hope Abramowski placed in the cooperative movement goes much, much farther than the hope inspiring other cooperativists. For Abramowski, cooperativism was not only supposed to transform the social system from a capitalist to a socialist-cooperativist one (as the School of Nîmes also expected), but the cooperative republic was additionally supposed to supplant the contemporary state and become a free, state-less society in the anarchist sense.[67]

Here we are coming to a neuralgic point in the history of cooperativism, where the fundamental divisions and internal ambiguities of the movement crystallize. It concerns the relation to the state understood as a class organization, and thereby to the class struggle as such. The anarchist strain, and even, as we have seen, the anarcho-syndicalist, form the clear context of Abramowski's intellectual searching: he indubitably based his doctrine of political change

---

67   O. Lange, *Socjologja i idee społeczne Edwarda Abramowskiego* [*The Sociology and Social Ideas of Edward Abramowski*], op. cit., p. 72.

on a bitter and multidimensional critique of the state, which, as part of the feudal and capitalist formation, was supposed in his view to disappear in the same manner as other creations of man had disappeared. Why? The cause is simple: the state constituted a sort of usurpation; the capitalist system had grown out of the original material of the human community. This community is in the primarily unconscious striving of every individual conscience toward fraternity with others, the making of cooperative relations, which in primitive societies were automatic and unconscious in nature but in modern societies require organic, deliberate social arrangements. For Abramowski, these were food and production cooperatives and voluntary vocational organizations through which the proletariat could express its will.

The state, according to Abramowski, is thus a neutral coercive formation. However, it is not a matter of coercion as such—in the form of an authority executing the law (the necessity of such coercion even after achievement of the communist state was emphasized by Engels)[68]—but a more fundamental kind, involving the basis of an individual's socialization: the coercion of belonging to a given organization.[69]

> The essence of a state and its raison d'être become "the oppression of individual differences," the realization of an "abstract human" model, molding the morality and consciousness of the individual [...]. With the aid of the external and internal—psychological—police, it tries universally to control everyone.[70]

Do we not find here the schema Marx discovered, and which after him sociologists such as Pierre Bourdieu named "symbolic force," enrolling individuals in a metaphysics of power with its hierarchies and truth promoted by one group against the truth of another group—the replacement of original "interdependence" by abstract forms of mutual "belonging"? Abramowski applies the same claim to other systemic forms, which place their hope in liberation within the state, including state socialism.[71] In his critique of the state fetishism of certain turn-of-the-century Marxists, Abramowski anticipated the totalitarian

---

68   F. Engels, *"O zasadzie autorytetu"* ["On Authority"], in: K. Marks, F. Engels, *Dzieła wybrane* [*Selected Works*], vol. 1, Warsaw 1949, Książka i Wiedza, pp. 597–600 [English translation at https://www.marxists.org/archive/marx/works/1872/10/authority.htm].

69   O. Lange, *Socjologja i idee społeczne Edwarda Abramowskiego* [*The Sociology and Social Ideas of Edward Abramowski*], op. cit., p. 64.

70   U. Dobrzycka, *Abramowski...*, p. 93.

71   E. Abramowski, "Kooperatywa jako sprawa wyzwolenia ludu pracującego" ["Cooperativism, as a Matter of Freeing Working People"], in: idem, Braterstwo, solidarność, współdziałanie [Fraternity, Solidarity, Cooperation], op. cit., p. 157.

atrocities of twentieth-century communism. According to Abramowski, the
state is

> ... a hundred-headed and hundred-armed Leviathan, nesting comfort-
> ably in all the old addictions of life [...] It has many different names and
> masks. It has been called the Roman Empire, a theocracy, the Holy In-
> quisition, Jacobinism, the National Convention, and today it is called the
> dictatorship of the proletariat and the people's labor state. The same—
> immortal and two-faced.[72]

Class Conflict and the Universal Entity of Cooperation

In the cooperative milieu in Poland in the 1920s and 1930s, the relation to the
state as an apparatus of class oppression and simultaneously the sole political tool (weapon) by which workers would complete the work of socialism
became a source of conflict.[73] The dispute was mainly between the representatives—such as Romuald Mielczarski, Stanisław Wojciechowski, or Edward
Abramowski—of a cooperativism closer to the old ideal of "work at the base"
and of the anarchist idea of freedom and mutual aid (being rather neutral in
terms of class and concentrated on a pragmatic but not political demarcation
of the route to developing the cooperativist movement) and cooperativists
(and cooperativist sympathizers) from the milieus closely associated with socialism and communism—the "classists."

Jan Hempel, one of the important thinkers of communist cooperativism, in
criticizing what he considered to be the utopian premise of the cooperative
movement, insisted on a return to the "true" premises of cooperativism, which,
as a tool of class struggle, in essence belongs to the labor-class movement:

> Workers' and farmers' cooperatives should work in close union with the
> whole labor-class movement. Instead of the toxic cooperativist ideology

---

72   E. Abramowski, *Idee społeczne kooperatyzmu* [*Social Ideas of Cooperativism*] (p. 99).

73   More on the subject of class cooperation: F. Kędziorek, *Nurty społeczno-gospodarcze w
      polskim ruchu spółdzielczym w latach 1918–1939* [*Socio-Economic Currents in the Polish
      Cooperative Movement in the Years 1918–1939*], Zakład Wydawnictw CRS, Warsaw 1969,
      pp. 140–148; more on the subject of the "class conflict" alone in Polish cooperativism:
      R. Okraska, *Od samo-pomocy do wizji nowego ustroju. Zarys dziejów rozwoju materialnego i
      ideowego spółdzielczości w Polsce do roku 1939* [*From Self-Help to the Vision of a New System:
      An Outline of the Material and Ideological Evolution of Cooperativism in Poland to 1939*]
      (p. 46).

they should be guided by the ideology of the fighting proletariat and all their activities should be subordinate to the general requirement of struggle.[74]

In this sentence, Hempel encapsules the entire discord between the old theoreticians of cooperativism of Abramowski's kind and cooperativism understood as part of the revolutionary communist movement. This discord is expressed primarily in the dichotomy between the two ideas discussed above: the paradigm of struggle deriving from post-Darwinist social evolutionism and the Marxist doctrine of class struggle, as well as from cooperation (mutual aid), whose substructures we find in utopian socialism, certain anarchists, and above all cooperativists.

According to Hempel, cooperativism, as the leading idea of the cooperative movement in Poland, operates in the name of bourgeois or outright fascist interests (fascism is after all the result of capitalist imperialism),[75] discouraging the working class from revolutionary struggle. Thus from the viewpoint of a communist activist, cooperativism is only a deception, because it obscures the picture of agonistic social relations—it is a pipe dream. This dream was created to inculcate in workers and cooperativists the conviction that thanks to hard work, solidarity, and associative democracy, capitalism could evolve and bear fruit of social justice on its own, without the aid of revolutionary forces. For the same reason, cooperativism does not oppose either the logic of capitalism—participating in the free market game and not breaking its rules—or the state, on whose help it depends and whose national-political coercion it supports. In Hempel's vision, cooperativism is part of the state-and-market metaphysics he is fighting.

The basic difference dividing "neutralists" from "classists" in their view of cooperativism's role in building the state and overcoming capitalism is in the strategy for acting: the former require action within the capitalist economy in order to replace its institutions from inside and the latter are guided toward a constant overstepping of capitalism, rejecting it, and not so much replacing as destroying it. According to the "neutralists" (or as Hempel called them, "independent cooperativists") cooperativism means the path of rebuilding the state and economy through inclusion of the largest possible group of

---

74 H. Janowicz (J. Hempel), *Utopia kooperatystyczna i jej apostołowie w Polsce* [*The Cooperativist Utopia and its Apostles in Poland*], Warsaw 1931, Robotnicza Spółdzielnia Spożywców Zagłębia Dąbrowskiego i innych spółdzielni klasowych [Workers' Consumer Cooperatives of Dąbrowski Basin and other class cooperatives], p. 23.

75 Ibidem.

"consumers" (and all citizens belong to it) in the structures of cooperation.
In this manner they called for the immediate reconstruction of the country's
socio-economic system.[76] The object of political change is not thus, in the
cooperativists' view, the proletariat, but the consumer—the universal figure.
The latter is potentially every member of society: the worker, farmer, bourgeois,
or intellectual.

Not all representatives of this "classic" doctrine had the same attitude to
the state. The majority, like the "classists," came from the workers' movement
but were not aligned so unequivocally with the official policy of the political
parties—doubtless much more with the Polish Socialist Party than with the
communists, as in the case of Abramowski. Many of them dreamt of a "cooperative republic," which as a sort of non-state would replace the oppressive class
structure of the contemporary political organism. All, however, were for the
idea of "general cooperation," open to all social movements and to members
inevitably deriving from various social classes: the idea according to which
cooperativism as a kind of "meta-doctrine" constitutes an instrument above
political divisions, not belonging solely to the working class, and certainly not
subject to solely political decisions. In this context, it is harder to produce a
more apt description than "pan-cooperativism."[77] They understood cooperation rather as an answer to the natural tendencies of man, who on account of
his needs is always a consumer, and by reason of belonging to a community,
develops only within it. Thus the direction of such cooperativism was determined by social universality and a democracy of "consumers"—participation
in a cooperative not by force of class and political affiliation but on the strength
of being at once a consumer and a citizen. Romuald Mielczarski called for
unification of the cooperative movement, claiming that

> Cooperation organizes consumers. Who are consumers? Everyone. Coop-
> eration organizes not only one group or another, one vocation or another,
> but people, because all people have needs and desire to fulfill them as
> best they can [...] a cooperative becomes a haven for all. The principle

76   This dispute even led to a temporary fracture within the movement—the Union of Work-
      ers Cooperative Associations formed in 1919 in opposition to the neutral Union of Polish
      Consumer Associations.
77   "In the twenty years of interwar pan-cooperativism it became the leading trend in Polish
      cooperativism. The pan-cooperativists included such outstanding activists as R. Mielczar-
      ski, Z. Chmielewski, and President S. Wojciechowski, as well as younger activists such as
      S. Thugutt and M. Rapacki" (Z. Chyra-Rolicz, *Z tradycji polskiej spółdzielczości II Rzeczy-
      pospolitej* [*The Tradition of Polish Cooperativism in the II Republic*], Warsaw-Poznań 1992,
      Ławica, p. 29).

of universality is in the movement's most fundamental interest. Unless the majority of the population cooperates, the victory of cooperation is unimaginable.[78]

The general subject of cooperation is something more than the communist ideal of the fighting worker, subordinating his activity to the party avant-garde, and thus acting in relation to a partly external force deriving from the enlightened proletariat and converted intelligentsia. The consumer expresses what is universal and quasi natural in a member of society: the needs and necessities characterizing human life, and thus joint participation and joint decision-making in organizing their fulfillment. It can be said that in the writings of the cooperativists the consumer is identified with the citizen, the subject of democracy, while democracy (in its strongly participatory, associative form) appears to be the "original," natural system, best expressing the "social nature of man." Cooperativists were thus members of the milieu (I hesitate to use the word "generation" here) to which Stanisław Brzozowski, Ludwik Krzywicki, Józef Karol Potocki (pseudonym Marian Bohusz), Helena Radlińska and others belonged; they were later called by some "community workers" or "culturalists," and by others simply the "democratic left." Although this group was often rather heterogeneous in its convictions and origins, the postulates linking it were freedom and justice; the attitude (contradicting the Jacobean vision of these ideals) was one of "deep empathy with the values of human dignity."[79] They were thus interested in universal freedom, but never of the kind that—as we remember from Alexis de Tocqueville—could quickly turn into equality before tyranny: justice, but not of the kind that would deny freedom. It was a matter thus of freedom as participation in government and justice as mutual aid. Leszek Kołakowski's description of a critique of communism formulated by Pierre-Joseph Proudhon, one of the pioneers of the associative idea, seems significant here:

> It thus appears that Proudhon (like Fourier, though his moral and philosophical premises are quite different) does not really wish to abolish property but to extend it. Communism, he believed [...] would never be compatible with the dignity of the individual and the values of family life.[80]

---

78 R. Mielczarski, *O zjednoczenie ruchu* [*On Uniting the Movement*] (p. 124).

79 A. Mencwel, *Etos lewicy* [*The Leftist Ethos*], op. cit., p. 70.

80 L. Kołakowski, *Main Currents of Marxism. Its Origins, Growth and Dissolution,* vol 1: *The Founders,* op. cit., p. 207–208.

Was that really what communists, on the order of Jan Hempel, held against the cooperativists?

Metaphysics and Consumer Democracy

For Abramowski—but other cooperativists as well, his companions, students, and followers—the principle of "mutual aid" grew to the rank of an ontological principle, conditioning the place of man in nature and society. Abramowski's ideas bring him near to Aristotle's teleological vision here. If a human being is nothing other than a political animal, a social being, then in meeting needs of an individual nature concerning what is closest to him, in economics (an area satisfying the needs of the body) and ethics (an area corresponding to spiritual and moral development), he is also taking care of social and political matters: he participates in the community. Cooperation in the most ordinary daily activities—communication, economics, science, etc., is the only path to meeting the original and inalienable needs of man. Man, as an individua,l is everything, but only in a community. Outside of it, as we remember from Aristotle, he is either a god or an animal.[81] A point at which the individual and the community meet is thus necessary: a point at which the particular factuality of contact with the world acquires the status of something supra-individual, approaching a "social sense." "Need has an indirect nature"—as Stanisław Borzym explains this aspect of Abramowski's thought—"it is shaped in the interaction of individual feeling and material-psychological social phenomena."[82] For Abramowski, the social sphere of needs is something that cannot be reduced either to the market—a place of competition and exchange—or to the sphere of work, understood exclusively as the realization of collective goals. On the side of the individual, however, need as the causal impulse of human action is the active side of personality, in which individual desire finds its expression in a collective manner of acting. By this same psychological theory, Abramowski bases himself on the way that collective activity manifests itself in individual minds, touching the deepest strata of the psyche, being on the order of the core of humanity. The sphere of needs is imprinted into what is pre-intellectual in the human soul, exceeding narrowly understood individuality, particularity.

---

81   Aristotle, *Polityka z dodaniem pseudo-arystotelesowej ekonomiki* [*Politics, Supplemented by Pseudo-Aristotelian Economics*], translated by L. Piotrowicz, Warsaw 1964, PWN, p. 8. [English translation at: http://classics.mit.edu/Aristotle/politics.html].

82   S. Borzym, *Abramowski—filozof epoki modernizmu* [*Abramowski—A Philosopher of the Era of Modernism*], op. cit., p. LI.

It is the root of the species before the individual and before society, in which at the same time the individual and society function as two members of the same process—collectivization, socialization, or, to use Abramowski's language, fraternity. He understood fraternity as a "deeper" process, non-sensual but acting on the senses, appearing in social activity but not reducible to it. The comparison that suggests itself in this place brings Abramowski and his sociological phenomenalism closer to the phenomenology if not of Edmond Husserl then at least of Alfred Schütz. Like Husserl, Abramowski seeks inherent metaphysical certainties, phenomena of a true social existence, functioning at the unconscious level of the species: "a feeling of the 'forgotten' type," as he writes.[83] It is thus a matter of the species rather than of the individual or social aspect—which combine with it in one ideal of fraternity. Abramowski's ideal, being "both a metaphysical experience of love and will,"[84] is close to Schütz's theory of intersubjectivity as a process in which objective social elements produce what is subjective—objectifying it again in the form of social identity. Love here signifies the mediation of one individual with another, a meeting in which will—the active creative element—gives birth to the entity "social individuality." Abramowski describes this process excellently, analyzing the experience of encountering beauty in art, or the moment of realizing social needs of a higher order:

> It would seem that because beauty appears exclusively in the individual sphere, in a person's inaccessible subconscious feelings, there can be no significant link between it and the highly social question of "fraternity." Nevertheless, this is not the case—not because a person's "sociability" is located outside of himself, but because it is embedded in his own soul; every individual, even when he is excluded from the human collective, can find in himself the "social being" of his personality.[85]

In this regard, there is no humanity for Abramowski outside of society and no society outside of the individual personality. Fraternity—the fundamental

83   E. Abramowski, "Metafizyka doświadczalna" ["Experiential Metaphysics"], in: idem, Meta-
     fizyka doświadczalna i inne pisma [Experiential Metaphysics and Other Writings], op. cit.,
     p. 590.
84   Ibidem, p. 581.
85   E. Abramowski, "Co to jest sztuka? (Z powodu rozprawy L. Tołstoja: «Czto takoje iskusst-
     wo?»") ["What is Art? (In Response to Tolstoy's 'Czto Takoje Iskusstwo?'")], in: idem, Wybór
     pism estetycznych [Selection of Writings on Aesthetics], selection, introduction, and edit-
     ing by K. Najder-Stefaniak, Kraków 2011, Universitas, p. 30.

relation of social lives—is the most elementary level of existence, its beginning and aim, nature and the ideal: *arche* and *telos*. All social ideals that do
not appreciate this fact are sooner or later condemned to failure—the ex-
cesses of disastrous individualism, leading in consequence to egoism, or to
the hypertrophy of collective tendencies—taking sovereignty from the real
social entity, from the human being, and stifling him in a totalitarian machine
of power. What is social reaches the deepest part of the individual, constituting his "conscience"—to use the terminology proposed by William I. Thomas
and Florian Znaniecki—his "social personality."[86] Accordingly—and there
is no contradiction in the statement—for Abramowski, the individual is the
bearer of historical rights, but the relation between the causal entity and the
mechanism of history can not be reduced to simple dependence. The basic
"environment of history" is the human soul; the active human mind immersed
in time is the tool of historical change. Thus the source of all social change is
nothing other than the social self—this is the tension that drives the pistons
of history.

The sole manner of social organization in which real social needs are realized but which does not result from the capitalist process of alienation,[87] the
illusion of needs, is cooperative democracy. It accomplishes economic tasks
while including individuals in the decision-making process and defining the
manner in which needs are to be satisfied—both in production and above all
consumption. Cooperatives are based thus on cooperation, self-government,
and solidarity. They personify, according to Abramowski, all the basic traits of
socialization, leaving room also for individual freedom and for the ideal of fraternity. Cooperatives are something more than organized forms of common
purchases or even production for the needs of the association. Combining
economic activity with social and political activity they constitute a kind of
breach in the structure of capitalism. Cooperatives are social experiments on
the living fabric of the community, in which the idea of exploiting individual
initiatives for the common good acquires a new dimension and the opportunity for realization. Cooperation and self-government combine here with making collective consumer choices, thanks to which the two figures separated by
liberalism—the citizen (as a member of the political community) and the consumer (the object of market play)—participate in the social process and again
become one. Cooperation is thus something more than a form of economic

---

86   W. I. Thomas, F. Znaniecki, *Polish Peasant in Europe and America,* New York 1958, Dover
      Publications.
87   Cf. E. Abramowski, *Zagadnienia socjalizmu* [*Issues of Socialism*], op. cit., p. 135.

organization; it is the forge of civil activity, in which economic activity implies civil behavior. As one of Poland's most important pre-war cooperativist activists, Romuald Mielczarski, said: "Cooperation is economically self-organizing democracy [...]"[88] Furthermore, cooperativists understand consumption as a civil activity in the strict sense. Cooperativism appears to them to be a form of economic system trying to reacquire consumption for conscious civil participation, unfetishizing the concept of "consumer" in order to establish a political subjectivity of a new type.[89]

A few years before his death, Abramowski began work on a program of "Friendship Unions"—special cooperatives that were essentially supposed to fulfill his dreams of unions based completely on the ideals of self-organization and self-help. "I imagine Friendship Unions," he wrote in 1912, "as neighborhood unions whose task is mutual aid in everything."[90] They were to be associations of various characters and functions, whose basic principle would be mutual responsibility and the largest possible unconditional autonomy, including from the authority of any central unions. How was the union, thus understood, to differ from cooperatives in the broad sense, of which we have been writing? In addition to the unions' fairly universal purpose—the possibility of these applications in various social and vocational environments—the difference is this: the basic task that Abramowski gives to Friendship Unions does not lie in the economic sphere (in collective production, services, or consumption) as in the case of other cooperatives, but in the sphere of ethics, that is, in adaptation to a new life, whose principles will be guided by cooperative socialism.

---

88   R. Mielczarski, *"Przed Zjazdem"* ["Before the Assembly"], in: idem, *Pisma [Writings]*, vol. 2, collected and edited by K. Krzeczkowski, Warsaw 1936, Związek Polskich Stowarzyszeń Spożywcow R.P., p. 220.

89   Adherents of cooperativist ideas saw in them an opportunity for the development of a new culture and education, which could become the source of a democracy freed from the ailments and aporia of traditional parliamentarism. In his important work for the cooperative movement, *Sklepy społeczne [Social Shops]*, Edward Milewski cites the words of Arnold Toynbee, which are an excellent apology for cooperation as a source of democracy: "What division of education remained for the cooperativists?—educating the citizen. I understand by this the education of every member of society in comprehending obligations toward other citizens and the entire society" (E. Milewski, *Sklepy społeczne [Social Shops]*, Lwów 1910, Nakładem Związku Stowarzyszeń Zarobkowych i Gospodarczych, p. 113. Translated from the Polish—Tr.

90   E. Abramowski, *"Związki przyjaźni"* ["Friendship Unions"], in: idem, *Braterstwo, solidarność, współdziałanie [Fraternity, Solidarity, Cooperation]*, op. cit., p. 218.

This adaptation must occur gradually as those social changes occur. Without that moral revolution, however, without that new conscience, the new social institutions can not develop and survive. The new social world can never live among the former people, breathing their moral atmosphere.[91]

Friendship Unions are thus associations realizing the postulate of general participation in order to prepare for the arrival of a new human being— "communal man."

The figure of a new human being appears both in cooperativist writings from the first years of the twentieth century (including the article "The Social Ideas of Cooperativism" of 1907 published in this volume), as well as in the series of lectures begun in 1917 and based on *Metafizyki doświadczalnej* [*Experiential Metaphysics*], the last, unfinished work of the philosopher. The inspirations for the idea came from varied sources and from the philosophical, political, and even religious doctrines with which Abramowski had become familiar in the course of his many years of studying the cooperative elements of the human psyche—the Gnostic and neo-Platonic figure of the new Adam, the Buddhist concept of spiritual liberation, the Christian doctrine of the Kingdom of God on Earth, Marx on overcoming the alienation of work, Bergson's philosophy of life, and finally, the Nietzschean ideal of the superman. The doctrine of the moral revolution that must precede the work of social revolution was the junction point of Abramowski's thought, concentrating all the elements of his planned reconstruction of society in the spirit of cooperation. It is true that the tone of the 1907 article differs considerably from that of the writer's lectures at the University of Warsaw's Institute of Psychology; nevertheless, their main trait remains the same. If, as has already been said, the basic element in the life of the species is the human conscience—the main point of the psyche, in which a synthesis of individual and social elements occurs[92]—the rebuilding of the social world must concern as many existential conditions of human life as does conscience: the ethical side of existence. Socio-economic change is thus not possible without moral change. According to Abramowski, the revolution will not happen by introducing appropriate institutional or organizational solutions—its source is conscience; thus only institutions whose aim is to introduce the new "ethical economy" (cooperatives and Friendship Unions) are capable of introducing the true revolution: and it will occur through hard work and education, without spilling blood, which only hampers its achievement.

---

91   E. Abramowski, *Metafizyka doświadczalna* [*Experiential Metaphysics*], op. cit., p. 595.
92   Ibidem, p. 597.

Prophetic and full of pathos, the language of *Experiential Metaphysics* is akin to Fourier's work in many aspects, producing a vision of communism on the basis of eschatological and metaphysical inquiries. In the case of Abramowski, as in the case of his ideological forbears, sober political calculation goes in tandem with a metaphysical, mystical, and even messianic mode of thinking. It is hard here to make a clear division, because for Abramowski, cooperativism constitutes the "practical" side of human aspirations toward succeeding stages in the biological and spiritual evolution of the species. In this context, the motto of the eighth chapter of *Experiential Metaphysics*, taken from Nietzsche's *Thus Spake Zarathustra*, takes on an entirely new meaning: "Man is a rope stretched between the animal and the Superman—a rope over an abyss." Just as animal life, which the human individual also shares, does not reflect the slightest degree of its specificity, so the new man, new citizen, and new, future democracy are not to be compared to any organism previously known to humanity. "What is great in man," we can add after Nietzsche, "is that he is a bridge and not a goal; what is lovable in man is that he is an *over-going* and a *down-going*."[93]

Conclusion: Attainable Utopia

It should come as no surprise that from Jan Hempel's viewpoint cooperativism was nothing more than a fantastical utopia, while its representatives in Poland—particularly Edward Abramowski, Romuald Mielczarski, and Stanisław Wojciechowski, propagators of the idea of a "cooperative republic"—seemed to him to be either calculating bourgeois cheats, deluding the working class with empty slogans, or thinkers and activists as politically immature as the first utopian socialists, believing that an historic social transformation could occur through appropriate social organization and education. There is no space here to continue considering the ideological differences that animated cooperativist circles in Poland at the time, but it is worth observing that Hempel's critique of cooperativism shows us the basic weakness and at the same time the value of the idea—its utopian nature. In criticism from communist positions, cooperativism is presented as an escapist ideology whose prescription for overcoming capitalism lies in institutions: in consumer associations, which are de facto an insignificant alternative to capitalist enterprise, or worse, maintain the logic of capitalism by operating within it.

---

93   F. Nietzsche, *Thus Spake Zarathustra*, translated by Thomas Common, Mineola–New York
     1999, Dover Publications, p. 5.

In his well-known work *Spotkania z utopią* [*Encounters with Utopia*] Jerzy Szacki made the differentiation between "monastery utopia" and "political utopia," placing it permanently in the vocabulary of historians of ideas. It seems that this dichotomy could also be helpful in appraising the utopian nature of cooperativism. As Szacki writes:

> The first of these borders on utopian escapism. An ideal appears. A group of people is found who are fixated on this ideal. They do not believe that society can be transformed now. They also do not believe that they can remain faithful to the ideal by participating in the life of this corrupt society. They decide thus to close themselves off as a group in order to protect a value they consider to be priceless [...] The monastery will not change the world; it creates an island. Political utopia begins [on the other hand] when someone—an individual or group—gives himself the task of changing society from the ground up.[94]

These first constitute moreover an attempt at suspending the temporary or local laws prevailing in an actual society, the creation of an imminent breach in the social and spiritual fabric of a given historical order; the latter, however, do the opposite—they are attempts to overthrow the existing society, to strike at its weak points in such a manner as to produce a permanent transgression of the existing conditions. Monastery utopias are characterized by an escape "inwards," while political utopias escape "outwards." The former are set on separation of the idea from the external world in order to survive till the inoculation of another, perhaps better, generation; the latter rely on faith in the possibility of an immediate, planned, and consequential change in the system—a revolution conducted by peaceful or violent means.

Where then should cooperativism be located, if we admit that it bears traits of utopianism? Should it be placed between these two poles of utopias desiring to change social reality? This question, asked from the inside—by the adherents of cooperativism—must in principle be treated as an attack on the doctrine, an attempt to reduce it to an insignificant fantasy, which perhaps expresses a certain longing and hope of humanity, the people, or the nation, but which is far from being a rational worldview. If it is asked from the outside, by opponents of the idea, it will be an attempt to emphasize the continuum of political rationality, which, in accord with their own system of values, excludes the cooperativists' mode of thinking. Leaving aside these extreme manners of viewing utopia, Aleksander Świętochowski, in one of the broadest studies of

---

94   J. Szacki, *Spotkania z utopią* [*Encounters with Utopia*], Warsaw 1980, Iskry, pp. 60–62.

the subject to have appeared to date in Poland, stated that "The internal value of the idea does not depend on its external manifestation."[95] Guided by this maxim, let us try then to treat the problem of utopia quite differently, by considering it rather as an intellectual product as valuable as other socially and culturally recognized phenomena in the history of ideas. Let us rather ask: What is the utopian function of the political idea that started the entirely pragmatic, rational, and down-to-earth manner of thinking that was cooperativism?

Doubtless cooperativists dreamt of complete social change, which in the course of time would cause the disassembly of the capitalist system from inside. The idea of associations which, in uniting their members around common work, consumption, and mutual responsibilities, become economically self-sufficient enough to be able finally to occupy ever more areas of social, economic, and cultural life contains many elements taken from the tradition of monastery utopia, as well as from Fourier's concept of *phalanstères*, or from "Owen villages." Within the capitalist formation, cooperatives and associations were to be a kind of breach, which would apply the new manner of acting and thinking within the occupied area, carrying it forward through work and education, and thus suspending the logic of the free market and private interest.[96] Nevertheless, in the case of the cooperativists, this mechanism of immanent labor, built within the very social fabric, was combined with faith in the transgressive strength of cooperation, the even messianic nature of its mission. Thus, in the same movement with pragmatists who were guided primarily by the ideal of grassroots work and the slow expansion of cooperative resources, such as Fr. Franciszek Adamski, Franciszek Stefczyk, Edward Milewski, or Stanisław Wojciechowski, could also be found revolutionary communists on the order of Jan Hempel or Bolesław Bierut, anarchist-leaning thinkers such as Jan Wolski or Maria Orsetti, and figures who inspired everyone but are difficult to classify, such as Edward Abramowski. Among them were also representatives of the most varied milieus and political doctrines—particularly socialists, but also anarcho-syndicalists, Christian democrats, communists, and even adherents of liberal economics, such as Edward Taylor. Cooperativism appeared thus as a

---

95   A. Świętochowski, *Utopie w rozwoju historycznym* [*Utopia in Historical Development*], Warsaw 1910, Gebethner i Wolff, p. 148.

96   "Every food cooperative that arises, every farmers' club, every common dairy, factory, bakery, etc., founded by an association—these are already the beginning of a new social system, its real, strong, true entry into our lives. The desired world of social justice, the world of fraternity and commonality, is not hidden in the mists of the distant future but is among us, within grasp, and can be established in every village, every factory settlement, every town" (E. Abramowski, *Kooperatywa jako sprawa wyzwolenia ludu pracującego* [*The Cooperative as a Matter of Freeing Working People*], op. cit., p. 162).

cross-divisional phenomenon, a kind of meta-doctrine linking the most varied groups and views in the hope of a better social world through the activities of cooperatives. This hope, as I showed at the beginning of this text, resulted from the dreams of "modern" people about the world, which through scientific knowledge and innovative social instruments can be ordered according to the laws of nature and reason. Their validity is nevertheless expressed only in the deeds and activity of the conscious subject. Cooperativism is thus an element—to use Jean-François Lyotard's by now classic definition—of a great modern narrative, and such narratives

> ...in contrast to myths, do not see validity in an original founding act, but in hope for the future, that is, in a certain idea awaiting realization. This idea (of freedom, "enlightenment," socialism, etc.) has a legitimizing value because it is universal. It organizes all layers of the human condition. It gives modernity its characteristic modality: that is the plan [...]⁹⁷

Cooperativism grew out of such a large project of modernity, founded both on utopian dreams and on a positivist program of deliberate familiarization with society in order to reshape it. Thus, in this sense it is one of the ideas that strode shoulder to shoulder through the nineteenth and twentieth centuries with the great political, scientific, and economic narratives. As such, it contains an integral element of utopia and yet it should not be treated exclusively as a beautiful but unrealizable dream. It should not be thought that the cooperativist utopia remained solely in the normative sphere, and, having nothing in common even with bringing about cooperatives or specific politics, could serve solely for appraising actualities. Every political idea contains a kind of utopian vector, placing the perfect world (even if this signifies the status quo) in the future, the past, or outside or inside society. In Ernst Bloch's terms, even the smallest "trace" of utopia, present on the margins of every political doctrine, sets political thought in motion and gives it the force to influence real decisions concerning the community.

> *Utopicum* is thus created for man, as a being desiring to change, a being to whom the world is given as potentiality, as a great δυνάμειον, existing according to the measures of possibility.⁹⁸

---

97   J.-F. Lyotard, *Postmodernizm dla dzieci. Korespondencja 1982–1985* [*Post-Modern Explained for Children: Correspondence, 1982–85*], translated by J. Migasiński, Warsaw 1998, Aletheia Foundation, p. 30. Translated from the Polish—Tr.

98   E. Bloch, "*Rzeczywistość antycypowana*" ["Anticipated Reality"], translated by A. Czajka, *Studia Filozoficzne* [*Philosophical Studies*] 1982, no. 7–8, p. 53.

The ideal of fraternity formulated by Abramowski, though far from political realism, contains all the components necessary to recognize it as a product of the modernist project of rebuilding the human world: in it, a philosophy concentrated on dynamism and intuitive understanding combines with a positive vision of the social sciences, particularly with psychology; metaphysical expectations as to the place of man in the evolution of the universe combine with a sober critique of all-encompassing projects for rebuilding society (for instance, criticism of the communist state and the dictatorship of the proletariat). Seeing in Abramowski's ideal of brotherhood a forerunner of Solidarity, Wojciech Giełżyński wrote about it thus:

It is a utopia. It is a myth. Yes, but a beautiful myth and utopia, which still defines human longing; an attainable utopia, since history creates solely people, and not some kind of independent historical laws.[99]

In this connection, utopia is not solely an ideal model, or worse, an aberration, or in the best case, a naïve or innocent longing for a better world. The utopia of cooperation appears rather as the principle of a "new political activity" going beyond the old methods of affirming or rejecting capitalism; it reflects a desire to develop the heritage of modern citizenship and democracy but at the same time to seek new forms of cooperation, based on ever more universal and inclusive values: thus the importance of the subject of universal cooperation—the consumer (treated as either a national or general figure).[100]

---

99 W. Giełżyński, *Edward Abramowski—zwiastun "Solidarności"* [*Edward Abramowski—A Forerunner of Solidarity*], London 1986, Polonia Book Fund, p. 56.

100 See the words of Andrzej Walicki, who in stating that the meaning of the word "utopia" is not limited solely to the narrow sphere of fantasy—is not reserved for a certain type of literary work—recognized the concept as a specific form of worldview: "It is related to a worldview by its all encompassing nature—great social utopias define a whole style of thinking; they open a complete new cognitive perspective; they give sense to history" (A. Walicki, *W kręgu konserwatywnej utopii. Struktura i przemiany rosyjskiego słowianofilstwa* [*In the Sphere of the Conservative Utopia: The Structure and Transformation of Russian Slavophilism*], Warsaw 2002, Wydawnictwo Naukowe PWN, p. 5). In the Polish context, the cooperativist utopia is linked with the viewpoint of a generation of writers, activists, and revolutionaries for whom the sense of history was contained in an uncompromising struggle for the dignity of man, the member of the community. We might risk the theory that that generation or group of people initiated the progressive Polish intelligentsia of the twentieth century: humanists cultivating a special "leftist ethos" (to use Andrzej Mencwel's description), which defined both the political and intellectual ways of thinking of many members of postwar intellectual circles—one example here would be Leszek Kołakowski, whose father was Jerzy Kołakowski (pseudonym Jerzy Karon), a theoretician, activist, and popularizer of cooperatives (cf. A. Duszyk,

If cooperativism is utopian, then it is a quite pragmatic utopia, whose guiding idea is the promise of hard work founded on the very basic fact of socialization. Consumer cooperatives, as elementary unions of cooperation, are essential starting points in the struggle for a better society and democracy, because in them individual initiative and social possibilities are most fully united; they are capable "of producing changes in the external world, of moving from the subjective to the objective field, of self-realization."[101] A cooperative is thus action, becoming, within which the discord between the idea and its realization is each time invalidated, because a cooperativist, as Abramowski wrote,

> not only speaks of a new social system, of a better and more just world, but is building that world [...] The desired world of social justice, the world of fraternity and community, is not hidden in the obscurity of a distant future, but is among us, is for the taking [...][102]

Every act, every activity of the community, opens a space for the appearance of a new identity, a new communal experience, a new awareness of "togetherness," exceeding previously known modes of co-existence.

E. Kołodziej, *"Historia radomskiej kooperacji 1869–1939,"* *Biuletyn Kwartalny Radomskiego Towarzystwa Naukowego* ["History of Cooperation in Radom 1869–1939," *Quarterly Bulletin of the Radom Scholarly Society* 2009, vol. 43, Section. 3, pp. 91–92). The historical continuity—unbroken in spite of the upheavals of the two world wars—between the critical intelligentsia milieus of partition times and the postwar intelligentsia (an important stage in the formation of the democratic opposition in the Polish People's Republic) constitutes one of the paths by which Polish cooperativism reached our times, without becoming a defunct idea but rather part of the cultural heritage of Polish democracy.

101   E. Abramowski, *Metafizyka doświadczalna* [*Experiential Metaphysics*], op. cit., p. 582.
102   E. Abramowski, *Kooperatywa jako sprawa wyzwolenia ludu pracującego* [*The Cooperative as a Matter of Freeing Working People*], op. cit., p. 162.

CHAPTER 2

From Self-Help to the Vision of New System: An Outline of the Material and Ideological Development of the Cooperative Movement in Poland to the Year 1939

Remigiusz Okraska

In Poland, initiatives based on group work and solidarity date back to the fifteenth to seventeenth centuries—there were, for instance, miners' fraternal or *Gewerkschaft* funds, as well as fishermen's companies. Community savings funds, fire insurance and granaries emerged in the eighteenth century. In 1816 (formally five years later) Stanisław Staszic opened the Hrubieszowskie Farmers' Society in the Zamość area (also known as the Farmers' Society for Mutual Rescue in Misfortune). This was the original system for the collective management of farming land and facilities (mills, granaries, fish ponds), for mutual savings (the Society's bank), and social aid.[1]

These initiatives departed, however, from the principles that modern cooperativism is based on. Such principles are, *inter alia*, a democratic and egalitarian mechanism for making decisions (every member of a cooperative has one and only one vote at the general assembly, regardless of number of shares bought); openness and universality (lack or unimportance of obstacles to joining the cooperative); self-help and dependence on one's own forces (the cooperative should be based on funds collected from the mass of members and on effective management of this capital); pro-social nature (cooperatives serve to improve the condition of the economically weakest classes); awareness of social role of cooperativism, and the related principle of dividing profits (allocating part for propagation of cooperativism ideals, cultural and educational activities, various forms of support for social initiatives, etc.).

The beginnings of the modern cooperative movement in Poland coincided with the period of the partitions. This left a strong mark on the movement's doctrine and on profile of its activity.

---

1 See: Z. Chyra-Rolicz, *Stanisław Staszic prekursor spółdzielczości rolniczej* [*Stanisław Staszic: Precursor of Agricultural Cooperativism*], Siedlce 2004, Instytut Historii Akademii Podlaskiej; H. Brodowska, *Towarzystwo Rolnicze Hrubieszowskie* [*The Hrubieszowskie Farmers' Society*], Warsaw 1956, Ludowa Spółdzielnia Wydawnicza.

It was Prussian partition where modern cooperative movement began the earliest, thanks to the freedom to associate which was acquired in 1848."[2] In the 1870s, inspired by Maksymilian Jackowski and the Central Farming Society, the beginnings of the farmers' club movement emerged in Greater Poland, Kujawy, and Kociew. The farmers' clubs pooled crops, making it possible to obtain higher sales prices; they acquired machines and equipment that were quite expensive for individual farms and hired them out according to need; they acquired products necessary for farming (fertilizers, seeds, coal, etc.) in wholesale amounts; and collectively insured the club members. They also conducted educational activities in the field of agriculture, hygiene, building, etc. In 1900 there were already 210 farmers' clubs in Greater Poland, Kujawy, and Pomerania; twelve years later there were nearly 400.[3] At the end of 1912, more than 14,000 farmers within the territory of the Grand Duchy of Posen (Poznań) alone were members of such clubs.[4]

The savings and loan cooperative movement was born in this same period. It furthered the development of crafts and farming, thanks to inexpensive, non-usurious loan for economic purposes. 38 Polish credit companies[5] had emerged by the year 1871—their development was so rapid that the representatives of 19 of them decided to create a central institution, the Union of Polish Labor Companies, for the movement. The initiative was in its infancy when it was given impetus by Fr. Augustyn Szamarzewski, who was chosen to be the patron (director) of the Union at the beginning of 1872. Fr. Szamarzewski was strongly inspired by the work of Schulze-Delitzsch, the pioneer of credit cooperativism in Germany. The leading role played by priests in the development of the

---

2 S. Wojciechowski, *Historia spółdzielczości polskiej do 1914 roku* [*The History of Polish Cooperativism to 1914*], Warsaw 1939, Spółdzielczy Instytut Naukowy, p. 25.

3 *Księga Pamiątkowa Związku Poznańskich Kółek Rolniczych wydana w sześćdziesiątą rocznicę założenia pierwszego kółka rolniczego w Wielkopolsce: 1866–1926* [*Yearbook of the Union of Poznań Farmers' Clubs, Issued on the 60th Anniversary of the Founding of the First Farmers' Club in Greater Poland: 1866–1926*], Poznań 1926, Związek Poznańskich Kółek Rolniczych, pp. 24–27.

4 *Rocznik Kółek Rolniczo-Włościańskich w Wielkim Księstwie Poznańskim* [*Yearbook of the Farming and Rural Clubs in the Grand Duchy of Poznań*], Poznań 1913, no. 39, p. 443.

5 W. Tomaszewski, *Pół wieku polskich spółek zarobkowych i gospodarczych w W. Ks. Poznańskiem, Prusach Zachodnich i na Gornym Śląsku. Ich powstanie, rozwój i organizacja od r. 1861–1910* [*Half a Century of Polish Labor and Farming Companies in the Grand Duchy of Poznań, Western Prussian, and Upper Silesia: Their Emergence, Development, and Organization from 1861–1910*], vol. 1, Poznań 1912, author's edition, p. 25.

movement in the Prussian partitions helped to overcome fears of rural people. At the same time, the idea of savings was propagated and the significance of cooperation among the weaker classes was emphasized. The program, as described some years later, was down-to-earth and realistic:

> The social question will neither be eliminated by even the largest possible number of savings and loan banks, nor by savings deposits themselves—this is certain. But the formation of a savings and loan bank could contribute to [...] stimulating the desire to save, the idea of savings among those who previously wasted more than one cent unnecessarily.[6]

In 1890 the Union of Labor and Farming Companies—as the association of Polish credit cooperatives in the Prussian partition was ultimately named—brought together 71 cooperatives, with the combined number of 26,553 members, which with family members made much about 100,000 persons.[7] The Union opened a bank, began to publish the biweekly *Social-Economic Movement*, and issued instructive and popularizing publications. In 1891, after the death of Szamarzewski, the organization was headed by Fr. Piotr Wawrzyniak who emphasized planned development of the movement and its expansion in areas without cooperative outlets. After nine years of such activity, almost 40 new cooperatives had emerged, and the number of members had grown by nearly 50,000.[8] When Wawrzyniak died in 1910, the leadership was taken by Fr. Stanisław Adamski. After around five years of his activities, there were over 200 people's banks, and there was one such cooperative for every 10,000 of the Polish population in Greater Poland.[9]

Other forms of Polish cooperativism in the Prussian partition had similar aims. There were parcellation companies (land banks) and the "Farmers' Cooperatives." Both types of cooperatives were connected organizationally and financially with the savings and loan cooperatives. The aim of the former was to compete with German colonization. "A company, acquiring a landed estate for parcellation, divides it into an appropriate number of parcels [...] The owners

---

6 Fr. S. Adamski, *Kasy oszczędności w obrębie towarzystw* [*Savings and Loan Banks in Societies*], Poznań 1904, Drukarnia i Księgarnia św. Wojciecha, p. 3.

7 S. Wojciechowski, *Historia spółdzielczości polskiej do 1914 roku* [*The History of Polish Cooperativism to the Year 1914*], op. cit., p. 49.

8 Ibidem, p. 66.

9 P. Spandowski, *Z praktyki spółek wielkopolskich. Cztery wykłady* [*The Practices of Greater Poland Companies: Four Lectures*], Poznań 1917, edition of the Związek Spółek Zarobkowych i Gospodarczych na Poznańskie i Prusy Zachodnie, p. 13.

of the parcels are entitled to repay the debt in installments of any amount."[10] From the middle of the 1890s to the outbreak of the war over 20 such entities were opened, with around 5,500 members.[11] The Farmers' Cooperatives, on the other hand, were trade cooperatives, usually emerging in connection with farmers' clubs for the purpose of selling farming materials and certain consumer items in a coordinated and modern manner. They began to be set up at the turn of the century. By the outbreak of the war, over 60 had been created, with nearly 10,000 members and continually increasing turnover.[12]

In addition to the cooperative movement in Greater Poland and Kujawy-Pomerania, there were similar initiatives in Upper Silesia. At the moment, the war began, 17 Polish savings and loan companies there had a combined total of around 13,000 members.[13] Nationalist activists and persons connected with the Church, including Karol Miarka and Adam Napieralski, editors of the *Catholic* journal, were also leaders and popularizers of cooperativism in the region. Polish consumer cooperatives were created in the 1870s on Miarka's initiative: in sum around 100 were established, although part of them quickly collapsed.[14]

When the war broke out, there were 297 Polish cooperatives of various kinds in the Prussian partition, with nearly 150,000 members.[15] To these should be added the number of Poles who were members of German cooperatives, particularly dairy ones.[16]

---

10   W. Bzowski, *Praca społeczno-gospodarcza wsi wielkopolskiej* [*Social-Economic Work in Greater Poland Villages*], 2nd ed., Warsaw 1921, s.n., pp. 20–21.

11   S. Wojciechowski, *Historia spółdzielczości polskiej do 1914 roku* [*The History of Polish Cooperativism to the Year 1914*], op. cit., p. 79.

12   S. Ochociński, *Podstawy i zasady wielkopolskiej spółdzielczości kredytowej do roku 1918* [*Bases and Principles of Greater Poland Credit Cooperativism to the Year 1918*], Poznań 1965, PWN, p. 123, tab. 7.

13   13 H. Tomiczek, *Spółdzielczość na Górnym Śląsku do 1922 roku. Przyczynek do historii spółdzielczości górnośląskiej* [*The Cooperative Movement in Upper Silesia to 1922: A Contribution to the History of the Cooperative Movement in Upper Silesia*], Opole 1967, 2nd ed., Instytut Śląski, p. 42.

14   Ibidem, pp. 33–34.

15   S. Wojciechowski, *Historia spółdzielczości polskiej do 1914 roku* [*The History of the Polish Cooperative Movement to the Year 1914*], op. cit., p. 97; S. Adamski, *Sprawozdanie Związku Spółek Zarobkowych i Gospodarczych na Poznańskie i Prusy Zachodnie za rok 1915* [*Report of the Union of Labor and Farming Companies in the Poznań and Western Prussian Areas for 1915*], part 3, Poznań 1916, Związek Spółek Zarobkowych i Gospodarczych na Poznańskie i Prusy Zachodnie, p. 62.

16   173 of such cooperatives appeared in the years 1880–1914 in the Polish lands of the Prussian partition. It is impossible to make a precise calculation, but several tens of percent

Given the conditions in the Prussian partition, it was found necessary to re-linquish one of the most important principles of cooperativism (while retaining the others), that is, the partial allocation of the profits for social purposes. Support for Polish cultural or educational initiatives risked retaliation or even delegalization by the Prussian authorities.[17] On the other hand, improving the lot of the poorest levels of society was strongly connected with concern for Poles as a national collective. Thus, the main aim of the Union was to create cooperatives adapted "either to the needs of defending the land, or the needs of maintaining the Polishness of cities."[18]

First, therefore, strong emphasis was placed on the principle of strength in unity. As a result, cooperative initiatives in the Prussian partition had a unified ideological profile not encountered in the other partitions[19] and almost all the cooperatives joined a central union. Nearly the whole of the Polish cooperative movement in the Prussian partition was concentrated in a few strongly connected institutions. Second, the leaders' interpretation of the movement in terms of national interest bore fruit in the almost complete relinquishment of creating consumer cooperative structures in competition with Polish commerce. The Farmers' Cooperatives were an exception; it was recognized that in the rural environment such outlets constituted more of a threat to private German trade than to Polish trade. But even in this case, it was argued in the spirit of the national interest that

---

of the members were Poles. See. S. Wrzosek, *Z historii spółdzielczości mleczarskiej w Polsce do 1939 roku. Problematyka ekonomiczna i organizacyjna* [*From the History of the Dairy Co-operative Movement in Poland to 1939: Economic and Organizational Issues*], Warsaw 1965, Zakład Wydawnictw CRS, p. 30.

17   S. Ochociński, *Podstawy i zasady wielkopolskiej spółdzielczości kredytowej do roku 1918* [*The Bases and Principles of the Greater Poland Credit Cooperative Movement to 1918*], op. cit., p. 136.

18   Cited after S. Wrzosek, *Z historii spółdzielczości mleczarskiej w Polsce do 1939 roku. Problematyka ekonomiczna i organizacyjna* [*From the History of the Dairy Cooperative Movement in Poland to 1939: Economic and Organizational Issues*], op. cit., p. 31.

19   This unity was raised to the rank of a leading principle: see Fr. S. Adamski, "*Ksiądz Piotr Wawrzyniak, wódz i krzewiciel żywotnych i zdobywczych sił społeczeństwa polskiego w dobie niewoli*" ["Fr. Piotr Wawrzyniak, Leader and Propagator of the Vital and Conquering Forces of Polish Society in the Time of Bondage," in: *Pamięci Króla Czynu. Z obchodu 25-lecia śmierci Ks. Patrona Piotra Wawrzyniaka w Poznaniu dnia 9 listopada 1935 r. i w Katowicach dnia 22 grudnia 1935 r.* [*In Memory of the King of Deeds: Commemorations of the 25th Anniversary of the Death of Patron Fr. Piotr Wawrzyniak, in Poznań, November 9, 1935, and in Katowice December 22, 1935*], Committee for the 25th Anniversary Commemoration of the Death of Patron Fr. Piotr Wawrzyniak, Poznań 1936, pp. 39–40.

In the time when the Farmers' Cooperatives emerged, scarcely two or three Polish firms were engaged in the agricultural trade [...] Our Farmers' Cooperatives teach people that it is possible to be a Pole and a good grain merchant at the same time. [...] And today, without exaggeration, it can be said that there is now major Polish grain commerce and, almost without exception, the people standing at its forefront went through the school of our Farmers' Cooperatives and their Union. In this manner, the Farmers' Cooperatives and the common agricultural work organized in them contributed to nationalizing the grain trade [...][20]

Consumer cooperatives developed only in Upper Silesia, where Polish merchants were few.

In our Silesia, around our little towns we have hundreds and thousands of merchants of various kinds who all live off the laborers and farmers, who maintain and feed the Polish population. [...] Go on to establish your own consumer companies! Show those centrist H-K-T-ers[21]* that it is not you who depend on them, but they do on you

—as an author popularizing cooperativism urged.[22]

The main current of the Polish cooperative movement in the Prussian partition should thus be defined as the cooperativism of smallholders. The movement mainly brought together farm owners, who constituted 60–70% of the total membership. Another dozen or more percent were craftsmen owning production real estate.[23] The remaining members were recruited among large landowners, clerics, the free professions, and merchants; around 10% were craftsmen bereft of workshops. It was a fully conscious choice. At the dawn of the movement, one of the founders stated that

---

20   Fr. S. Adamski, „Rolniki" a rolnictwo. Referat wygłoszony na jubileuszowym Sejmiku Związku Spółek Zarobkowych i Gospodarczych" ["The Farmers' Cooperatives and Agriculture: A Report Given on the Jubilee Assembly of the Union of Labor and Farming Companies"], Poznań 1922, edition of the Związku Spółdzielni Zarobkowych i Gospodarczych [Union of Labor and Farming Cooperatives], pp. 4–5.

21   * Members of the German Eastern Marches Society, from the names of the leaders: von Hansemann, Kennemann, and von Tiedemann—Tr.

22   J. Krzyżowski, O spółkach [On Companies], Katowice 1903, Górnoślązak, p. 12–13.

23   S. Ochociński, Podstawy i zasady wielkopolskiej spółdzielczości kredytowej do roku 1918 [The Bases and Principles of the Greater Poland Credit Cooperative Movement to the Year 1918], op. cit., p. 139, tab. 8.

They [the savings and loan companies—R.O.] are, without exaggeration, the anchor of salvation, the foundation of our emerging middle classes [...] They should be the channels drawing in every Polish cent that lies among us unused, in order to revitalize small industry, Polish work and entrepreneurship.[24]

Such attitudes were influenced by both the objective situation, that is, the social-economic structure of the region, and the doctrine of preserving the "Polish state of possession" in these lands.

In terms of ideology, national solidarity was combined with the expansion of Polishness through collective activity, organic work, and social-minded Catholicism, in the spirit of the *Rerum novarum* encyclical. Concern for the national community went along with the perception—typical of Catholic social thought of those times—of "great" capitalism as a menace to the community, to native production facilities, and the connected moral-cultural order. A system based on private property was considered desirable but needed to be supplemented by the economic self-help of the weaker classes. In 1875 in one of his reports Fr. Szamarzewski claimed that

Our world must work with small capital sums—restore itself to being, property, position, and importance [...] The whole difficulty of our position consists in that we must achieve, by our small change, the same goal that capitalists achieve with ease by their large resources [...][25]

The biographer of another leader of the movement wrote that

Polish companies in the Prussian partition are the triumph of financial self-help over usury; it is a stream of invigorating gold directed to farmers' fields, to the craftsmen's workshops, to the merchants' storehouses, to support those falling under the onslaught of the enemy in all estates [...][26]

---

24 M. Łyskowski, *"O zakładaniu u nas rozmaitych spółek ludowych. Rzecz powiedziana na Sejmiku Spółek Zarobkowych Polskich w Poznaniu roku 1876"* ["On the Founding Among Us of Various Folk Companies: A Speech to the Assembly of Polish Labor Companies in Poznań of 1876"], Poznań 1877, J.I. Kraszewski edition, p. 26.

25 Cited after: J. Kosik, *O spółkach Ks. Augustyna Szamarzewskiego pod zaborem pruskim w latach 1872–1891* [*On the Companies of Fr. Augustyn Szamarzewski in the Prussian Partition in the Years 1872–1891*], Wrocław 1992, Wydawnictwo Uniwersytetu Wrocławskiego, p. 28.

26 Fr. K. Zimmermann, *Ks. Patron Wawrzyniak* [*Fr. Patron Wawrzyniak*], Kraków 1911, author's edition, pp. 12–13.

In the Austrian partition, the Polish cooperative movement was somewhat different. The forms of activity were more varied and there was a lack of organizational and ideological-political unity. A considerable similarity, on the other hand, could be observed in the matter of aims—they were equally specific, practical and moderate.

The first cooperative initiatives were savings and loan banks in Galicia, as well as farmers' clubs. Their establishment was encouraged by the priest-politician Stanisław Stojałowski, who emboldened the peasants to social activeness. His activities resulted in the creation, in 1882, of the Society of Farmers' Clubs, which was composed of 30 clubs, mainly farmers' ones. The development of the organization was rapid. After a decade there were 825 clubs with nearly 35,000 members. In 1899, as the result of removing inactive members from the rolls, the number fell to 529 clubs with 26,000 members, but from that moment on the statistics and audits reflected the facts: at the end of 1913 there were 1,862 clubs united in the Society of Farmers' Clubs, with over 79,000 members.[27] They engaged in activities similar to those of their Greater Poland counterparts, although, as a result of the high margins of private trade, more emphasis was placed on the creation of their own shops with agricultural and farm products. In 1913 there were nearly 500 cooperative shops operating in connection with the clubs; as many shops were let to merchants again. Their prices were controlled; and there were also 86 wholesale warehouses.[28] The clubs were not uniform in political terms. Although the slogan of social and national solidarity was raised, the emancipation aims of the peasants resulted in conflicts between the Polish People's Party and conservative landowning circles, and then with the National Democrats.

The beginnings of savings and loan cooperativism in the Austrian partition date from the turn of the 1880s to 1890s. The first "advance-payment societies," which were based on the Schulze-Delitzsch model (a fairly large territorial reach, limited liability of the members), began to operate in Lwów and Kraków, achieving success that inspired similar initiatives. After a few years there were several dozens of them. In 1874 the Union of Labor and Farming Societies in Lwów was opened—the movement's first central

---

27   A. Gurnicz, *Kółka rolnicze w Galicji. Studium społeczno-ekonomiczne* [*Farmers' Clubs in Galicia: A Socio-Economic Study*], Warsaw 1967, Ludowa Spółdzielnia Wydawnicza, pp. 78 and 80.

28   S. Wojciechowski, *Historia spółdzielczości polskiej do 1914 roku* [*A History of the Polish Cooperative Movement to 1914*], op. cit., p. 139; A. Gurnicz, *Kółka rolnicze w Galicji. Studium społeczno-ekonomiczne* [*Farmers' Clubs in Galicia: A Socio-Economic Study*], op. cit., p. 275.

institution. At the beginning, the societies' members were craftsmen; before long there was an influx of farmers. In addition to the desire to provide self-help, an important factor was combating usury—a problem that was connected with strong Polish-Jewish antagonism. Expensive credit—which could even reach several hundred percent—prevented economic development, and not infrequently produced—or deepened—the debtor's abject poverty. The harmfulness of usury in the ethnic-religious context was emphasized not only by cooperativists connected with solidarist-nationalist milieus but also by those from the progressive-leftist camp.[29] Naturally, the poorer Jews also sought help in the cooperative movement. In 1901 Jewish cooperatives opened the General Union of Self-Help-Based Galician Labor and Farming Societies—also according to Schulze's model. It observed cooperative principles, promoted the struggle against usury, and criticized Jewish pseudo-cooperatives (called "little family banks"). At the end of 1912, it had 582 affiliated societies.[30]

The development of Polish advance-payment societies occurred as follows: after twenty years, the Lwów Union had 130 affiliated cooperatives with 136,000 members. Around 1905, only slightly larger number of companies had twice as many members. In 1912, there were already 235 companies, with nearly 350,000 members.[31] In that year, two-thirds were farmers; 13% were white-collar workers; not quite 9% were craftsmen; and over 6% were merchants and traders.[32] In addition, a quantity of societies existed that were not associated with the Union. Some of these were pseudo-cooperatives, hiding commercial activity

---

29   Cf. J. Bek, *"Polski Związek Stowarzyszeń Zarobkowych i Gospodarczych we Lwowie"* ["The Polish Union of Labor and Farming Societies in Lwów"], in: *Ruch współdzielczy na ziemiach polskich* [*The Cooperative Movement in Polish Lands*], Lwów 1916, edition of the *Czasopism dla Społek Rolniczych*, pp. 125–126. Bek was an ex-activist of the socialist movement and a collaborator of the cooperativist theorist E. Abramowski, who was inspired by leftist ideas.

30   *"Żydowskie stowarzyszenia na samopomocy oparte w Galicji"* ["Jewish Self-Help Associations in Galicia"] in: *Ruch współdzielczy na ziemiach polskich* [*The Cooperative Movement in Polish Lands*], op. cit., p. 213.

31   R. Witalec, *Spółdzielczość kredytowa systemu Schulzeego w Małopolsce w latach 1873–1939* [*Credit Cooperativism of the Schulze System in Lesser Poland in the Years 1873–1939*], Warsaw—Rzeszów 2008, Museum of the History of the Polish People's Movement—IPN. Commission for the Prosecution of Crimes Against the Polish Nation, p. 131, tab. 20.

32   *Polskie kooperatywy kredytowe i kasy oszczędności. Rozwój i stan obecny na obszarze ziem polskich* [*Polish Credit Cooperatives and Savings Banks: Development and Present State in the Polish Lands*], edited under the direction and with the collaboration of J. Michalski, Lwów 1914, main supply in Gubrynowicz i Syn Bookstore, p. 47.

behind lofty slogans, but there were also small local cooperatives. In 1912, there were 1,340 of them, with nearly 670,000 members.[33]

The Schulze model, which was based on relatively high member shares, proved viable among the rural population in comparatively wealthy Greater Poland. In poorer Galicia, many peasants remained outside the system of convenient credit. This was changed by the activity of Franciszek Stefczyk, who was connected with the farmers' clubs and grafted Friedrich Wilhelm Raiffeisen's model on Polish ground (small territorial reach—a commune or parish, symbolic share size, unpaid work of board members). First such cooperative emerged in 1890. After nearly a decade the so-called Patronat, the organizational centre of the movement, was opened. At the beginning it united around 60 cooperatives, with not quite 8,000 members, but after five years there were over 500 cooperatives and around 85,000 members. At the end of 1913 the Stefczyk Banks, as they were called, comprised nearly 1,400 cooperatives, with over 320,000 members. In 1909 over 90% of the shareholders of these cooperatives were farmers, and over 4% were craftsmen.[34]

The Patronat's care and support encompassed dairy cooperatives as well. Thanks to the organizational work and instruction of Zygmunt Chmielewski, this sector had also developed over the course of not quite a decade: in 1913 in the Austrian partition there were 73 dairy cooperatives, with 104 branches and over 14,000 members.[35] The Union of Labor and Farming Societies performed a similar role in regard to consumer cooperatives. Toward the end of 1912, the Union had 22 such cooperatives, with over 5,400 members. In addition, there were 69 unassociated cooperatives, including 45 belonging to labourers. Ordinarily cooperatives were based on milieus associated with the socialist movement. Toward the end of 1912, the union and unaffiliated cooperatives established the Unification of Consumer and Consumer-Production Societies, which entered the composition of the Union as an autonomous section. Jędrzej Moraczewski, an activist and socialist parliamentarian, was selected for a chairman.[36]

---

33   R. Witalec, *Spółdzielczość kredytowa systemu Schulzeego w Małopolsce w latach 1873–1939* [*Credit Cooperativism of the Schulze System in Lesser Poland in the Years 1873–1939*], op. cit., p. 151.

34   T. Kłapkowski, *Patronackie spółdzielnie rolnicze w Małopolsce* [*Patronat Agricultural Cooperatives in Lesser Poland*], Kraków 1927, Wydawnictwo Społdzielczego Instytutu Naukowego, pp. 131–132.

35   Ibidem, pp. 181–182.

36   E. Milewski, *"Stowarzyszenia spożywcze w Galicji"* ["Consumer Associations in Galicia"], in: *Ruch współdzielczy na ziemiach polskich* [*The Cooperative Movement in Polish Lands*], op. cit., pp. 177–181.

The range of the movement in the Austrian partition also included cooperatives connected with other milieus (among these there was the group of crafts-production associations, which in 1912 counted 31 cooperatives and over 2,500 members) and the cooperatives from Cieszyn Silesia and Zaolzie. Among the latter, the consumer cooperatives connected with the socialist movement were fairly dynamic (toward the end of 1911 there were 28, with over 8,000 members), and the local counterpart of the Stefczyk Bank also expanded (at the end of 1912, there were 12,500 members in 98 cooperatives).

On the eve of the First World War, the number of cooperatives in this partition was estimated to be over 2,000, with nearly 750,000 members.[37] In addition to the consumer cooperatives, which brought together wage labourers, it was possible as in Greater Poland to speak of a cooperative movement of the middle classes—with the difference that in Galicia smallholders were poorer on account of the fragmentation of land structure in agriculture and the miserable condition of the majority of the towns (crafts).[38]

In the ideological sphere there was also a similarity. The aims of cooperatives were formulated pragmatically and specifically: to improve the economic condition of the middle classes and to gather the capital necessary for the development of farms or workshops. The ideology of national solidarity was dominant, and the German-Polish antagonism known in Greater Poland was often replaced in Galicia by a similar attitude toward the Jewish population.[39]

In terms of ethics, thinking inspired by the Christian principle of neighbourly love dominated, for instance,

> Members of a company based on the principle of "strength in unity" will be bound by ever closer ties of brotherly love. How often has meanness been born in a peasant's heart and he has been overcome by helplessness on seeing that no one would extend a helping hand to him in his difficult situation? [...] When [...] he sees that wealthier people are entering the company, who do not themselves need help, and are contributing their

---

37 S. Wojciechowski, *Historia spółdzielczości polskiej do 1914 roku* [*The History of the Polish Cooperative Movement to the Year 1914*], op. cit., p. 162.

38 In 1912, the average sum of savings in cooperative banks in Galicia was almost three times lower than in the Prussian partition. The author's calculation on the basis of *Polskie kooperatywy kredytowe i kasy oszczędności. Rozwój i stan obecny na obszarze ziem polskich* [*Polish Credit Cooperatives and Savings and Loan Banks: Development and Present State in the Polish Lands*], op. cit., p. 101, tab. XIV.

39 Cf. for instance, Fr. W. Owoc, *Rzut oka na kasy systemu Raiffeisena* [*A Glance at the Raiffeisen Credit Union System*], Rzeszów 1898, author's edition.

coins to the company only in order to save the economically weaker and poorer, he will be convinced that it is not solely self-love that prevails in the world, but that an active love of one's neighbour still has its place.[40]

The most meritorious activist of the Galician cooperative movement, Franciszek Stefczyk, accepted the capitalist, free-market system. Among its faults, he listed individualism and egoism, whose remedy was supposed to be cooperativism.

In Stefczyk's vision, it should also counteract class antagonism, creating social harmony.[41] Concluding one of his essays, he stated that

we believe the Raiffeisen system [...] having been adopted in our country, will pave the way to the further spread in economic life of principles and ideas that are more in accord with the sense of civic and Christian duty than the doctrine still prevailing today, which, hiding under the beautiful slogans of freedom and equality, leaves the weakest persons at mercy and exploitation of the stronger and more cunning. A very strong movement has commenced against today's still dominant trend of political economics, which prevents any social or religious considerations from influencing the national economy, and which seeks and sanctifies individual interest and egoism. The humble mayor of Heddesdorf preceded it in deed by a few decades. The work he created is also a protest against the principles of the Manchester school [that is, economic liberalism— R.O.]; it is an expression of the economic harmony of man's activity with his social and religious obligations.[42]

Solely the consumer cooperative movement in Galicia was marked by different views. Their main exponent was Edward Milewski. He propagated consumer, production, and housing cooperatives, that is, those currents that best expressed the needs of wage labourers. Cooperativism for him was a path to egalitarian system in which the means of production and profits were

---

40   *O spółkach pożyczek i oszczędności systemu Raiffeisena* ["On the Raiffeisen System of Savings and Loan Companies"], in the *Głosy Katolickie* [*Catholic Voices*] series, no. 8, ed. 3, Kraków 1908, Wydawnictwo Apostolstwa Modlitwy, p. 27.

41   J. Skodlarski, *Franciszek Stefczyk (1861–1924). Pionier spółdzielczości kredytowej w Polsce* [*Franciszek Stefczyk (1861–1924), Pioneer of Credit Cooperativism in Poland*], Łódź 2010, Wydawnictwo UŁ, pp. 50 and 54.

42   F. Stefczyk, *O spółkach systemu Raiffeisena* [*On Companies of the Raiffeisen System*], Kraków 1890, G. Gebethner i Sp., p. 146.

socialized—gradually "bought out" by the masses organized in cooperatives. In contrast to Stefczyk, he viewed class conflict as an intrinsic element of capitalism, which could be eliminated by a change of system, introducing "social harmony" by abolishing exploitation.

> Cooperativism is the antithesis of capitalism; it raises the well being of the group, the level, the class, the whole. It contributes to an equal division of incomes. It protects the worker and the consumer from the exploitation of oligarchs. It frees society from the tyranny of the trust millionaires, the vampirism of the cartels. It serves to free the masses and the individual,

he claimed in 1910.[43] Milewski's views were the exception in Galicia, though, and he had few followers. Nevertheless, his ideas were close to those of the main current of cooperativism in the Russian partition.

The cooperative movement in the Kingdom of Poland developed last. This resulted from the political situation—the lack of civil liberties was accompanied by bureaucracy and suspicion of all Polish initiatives. Authorization of a cooperative could take as much as several years, during which the political police would analyze the "orthodoxy" of the founders, and formalities were handled by civil servants in St. Petersburg. The result was the negligible development of the cooperative movement. In 1869 the first consumer cooperative arose; a few more emerged in later years. Nearly all of them vegetated, not finding support in the movement of similar initiatives.

The situation changed at the turn of the century. Economic development forced administrative changes in the question of savings and loan cooperatives, and the revolution of 1905 brought political liberalization, including the law on associations of 1906. This made it possible for the movement to develop broadly and rapidly. The situation was facilitated by three phenomena: the earlier theoretical and popularizing preparations (numerous articles in the economic and popular press, brochures, lectures, etc.); sympathy for the idea of cooperativism among the intelligentsia engaged in social issues; and, paradoxically, the movement's late beginnings, which allowed it to learn from the mistakes of others.

In 1903 there were already 28 mutual savings and loan associations of the Schulze system, with nearly 20,000 members. A decade later there were 95

---

43 E. Milewski, *Sklepy społeczne (rzecz o kooperacji spożywców)* [*Social Shops (On Consumer Cooperativism)*], ed. 2, Warsaw 1930, Związek Spółdzielni Spożywców Rz. P., p. 139.

associations, with around 50,000 members.[44] At the same time, the banks of the Raiffeisen system were developing: in 1903 there were 99 savings and loan associations, with over 60,000 members, and in 1911 there were 315, with 260,000 members, and also, respectively for those years, 13 and 38 credit associations, with 8,000 and nearly 50,000 members.[45] The total number of members of savings and loan cooperatives amounted to nearly 550,000 at the end of 1912.[46] In 1910 a central financial institution of the movement, the Cooperative Associations' Bank, was established.

Agricultural cooperativism had an entirely different genesis. In the autumn of 1904 the illegal Polish People's Union was established, combining demands for independence with a program of emancipation for the peasant class and the call for radical social reform. Its main ideologue was Edward Abramowski, a former activist of the socialist movement. He expressed the idea that social revolution, if it is to succeed, must be preceded by a moral revolution, a transformation of the system of values and ethical norms, and the best practical path to the emergence of a new type of person was collective action, active self-help, and solidarity.[47] Under his influence, in January 1906 the first congress of the PPU adopted the principle of indicating cooperativism (credit, trade, and production cooperativism) as the desired economic organizational form for the peasant stratum.

The "Draft Program of the Polish People's Union" also announced that:

The transformation of the entire country into such a cooperative republic is the basic aim of the people's party; in order to attain this goal, it will strive not through bureaucratic reform, imposed from above, but by independently reforming society through the method of cooperativism in all areas of culture and the social economy.[48]

---

44 *Polskie kooperatywy kredytowe i kasy oszczędności. Rozwój i stan obecny na obszarze ziem polskich* [*Polish Credit Cooperatives and Savings and Loan Banks: Development and Present State in the Polish Lands*], op. cit., p. 82, tab. x.

45 Ibidem, pp. 85–86, tab. xi and xii.

46 Ibidem, p. 93, tab. xiii.

47 E. Abramowski, "*Socjalizm a państwo. Przyczynek do krytyki współczesnego socjalizmu*" ["Socialism and the State: A Contribution to a Critique of Modern Socialism"], in: idem, *Pisma* [*Writings*] vol. 2, ed. K. Krzeczkowski, Warsaw 1924, Związek Spółdzielni Spożywcow Rzeczypospolitej, particularly pp. 326–345.

48 "*Projekt programu Polskiego Związku Ludowego*" ["The Draft Program of the Polish People's Union"], in: J.S. Brzeziński, *Polski Związek Ludowy. Materiały i dokumenty* [*The Polish People's Union: Materials and Documents*], Warsaw 1957, selected and with an introduction by Czesław Wycech, Ludowa Spółdzielnia Wydawnicza, p. 243.

These ideas were developed in two of Abramowski's popular brochures: "A General Conspiracy Against the Government" and "Our Policy." In the second one, the author advocates "economic companies," that is, farming cooperatives of a trade, processing, and production character; the development of consumer cooperativism for the whole population; and also savings and loan companies.[49]

This program was accompanied by invigorated activity among the rural people, who, in spite of obstacles, had managed to establish 40 farming cooperatives by 1904.[50] Although the Polish People's Union was broken up by the police, there was no way to hold back the activeness of the rural people. After liberalization of the regulations on associations, the Central Agricultural Society, which was dominated by landowners, began to support the formation of farmers' clubs. Part of the radically oriented peasants, who came chiefly from the Polish People's Union, established the independent Stanisław Staszic Association of Farmers' Clubs. The Central Agricultural Society's program was one of national solidarity, and for it the clubs were only one form of improving agricultural and rural areas, while the Staszic Association stressed the necessity of emancipating the peasant class and treated cooperativism as a method for far-reaching systemic transformation in the spirit of social justice. The form of activity of both organizations was similar to that in other partitions. By the outbreak of the First World War over 1,200 clubs, with around 60,000 members, had been established under the Central Agricultural Society's patronage, and there were nearly 140 "Staszic" clubs, with over 6,000 members.[51] The Staszic clubs conducted considerably more non-economic activities, that is, educational, cultural, and so on.[52] This was accompanied by an ideology which the people's journal *Zaranie* [*Dawn*] expressed through the slogan "by ourselves," meaning self-help and solidary cooperation while working on emancipating the peasant class. Cooperativism was treated as a key method in this process, and considerable space was devoted to its promotion in the pages of the journal (including contributions from the pen of the later well-known writer, Maria Dąbrowska).[53]

---

49 E. Abramowski, *"Nasza polityka"* ["Our Politics"], in: idem, *Pisma publicystyczne w sprawach robotniczych i chłopskich* [*Journalism on Labor and Peasant Affairs*], "Społem" Warsaw 1938, Związek Spółdzielni Spożywcow R.P., pp. 266–267.

50 J. Bartyś, *Kółka rolnicze w Królestwie Polskim* [*Farmers' Clubs in the Kingdom of Poland*], Warsaw 1974, Ludowa Spółdzielnia Wydawnicza, p. 49.

51 Ibidem, pp. 64–65.

52 M. Malinowski, *Chłopski ruch zaraniarski w b. Kongresowce przed pierwszą wojną światową* [*The "Dawn" Peasant Movement in the Former Congress Kingdom before the First World War*], ed. 2, Warsaw 1948, Spółdzielnia Wydawnicza Chłopski Świat, pp. 59–70.

53 W. Piątkowski, *Dzieje ruchu zaraniarskiego* [*History of the "Dawn" Peasant Movement*], Warsaw 1956, Ludowa Spółdzielnia Wydawnicza, pp. 79–88.

These initiatives came from a broader ideological and political camp which included the leaders of emancipatory initiatives among the rural and local people and members of the leftist intelligentsia. A number of the leaders were former activists of the Polish Socialist Party who had grown disappointed with political and party methods. In 1905, the Union of Social Self-Help Societies emerged in Warsaw with the participation of Abramowski, among others. In contrast to political activity, the Union offered "culturality," a grassroots trans-formation concerning both the "bases" and the "superstructure" in the spirit of the above-mentioned concept of moral revolution.[54] On Abramowski's initia-tive, a cooperativists' section was established in connection with the Union; the section was transformed into the independent Cooperativists' Society shortly afterwards. Its aim was to promote the principles of cooperativism and to aid others with cooperative initiatives. The broader goal was not lost from sight. According to an announcement of the organization's establishment:[55]

> The society approaches cooperativism from three angles: 1) as a training ground for the people in socio-political terms, where they can learn the bases of democracy—the ability to manage themselves and the collective resolution of their affairs in order to free the nation from bureaucratic and government oversight; 2) as a social institution capable of raising the material well-being and intellectual culture of the people; 3) as a passage to a higher economic system based on the principles of commonality and social justice

In 1906, the Society began publication of the journal *Spotem!*, which propa-gated cooperative ideals (the title was thought up by Stefan Żeromski); it orga-nized lectures and courses, and published books and brochures, including the most popular text in Poland that propagated cooperativism—Abramowski's *The Social Idea of Cooperativism*. Consumer cooperatives in particular were much more often considered to be the most universal and devoid of barriers. Every person is a consumer, even a person who does not have a workshop, sav-ings or other assets. Consumer cooperativism was also, in the opinion of the Society's founders, the most effective in terms of transforming the system.

---

54   H. Radlińska, *"Związek Towarzystw Samopomocy Społecznej"* ["The Union of Social Self-Help Societies"], in: Ibidem, *Pisma pedagogiczne [Pedagogical Writings]*, vol. 3: *Z dziejow pracy społecznej i oświatowej [From the History of Social and Educational Work]*, Wrocław 1964, Zakład Narodowy im. Ossolińskich, pp. 305–313.

55   Cited after: *"Aneks,"* ["Annex"] in: F. Dąbrowski, *Historia Towarzystwa Kooperatystow [History of the Cooperativists' Society]*, Warsaw 1931, Towarzystwo Kooperatystow, p. 48.

The capitalist system, with its miraculous technique and fantastic trade organization, appears to be an invincible fortress. And yet in that fortress, where it appears to be armored, an unprotected point is found [...]. The weak side of capitalism, that makes it possible to overthrow, is sales. [...] If the profit of capital is realized through sales, it ensues that in the capitalist system the master of the situation is the recipient of goods—the consumer. [...] Nominally the master of the situation, he is the plaything of capital, because he is not part of an organization. But from the moment when he understands his strength and wants to organize with others, from being the servant he becomes the actual master of capital,

wrote one of the leaders of the movement a decade later.[56]

The Society quickly became the organizational backing for the consumer cooperative movement. In autumn 1908 a congress of consumer cooperatives was called, where the Information Office of the Consumer Associations of the Cooperativists' Society was formed. Romuald Mielczarski and Stanisław Wojciechowski were chosen for secretaries of the Office. After a year and a half of waiting for the authorities' permission, at the beginning of 1911, the Warsaw Union of Consumer Associations was established and joined by cooperatives from all over the partition. On the eve of the First World War, the Union counted over 40,000 members in nearly 300 cooperatives. In addition, quite a few unaffiliated cooperatives were operating. In total, there were then around 1,200 consumer cooperatives with 140,000 members.[57]

Dairy cooperativism also developed, due, among other things, to the arrival from Galicia of Zygmunt Chmielewski, who was an instructor at the Central Agricultural Society. From 1910 several dozens of cooperatives were established annually, and at the outbreak of the First World War, there were over 200 dairy cooperatives with around 10,000 members.[58]

According to estimates, at the start of the war the entire cooperative movement in the Russian partition comprised over 1,400 cooperatives, with around 680,000 members.[59] This was a broad movement in intellectual terms,

56   R. Mielczarski, *"Cel i zadania stowarzyszenia spożywcow"* ["The Aims and Tasks of Consumer Associations"], in: idem, *Pisma* [*Writings*], vol. 2, selected and edited by K. Krzeczkowski, Warsaw 1936, Związek Polskich Stowarzyszeń Spożywcow R.P., pp. 225–226.

57   A. Światło, *Polska spółdzielczość spożywcow w latach 1869–1925* [*The Polish Cooperative Movement in the Years 1869–1925*], Warsaw 1972, Zakład Wydawnictw CRS, p. 36.

58   J. Bartyś, *Kółka rolnicze w Królestwie Polskim* [*Farmers' Clubs in the Kingdom of Poland*], op. cit., pp. 321–327.

59   S. Wojciechowski, *Historia spółdzielczości polskiej do 1914 roku* [*The History of the Polish Cooperative Movement to the Year 1914*], op. cit., p. 252.

politically varied, and boldly formulating aims of a systemic nature. Its most
active part was the milieu of a leftist-progressive provenance, where even adherents of Marxism (Ludwik Krzywicki,[60] for example) could be encountered.
Egalitarian and civic ideas were strong in that milieu and attention was paid
to the disadvantaged situation of groups deprived of rights for non-economic
reasons, for instance, women.[61] In the question of usury or the role of private
trade, the role of the Jewish population was much less emphasized, while the
backward economic structure and harmful role of intermediaries as such was
stressed. Cooperativism was promoted as an alternative, without ethnic or religious discord. In addition, the cooperative current also occupied an important
place in the activities of the National Labour Union, that is, a centrist-solidarist
group deriving from the National Democrats.

The National Democrats similarly did not avoid these kinds of ideas and
practical activities; one of the leading propagators and theoreticians of agricultural cooperativism was a well-known National Democrat activist, Stanisław
Grabski. The Christian Democrat current was also strongly represented; the
party's best known figure was Fr. Wacław Bliziński from Lisków near Kalisz.
Lisków was called the "cooperative village" because the poverty-stricken and
backward locality blossomed in a short period due to the consumer cooperatives, farmers' clubs, dairy cooperative, and mutual insurance society founded
there at the priest's initiative.[62]

The First World War was naturally painful for the cooperative movement
in organizational and economic terms, yet it did not harm the movement's
long-term growth. In the early days of Poland's independence, cooperativism

---

60   Ludwik Krzywicki, *"Kooperacja spożywców: podsumowanie"* ["The Consumer Cooperative
      Movement: Summary"], in: idem, *Stowarzyszenia spożywcze. Ustęp z dziejów kooperacji*
      [*Consumer Associations: A Passage in the History of the Cooperative Movement*], Warsaw
      1903, Nakładem Członków Stowarzyszenia Spożywczego Pracowników Kolei Żelaznej
      Warszawsko-Wiedeńskiej [Published by Members of the Warsaw-Vienna Railway Em-
      ployees' Consumer Association].

61   *Znaczenie kobiety w ruchu spółdzielczym* [*The Importance of Women in the Cooperative
      Movement*], Warszawski Związek Stowarzyszeń Spożywczych "Społem," Warsaw 1912
      (brochure); analogous tendencies in the Staszic Farmers' Clubs Society are described by
      J. Bartyś, *Kółka rolnicze w Krolestwie Polskim* [*Farmers' Clubs in the Kingdom of Poland*],
      op. cit., p. 131.

62   W. Karczewski, *Lisków. Dzieje jednej wsi polskiej* [*Lisków: The History of One Polish Village*]
      s.n., s.l., s.a., pp. 35–43, 55–59, 74–77; W. Bliziński, *"Działalność spółdzielni i organizacyj rol-
      niczych w Liskowie. Referat wygłoszony na Zjeździe Spółdzielni w Wilnie, w dniu 18 grudnia
      1927 roku"* ["Activity of Agricultural Cooperatives and Organizations in Lisków: A Report
      Delivered at the Cooperatives Congress in Wilno on December 18, 1927"], Warsaw 1928,
      Związek Rewizyjny Polskich Spółdzielni Rolniczych.

was already a strong and well-formed movement. The new conditions provided complete freedom to associate and propagate ideals. Leaving aside ideological differences and aims, the cooperative movement as a method of farm management enjoyed the support of many currents and political milieus in the reborn state: socialists, peasant party activists, Christian Democrats, part of the National Democrat and Piłsudski milieus, and not excluding even liberal economists, who considered this method of expanding the business activities and improving the economic conditions of the poorest classes to be worthy of recognition, and not in opposition to market mechanisms (open access to cooperatives, lack of state subsidies, etc.).[63] The cooperative movement enjoyed the support of the authorities and highest level civil servants. At the beginning of the 2nd Republic, the movement's well-known activists occupied high public positions (Stanisław Wojciechowski—president of the Republic; Zygmunt Chmielewski—minister of agriculture; Franciszek Stefczyk—director of the National Agricultural Bank and chairman of the Main Land Office; Józef Bek—undersecretary in the Ministry of the Interior and member of the Tribunal of State; Fr. Stanisław Adamski—adviser to Prime Minister Władysław Grabski on currency reform), or belonged to the academic elite (Zofia Daszyńska-Golińska, Ludwik Krzywicki), or cultural elite (Stefan Żeromski, Maria Dąbrowska); they were lecturers in leading institutions (the University of Warsaw, the Jagiellonian University, Warsaw School of Economics, the Main School of Rural Economy); they were members of the Sejm and Senate, and so forth. A large part of the political, social, cultural and academic elite of the 2nd Republic sympathized with the cooperative movement, while the intelligentsia, of varying ideological and political leanings, was particularly engaged socially.

The act on cooperatives had already been adopted by 1920; it carefully regulated the operating principles of this sector. The Cooperative Council also arose at the time. As the advisory institution connected with the Ministry of the Treasury, it was composed in two thirds by representatives of the cooperative movement. It supervised cooperatives that were not affiliated with any central institution. In 1929, at the initiative of the Ministry of Agriculture, the State School of Farming Cooperativism was established in Nałęczów.

The movement itself created institutions going beyond the economic and organizational sphere. In addition to the Cooperativists' Society, which continued its work, the Cooperative Scientific Institute was created in 1919 on

---

63   Cf. inter alia: E. Taylor, *Pojęcie współdzielczości* [*The Concept of Cooperativism*], Kraków 1916, Akademia Umiejętności; A. Krzyżanowski, *Związki rolników* [*Farmers' Unions*], Kraków 1905, s.n.

Stefczyk's initiative. This was an outlet for research and education, as well as for popularizing issues the cooperative unions had not touched. In ideological terms it was pluralist, bringing together people from various currents of the co-operative movement.[64] In 1935 the Cooperative Women's Guild was established in Poland, with the aim of propagating cooperativism among women who were underrepresented in the movement.[65] Beginning in 1925, Cooperativism Day was organized annually; its commemorations throughout the country were co-ordinated by a team of representatives of various central institutions. In 1923, the Trade Union of Cooperative Employees, which represented the interests of persons employed in cooperative outlets, was established (a decade later it had around 1,800 members and at the moment the Second World War erupted, it had 3,800).[66] In 1931, on the initiative of the Union of Consumer Cooperativ-ism, a Cooperative Secondary School was established in the capital. With the collaboration of various currents in the cooperative movement, more than ten educational institutions, whose programs covered specialist and ideological aspects of cooperativism, were operating in the second half of the 1930s.

The cooperative press in 1935 consisted of 6 weeklies, 6 biweeklies, 22 monthlies, and several publications that appeared less frequently. The annual print runs of these periodicals was over 1.7 million copies for the Polish coop-erative movement and around 700,000 copies of journals of the cooperative organizations of national minorities.[67] In 1936 alone, central consumer coop-erative institutions issued over 150,000 copies of popularizing non-periodical publications and sold around 115,000 copies of books and brochures propagat-ing cooperative issues.[68]

---

64   S. Surzycki, *Spółdzielczy Instytut Naukowy (dziesięciolecie istnienia 1919–1929)* [*The Coop-erative Scientific Institute (A Decade of Existence 1919–1929)*], Warsaw 1929, Wydawnictwo Społdzielczego Instytutu Naukowego.

65   Z. Chyra-Rolicz, "*Kobiety do spółdzielni. Liga Kooperatystek w Polsce 1935–1944*" ["Women to the Cooperatives: The Cooperative Women's Guild in Poland, 1935–1944"] *Nowy Obywa-tel* [*New Citizen*] 2011, no. 2.

66   *"Pracownik Spółdzielczy'—numer jubileuszowy, wydany z okazji dziesięciolecia istnie-nia Związku Zawodowego Pracownikow Społdzielczych Rzeczypospolitej Polskiej 1923–1933"* [*The Cooperative Employee—A Jubilee Issue on the Occasion of the First Decade of Existence of the Trade Union of Cooperative Employees*], Warsaw 1933; W. Rusiński, *Zarys historii pol-skiego ruchu spółdzielczego* [*Outline of the History of the Polish Cooperative Movement*], part 2: 1918–1939, Warsaw 1980, Zakład Wydawnictw CZSR, pp. 195–201.

67   W. Rusiński, *Zarys historii polskiego ruchu społdzielczego* [*An Outline of the History of the Polish Cooperative Movement*], op. cit., pp. 264–265.

68   *"Społem" Związek Społdzielni Spożywcow Rzeczypospolitej Polskiej, Statystyka spółdzielni związkowych za rok 1936* [*Społem Union Cooperatives Statistics for 1936*], Warsaw 1937, p. XXV.

Naturally, economic and organizational activity remained essential. Several basic tendencies can be discussed in this regard: 1) a two-stage process of consolidating the movement; 2) the comparatively large, although not homogenous, growth in the number of cooperatives, the member base, and other assets; 3) the development of cooperativism in other areas. These processes were accompanied, among other things, by quarrels and debates of ideological nature, crystallizing the identity of specific currents of cooperativism, and also drawing new social milieus into the orbit of the cooperative movement.

In the first years of independence 16 supervisory institutions—that is, the organizing centers of the cooperative movement—were functioning in Polish lands. This meant that the movement was fragmented, which was understandable given the partitions from the country's past, but harmful from both the ideological and practical viewpoints (fewer economic possibilities, higher costs, mutual competition).

At the beginning of 1924, three supervisory unions of the Schulze-system savings and loan cooperatives in all the former partitions united in an organization by the name of the Union of Cooperative Unions in Poland. It affiliated over 600,000 persons in 930 cooperatives. The member composition was varied; not quite half were farmers. The average amount of savings deposits shows that the Union's members were the wealthier part of the smallholder class. A few weeks later, six of the largest organizations of the Raiffeisen system established the Association of Agricultural Cooperatives' Unions. It brought together nearly 2,300 cooperatives with over 600,000 members. Nearly 90% of the members were farmers; most were smallholders.[69]

In both cases the unification had more to do with ideological milieus than with economics. Although the Union and the Association were dominated by savings and loan cooperatives, they had also been continuing the model of affiliating the regional farmers' clubs, rural trade cooperatives, dairy cooperatives, and so forth, in these central institutions from partition times. Initially, the consumer cooperatives began quite differently. The leaders of the Union of Polish Consumer Cooperatives strove to unite all consumer cooperatives in one central institution, but already by the spring of 1919 the Union of Labor Cooperative Associations, which also used the name Union of Labor Consumer Cooperatives, emerged. It was created on the inspiration of leftist milieus— the Polish People's Party, the communists, and smaller organizations.

The creators of "labor" cooperativism, which was also called "class cooperativism," criticized the existing central institution of consumer cooperatives

---

69   W. Rusiński, *Zarys historii polskiego ruchu spółdzielczego* [*An Outline of the Polish Cooperative Movement*], op. cit., pp. 38–40.

for its "petit bourgeois" character. The Union of Polish Consumer Cooperatives stood on "neutral" ideological ground. According to the accepted doctrine, these cooperatives were of a "universal" or "general" nature, as was often emphasized in their names. They were based on absence of barriers to joining. It was assumed that everyone who was a member of a cooperative and was making purchases there was contributing to the accomplishing of the Union's aims, that is, the replacement of capitalist economics and private ownership of the means of production by a slowly emerging "cooperative republic" (as this futuristic vision was called). For this reason, the "neutral" current avoided engagement in current politics, connections with parties, and the propagation of specific ideological or political currents.

The "classists," on the other hand, considered "universalism" as blurring the cooperative movement's identity and obscuring its social goals; in the economic dimension they considered it a manner of making cooperativism into an unimportant element of the free market economy. The Union's initial platform announced, among other things, that:

1.   Consumer cooperativism is a proletarian economic movement, creating an open association based on self-help and aiming to organize the whole social economy for the aims and needs of the working people.
2.   This movement is part of the great emancipating labor movement which aims to overthrow capitalism—abolition of wage labour, socialization of production, and exchanging the system's foundations for those of the socialist system [...]
3.   Consumer cooperativism, on account of its economic idealism, has nothing in common with agricultural associations of producers, nor with credit cooperatives, because they are based on the privilege of owning land or other means of production and display a clear tendency to transform into associations of larger or smaller capitalists.[70]

In practice this meant the expectation that cooperatives would stress ideas critical of the existing order, organizationally support other forms of activity of the labour movement, place strong emphasis on shaping the total worldview of members in the leftist spirit, and not accept persons from outside the working classes (and the unemployed).

---

70   *Jak powstał i czym jest Związek Robotniczych Stowarzyszeń Spółdzielczych* [*How the Union of Labor Cooperative Associations Arose and What it Is*], Warsaw 1919, Wydawnictwo Związku Robotniczych Stowarzyszeń Spółdzielczych, pp. 4–5.

What one side of the conflict considered an advantage, for the other was an attack on their declared principles. "Universality," for the Union of Polish Consumer Cooperatives signified the quicker realization of their intended purpose, and for the Union of Labor Consumer Cooperatives it was a form of concession toward the petit bourgeois and collaboration with the capitalist order. For the "classists" the strong ideological identity and cohesive worldview of the members was one of the main advantages of the movement, while from the viewpoint of the "neutralists" it meant breaking up the unity and effectiveness of consumer cooperativism. The "neutralists" also pointed out that the main accusation of the "classists" was dubious. At the height of the conflict they explained that

> In 1921, in the cooperatives belonging to "Społem," there were 248,621 members in total. Of these, the largest number were labourers—as many as 117,900, or 47.4% of the total; next were farmers (the vast majority of whom were smallholders or landless)—101,838 members, or 4%; and finally, there were the "others" (civil servants, members of the intelligentsia, petit bourgeois, "gentlemen," priests)—scarcely 28,883 members, or only 11.6%.[71]

At the beginning, the Union of Labor Consumer Cooperatives grew rapidly, having around 170,000 members at its peak (the Union of Polish Consumer Cooperatives then had around 350,000), but before long it fell into a crisis. Its members were poorer; it had a smaller territorial reach and less well-prepared specialists; and there was a conflict between the socialists and communists in the management. In 1924 the Union of Polish Consumer Cooperatives had member contributions of 1.7 million zlotys, while the Union of Labor Consumer Cooperatives had scarcely 41,000. The annual turnover in goods of the "neutralists" was over 20 million—of the "classists," not quite 2 million. The trade costs of the first were around 3.5% of turnover, and of the second 9.3%. After the communists were eliminated from the management of the Union of Labor Consumer Cooperatives, and as a result of the worsening condition of this central institution, at the turn of the year 1924 to 1925 unification talks were

---

71   J. Wolski, *O zjednoczenie ruchu spółdzielczego w Polsce* [*On Unifying the Cooperative Movement in Poland*], Warsaw 1923, Wydział Propagandy Związku Polskich Stowarzyszeń Spożywcow, p. 33. At the end of 1923, these proportions supported Wolski's argument even more strongly: laborers—52.6%, rural-farming population—44.5%, others—2.9%. See A. Światło, *Polska spółdzielczość spożywców w latach 1869–1925* [*Polish Consumer Cooperativism in the Years 1869–1925*], op. cit., p. 157, tab. 10.

held with the Union of Polish Consumer Cooperatives. On April 26, 1925 there took place a unifying congress of the three organizations: the Union of Polish Consumer Cooperatives (614 cooperatives and 308,000 members), the Union of Labour Consumer Cooperatives (114 cooperatives and 168,000 members), and the Central Union of State, Municipal, and Social Employee Cooperatives (44 cooperatives and 32,000 members). In this manner the Union of Consumer Cooperatives of the Republic of Poland was established. In 1926 the Central Union of Consumer Associations of Christian Labour Cooperatives also announced that it was joining; then an agreement of far-reaching cooperation with the Central Union of Army Cooperatives was concluded on the basis of autonomy. An enormous dynamic institution emerged, uniting over 850 associations and 550,000 members, and having 1,670 shops and 200 production facilities of varying sizes.[72]

In this manner, the previous "old" branch of the Polish cooperative movement became concentrated in three main organizational-economic institutions. In 1926 the only larger central institution aside from these was the Union of Construction Cooperatives;[73] however, before long it also entered the Union of Consumer Cooperatives of the Republic of Poland. Central cooperative institutions of national minorities (Ukrainian, Jewish and German) were also functioning. On January 1, 1926, the Union of Ukrainian Cooperatives in Lwów had 1,029 affiliated cooperatives (mainly agricultural and trade cooperatives); the Russian Union in Lwów had 94 credit cooperatives; 5 unions of cooperatives belonging to the German minority encompassed 864 cooperatives (including 598 credit cooperatives, 136 dairy and/or egg cooperatives, and 50 agricultural and trade cooperatives); and 2 Jewish unions had 598 cooperative entities (including 524 credit cooperatives).[74] There were still quite a few unaffiliated

---

72   For more on the conflict between the Union of Polish Consumer Cooperatives and the Union of Labor Consumer Cooperatives and its conclusions, see R. Okraska, *"Marzyciel i realista. Romuald Mielczarski i spółdzielczość spożywców w Polsce"* ["Dreamer and Realist: Romuald Mielczarski and Consumer Cooperativism in Poland"] in: R. Mielczarski, RAZEM! *Czyli Społem. Wybór pism spółdzielczych* [*TOGETHER! That is, Społem: Selected Writings on Cooperativism*], Łódź—Sopot—Warsaw 2010, Stowarzyszenie "Obywatele Obywatelom," pp. 154–162.

73   K. Weydlich, *Ruch spółdzielczy w Polsce w latach 1914–1926. Zagadnienia dotyczące współdziałania grup i typów spółdzielni oraz zmiany zaszłe w ustroju ruchu* [*The Cooperative Movement in Poland in the Years 1914–1926: Questions Concerning the Cooperation of Groups and Types of Cooperatives and the Changes That Have Occurred in the Movement's System*], Krakow—Poznań 1927, Spółdzielczy Instytut Naukowy, pp. 216–225.

74   F. Dąbrowski, *Spółdzielczość w Polsce* [*Cooperativism in Poland*], in: *Kalendarz spółdzielczy na rok 1927—Społem* [*Cooperative Calendar for 1927—Społem*], Warsaw 1927, edition of the Związku Spółdzielni Spożywców R.P., p. 114.

Polish and minority cooperatives. However, their percent in the total number of cooperatives had declined.[75]

To the end of the 1920s it was possible to speak of the developmental trend of the cooperative movement. The number of cooperatives grew. Usually the amount of turnover, shares, and other assets—for instance, real estate—and the number of members also increased (although in this question contrary trends could appear, particularly in regard to consumer cooperatives, where a fairly restrictive policy in regard to inactive members was conducted). In 1926 there were 3,684 consumer cooperatives in existence. Three years later there were 5,782, of which 2,460 and 3,755 respectively were in unions. The number of total members for these years was 774,489 and 814,749.[76] In 1925 there were 997 agricultural and trade cooperatives, and in 1928 there were 1,101. For the union cooperatives in this branch there were respectively 256 and 301 entities, with around 100,000 members in 1929.[77] In 1926 there were 788 union dairy cooperatives, and in 1929 there were 1,362, with 81,913 and 222,506 members respectively.[78] In 1925 there were 3,274 savings and loan cooperatives, and in 1929 there were 5,661. In 1929 the Union had 636 cooperatives of this type, with 492,000 members, and two years later it had 697 cooperatives with 567,000 members, while the Association had 2,274 cooperatives and 506,000 members and 2,775 with 707,000 of them.[79] At the end of 1927 there were 1,259 Stefczyk savings and loan banks alone, with 525,000 members.[80] The scale of their co-operative economic activity was significant: for instance, in 1927 Union, Association, and unaffiliated agricultural and trade cooperatives accounted for nearly 24% of the national turnover in fertilizer.[81]

---

75   In 1924 they were 43.1% of the total, by 1930 only 35.1%. After: W. Rusiński, *Zarys historii polskiego ruchu spółdzielczego* [*An Outline of the History of the Polish Cooperative Movement*], op. cit., p. 68.

76   Ibidem, p. 78.

77   E. Rudziński, T. Kłapkowski, "*Spółdzielczość rolnicza*" ["Agricultural Cooperativism"], in: *Pięć lat na froncie gospodarczym 1926–1931* [*Five Years on the Economic Front 1926–1931*], vol. 1, Warsaw 1931, Wydawnictwo Drogi, p. 198, tab. 3.

78   W. Rusiński, *Zarys historii polskiego ruchu spółdzielczego* [*An Outline of the History of the Polish Cooperative Movement*], op. cit., p. 105.

79   Ibidem, pp. 94–95.

80   *Zjednoczenie Związków Spółdzielni Rolniczych Rzeczypospolitej Polskiej na Powszechnej Wystawie Krajowej w Poznaniu* [*The Unification of Agricultural Cooperative Unions of the Republic of Poland at the General National Exhibition in Poznań*], May-September 1929, s.l. 1929, s.n.

81   F. Kędziorek, *Nurty społeczno-gospodarcze w polskim ruchu spółdzielczym w latach 1918–1939* [*Social-Economic Currents in the Polish Cooperative Movement in the Years 1918–1939*], Warsaw 1969, Zakład Wydawnictw CRS, p. 46, tab. 25.

In independent Poland cooperativism developed in other branches and milieus as well. In the second half of the 1920s, the central institutions of consumer cooperation and the Raiffeisen savings and loan system launched activities to promote and support student cooperativism, and in 1928 the Cooperative Section of the Union of Polish Teaching was established. Their efforts brought results. According to estimates, in 1936 there were around 4,700 student trade (consumer) cooperatives and around 2,000 school savings banks (having the nature of savings and loan cooperatives).[82] The development of housing cooperativism—both construction-investment and tenant-administrative types—was significant. At the end of 1922 there were 18 construction cooperatives and 72 housing cooperatives. Eight years later, careful estimates spoke of over 850 such associations.[83] These were usually not very large cooperatives, frequently involving a single building, but nevertheless the development of the movement was rapid. In 1929 a small part of all the cooperatives of this type—the 49 belonging to the Union of Consumer Cooperatives of the Republic of Poland—alone had over 6,000 members and around 5,200 housing premises.[84] One model initiative was the Warsaw Housing Cooperative which was established by leftist activists in 1921. It built settlements in Żoliborz and Rakowiec and in the mid-1930s not only provided a place of residence for over 5,000 people but was also a deliberate, holistic "organism." It made use of innovative, pro-social architectural and urban designs, the support of working class institutions (trade unions) and other cooperative branches (such as the Cooperative Construction Enterprise, which was established in 1928 in the form of the collective membership's cooperative and was involved in investment work on a large scale), extensive administration by the inhabitants, invigorated socio-cultural activity, and numerous forms of cooperative and self-help services for inhabitants, as well as the WHC milieus' participation in initiatives to reform housing in a pro-social spirit. Although this was a local cooperative, its example shone throughout the country, inspiring other initiatives. At the end of 1927 it had 345 members, and a little over a decade later there were 2,283.[85]

---

82   F. Dąbrowski, *Spółdzielnie uczniowskie* [*Student Cooperatives*], 2nd ed., expanded and supplemented, Warsaw 1936, Nasza Księgarnia, pp. 61–64.
83   W. Rusiński, *Zarys historii polskiego ruchu spółdzielczego* [*An Outline of the History of the Polish Cooperative Movement*], op. cit., p. 83.
84   Ibidem, p. 85.
85   *Sprawozdanie Warszawskiej Spółdzielni Mieszkaniowej za rok 1927* [*Report of the Warsaw Housing Cooperative for 1927*], Warsaw 1928, p. 5; *Warszawska Spółdzielnia Mieszkaniowa. Sprawozdanie z działalności w roku 1938* [*The Warsaw Housing Cooperative: Activity Report for 1938*], Warsaw 1939, p. 5.

Development processes were interrupted by the worldwide economic crisis which reached Poland at full strength in 1930. The result was collapse of entire economy, including cooperative enterprises. In many areas, cooperatives lost members, either because they left the cooperative or were crossed off the rolls due to lack of activity; member shares, savings deposits, and trade turnover decreased; and in the case of investment or production cooperatives, work collapsed and some of the enterprises failed.

Under pressure of the crisis many reforming activities were undertaken. As a result of pressure from the ruling Sanacja camp, changes were made in the organizational structures of Polish cooperativism. This resulted from the state's establishment of measures to make the cooperatives more effective in exchange for credit to overcome the effects of the crisis. The ruling camp wanted to have more influence on the cooperative movement and to connect it with the socio-economic policy of the state. Initially, the leaders of the cooperative movement were not willing to adopt the government propositions. The authorities retreated from the attempt at stronger interference in the movement's internal affairs, although they forced several new solutions through. The essential one among these was the gradual merger of the unifying bodies and putting order into the movement's structures, particularly on the basis of a kind of economic activity. In 1934 the Association, which had previously had a federalist structure, was centralized. At the beginning of 1935 the Union and Association merged in the Union of Agricultural and Farming-Labour Cooperatives, and thus all the union savings and loan cooperatives found themselves in one organization. The consumer cooperatives that had previously belonged to the Union were gradually joined to the Union of Consumer Cooperatives of the Republic of Poland. The exception which was partially conditioned by politics (the civil-servant class being the support of the ruling camp), was the transformation (in 1934) of the Union of Housing and Housing-Construction Cooperatives, which had existed since 1931, into the Union of Employee Cooperatives and Associations. It became the central association of housing and construction cooperatives, and also of the labour cooperatives and labour savings as well asloan cooperatives. The Central Union of Army Cooperatives retained its independence, although it was strongly connected with cooperative central institutions in the sector. As a result, toward the end of the 2nd Republic, Polish cooperativism was united in several strong organizations.

The post-crisis period was marked by a return on the path of development. At the end of 1938, there were almost 5,600 savings and loan cooperatives. In 1937 there were 1,408 dairy cooperatives, which meant a growth of over 130 cooperatives in comparison to 1933, while the number of members in this period grew from slightly over 300,000 to nearly 630,000, including 210,000 new members who joined union cooperatives.[86] Housing cooperativism in 1933 comprised 189 cooperatives with not quite 15,000 members, and at the end of 1937 it had 252 cooperatives with 22,000 members,[87] of which union cooperatives, whose premises were inhabited by over 34,000 persons, had 12,500 members.[88] In 1936 alone, the Union of Labor Cooperatives and Associations acquired 180 new cooperatives, including 38 housing cooperatives and 130 savings and loan cooperatives.[89]

At the beginning of 1938, it had around 150,000 members.[90] In the 1933–1938 period over 1,000 cooperatives were added and this despite transformation of the smaller ones into larger branches. In 1937 the union consumer cooperative movement had 60 warehouse branches throughout the country and employed nearly 1,200 persons which meant that the Union of Consumer Cooperatives ("Społem") of the Republic of Poland—this was its official name from the middle of the 1930s—was one of the largest trading enterprises in Poland of those days.[91] At the end of 1937 Społem-affiliated cooperatives were employing over 6,000 persons.[92] At that moment they had 2,731 shops[93] in sum and over 500 pieces of real estate at their disposal.[94] Before the start of the crisis—in addition to slightly over 200 local enterprises (butcher shops, bakeries, etc.) belonging to affiliated cooperatives—the Union had two large consumer goods facilities in Kielce and Włocławek; toward the end of the 2nd Republic it also had warehouses in Gdynia and Dwikozy and a factory (bought just before the Second World War) in Toruń, and its number of local cooperative workshops

---

86   W. Rusiński, *Zarys historii polskiego ruchu spółdzielczego* [*An Outline of the Polish Cooperative Movement*], op. cit., p. 154, tab. 42 and p. 180, tab. 59.

87   85 Ibidem, p. 148, tab. 38.

88   Ibidem, p. 171, tab. 55.

89   "*Sprawozdanie Związku Spółdzielni i Zrzeszeń Pracowniczych Rzeczypospolitej Polskiej za rok 1935, Biuletyn Związku Spółdzielni i Zrzeszeń Pracowniczych Rzeczypospolitej Polskiej*" ["Report of the Union of Labor Cooperatives and Associations of the Republic of Poland for 1935," *Bulletin of the Union of Labor Cooperatives and Associations of the Republic of Poland*], December 1936, no. 15, p. 22.

90   S. Oksza, *Przez spółdzielczość do gospodarczej niezależności Polski pracującej* [*Through Cooperativism to the Economic Independence of Working Poland*], "Społem" Związek Spółdzielni Spożywcow R.P., Warsaw 1938, p. 42.

91   J. Jasiński, "*Rozwoj Hurtowni w okresie 1918–1938*" ["Wholesale Development in the Period 1918–1938"], *Społem!* 1938, no. 21–22.

92   "Społem" Związek Spółdzielni Spożywcow Rzeczypospolitej Polskiej ["Społem" Union of Consumer Cooperatives of the Republic of Poland], *Statystyka spółdzielni związkowych za rok 1937* [*Union Cooperative Statistics for 1937*], Warsaw 1938, p. XVI.

93   Ibidem, p. XIX.

94   Ibidem, p. XXVIII.

and production outlets had grown to around 350.[95] At the end of 1938, the union had nearly 400,000 members (in around 1,800 cooperatives), which meant that it had exceeded the 1928 pre-crisis number.[96] In 1938 the whole of the consumer cooperative movement accounted for over 15% of the national turnover in matches, nearly 10% of salt, 10% of rice, and over 5% of tea and sugar.[97]

The 1930s was also a decade when cooperativism developed in new areas. The "atypical" cooperatives included ones in orchardry (5 in 1937); animal husbandry and sales (9); vegetable crops (2); beekeeping (93); the production of spirits (2); distilleries (12); mills (4); grazing (5); fishing (2); publishing (several); and innovative individual initiatives in, for instance, brewing, cold cuts, fruit processing, sugar products, bentwood furniture, theatre, and tourism. The cooperative bookselling movement developed in the years 1929–1938 in particular; at the end of the period there were over 30 such cooperatives, with nearly 4,500 members.[98] In 1937 there were 21 electrification cooperatives. Within two years of 1936, 5 healthcare cooperatives (medical clinics) had emerged.[99] "Folk industry bazaars"—cooperatives that organized the wholesale and retail sale of rural handicrafts—were an original idea. There were 6 such cooperatives in 1936.[100] Craft and piece-work cooperatives developed, and provided raw materials to their members or organized the sale of products. Labour or production cooperatives also developed. In 1935, over 400 of them were functioning; on the eve of the Second World War, there were nearly 550 (usually not large ones).[101] Among them there were glassworks, quarries, tableware

95   J. Żerkowski, *Spółdzielczość spożywcow w Polsce 1918–1939* [*The Consumer Cooperative Movement in Poland 1918–1939*], Warsaw 1961, Zakład Wydawnictw CRS, p. 62.

96   "Społem" Związek Spółdzielni Spożywcow Rzeczypospolitej Polskiej ["Społem" Union of Consumer Cooperatives of the Republic of Poland], *Statystyka spółdzielni związkowych za 1933 rok* [*Union Cooperative Statistics for 1933*], Warsaw 1934, p. XIII, tab. 1; J. Żerkowski, *Spółdzielczość spożywcow w Polsce 1918–1939* [*The Consumer Cooperative Movement in Poland 1918–1939*], op. cit., p. 64.

97   F. Kędziorek, *Nurty społeczno-gospodarcze w polskim ruchu spółdzielczym w latach 1918–1939* [*Socio-Economic Currents in the Polish Cooperative Movement in the Years 1918–1939*], op. cit., p. 34, tab. 14.

98   W. Rusiński, *Zarys historii polskiego ruchu spółdzielczego* [*An Outline of the History of the Polish Cooperative Movement*], op. cit., p. 187.

99   I. Solarz, *Spółdzielnie zdrowia* [*Healthcare Cooperatives*], Warsaw 1938, Związek Spółdzielni Rolniczych i Zarobkowo-Gospodarczych R.P., pp. 93–94.

100   S. Miłkowski, *Spółdzielczość przemysłowa wiejska* [*Folk Industry Cooperatives*], Warsaw 1938, Związek Spółdzielni Rolniczych i Zarobkowo-Gospodarczych R.P., p. 22.

101   Z. Chyra-Rolicz, *Z tradycji polskiej spółdzielczości II Rzeczypospolitej (idee—fakty—dokonania)* [*From the History of Polish Cooperativism of the Second Republic (Ideas, Facts, and Achievements)*], Warsaw—Poznań 1992, Ławica, pp. 80–82.

producers, a button factory, a tannery, firefighting-equipment producers, and multi-sectoral cooperatives for the disabled. Part emerged due to the support of the Society for the Support of Labour Cooperativism.[102]

In the last years of the 2nd Republic, the state of the Polish cooperative movement and the cooperative movement among minorities was as follows:

> We presently have in Poland 14,000 cooperatives of various types, with a total number of over 3 million members. The capital of these cooperatives (shares, resources, and other assets) amounts to a quarter of a billion zlotys, and the total sum of the balance to 2 billion zlotys. Over 35,000 persons are employed in cooperative shops, offices, and production facilities. Cooperatives in Poland are grouped in 11 central unions, of which there are 5 Polish unions, 1 Ukrainian, 1 Russian, 2 German and 2 Jewish. The number of "wild" cooperatives (unaffiliated with unions) does not reach 1,000 and is quickly decreasing. Around 8,000 cooperatives belong to Polish unions. [...] Among our national minorities, cooperatives have expanded most among the Ukrainians. The Central Union of Ukrainian Cooperatives in Lwów affiliates around three and a half thousand various, mostly rural, cooperatives.[103]

The post-crisis period was also the time of important change in doctrinal sphere. Among the main ideological-organizational centers of the movement, only that part of the Union of Agricultural and Farming-Labour Cooperatives that was connected with the Greater Poland savings and loan cooperative movement persisted in the position that cooperativism was solely a manner of increasing individual well-being. The second wing of this union—that is, the former "Stefczykers"—retained solidarity and defense of smallholders as a basis, but capitalist conditions were criticized with increasing force. The need for the state to support individual farming began to be stressed. In spite of unification, the dispute between the adherents of these currents continued. In one of the Union's official publications, accusations were even leveled at its own Greater Poland organization of concentrating on "money-grubbing" and organizational-technical modernization while losing sight of the broader goal:

102   J. Wolski, *Sprawa kooperacji pracy w Polsce* [*The Question of Labor Cooperativism in Poland*], Warsaw 1937, Towarzystwo Popierania Kooperacji Pracy.

103   J. Wolski, *"Do młodzieży o spółdzielczości"* ["To Youth, On Cooperativism"], (Speech on Cooperativism Day), Warsaw 1938, Centralny Komitet Dnia Spółdzielczości w Polsce, pp. 13–14.

Cooperativism is a great school of coexistence and collaboration. Through it, the village takes its fate in its own hands and begins to direct its own economic affairs. Cooperativism in the Poznań area does not educate people; it rather connects them with outside workplaces, with workplaces that keep clients solely and exclusively through money.[104]

The evolution of views of the two leaders of the cooperative movement, Zygmunt Chmielewski and Marian Rapacki, are typical. The first, the organizer of dairy cooperativism and one of the leaders of farming cooperativism, represented the earlier moderate position in the question of the movement's aims and ongoing tactics. Among other things, he worked with landowning circles, for which he was not infrequently criticized by cooperativists of more radical views. The economic—and simply civilizational—collapse of Polish villages in connection with the crisis caused him to adopt an anti-capitalist position by the second half of the 1930s. He advocated the abolition of exploitation, and postulated a planned economy and radical agricultural reforms (parcellation of farms above 50 hectares, and in regions of more productive agriculture, even farms above 20 hectares).[105] He also considered that although too much government interference could in fact have negative effects, from the viewpoint of cooperativism, statism in itself should be appraised positively as it lessened the significance and influence of private capital.[106]

The evolution in the views of Rapacki, who had been the chairman of the consumer cooperatives' central organization since 1926, is even more significant. He differed from many leaders of this current in terms of thelack of connection with the socialist movement; on the other hand, he was a prominent activist of the National Labour Union, a moderate and solidarist party for several years.[107] After becoming the leader of the Union of Consumer

---

104   *Zjednoczona spółdzielczość rolnicza* [*United Agricultural Cooperativism*], Warsaw 1937, Związek Spółdzielni Rolniczych i Zarobkowo-Gospodarczych R.P., p. 108.

105   Z. Chmielewski, *Przyszły ustrój gospodarczy wsi Rzeczypospolitej Polskiej* [*The Future Rural Economic System of the Republic of Poland*], Warsaw 1938, "Książnica dla rolników," C.T.O and K.R., particularly pp. 11–12, 17–19, 38–39.

106   Z. Świtalski, "*Polska myśl spółdzielcza okresu kapitalizmu (pięć programów)*" ["Polish Co-operative Thought in the Period of Capitalism (5 Programs)"], in: *Myśl spółdzielcza doby współczesnej. Materiały z konferencji zorganizowanej przez Spółdzielczy Instytut Badawczy w dniu 6 grudnia 1973 r.* [*Contemporary Cooperative Thought: Materials from a Conference Organized by the Cooperative Research Institute on December 6, 1973*], J. Kleer, T. Kowalak (ed.), Warsaw 1976, Zakład Wydawnictw CZSR, pp. 94–95.

107   Z. Pawluczuk, *Spółdzielczość w myśli programowej i działalności polskiego ruchu robotniczego w latach 1892–1939* [*Cooperativism in the Platform and Activity of the Polish Labor Movement in the Years 1892–1939*], UMK, Toruń 1977, pp. 78–87.

Cooperatives of the Republic of Poland, he adopted a position in accord with
the main principles of the "neutral" current of cooperativism, speaking of the
gradual, grassroots replacement of successive areas of free market economy
with cooperatives and their unions. Observation of the results of crisis drove
him to become radical. In 1936 he gave a speech that reverberated widely. His
point of departure was a claim similar to one of Karl Marx's:

> From the moment that a given formation of the political system ceases to
> satisfy the needs of a given society in the best manner, from that moment
> the desire to find a better form naturally arises in every society.[108]

Then he painted a picture of capitalism as a system that had lost its ability to
meet the needs of the masses, with the result that civilizational collapse was
threatened. The way out of the danger was to rest the economy on the primacy
of satisfying needs. This was contrary to the interests of the possessing classes,
thus their resistance should be broken by the force of the state apparatus and
private production capital should gradually be expropriated from its owners.

In effect, the leader of consumer cooperativism formulated a socialist
program according to the reform model. Rapacki's concept was attacked by
conservative milieus and adherents of liberal economics, but was appreciated
by the Polish Socialist Party, the left wing of the People's Party, and the Sanacja
left.

As a result of the crisis, the relations of a large number of cooperatives in
regard to the state also changed. As a result of the collapse of liberal capitalism, the cooperative movement faced serious difficulties (loss of members
and shares, diminishing turnover). Cooperativists began to announce that

---

108   M. Rapacki, *Program gospodarczy spółdzielczości spożywców. Referat wygłoszony na
      Zjeździe delegatow "Społem" Związku Spółdzielni Spożywcow RP dnia 14 czerwca 1936 roku*
      [*Economic Program for Consumer Cooperatives: A Speech Given at the Congress of Dele-
      gates of the "Społem" Union of Consumer Cooperatives of the Republic of Poland on June 14,
      1936*], Warsaw 1936, "Społem" Związek Spółdzielni Spożywcow R.P., p. 2. Marx: "At a cer-
      tain stage of their material development, society's production forces come into conflict
      with the existing relations of production or—what is only the legal expression of this—
      with the relations of property, among which they have previously developed. From forms
      that develop production forces these relations change into their shackles. Then a period
      of social revolution occurs." (K. Marx, *"Przyczynek do krytyki ekonomii politycznej"* ["Con-
      tribution to a Critique of Political Economy"], in: K. Marks, F. Engels, *Dzieła wybrane.
      W dwoch tomach* [*Collected Works: In Two Volumes*], vol. 1, Warsaw 1949, Książka i Wiedza,
      p. 338) Translated from the Polish.

state economic intervention and its stabilizing role had a positive impact on the whole economic system. They considered that if the modernization of Poland and overcoming its civilizational backwardness had not been to last many decades, a broad investment, organizational and regulatory action on the part of the state would have been necessary. Cooperativists began to view their movement as one of the elements in a planned, rational state policy, opposed to the chaotic acts of private entities which were not directed by social interest. Cooperativism, in their view, was a bulwark against the totalitarian tendencies displayed in that period by the USSR, Germany and Italy, whose realities they implacably criticized. The cooperative movement and the state should together push Poland on the path of economic and social modernization, to make it a strong and rich state, to ensure economic independence, and also to guarantee the pro-social face of the system and its democratic nature not only in the political sense, but also through the participation of the masses in ownership and management of the means of production.

> Major discretionary centres must arise here, in the country, and not as at present, outside the borders of the Republic, and must be guided by the will of the Polish collective and not international and capitalist forces [...]

concluded a well-known activist of consumer cooperativism.[109]

---

109   J. Jasiński, *Rola spółdzielczości w rozbudowie gospodarstwa narodowego w Polsce* [*The Role of Cooperativism in the Expansion of the National Economy in Poland*], Warsaw 1937, Społem, p. 63. Similar ideas were expressed at the time in articles and the larger publications of the cooperative movement, mainly in the milieus of consumer, housing, and labor cooperativism.

PART 1

Cooperativism and Democracy

∴

CHAPTER 3

The Social Ideas of Cooperativism[1]

Edward Abramowski

1   Associations and the State

Today, when the attention of society is preoccupied with state reforms, when various parties are mutually striving to put forward a program of demands that will ensure the best laws and civil liberties, it is worth remembering that there is a form of communal life existing outside of the state structures, one which is capable not only of meeting all the requirements of society but also of ensuring the best and broadest civil liberties. This form is an association.

The furthest reaching constitutions of democratic states, the broadest concept of representation of the people never achieves—and can never achieve—such a protection of liberty, such respect for the individual will in regard to the collective, as characterizes associations. Furthermore, in no form of state organization do we find such an ease of adapting to the conditions and necessities of life, to newly emerging ideas and movements, as in associations. Thus we can boldly state that given the ever multiplying questions of human life—its increasing variability, its richness of types and trends, the developing individualism of groups and persons, who subordinate themselves with ever more difficulty to general norms—the association type of social organization is the type of the future, the heir to the modern State. Those modest "statutes" of various consumer, agricultural, and credit cooperatives, which we have grown accustomed to overlook, to treat as parochial policies of small deeds and small people, yet conceal in themselves the seed of a new political idea, which could in the future supersede all state "constitutions" and "representations," as unnecessary relics of bondage.

To understand this, let us look at the organizing principles of cooperative associations. We could take, for example, the statute of any of the consumer, mutual-aid, labor, or other kinds of associations that have branches throughout Western Europe; everywhere we see the same constitutional structure, adapted to various goals.

---

1   Edward Abramowski, *"Idee społeczne kooperatyzmu"* ["The Social Ideas of Cooperativism"], on the basis of: idem, *Pisma* [*Writings*], vol. 1, K. Krzeczkowski (compilation and introduction), Warsaw 1924, Nakładem Związku Spółdzielni Spożywców Rzeczpospolitej Polskiej [Published by the Union of Consumer Cooperatives of the Republic of Poland].

Thus, above all, the legislative power in an association belongs to the entirety of the membership, both men and women. Only resolutions of the general assembly, adopted by majority vote, are binding on the association. These resolutions are continually dependent on the will of their creators and if, after a certain time, they appear to be inconvenient, the next assembly can repeal them and replace them with others. All members can take part in creating resolutions, and in improving or critiquing them. The right of private initiative is unlimited here: every personal talent and energy, every idea emerging in someone's mind, can find an appropriate creative field and by strength of persuasion enter the life of the association. Legislation—if that state-level term can be used for free associations—is thus here in continual contact and continual dependence on the needs and convictions of that whole for which it arose and for which it functions.

The executive authority, that is, the management and administration of the association, is chosen by the general assembly for a limited time and remains under the dual control of the association: under the control of the general assembly, to which it must present a detailed report of its activities, and under the control of a committee chosen for this purpose by the assembly. The role of the management is usually limited to performing the tasks entailed by the association's permanent functions. However, if the association becomes convinced that this performance does not agree with the spirit of its resolutions and aspirations, it can at any moment subject it to severe censure and change the composition of the management.

We have here thus all the basic traits of a democratic constitution in its most developed form: the highest legislative power rests in the hands of the whole; the right of initiative belongs to everyone; there is absolute freedom of criticism and propaganda; the executive power, established by direct elections, is responsible to the whole for all its actions and controlled by majority will in regard to fundamental reforms. Only a few republican countries, such as Switzerland, and a few states of the United States of North America have attained such a degree of democratic development in their state structures. However, there too the political rights of citizens, such as, for instance, the right of initiative and control over the executive power, are to a considerable degree limited and never reach the plenitude that exists in the constitutions of associations.

Seen from this angle, associations appear to be non-territorial republics with a perfected democratic form, embodying human and civil rights within wider boundaries than any state democracy has managed to this time to achieve.

Between the association and the state, even the most democratic, a fundamental difference appears of immeasurable significance for the future of society. Namely, that an association is a voluntary union of people, created on the grounds of the natural commonality of needs, while a state is a coercive territorial entity, by the law of the land, which rules a person because he resides within it. It never gives its citizens the freedom to avoid its rules and regulations, the freedom to voluntarily belong or not belong to its structures. True freedom of the individual becomes here an unattainable utopia. Even in the most democratic states, only a simple majority of representatives or of the people decides, and minorities, even very large ones, can have laws imposed upon them that are in the highest degree inconvenient. Nevertheless, they must remain within the framework of the common entity, adapt themselves to its decrees and bear its common burdens.

In addition, while associations usually have as their aim the satisfaction of some one category of human needs, a state strives to encircle all needs, the whole human being. It regulates not only the conditions of security and defense, but also of manners, religion, education, private and public behavior, economic conditions, hygiene, and morality: all is connected to the state's interests and everything could threaten the foundations of its existence. It thereby results that state legislation must be rigid, difficult to change, and hard to adapt to the needs of life. The complicated mechanism of the state, which encompasses the most diverse human elements and questions, must make serious calculations over every change. Reform in one area must be evaluated from various external viewpoints and sometimes military considerations or the interests of colonial, financial, or diplomatic policy will make it impossible to conduct reforms in economic, cultural, or educational spheres.

The result of all this is that even the most democratic state is becoming less capable of resolving social issues, which are mutable, diverse, and rapidly evolving. These questions, multiplying with the progress of history, require a flexible, spiritualized organization, where there is the least possible routine and pattern and the freest possible thinking and natural selection. Such a structure is to be found in associations.

And here we are witness to a curious process: even though the idea of "nationalization," from above and below, is gaining strength, its antagonist—the democracy of associations—is also spreading, so that today we find practically no area of social life, no collective issue where the two forms do not appear simultaneously. We have thus a state economic policy and a federation of consumer cooperatives striving to regulate production and the market in accord with consumer interests; state labor legislation and the legislation of vocational unions protecting the worker against exploitation; state insurance for old age and the insurance of mutual aid societies and consumer cooperatives; a state agrarian policy and agricultural associations undertaking the same tasks of raising the culture and well-being of country [farming] people; state schools and universities beside free schools and universities; state credit beside the credit of savings-and-loan societies, Raiffeisen banks and many other such; and so on in every area of life and interests.

Not only two different forms of social organization appear here, but also two different ideas, two different directions of the human soul: one that desires to cramp life by law and subject its natural diversity to forced and uniform norms, and another that wants to make law subordinate to life, to make it dependent and adapted to the variability and richness of human types, to what in comparison to it is important, primary, and sovereign.

2   Democratic Culture

At every historical turning-point, when the harbingers of a new world appear—the nameless great ideas, belonging to everyone and no one—then criticism of individual life also appears, the first breeding ground of internal perplexity. The ideas seem so enormous and at the same time so distant and foreign to dull everyday life. There, in the world of ideas, the eternal dreams of mankind exist: brotherhood, prosperity, liberty; Isaiah's prophecy of beating swords into plowshares and the evangelical announcement that the temple resides in the secret hiding places of the human heart are resurrected. But before the image of this beauty crawls shameful, dirty life; a life of profiteering, self love, coercion of the weak; a life of chancelleries, courts, markets, and poorhouses; a parade of petty cares and ambitions, of shuffling thoughts and feelings.

And suddenly, before everyone who has felt the waft of the new ideas, the question appears of individual life—its improvement and ennoblement: the invincible, necessary postulate that a new social world requires new people.

Free institutions can not arise from slave natures. Democracy can not arise from social robbers and parasites. A just society can not be born to people who only chase profits or luxuries. Even if we were to turn the question around and claim that political institutions of a new type are capable of improving people and reorganizing life, even then the question remains of what forces can extract these institutions from nothingness, can organize, maintain, and vitalize them in the spirit of rebirth? From whence shall we take these legions of individuals capable of creating social evolution, these masses with advanced human and civil consciences, without which political democracy is only a fiction, a name without content, a whited sepulcher of the Pharisees?

Democracy only arises where the mass of people need it. It appears as a reaction against the acquisitiveness of the state, as an essential defense of natural institutions: the organized economic and cultural interests of the people against bureaucracy.

If the Swiss people, with such logical resistance, defend their democratic arrangements against the various claims of the central government, if they have managed to broaden those arrangements to the furthest boundaries of political liberty, then we should remember that their defense of democracy was defense of their own life. The political constitution they formed has a natural broad base: a thousand different associations, clubs, and unions; a thousand natural economic, trade, labor, or cultural organizations; democratic customs, habits of equality, and respect for human dignity are rooted in the whole civilization of this people; the custom and ability to arrange their affairs and collective needs independently; strongly developed civil consciences and, what is inseparable from this, distrust of bureaucracy.

All this creates a democratic culture, the first and essential condition of democracy and political independence.

The Polish people do not yet have such a culture. This is not a modern society, organized in various free associations and unions, but until recently a loose collection of individuals waiting to see what reforms would be given them, along what new lines the state would order their life to flow. Without their own social institutions, which could be developed and improved, they have expected only police reforms. And this lack of independence has sunk so deep in the national character that even leading spirits or party programs have been unable to attain to any other social postulates than those contained in the formula of "what is wanted from the state."

We have grown accustomed to considering ourselves as material that someone else moulds into various shapes; on every occasion we have offered ourselves: "make of us this or the other thing; make us into a constitutional, democratic, of social-democratic society; reform our schools and hospitals; protect us against poverty and exploitation." Political wisdom was entirely contained in these pleas or demands for reform. All ideals bowed before one: The State-Providence. It was to think and act for us, to feed us, heal us, and protect us. And that's what we called "democracy."

On the way to such politics all other kinds can be created, only not democracy. Democracy primarily requires a strong sense and instinct of social self-aid. It requires people who know not only how to demand reforms from the state but also how to conduct those reforms through the help of their own institutions. It requires the ability to independently organize social interests. It requires the development of associations encompassing various areas in the economy, culture, work protection, and health. It requires, finally, people who are strongly individual; it requires a distinct need to live according to one's own norms while respecting that independence in others. Without these moral and social conditions, democracy can not be created.

Even if the most far-reaching reforms were elaborated in the council of ministers or the Duma—even if we obtained political institutions of self-government based on universal suffrage—we would unfailingly change them into rule by bureaucrats and representatives of elections, centralized some-where far from the people and completely adapted to society's democratic immaturity ... if the work of creating democracy from below—that free de-mocracy of associations—were to be neglected by us.

The creation of democracy through society alone, the creation of its essence, its inner strength, simultaneously involves the healing of life and the moral liberation of people. There, where self-help institutions, cooperatives, peasant companies, and trade unions are developing, where independent centers of education and culture arise, there too deep changes in the habits and souls of the people must—and are—occurring in the upbringing of children, in physical and moral hygiene, in the understanding of life tasks and happiness. Above all, people then create the conditions of their existence for themselves. Goals appear in the lives of individuals, where formerly none existed; the sense of independent creation and human solidarity appears. The remnants of the slave spirit and the spirit of the modern "profiteer," unable to understand profit without harm, disappear. New categories of moral and social enjoyment ap-pear and drive out the mindless boredom of luxuries, debauchery, and drink-ing. In a word, a new culture and new type of person is created, the kind that fundamentally distinguishes a democratic society.

A member of a free association is a person who creates life by the force of his own mind, character, and heart—and this is the citizen of democracy. An individual who walks with the mass, in the herd, is a passive pawn in the hands of bureaucracy and party leaders, a slave to life conditions. Such a person is characteristic of an unfree society.

These two basic outlines define the whole psychological and moral differ-ence; they adapt for themselves ideas, feelings, conscience, needs and lifestyles, desires and ideals. The democratic character demands above all freedom to create; the slave type—"bread and circuses"; the first tries to improve himself and better his life, the second requires it of the state.

In the democratic character, the need for bitter complaints and grumbling, the discord between individuality and conditions, between the ideal impressed in the mind and real life disappears, because a member of a free association is able to create his life and adapt conditions to his individuality. A perfect unity of thought, feeling, and action—the prerequisite for a healthy and fully developing individual—is produced here.

In the slave type, however, there is an entire abyss between the ideal and reality, between individuality and conditions. A person falls into a life pattern that others have created for him by force; his unavailing adaptation to it tires him; his individuality is castrated in the most various ways; he is drilled in various concepts and morals; he loses all contact with his latent desire to act—and as a result is warped into a sickly, degenerate, and incomplete character.

Cooperativism sees its most important task—the deep essence of the democratic culture it spreads—in this moral transformation of the person from slave to free creator of life.

Every consumer cooperative, every farmers' company or trade union, becomes a live center and school of that culture, a school where people learn by deeds about a new science of liberty. Those who have previously done nothing more than accept the orders of their superiors or the alms of their benefactors—who have been ruled and civilized in someone else's mould—must here, in cooperatives and unions, govern themselves and decide about all their own affairs: the conditions of their employment; the management of their funds, workshops, and shops; the needs of their schools, libraries, hospitals, and security. They must not only advise on this but also create it all, forming institutions, adapting them to their tasks and characters, and contributing their own initiative, enthusiasm for creation, and perseverance. Then the social institution ceases to stifle a person and becomes an obedient tool in his hands, allowing him to convert need and conscience, his thoughts and feelings, into reality: allowing him to be a creator.

This, in the understanding of cooperativists, is what the idea of democratic culture is based on.

3   The "People's Labor State"

In wanting to demonstrate the idea of a "people's labor state" as it is outlined in cooperativism, we must begin with what constitutes a common historical and moral source of cooperativism and of contemporary socialism, namely, the first aspirations of the labor movement.

The struggle to free the working classes appears in world history as a collective protest against human injury. This is its departure point. In the concepts that were adopted and announced as its ideals, it was never a matter of changing one system of exploitation for another; the social question was never to be answered in such a manner that the working classes would occupy the position of the bourgeoisie and later enslave some other part of humanity. On the contrary, clearly and simply, exploitation itself, of every kind and against whomever applied, was supposed to be abolished. This was a strong and vital idea before which all concepts of class and divisions of people in the new system had to disappear, and as a result any interest appearing to pertain purely to workers, to a class, changed into a general human interest, into the natural law of every human being to a free life and development.

Correspondingly, the economic ideal of the working classes was formed. A social movement that protests against human harm and fights all kinds of exploitation has to include, among its furthest reaching aspirations and reasoned aims, the transformation of capitalism into a type of social economy in which neither the production of riches nor their trade and use requires the oppression of one part of society by another, and where there can be no room for profits extracted at the cost of others' work and poverty. Such an economy, in today's conditions of large industry and world trade, can only result from the common possession of national resources, the conversion of everyone into co-owners with uniform rights.

However, the economic idea could not remain in such a generalized form. Of necessity, as a real policy for the workers' movement and socialism evolved, the economic idea had to be combined with the entirety of social issues, to have its essence and details explained, and to conduce to the formulation of cultural, ethical, and, in particular, state-political aims. This led to the creation of the idea of a "people's labor state," which in recent years has found a codifier in the person of Professor Menger.[2] As it emerges, Professor Menger has the uncommon merit of being entirely frank and logical, thanks to which everything that was previously unsaid in socialist programs and about which people were ashamed to speak and think clearly has been openly expressed as the completely developed idea of state socialism.

What is a People's Labor State?

It can be defined by the following two statements: (1) it is the democratization of a state through legislative support for universal suffrage and by broadening the executive power's principles of responsibility to the voters; (2) it also involves extending the state power to all activities of social life, putting agriculture and industry, labor protection and health care, child-raising and education, in the hands of the state.

---

2   Anton Menger (1841–1906) was a professor of civil law at the University of Vienna. He was also an activist of the social-democratic party, a critic of liberal economic concepts and systems and an adherent of strong state intervention in social life and economic relations. He was the author, among other works, of *Neue Staatslehre* (1903), to which Abramowski refers.

The democratization of governments, in the broadest sense of the term, does not constitute the essence of a "people's labor state." Menger even declares that

> It would be proper if the legislature of the people's state consisted of two chambers: the chamber of deputies, always liable to democratic currents, and an aristocratic chamber, which should include not the most useful but the best members of the state ... The most outstanding representatives of science, art, and literature, he says further, "must find places in that Chamber, by means of election or appointment."[3]

We find a much more characteristic limitation of democracy in socialism's operational programs, which, consciously, entirely exclude postulates of direct legislation by the people—initiatives and referendums—and respond to such aspirations as political decentralization and giving women the right to vote with great caution, unwillingness, and reservations about the "maturity of the people."

However, to properly evaluate the "democracy" of that labor state, it is necessary to look at its other side, which is formulated as "nationalization of the economy." Only in the combination of these two does the "people's state" of socialism acquire its true form and reveal the kind of civil liberty it would guarantee.

The people's labor state rests on the assumption that the moral, family, and economic interests of people are considered to be a public good. As a result, as Menger says:

> It will be necessary to nationalize the private-public order, that is, to change a private right into an administrative right and to achieve the latter by official means, through the intermediary of its organs. Thus all property and private-family relations, not excluding even the private ownership of foodstuffs, should be regulated by administrative means (p. 224) ... A designated quantity of means to satisfy the requirements of life and a designated period of work—this is the principle of the state distribution system in regard to individuals (p. 147).

To correspond with this economic principle, the organs of the people's state will have to be divided into offices of the public and economic order.

---

3   A. Menger, *Nowa nauka o państwie* [*A New Science of the State*], translated by H.S. Kamieński, Lwów 1904, Polskie Towarzystwo Nakładowe, pp. 263–265. Translated from the Polish—Tr.

The task of the first will be to maintain the existing relations of force and keep the peace and public order; the second would govern economic affairs: the production, distribution, and consumption of goods and services.

The first entities would be similar to today's courts and administrative offices; the latter organizations, to today's state enterprises: the post office, the railway, etc. (pp. 273–274).

In accordance with the nature of the people's labor state, the major part of the state's activities would have to fall to the economic organs. The task of these latter would be to determine the type and extent of work to be performed by each individual, as well as to resolve the amount of material goods and services to be distributed to each citizen of the state ... In spite of its predominantly technical nature, the economic organ would be considered an administrative office of the state, and every citizen would have to adhere to its decrees, while retaining the right to submit complaints to the competent economic office or office of the public order (pp. 276–277) ... Universal obligatory work creates the basis for a new concept of offence ... Every citizen who would threaten the bases of this form of state through his illegal recoil from work would be subject to punishment, regardless of his social position (p. 220).

This system, which changes economic life into the legal-bureaucratic order of the state, necessarily also requires considerable restriction of local self-government and workers' associations.

In a labor state, the people's communes, in regulating economic affairs, would oppose each other to a certain degree, as independent individualities. It would be entirely erroneous, though, to identify their relations with the relations between individual persons engaged in economics in our system. In truth, while material goods would be created and consumed within that one district, it would naturally be independent and autonomous. But every exchange of goods and services between two autonomous communes would have to take place under the supervision or direction of the economic offices .... In our system, the right of freely changing residence would also be significantly limited in the people's labor state ... Moving to another commune could only be allowed, in the ordinary course of events, if the commune from which the individual was moving freed him from his obligatory work, and the commune to which he was going gave him the right to live there. But even if the interested parties did not all agree, the supervisory economic power would have to have the right to consider requests to change commune affiliation (pp. 287–289).

Every larger commune, whose economic life represents a difficult-to-control diversity, must combine people of one trade into groups of workers. Both indirect creations—the communes and the groups of workers—should be considered only as administrative institutions. Thus the members of a group actually possess the right to exist in respect to the commune, but they cannot demand that income from work performed by the group be divided among them in accordance with any kind of measure. A group of workers is established or dispersed by decree of the commune. The commune also decides which members are to be included in a group and the distribution of the tools of labor. In this the institution differs from Fourier's system, which relies on the inclination of members toward a certain trade and not on external authority. The dissimilarity between the working group and the workers' associations of Blanc and Lassalle[4] can also be seen, as the latter were to be created through the voluntary combination of members.

The district appoints and dismisses the heads of the groups of workers. They are responsible for the work performed by the group. But they must also possess the authority to direct the work of the members and to impose disciplinary penalties on lazy or surly workers, with the latter reserving the right to bring a complaint to the organ assuring order. These same methods must also be practiced if the commune itself were to direct the work of its members, without the intermediary of the workers' groups. Only when the labor state acquires an entirely established form will it be possible to shape the workers' groups in a more democratic spirit (pp. 291–293).

In general, "the task of public organization would be the orderliness of social work; private initiative would be left a very limited field of operation. Moreover"—Menger assures the reader enigmatically—"it would develop in the area of morality"(!) (p. 165).

---

4   Louis Blanc (1811–1882), a French socialist, politician and historian, he participated in the Revolution of 1848 in Paris, and was one of the precursors of the cooperative movement; Ferdinand Lassalle (1825–1864), a German-Jewish socialist and political thinker, he initiated the international-style socialism in Germany; a co-founder of the first German socialists party – *Allgemeiner Deutscher Arbeiterverein*. Lassalle was considered one of the founders of social democracy, he opposed the revolution.

However, this limitation on individual freedom would not in the least ensure economic equality. Menger, adherent and legislator of the "people's state"
is clear on the subject. "In the people's labor state," he says,

> there will always be contradictions that make it impossible to equalize all
> citizens in economic terms. Here, above all, the contradiction between
> the rulers and the ruled—or, if you will, between the managers and the
> managed—should be taken into account, given that in a people's labor
> state it will appear in even sharper form than in today's social system,
> because the state's activity will encompass the entire economy. The expe-
> rience of all time teaches us, though, that rulers have always taken advan-
> tage of their dominance to ensure themselves an economically privileged
> position in life (p. 95).

And now let us see what the moral life of the citizens of the people's labor state
would look like on this foundation of state economics. It becomes a general
rule that upbringing, education, and religion are transferred into the hands of
the state bureaucracy. "If the state," says Menger,

> declares itself for the system of combined economies, it will be most ad-
> vantageous if the feeding and raising of children should be a function of
> the state organs and occur in separate buildings designated for the pur-
> pose. Since in the people's labor state every private right is generally con-
> verted into an administrative right, the question of who is to care for the
> spiritual, moral, and physical development of children will be resolved by
> administrative decision (p. 201).
>
> Since private property in the people's state will be very limited, the
> state can prevent the activities of religious associations by a simple refus-
> al of material means. But similarly, automatic means of coercion should
> not be used in matters of conscience in the new social system; on the
> contrary, the satisfaction of religious needs, which nevertheless can not
> be refused to the followers of the revealed religions, should be considered
> as part of the right to existence. The people's labor state is thus obligated
> to render to religious associations the material goods and services neces-
> sary for the performance of their rites, but it also has the right to organize
> these associations and extend its influence over them. Our state today
> gives the masses a predominantly religious upbringing in their youth
> and subsequently leaves them entirely to the influence of the church,
> remembering them in the further course of their lives only when it is a
> matter of property tax or blood. The people's labor state, however, in ac-
> cord with the nature of its whole organization, will care for the individual

throughout his life with the aid of various scientific, aesthetic, and moral educational measures (p. 308).

This is what the legal contours of the people's labor state, logically derived from the programs and political actions of today's socialism, would look like.

In life, these laws would appear as follows: the government has all the land at its disposal and lets it for cultivation to farmers or agricultural companies, sets the length of the lease, the conditions, and the price of agricultural products, and issues detailed decrees as to the manner in which the farm is to be run. Legions of government inspectors watch to make sure the decrees are fulfilled and any transgression of the regulations could deprive the farmer of the land he occupies. Similarly, the settlement of farming people and matching the number of hands to the needs of cultivating the land would occur on the basis of government decrees, in accordance with the requirements of the entire national economic system.

With factory production it would be the same. Factories, like the land, would be the exclusive property of the state; consequently the government would be the main administrator of the entire production. Perhaps it would give factories to workers' unions to run; but in any case it would have to reserve for itself the highest administrative power. Designating the quantity and type of production, setting wages and the length of the working day, closing unnecessary factories or transferring them to a more appropriate place, all this, as matters concerning the general plan for the entire national production, for which only the government would be responsible, would have to belong exclusively to the government.

The ministry would keep extensive and detailed statistics, according to which it would set the norms for production and wages. For each branch of industry a necessary number of workers would have to be found; and if those hands could not be found willingly, it would be necessary to apply coercive, police measures to satisfy the requirements of production. The state, in order to respond to the difficult question of supplying society with all the products relative to its real needs, without wasting strength and riches, would be forced to organize the workers on the model of an army, to establish an obligatory work service and the average length of its duration in the life of an individual. There would also have to be, in accord with industrial and agricultural statistics, a draft of working people, with a precise specification of the number of workers needed for each branch of production. If it emerged, for instance, that there were too many volunteers to work in agriculture and too few to work in the mines, then the government would have to refuse to accept the unnecessary agricultural workers and instead to venture some other means—higher remuneration, distribution of honors, or as a last resort, a draft—to draw the necessary number of workers to the mines, as otherwise the whole system of state production could collapse. Such a classification of people in various occupations, according to the numbers needed for production, would occur quite often in contradiction to natural abilities and individual desires. And there would be nothing to do about it, as every branch of production would have to have the essential quantity of human sacrifices in order for the entire national economy to run successfully.

From this we see that the government of the collective system, as understood by state socialism, would have enormous control over individuals. In very many cases, it would decide people's lot—the kind of work they do—and thus about their lives; it would always have to decide regardless about the length of obligatory service in industry or agriculture, the norms of remuneration and work, methods of production, and divisions of wealth. No workers' unions could organize independently of the state collectivism, which would encompass everything in a uniform system of centralized economy, based on precise, detailed statistics about production forces and the needs of society. Everything would have to be regulated here like in the most perfect mechanism and be subject to the same general rules. No deviation of an unauthorized group or workers' association could be allowed. A single state authority, responsible for the whole economics of the society, would make decisions about its fundamental matters and would have to have a strong hand, and obedient citizens, so that its laws and smallest economic decrees would be obeyed conscientiously and precisely.

It is also clear that the government of the people's labor state, being not only a political government but also an economic one, would have to have an enormous army of civil servants at its disposal. There would have to be countless numbers of state inspectors, caretakers, technicians, accountants, statisticians, experts, etc., taking direct care of every industrial enterprise, every agricultural estate. This whole new economic bureaucracy, whose numbers would exceed today's state bureaucracy by a hundredfold, would be, like it, dependent only on its superior authority, that is, on the government. It would not adapt itself to the will of persons working in a given factory or farm but exclusively to the orders of its ministry, because otherwise disorder and confusion would prevail instead of efficiency and order.

Moving to matters of culture, we find a state monopoly there too. In minimal socialist programs it figures primarily as obligatory free education, in maximal programs (as in the case of Menger) it is extended to the whole of human behavior. As a result, bureaucracy grows even more and centralizes in its hands a huge quantity of schools and educational facilities, which, being obligatory and free of charge, in practice entirely eliminate free schools, in spite of the freedom of education guaranteed in the constitution. Such an important— such a basic—matter for society as people's upbringing becomes the privilege of the government. Bureaucracy acquires the exclusive right to shape people's youth. It will indubitably shape that youth according to its programs and view of life, watching carefully to make sure that no rebellious ideas, no unorthodox deviations in regard to new concepts, should make their way into education; in time a kind of citizen would be molded who would be completely in agreement with the prevailing system of life and morally suited to obedience.

Thus on closer inspection that beautiful commonplace of the future, that a management of things will replace ruling the people, shows that under the mask of those administered "things" it will always be living people who are managed.

To objections to the rather excessive predominance of the government in such a system, the defenders of state collectivism usually respond that it would be, after all, a people's state, as democratic as could be, ensuring each citizen the ability to influence the government and combat any abuses of power. "The state will be you yourselves" the agitators argue.

But in this they are most mistaken. In a democratic state, a majority of votes is used to resolve everything; a minority, even if it constitutes a significant part of the nation, has no way in which to resist the majority and must be subject to its governments and laws regardless of how harmful they may be for it. A person whose needs and ideas are contrary to the voting majority will be as fettered by the law as in any other state.

Moreover, in a democratic collective state where the government will be the manager of the land and industry, such a major part of society will be directly dependent on the government, such a mass of people will be state officials raised in the bureaucratic discipline, that at every vote, whether for representatives or new laws, the government will be ensured of a large moral advantage and will be able much more easily than today to bring its candidates to parliament, makes its bills into law, and stifle opposition. We can see now in democratic countries that the entire civil servant class—the holders of various state monopolies, the magistrates, the railway service, the post office service, teachers, etc.—are the most intimidated element of society in political conflicts with the government; they are afraid to undermine their authority and are accustomed to obedience; they follow their bosses' directions not only in voting but even in private and social life, and adapt themselves to government policy. Let us imagine that the civil servant class, which is constantly dependent on the government, is ten or a hundred times more numerous than at present, as would be necessary under collectivism, and we can easily conclude that in such a society, bureaucratic throughout, opposing the government and succeeding in that opposition would be unusually difficult. In that heavy, barracks atmosphere, in which life is everywhere imbued with an element of official discipline and obedience to authority, the exercise of civil liberties would be practically a fiction. The moral influence of the state, its power, inserting itself into every opening of human life, tracking a person from the very cradle to old age, in upbringing, education, work, in the family and in the economy, in spite of all the written constitutions, would paralyze the simplest movement of freedom, would stifle rebellion in its breeding ground, in the very soul of a person, without need even to have recourse to armed force.

It is clear that when presented in this manner the question of "liberating" the working class becomes ironic, a slap to that class by falsifying their ideals and historical aspirations. In becoming the handwork of the police state, economic commonality—the commonality of riches and cultural attainments—becomes at the same time an extension of slavery, which is so discordant with the needs and development of today's human being. Perhaps people would gain then in certainty about the morrow, in satiety, in hours free from work, but it would all occur at the cost of freedom and to the detriment of the soul. A person subjected from infancy to old age to the decrees of the state, raised and nurtured by it, for whom bureaucracy designates occupation, work, and type of life, would not be able either to create cultural achievements or to benefit from them. It would kill his self, his individuality, his creative being.

Such a position of the individual does not lie at all in the interests of the working classes and no social end requires that prosperity and economic justice should be achieved only on condition of relinquishing freedom. There is nothing of the kind either in the history of development or in the nature of today's social economy that would prove that man cannot get rid of capitalist exploitation other than by submitting himself, body and soul, to the yoke of democratic bureaucracy. These are all false concepts and as if deliberately distorted in some social caricature of the great idea of liberation which the proletariat has brought to the world.

Let us remember the source of the working classes' struggle: it is a protest against human harm. If it is considered to be a proper thing that people can be condemned to hunger and poverty, worked beyond their strength, deprived of the liberty to take advantage of life and civilization—if it is accepted as a necessary thing that for the benefit of some the lives of others should be broken under the yoke of exploitation, that children should be condemned to handicaps by which society will in time take all the joy from life—if today's order were felt and considered in this manner then at this moment there could be strikes of workers demanding higher wages or movements of peasants demanding land—as has occurred in all times—but there would not be today's worker movement, that movement that has created an invincible weapon of universal solidarity, knowing how to stand disinterestedly in defense of every injured person and to kindle the fire of struggle against every oppression, and above all there wouldn't be that ideal of economic communality which, in calling all people to fraternal coexistence and the use of nature's and civilization's gifts thereby destroys all separateness and class interests, and in the place of class interests advances the interests of human beings.

This position of the workers' movement must correspond to its political ideal as well. Today's (police) state has developed along with capitalist exploitation, with that economic coercion that characterizes every action, every movement of bourgeois economics. It is obvious that the exploitation of one person by another, the exploitation of the masses by one class, which expropriates to itself the right of ownership to the land and products of work—to the injury of others, who are forced to work by hunger, in spite of surpluses of food—that all these well-known procedures of today's economics could not be practiced if it were not for the strong state authority and legislation protecting the order of ownership. Without a police state, more or less frequent cases might occur of the exploitation of the weaker by the physically strong, the stupider by the more mentally able, the exploitation of individuals by a group, imposing obedience through numbers; but there could not be continual exploitation changed into a social system—today's type, where the exploiters are not those who are the more numerous, who have better muscles or more developed minds, but are only those less numerous persons who have managed, by whatever means, to become owners of capital. Such exploitation can only persist in a strong state, by the artificial force of the government and its executing organs, and this is why the development of capitalism entailed the perfection, strengthening, and extension of the mechanism of state control.

But that mechanism of perfected legal coercion is quite unnecessary in the system of economic commonality, which excludes all legal exploitation. The system of commonality has its natural bases in the needs of life; it depends not on harm, but on common interests; and where there is a natural accord of interests, legal compulsion and police assistance usually turns out to be unnecessary. No company or association whose members are uniformly interested in a common aim requires this duress, nor do workers, who organize voluntarily in unions to obtain better wage conditions, or peasants, who help each other to cultivate the land and organize mutual credit, or any other group of people coming together voluntarily for the purposes of mutual aid, education, care of the ill, etc.

Basing ourselves thus on the social nature of this system of commonality for which the working classes are struggling, it would be proper to present the claims that are directly opposed to those advanced by today's theoreticians of socialism: namely, that instead of requiring the nationalization of life, the system of commonality, because it abolishes exploitation and class struggle, also abolishes the social need for the state as an organization of coercion and clearly calls for reducing legal compulsion to a minimum and its replacement wherever possible with a new type of social organization in accordance with the economic principle of commonality.

What is this new type of organization that could replace today's state? Associations are such organizations. Simultaneously with the development of the workers' movement, with progress in the economy and production technology, a new form of social organization is also developing in all areas of life. It is developing even though the state is gathering into its hands an increasing number of tasks and functions and—it is worth noting—the same social tasks that the state undertakes are also undertaken by associations of the people.

The standardization of factory relations and protection from exploitation, with which state legislation is increasingly involved, have also been assumed by trade unions and it should be acknowledged that so far they have protected workers' rights more effectively and extensively than has legislation. In farmers' affairs, in addition to the state protection of agriculture and small property owners in the shape of agricultural credit, land banking, and other means intended to raise the agricultural culture of small property owners, there are also agricultural associations of various types, farmers' clubs engaged in improving cultivation, trading companies, joint-purchase companies, companies for the production and transport of crops, people's banks, and mutual savings and loan banks, acting in an extremely wide sphere and aiming to improve the prosperity and social culture of farmers. In the reform of trade and industry, where to this time the state has generally taken very timid steps, consumer cooperatives are appearing which place trade directly in the hands of the people and at the same time create common enterprises belonging not to capitalists but to people's associations. In the sphere of old age and accident insurance, in work on public health, in matters of child-raising and education, we see the same everywhere: alongside the government and philanthropic institutions, hundreds of various associations are appearing that conduct these same tasks of hygiene, security, and education by their own forces and own creativity.

In connection with this fact an entirely justified question arises: shouldn't the political ideal of the working classes be sought in this organization of voluntary associations? Are they not the building blocks of which a true people's republic is being formed before our eyes? At the outset we can predict that if we were to answer this question affirmatively—if we became convinced that the future republic of liberated people must rest on voluntary associations

rather than the state-bureaucratic structure—then many things in today's socialism and workers' movement would have to change.

Above all, the idea of the historical aim of the workers' movement, the
joint ownership of factories and land, would have to change. Joint ownership
would then cease to mean placing industrial and agricultural enterprises under state management, and would instead take a more realistic form: industrial
enterprises belonging to various people's associations and administered by
them (as can be seen today in the example of many food-production enterprises); and agricultural enterprises as associations of private farms conducted
through the common forces of farmers' unions (of which we can see the beginnings in today's farming, business, and credit associations).

In connection with the above, the policy of the working classes, its direction
and bearing, would also have to change. Instead of striving for a democratic
state of a bureaucratic-police nature, which would concentrate all economic
and civilizational matters in its hands, the aim would be quite opposite: a democratic state with the most limited state power and leaving the greatest possible room for the voluntary activities of social self-managed organizations, for
people's associations, and private initiative. The focus of socialist policy would
shift from parliament and ministerial offices to non-governmental social life;
the new system would be built not there where new laws are made, but in that
broad, free sphere of life where various associations, unions, and cooperatives
arise: where the working people are themselves creators.

The morality of the socialist movement would also change. Instead of in-
tolerance, party discipline, and the imitation of police methods in converting
people, instead of neglecting the moral perfecting of mankind as worthless
for current politics, socialism—building a new social world through people's
associations—would everywhere raise and develop new elements in the human soul. Its activity would require broad tolerance, respect for the freedom of
every person, and consideration for diverse needs, feelings, and ideas, because
only in such an atmosphere of freedom could associations develop as a natural
creation of life. It would also require feelings of fraternity and individuality to
be formed—these two cardinal virtues by which people's associations could
essentially transform the world.

In this work of building the future the labor movement can not be indifferent to the kind of human being involved. The movement can not then make
use of people with exploitive and self-loving instincts, with the traits of police-
men or slaves; it must create a new human being and as a result would give the
world not only a new organization and new social economy but something
even greater, a new soul—the soul of a free creator, viewing life as a great act
of brotherhood.

4   The Idea of Liberation

The history of an ideal can be strangely sad. Begun in some unnamed human depths, in some divine vision of injury, struggle, and suffering, it comes into the world clear and simple, as an eternal thing. It comes joyous and pure, like a true creator of new life. It promises everything, resolves all contradictions and conflicts, on one condition—sincerity.

In the meantime, its enemies are on the watch—knowing, cunning enemies—the habits of age. And they do not fight it, knowing that struggle frequently beautifies and strengthens an opponent, rather they adapt, pervert, and parody it. And the joyous ideal dies a monstrous, comical death.

This is what is happening with socialism, in both its social and its individual-psychological history.

In its social history, there were times of "utopia" when it was believed that socialism was to be the work of people of "goodwill," freeing the workers "by themselves"—the creation of a new free life, through the strength of the ideal itself, by the strength of living examples which would appear as oases of liberation in the desert of the capitalist world of exploitation and bondage. It was believed then too that socialism meant not only an economic community ensuring everyone of prosperity and equal rights, but also freedom, the unlimited freedom of nations, groups, and individuals, abolishing all coercion, all collective compulsion of the individual, of the codex over living hearts and minds. It was also believed that its task was not only to transform relations between people but to transform the individual through the birth in his soul of the undying religion of brotherhood. Then came the time of real politics. The work of people of "goodwill" became the work of "the dictatorship of the proletariat," and later of the social-democratic parliament. The economic community of free communes was transformed into forced "nationalization," and state vodka, tobacco, railway, post, etc. monopolies became the sole inheritor and live example of a "liberating" communism. Socialism was announced as the new track along which evolution was striving toward liberation, but as the examples were not very encouraging, it was promised that they would be improved and perfected by a democratized state, blaming all socialism's faults on the lack of universal suffrage. This suffrage is to create a true people's representation; this representation, as the unlimited administrator of all, will declare the nationalization of industry, agriculture, trade, child-raising, education, division of tasks, and division of products, and place it all under the management of various people's ministries, of new police in revolutionary colors.

In this setting, the matter of liberation—"freedom"—turned out naturally to be a dangerous thing, often reactionary (for instance, on the order of the

French congregations), a "bourgeois" idea that could not be allowed to inter-fere in the people's labor state. "Fraternity" became even more dangerous as a clerical-Christian soporific of class antagonisms, while as an ideal it became useless in regard to the fraternal codices of the future people's state. And here begin the tragic and simultaneously comic death throes of former beliefs, the pitiless dialectic of a thesis that has consumed itself: freedom leading to the spread of bondage and its fighters in the French parliament dictating to police prefects the most effective rules for tracking down banned religious associa-tions and free teaching.

In the history of individual-psychological socialism, in the histories that sur-vive in the souls of its adherents, a similar process is occurring. Because social ideas state that justice and collectivism are to be the work of the new people's state, therefore, for as long as that state does not exist, it would be utopian and barren dreaming to create models of justice and collectivism in the current conditions of life. Adherents of the ideal, instead of busying their minds with reforming human relations, should adapt themselves to the existing relations and direct all their strength to where a new state is being built, that is, toward the political, electoral, parliamentary or other struggle; they should exploit all the bitter hatred, the filth of life, all the methods of struggle and ruling prac-ticed in today's society, so that the anticipated, all-powerful "liberating govern-ment" should at last arrive from this revolutionary work. For the time being it is necessary in practice to give up one's "ideal" prejudices against the bourgeois state and make use of all its means to fight one's opponents. It will be neces-sary, moderately and "dialectically," to announce the principle of freedom in order to know how to transform it handily into a knout for reactionary en-emies; it will be necessary to be discreetly quiet about dangerous postulates of respecting individuals and the brotherhood of man, as real politics will require flouting these utopian ideas at every step.

In this manner, an authorized betrayal of ideas—raised to the significance of political wisdom—is created: a conflict between professed ideas, con-science, and life. A new type of human is created—apostles of hypocrisy and its unconscious adherents.

Who does not know people who quite openly avow the ideas of social jus-tice and fraternity and at the same time make use, as calmly as can be, of all the arcana and conveniences of the courts, police, and markets: people con-testing payment, starting civil affairs, reporting to the police about thefts, re-gardless of the kind and dimension of calamity and poverty that will result for someone from these innocent, legal, paper formalities? Who doesn't know of an opponent of exploitation, an honorer of the idea of respect for human dignity, who does not simultaneously load his domestic service with day-long work, brutally stifles the individuality of a child, and strives to climb higher on the rungs of the social hierarchy?—None of this prevents him, in conversations, in gatherings, or in writings, from ardently condemning the various evils of the capitalist system, from believing intellectually in the arrival of a social transformation, or from being moved by a reading of Hugo's *Les Miserables* or Tolstoy's *Resurrection*, and recommending them as books serving the propagation of morality.

In youth, it was different. Every new idea that passed then through one's mind became the beloved of one's whole soul; all the gifts of life were laid at her feet, all the benefits, pleasures, and sufferings. It was not only a postulate of the mind but also of the conscience, not only a vision of the future but also a living truth to be lived by and acted upon. Each day of life was hers.

Politics had its way, however; it created old age. The period of maturity arrives and those beautiful, exhilarating beliefs change into calcified dead ideas, which no longer rule an individual's personal life and create nothing in it. Closed in the purely mental sphere, they only come alive when there is a need to speak and argue about politics; in the depths of souls, in what is created by daily life, in the practical will and conscience, the old, theoretically hated ideas reign completely, sneering quietly at their predecessors from the bankrupt ideals of youth. And thus a person becomes like those French prisons above which is written, in large letters, "liberty, equality, fraternity."

This type of hypocrisy develops in people through upbringing alone and the great forces of youth are required in order to overcome such influences. I remember a painting seen once in a gallery: Christ is speaking to the crowd, his eyes filled with the vision of his kingdom, while before him stands a monkey, who mocks and comments on his words. On the faces of the people can be seen confusion, conflict, unease; it is clear that the monkey is beginning to have an effect and has overwhelmed some entirely.

During the entire period of "upbringing" the same thing happens. We receive the legendary beauty of the word, from which even the deformations of the catechism cannot take the strength and charm, verses of the immortal Sermon on the Mount about giving away riches, about courts and condemnation, about the pointless cares of the day, about those who do not have to have their princes, on the one commandment of love and brotherhood, on the one sin—harm. But beyond, the monkey is always standing; sober, practical people are standing, who comment on these words and try to square them with the requirements of life as understood in their fashion; they comment in such a manner that harm becomes the rule, the normal atmosphere of the conscience, and brotherhood—is alms.

That same "monkey" also has an influence later, and even more effective-ly. When the bright figure of the Nazarene passes before our eyes and in its place appears the vision of modern justice, enchanting all young feelings and desires, when gazing at the beloved model of the Resurrection, we decide to materialize its beauty in the life around us, then too that practical "monkey" appears and tries to convince us rationally that our Resurrection was possible only in the past, in another social system, that only an ignoramus, a utopian not understanding the materialist view of history, could think of transforming his morality while the old social and economic bases persist; that we should even, not wanting to enter on the fatal road of utopia, remain adherents of the morality of this system in which we live, and adapt our personal life to it, in order to have the strength to proclaim ideals.

And the "monkey" almost always wins.

This is the sad history of a joyous ideal. Desiring to characterize the fate of the idea of social rebirth in one image, it could be said that it is held in bondage by a Hobbesian Leviathan, a hundred-headed and hundred-armed Leviathan nesting comfortably in all the old addictions of life, in all the filth that force has birthed in human souls, in all the hatred that slavery has conceived. It has many different names and masks. It has been called the Roman Empire, a the-ocracy, the Holy Inquisition, Jacobinism, the National Convention, and today it is called the dictatorship of the proletariat and the people's labor state. The same—immortal and two-faced.

Those who have experienced the same in their thoughts and feelings will not be surprised that I raise the issue of freeing the ideal. It has to be freed from politics, which castrate it and rework it into some chancellery ideal of a future people's bureaucracy—from politics, which orders it, the child of freedom and fraternity, to proclaim coercion and hatred. The apostles of hypocrisy and their sad science of the world's rebirth by police methods must be countered by the "joyful wisdom" drawn from the youthful era of the ideal.

5   "Joyful Wisdom"

What is this joyful wisdom? Above all, it says this: do not lie to your soul. If, in your social convictions, you disapprove of exploitation and coercion, of own-ership at the cost of the hungry, and the codices that support it, then let your personal life proclaim the same. Let them know you by your life. Not only the beauty and worthiness of the ideas you profess require it, but also the ability to create world history.

Every social institution, both customary and legal, lives only in people, in their needs, habits, beliefs, and feelings; it lives until it finds itself alone in the human conscience. When needs begin to vanish, and beliefs and feelings change, then the institutions that lived by them die their natural, inevitable death, and no ministerial edict or efforts of reaction by the rulers can save them. In those small, minor human changes—internal, psychological changes, from the beginnings of a new conscience, which in some other manner begins to provide norms for man's everyday behavior and his relations with people— there is a powerful breath of death and social rebirth. Institutions that are only combated politically can live again and reign anew, but institutions that are fought against morally, whose sources of needs and feelings have dried up, are truly dead. And therefore you should above all create a new human being: a truly new one, that is, not only with new ideas, but also with a new conscience. Because it is not a chancellery of ministers and prefects, but the new human who is the world power; from him will be born new life, new forms, and a new system. Therefore too, do not lie to your souls—because in ordering them to maintain the old forms of life, you destroy the start of that new social world whose arrival you herald—and you proclaim a falsehood.

Furthermore, it says: allow your souls to adopt, simply and clearly, that ancient idea of the "brotherhood of man" if you want to find an aim and the beauty of life, if you want to attain to eternal matters in your own selves. This idea can not stand theories and reasoning: it is larger than reason. It is adopted directly, as a gift without price or reward. Its exclusive property, which no other possesses, is that it must simultaneously be life and an entry to all the simplest human relations, without any reservation and conditions, not being the hand-maiden of any other aims, personal benefits, or social aspirations. It must be absolutely free and made through the free creation of life. Only then is it itself and its true visage can be known, freeing individuals from their personal cares, fears, and poverty.

By returning to individuals their lost dignity as life creators, we simultane-ously change the existing postulates of social policy. Instead of expecting that a new messiah will appear—a people's state, whose bureaucratic cadres will col-lar all issues and bring about community and fraternity by edict, suppressing the new rebel in the old manner by reaction—let us make creating the "world of the future" today's task: the present, free task of people of "goodwill." The whole essence of cooperativism is contained in this understanding of life as a voluntary act of brotherhood.

In the existing capitalist society there are conditions, forces, and forms that make constructing a new society based on economic community and workers' democracy possible.

These are primarily consumer cooperatives, which, by placing market and merchant capital in the hands of the associated persons, allow them gradually to become the owners of workshops, factories, mines, or large farms as their collective property. These cooperatives are open to all and require, in their own interest, unlimited expansion. The natural antagonists of monopoly, they bring the ideal of "nationalization" to life by changing the workers into co-owners of all enterprises, adapting production to the interests of consumers in general, making "surplus value" the common property[5] of the associated persons, and giving economic self-government to the people. What differentiates the ideal from state "nationalization"—with which our idea has become bound—is solely that it does not take place by compulsion, under the orders of bureaucracy, but voluntarily, through people's natural interest and the strength of the very idea that in bringing about economic community it does not simultaneously kill freedom, the spirit of initiative, self-help, or personal bravery, but on the contrary, it requires all that and expands, increases, instills, and creates not only social democracy but true democrats, that is, independent people.

There are also farmers' agricultural cooperatives, which in connection with loan cooperatives strive for the natural transformation of self-centered peasant farms, which struggle continually with poverty, into cultural, associated farms. They begin with the common possession of agricultural tools and develop toward common dairy, fruit, or livestock production, undertaking at last common grain sales and common mills, and proceeding in that direction, by force of the natural interests of smallholders achieve a higher economic culture and prosperity, closely combined with an ever increasing extension of association in various aspects of the rural economy. In other words, they enter into agricultural collectivism—into a collectivism that does not destroy the individual farm, does not change their farms into "colonized" state farms, but instead is essential collectivism in its democratic, voluntary meaning, while providing all the advantages of the agricultural techniques of large farms and allowing the mass of farmers to reach the highest agricultural and economic culture—not on the principle of market competition, entailment, or parcellation, but on the principle of association and solidarity.

---

5   The author has in mind the basic principle of cooperativism which requires the annual division of profit between all members of the cooperative. Usually a certain part is divided and the remainder is designated for the recapitalization and development of the cooperative. In consumer cooperatives the part that reaches the members of the cooperative is called the "return on purchases" and everyone in the cooperative receives a return in proportion to the amount spent on purchases in the cooperative's outlets.

There are also workers' syndicates in which this new system of the future is beginning to form. They have created the institution of a collective wage contract, which guarantees workers not only security from capitalist exploitation, but also gives them a certain participation in the management of industry and ensures the consideration of their particular interests in industrial matters. Not stopping here, syndicates further strive to acquire complete management of their trade in order to transform themselves into companies that take over the entire work from entrepreneurs on set conditions, with the entire organization of that work, the internal division of wages and occupations, being under the control of the syndicate. In this role, the syndicate desires to produce a communist equality and abolish the hierarchy of workers and the inequality of remuneration in regard to the scale of work, and to divide the whole production of the collective, as a company, among all. In this manner, capitalist industry passes into the hands of new administrators and the managers of independent workers' companies, which govern themselves by the entirely new life principle of brotherhood. They are creating real bases, among the working class itself, on which the new organization of social economy will be able to rest.

From these foci of life will be formed the future of the world wherein man is to be freed through brotherhood. Doubtless the Junker ideal of social barracks, saving mankind by Jacobin methods, the dreamed-of dictatorship of people's parliaments, will continue to oppress slave minds, the harassed souls of those whom life has not permitted to see and love the beauty of freedom and the creative power of man. But it is also certain that the "joyful wisdom" will find its apostles and adherents, that in addition to the policy of "nationalization," a young, vital world will be created of institutions for the improvement of life and of people knowing how to create them.

CHAPTER 4

Clasped Hands

Maria Dąbrowska

With or without the Idea[1]

In those same spheres where every independent attempt of the masses to improve their existence is discouraged as materialism deprived of ideals, rather
strange accusations are leveled at cooperativism for its very ... idealism. As I
mentioned in my book *Rozdroże* [*Crossroads*], such accusations were made,
among other times, in 1936 during that great discussion in the Association of
Educated Farmers after a report by Colonel Dżugay on Czech cooperativism.
The object of attack there was again mainly consumer cooperativism and its
role in the countryside, but above all its idealism, which was supposedly typical only of it and was unnecessarily infecting the agricultural cooperatives,
which were free—again supposedly—of all spirituality.

Cooperativism, it was then said, is a method of doing business and nothing
more. There should be a radical and rapid break with the attitude of the good
souls of Rochdale; it's a naïve anachronism. Cooperativism has long ceased to
be a source of worldview, and we're still stuck in the ideological beginnings of
the movement.

To say such things is practically the same as if they were to say to a Christian
that it was necessary to break with the tradition of the Bethlehem stable, that
Christianity had ceased to be a worldview source and that the Church should
only be an efficient organization of ecclesiastical interests and not also—in
accordance with the spirit of the first Christian communities—a still living
apostolate.

To break with the tradition of the Rochdale pioneers or in general with the
idea of social justice (because this is what is involved), means breaking with
the light that warms and illuminates all the activities of cooperativists with
that moral strength that helps them to persist in hard positions of often thank-
less work, requiring—like every sacrificial and daily toil—strong spiritual support. Never mind that those "good souls" of Rochdale gave the cooperativist

---

1 Maria Dąbrowska, *"Z ideą czy bez idei"* ["With or without the Idea"] and *Ręce w uścisku*
["Clasped Hands"], in: idem, *Ręce w uścisku: rzecz o spółdzielczości* [*Clasped Hands: On the
Cooperative Movement*], Warsaw 1938, J. Mortkowicz, Towarzystwo Wydawnicze [J. Mortkow-
icz, Publishing Society].

movement precisely that sober and practical method of proceeding that allowed them to develop such a successful and vital business. The weavers of Rochdale were distinguished not only by their idealism but above all by their will and ability to act. To depart from their tradition would be to depart from the tradition of something very rare and very much desired by people—the happy combination of idealism with real life effectiveness.

To take sobriety, practicality, and reason from cooperativism would mean plunging it in the hazy barren social mysticism of its "prehistoric" times. To take the idea away from cooperativism would be the same as taking spirituality from love and demanding that it be solely a sensual pleasure.

Today even the advertisements of private shops invent an "idealism" for themselves, simulating an impoverished metaphysic, promising clients success in life and often, and less importantly, spiritual benefit.

Cooperativism deprived of idealism and condemned solely to absorption in immediate material interests would lose that valuable stimulus to its entrepreneurship and, desiring only to do business, would begin to do bad business and soon would be defeated by better—being unscrupulous—specialists in doing solely business.

Charles Gide[2] in the work *Cooperativisme* tells the story of a cabin boy who is ordered to climb the mast for the first time. He looks at his feet, unable to take his eyes off the deck and the rungs on which he is stepping. Before long his head begins to spin; he nearly falls. Seeing him close to fainting, the more experienced sailors shout to him: "Look up, or you'll fall!"

For cooperativism, the idea that supports it is like this upwards view, which is necessary to maintain balance in difficulties and in climbing steep and distant heights.

Not only has cooperativism not ceased to be a source of worldview, but on the contrary, in achieving its aims, it has increasingly solidified as a view of the world, leaving a mark on the whole life of its adherents.

And the heart of the matter is that that worldview does not please certain spheres, which are unable to accept that something outside of themselves might become a source of social worldview. In the discussion mentioned above, and also in many other press statements, this cooperative view of the world is defined as "saturated with the spirit of socialism[3] and social radicalism,

---

2   Charles Gide (1847–1932), French economist, outstanding theoretician of cooperativism, creator of the "School of Nimes," which propagated the idea of 'pan-cooperativism', author of *Kooperatyzm* [*Cooperativism*], translated by S. Thugutt, Warsaw, 1937.

3   Signs of dangerous "collectivism" or "communism" are additionally seen in cooperativist economics themselves and above all in their collection of 'social funds', whose essence and mechanism of establishment we have already discussed here at length. It is clear that

which"—as it was expressed—"has nothing to do with cooperativism." On the contrary, those things have a great deal to do with cooperativism, although not in the sense in which opponents try to persuade cooperativists that they do. Cooperativism is radical, because it radically changes the method of organizing trade and the idea of economic abilities and organizational talents in the world of work. It is revolutionary because it introduces into economic life not only new and different elements, but also transforms human souls, helping them to the full revelation of their humanity, which civilization has hitherto squandered and currently, additionally, holds in low esteem. But the radicalism of cooperativism is positive and creative and its revolutionariness is peaceful and constructive. In a similar sense, Christianity was radical and revolutionary, propagating a new order among the old.

And as to socialism, cooperativism in itself emerged in part from socialism and retained some of its postulates, such as condemning profit without work, excessive competition, exploitation, and the harm of one person by another. But what of it? Were we to want cooperativism to glorify all those indubitably bad things by which it lived and on which it based its development? After all, even the most virulent enemies of socialism have objected not to its involvement with the injured but mainly to its doctrine of class struggle and the materialist view of history, and to its tactics, which envision violent revolution, dictatorship, and the complete nationalization of production.

Cooperativism does not contain any of these things in its program or in its ideas. It does not engage in historiosophy at all; it does not set itself final goals in the doctrinaire sense; it does not proclaim a revolution, but on the contrary, it evolves organically and harmoniously in the old system, like a child in the lap of its mother—whose replacement, if it occurs, will be by the natural and necessary human order of things. It also retains full respect for human personalities and socializes economic life only to that degree to which it can be socialized without damage to the freedom of individual life.

If cooperativism borrowed from socialism its spirit of social justice and love of the oppressed worker, Christianity and Catholicism (and particularly its doctrine as developed by the medieval fathers of the Church) took more than a little from the pagan philosophy of the ancient sages. And what of it? Were they less Christian and Catholic on that account?

---

without these social funds the entire cooperativist movement would be in the pockets of private banks and suppliers and would only be their branches. The whole material strength and resilience of the movement lies in these social funds. And if their collection is to be called "communism" then the assets of all institutions or associations saving for the common good of their members constitute "communism."

Socialism—that is a very serious and multifaceted matter. It is a research discipline, a certain spiritual attitude, an ethical system, and a method of proceeding. Regardless of its future fate, it has had an immense influence not only on the working masses but on political economy and sociology, on art, on the views of thinkers in all camps, on methods of governing, and on all programs of the most opposing parties. Even nationalists, racists, and totalitarians use the ideas, terminology, and tactics created by socialism. We have, after all, "national socialism" and nationalist "social radicalism"; a little while and we can expect the slogan "fascists of all nations unite." Well, and the nationalization of everything, including human souls, has been announced not only by red fanatics but also by brown, black, and orange ones, and moreover all of them have introduced solely a great parody and caricature of socialism.

Here a small intermezzo about the relation of cooperativism to the state is offered.

If cooperativism has deviated rather far from socialism in anything it is in its relation to the concept of the state. While never fighting with the state, anywhere, cooperativism does not share the socialist faith in the providential mission of the state as the unique element called to organize society properly at all levels of life. Contrarily, it sees the real and reliable element of order and the organization of collective life in voluntary associations of citizens. Once cooperativism even imagined that various related groups of such associations would largely be able to replace the state: at least in regard to the internal socio-economic-cultural life of the nation. Ideas of this type were at one time elaborated by Kropotkin, and then here in Poland by Edward Abramowski in his concept of the Republic of Cooperatives. Today cooperativism does not predict what will be the final extent and result of its own development. Not because it has relinquished the realization of any of its possibilities. But, being a great realist, it must take into account the state structure's enormous expansion everywhere, and being naturally as much opposed to totalitarianism, or even to the growth of statism, as it is capable of judging each phenomenon properly, it recognizes the usefulness and sometimes the necessity of the democratic state's moderate interference in this or that area of economics previously left to private initiative.

On its side, the state not only does not persecute cooperativism but relates to it with goodwill. This goodwill is sometimes more dangerous for cooperativism than the simple hatred of enemies. It becomes a sort of friendship like in the fairy tale about the bear's favors. The modern state, with its desire to have a finger in every pie, is a little too eager to regulate and control cooperativism; it wants too directly and immediately to draw benefits from cooperativism and is too inclined to inform it of its tasks and obligations.

But there is nothing to control here. The attitude of cooperativism—and Polish cooperativism in particular—to the state is unreservedly positive and loyal. This is shown not only by the pedantic fulfillment of obligations to the state (cooperativism is one of few economic organizations not to be behind with its taxes), not only the funds paid by it for state and public purposes, but also by the names of our most outstanding cooperativists, who have themselves taken such an impressive part in the construction of our state. I will only mention here Stanisław Thugutt, deputy, twice minister, and soldier of the war of 1920, which left him an invalid; Stanisław Wojciechowski, minister of internal affairs and president of the Republic; Zygmunt Chmielewski, organizer of our Ministry of Agriculture and for a long time undersecretary of state in it; Fr. Wacław Bliziński, deputy and for years director of a department in the Ministry of Religious Faiths and Public Education; and finally Dr Franciszek Stefczyk, minister and high dignitary in various state institutions.

As to the excessive interference of the state in cooperative economics, if it were not that the grand master of all things is the entity that controls the armed forces and police, cooperativism could be for every state and government a great instructress in efficient economic activity undertaken for the common good and conducted according to plan and with a leading idea. It is obviously a misconception that the sense of rational foresight and ability to plan should be the spiritual monopoly solely of the state authorities. These properties exist within society itself and do not need to be imposed on it from above. And cooperativism is the best example of how a voluntary association, based on a real community of interests, is able to use that planning ability significantly more adroitly than a state, with its method of coercion and injunction.

Cooperativism, whose distinguishing trait is the ability to make use of the good side of every economic system, is organized, as we have said, on the basis of the liberal principle of freedom to establish enterprises. But having arisen on this basis, from the beginning of its existence it adopted the plan of subordinating egoistic aims to social interests, replacing unlimited freedom with organized and responsible freedom, curbing economic chaos by a regulated, planned, and foresighted economic order. Cooperativism used these methods long before the state began to see in them a panacea for all deficiencies. Even the concept of modern compensatory trade grew out of cooperation. Polish cooperativism adapted it when it was forced to regulate its debts to English consumer wholesalers, long before the Polish state finally decided on that path. The difference, however, lies in that cooperativism adapts all these methods significantly more rationally. It takes much greater account of the requirements of the circumstances and at the same time keeps in sight the aims that greatly favor life and mankind, while the contemporary state, in its economic planning and its supposed subordination of everything to general purposes, has only one aim—a general aim in fact but also a fairly grim one, because it leads most often not to the flowering of life but to war and death.

Clasped Hands

This cooperativism differs in practice from socialism in that it does not constitute a political party; it is open, as we have said, to all, regardless of convictions. The condition for acceptance is solely to abide by the statutes of the cooperative. As has been said, these statutes are of a type that does not make cooperativism an alluring proposition for the rich, for speculators, or people desirous of fishing in troubled waters. They do, however, make it of value for every working person, whether he is by preference or views a socialist, populist, nationalist, or conservative. But this, precisely, is what sticks in the throat and galls the eyes of our rightist element. They want cooperativism to rid itself—and rapidly—of "socialist and radical elements," or even those that are moderately democratic. Thus it desires to exclude from cooperativism those who did most for its establishment and development: those, moreover, who were perhaps the only ones in Poland to prove that they were able to rise above partisanship without relinquishing their views. Those who made clasped hands the sign, emblem, and symbol of cooperativism and who, in the same matter, frankly, loyally, and fraternally extended their hands to all people of goodwill. They extended their hands and were not disappointed. The number of people who were waiting for an outstretched hand turned out to be infinitely more than had been imagined. Workers and peasants of the most moderate convictions, priests, and members of the intelligentsia never having had anything to do with the socialist party came to cooperativism together with the socialists, seeing in this work a safe sphere in which to unite such broad layers of the nation as would have been impossible on any other level except national defense. The rainbow cooperative standard became for them all the symbol of a real harmonizing of the contradictions dividing the world of work. And the world of work is everywhere—including in Poland—the overwhelming majority of the nation. In whose interest could it thus be to break apart such a valuable and real beginning of the consolidation of Polish society? Of this consolidation in particular, which brings together—not in showy slogans but in real life interests—producers and consumers, wage-earners and owners of small workshops, country people and city dwellers?

The opponents of the socialists and democrats are afraid they could be infected by the ideology of the cooperativists, who are sustained by other views. Why do socialists and democrats not fear being infected by a different ideology when they extend their hands in harmonious cooperation with every honest person, not asking for his party identification? Are we really only capable of building ever more ghettos, divided from each other by the barbed spirit of hatred? Instead of rejoicing that even a modest area of work has been found where the majority of the nation can unite without destroying the colorful diversity without which you don't have life?

Even taking the viewpoint of the poltroons who see the vanguard of communism and revolution in every more enlightened person, shouldn't their fears be calmed when people inclined to radicalism gather together for positive, creative work instead of building barricades? And when, in common with the non-socialists—and thus exposed to their influence to the same degree as they are to socialist influence—they work to raise the prosperity and enlightenment of the masses, which of these things best secures them against outbursts of despair? Unless a certain kind of opponent of cooperativism absolutely needs it to be as desperate and rebellious as possible, in order to hate and persecute it. But we have no right to ascribe such sentiments to them.

When all other arguments against cooperativism are exhausted, it is accused of … internationalism. There is indeed the International Union of Cooperatives, to which both our "Społem" and our Union of Agricultural Cooperatives belong.[4] This is enough so that certain elements of our press and our Sejm are ready to incite opinion against them, because recently, as a result of more omnipotent currents dividing nation from nation, it has become common belief in less enlightened circles of society that internationalism is in itself something bad, criminal, and threatening the welfare of individual nations. Meanwhile, the word "internationalism" is not a moral, negative, or positive idea. From the ethical point of view, internationalism can be good, bad, or neutral. Certain preferences that spontaneously engulf all or many nations, such as fashion, some dances, social forms and customs, certain cults or hatreds that are infectiously shared by the majority of people throughout the world—these are international. Usually all art is international and every nation strives and very much desires that its national art should become international.

An international band of bandits, cheats, or forgers is a bad thing that everyone should avoid. By these same rights, certain international machinations of large capitalists, market speculators, or arms manufacturers are evil,

---

4   The International Union of Cooperatives unites national unions of cooperatives in forty countries, constituting a force of 96,436 cooperatives with 29,600,000 members.

but they are not in the least so passionately condemned by public opinion as other "internationalists," even though the machinations are sometimes such as to plunge many countries—which are sometimes very far removed from the source of such intrigues—into the abyss of bankruptcy, calamity, and wars.

There exists, however, an enormous range of generally acknowledged international agreements, which are not in any sense bad and cannot be called foul even though for one reason or another their influence might merit critique. The Postal Union of all the countries of the world is international and the air, water, and railway communications network is international too. World trade was international for a long time, and those who are today against the International Union of Cooperatives are simultaneously demanding with no less enthusiasm the restoration of private international trade. A quantity of research institutions and professional associations are international in nature. The Federation of Defenders of the Homeland and the Federation of Women with a Higher Education are also international. The PEN Literary Club is international, as is the League of Nations, which indeed did not succeed, because the world had not matured to that degree, but if it had succeeded no one would have called submission to its decisions and directives the influence of "foreign agents." The Catholic Church is and always has been a powerful international body and in the times when it was still fighting for secular power over the world, our Bolesław the Bold[5]—who, as we know, stood on the side of Pope Gregory VII, in contrast to Bishop Szczepanski, who sided with Heinrich IV—by ceremonious act *gratuita devotione* offered the ownership of all Poland to that holy international body.

Why, given the number of the most various, and variously sanctioned, international bodies, should only organizations in the world of work be deprived of the right to international agreements or contracts?

I do not claim that foreign agents do not exist and are not operative. In order to believe that, it is enough to know the history of Poland's downfall and the sinister role played by the bribery of neighboring countries. But if anything is a guarantee of independence from "foreign agents," it is precisely the internationalism of a given union, institution, or activity. International associations are loyal agreements of representatives of all nations in the spirit of equality among peers and the vote of every nation can influence the decisions or activities of such associations in the same measure. Foreign agents only appear where one country is engaged in covert activity with the view to its own interests or the preservation of its influence in one or several other countries. We in

---

5   Bolesław II the Generous, also known as the Bold and the Cruel (c. 1042–1081 or 1082), Duke of Poland from 1058 to 1076 and third King of Poland from 1076 to 1079.

Poland are well aware which countries have their agents in the world, and perhaps here too, and are trying to have their adepts and to maintain their influence. However, this is a matter that has nothing in common with international unions or institutions. And only a kind of primitive magical thinking—proper to primitive peoples, and also certain journalists and deputies of supposedly civilized peoples—a kind of thinking incapable of comprehending the essence of the phenomenon and of historical processes, could confuse the things.

To return to the matter at hand, if the socialist movement is international, as the capitalist world is international after all (only in a worse, cosmopolitan, sense), this is not sufficient reason to vilify socialists. It is possible, nevertheless, to understand a certain resistance and passionate emotional coloration in connection with the socialist international entity, which is generally disposed toward revolution and capable of directly threatening the prevailing system. It is difficult, though, to understand the bitterness directed at the International Union of Cooperatives, which is an agreement between open, apolitical, economic associations. Not only does this Union not impede or damage the national nature of the cooperative movement in individual countries, but in general it does not interfere in their internal or national activities. It solely regulates affairs relating to the international cooperative trade, and the assemblies of the Union, like all international occupational assemblies, discuss the best methods of cooperative work, share the experiences of various nations with cooperativism, and so forth. Thanks to the assembly of representatives of the International Cooperative Union in Warsaw (which produced a fair amount of hostile clamor), the Polish cooperative movement had the opportunity to present itself in such a manner that it significantly raised foreign opinion about the value of Polish business. Thanks to this assembly, skeptical foreigners were able to see not only official Poland but also everyday, working Poland, from its best side. And they left edified and delighted, without knowing how much the unfortunate "Union" had to suffer for having raised Poland so high in their eyes.

CHAPTER 5

Solidarism as a Doctrine of Democracy[1]

Jerzy Kurnatowski

The war has greatly weakened the principles of democracy while simultaneously creating a whole range of democratic countries. In addition, democracy throughout nearly the whole of Europe is undergoing a serious crisis. On the one hand, there is a monarchic, clerical, almost medieval reaction; on the other, communism is emerging and under the mask of a far-reaching progressiveness is drawing European civilization back into a state of some kind of premedieval barbarism, so to speak.

In undeveloped, unbalanced societies this pendulum swing between the extreme right and the extreme left, which is basically also the very extreme right, is violent and without gradation. In Russia, the white tsardom of the Romanovs was followed almost immediately by the red tsardom of Lenin; Kerensky's democratic government lasted a very brief time; in Germany, namely in Bavaria, after the former monarchy we have the red communist terror of Kurt Eisner, and after him the military-nationalist government of von Kahr; the same occurs in Hungary—after the Habsburgs, Bela Kun, after Bela Kun, Horthy.[2] Communism is a kind of heir to absolutism, and at the same time its herald. Communism tries, on a small scale, to play the role of Jacobinism, which arose in consequence of the absolutism of the Bourbons and prepared the way for the absolutism of Napoleon. Even in societies with old established democracies, communist currents are appearing, as the fumes of war, a

---

1   Jerzy Kurnatowski, *"Solidaryzm jako doktryna demokracji"* ["Solidarism as a Doctrine of Democracy"], Warsaw 1922, Nakładem Polskiego Zjednoczenia Mieszczańskiego Narodowo-Postępowego [Published by the Polish National-Progressive Townspeople's Union].

2   Kurt Eisner (1867–1919) was a German politician, member of the Social Democratic Party of Germany and from 1917 of the Independent Social Democratic Party of Germany. He was the leader of the November 1918 revolution in Bavaria, which resulted in the establishment of the Free State of Bavaria. Gustav Ritter von Kahr (1862–1934) was German conservative. In 1923 he created the triumvirate whose forces smashed the march of the NSDAP during the Munich putsch. He was murdered by the SS during the Night of the Long Knives. Bela Kun (1886–1939) was a Hungarian communist, leader of the Hungarian Republic of Councils in 1919. Miklos Horthy de Nagybanya (1868–1957) was a Hungarian admiral and regent of the state in 1920–1944; in 1919 he abolished the Hungarian Republic of Councils, introducing the first rightist dictatorship in Europe after the First World War.

symptom of the mental and economic balance disturbed by the war. The war destroyed an enormous mass of goods and thus decreased the sum of riches to be divided among the whole of humanity, while at the same time derailing the lives of large multitudes of people, making them unaccustomed to work, weakening them and making them unfit for it, thus lessening production capacity and increasing the desire for more rapid improvement in economic conditions. It seems just that the terrible war effort should be rewarded with somewhat greater prosperity. The expectation of improved living conditions is thus greater and more impatient today than before the war, and the possibility of satisfying it very much less. In this state of mental discord, all crazy ideas for the betterment of mankind easily find an ear, even though they obviously only magnify the chaos and make it impossible to exit the vicious circle of increased desires and reduced chances for their fulfillment.

This base exists even in England, where we have communist writings, and even in France, where the parliamentary group of communist deputies comprises over a dozen persons—not to mention that very many persons and groups, while deliberately rejecting any connection with communism, are nevertheless actually campaigning along its line.

The principles of democracy are in danger and with them the whole of our civilization, which is linked to democracy by a thousand unbreakable ties.

The old classic formula of democracy from 1798 is "liberty, equality, and fraternity"—citizens of the nation and the nations of mankind. Today that formula is insufficient because it encompasses only the political side of the question, its electoral—in a sense philanthropic and international—side, but avoids the whole tangle of socio-economic questions: everything concerning work, production, poverty, and the distribution of goods.

The need to adapt the democratic principles from the end of the eighteenth century to contemporary conditions was first sensed long before the war in France, where the republican system, struggling with monarchic reaction on the one side and anarchy on the other, relied on a social doctrine corresponding to the principles of democracy. That doctrine is solidarism, with which the worthy names of Léon Bourgeois, Emile Durkheim, and Karol Bougle[3] are associated.

At the moment when solidarism arose, the theory of conflict held undivided sway in the world of ideas: the Darwinian struggle for survival, which

---

3   Léon Bourgeois (1851–1925), French lawyer and politician, prime minister in the years 1895–1896, winner of the Nobel Peace Prize, theoretician and one of the initiators of the League of Nations, propagator of the idea of solidarism; Karol Bougle—most likely the author is speaking of Célestin Bouglé (1870–1940), a French philosopher, colleague of Durkheim's, and author of a work on the caste system in India.

liberal economists transported to the social context and adopted as the basis of their apology for free competition unhampered by any curb of the state or social structures; the class struggle of Marx; finally the racial struggle, which was actually formulated by the Frenchman Gobineau but was developed and perfected in Germany in the numerous Gobineau Societies which emerged in that country. In the second half of the past century, ideas of conflict resounded everywhere in the kingdom of thought and prepared the psychological foundations for war, which was soon to pour over humanity in a bloody wave. These ideas explained both the past and the present, and were also supposed to point to the future. We find them in sociology, in political economics, and in international and social policy.

These ideas were opposed at the end of the last century in France. People began to question whether the world truly holds nothing but conflict—class conflict, racial conflict, conflict among individuals—whether only the idea of conflict was the key to explaining the past and foreseeing the future, and whether in fact it alone could be a practical regulator of our activity and source of our moral imperatives.

The dominant factor in development is not conflict but firstly and above all the division of work and the resultant exchange of goods, says Durkheim, and proves the claim in his works by summarizing, without attempting to generalize, the vast quantity of sociological material that has been collected. A primitive society is a society where everyone is like everyone else and everyone does the same thing. This original homogeneity then hatches castes, which in the beginning are groups devoted to one kind of work and as a result achieving greater perfection at it. These specialized groups exchange the products of their work between themselves and this system allows a much greater number of people to live within the same territory than previously. It is proper if the warrior caste occupies a particularly elevated position, because under cover of the protection the caste provides the whole of society other groups can relinquish the toils of war: they can work in their occupations and exchange the products of their work between themselves. M. Bougle, in his excellent work on Indian castes, gives a picture of a real network of inherited castes of craftsmen, smiths, masons, doctors, and farmers, who live under the care of the military caste, which defends all from the attacks of nomadic tribes of the desert, and of the priestly class, which creates the philosophy of this system and surrounds it with an aureole. The society maintains it and develops because in its internal relations the elements of conflict have been reduced to a minimum and been replaced by the productive work of specialized groups who exchange between themselves the products of their work, giving one another in this manner more or less equivalent services. It is not the element of conflict that dominates here but the element of solidarity; the solidary relation is a relation that is beneficial to all sides participating in it while harming no one. Already at the dawn of civilization's development, it was not the struggle of individuals or groups among themselves that predominated but the collective organization of work, which allowed a more intensive exploitation of nature and multiplied the quantity of riches in general use.

In a modern society the function of castes is filled by classes, with production and trade being organized by some and executed by others. The moment of conflict comes to the fore when a given caste or class continues to benefit from services received for its functions but no longer fulfils those functions. Then it becomes a parasite; it receives more from society than it gives in exchange and then it is necessary for another social group to replace the former in its functions. But let us not forget that this process occurs gradually: former groups slowly lose the talent for their functions; new ones slowly acquire it. In less developed societies, the legal norms adapt to these changes spontaneously, but in a free, enlightened society the role of legislators, based on intelligent public opinion capable of scientific and objective understanding of social phenomena, consists in regulating the division of social work, that is, the legislator should *de jure* force the former class to relinquish those functions that it *de facto* no longer performs, and deprive it of the privileges it possessed on that account, while the new class should be allowed to perform only such functions as it knows how to perform—for whose performance it has already shown a certain ability. A legislator should base his judgments on extremely careful analysis; of two evils it is better that a given function, which is necessary to the life of the whole, is done ill than not at all. In order to be a change for the better the transformation can only occur, so to speak, on the margins of "permanent relations": "*Il n'y a de révolution que dans la tradition,*" says Proudhon, expressing the same idea tersely if imprecisely. For Proudhon, revolution is change, a kind of moment that destroys tradition; in reality, change is a permanent factor in survival and the division of work and exchange of services is the basic backdrop of social development.

Change, in order to be creative, must not hinder the action of the law of the division of labor; it must not weaken production or slow the tempo of exchanges of services: these are the minimal conditions that should be set from the viewpoint of rational progress, because it should rather intensify all these factors, leading simultaneously to a more balanced and just division of profits.

Post-war French syndicalism, headed by Maxime Leroy,[4] while remaining unusually critical of social revolution, announced a "socialism of the institution." Syndicalism stood for the "technique of the institution." The introduction of new economic arrangements

---

4 Maxime Leroy (1873–1957), French syndicalist, lawyer and historian, in the twenties one of the ideologues of the Confédération générale du travail (CGT).

can not be the result of expecting catastrophes and leaving to the catas-
trophe itself the task of defining the new order and new balance ... The
idea of attaining power and only then issuing rights—this is the idea they
so often make up for themselves about the revolution.

It is not, however, the idea of contemporary syndicalists. On the other hand, they
are characterized by the "constructive" attitude of "experimenting observers." In
Leroy's opinion, "the promoters of intelligence should teach all social categories
to use intelligence the way a physicist uses a scale, a thermometer, or a number,
with the only concern being the precision of the weight, degree, or sum."

I doubt whether precisely those institutions that the syndicalists primarily desire gradually to establish—namely, industrialized autonomous government offices, free from outside influences, administered by state delegates,
intellectual employees, workers, and users—are the most practical. I think
rather that the tried path of cooperatization, municipalization, and nationalization should be taken first: with extreme caution in the last two cases obviously, in regard to exceedingly well-justified fears today of creating a parasitical
and ineffectual new reigning class in the form of a bureaucracy.

I don't want to delve into the details of these questions here. I only wish to
declare that attempts to create new collective economic institutions are not at
all contrary to the doctrine of solidary evolution as understood by Durkheim,
so long as the new institutions perform their functions at least as efficiently
as the former. This is of course most visible in the case of free competition
between enterprises based on the principle of private property and enterprises
based on the principle of collective property (and being thus cooperative, municipal, state, or national enterprises).

It is important here that these changes should occur with the attitude of
"experimenting observation" and that the same scientific caution should be
applied to sociological experiments as is used by physicists or other representatives of the sciences in their field.

The basic sociological law, or, if you prefer, the basic trait of social development, is the still growing productivity of labor, the still intensifying exploitation of nature, the still diversifying division of labor, and the still increasing
exchange of services. New institutions of economic democracy are only as
progressive—that is, capable of increasing the sum of riches—in so far as they
are organized with these conditions in mind. With this reservation and within
these limits they are desirable from the solidary point of view.

Thus solidarism counters the brutal and imprecise theory of class conflict
with a scientific doctrine of creating new, more efficient, and more just economic institutions, requiring solely that they reckon with the incontrovertible

laws of sociological evolution. Bacon's *"naturae imperator, nisi parendo"* should be adapted to social experiments as well: *"societati imperator, nisi parendo."*

The formula of class conflict does not compass social relations, either dynamically or statically. At this moment they are continually repeating to us that the relation of the bourgeois with the proletariat, the entrepreneurs with the workers, is based on the element of class conflict. I will pass over the fact that among entrepreneurs there are collective entrepreneurs: the state, towns, and cooperatives that today are administered by "socialized means of production," and thus fighting against those entrepreneurs and taking from them the possibility of producing is to combat the socialization of the means of production, that is, fighting the goal that class struggle has set itself. Moreover, an ordinary private entrepreneur is producing for the market, that is, for a broad mass of customers, and obviously the more they earn, the richer they are and the more they will buy. The expenditure that industry incurs on increased wages of the workers is reflected in the increased sale of goods. As a matter of course, the shortened working day also does not decrease productivity: a person who works less is less tired, is stronger and healthier, and thus works more intensively. Reducing the time is compensated for in increased human energy. On the other hand, if the industry doesn't go well, if the factory owner doesn't have income, it is clear the worker will suffer from it because he will lose his wages or will receive them in reduced form. Contrary thus to the unilateral theory, the interests of the factory owner and the worker are frequently solidary; there are many more points of contact than of divergence between them and disputed issues can be regulated by courts of arbitration without recourse to striking, which is economic war and—like every war—harms both sides. In addition, the whole matter of hours and wages is loosely related to the creation of new institutions of collective economics, where there are performance as well as management factors, and the same questions of time and wages appear there the same as in private enterprises.

Racial conflict is also not an exponent of history. Nations do not solely fight among themselves; they also trade, and above all, learn from one another. In terms of economics, a damaged and impoverished nation is unable to purchase the goods produced by rich nations and will lessen their wealth. Wealthy nations need a whole range of things they are unable to produce themselves and thus stimulate the ranks of poor nations to production. The wealth of one nation raises the level of wealth of all, while the poverty of one impoverishes all.

We find a chain of positive interdependence, like a chain of negative interdependence, both in international relations and in interhuman relations. The chain of positive interdependence—the fact that the wealth of one produces the wealth of another, the education of one raises the intellectual level of another, etc.—constitutes those bilaterally advantageous relations that harm no one and are called "solidary." Furthermore, due to differences of soil, climate, and talents between nations, a division of work arises that eliminates competition, sometimes partially and sometimes entirely. Poland, which produces rye, does not compete in the production of foodstuffs with Italy, which produces oranges. But even among industrialized nations there is a certain division of labor: France produces luxury items, England produces quality items, and Germany produces mass items, which are less durable but cheap. These countries are markets for each other's goods. Before the war, France sold considerably more of its products to England than to its own colonies. In such conditions war is the most obvious ruin both for the vanquished and for the victor, because the vanquished country becomes a reduced market for the victorious country. The most striking illustration of solidarism imaginable is the terrible crisis that the rich and victorious countries, England and America, are experiencing at this moment because in impoverished post-war humanity they are unable to find sufficient purchasers for their goods. The worse matters are for a backward nation, the more the privileged ones lose by it. The worse for one, the worse for another, the better for one, the better for another—this brief formula comprises the whole of solidarism, in inter-class relations as well as international and inter-individual ones, and although it is not always applicable, it is nevertheless generally much truer than the brutally popular paradox "the worse for one, the better for another"—a paradox that has taken on the robe of science and which has been propagated as the basis for all social relations. In international relations war has a raison d'être only in regard to tribes living from plunder—tribes whose normal activity and source of maintenance is only war and who can only be held in check by violence.

But humanity is not only the sum of classes or nations, the sum of certain groups or others; humanity is above all the sum of individuals. In inter-individual relations both negative and positive interdependence appears with entire clarity and entire obviousness. The ills of individuals here become, with fatal force, the ills of all; the good of individuals is the general good. The basic principle of solidarism, "the better for you, the better for me," becomes visible here with nearly mathematical precision.

The ills of individuals are disease, poverty, ignorance, or laziness. Every such individual ill reflects a thousand-fold on all other individuals, on the whole society. An individual's illness is contagious; in order to get rid of the illness it is necessary to remove its source: dirt, poverty, and uncouth and unhygienic habits. To the degree that this is not done, the illness, like a flame during a drought in the forest, will jump from one person to the next. That a Russian peasant is dying of hunger somewhere by the Volga would not seem to be of concern to us Poles. Nevertheless, at the moment when Poland becomes a sanitary dike against the overflow of Russian typhus and when the health of all Europe depends on maintaining that barrier, it will not require any particular sharpness of intellect to understand the iron law of the interdependence of ills. The disease threatens the lives of the infected and the lives of all who have contact with them. But even an ordinary, non-infectious disease is not at all an individual matter. A sick person does not work, does not multiply the general wealth, and his absence from the workshop slows that workplace. Therefore it is in the general interest to shorten the period of illness to a minimum, to cure it at once, effectively, or to prevent it ahead of time where possible, because the more a disease spreads the greater havoc it wreaks both on the sick individual and on the whole society.

Moreover, disease is a good guide to poverty, as well as contrarily: poverty is a base for illness. The poverty of individuals is also not at all their individual affair. A poor person spends little and thus reduces the market, for which all production is working. A poor person eats poorly; his organism is weakened and becomes a receptive ground for ailments and contagious diseases, which are dangerous for all. Poverty in turn is a good conductor to crime. The enormous percent of crimes occur as the result of poverty. Society must defend itself against crimes and must maintain the costly apparatus of police and courts; it must feed the prisoners and keep buildings for them. If society were to eliminate such an important source of crime as poverty it would free itself in large measure from its result—crime. Perhaps with time this preventative method would even emerge to be cheaper than today's method of treating moral ills when they have already acquired the threatening form of crime, which is dangerous for all.

Poverty, and even illness, is yet in large part the result of ignorance, laziness, weakness of character, and intellectual and moral backwardness. An ignorant and lazy person is not only a misfortune for himself and his family he is also a bad co-worker for all those who work with him. Nations composed in the majority of ignorant and lazy people must give way to others. Ignorance contributes excellently to the spread of diseases. Laziness, together with ignorance, pushes a person along the line of least resistance in life and directs him to the path of crime, which is outwardly easier and less requiring of effort. The chain of interdependence in ill, the chain of disease, poverty, crime, and ignorance, is incredibly strongly linked. One can search for what is cause and what result in it, but one can not fail to see the bond or deny the need to combat every link in the chain simultaneously by the aid of specific methods.

The chain of interdependence in good, that is, the solidary chain in the narrow sense of the word, is equally strongly linked. A healthy person will not infect anyone, is able to work, can multiply the general sum of wealth, and can consume a great deal and thus increase the size of the market. A person with sufficient means to maintain himself will not as easily give in to the temptation of crime, and will not save excessively, which promotes production. Not only can an educated and industrious person take care of himself easily, without being a burden on anyone, but is a desired, often essential, work colleague for others. As a matter of course, educated and industrious nations advance to the fore, taking leading positions in the exploitation of nature, which, in spite of all the battles and discord between people and groups of people, remains the dominant factor in humanity's development.

The chains of good and bad interdependence are facts. Stating and becoming aware of these facts presents the practical question of how the chain of bad interdependence should be transformed into the good, solidary chain. And here what stands out at once is the circumstance that the larger the chain of bad interdependence, the more everyone is exposed to the danger of being drawn into it. The more ill people, the easier it is to catch a disease. The more criminals, the easier it is to become a victim. The more stupid and lazy people, the hardier it is to work oneself, because in a society based on a division of labor, it is impossible to do anything alone. Everyone is exposed to the risk of other people's illnesses, criminality, and ignorance and thus everyone who wants to insure himself against this risk should cooperate in combating these phenomena. A society pretending to culture is above all a mutual insurance society against illness, poverty, crime, ignorance, and their effects. No one can be freed from belonging to that society and from incurring on its behalf certain burdens, because no one is free of risk. The healthiest person can, for instance, fall ill of typhus and die, just as the richest person can become bankrupt and impoverished. No one is served by removing himself from the general insurance institution; therefore society's executive organ, that is, the democratic state, is free to organize this association on the basis of legal, binding compulsion.

The whole system of social reform, which is not in the interest of this or that class or party but expresses the most important shared needs of all society, results from these premises. A system of charity for those who are entirely unable to help themselves, an insurance system against diseases, disabilities, inability to work, old age, and unemployment, applied not only to workers but to the entire working-but-not-wealthy portion of the population—these are the practical effects of solidary postulates. As a result, every human, at the moment he finds himself on poverty's threshold, will find society's outstretched fraternal hand to save him from tumbling into the abyss. And I will say it again: since saving every individual from dire poverty is in everyone's interests, thus all—that is, the entire society—should contribute to that rescue, and for this purpose the executive organ of society, the state, should collect contributions—justly, in accord with each person's ability to pay. To the degree that private associations are properly combating poverty, the state should merely support them; wherever their activities do not reach, it should replace them. In no case should anyone in hard circumstances be left to the mercy of blind fate, which can entirely overcome a failing individual and cause both an individual and general loss.

No less important is general security against ignorance, which requires the creation of a whole network of schools of various types and degrees, organized in such a manner that everyone receives the highest education possible for his talents; moreover, the funds for educating the non-wealthy should of course be covered by the state.

The view of society as a mutual insurance company against poverty and ignorance—a universal insurance company, that is, because absolutely no one is free of the risk of poverty and ignorance or their effects—accords with real conditions and furthermore authorizes the state to organize that company, or in other words, to guarantee everyone a certain minimum of material and intellectual-moral existence.

But beyond that minimum, the coercive role of the state ends. Life must be given strong foundations, and this can and must be done deliberately, but beyond these basics, the expansive, diverse, and often unconscious play of social forces is much more capable of increasing life momentum than a detailed foresight.

In inter-individual relations the elimination of poor people and ignorant people will naturally produce an increase in positive interdependence. Human life is of necessity altruistic and the more intensive it is, the more altruistic. Everyone produces for others and the more that is produced the more others provide goods of all types. Everyone consumes goods produced by others and the more intensively one lives, the more goods are consumed. The elimination of poverty and ignorance, that is, of people who consume little and produce little, increases the general momentum of life. Finally, it has been correctly noted that not only in human life but in life in general, the element of unconscious altruism, or the element of solidarity, plays an enormous role. An animal that eats ripe fruit from a tree does not cause the tree any harm and benefits itself. From animal and plant life a thousand examples of solidarity have been collected, such as, for instance, the well-known case of flowers fertilized by pollen which bees unwittingly carry from flower to flower as they seek nourishment in the calyces. The most enduring animal species are those that live in organized societies, care for their offspring, the females, and the elderly, and have a certain division of labor, that is, a certain involuntary altruism.

The natural momentum of life upwards occurs spontaneously, so long as it is strengthened at the base. That base in human inter-individual relations is combating poverty and ignorance. In human international relations such a guarantee of the cultural minimum of existence should be the League of Nations. It is not in the least a coincidence that M. Léon Bourgeois, creator of the theory of social solidarism, is one of the main theoreticians of the League of Nations. Is it necessary to prove that for as long as the threat of war hangs over nations, the whole intricate network of securities, organized on the basis of ne state, is continually exposed to danger? Is it not obvious—given the whole interdependence of the fate of all people—that that network can be perfected only on the international scale? Without the need for numbers, is it not clear that if humanity, after the terrible destruction of war, continues unproductively to waste billions on arms, there will be a lack of funds for the establishment of productive workplaces?

International solidarism, whose practical expression is the League of Nations, is thus an essential complement to national solidarism, which has a system of social insurance and a proper school system to combat poverty and ignorance. For solidarists, it is also only a matter in international relations of strengthening the bases, of avoiding wars and replacing them with arbitration, while leaving the further development of relations to the effects of the mutual benefits that will be brought by further rapprochement.

The position of solidarism in inter-class relations is similar. Solidarism desires peaceful evolution; it desires to avoid civil wars, strikes, lock-outs, social revolutions, and everything that slows production and decreases the general quantity of wealth; it wants to replace taking up arms or laying down tools by formal courts of arbitration. Solidarism looks favorably on the new institutions of collective enterprise and on collective control of the functioning of private enterprises, though always with the condition of undiminished production, undiminished efficiency of the economic apparatus. It looks favorably on all collective enterprises so long as they correspond to the spirit of that "technique of institutions" that Maxime Leroy characterized; solidarism does not prejudge the future road of social development. As everywhere, here too it is a matter only of finding peaceful and cultural bases for development. Solidarism is not collectivism, and is not thus, for instance, cooperativism. Cooperativism foretells the result of the development of cooperatives; it supposes that the end of that development will be the socialization of the means of production through their cooperatization. Solidarism looks favorably on cooperativist efforts, but does not prejudge their result. Of course it is possible to be simultaneously a solidarist and a cooperativist; that is, to have a certain minimum program and to understand, or believe, that it is possible to reach a certain maximum by the method that program professes. It is also perfectly possible to be solely a solidarist, without being a cooperativist; that is, it is possible to suppose that cooperatives will not reach their integral point of development in spite of the possibilities that solidarism provides to that end.

If someone considers the district, state, or trade union as the vehicle for socializing the means of production rather than the cooperative, then that person—in so far as he recognizes the methods and principles of solidarism—can simultaneously be a solidarist.

Personally, I am simultaneously a solidarist and a cooperativist, but I perfectly understand those who want to be only solidarists, who without foretelling the ends of social evolution, desire above all to guarantee peace and the continuity of work in inter-class and international relations, who desire to give every individual a minimum existence and minimum education in order that the idea of brotherhood, which has been so long expressed and has remained empty to this day, should at last acquire the real and definite substance that is the essence of democracy.

CHAPTER 6

On Uniting the Movement[1]

Romuald Mielczarski

I am to report on the subject of consolidating our movement. There are two reasons why this question must be on the agenda of our congress. To start with, consumer cooperatives from all areas of Poland, which a few years ago, still had to lead separate existences, are meeting together for the first time. The second reason is that the postulate of the movement's unity has been called into doubt by certain factions of cooperativists.

For me, a cooperativist honoring the Rochdale principles, the necessity of the movement's unity results from the very premises of cooperation. Thus, to prove the necessity of unity in our movement we will have to stick to those premises. For many of you, this will in truth be preaching to the converted, but the repetition of well-known things is unavoidable.

Consumer cooperation—and that is the only form of cooperation I consider to be important—emerged, as we know, in England and not elsewhere. Why first in England and not elsewhere? Because England is where capitalism first developed in full. As can be seen, cooperation is the child of capitalism.

We are all familiar with capitalism because we live in its atmosphere. Like everything with which we have grown up from our earliest years, this system seems eternal to us. But capitalism is scarcely a few centuries old. It is true that various seeds of capitalism are to be encountered in remote antiquity, but it began to develop seriously only at the end of the fifteenth century, and began finally to rule at the end of eighteenth and beginning of the nineteenth century. It is worth emphasizing that capitalism began with credit and trade, from whence the rich moved into industry and agriculture, controlling in that manner the whole of economic life.

---

1 Romuald Mielczarski, *"O zjednoczenie ruchu"* ["On Uniting the Movement"], in: idem, *Pisma* [*Writings*], vol. 2 and *O naprawę Rzeczypospolitej* ["On the Improvement of the Republic"], in: idem, *Pisma* [*Writings*], vol. 1, K. Krzeczkowski (compilation), Warsaw 1936, "Społem" Związek Spółdzielni Spożywców Rzeczpospolitej Polskiej [Union of Consumer Cooperatives of the Republic of Poland].

The trait that distinguishes capitalism from other past economic systems, whose remains are still coexisting with it, is that the whole of its economic activity is calculated in terms of profit. In capitalism, every credit, trade, industrial, or agricultural enterprise has the owner's profit as its goal.

It should be stated that capitalism brought about a complete upheaval in economic relations and that in many respects it was more advantageous for humanity—an unprecedented division and coordination of work has developed, science has been utilized, various natural forces have been discovered and used, a whole range of new needs has been created and developed, a quantity of means for their satisfaction has been produced. Capitalism, however, has a deadly sin on its conscience—in leading gradually to the proletariatization of formerly independent possessors of the means of production, it has divided society into two classes, which remain in continual war with each other, either openly or covertly, and has created an unprecedented inequality of wealth.

In the first period of the development of capitalism, only hymns of praise were heard. However, when the antagonism of the two battling classes and the inequality of wealth began to be ever clearer and at the same time the inequality of rights and obligations began to strike the mind, the hymns of praise began to subside, while ever louder criticisms arose and doctrines aimed at reconstructing society, either partially or entirely, began to be produced.

One of the doctrines aimed at the entire reconstruction of the economic system is consumer cooperation.

The cooperative doctrine in today's form is not in the least the discovery of one or a number of ingenious minds but the result of collective trials, attempts, and experiences of spontaneously formed consumer associations. More than other doctrines, cooperation owes its present-day substance to former defeats and failures.

What is the essential substance of cooperation? Cooperation states that, even though it may seem very strange at first sight, the existence of capitalism is entirely in the hands of consumers and this unjust system can be gradually ousted by the cooperative system, if only consumers, uniting in consumer associations, take trade and production into their own hands. If one thinks of banks, disposing of enormous capital, of mines, foundries, and factories, and finally about the great warehouses of goods at the disposal of capitalism, the cooperative idea seems simply mad. Nevertheless, as life shows and has shown, this mad idea is the most certain path to liberation from capitalism. Capitalism indeed possesses terrifyingly large means in comparison with the consumer. It is an enormous Goliath matched with a miserable David. We must remind ourselves, however, that all that wealth at capital's disposal is nothing other than collected profit.

Let consumers, organizing in their own associations, step by step deprive capital of profit and let that profit be changed into common capital, and the relation of forces will change overnight in favor of the consumers. Capitalism will lose ground and cooperation will gain it. This is precisely what consumer associations are doing. Consumers in one locality are joining together in associations and beginning with the founding of a retail shop or shops. Associations obtain the profits that previously went into the pockets of the shopkeepers. These profits are partially converted into common capital; the current assets of the association are increased, which gradually allows it to satisfy to an ever greater extent the needs of its members and thereby to increase the dimensions of the common surplus. To strengthen its current assets the association accepts contributions from its members. These contributions previously supplied private banks; presently they are strengthening the position of consumers. Controlling local trade to a certain extent, the association proceeds to organize production of a local nature. And again the profits previously obtained by industrial capital remain with the association. Consumer associations from around the country join together in one national union for the purpose of conducting warehouses, imports, and later production, banking, and insurance as well. And again the additional profits that previously strengthened the wholesalers, importers, industrialists, banks, and private insurance companies are converted into the common property of organized consumers.

If in our imaginations we extend this slow evolution, at the end of the road we see the Cooperative Republic and a new system in which the whole economic activity will be calculated not in terms of profit but of satisfying social needs.

Cooperation organizes consumers. Who are consumers? Everyone. Consumers organize not one group or another, one trade or another, but people, because all people have needs and desire to satisfy them as best they can, with the least effort. For the legitimate and strictly democratic preservation of its system and to secure itself against individuals whose professional interest could be in opposition to the successful development of the association, a cooperative may, by rule or statute, not accept certain categories of persons as members. With this reservation, the cooperative stands open to all. The principle of universality is in its fundamental interest. Without the accession of the majority of humanity to cooperation, it is not possible to imagine cooperation's victory.

Certain factions of cooperativists are opposing the principle of universality, considering that cooperation would thereby lose its class character. I consider this accusation to rest on a misunderstanding. If through "class nature" we are to understand a negative attitude to capitalism, then every consumer cooperative is of a class nature because its very establishment constitutes a break with capitalism. I will say further that in this sense the universal cooperative has a more class nature, because it more quickly and effectively combats capitalism than the most red, closed cooperative. If, however, by "class nature" we are to understand participation in the political struggle, then no cooperative is of a class nature, because the exclusive field of action for cooperation is the area of the economy.

In its struggle with capitalism, the cooperative finds itself in the identical position as every capitalist enterprise in relation to others. Cooperation "competes" with capitalism. As a competitor of capitalism, cooperation, in order to conquer, must in every respect show its economic superiority. We must never forget this truth. We can not submit to the illusion that the cooperative, solely because it is a consumer entity, and thus an organization having a market somehow regulated and ensured in advance, need not concern itself with competition. The idea of all consumers from the beginning of the world has been to satisfy their needs the most fully at the lowest cost. Due to this consumer attitude, capitalism supplanted its predecessors—primitive communism, the family system, and the craft system—even though it is indubitably much less equitable in terms of the division of material goods, because it was able better and more cheaply to satisfy consumer needs. The ideal, just system will never triumph permanently if it is not economically effective. We can rebel all we like against such a course of events, but we will never be able to change it. Thus if we want cooperation to triumph, we must organize cooperatives in such a manner and give them such traits as will allow them to meet people's needs better and more cheaply than capitalism can. This is obviously neither the time nor the place to list the detailed conditions that give cooperation the advantage over capitalism.

I will pause to mention just one condition, because it is the subject of my report—the unity of the movement.

The unity of the movement—and through that unity I understand one cooperative in a given locality instead of several dispersed ones and one countrywide union instead of several separate ones—is the most important condition for the success of the movement. Each of you, whoever has even superficially read social economy—and every social activist must learn at least the rudiments of that science—knows that the main cause thanks to which capitalism beat its predecessor, the craft system, was the size of enterprises. Thanks to large sizes it was possible to sell in bulk in advance and later to produce and sell in bulk, and in the mass production and sales it was possible to apply a better and improved division and coordination of work, to utilize inventions and scientific discoveries, and in this manner to improve technology to an unprecedented degree. Similarly, cooperation must aim, with all its force, for the size of its undertakings to exceed the size of private enterprises. Only absolute unity can give cooperation these large dimensions. In order not to bore you longer with theoretical proofs, I will offer several examples from our movement that show exactly how the lack of unity has a negative effect on our competitive ability.

First example: The lack of unity leads to high purchasing costs and high trading costs. In places where there are several or a dozen or more cooperatives instead of one, as is the case in nearly all the larger cities and towns, every small cooperative buys goods separately, transports them separately, stores them separately, and distributes them separately; each has a separate director, a separate management board, separate staff, a separate warehouse. It is obvious that in such circumstances purchasing power is diluted and thus the price of buying goods must be higher and the costs of trade higher per item than when there is unity.

Second example: The lack of unity makes the rational location of shops impossible, resulting in high inventories and lower purchases by members. One large multi-shop cooperative introduces specialization in its shops. Shops with articles of the type purchased daily in small quantities are located at points where there is the largest concentration of members; shops with haberdashery, textiles, stationery, cooking utensils, and such like articles, bought periodically, are located in the most central parts of town, while shops with meat and vegetables are located in another part; storehouses for coal and fuel are located closer to the railroads; and milk and bread are predominantly transported to the door. Where there are several or over a dozen small cooperatives instead of one multi-shop cooperative, there is no speaking of the rational placement and specialization of shops. In this case, the shops of one cooperative are entirely copies of another; all are far from the homes of members and all are disproportionately overburdened with inventory. The result is that cooperatives continually suffer from a lack of working capital, because simultaneously member purchases are negligible and the cooperative owes its existence principally to the accidental purchases of the public.

Third example: Lack of unity prevents the production of the most important articles and limits members' purchases to articles that are less necessary. I have wondered for a long time why purchases by members in our cooperatives are only a small part of their household budgets. One of the causes is indubitably the inappropriate placement of shops. The most important reason lies in the fact that our cooperatives do not primarily sell the most basic articles of food, such as bread, meat, lard, milk, butter, potatoes, and vegetables; they do not sell them because the sale of these articles simultaneously requires their production. For as long as our cooperatives do not undertake the production of these articles, the whole of their sales must of necessity be limited to sugar, coffee, tea, soap, and colonial products—articles which are indeed important, but which constitute only a small fraction of the household budget. Without the production of basic food items, the further progress of the movement is not possible, and the organization of production requires unity.

The greatest problem of our movement is the fragmentation of our cooperatives on the spot. This fragmentation existed before, but it was limited. From the moment when several national unions arose, with each striving to create its own cooperatives, the fragmentation has increased and is now threatening to transform a movement about great social ideals into cooperative shopkeeping. We will be able to speak of stemming this fragmentation and creating the unity we badly need only when, in place of several battling national unions, one arises that all the other local unions join.

Cooperation is a great movement which will bring direct benefit to the consumers taking part in it and is simultaneously a broad highway leading humanity toward a more just, more humane system. This movement, in order to attain its immediate as well as its ideal goals, must create an organization and techniques that will give it an advantage in the competitive battle with capitalism. Only the complete unity of the movement can give cooperation such organization. Unity is the requirement for the movement's success.

Cooperation for the struggle with capitalism is organized by consumers. All people are consumers. All people are thus interested parties in the development of cooperation, but the proletariat is the most interested. The proletarian is injured by capitalism, both as a consumer and as an employee. Thus in appealing to all consumers to bring about the unity of the movement, I am appealing above all to the proletariat. Without unity there is no cooperation and without cooperation there is no liberation from capitalism.

Resolution

On the consideration that cooperation, in order to achieve both its immediate aims as well as its ideal goals, must possess techniques and organization that will allow it to compete effectively with capitalism, and that such organization and techniques can be given only by the complete unity of the movement, the 1st Congress of Consumer Associations of the Republic of Poland calls for:

(a)   consumer cooperatives in one locality to merge in one association;
(b)   nation-wide unions to merge in one national union;
(c)   local unions to join the Union.

On the Improvement of the Republic by Reason of the Election of Mr. Stanisław Wojciechowski to be President of the Republic

Dear Stach,

I am glad, truly glad, and my joy and pride is shared by the whole Polish cooperative movement, that the difficult and responsible position of President of the Republic has been entrusted to you, the first cooperativist in Poland.

I am glad as a citizen, because I am convinced that in the period of forming our statehood, you, raised in the principles and methods of cooperativism, will be the best Builder of the Republic.

Poland has all the gifts to become a great state, wealthy and prosperous, because it has great natural resources and a valiant, talented population, with noble drives, longing for order and regularity, eager for work. We do not know how to govern and direct ourselves is all. We must develop this organizational sense in ourselves at any price, in order for bountiful nature and the population to form a beautiful whole.

From the lowland, where the whole is viewed with difficulty but details with complete clarity, you have risen, as President, high, where it is easy to grasp the whole but the possibility of observing details directly is lost. And the life of the state, like the life of people, is composed of details. In the government, Sejm, and senate you will have a powerful source of information, but it will never replace direct contact with life. And you, in order to lead properly, should and must see clearly. As the representative of the Majesty of the Republic you will of necessity be hampered by ceremony, but do not allow yourself to be cut off from the world and do not break, Heaven forbid, the cordial bonds with people with whom you worked in various areas. Those thousands, scattered about the various corners of the Republic, who sincerely wish you the best, will come disinterestedly to your aid, so that you always see clearly and in accord with reality. The longing of all Polish citizens is for a permanent, strong government.

A government is strong when it is the faithful reflection and executor of the opinions and desires of the vast majority.

Whether you form it of parliamentarians or in another manner, remember that it should be composed of people of high morals and strong character, who are fond of the kind of work that is entrusted to them and are well aware of the country's needs and the wishes of the population. A government formed of such people, on the basis of a definite program, harmonized in part and in whole with the country's needs, will be strong because the whole light of opinion will be behind it.

The most able government will be powerless without good executors. The principles of a good administration can be summarized as follows: a small number of members, with a high moral level, a set range of activity, independent decision making within this range, as few conferences and as little paperwork as possible, rapid and clear decisions. The administration, from the top to the lowest rungs, should be animated by the pure spirit of democracy and aware that the nation is not for it, but it is for the nation. The formation of our administration in these principles and in this spirit is one of the country's most important needs.

The Republic's misfortune is the poverty of its treasury with the comparative wealth of its citizens. Stabilization of the mark and its replacement with the zloty is a cardinal condition for the improvement of the Republic. The instability of the mark is the main, if not the exclusive, cause of economic chaos and speculation and a source of general demoralization. The mark can be stabilized permanently only with a regulated budget. The state's revenues can be raised very well by raising land and real estate taxes, divided among tenants, to the pre-war height, raising the tax on profits from trade and industry, raising customs and railway tariffs, introduction of variable export levies on sugar, wood, crops, and eggs (depending on the situation), and increasing the profitability of state enterprises by making them independent and basing them on strict trade principles. Before this happens, a repetition of the levy is indicated.

In expenditures, serious savings can be introduced. It is necessary, above all, to lower the number of civil servants, whose work is in contrary relation to their number. Directors of departments and heads of divisions should be encouraged seriously to consider whether with a better division and intensity of work and more efficient methods it wouldn't be possible to significantly reduce the number of personnel. The procurement system of the central state institutions should be fundamentally revised, because material costs are a major part of the budget.

The state is the largest recipient of agricultural and industrial articles. It is not a neutral matter in procuring these items whether it acts like a housekeeper and buys at tenth hand or goes directly to the producer. The creation of a central procurement office for state institutions, observing the prices on national and foreign markets and keeping in direct touch with producers, would indubitably reduce the material expenditures of the state and would contribute, to universal joy, in reducing the number of parasites preying on the state.

Every effort should be made to return the country's finances to health. Certain expenditures, however, should on no condition be subject to limitation. Among these are expenditures for universal education and Polish science. Poland has the most unfortunate borders in the world and most unfortunate neighbors to the east and west, who for a long time yet will not forget that we were their subjects. One guarantee of our independence is a valiant and intelligent army, but no less a guarantee can be given by creative Polish scholarship. The more secure we are, the higher the Polish soul rises, the further and more intensive the rays of Polish culture, the sooner we will become, from passive recipients, the joint creators of European civilization. And in the event of war—from which God protect us—in science we will find the aid that will determine victory.

The Republic must take all its citizens into account, and those who have lost the ability to work for reasons not of their own fault, should be assured of the means of existence. Thus when the currency is stable and the treasury full, think about social insurance.

To a cooperativist, who was a pioneer of cooperativism in Poland, I don't need to write about its desiderata. Cooperation is an expression of the world of work's longing for a new social order based on brotherhood and justice. What has been created to this time in Poland is far from the ideal and very small, but already that something is an important factor in economic life in Poland, and when party passions subside, local separatisms are blunted, personal ambitions fall silent, and the whole of the cooperative movement is united in one union, hat something will be a powerful factor in Poland's economic rebirth and a great, always living, source of creative democracy.

The cooperative movement is born, grows, and matures by its own strength, but it feels the fate and misery of the country with the greatest sensitivity. The war increased its ranks, but made it poorer. The crisis of provisions in the first years of independence forced it to borrow from abroad, and the financial crisis deprived it of the dominant part of its operating capital. The cooperative movement thus needs the friendly aid of the state; the matter of changing the law on cooperatives and producing a separate law on the taxation of cooperatives is also urgent.

I am glad that after Józef Piłsudski,[2] who played a powerful part in resurrecting and defending Poland, fate has designated you, dear Stach, to continue its construction. I am heartily glad because I have a deep belief that you, a cooperativist, will most easily manage to turn your attention from the sphere of empty power struggles to the sphere of great economic questions.

---

2 Józef Piłsudski (1867–1935), a Polish statesman and military commander, in early life one of the leaders of the Polish Socialist Party (PPS); a co-founder of the Second Polish Republic in 1918, 123 years after it had been taken over by Austria, Prussia and Russia; "Chief of State" (1918–22), "First Marshal of Poland" (from 1920), and after the May 1926 Coup d'État *de facto* the first person of the state and an important figure on the European political scene.

CHAPTER 7

Through Cooperatives to the Future Order[1]

Zofia Daszyńska-Golińska

Is the Future Social Order Distant?

Cares, problems, high prices, the exploitation of merchants—these fill the day of every person. We live, however, in the hope that the future will be different and that the country of our children will blossom with the flowers of happiness. Thus, one of the most important questions that the proletariat asks itself is: What will the future social order be like?

We believe that it will be better, more just, that the wealthy landowner and capitalist will cease to lord it over others and the poverty of the overworked laborer will end. Nevertheless, it is not easy to create such a promised land in which people will be happy, free, and rich. How are we to change all the ills? How are we to combat the might of capital and eliminate private entrepreneurs? For this not only wealth and strength—which can be obtained through revolution—are needed, but skills and work are also necessary in order to build a new world in place of the one destroyed.

It is not possible to imagine the future system in all its details; we do not believe, though, that it is a fairy-tale. On the contrary, every day could bring us closer to it on the condition that we take advantage of each day. Today, already, new forms of enterprise are being created: there are factories, warehouses, and farms, which do not belong to private wealthy persons but to working people. The people themselves created them; they maintain them by their own work and money; they manage them through their own officials. Looking at the great expansion of these institutions whereby the people help themselves, that is, *institutions of mutual aid*, we have to believe that we are binding ourselves together in the future system and that it is not a pipe dream *but is already dawning today*—and is not far away. Self-help and collective action, that is, co-operativism, has placed great strength and capital in the hands of the workers

---

1 Zofia Daszyńska-Golińska, "Przez kooperatywy do przyszłego ustroju" ["Through Cooperatives to the Future Order"], 4 edition, Warsaw 1921, Nakładem Wydziału Propagandy Związku Polskich Stowarzyszeń Spożywców [Published by the Propaganda Department Union of Polish Consumer Cooperatives].

themselves—not only in distant parts, in the wide world, but here in Poland too.

The war, which destroyed industry and private trade, has given new impetus to cooperatives.

It is about these cooperatives and the principles on which they rest that I am going to speak here. My readers will be persuaded that the cooperative system eliminates exploitation and the rule of private capital, brings better living conditions, and could become the manner of producing and distribution—the form of existence—that will prevail in the future order.

Competition and Cooperation

Today the Latin proverb "Man is a wolf to man" is being proven true. Greed, jealousy, intrigue, the crushing of the weaker by the stronger, the exploitation of the worker by the employer—these are the generally prevailing principles. Class struggle pits organized laborers and the no less solidary capitalists against each other and everyone vigilantly guards the interests of their class. *But this struggle is already a great step forward, because it relies on organization.* The solitary worker does not fight, he only suffers. When he requests higher pay, when he requires humane treatment from his overseer, they let him go, starve him, and thus crush him. Organization gives him strength. In an organization it is not struggle that prevails, but mutual understanding, common goals, and cooperation to achieve those aims. We have thus proof that there exists another principle, and that is *"man is a brother to man,"* in other words, a faithful companion through thick and thin.

Such fraternity should encompass not only the people of one class but should reach further. As citizens of the Polish state we have common interests. Everyone wants to maintain its permanency, strength, and wealth, and thus to abolish dishonest and unscrupulous acts. As cooperativists we feel our nearness to honest people of other nations, who want to improve their lots and that of their homeland by this same path. Let us come together then and consider not only what differentiates us but also, with the same strength, what unites us, and we will form a society of honest people. This society might be not only a national society but could reach to other nations. It opposes the fraternity of decent citizens to the desire to exploit their weaknesses. Organization makes us aware of our strength and gives us the means of defense.

Human Needs

The aim of every gainful employment is to satisfy needs. When the time and strength of the working people have been subordinated by the owners of capital and land, each person must think about satisfying those needs on his own. We buy every good at a price that is three, four, or sometimes ten or one hundred times higher than it costs in the factory or workshop. The farmer, controlled by the profiteer-intermediary, has forgotten about the needs of the city and the industrial workers, whose products are, after all, necessary to him.

Think how many people live from trade. Above all, there is the wholesale merchant: a substantial man disposing of large amounts of capital and sending out agents with samples to praise his goods. Then there are large merchant warehouses, which supply the smaller shops; and finally there are peddlers, vendors, smugglers, their helpers, and so forth. We maintain, and often enrich, all these people in making our modest purchases. In addition, the poorer the individual, the worse goods he receives. He is concerned to buy cheap, and thus he receives meat scraps, bread baked with bran and shorted in weight, coffee mixed with burnt beans, coal in which there are stones, clothing that has been used and not disinfected and will give him disease, and so on.

Women, who spend the meager cents that have been earned, know best what it means to be dependent on merchant capital. For them, the ideal should be to finally manage to buy cheap, without being cheated or exploited. Is there a means to achieve this?

Consumer Associations

The cooperativists have thought of this.

Cooperatives, that is, consumer cooperatives, are sales outlets created by the consumers themselves. Everyone, rich or poor, worker or capitalist, is a consumer and everyone can be a cooperativist who wants to make the effort. For this purpose we establish our *own* shops and supply them *ourselves* with all the basic necessities.

The capital necessary for establishing the shop is not large. At the beginning it is enough to rent an apartment, buy goods, and find an honest person to take care of the sales. Such a person should be properly paid, in order to be able to give his entire time to the association. He need not be a professional merchant, but should be an honest, diligent, and wise employee, in order not to be cheated and not to cheat buyers.

If, for example, *100 persons each contribute 1,000 marks, that will already be 100,000*, and the majority of our small shopkeepers begin with less capital. 1,000 marks could be paid gradually, for instance, at 50 marks per week. These marks won't be wasted, because trade brings profit, and customers and members will increase, and every customer is a co-owner, because he has his share. To the degree that prices rise, supplementary payment will have to be made to the share. Similarly, the association can require the deposit of a higher sum if it is needed to make a larger purchase.

In today's post-war conditions, there are few goods and they must be acquired when the opportunity arises, with no delay in payment, though this can sometimes be burdensome. The money will be returned in the form of cheaper goods, but care must be taken that it is properly used. The shareholder *must take care of his shop*. Above all, he must buy only from the cooperative association. Every purchase increases turnover and gives profit to one's own little shop. The cooperative must establish a board of management and a supervisory council, which without remuneration but only out of a sense of civic duty will oversee that sales are being managed honestly and that the cashier isn't siphoning the assets. All should be concerned to find cheap and certain supply sources, to establish low prices, and acquire only those articles that will find customers.

It has been found that at the beginning only a few paid people are sufficient; the cooperativists themselves think about all the rest.

They make their decisions at the General Assembly, which is convened, for instance, every half a year, and in which every member of the cooperative has one vote. Every member, whether he has purchased one share or many, votes and decides not as the owner of capital but as a full-fledged member. In a joint stock company, a member is only the representative of capital. His needs or aptitudes are of no concern, only capital. If he has contributed half the capital in shares, he has half the votes. A *cooperative operates differently*. A member is able to acquire only a few shares, and at the shareholders' meeting he will have the same influence as the holder of a single share.

What Benefits Does a Cooperativist Receive?

The benefits are comprehensive. The company goods are sold at a low price, because no one is interested in profit but only in covering the costs. This frequently forces private merchants to lower their prices.

Defective goods are a plague for consumers. Currently, after the war, profiteering has gained the ascendancy and the adulteration of goods has reached monstrous dimensions. Butter, cheese, and milk are adulterated. So much water is added to butter that scarcely the fifth part remains of all the proper fat in cream or sour cream, and a pound packaged as butter cream costs hundreds of marks. In the cities, special workshops have been established to test food, soap, medicines, and so forth. In 1917, such a workshop in Warsaw made 4,531 analyses (of the composition of goods). It emerged that 964 samples were unusable and 1,035 were adulterated. This means that out of 100 items bought by a Varsovian, 45 were adulterated or harmful—that not only dairy products but also bread, barley, fat, cold cuts, meat, coffee, candies, carbonated waters, soap, medicines, and so on, are falsified and the money we spend on them brings us harm, not benefit.

In a cooperative, only good products are sold, not defective ones, because no one will adulterate merchandise for himself. Weights and measure will be accurate, because every shareholder has the right to make sure of it.

With the passage of time, the shop will grow and be located in better premises; it will acquire goods direct from the factory and thus better and cheaper ones; the service will be conscientious, the packaging clean, and shareholders will increase. After a year it will turn out that profit has accrued, which: (1) is paid as a percent to the shareholders, that is, as dividends, and (2) is put into expanding the shop.

This is not all, though. With every association purchase, even selling at a lower price than in the neighboring shops, some small amount is earned. The most is earned by those who have spent the most in purchases. These are not the richest members but usually the ones who have most faithfully bought in the cooperative—those who went to it even for purchases worth pennies. The cooperative pays each person as much as it earned from him. A surprised housewife, who has made purchases in the cooperative shop all year and was happy to have good, cheap goods and paid—for instance—80,000, will receive 4,000 marks at once. How useful this sum will be to buy clothing or household equipment!

The Principles of Consumer Cooperatives

1. In a cooperative, purchases can only be made with cash. This prevents the possibility of members becoming indebted. It accustoms them to buying only articles that are necessary and to making expenditures accord with income. It clearly shows that if income is too small then a person should seek other earnings or ask for higher wages.

2. Whoever has bought a share must make purchases in the cooperative. Otherwise, the cooperative will not develop, shares will not bring interest, and the cooperative will always remain one small shop.

3. Making purchases in the cooperative results in savings, because any extra paid for an item is to the benefit of the purchaser. And therefore, *whoever buys more, saves more*. It will be paid back to him at the end of the year.

4. A shareholder is a co-owner in the cooperative and should be concerned with its development. He has the right to be, because the cooperative is managed by the general assembly, at which each shareholder can speak and vote.

5. *Low interest is paid on shares*, usually not more that 5 percent.

6. *At the end of the year or half year, the return on purchases is calculated and distributed to each person according to the sum he expended on purchases.*

7. *Shareholders, in caring for the development of the cooperative, should not require the entire surplus (profit) but should leave at least part for the expansion of the enterprise.* This will be *reserve capital.*

8. *The reserve capital goes to expand the shop and to buy a larger quantity of goods, and to construct premises for the cooperative* in order not to pay rent and to have a place for other common institutions such as a savings association, a reading room, a library, community rooms, association rooms, and so forth.

9. *Cooperatives in Poland are free to sell to non-members.* It is the same in other countries. In Belgium and England, anyone can buy in cooperative shops, but naturally only members benefit from the profits. Similarly, it is possible and proper to sell goods acquired in limited amounts only to members. Thus it is necessary to put in for a share and complete it at the proper time, in order to have the right to buy everything the cooperative offers. Since a cooperative, in the present difficult conditions, can not always be supplied with all goods, the custom has been adopted of writing on a blackboard the names and prices of the article that can be acquired on a given day. The prices of goods are uniform for all buyers.

10. *Every shareholder, in his own interest, should be concerned for the cooperative to acquire the largest possible number of members.* The larger the cooperative, the better it can be run and thus the lower its prices.

11. *Shareholders,* when the shop succeeds and turnover grows, *should take care to create new associations for building homes, granting loans, establishing bakeries, pharmacies, a shoe or clothing factory, and other such facilities.*

12. *Shareholders should remember that every cooperativist is closer to them than whoever looks on indifferently at their measures and strivings; they should feel like a family, where each member helps the others.*

The Progress of Consumer Associations

Adoption of these 12 commandments has made cooperativists into a power. The cooperatives scattered around various countries today are counted among the world's largest enterprises. They have wonderful palaces, ships, lands, factories, a quantity of housing for their members, savings and loan banks, and schools.

Cooperatives look after the entertainment and spiritual life of members by arranging lectures, theater presentations, libraries, reading rooms, joint travels around the country and abroad, and so forth.

Undoubtedly, more than one such company has collapsed, or was unable to develop. The usual cause here, though, was lack of adherence to the above-mentioned principles. If cooperativists are concerned only to raise their personal income—if, at the end of the year, without consideration for the development of the cooperative, they scrape off the entire profits—then the cooperative will be unable to grow or to compete with private traders. This is culpable negligence, which has produced the downfall of many cooperatives in former Galicia. The admission of members who only take shares but do not care for the cooperative or buy goods in it is equally harmful. Such members are rather ballast. It is better to borrow money from them and later to return it, than to give them membership rights of which they will not make proper use as they do not care about the success of the enterprise itself.

It will cause great difficulties if the cooperativists belong to different social levels. A working-class family will be happy to eat sausage or fat pork. Professors, who pore over books and could be harmed by an excess of fats, will want other goods.

Their requirements in shopping will thus vary. It will also be difficult to establish those relations of mutual aid which among cooperativists create a provident whole, caring for the success of every individual. Thus cooperatives that are solely or primarily composed of workers develop better, because the needs of working-class families are simple and stable, and workers who belong to trade unions and labor parties are accustomed to solidarity and mutual aid.

Solidarity and a good understanding of their own interests have given cooperatives strength and created the above-mentioned wealth. It is hard to believe that from the minor sums paid in mostly by poor people capital has been accumulated that today is counted not in the millions but in the billions. If, however, we take into consideration that before the Great War there were over 20 million cooperativists in various countries and from that time cooperatives have developed and acquired masses of new members and that each of these members, even the poorest, is continually making purchases in the cooperative and expends there annually probably a couple thousand, the calculation is easy.

The beginnings were difficult and modest, though; let us talk about them, in order to convince our companions that in our country too the might of cooperatives is possible and that it depends on us alone whether they will develop. In Poland, the growth of cooperatives has been rapid, if only because our private trade is in general badly conducted and should give place to cooperative trade.

Belonging to a cooperative has become a necessity in cities, where it is so difficult to obtain food and materials. This should not stop, even when normal times arrive. Since cooperatives have survived the most difficult period, let them teach us self-help and let them bring about, finally, better economic relations.

The Beginnings of Cooperativism

At the beginning of the nineteenth century, the originator of the idea of the cooperative, the great English reformer Robert Owen, decided to improve social life and "abolish the abnormal and shameful practice of buying cheap and selling dear."[2] Owen's projects encouraged the English working class to think and experiment. The most wonderful of these attempts turned out to be the consumer cooperatives established by the impoverished flannel weavers of Rochdale, who are often called the fathers of English cooperativism.

The cooperative association in Rochdale was founded in 1830 under the influence of Owen's teachings. This was a period of faith in production cooperativism, with the idea of supplanting private factories with cooperative ones. Rochdale, a locality inhabited by 7,000 hand weavers, made the attempt. Gathering a small amount of capital, they established a flannel factory, which yet developed slowly and finally, as a result of a crisis, had to be eliminated. The workers were out of work; they had eaten up their savings and looked helplessly at the future. However, the energy and resourcefulness of a few dozen individuals rescued them from poverty. One of them, the thinker Charles Howarth, who was a pupil of Owen's and whose ideas saved cooperativism, decided to strive for a just division of profits and capital. Thus the idea of justice appeared alongside joint action as the basis of reforms, and taking control of economic life was begun by the transfer of trade operations into the hands of the consumers themselves.

---

2   Translated from the Polish.

The principle of income through purchases was adopted, meaning that the trade profits were to be divided among the purchasing members in relation to the sum expended by them in their own cooperative, that is, their consumer association. In this manner capital is created that can serve as the capital of a future production facility or be returned in the form of dividends.

In accord with the above principle, in 1843 a humble shop was founded with the tiny capital of 28 pounds sterling, that is, 280 gold rubles, contributed by 28 unemployed weavers. After 30 years (in 1877) the number of members had reached 8,892, the capital to 2.5 million rubles, and pure profit amounted to around half a million annually. The cooperativists built themselves a wonderful building and erected 19 even larger ones in the vicinity for branches of their association.

Today these are wealthy people, because around 20 million rubles in the form of dividends has been paid to them. More importantly, they understand the need for education and the best proof of this is the placement in their main building of a rich library, a research facility, telescopes for studying the heavens, microscopes for the use of members, a reading room with journals and newspapers, lecture rooms, and all kinds of scientific help.

The association in Rochdale has its own bakery, tobacco-products factory, slaughterhouse, and tailor and shoe-making workshops. From savings on purchases an income is created that makes it possible to pay 10- to 15-percent dividends.

However, the greatest reward for the pioneers is that the principles that are adopted today by consumer cooperatives were their invention, and the name of the Equitable Pioneers of Rochdale is known in every country and every part of the world where cooperative thinking has penetrated.

Grateful cooperativists erected a statue to Owen in 1902.

Cooperative Associations in England

Let us take a closer look at the cooperative movement in the country where it has seen the greatest development to the present day.

In the countries of Great Britain (in England and Scotland), which could be called the fatherland of cooperativism, there were 1,582 cooperative associations in 1907. Their number is currently not growing, because cooperatives understand the advantages of turnover on a large scale and are concentrating their capital. Instead of several associations, one larger and richer one emerges. The English cooperativists have not stopped there and cooperatives have continued to make progress.

The statistics that we have from the year 1919 tell us that in the countries of Great Britain, that is, England with Wales, Scotland, and Ireland, 1,357 consumer associations have been counted, with 4,151,000 members. These associations disposed of share and loan capital of 740,500,000 million gold rubles, annual trade turnover amounted to nearly 2 billion in this same currency (1,990 millions) and net profit from goods amounted to around 204 million gold rubles. During the war the number of members grew by over one million.

The countries of Great Britain did not lack grain, meat, leather, or fabric on account of the war activities, because this great power was able to increase shipments from its overseas colonies, from Australia, or India. Cooperatives were joined not out of necessity, to feed oneself, as often happens in our country, but out of the conviction that this is so far the best and highest form of economic organization. It is not surprising that 130 to 1,000 employees were needed to serve customers and their pay amounted to 142 million gold rubles. These huge figures prove that nothing could stop the progress of cooperative associations. And yet they went through good years and bad. The crisis and the accompanying unemployment and impoverishment made members' purchases more difficult; merchants colluded to harm them; wholesalers refused to sell to them. This could not last long, though, because personal interest compelled wholesalers to sell to those who were acquiring goods for tens of millions of customers. Cooperative headquarters make purchases direct from the factory and thus at the lowest price and with the advantage of the discounts that factories make for their largest clients. Such goods as grain, tea, and coffee are transported in their own ships. They also establish factories that produce for them directly. Thus there is an enormous steam mill in Silverton, a bakery and shoe factory in Leicester, and a clothing factory in Leeds; they make sponge cakes, cake, plum butter, canned goods, pickles, butter, chocolate, cocoa, soap, glycerin, candles, faience, furniture, cigars, and many other articles that members need.

Cooperative Federations and Warehouses

Control of retail trade gives consumers little benefit, unless they can manage to take the wholesale trade into their hands. Wholesalers are those sharks of capital who buy grain or cotton direct from the agricultural producers, drive cattle from Ukraine, buy up leather, receive millions of eggs through their agents, control coal, in a word, they rule the small merchants and make consumers dependent on them. The continual aim of the cooperativists is to buy at the source, that is, from the producers themselves, and to create their own wholesale enterprises.

In every country of Great Britain there are cooperative wholesalers that purchase from the producers. The agents of these wholesalers are sent even to the United States of North America, or to Canada after grain and flour; they travel to Greece to buy fruit. The wholesalers have enormous buildings for the storage of grain and tea, their own docks for the unloading of goods, five ships for their transport—in a word, they are a power with which even the wealthiest capitalist producers must count.

The wholesale enterprises emerged almost simultaneously in 1863 and 1864, and since that time the English and Scots have affiliated nearly all the consumer associations in their country and tripled turnover. Last year, the turnover of the English wholesaler reached 893 million gold rubles, and the Scotch one 248 million. The Irish wholesaler serves agricultural cooperatives. 588 associations belong to it.

On the English model, wholesale enterprises have emerged in other countries, as well as in Poland, of which we will speak below.

Individual associations can only exceptionally manage first-hand purchases. They have rather too little capital and do not have people who are versed in both the domestic market and global trade. What is needed here is a broader organization. Thus local associations create unions, which join in national alliances.

Great Britain has such an organization, where consumer associations combine in the national unions of England, Scotland, or Ireland.

Since 1869 they have formed a Union. The aim of the Union is to render cooperatives every assistance, influence legislation relating to cooperative associations, and to spread the cooperative idea. In addition to these aims, in regard to the outside, the Union attempts to manage its trade and industry on the principles of justice, honesty, and order. The Union is directed by a Central Board, and every year at Pentecost cooperative delegates gather for a general meeting. This parliament of cooperativists also draws delegates from other countries; deputies and journalists, scholars and social activists, come to listen to the sessions.

The annual congresses discuss affairs that are common to the cooperativists of all three countries.

Consumer Cooperatives in Germany, Belgium, and Switzerland

Other countries in which the cooperative movement is today developing with force followed England's example.

The largest among several central cooperative organizations in Germany is the Central Union of German Consumer Cooperatives. In 1914, it had 1,717,000 members. Wholesale turnover reached the sum of 152 million marks. The war, and Germany's defeat, depressed this movement for a certain time. But already in 1919 German cooperatives were showing great growth. Wholesale turnover is attaining close to 1 billion 76 million marks, and production facilities are putting out products with a value of 179 million marks.

The largest German cooperatives are in Hamburg and Wrocław. In Hamburg, a company named "Production" has 100,000 members. Its buildings have been erected in the largest municipal squares. It has 47 branches around the city. The cooperative has even reached into the countryside and has shops within a 50-kilometer range of the city.

"Production" owes its rapid development primarily to the fact that the city is large and wealthy. A first-rate port gives employment to a large working-class population, which is hired for the loading, unloading, and building of ships. In addition, it furthers development that the members do not collect their dividends, but deposit them in a bank as savings and endowment capital. The cooperative was thus able to organize a bakery and a slaughterhouse, to construct three buildings with apartments for workers, and to buy 6 lots for the construction of more.

The Lipsk-Plagwitz cooperative is also developing successfully and counts tens of thousands of members. These cooperatives are the work of laborers who have managed them honestly and efficiently.

The situation is similar in Belgium, although in order to be accepted as a member of one of the large Belgium cooperatives it is necessary to accept the program of the Belgian socialists.

In Belgium's beautiful capital Brussels and its suburbs, a cooperative association has built 6 huge buildings that provide shops, meeting rooms, and coffeehouses, and testify from afar to its wealth.

In Switzerland, where scarcely 3,753,000 people live, 355,000 belong to cooperatives. Moreover, counting cooperativists with their families, more than one third of the entire population makes purchases in cooperatives. Where every third individual is a cooperativist, cooperatives must do well. The turnover of cooperative associations has reached 260 million franks. The Swiss movement emerged at the end of the last century; today it has a model wholesale enterprise.

Switzerland is inhabited by four nationalities: German, Italian, French, and Romansch people live together in harmony and as cooperativists work in a common Union. They publish a paper devoted to cooperativism in the language of each nationality; they have created a headquarters for sales and thanks to this harmony and perseverance they are growing in wealth and strength.

Cooperative Factories

The reader might rightly ask me the question: Why don't cooperativists found factories and cooperative workshops at once?

After all, that would be the best way to achieve the workers' aims to take control of production.

Yes, undoubtedly, the workers want to free themselves from capital and be free workers. Cooperativism is aiming for this and believes that it will achieve it. The difficulties, however, are great. We must try to look at them full on.

In order to found a factory, a large amount of capital is needed. From a small amount of capital—a couple or even several hundred thousand—a small factory or even workshop can be established. But a large factory requires land, buildings, machines, raw materials, and thus huge expenditures. As there is a lack of cash for all that, the enterprise will hardly thrive and if it gets richer, it will be by underpaying its workers. We see too that in large factories the pay is higher than in small ones, and the sanitary conditions are much better. Cash can partly be replaced by credit, but a worker will not be granted credit, and a workers' association, which affiliates impoverished people and those who live from day to day, will not receive it either.

The second difficulty is the system in today's industry. It produces primarily for distant and unknown markets. Time is necessary in order to master this market. And during this time the factory will require considerable expenditures—where are they to be acquired? It is also necessary to know the prices, the transport conditions, that is, the shipping conditions, to have specialists who will skillfully manage the factory, technical directors, etc. All this makes the establishment and management of a cooperative factory difficult or often impossible. Workers have yet too little organizational skills; there are not enough technicians and the necessary experts.

The hope of being independent is alluring, though.

Cooperative unions in France, and even in practical England, started production companies. The failures and bankruptcies were numerous. After a temporary blossoming—as was enjoyed, for instance, in France around 1880 by the cooperative workshops of various crafts—they declined.

Nevertheless, producers' associations, particularly when it is a matter of crafts, exist and continue to be established. On the other hand, in England, which is a country with highly developed factory production, producers' associations have made very slow progress and their number is diminishing. In 1919 there were 95 companies, with 40,000 members. They employed scarcely 11,000 workers.

If we compare the numbers of this cooperative activity with consumer cooperatives, we are obliged to say that the latter is the road to victory over private capital and to replacing it with social production. Let us compare the two types of cooperative activity. For 1 member of a production cooperative, there are 100 members of a consumer cooperative. For 1 employee of a cooperative whose aim is production, there are 11 hired by a consumer organization. It is better thus to obtain one's own workshops and factories more slowly, by an indirect path, and to develop them later in the circle of assured customers, that is, the cooperative's own members.

This has worked very well in Norway. This highly civilized but little populated northern country understood that to be a cooperativist means more than just buying goods in a consumer cooperative at lower prices than in private trade. Norwegian cooperativists energetically undertook to establish their own production facilities with the capital collected by consumer cooperatives. They thereby possess their own bank, mill, bakeries (33), butcher shops, shoe-making workshops, and tailor shops. Wholesalers run a factory for tobacco goods with an annual production of over 1 million Swedish crowns and a margarine factory from which millions of kilograms of that fat are dispatched. As Norway has scarcely 71,000 cooperative members, this can be considered an example of how far the organized action of cooperatives conscious of their aims and ends can go.

In Italy, on the other hand, there is an extensively developed movement to found production and work cooperatives. These are unions of cooperativists who join together in order jointly to found a factory or workshop, lease agricultural land, or undertake the execution of some work. Labor unions have undertaken such large enterprises as the construction of railways, canals, and roads, and everywhere they have been able to meet their obligations. In 1919, 2,351 production and work cooperatives were counted in Italy.

Causes of Success

A union of consumer associations proceeds to organize factories when it has the capital and members. Most often, a bakery is founded. Even the smallest association is capable of assuring the existence of a bakery, because every family needs bread. The amount of the daily production can be established beforehand. If a family composed of 5 persons eats 3 kilograms of bread daily, then a cooperative with 1,000 members can set up a bakery whose daily production of 3,000 kilograms will allow it to exist. It will be possible to supply the bakery with mechanical equipment when the daily production rises by 4 or 5 times. This can be done if the number of members of the cooperative grows.

Along with that growth in the cooperative it will be possible to go further and establish a mill. Then the cooperative will not buy flour, only grain, by which there will be savings and earnings for its members and here the amount of milled products can be foreseen, because the flour is acquired by the cooperative's own bakery.

With further development, a shoe factory can be set up, because the members and their families must buy shoes and boots and it is not difficult to calculate how many a year.

Cooperative associations connected with a labor party, for instance, in so far as it has capital, can establish a printing shop, because the party will print newspapers, brochures, fliers, and books. Work for the printing shop is assured.

Because individual associations do not have sufficiently large amounts of capital to establish large factories, this is usually done by unions of cooperatives or wholesalers. They have a great advantage over private factories or workshops because they know for whom they are producing and in what sizes. They count above all on their own members. Capital accrues. The English cooperative associations had a net profit on income over expenditures in 1913 of 128 million gold rubles; in 1916, 163 million; and in 1919, 204 million. There was thus capital for their own factories. In France, where production cooperatives have previously maintained themselves independently of trade cooperatives, the value of their production is calculated at 14 million francs.

Both individual cooperative associations and wholesale enterprises need capital in order to establish factories and workshops. You already know, readers, when it can be obtained:

1. Only when all the members of a cooperative make purchases in it, that is, increase turnover.
2. Only when the members are sufficiently selfless to relinquish part of the profit and create capital out of it.

Capital and the Sales Market

Capital is the first condition for the emergence of cooperative factories. Consumer cooperatives can and do collect large amounts of capital. It is even easier for unions of cooperatives and wholesale headquarters to do so.

In addition to the examples above, I will give some others. After ten years a Hungarian wholesale headquarters named Hangya had turnover of 4,800,000 rubles, and its endowment capital, which could be used to found factories, amounted to 110,000 rubles. By 1908 in Germany, consumer associations had established 8 bakeries, 4 factories for men's clothing, 2 printing shops, a shoe factory, a furniture factory, a cigar factory, a sauerkraut production plant, and a brewery. They employed 2,449 male and female workers. The cooperative wholesale printers had 3 rotary presses and 3 jobbing presses.

Another prerequisite, as mentioned above, is an assured market. A cooperative factory must know from the outset for whom it is producing; it must have a circle of buyers, that is, customers, in order for the goods not to lie in store. This is called a sales market.

Private factories often produce at random. They seek customers in African colonies or Asian markets, and this is one of their difficulties. In the place where the factory has been established, another may appear, belonging to a cleverer factory owner who may be better able to persuade the population to buy his goods, or he can lower the price, and the sales market will collapse. The base was fragile and bankruptcy threatens.

The strength of a cooperative factory is the certainty of the sales market. Its existence is not built on the amount of its capital, the skill of its agents, or the underhand overtaking of a competitor. Its basis is an exact calculation of members and their needs. Honest production and lack of desire for dishonest profit affects the quality of the goods and satisfies customers. They also, however, have responsibilities. They must not be lured by private merchants or agents. They can not try new firms. They must buy everything in their own company, because only then do they deserve to be called honest cooperativists, and this is a very beautiful and honorable name—the name of people who are constructing their freedom and wealth by their own efforts.

Housing Cooperatives

As a result of the war, housing poverty has reached such dimensions that neither private capital nor state aid can deal with the situation. The combatant countries lack capital and people for construction purposes. The neutral countries, such as Holland or Switzerland, feared the kind of invasion that Belgium endured. In Poland, both in the Kingdom and in the former Galicia, hundreds of thousands of buildings were destroyed and burned due to war activities and enemy destruction. At the same time, the population growth, even though slowed by the war, turned out to be greater than the losses on the battlefield. The lack of apartments is universal; nowhere is it so great as in Poland, where in Warsaw itself it is necessary to build no less than 300,000 apartments for the needs of the population presently living there.

But even before the war, the housing situation was one of the greatest ills to be obviated by a cooperative.

Small apartments, the only kind that working-class families can afford, are ordinarily located in basements or attics. The residents are troubled by lack of light, lack of air, and lack of cleanliness, by unlit stairs and corridors, by damp and cold, or excessive heat. These apartments are usually expensive and over-crowded and a family can consider itself fortunate if it does not have a sub-tenant. The life of a worker—particularly a woman worker—who is able to pay only for a bed, that is, overnight accommodation, and on holidays and Sundays has nowhere to take shelter, is hard. Those persons who can spend the least time at home, who deserve to rest after work, do not find any conveniences or pleasure in their homes.

Thus one of the most important tasks of cooperatives is to build homes for their members. Cooperatives in Germany, England, France, Belgium—in a word, everywhere the cooperative movement has developed—have under-stood this and are undertaking to build workers' homes.

The construction of homes can be undertaken by consumer cooperatives that already exist or unions of cooperatives or wholesalers, or by construction cooperatives that are created exclusively for this purpose.

In Switzerland in 1919 cooperative associations undertook to construct homes for the purpose of providing cheap apartments. The Swiss union also established a special cooperative association for the purpose of providing furniture.

The construction business is one of the most secure, because in every country the lack of housing is felt by the working classes. There are tenants, or later co-owners, who are only waiting to move into the houses that are built for them. With the rent, even if it is lower than that required by private own-ers, they receive interest and a useful and lasting placement of capital. It is best though if the rent is calculated so that in part it at once pays the building capital and after a dozen or couple dozen years the tenant becomes the owner or co-owner of the cottage or apartment building in which he lives.

If entrepreneurs, who build for profit, do well by such a speculation, then why should it not be undertaken by a wealthy cooperative association, which after all does not have profit but rather the good of its members as its goal?

Poland can be proud that in the war years (1917/1918), the Patronat Construc-tion Cooperative was founded, with 70,000 members. The majority of these are people ruined by the war.

The aims of the construction companies and associations connected with the Patronat are to provide building materials to members and non-members (once the requirements of the members have been met). They thus found their own brick yards, lime kilns, tile yards, concrete plants, carpentry shops, locksmith's shops, and saw mills; they exploit peat bogs; operate warehouses for building materials; are active in housing settlements; rebuild ruined headquarters, and so forth.

Let me give a few numbers as proof that Patronat is already operating and developing in spite of the great difficulties. During the last 2 years, 148 brick yards, 57 concrete plants, 27 saw mills, 16 lime kilns, 12 carpentry shops, 76 shops and storehouses of construction material, 40 tile yards, 3 metal factories, and 9 masonry enterprises were built and put into operation. Wood is felled on 35 forestry lots and peat is harvested in 3 localities. Given our needs, Patronat's activity should grow a hundredfold.

Garden Cities

The most pleasant and healthy human settlement is formed of small houses, designed for one or two families, among greenery and gardens. Such houses can be built in the city suburbs, if appropriate land is found for a colony, and a railway, steamboat, or tramway makes it possible to reach the city rapidly at the right hours.

Such a garden-city project was undertaken by German cooperatives and built near Berlin. A similar project emerged in the far west of North America. In a country called Mexico, cooperativists bought around 300,000 *morgens*[3] of land. The land there is cheap, the climate is delightful, and the soil is fertile. The purchased land was supposed to be divided into lots of 5 to 20 *morgens*, which the cooperativists would farm. 6,000 *morgens* were set aside in the center for the entire town, which was to be arranged according to the cooperative system.

150 cooperativists from German Switzerland also managed to found the garden city of Freidorf (Free Village), whose inhabitants are exclusively confirmed cooperativists, the employees of a Swiss cooperatives' union. The work was completed in the course of 2 years, so skillfully that the rent for one family in a house with a garden is to come to solely 850–1,500 franks per year. On a square of ground that has been set aside a Community Center is to be built, with a meeting room and gymnastics room, with premises for food shops, a clinic for

---

3   ½ to 2½ acres—Tr.

sick people, a café and a restaurant. Alcohol will not be served in the eateries. In the cooperative's schools, the future generations are to be raised in cooperativist principles and are to be introduced to social work from earliest youth.

But this is a dream, you will say. A city without private owners of land and factories—is that possible? This dream has already been made real by cooperativists in England. The garden city of Letchworth, which had 5,000 inhabitants in 1908, exists there. Workers' houses are built only in gardens, and workers are employed in 12 factories which the cooperativists founded. Could such a colony not be established near Warsaw, Kraków, or Lwów? It would give health to our children and better, brighter conditions of existence for us elders.

Cooperative Employees

In cooperatives, as everywhere in the wide world today, the question of labor appears.

Where the workers are the cooperativists themselves, they appear as owners of their companies. These companies need personnel for service and sales, workers for their factories and workshops. The same cooperativist who is co-owner of the association could be employed by it as a worker in a mill, bakery, printing shop, or shop assistant. As a cooperativist he makes purchases, is eligible to join the management, control profits, receive dividends, and use the cooperative's equipment. As a worker he must be concerned, for himself and his companions, with the maintenance of good work conditions and high pay.

Nevertheless, the fact that being a worker, he works for himself, that is, for his own cooperative, and that the factory or shop is run by cooperativists and thus people who are close to him, gives him satisfaction and better living conditions. In addition, a cooperative association that operates on the principle that all exploitation must be eliminated and that a just system must be introduced in the world must recognize the workers' desire to organize and seek the highest possible pay. Otherwise they would undermine their own ideals and own existence, and the working class would correctly turn away from them.

Cooperatives only accept union members as workers. In every occupation they try to pay according to the price set by the trade union, and more if business goes well.

The disputed issue arises of whether workers should participate in profits since they receive part of the profits in making purchases. But after all, they have the incontrovertible moral right to part of the profits of the enterprise for which they work, because that enterprise belongs to the cooperative, that is, to themselves in part. They are contributing not only money, thoughts, and loyalty to the company, but their work, directly, all the time, and thus acquire greater rights than others to part of the proceeds.

Not all cooperatives today are adopting this position. In England, workers generally do not share in the profits. In Belgium, in calculating dividends, 2–3% is allocated for division among the workers.

The Life of Private-enterprise Workers and Cooperative Workers

Nearly the saddest side of a worker's life is his job insecurity. From one week to the next he could be a worker without work. This is the result not solely of his dependence and the caprice of his supervisor or the factory owner but lies in the nature of present-day enterprises.

It is enough for a factory to lose its market, or a new, wealthier competitor to arise, or a new machine to be invented to replace human hands, and already the factory's workers can find themselves out on the street. When a crisis comes, and with it the inability to sell off goods or get credit, it is most often the workers who suffer, because the factory owner loses his profits, but they lose their job and earnings.

Many fewer disasters of this kind threaten the workers employed in cooperative factories. Above all, here the workers are not subject to the arbitrariness and freedom of the business owner. The workers themselves make sure of it, because they are in the cooperatives' management boards. A cooperative hires only workers belonging to a trade union, who have thus a defender.

In addition, cooperative factories create items of general necessity. In good or bad times, people need bread, shoes, soap, candles, and so forth. Factories emerge not when one person wants to make money from them, but when the members of a cooperative need their products. They work for a known circle of customers. Therefore, they are less threatened by a crisis than private factories. They do not need to fear competition because in every country cooperative associations are already forming unions and will not interfere with one another. Production and sales are even regulated between country and country. Cooperative production thus eliminates randomness and the risk associated with it.

Therefore the life of workers employed in cooperative factories rests on certain bases. It is thus in the interests of the working class to establish the largest possible number of cooperative factories and workshops.

Agricultural Companies

Cooperatives enjoy great success in the countryside among farmers, and particularly among the wealthier ones. Only in very rare instances do they manage to cultivate land by their common efforts and at their joint risk. But even the small farmer understands today what an association and common action in the matter of purchases or sales can give him. It is a matter of purchasing the items necessary for cultivation, and thus farming tools, and machines—which are bought by the cooperative and loaned to members—seeds, fertilizers, breeding bulls, and so forth. They thus create storehouse cooperatives for the trade in grain, and agricultural-commercial cooperatives, which buy direct from the factory all those items needed by their members. In addition, these companies stay informed about the prices of grain, potatoes, and cattle, and facilitate the sale of the products produced by their members. Small and larger farmers join together in the storehouse cooperatives. However, cooperatives do best where there are the least differences in wealth among the farmers. They run dairy farms, trade in pork, sell eggs, and have multi-millions in turnover. At the head of agricultural cooperativism stands a country of small farm properties, Denmark. The wellbeing of this country rests on production and consumer cooperatives, and in particular the production and sale of butter, meat products, and eggs. No butter in Europe equals Danish butter, which attains such high prices that it is considered a luxury item in its own country and is chiefly exported to England, that is, to where they can receive the most for it. Similarly, in export trade, Denmark sells the most highly valued eggs on the egg market. In Denmark, towns have emerged that are rural in nature and whose inhabitants are chiefly occupied in the processing and sale of agricultural products. They make milk into butter, make meat preserves, and weigh, measure, and sell eggs, chiefly for export. These enterprises are founded and conducted by cooperativists.

Before the war in Germany there were 18,000 agricultural cooperatives, with over one and a half million members. Sales turnover reached nearly 5 billion marks, and the sale of products by cooperatives reached 268 million.

Butter-making Cooperatives

The largest success among agricultural cooperatives has been achieved by butter factories. Every farmer has a cow. The poorest have one or two cows. The production of butter at home, in a farmer's own churn, does not pay, because it is difficult to find buyers and the product is less pure and good. Butter factories

are thus established in the countryside and the partners are all the local owners of cows. They provide milk to the factory at a set price, and the factory
processes it and takes care of sales.

In addition to Denmark, which owes its success in large measure to the
cooperative trade in butter, cooperative butter-making has also developed
in Holland. The famous Dutch cows and pastures were unable to ensure the
prosperity of farmers until cooperative factories undertook the matter. Formerly, from 100 liters of milk scarcely 3 kilograms of butter were made on home
churns. Today twice is much is obtained in factories. For as long as production
was run by private factories, the farmers were subject to terrible exploitation.

This was 25 years ago. Farmers decided to establish a cooperative and found
a butter-making plant. This determined their future. Before the war there were
589 butter-making cooperatives in Holland. Each of them processes 600–700
million kilograms of milk, which gives around 14 million kilograms of butter.
The production is great, and the wealth of the farmers is growing with every
year. Dairy cooperatives in Siberia, where the Union of Butter Cooperatives
arose, have also developed on an enormous scale.

The progress of butter-making cooperatives in the former Galicia has been
distinct. There are already 23 of them. The largest, which is in Rybna near
Kraków, processes around one and a half million liters of milk a year. The butter was snapped up. The village changed in appearance. The farmers grew in
wealth; they now raise an increasing number of cows, which in their own interest they must feed better and keep in cleaner conditions. Butter-making cooperatives also developed in the former Kingdom; we had the hope thus that the
country would follow the example of Denmark and butter-making cooperatives would become one of the sources of its wealth. The war broke up many of
these organizations and the great loss of cattle caused milk products to rise in
price and for there to be insufficient amounts even for the needs of the country.

Consumer Cooperatives in Poland

Consumer cooperatives, which, as numerous examples have shown, have
given the beginnings to cooperative production outlets and housing cooperatives as well, must be placed first in the cooperative movement. These cooperatives have been tested through the nearly eighty years of their existence; they
have not failed in any country, and the principles of the Rochdale pioneers,
like an unshakeable rock, have allowed them to survive even the difficult war
period.

This is why we must consider whether Polish society has not fallen behind others, and whether in fact the path of cooperativism is bringing the future order closer to us.

The history of cooperatives before the war, like all manifestations of collective life, followed various paths in the different partitions and had to adapt to the existing legislation and the living conditions imposed on Poles. Generally, it should be said that they developed successfully only in the former Congress Kingdom, both in the countryside and in the towns. In Galicia, cooperatives led a consumptive life; they were dilapidated and did not meet with proper understanding because the industrial working class was not large and farmers were concentrated around farmers' clubs. On the other hand, the cooperative movement in Cieszyn Silesia expanded briskly among workers. In the Poznań area and Pomerania, society's entire attention was absorbed by the struggle against German culture. In order not to create difficulties for Polish merchants, consumer cooperatives were not founded.

But cooperativism in the former Congress Kingdom is also of very recent date.

Up to the year 1905 it was necessary to receive permission from the ministry in St. Petersburg for the establishment of a cooperative association in the Kingdom. This hampered the matter or made it impossible, and cooperatives scarcely had 81,000 members together. Only when the government expanded the "normal law," did the movement at once begin to flow more broadly. This was furthered by the workers' self-knowledge, awakened during the revolution, when lock-outs taught them to count only on themselves. For this reason, it is mainly workers and farmers who belong to cooperatives.

On this basis the cooperative movement could boldly begin to build. Several brochures and the journal *Społem*, meaning "together, in accord," which was devoted to cooperative issues, stirred such interest that before the war there were 583 consumer cooperatives in existence. The number of members in these cooperatives amounted to 110,000, share capital to 2 million, and turnover to 35 million marks.

In Galicia, the movement had barely sprouted. The shops belonging to farmers' clubs in the villages were changed into cooperatives. The cooperative in Nowy Sącz was the first; in Kraków a Catholic egg cooperative, two shops, and a bakery developed well, as did the socialist consumer cooperative "Naprzód"; workers' cooperatives in Nowy Sącz and Przemyśl blossomed. These were positive beginnings; they required perseverance and understanding of the affair. Optimists predicted the development of cooperativism and dreamt about combining the movement in the three partitions.

No one, however, expected the enormous progress made by cooperativism during the world war or the movement's development in independent Poland. This prosperous situation is best shown by a comparison of the figures from 1914 and 1920 (see Table 7.1). I can't give exact statistics here, but the calculations give a picture that is close to the truth.

These figures reflect the history of each partition and augur a bright future. The number of cooperatives has grown almost threefold in the Congress Kingdom and fivefold in the former Austrian partition. At the same time, the number of members in these associations has increased tenfold. Perhaps the main objection we could still make about them is that they are rather too small as organizations. While in England there are 3,000 members per 1 consumer cooperative, in the former Russian and Austrian partitions there are scarcely 375. Efforts should be made for cooperatives to create larger memberships. And if more sales outlets need to be created, it is better to found another branch than to establish a new cooperative. But the former Prussian partition, where people have the most economic training and preparation to organize themselves in credit cooperatives, is already approaching the English norms and has around 1,900 members per cooperative. In industrial regions, it should be expected that cooperatives with a large number of members will predominate. It was indicated at the congress of the Union of Polish Consumer Associations

TABLE 7.1   *Through cooperatives to the future order*

Region	Number of cooperatives		Number of members in thousands		Turnover in millions of marks (1 ruble = 2.16 marks)	
	Year					
	1914	1920	1914	1920	1914	1920
Congress Kingdom	1250	3500	110	1100	35	
Galicia and Cieszyn Silesia	100	500	32	200	5	+2,000
Greater Poland, Upper Silesia, Pomerania	–	36	–	68	–	
TOTAL	1,350	4,036	132	1,368	40	2,000

in Łazy in former Cieszyn Silesia, presently Czech Silesia, that the Union had 19,638 members, in 6 cooperatives, and maintained 53 shops. There were then 3,273 members per cooperative, and 375 per shop. In the present difficulties of making purchases, small shops prosper many times better than large ones, although the principle should be not to fragment the movement. Principles, though, are created for normal conditions and we still live in a period of war shortages.

We also have very large organizations. "Zgoda" in Poznań has 11,000 members and 7 shops. The Regional Association in Bielsk (the Białystok voivodeship) has the same number of members and 44 shops. "Jedność" in Częstochowa has 8,500 members and 33 shops; a bazaar with goods sold by the ell, shoes, and dishes; two cafeterias; a model bakery; a slaughterhouse; a shoe-making workshop; a lumberyard; a petroleum reservoir; a car; horses; and 4 buildings. There are large and well-stocked cooperatives in Łazy, Łódź, Pabianice, Sandomierz, Gniezno, etc.

The development and wealth of these cooperatives places Poland among those countries of which the French theoretician of cooperativism, Charles Gide, said that "they will be able to solve the social question, having reached the highest level by way of cooperativism."

Legislation and the Organization of Cooperatives in Poland

On October 29, 1920, the Sejm of the Republic passed a special law on the formation and management of the associations and companies generally known as cooperatives. This term signifies joint activity and has been accepted by language experts.

The law will be binding throughout the country and within two years of its entry into force all cooperatives must make their statutes accord with it.

By a "cooperative" the law understands every enterprise (factory, workshop, shop, construction company, etc.) based on member shares. Every cooperative must be registered in a court and then will have the right to buy, sell, donate, build houses, acquire land, etc. It is responsible as a legal person, without burdening the assets or income of the members for debts. At least one tenth part of the annual profits must be transferred to a reserve fund. A dividend on paid shares can be allocated from the part of the profit intended for division, and the rest divided between the members.

During the drafting of the present act, cooperativists requested the inclusion of a provision to the effect that the remainder of the profit after covering the part designated for the reserve fund and the share dividends should be divided "among members solely in the proportion in which each met his household needs in the cooperative during the accounting year." This provision, which is in accord with the principles of the Rochdale pioneers and is applied in cooperatives in nearly all countries, would have assured consumer cooperatives of first place among cooperatives. It was not passed.

The law provides for an obligatory audit at least once every 2 years by a competent auditor. It also establishes the institution of the Cooperative Council, whose responsibility will be to cooperate with society to create the best development conditions for the cooperative movement. A common law on cooperatives for the entire country should help in uniting the efforts of Polish cooperativists. The creation of a uniform movement directed from one center is a major goal and desire of the movement, as has been expressed at congresses of both universal and labor cooperative associations.

At the same time, cooperatives in Poland are erasing the traces of the former three partition distinctions and war destructions. Cooperatives throughout the country are grouping together in the Union of Polish Consumer Cooperatives, the Central Union of Food Cooperative Associations of State Railway Employees, the Union of Labor Cooperative Associations, and in the Central Headquarters of Consumer Associations of Christian Workers. These four organizations encompass cooperatives throughout the territory of the country. The strongest of them is the first, which has existed since 1911, and which a year ago had 709 associations and 280,000 members, while 328 associations and 235,000 members belong to the 3 remaining unions. In the railway association, turnover for individual cooperatives was the highest, reaching on average to 650,000 marks for half a year (in 1920), while the largest number of members per cooperative—an average of 1,500—appears in worker—"class"— cooperatives.

The regional unions of food associations, that is, the groups of associations in the former Kingdom, Silesia, and Galicia, are also developing prosperously, as are unions encompassing the cooperatives in a single territorial area, such as a *powiat*, for instance.

The former includes "Proletariat" in Lesser Poland, which affiliates labor associations, the Union of Polish Associations in Cieszyn and Poznań, "Jedność" [Unity] in Lwów, and so forth. There are 20 regional unions. Each brings together several to several dozen associations, and tries to feed its region, to conduct educational work and promotion. Some, such as the Regional Union in Biłgoraj, run their own warehouses, have tens of thousands of members, and construct their own buildings.

The Union of Polish Consumer Associations, with headquarters and a wholesale enterprise in Warsaw, is prospering. Production is already underway, starting with a soap factory in Kielce, where the Union had its own real estate.

Given the difficulties with finding premises for storehouses, shops, and educational purposes, the Union is acquiring land, constructing buildings, and is already the owner of real estate in all the larger centers except Łódź, that is, in Będzin, Częstochowa, Włocławek, Łomża, Kielce, Radom, Końskie, Ostrowiec, Lublin, Ołtarzew, and in Warsaw.

With appropriate headquarters, our cooperatives can arrange community centers, libraries, reading rooms, courses, and lectures. After all, no less important than the provision of quality goods at low prices is the shaping of people into able managers of cooperatives, or at least into members who are conscious of the cooperative's aims and faithful in fulfilling the duties of a cooperativist. In order to educate people and at the same time to maintain the movement on a scientific level, Polish cooperativists publish numerous magazines, books, and brochures, and distribute them at very low prices among cooperative members.

It can be stated with pride that the cooperative movement in Poland is making rapid and universal progress, that it is replacing private trade with increasing skill, and that new members are continuing to join.

This is a great deal, but it is not enough and not all. We are aiming not to improve our living conditions but at their fundamental reform and even to transform the bases on which they rest. If this is to be achieved by way of cooperativism, the first aim must be to have one great unified movement that would encompass the whole country and affiliate cooperatives linking people of various occupations, and the inhabitants of town and country, under a common management. Only this way can cooperativists control wholesale trade, acquire their own factories, and with time eliminate the rule of private capital in replacing it with cooperative capital.

In Poland, this is not at all a more difficult task than anywhere else, because we are in a period when the country's economic life is being built and we should give modern and equitable bases to this new life.

The Internationalism of the Cooperative Movement

Like all great democratic movements, cooperativism is international.

I have presented examples of this movement in various countries to the reader. The movement is growing stronger and everywhere is developing on the same principles. Where there is a common international idea, where there is a common evil that must be fought, efforts must also be combined.

Today we have a strong cooperative movement in all the countries of Europe, in America, and in Japan. The principle is increasingly acknowledged that human needs and not profit should be the aim of economic life and that organized consumers can and should direct production and determine its paths.

The common idea and path is the principle of mutual aid through cooperative joint action. The common enemy is private capital in trade and industry, which should be combated. Today, millions of cooperativists have declared their intent to combat capital and are themselves thinking about providing goods to consumers, are themselves forming companies, buying in goods, building homes, and spreading healthy thinking and education. Companies are organizing factories and undermining the existence of private entrepreneurs. No one can accuse them of acting dishonestly, because this is happening with the general good in mind.

However, as today's trade is international and it will always be necessary to bring certain goods from distant countries, the great International Cooperative Alliance was formed and has been in existence since 1886.

The idea of the internationalism of cooperatives came from England and gradually swept across all Europe. Wherever the cooperative movement exists and wherever individual cooperatives create common associations, unions, or federations, a need emerges to make agreements with cooperativists of other countries. Trade relations with foreign wholesale cooperatives are thus established and goods are bought from them and not from the private suppliers of a given country. Reports on the movement, periodicals, and books are exchanged; delegates are sent to international congresses; and finally, there is permanent participation in the works of the cooperative secretariat.

In the first years of its existence the ICA wanted to see in cooperativism a means to reconcile labor and capital through the participation of workers in profits and enterprises. After a dozen or more years, the Rochdale principles triumphed and it was decided at the Congress in 1902 to support consumer cooperatives above all, because they are the organizations that create factories with cooperative capital, cooperative farms, and so forth. It is not out of the question that another, more perfect, form of cooperative organization will appear; in the meantime, we must stick with the one that has shown itself to be so well conceived that it is progressing through war and peace throughout the world.

To 1910, that is, up to the international congress in Hamburg, there were also disputes over whether the cooperative movement should be connected with political parties, or whether it should be independent of politics. In England, the cooperative movement was always a movement of consumer cooperatives and did not concern itself with the convictions of its members. In Belgium, meanwhile, socialist cooperativism developed separately from Catholic cooperativism. But alongside party and faith cooperativism, there is a nonpolitical movement based on common needs and economic aims and on the uniform humanitarian sense of all decent people, whether they are under the red, the white, or the blue-and-white standard. And this movement is conquering. Common sense inclines people to join together for the sake of their economic and moral interests. Since 1910 the international cooperative movement has been based on nonpartisan grounds.

Cooperativism as a Form of the Future Order

Looking about at the cooperative world, knowing what it is and what its principles are, we can return to our first question: How should the future social order, after the removal of private owners of capital, be pictured?

The answer is easy, because the successors have already appeared in their place, and they are the masses, organized in cooperatives. Cooperativists have created companies that engage in trade and supply consumers with all the products they need. The cooperative companies establish ever more factories and workshops. These factories rest on firm foundations, because they know for whom they are producing and in what quantity. Cooperatives already have enormous capital; they are entering into relations with one another in every country; they have international connections. Instead of chaos in production they are introducing order. Instead of exploitation, advertising, and bad and adulterated products, they have the aim of honestly supplying the needs of the broadest masses.

The foundation of trade and industry based on private capital is only money and dirty, greedy egoism. The basis of cooperative trade and industry is an intelligent, provident person occupied with the idea of the public good. In tearing down the current order, he is erecting a new one in its place. Cooperation and solidarity will replace competition. Great human beings, the community, are building the bases of their own freedom and wellbeing.

Cooperatives destroy today's economic arrangements, but they destroy them through peaceful work.

Puławy, August 1921

PART 2

The Aims and Functions of Cooperativism

∵

CHAPTER 8

Woman, Whose Name is Millions (On the Responsibilities of Women in the Cooperative Movement)[1]

Maria Orsetti

1

Everyone knows how hard it is in today's times of poverty and unemployment to find gainful employment with sufficient wages to maintain oneself and one's family. On the other hand, to spend the money earned seems unusually easy and without any particular social significance. Just have money and everything is available! Doubtless for a person who has money galore, spending it causes no difficulty, but how different the matter looks for the great majority of families in the mass of laborers, where the mother of a family, being forced to lead a constant, quiet, but heroic struggle against the threat of hunger and abject need, must spend every smallest coin carefully in order with scant funds to provide for each family member and plug the most urgent holes in the household budget.

In all civilized countries the task of spending money to maintain the family falls to women, particularly in towns and industrial areas. This task is the more difficult the harder the living conditions and the more earnings shrink, prices rise, or unemployment threatens. The rational expenditure of money is no less important for the good of the family than the gainful employment of the family head. It can not be said which of these functions is more important as they complement each other like, shall we say, a key complements a lock, or a lock complements a key.[2]

---

1 Maria Orsetti, "*Kobieta, której na imię milijony. Rzecz o zadaniach kobiet w ruchu spółdzielczym*" ["Woman, Whose Name is Millions: On the Responsibilities of Women in the Cooperative Movement"], Kraków 1933, Wydawnictwo Stowarzyszenia „Służba Obywatelska" ["Civil Service" Association Publishing House].

2 It should not be forgotten that a housewife is often also a laborer, working in industry, trade, agriculture, or domestic service, or engaged in piece work such as washing, cleaning, sewing, etc. There are around 30 million women employed in Europe (piece work eludes all statistics). Our brochure concerns the work of women in her function of managing the household. Our proofs are not the least undermined but are rather strengthened by the fact that numbers of

Spending also has great importance for the whole of economic life.

Every human being, whether man, woman, or child, is a consumer, because each eats bread, wears out shoes, uses soap, and must satisfy many other needs. But among consumers a woman, as a housewife, plays a special role because she is concerned not only for her own needs but also for the needs of the entire family: she does the daily shopping, prepares food, washes linen, and takes care that clothing and household equipment should last as long as possible. In a word, the housewife is not only a consumer but more importantly the organizer of family consumption.

In Vienna a few years ago some large shopping bazaars where everything is available conducted an interesting experiment. The salesclerks were asked to mark the cash register receipts for a couple of days with appropriate letters for the sex of the buyer. And what was discovered? 80 of 190 customers were women. Even so-called men's items, such as men's shoes or hats, were purchased in half the instances by women. Only the purchase of jewelry items, and doubtless other luxury articles, were chiefly made by men.

But luxury items do not have any broader social significance. If similar research were conducted in a shop selling solely food, the result would indubitably be even more striking.

Let us try to imagine that whole mass of basic necessities—food, clothing, fuel—which through a chain of intermediaries make it into the humble shopping baskets of the millions-strong multitude of women before fulfilling their intended purpose, that is, are consumed or used.

And on the other hand, let us imagine that stream of money that constitutes the lion's share of workers,' clerks,' or craftsmen's earnings, which women return to circulation by a reverse path when they acquire cabbage, salt, herring, etc., for pennies, distributing it among peddlers, merchants, bakers, etc.

What enormous sums come into play here is shown by a calculation made for Germany. There are 15 million households in that country. It is estimated that they use around 70–80% of the country's entire production, which represents 35–40 billion German marks, or more than two times as many billion Polish zlotys. Such an enormous sum is hard to imagine. Note that it is more than forty times the budget of the Republic of Poland in recent years.

---

these women do not give 100% of their strength and time to housework, but only, let us say, 50%, while simultaneously being gainfully employed. Information about the employment of women can be found in Halina Krahelska's book: *Praca kobiet w przemyśle współczesnym* [*Women's Work in Contemporary Industry*], Warsaw 1932, Instytut Gospodarstwa Społecznego [Institute of Social Economy].

Woman thus, taken as a mass, as the main purchaser of articles of basic necessity having a decisive importance for the economy of every country, distributes life force to businesses and industries according to her discretion and it lies in her power to make some thrive and others to falter in their development.

Therefore, basically the responsibility for what is produced and in what conditions production occurs falls to woman. Unfortunately, the average woman-housewife generally feels so weak and defenseless, so burdened by material cares, that she does not even suspect the hidden existence in her shopping basket of a force which concentrated and consciously directed strikes at the most sensitive side of capitalism and could be the lever for important change in human relations. All entrepreneurs are after her purchasing power.

Through clever advertising, on which they spare no cost as it will ultimately be borne by the consumer, businesses try to attract the most buyers, to make them the proper suggestions. The art of selling, that is, of pushing on clients what they do not absolutely need, has become a true art and is even taught in schools where youth is trained in the merchant trade. And the number of moving live ads, that is, of agents traveling around the country and going door to door in search of customers, is incredibly high. Thanks to the battle over where and with what a woman will fill her shopping basket the cost of distributing goods is becoming huge and sometimes exceeds the cost of production itself. And this is all because a warehouse or factory without clients is a useless rubble heap of old iron and bricks, a feeding ground for rats and mice.

Of course, purchasing power, if it is fragmented, atomized, so to speak, among individual shopping baskets has no significance as a tool for social reconstruction. The individual basket is as weak as an individual ant far from the ant hill, as a single blade of grain blown by the wind, as a water drop separated from Niagara Falls. But nature teaches us through a thousand examples that cooperation—mutual aid—is the strength of the weak. The flocked migrations of birds, the wonderful works of societies of ants, bees, or wasps, and the helplessness of large animals in comparison with the solidary attitude of the tiny ones, and so forth, are eloquent testimonials to this fact. Thanks to this tried path of mutual aid, an economic power could arise from shopping baskets, because as it says in a Belgian workers' song, "There are more of us than blades of grass in a meadow."

Thus if a woman wants to throw her purchasing power onto the scale in the fight for a better future, for humane living conditions for all, she must combine her strength, that is, unite with other shopping-basket managers; she must join the organizations leading that struggle by creating economic outlets based on principles that are directly opposite to those of capitalist enterprises. These organizations are cooperatives of all types, and above all, *consumer cooperatives*.

2

Nearly a hundred years ago a handful of weavers in the town of Rochdale in England, faced with dire poverty in spite of the unprecedented development of production and the unexampled enrichment of business owners, began to think of ways out of the trap and to seek means to improve the situation of the working class.

The fruit of these debates and considerations can be summarized in the following words: Let's be our own dealers and manufacturers! Let's take our affairs in our own hands! Let us not give our hard-earned wages, our purchasing power, to private businesses which are based on the egoistical principle of profit and exploitation. Let us create our own distribution and production outlets based on principles of mutual aid and with the sole aim of best meeting human needs and thus the general good.

In other words, it was a matter of creating a new form of ownership, the mutual ownership of associated consumers, a kind of ownership that without infringing on personal liberty would serve everyone and harm no one, just as the sun shines for everyone and warms everyone.

What feelings and intentions animated these people can be seen from the name they adopted of "Equitable Pioneers."

As befits solid builders, they set about their work on the basis of a considered plan and precise operating principles.

These famous principles, known as the "Rochdale Principles," have victoriously withstood the test of time and today in the main serve the cooperative movement around the world. The plan for organizing consumption comprises a couple of levels: certain cooperatives are engaged in the retail distribution of goods; an association of cooperatives, that is a cooperative union, operates on a wholesale basis. Production, as well as wholesaling, is undertaken by individual cooperatives, depending on the nature of the product. Where a source of raw materials is hard to obtain, as in the most important areas of agriculture, the associated consumers strive to establish direct relations with farmers' organizations.

The Rochdale pioneers foresaw the necessity of conducting educational activities along with their economic activity, because the democratic structure they had given their cooperative meant that every member would have an important influence on its future. The cooperative movement can not thus be satisfied with wise managers, it requires wise members to no less a degree.

The little cooperative shop, which began in poverty with the penny contributions a handful of brave founders had collected perseveringly over the course of an entire year and which opened only once or twice a week for the first few years, in the late evening, so that board members could visit it themselves after finishing work at the looms, proved expressively that the power of the shopping basket is not an unreal fantasy. Today the cooperative movement in England and many other countries has become a powerful factor influencing general economic life in the interest of consumers, that is, the whole. Here are a few examples:

The cooperative movement in Great Britain today encompasses over 6 million members in around 1,200 consumer cooperatives, employing more than 200,000 members of both sexes. It is the largest producer in the country, conducting through its wholesalers more than 200 factories in forty branches of industry. It has its own ships and sources of raw material throughout the world: farms and coal mines in England, tea plantations in Asia, palm forests in Africa, grain fields in America. Members have been saved colossal sums which have come back to them either in the form of individual returns or in the form of social and educational services, and all of this has been achieved without external aid, without a cent of help from the state, thanks solely to the hidden power of the shopping basket.

The movement in Sweden is comparatively young, but it has glorious moments in its history. Over and over the might of capitalist cancers—a millers' trust, a margarine-producers' trust or rubber-products trust—burst out against the solidarity of united market baskets. A modern duel between David and Goliath. The Swedish wholesaler is now the largest producer of flours; it supplies one fourth the needs of the entire country.

A Swiss wholesaler likewise possesses the largest mill in the country, the result of long struggles with private mills, which boycotted cooperative bakeries on account of their depressive influence on the price of bread.

Formerly, cities were conquered by the sword; today cooperatives are making peaceful conquest. For example, the General Cooperative in Basel made a real conquest in uniting 85% of the population of the town and surrounding villages and exerting a decisive influence on local economic life, thanks to its dense network of shops, pair of production facilities, and farm.

We could say the same of Vienna, Helsinki, Dresden, Berlin, London, Edinburgh, and to a more modest extent about Łódź, Pabianice, Częstochowa, Żyrardów, Borysław, or Żoliborz in the Warsaw suburbs, where in spite of the building crisis a cooperative settlement grew as if by magic in times when no one thought of addressing the indescribable housing poverty of the capital's laboring classes. And although housing cooperativism can not avoid seeking external credit, it is nevertheless an example of the solidarity of forces of the economically weak.

3

On the premises of many of our cooperatives, beautifully made inscriptions announce that "Without women there is no cooperativism." In theory this elementary truth is recognized everywhere that pulses with social life, but unfortunately it is not always the case in practice.

Abroad, it might have seemed until recently—and to this time still in Poland—that cooperatives were the work exclusively of men; they are the initiators, the founders of cooperatives; they are usually the overwhelming majority of members and rule indivisibly in management organs.

In actuality, even in these cases the development of a cooperative is directly dependent on women, who more or less consciously and sometimes entirely accidently bring their purchasing power to bear. But this fact is not obvious and thus the above illusion exists.

What are the factors that, in spite of all this, hamper women-housewives from occupying their proper position in the cooperative movement, given that the division of labor requires them to perform the same functions for the individual household that the cooperative fulfills in a broader extent for the associated households?

What is the reason for such a simply humorous situation being the order of the day in our cooperatives, where a woman, the wife of a member, even though she makes purchases in the cooperative throughout the year, is not allowed at the cooperative meetings except as a favor, as an outsider, as a guest without the right to vote, and is deprived of the ability to express her desires, plans, criticisms—in a word, to collaborate in improving the cooperative? And although cooperativism combats intermediation in general, attempting wherever possible to establish direct relations between interested parties, a woman—the wife, mother, or daughter of a member—has no other way of expressing her opinion than through the intermediary of a man.

Thus, even with the best of will, the directness of women's voice is lost; the whole receives her information only as a muffled echo. The ability to have a regular influence on the cooperative's management bodies is thus almost closed to women.

Before we consider the causes of this unusually negative phenomenon for cooperativism, we must make the reservation that this handicapping of women in the cooperative movement is not at all the result of anyone's intentional ill will. On the contrary, it must be admitted that the cooperative movement has even done so much for women's affairs in general that it is rather a pioneer of women's rights in its sphere.

Given their practical genius, the Righteous Pioneers of Rochdale were aware of the importance of having women-housewives participate actively in the cooperative. For those times, the Rochdale association took very serious steps toward equality of the sexes, not only in not placing barriers to women's membership but even supporting it in certain cases (the drunkenness or indolence of a husband). Contrary to the law of the time, which denied married women the right to administer their property, returns were paid into the hands of women with the intention that the money would be used for the good of the family and not squandered.

What is more, the general atmosphere of enthusiasm excited by the founders of the Rochdale cooperative also encompassed women, who "were proud," as the chronicler Holyoake claims, "that they were taking part in an association which thanks to the principle of selling for cash was liberating the working class from the yoke of shop credit."[3]

Almost all the other cooperatives, both in England and in other countries, have followed the example of the Rochdale cooperative; everywhere there is formal equality of the sexes; that is, there are no obstacles to women joining as members.

There is a difference of opinion as to why women take a more or less weak organizational part in the cooperative movement.

Some—and they are the majority—are inclined to place the entire fault for the existing arrangement of relations on women themselves, claiming that they do not know how to make use of the equal rights given to them by the cooperative movement, which as a rule does not make any restrictions as to gender in regard to membership. Nor are there any restrictions of this kind in cooperative legislation or in the cooperative statutes, other than as an exception. Therefore, if a woman acquires individual membership all the positions in the movement without exception are open to her in principle. The low level of interest and participation of women in the cooperative movement can be ascribed to the general socio-economic conditions of women's lives, which box their interests within the narrow walls of the household and develop in them the traits of passivity, timidity, and lack of socialization. These traits of women's mentality become obstacles preventing them from making proper use of the equal rights given to them by cooperativism.

This explanation indubitably contains part of the truth but not the whole truth. If, however, we take a deeper look, the matter of equal rights in cooperativism does not seem as ideal and, in addition to the above reasons, there are reasons connected with the system of cooperativism itself. It is namely a matter of the nature of membership. Superficially, a member of a cooperative is a person who signs the proper declaration, makes the required contribution, and is entered on the cooperative's register. A member joins a cooperative in

---

3 Translated from the Polish—Tr

order to satisfy his needs by its help. But we note that when the father of a family, or most often a mother, does the shopping, he or she is shopping for the whole family.

With the exception of single people, individuals satisfy their most important material needs (food, housing) not in isolation but collectively, in a household, that is, a group of people sharing a hearth. Notice that cooperatives first of all distribute food, whose cost absorbs the lion's share of the budgets of non-wealthy families; we must conclude that the true elementary cell of the cooperative, its member, is the household, and the person registered as a member appears in the character of family representative. We must thus view the cooperative as an association of households for the purpose of the common supply of goods, for satisfying needs connected primarily with nutrition.

In this light, the fact of men's enormous dominance among members is explained simply in that men represent the family to the external world by force of custom and therefore become members of cooperatives. The custom that the family is represented solely by the father of the family is connected with the fact that the family does not yet have a democratic structure, or rather that it has a monarchical structure, even though there is a clear evolution in the direction of democratism. We are moving increasingly far from the times in which the father of a family held unbounded power over all household members.

In order to meet the requirements of democratism and social justice, the family would have to be represented by its two equal mainstays: the father of the family as the main breadwinner and the mother of the family as the director of the household economy. Only if households were thus represented in cooperatives would it be possible to speak about the true equality of women.

To this time, the above postulate has been realized by only two countries: Switzerland and Norway.[4]

Like all lies, this internal contradiction also avenges itself in life. The cooperative's democratic construction, the equal rights of all members, becomes deceptive given the undemocratic representation of its basic units. The cooperative principle of "taking affairs in your own hands" is not completely implemented. A wall of distrust arises between the women who shop and the men who run the cooperatives. The basic requirement of all democracy—equal

---

4 Swiss cooperatives apply the right of substitution for both spouses, which means that either the father of the family or the mother, according to their decision each time, has the right to represent the family at cooperative meetings. In Norway, cooperatives in cities have adopted the principle of "dual vote per family," by which both spouses are simultaneously entitled to take full part in meetings.

rights, equal obligations, equal responsibility for all—is overturned here: men have the rights but not the most important responsibility, because the function of shopping is not within their competence; the majority of women have the obligation, but do not bear the responsibility publicly, because they are deprived of the right.

This lack of actual equality for women must be felt consciously or unconsciously as an injury, as a discord between cooperativism's ideals and their realization. This inevitably contributes to the cool, indifferent attitude of most women toward cooperativism, and such an attitude, as we know well, is not easy to overcome. It is entirely understandable. The vast majority of women who buy in cooperatives are deprived of rights. In the consumer cooperatives associated in the Union of Consumer Cooperatives of the Republic of Poland, for ten women shoppers there is approximately one woman member; four belong to the family of a member, and five are entirely accidental, the result of the proliferation in our cooperatives of the mistaken habit of selling to non-members.

Is deeper interest possible in such conditions? Is it really possible to take an interest in an organization on whose development one has no influence? Setting aside here the question of selling to non-members, which is a deviation from the principles of cooperativism and a symptom of disease in the cooperative movement, the role of women—the wives of members—could be compared to the laborers' role in building a house: they solely bring bricks and mortar to the master craftsmen while someone else thinks about the plans and the construction.

Formally, everything appears to be in order, because in all countries, with the exception of the two mentioned above, by practice the movement silently recognizes individual membership. It is a truly regrettable complication that by custom men are registered as members while women are thereby set aside, but nevertheless equal rights exist. A woman, if she wants, can register as a member.

These are the systemic difficulties. Eliminating them is not easy as it would require a change in cooperative legislation. In any case, it is important to recognize the state of affairs and seek an answer, even if an imperfect one.

One such imperfect—because unilateral—solution is the method of the Austrian cooperatives, which encourage membership in the name of the wife rather than the husband. This method, when pushed to its ultimate conclusion, would lead to exclusivity, only in the opposite direction than at present. Yet cooperativism is a matter for all—men as well as women—who long for a different system. All should have the ability to use their talents and good will to meet the great challenges facing the cooperative movement.

Other solutions are found in English cooperatives. We will discuss these a
little further on.

4

As a barrier to the real equality of women in the cooperative movement there
is still the point, of a psychological nature, that a person or group enjoying a
privilege is not usually inclined to relinquish it voluntarily. To a certain degree this also concerns men, who to this time have occupied a monopoly position in directing the movement. An exceedingly characteristic expression of
faith was made in this regard at the International Conference of Cooperative
Guild Women in Vienna by an outstanding cooperative activist, from a country
where cooperativism is very backward in terms of women, saying that "men's
thinking must slowly be changed. Men still think today that they are the crown
of the work of creation and that women are subject to them!" and the outstanding English cooperativists, Acland and Jones, wrote in their well-known
booklet *Working Men Cooperators* that "the male gender has perhaps a rather
excessive tendency to consider his own opinion to be of more value than that
of the other sex."[5]

In spite of the abundance of high-sounding phrases with which the cooperative press is filled and the ceremonious speeches of leaders of the movement about the need for the active participation of women, in reality, here as
elsewhere, woman must struggle for her equal rights.

Separate women's propaganda organizations, which are called Cooperative
Guilds abroad and Active Cooperative Women's Clubs here in Poland, have
turned out to be necessary in this struggle. Their raison d'être as separate organizations also derives from the fact that in cooperative organizations that are
mixed in terms of the sexes only very few women have the opportunity to become socially adept, and additionally, the more critical and practical attitude
of women to cooperativism requires a different approach to a range of questions, and finally, as experience has shown, a woman can more easily be spoken to and persuaded in a womanly fashion. This direct influence of woman on
woman can not be replaced by any other propaganda method.

The separateness of women-housewives' organizations for the defense of
their interests in cooperatives should not offend anyone, just as presumably no
one doubts the need for a separate vocational union for child-minders, nurses,
or midwives. The need for a separate Cooperative Women's Guild could be

---

5   Translated from the Polish—Tr.

seen as transitional. When the great task of breaking down the internal and external barriers to activating and socializing housewives has been completed, then that separateness may appear useless, but at the moment that is a matter of the distant future.

To avoid misunderstandings let us clearly emphasize that in speaking of these types of women's organizations it is not a matter, naturally, of cooperatives solely for women, but of accessory organizations with exclusively educational-propagandizing aims or special tasks.

We wish to show how positively the Cooperative Women's Guild understands the struggle for factual equality in cooperativism through the example of the oldest and most worthy of them, the English Guild, which happens in 1933 to be celebrating its fiftieth anniversary.

Today the English Cooperative Women's Guild is a powerful and influential organization with more than 1,500 branches strewn throughout England (in Scotland and Ireland there are separate leagues), bringing together 72,000 women. But do not think that it was always thus. On the contrary—and this is unusually interesting—the Guild's beginnings were extremely humble. It suffices to mention that the first proclamation in 1888 was "there are seven of us!" This proclamation, which stimulated the emergence of the Guild, raised the lack of real equal rights for women, because even though women were allowed to become members in those times, the arrival of a woman at a meeting produced astonishment and no one yet dreamt of their participation in cooperative management boards.

Here are the words in which the first women pioneers of the Guild express their indignation:

> What is required of men when it is a matter of establishing or supporting the cooperative organization? Come! Help! Vote! Criticize! Act! What is required of women? Buy! This summarizes the particular field of work designated for women .... We must, of course, as far as possible, buy everything in cooperatives, but is that where our obligations end? They can require of us only that we buy, but can we not ourselves go further? Why could we not have our meetings, chats, and discussions?[6]

The spark lighted by this proclamation landed in flammable material, spreading the flame outward in a rapidly increasing circle. But this was a fire that did not spread by destruction; on the contrary, it aroused a creative force, bringing encouragement and the desire to act. At the beginning the initiators of the Guild set themselves a modest task: "we will get together with our needlework,

---

6 Translated from the Polish—Tr.

read something about cooperatives, and chat about the current affairs of our shop." Furthermore, the social activity of the Guild was initially rather philanthropic: sewing clothing for the poor, providing layettes for poor mothers, and visiting the poor in hospitals.

Before long, however, they realized that not much could be achieved by means of clubs of a social and philanthropic nature. It was understood that the aims of cooperativism do not end in giving immediate benefit to the members—in a little cheaper and better bread or tea—but that its aims are incomparably higher: the creation of a new form of social property that could serve as a model and example for the system of the future. It was realized that a woman who wanted to participate in these great struggles between the new form of economic life and the old must above all *educate* herself.

Women of the cooking pan and washtub—and these are after all the great majority, who are predominantly busy all day with a thousand minor, recurring, never-ending daily chores—do not usually have the means to expand their interests, to acquire the necessary knowledge to orient themselves in the complicated web of present-day socio-economic relations. This was the problem the Cooperative Women's Guild took upon itself to address.

It can be stated without exaggeration that the main point of the Guild's program is summarized in the command: "first educate yourself; then educate others!" All the Guild's efforts and even its manner of organizing are designed to ensure that there are no passive members, to give each one the possibility to develop socially, to expand her interests beyond the walls of her own kitchen. This is strongly emphasized in one of the Guild's reports, where we read that

> Sometimes, of course, we are asked the question: what good are our Clubs doing?... We could, of course, point to the practical results, such as the growth in the number of our members, the improvement in their loyalty, but above all our desire is to complete a work whose results can not immediately be seen. If we contribute to the intellectual development of women, if we provide them with a field for the realization of that faith— then future generations will reap the harvest of our sowing.[7,8]

---

7   We must maintain a certain balance between the two tasks of enrolling new members in a cooperative and education; it is not good that one of these tasks is neglected; both must supplement one another. If we are satisfied with enrolling members and neglect the educational side, deepening social awareness, not much will be made of such human material for the cause of cooperativism—at the first blast of circumstance the cooperative will collapse. A cooperative that exclusively educates and teaches will perhaps not lose members but will not contribute much to increasing the reach of cooperativism, to its expansion. Work at improvement and work at extension must go together.

8   Translated from the Polish—Tr.

In order for housewives to receive education, they must have time for it, and they will have time for it if work in the household is done in a rational manner, that is, one that saves time and strength. Women must abandon antediluvian methods of cooking, washing, etc. As long as home economics is not added to the programme of all schools, the Guild must fulfill this task by organizing various practical courses in cooking, sewing, washing, etc., and by appropriate exhibitions and demonstrations of, for instance, the rational equipping of a kitchen, an apartment. These questions interest all housewives and they can most easily be reached by this path.

Thus as a parallel aim to educational and propaganda actions, with the passage of time the question of improving household management came to the fore in the English Guild's program, along with the expression of housewives' needs and the struggle for the reforms they desire in their own lives, their family's lives, in the district, and in the country. The Cooperative Women's Guild is predominantly an affiliation of women who are not gainfully employed outside the home. No one was concerned with the interests of this previously unorganized and little-conscious social layer, while legislation for the protection of labor entirely omitted it, even though, for instance, there is often more danger to women's health in hauling bags of coal and pails of water and cooking and washing for a numerous family than in performing some of the lighter kinds of factory work.

Not being gainful employment, housework in our materialist times is underappreciated and not considered an occupation in general opinion or even in official statistics.[9] To increase respect for housework in the consciousness of women, above all, and to ensure them greater influence on shaping general affairs that in some manner concern them—this is the previously untouched area of social work that was undertaken for the first time by the English Cooperative Women's Guild.

In the work conditions of housewives it is easiest to reach them through direct words: chats, discussions, readings, courses. Thus the power of the direct word has become the Guild's main weapon, and work on educating speakers is a continual concern. The Guild could not be satisfied with the narrow handful of speakers among its members who, thanks to a better education, were not caused particular difficulty or emotion by speaking in public. It was necessary to seek the hidden, unexploited oratorical talents of the ordinary members who had previously kept silent in public affairs. The dense, elaborate network of conferences and courses covering the entire country is aimed at the annual

---

9   In certain countries the instructions for population polls require the work of a housewife to be described as "being in her husband's keeping."

preparation of new successions of speakers. As a result of this systematic action, the English Guild has at its disposal hundreds of women speakers who are at every moment ready to participate in the meetings of neighboring clubs. The condition for all mandates in the Guild organization is the candidate's activity in the above field.

The English Guild's method of work is interesting. The annual Congress of the clubs' representatives (every club has the right to one representative for 25 members) chooses a couple of topical social or cooperativist issues that require direct practical action. Nevertheless, for the moment, the Congress does not express any opinion, put forward any conclusions, or take any practical steps. The point is that the given issues should be fundamentally understood and discussed by all the clubs. The clubs are aided by speakers who have the possibility of becoming more deeply acquainted with a given issue at special one or two-day courses devoted to the questions chosen by the Congress. In addition, the secretariat of the Guild is continually supplying its speakers with appropriate literature. After a year, when the matter has matured in the general consciousness, the Congress of the Guild expresses its opinion and makes the appropriate decision about practical action. Then the clubs set themselves to its realization. By what path? The slow but sure road of convincing public opinion of the correctness of the position adopted. And because the given question is raised simultaneously by a large number of the Guild's members around the country, both in the press and at meetings, and as this is ordinarily done with vast energy and enthusiasm, the Guild's propaganda campaigns have a great influence and have achieved a number of important results. Here are a couple of examples.

Above all the Guild's propaganda has been directed at removing the formal obstacles which, as we saw above, obstruct women's active participation in cooperatives. The Guild's solution consists in propagating "open membership," that is, the admission of persons from the same household as individual members, where previously there had been restrictions in this regard in many cooperatives.

The principle of "open membership" gives rise to many reservations; it after all creates members who are predominantly fictional in terms of shopping and favors the wealthiest families, for whom the payment of a second share is not a difficulty. Nevertheless, it should be admitted that this principle is well adapted to English conditions and has given the Guild's clubs a rewarding field for specific propaganda. The struggle was long and fierce, particularly within the terrains of those cooperatives where men were not inclined to relinquish their previous privilege of entitlement to membership. The persistent propaganda of the Guild triumphed over all difficulties. The principle of "open

membership" is today a generally accepted principle in the English cooperative movement.

The difficult campaign led by the Guild for years to improve working conditions for the employees of cooperative factories and shops had very momen-
tous effects. The Guild's position in this matter is well characterized by the
following passage from one of its publications:

> We are all buyers; it is in our interest that prices be low provided they
> are honest. But it is not in our interest to acquire products cheaply as the
> result of insufficient remuneration for work ... We understand well the
> responsibility upon us. As co-owners and employees we strive for model
> working conditions; as mothers we desire our daughters and other girls to
> have good working conditions; as organized progressive women we wish
> to further the cause of women.[10]

It was no secret that at the end of the last century work conditions in English
cooperatives left much to desire. The Guild called attention in particular to the
work conditions of women employed massively in the cooperative movement.
It put forward demands for so-called minimum wage norms for women, below
which no cooperative would have the moral right to go. The Guild's action in
this affair is a model of action conducted with equilibrium and persistence.

It began with the scrupulous investigation of the working conditions in
many cooperatives. It was confirmed that there was complete chaos in this
regard and that in 70% of cases, women's pay was below the level of a 'living
wage' as is said in England.

Acquiring the moral support of the Union (that is the Union of English
Cooperatives) for the Guild's draft of a minimum-wage scale—with the wage
automatically rising with age to avoid the negative aspects of arbitrary promotion—did not cause any great difficulty. However, if the Guild had been
satisfied with the favorable position of the Union Congress, this important
resolution would have remained on paper.

The Guild's clubs proceeded to win over each cooperative separately on
its own terrain. The members of the Guild fought for their postulates not by
means of force, not through the organized strikes of employees, but by means
of conviction, by influencing opinion at general meetings. They had to learn to
rebut various arguments: for instance, it was generally claimed that cooperatives would be brought to bankruptcy if higher wages were paid. But the brave
women cooperativists did not allow themselves to be deterred and stubbornly

---

10   Translated from the Polish—Tr.

defended their view that injury to employees could not bring success to cooperatives. They had the satisfaction of seeing an increasing number of cooperatives on the honor list of those that had been convinced.

In its attempts to improve working conditions in cooperatives, the English Cooperative Women's Guild gave clear proof that its criticism was not solely a verbal critique but the criticism of action by instantly proceeding after its victory to a campaign to "push sales." The stimulus was the fear that the increase in costs due to increasing wages might have a negative impact on cooperatives' economic performance.

If today the working conditions in English cooperatives stand out positively and are to a degree considered model, if English cooperativism became a pioneer of reforms such as the minimum wage, the eight-hour day, the English Saturday, vacations, and so forth, which with time became legally binding on broader reaches of the working class, it is to a considerable degree due to the English Cooperative Women's Guild.

Care to have the proper assortment and origin of goods has also been a lasting concern of the Guild. Naturally, it is a matter of cooperative production above all. If a cooperative shop neglects this responsibility and gives priority to the products of private firms, the local Guild, with youthful enthusiasm, organizes a quiet storm, that is, its members daily repeat their demands in the shop until they are effective. In their day, when the safe manufacture of matches was topical at the end of the nineteenth-century, the Guild announced a boycott of all matches except so-called Swedish ones and called on the Cooperative Wholesaler to supply exclusively the latter.

Another case with great social importance was the Guild's campaign in the matter of milk—its increased consumption and improvement in quality, and placing the production and distribution of milk under public control, in which the Guild gave priority to cooperative over municipal inspection, as being less subject to political fluctuations.

"Our members," we read in one of the brochures published on this subject, "can not provide a more valuable social service than to campaign in their cooperatives for the introduction and eventual extension of milk delivery."[11] In this area the Guild achieved important successes, as currently one fifth of English cooperatives have such a department, and certain of them regulate the price of the milk market, being the main supplier of the vicinity. Lately the sale of milk in cooperatives has achieved such dimensions that the English Wholesaler has been able to open, without fear of the crisis, a glassworks to make milk bottles.

---

11   Translated from the Polish—Tr.

The newest phase of the Guild's milk campaign is directed at encouraging school authorities to supply free milk to all children during school activities. In as far as possible, local cooperatives provide the milk for schools. This campaign has already had significant results.

The results of the English Guild's half a century of work and struggle in the cooperative movement can be summarized in the two words "buyers and producers" which appear on a jubilee brochure and which the women have merited. In place of semi-conscious consumers, the Guild is raising increasing hosts of women from their cooking pots and washtubs to a creative and constructive role.

The outstanding English experts in social relations, the Webbs, have made the following testimonial to the English Guild:

> The Guild has had a visible influence not only on opinion in the world of work but also on parliament and government institutions: an influence which is out of all proportion to the number of its members and which is indubitably surprising given the modesty of its budgets.[12]

5

The same conditions that led to the establishment of the English Guild have been repeated with inevitable necessity in the cooperative movement in other countries. Today in almost all countries where cooperativism is highly developed, organizations of cooperative women are active, although they are quite diverse in terms of their manner of organization and extent of activity, depending on local conditions. For example, the Austrian Guild has achieved such a position in the movement that women direct all the educational-propaganda work in three of the largest cooperatives.

In 1922, an international organization called the "International Cooperative Women's Guild" was established; it presently unites 14 organizations, including the Ukrainian organization in Poland. For the Polish clubs, which are not yet organized into a national organization, this is a very instructive example. The chair of the International Guild is in Vienna, while the secretariat is in London. The secretariat also maintains contact with many countries outside of Europe where women are in the process of organizing, for instance, in Japan, India, Australia, and the United States. The International Guild holds its conferences

---

12   Translated from the Polish—Tr.

every three years. They draw a considerable number of representatives both from the organized countries and from those that are not organized but are characterized by great vitality.

6

It would be worthwhile, finally, to consider how women's affairs look in the Polish movement. Unfortunately, not much has changed in this regard since the times when Edward Milewski characterized the matter as follows in the first edition of *Sklepow spolecznych* [*Cooperative Shops*] of 1911:

> In principle, the matter of women's participation was resolved long ago, but in actuality it should be said that women have shown little interest in cooperativism and take little part in the life of associations. In rare cases, women have been appointed to the boards or supervisory councils of associations. Yet a well-understood principle of the democratism of the consumer cooperative system requires women to participate equally with men in directing and management. Consumer cooperatives join everyone in a common concern. It is thus proper that all—both men and women—participate in the life of that concern, availing themselves of its uniform rights and responsibilities (2nd edition, pp. 78 and 81).

Significantly, the statistical data at our disposal completely confirms that women occupy a very modest position in our movement, both in terms of membership and of participation in management organs. It is not even known how many members of consumer cooperatives affiliated in the Union of Consumer Cooperatives of the Republic of Poland are women, because very few cooperatives take the trouble of specifying the sex of their members. Even the most optimistic estimation of the number does not exceed 20%; that is, there are four men for every woman, which means that four women make purchases in cooperatives while devoid of rights—in other words, they are purchasing machines.

In general, it should be said that in our movement the subject of campaigning among women is neglected and means by which women can develop themselves practically do not exist. Nearly all the cooperative courses and the Cooperative School are aimed at training shop employees and are available only to boys, even though women are decidedly predominant among shop clerks in urban cooperatives. In comparison to other countries such as, for instance, Czechoslovakia, Sweden, Norway, Holland, Belgium, Switzerland, or even peasant Estonia and Bulgaria, not to mention Great Britain and Austria, Poland's neglect in this regard is gross and who knows whether this sad fact might not be the main reason why our movement is not keeping pace with abroad and has even recently shrunk organizationally and lost some of the enthusiasm of the early period.

However, there is no longer reason to doubt! In the last few years something has begun to move among women themselves and independently clubs are arising with the eloquent name of "Clubs of Active Cooperative Women." Some of them, such as the Club in Nowy Sącz connected with Railway Workers' Self-Help, in Łódź in affiliation with the General Consumer Cooperative, or in Warsaw in association with the Warsaw Housing Cooperative, already have considerable achievements to their name.

The current difficult situation of cooperativism in Poland, which is not solely the effect of the economic crisis but also of increased attacks by merchants—directed even against children from cooperatives in public schools—and of threatened amendments to cooperative law to take independence from cooperatives and subordinate them to bureaucracy, should infallibly be the "reminder" that will bring together every resource of energy and enthusiasm for cooperativism and not pass by those who are still slumbering unconcerned in the masses of housewives.

7

It is probably not necessary by now to explain the apparent oddity of the title of this work. To summarize the main idea at its basis, let us say the following: We live in times of change, in which people must proceed to the conscious guidance of economic forces. Along with the growth of capitalism these forces have slipped from all social control and are acting as if they were impersonal, as is reflected even in the use of language: "grain is falling," "prices are rising," and so forth.

Humanity has every resource in sufficiency. There is no lack in the world either of raw materials or sources of energy, of hands and minds eager to work. The achievements of contemporary science and technology have opened unrealized opportunities for increasing everything necessary to man, both materially and spiritually.

Neither outstanding, ingenious individuals nor the extensive plans of the Roosevelts and brain trusts will be able to do much to govern the economic forces, to harness them to the service of the general prosperity, if they do not carry the masses. The conscious participation—that is, the work or ideas—of all who participate in economic life is indispensable. This is particularly the case for the millions of women who organize household consumption and thus the domestic market of the country.

Nevertheless, before this great feeling of social responsibility reaches the consciousness of millions of women it is necessary to create tens, hundreds, and thousands of women pioneers, to expand by word and example the idea of participation, the idea of fraternity in the economic field, as the indispensable condition for the development of full humanity. More than one of our young-spirited readers will undoubtedly find herself in that number.

CHAPTER 9

The Social Aims of Cooperatives[1]

Stanisław Thugutt

The ultimate aims of cooperatives have not yet been defined. The lack of a generally recognized scholarly definition of the cooperative movement, or at least of a uniform legal definition of cooperatives in different legislation, is equally a contributing factor to this state of affairs. Without entering into detail, it is enough to indicate that the former scientific and legal definitions have been confined to encompassing the cooperative's external traits—the volatility of capital and staff, the type of liability; in addition they either state that cooperatives are economic organizations intended to improve the prosperity of their members or are simply silent on the issue. Indication of aims that are not solely material are more frequently encountered in more recent definitions, but the social position of the cooperative is still not established. Among legislative acts, solely the Soviet act states clearly that the aim of a cooperative is work to realize the communist system—a precise definition but connecting cooperativism with only one trend, or rather with only one of the branches of a trend. The comparatively most far-reaching and at the same time broadest definition is contained in the resolution of the International Cooperative Congress of 1910, which sees in cooperativism a social movement aiming to protect the interests of labor through the creation of economic associations based on self-help. However, this definition in individual countries has remained predominantly a dead letter or a point of dispute, over which there are quarrels, which have led to divisions. Further, interpretation of the social aims of cooperatives is usually left not only to individual organizations but to separate members.

The causes are various. The main—if insufficient—one is that from its beginnings cooperativism was predominantly an empirical movement, not seeking theoretical foundations for its exuberant growth. Even if certain philosophical conceptions stood by its cradle they did not help the young movement to a clear outline of its social profile, perhaps because in calling almost exclusively for the creation of production cooperatives they pushed it along a road where cooperativism did not go or went in a lesser degree. Later, when

1 Stanisław Thugutt, *"Społeczne cele spółdzielni"* ["The Social Aims of Cooperatives"], *Spółdzielczy Przegląd Naukowy* [*The Cooperative Movement's Academic Review*] 1931, no. 7.

consumer cooperativism began to grow with unprecedented speed, theories for it also began to be produced.

This happened in a period of increasingly dramatic disputes between capital and labor, in times when socialism began to give many people sleepless nights. Abusing the theory of cooperatives' classlessness and seeking in cooperatives an expression of social solidarity, attempts were made to use cooperativism as an antidote against "subversive" currents. This was the easier done because the socialism of the time regarded the cooperative with unqualified and open contempt. Growing in this manner, the cooperative movement took under its wing millions of people, of which a certain part—not a large number—were for one or another reasons antipathetic to all social radicalism, while the rest, the mass, were passive or kept their sympathies and social views for private use.

In recent times, in the post-war period, a new phase of internal development is beginning to appear in cooperativism. To a certain degree this is occurring as a result of socialism's acceptance of cooperativism, drawing it into the orbit of its activities and using it for its aims. Above all, however, a certain psychological maturity has begun to appear in the cooperative movement, which is paying closer attention to the conclusions advanced by life, to the phenomena that are the test of theory. These phenomena jump to the eye; the conclusions are easy. But under their influence more than one thing must be changed in the battle plan and more than one thing must be eliminated from the movement's manner of thinking.

It would be appropriate, given its age, to begin with the principle of the cooperative's classlessness. Never mind whether it ever had a value of any kind; following the beaten path of cooperativist empiricism, it is enough to consider what kind of value for use it could have today. The most superficial acquaintance with the cooperative movement supplies the answer: none. The personal composition of cooperatives could be very diverse in terms of class, yet as a rule one class is excluded—the class of capitalists. It is not at all excluded on principle. Only the Soviet consumer cooperatives are closed to persons living off the work of others and in general to all citizens not possessing full political rights. Elsewhere the principle remains untouched; it is simply not applied. If credit cooperatives, the least cooperative in the spirit of cooperatives, were removed from the total of all the others, particularly consumer and agricultural cooperatives, nearly all the members would belong to the world of labor. But capitalism, which is no less elitist than medieval feudalism, is bringing them ever more to one level, establishing the dogma that the world is divided into the possessors of capital, aspirants to its possession, and others, who are no longer even aspiring to such possession.

Of course, exceptions occur. For summer residence or in a manufacturing district capitalists can be found who are members of cooperatives purely for practical convenience. They buy barley, sugar, and flour, and are "dead" members. The capitalist's mental attitude, shaped by the efforts of an entire life and directed toward other goals, is strikingly different than the essence of the cooperative.

Never mind that his needs can only partially be met in the cooperative, as cooperatives are organized and calculated for the needs of poor people or those on the borderline with poverty and the most modest beginnings of wealth. More than the humble assortment of goods, the cooperative will repulse him by its atmosphere, its internal organization. It is nearly the only place in the world where on entering he must leave his wallet at the door as a thing devoid of all use. He is not allowed to acquire more than a small amount of shares; if he were to acquire even a majority, he would have no more than one voice in the general assembly. The capital placed in these shares gives a poor return and can not be improved either by persuasion or pressure; the low standards of interest are imposed by statute and sometimes even by law. In the end, cooperatives provide something in the nature of profits—although it is not even called profit—but in the distribution of those differences in wholesale and retail prices his capital turns out again to be useless. It can easily happen that when the rebate is paid, he will receive a lesser sum than the janitor of his home, who buys everything he needs here, while he buys only a few items. Furthermore, a considerable part of these strange "profits," being put aside, cease to be anyone's property, becoming social capital not only in name but in reality. Even in the case of withdrawal, even in the case of the cooperative's liquidation, this money will not return to him; he will lose it irrecoverably and namelessly, without any equivalent pleasure, use, or glory. The only thing that he could gain in a cooperative is a position in one of its management organs. Leaving aside, however, that such a position is usually very poorly paid or entirely unremunerated, it would emerge before long that it is not very suitable for him as all his methods and understandings, all his vocational training, differs fundamentally from the methods used in cooperativism. In a cooperative, buying and selling is done differently; clients are attracted differently, and profit, which plays a different role than in capitalist enterprises, is differently acquired.

It is not surprising that as the outcome of these causes, the capitalist classes are generally neutral, if not outright antipathetic, in regard to cooperativism. In addition, this cooperativism is slowly but continually eating away at the roots of their existence, and in this connection that distaste is fanned into a state of enmity. In general it is a masked enmity; cooperativism is borne like an unavoidable evil, bad weather, or an incurable disease. From time to time, however, it bursts into real flame. Not long ago one of the English chambers of commerce forbade its members, in a severe memorandum, to acquire anything at all from cooperatives.

This antipathy or enmity is not at all an individual feeling, deriving from personal views or preferences. It does not concern some particular cooperative action about which there could be an understanding with mutual benefit, an end to the conflict through compromise. There can be no permanent compromise between cooperativism and capitalism; it is a struggle for survival. Whether it will be conducted brutally or by outwardly peaceful methods is a matter of indifference in regard to the final result. It will always be, at the least, the classic struggle of two hares over the meadow grass that feeds them. If we were to take the narrowest of all definitions of cooperatives and simultaneously the one with the least drastic social aims, if we saw nothing more in a cooperative than an organization striving to improve the home economics of its members, the effects of its activities would not be the less inimical for capitalist enterprises. Every new cooperative removes a range of intermediaries, which act as parasites on consumers with the help of capital; it blocks the road to the emergence of new manifestations of mediation. When a cooperative, raising itself to a higher level of organization, begins to produce, it eliminates not only merchants but also manufacturers. When a bank is established, intended exclusively for the service of the cooperative, it scratches the last wall of the capitalist fort. The capitalist hare must leave the meadow for the exclusive use of the cooperative hare.

The cooperative's methods of acting and its internal organization, which are contrary to the spirit of capitalism, are not a matter of accident. They flow from the very nature of cooperativism and can not be separated from it. Gaining ground step by step, cooperativism introduces its system and its views of human relations. Its system is economic democracy, to the extent achievable within a foreign, undemocratic system. Within the confines of the cooperative itself, a member can shake off poverty and achieve a certain modest prosperity, but he can not enrich himself at will at the expense of other members. To prevent him from doing so, resolutions are introduced about the equality of votes, about low interest rates on capital, and on the variable division of profits, which sufficiently hamper him.

They hamper him, it is true, solely within the limits of relations with the organization, outside of which he is left all freedom of action; they hamper him imperfectly because in the nature of things a cooperative, being a voluntary organization, does not possess serious means of coercion. However, the influence of this system, in which the member of a cooperative agrees to accomplish a very serious portion of his life interests, should not be underestimated. If his relation to cooperativism is honest, if he enters it with faith in the objective of its actions and does not lose this faith after a longer stay, far-reaching changes doubtless occur in his psyche. He sees that the world is not a jungle in which all hunting methods are allowed in the chase after profits. He feels satisfaction from the creation of another kind of capital—not personal, not predatory—which in the further course of events is a source of creativity while ceasing to be a tool of exploitation. He relinquishes the mad race for great wealth, in which so many participants fall by the wayside and are lost. He prefers rather to march quietly in a compact group toward mutual benefit, even though it may be significantly more modest. An instinct of sincere solidarity arises in him; he does not apply it there where his wages are concerned, knowing they are the result of the struggle of two forces with contrasting interests, but to those like himself who are working people, with whom he has connected himself by honest contract.

Slowly, a newer, different, and better world emerges before his eyes. This new world is built on entirely different foundations than the old world of capital. The statement that there is no essential difference between capitalism and cooperativism would be the same as saying there is no difference between a tumor and the still healthy tissues of the organism in which it develops. It is insignificant that cooperativism and capitalism sometimes use the same means, the same tools. A tool is a dead thing; what is living is the will that uses it; what is living is the aims to which it strives. If a cooperative, like a stock company, uses private capital, if it even rewards it, these are subsidiary phenomena in its life. Firstly, there are non-share cooperatives; furthermore, the essential thing in comparing a cooperative with a stock company is not the collection of shares, but the creation of social capital, which is impersonal and entirely harnessed. Without too much fantasy it is possible to imagine a time when cooperatives, possessing great social capital, will lower the interest on shares to zero; the same could happen as a result of the growth of cooperative awareness in the members. In addition, from the first moment when consumer cooperatives began production, a condition of their existence and development was the prior organization of purchasers. Today capitalist enterprises are beginning outwardly to do the same, sharing markets and organizing sales. And yet between the cartel that arises to maintain prices at a high level and which uses barbarian means to destroy excess production, and cooperatives, whose purpose is to satisfy its customers' essential needs, the similarities in this case are purely external. In their deepest essence, in premises and aims, cooperativism is at least a-capitalist.

There can be serious doubts as to whether it can remain such. The present moment is not at all idyllic; there is furthermore no quiet development of long-term economic relations. The serious shock of the war is forcing both capitalism and its opponents to change more than one position, to seek for new roads. The old acknowledged truths are fading and weathering; from the slow road of hard experiences and sufferings new ones are being born. The relation between work and capital, the matter of wages and payments, is increasingly attracting general attention and is becoming to a considerable measure the core of contemporary world history. Preserving complete neutrality on such a burning issue is becoming ever more difficult, even for persons who are sufficiently wealthy not to have to struggle to maintain themselves and who are completely indifferent to social questions. It is entirely impossible to maintain neutrality in such conditions for an economic institution such as a cooperative. If its task were even only to sell products to its members at lower prices the task would equal the raising of the real value of wages and would thus find itself at the heart of the dispute between those fighting with one another over the distribution of class incomes. Only a small insignificant group of theoreticians, who are less concerned with their social position, can be neutral. The cooperative movement, with its tens of millions of members, enormous distribution of goods, and no less enormous production facilities, can only create a fiction of neutrality which would clearly be contradicted by its activity and very existence. Striving to lower prices is a battle with cartels and further on a battle with entrepreneurs who strive to lower wages to the level of the minimum cost of living. Seeking a rational relation to buyers is a struggle in which merchants try to induce purchasers' needs, whereas the cooperative arises in order to meet them. Let us pass over the already elementary fact of taking clients from intermediaries and capitalist producers. No, cooperativism can not become a-capitalist. It must betray its foundations or display its anti-capitalist face. To follow the line set out, established by the very nature of things, and to proclaim neutrality, would be to put on a mask that hides nothing and deceives no one.

Why, in any case, should it be neutral? It takes two sides to agree to a truce. Unfortunately, in this battle, capital can not stop, because it is not a matter of its views, habits, or preferences, but of its life. This is shown by a cool analysis of economic relations and confirmed by daily practice. It is time to introduce an amendment to the purely abstract theory in which cooperativism is the organization of all consumers and to say without obfuscation that it primarily brings together those people whose consumption is in a deplorable state and who, at the world's great banquet, sit at the very end of the table. If, in accordance with the truth, we state that cooperativism is the weapon of labor in the struggle for existence, neither its ideology nor its situation will be changed.

However, the determination with which its members will serve the issue will change and increase. This is a detail of first importance. It would be an unforgivable error to imagine that cooperativism is a cleverly devised machine which can complete its task quite automatically. It would be simplistic to believe that social justice can be smuggled in like contraband. We correctly call a cooperative not so much a capital company as an association of people. In saying this we state that without ceasing to be an economic phenomenon it is at the same time an ideological association. If this is so, two things are needed: an idea that would draw people toward it with irresistible force and the readiness of the members to serve that idea. Such an idea can not be solely the highest possible sum of returns on operations performed. That idea is right, fair, and worthy of all support, but it is not yet a star that the crowds will follow. The temporary improvement in the prosperity of one member, or even of all members united in a cooperative, is only a personal affair. The general affair, raising the organization to a higher level, will be the continual maintenance of the prosperity not only of members but also of people having the same needs as members, protecting them against exploitation. It is not a matter here only of exploitation by intermediaries but of eliminating profit—in the sense of capitalism and thus in the sense of the privilege that possessing capital bestows—from the surface of life in general. If it were otherwise, why would cooperativism strive to reach the sources of evil by creating its own production, by saving social capital that will bring none of the members any direct benefit? If we were to surmise theoretically that cooperativism had taken control of the world's whole production, and that its social capital exceeded by multiple times the individual shares of its members, it would be indisputable that we would have covered a good part of the road toward rebuilding the social system not for the partial use of members but in the name of social justice, which was the ultimate conscious or unconscious aim of the efforts of millions of cooperativists.

It would be an empty and barren activity to start dithering over whether this is at all possible. No aim can be entirely achieved, just as no fuel can give off one hundred percent of the heating energy contained in it. The important thing, as always in social phenomena, is not achieving a goal, but the striving toward it. That defines the path; that creates a certain mental attitude.

It is much more important to know that cooperativism will not be alone on its long journey. Trade unions, socialist parties, and thinkers of independent concepts will accompany it toward the same aims. This does not mean that cooperativism is the same as socialism, which is also in truth a system aiming at the socialization of the tools of labor, but it is furthermore a world closed in on itself, having its traditions, customs, and methods. Similarly, the trade unions are not identical with cooperativism, just as trade unions are not the same as socialism. Each of them defends the interests of the world of labor in a different manner. Perhaps these parallel paths will one day run together into one. It is useless to predict when that might happen. At the moment joint action is sufficient.

In particular, the cooperation of trade unions with cooperativism is natural and in many countries strenuous efforts are being made to that end. Cooperativism's relations with political parties are more difficult and sensitive. The methods in them are different; the types of people are different. The desire of political parties to subordinate cooperativism to itself is as unsuitable as would be the desire of cooperativism to make a party its instrument. Of course, the issue of the political system is not a matter of complete indifference to cooperativism. From the moment power falls into the hands of representatives of militant capitalism, the cooperative movement will find more than one large stone in its path. But the struggle for power is not a matter over which cooperativism should yearn, if only because it might be led from its proper path. Cooperativism is one of the expressions of striving for freedom, because only freedom provides the opportunity to eat one's fill. Thus cooperativism is not solely a road toward democracy but democracy's realization in its domain. Whoever says that cooperativism can achieve its goals only in a capitalist system should remember that socialism can be preserved only in the event of cooperativism's ultimate victory. Thus interdependence is to be concluded, not subordination. It would be vain to dispute which road is shorter and better. The foot soldiers do not usually keep up with the cavalry, but in battle they play a decisive role.

The life techniques of cooperatives and the minor benefits they provide are things of great importance. But it should not be forgotten that the broad masses of consumers, maltreated by post-war relations, are seeking higher ideals in which to believe, for which they can struggle and dedicate themselves.

***

It would seem, at first glance, that there is a serious lacuna in this entire reasoning. There is, after all, a great branch of the cooperative movement, which in some countries is growing elementally from day to day and which ought not to feel the class antagonism to capitalism because it is deeply rooted in it. This branch is agricultural cooperativism, whose members are predominantly owners of capital in the form of agricultural lands, to which by the way they are passionately attached. Their opposition to capital would be opposition to their own interests, which usually—even if such opposition is proper—does not augur success in the long term. It would be even less possible to allow two fronts in cooperativism and in its ultimate aims, modified by the interests of certain categories of members.

Fortunately, there is no need for the cooperative program to cleave. Even if small farmers are capitalists, they are capitalists of a special kind. Their capital, tied up in agricultural affairs, is most often so insignificant that its interest, even in years of prosperous agricultural conditions, does not play an important role in the income of landowners. The real profit and at the same time means of earning a living is in their work and this one aspect designates a place for them in the great social dispute over the division of revenues.

There is another consideration. Living far from town centers, being little acquainted with industrial and trading affairs, the small farmer will always be the classic victim of exploitation by intermediaries until he reaches for the weapon of cooperative defense. Both the harvest of his work and everything which he must, in increasing degree, purchase from factory production comes to him through a series of hands and at extortionate cost. He pays it twice: to factory owners, before his cooperative's union or other cooperatives obtain their own production, and to the intermediary, whose entire existence lies in the capitalist system.

These are the reasons—not to mention the political reasons—why there must be, entirely naturally, an antagonism between large capital and the world of work in agriculture. It is true that in recent times there has been considerable talk of a planned amelioration of friction, of strengthening the purchasing power of consumers in the mutual interest of both sides. To this time, these aspects have predominantly remained as theory. Without predicting final outcomes, it is possible to doubt whether they will stand the test when there is a continually growing battle for existence within the capitalist camp itself. At any rate, even in the nearest stages their realization will depend largely, if not exclusively, on the pressure of growing awareness of the separateness of their interests in the working classes in general and the cooperative movement in particular.

CHAPTER 10

A National Ideology of Cooperativism[1]

Stanisław Wojciechowski

The main purpose of man on earth is to do good to other people, to spend one's whole life trying to better the lot of one's neighbors, and even to attempt to ensure that the charitable acts of one's life bring happiness to future generations.

On the occasion of a nationwide school questionnaire thirty years ago, Stanisław Szczepanowski[2] wrote in *Słowo Polske* [*Polish Words*]: "A person is only a person if he lives in service of an idea. Without it, he is at most a human ox, regardless of how blue his blood and how refined."

"Even in the economic movement, what we most lack is not money or education but character."

Complaints about a lack of idealism and lack of character are being made now no less than in the times of degrading bondage. They are not an expression solely of the shortcomings of our national life alone; we hear them in countries that are happier than ours, even in American, which is saturated with gold and a flourishing industry.

Extravagant greed and the desire for consumption risk producing man's complete materialization, the predominance of personal and class aims over national ones, the neglect of ideas about the future for temporary benefit today.

An increasing number of people regard public affairs as a sort of stock company whose purpose is to pay dividends to each of its stockholders; they take that much interest in it and are ready to abandon it when there is no profit.

Warning voices say: what is the nation becoming, when rationalism and materialism cool the heart, stifle the conscience, loosen the ties of obligation, and a crisis or war constrains the satisfaction of expanding personal needs?

---

1 Stanisław Wojciechowski, "*Narodowa ideologja spółdzielczości*" ["A National Ideology of Cooperativism"], Lwów 1928, Nakładem Związku Stowarzyszeń Zarobkowych i Gospodarczych [Published by the Union of Occupational and Farming Associations].

2 Polish economist, engineer, petroleum entrepreneur, deputy of the Austrian parliament and the diet of Galicia, proponent of the industrialization of Galicia, founder of the Folk School Society, called "a romantic among positivists." Most important works: *Idea polska wobec prądow kosmopolitycznych* [*The Polish Idea and Cosmopolitan Currents*] (1901), *Nędza Galicji w cyfrach i program energicznego rozwoju gospodarstwa krajowego* [*Galicia's Poverty in Numbers and a Programme for the Vigorous Development of the National Economy*] (1888), *Nafta i praca—złoto i błoto* [*Petroleum and Work—Gold and Mud*] (1886).

Will it be possible then to regulate economic life, to stop unruly egoisms, if previously higher motives of action, such restraints as religion and patriotism, have been degraded? A person is a person if he lives in the service of an idea. And a group of people is a nation only if the citizens are bound by mental ties and not merely by money interest. On the basis of the Polish ideological question, higher motives of acting in public life have particular significance.

We can not complain of a lack of ideas. Whenever some doctrine is hatched abroad, it at once finds a group of enthusiasts to import it to Poland, almost like patent medicines, which are equally praised.

We also have no lack of indifferent materialists who cultivate egoism of the worst sort. This kind of person appeared among us even earlier than abroad, contaminated our public life, and led the Republic to its downfall. Piotr Skarga[3] once pointed to them, saying

> You love your individual benefit while the common one you wreck and imagine you have done yourself well...Greed and a narrow heart attached to its own benefit dissipate all good advice. Do not restrict or confine love to your homes and individual benefits; do not confine it in your chambers and moneyboxes!

Poland has suffered, and still suffers, not from a lack of hot heads and cool hearts, but above all from a lack of moderation, from the rift of reason and heart in the life of its citizens.

At times in Poland wild enterprises have been undertaken which had no chance of being maintained, were ill prepared, and unsupported by the organization of national forces.

At other times, cold prudence came to the fore, repelling the young generation with its chill, ordering the renunciation of dearest hopes and passive submission to the waves of fate.

Our heroism at times aimed very high, but the thin flame was quickly extinguished, or we floundered again in heavy materialism; we gave predominance to personal goals over general goals, without concern for the future of the nation. This division of mind and heart, the lack of continuity in the life of the nation is a most dangerous of diseases, ruining the health of families and of the Republic. Our entire past and future demands a continual tie between national

---

3   Piotr Skarga (1536–1612), a Polish Jesuit, theologian, preacher and polemicist. He was a leading figure of the Polish Counter-Reformation, the author of *Kazania sejmowe* (*Sejm sermons*). He was an advocate of reforms of the Polish-Lithuanian Commonwealth, he wanted to strengthen the king's power against the parliament (*Sejm*) and the nobility (*szlachta*).

obligations and the daily life of citizens. We need new people—Poles—in whom understanding does not cool the heart and the heart does not require reason to be silent. We fell by anarchy, because anarchy was in our crooked souls.

Poland's need was expressed by Mickiewicz[4] in the words: "in so far as you improve your souls, so far you improve your rights and extend the borders."

The rebirth of the nation must begin with the rebirth of its daily life, with constant work on the personal bravery of citizens, on forming their characters.

Rebirth is active patriotism, fed by daily activities, requiring each thought and action to accord with the good of the nation. In literature and journalism we find models of modern Poland, the kind that is needed for Poland's preservation but also for it to grow in culture and prosperity.

Offering models is not enough. Feelings come alive, characters are strengthened, only through continual exercise, in daily practice, in the idea of national obligation actively grappling with laziness and selfishness, ineptitude and incompetence, coxcombry and lack of civil courage.

Religious and patriotic feelings have greater intensity than economic factors, but they do not act as directly and continuously as the latter.

The conditions in which a person lives, works, and acquires the means of existence have a predominant influence on shaping his character. They can fortify the feeling of obligation and will or offend and destroy it.

The organizational structure and morale of economic enterprises could strengthen or weaken the development of a nation's forces, hidden in its depths. The economic relations in a country influence the shaping of characters and strengthening of national ties in the community to no less measure than school and family.

Perfecting the creation and division of riches, increasing savings which could be used to facilitate work or future production, developing technology and industrial organization—all this raises the Nation. The growth of the population, in connection with its poverty, which forces it to work by outdated methods and means, could produce such a weakening of characters that the nation will lose its energy, its ability to develop a better organization and effectively counteract the industrial expansion of foreigners. Thus it can not be

---

4   Adam Mickiewicz (1798–1855), a poet, dramatist, essayist, publicist, translator, professor of Slavic literature and political activist. He is regarded as a national poet in Poland, Lithuania and Belarus; one of the greatest European Romantic poets and dramatists called the "Slavic bard". Main works: poetic dramas *Dziady* (*Forefathers' Eve*) and *Konrad Wallenrod*, and an epic poem *Pan Tadeusz*. These served as an inspiration for uprisings against the three empires – Austria, Prussia and Russia that had partitioned the Polish-Lithuania Commonwealth out of existence.

a neutral matter whether the population earns more than it consumes, whether its savings are directed toward strengthening production, whether it is not falling victim to the usuries and parasitism of foreigners and its own outsiders, for whom the nation is nothing and business everything.

These considerations require that the organization of the nation's economic life be addressed in order to increase its strength as far as possible, in order that private economic interests do not act against the interests of the whole. The faith of the nineteenth century in the charitable results of the free play of interests, in rational egoism, in the individual's concern for his own interest leading to concern for the interests of the whole has long been buried by science and life experience.

Egoism could be the chief right only in a declining society. An individual is not free in the sense given by nineteenth-century rationalism. Above the individual is the nation, the live mental community forming since the most ancient times, continually increasing its solidarity together with the growing share of activities and relations of succeeding generations.

Our existence is not the result only of our activities; it is also formed by the sacrifices, hardships, foresight or fecklessness of our ancestors. In the same way, the existence of future generations depends on our work and forethought. For this reason the nation requires the restraining of its members' freedoms, in order to insure the greater independence and better future of the whole community. Without sacrifice of freedom, the individual can not acquire wealth or work; in general, without intentional sacrifices, human society is unthinkable.

The strength of the nation is expressed primarily in the strength of its civic responsibilities, in increasing punctiliousness in performing those duties, requiring the individual in ever greater degree to make his needs conform to the needs of the nation in all areas of life, not excluding the economic sphere. If economic life is not governed by the spirit of national obligation, it can overthrow the nation's existence, and with it, the citizens. Skarga pointed it out to the materialist Polish gentlemen, saying "Who serves his Fatherland, serves himself, because all his good is contained in it."

In the idea of a great community, such as is constituted by a nation, mental ties draw their strength from a common origin, from the coexistence of a series of generations, from tradition, faith, behavior, and concern for an imperishable existence. In the idea of the cooperative, which aims to improve production, savings, and the division of wealth, the material tie predominates. In the classic Rochdale cooperative, Smithies, one of the pioneers, said that

> many of our well-wishers express the fear that we place too much importance on making capitalists of ourselves, but my experience of sixteen years among workers has led me to conclude that to arouse them

to common action it is necessary to bind them together with the golden bonds of their own labor.[5]

The first experiments in cooperativism, undertaken over a hundred years ago in the West, produced doubts. They were in truth a desirable reaction against economic liberalism, which entitles the materially strong entity to exploit the living forces of the nation unlimitedly, but they were subject to rationalism: they tried to organize their followers non-nationally, in the form of new unit-phalanxes and communes, based on reason.

Experience has taught us that it is not possible to make the leap to a new society, even though it has been most rationally planned in all its details. Human individuals can not be treated abstractly, as if they were all uniform. People must be taken as they are in reality, in this environment, this civilization in which they grew and live.

The initial universalism of cooperativism quickly died down. Since that time it has adapted itself to the mentality of the nation in which it is propagated by its adherents. In spite of uniform economic aims in the field of consumption, production, or agriculture within the same national borders, even within the same land, the basis of the organization is the mental tie. Every nation understands the ideology of cooperativism in its own manner. In the Czech lands the Czechs organize themselves separately; the Germans organize separately; in Poland the Poles, Ruthenians, and Jews organize separately, creating their own unions, banks, and wholesalers. In spite of the officially affirmed universality of the cooperative's economic goals, the boundaries are everywhere defined by the national tie, for the creation of a neater organization and the avoidance of losses and turmoil resulting from different mentalities and national aims.

Everywhere the cooperative movement is increasingly becoming a national movement with the goal of strengthening the nation, creating in it greater cohesion and resilience to the unifying influences of international capitalism and rationalism.

The recently deceased, long-time prime minister, Luzzatti, founder of Italian people's banks, said at the congress in Cremona that

> [In] 1862, when Lombardy had just been freed from the foreign yoke, we propagated the idea of mutual, liberating aid. Before the fear of socialism emerged to stimulate reform, we understood and declared that the political liberation of the homeland would be barren if we did not combine it with the economic and social liberation of the working and suffering people...Our cooperative credit institutions have played a wonderful part in

---

5   Translated from the Polish—Tr.

the history of the people's economy. Nevertheless, they are growing quietly and without external commotion, which is a sign of real strength...It
seems to me that the future of many states—and our dear homeland is included in that number—is very little dependent on the persons heading
government and parliament, those momentary expressers of the passing
current. The happy future of the people is maturing in cooperative institutions and in new searches for solutions to the social question.

The first patron of a cooperative in Wielkopolska, Fr Szamarzewski, said in
1874 that

> The whole question of our generation will be resolved if we do not de-
> ceive ourselves and if we understand that we are living in the Copper
> Age—if we can manage with copper coins. Our world of workers must
> restore for itself life, property, position, and significance, and struggle
> with diverse competition by means of small capital sums. The whole dif-
> ficulty of our generation lies in having to achieve with small coins a goal
> that capitalists can easily acquire with their large resources. It is a great
> task, an eternal task, because our small coins, like drops of water in our
> hands, must pour by our common efforts into one great current so it nev-
> er ceases to be called a current...Through such collective work abnormal
> relations must cease; work invigorated by thrift must rise in value, and
> strengthened by a new source, neglected property and fading life must
> emerge, to the benefit of spiritual and material relations.

Our theoretician of cooperativism, Edward Abramowski, wrote in 1910:

> For other nations cooperativism is only a force for further social develop-
> ment in the direction of justice; for us it is yet something more, because
> it is also a force for national defense, a force that could defend us against
> elimination and destruction.

Enough of these citations from people who are of various camps but are of the
uniform opinion that cooperativism is a powerful factor in the material and spiritual rebirth of the nation. The ideology of cooperativism is becoming continually more national. It is being permeated by the idea that embodying national
responsibility in institutions adapted to the daily needs of our life is a necessity.

The nation is the highest community of minds. A cooperative is a material
organ of that community, working in various fields of the national economy,
sometimes with the aid of diverse methods but with the single aim of raising
culture and the well-being of the nation.

And in the cooperative movement, as everywhere, in the whirl of life, there can be turns to the left or right, whose aim is solely to strengthen a certain group or class at the cost of others; even the diversity in manner of seeking members can be clothed in different ideologies; some will give primacy to the material interests of the members, others will place greater emphasis on the collection of unshared reserves.

The differences deriving from the transfer to the cooperative movement of class ideologies born elsewhere can not endure in the long term; as foreign ac-cretions they soon disappear under the pressure of the progressing democracy of life, the increasing importance of work and the national tie, which is psy-chologically stronger than any doctrine based on rationalism or materialism.

The history of the cooperative movement at home and abroad is full of such examples. No social movement is as easily freed from the barren formulas of doctrine as the cooperative movement. In its historical development coopera-tivism aims to consolidate the nation, oppose the antagonisms that give birth to the development of large enterprises and remove the danger of the nation's division into two camps: the few, who are materially very strong, and the mass-es of wage earners, bereft of property. Cooperativism not only protects small property from decline but favors its spread, particularly in agriculture, without in any way debasing production techniques. Cooperatives adopt the various functions (sales, processing) of minor enterprises for their better fulfillment in accordance with the requirements of technology and the market without impinging on the most valuable guarantee of an individual's independence—working in his own workplace.

It is not the amount of resources collected in a country that decides its wealth but the quality of their division, their spread. The healthiest social rela-tions prevail where there are no striking differences in wealth. A more efficient organization of economic life furthers this end and weakens the bad effects of possible upheavals. We have an example of this in Denmark, thanks to its several decades of cooperative work.

But perhaps in propagating the idea of the democratization of wealth by aid of cooperatives in order that the greatest possible number of Poles should become capitalists we are acting contrary to the guidance of science, which supposedly makes industrial development dependent on a far-reaching con-centration of large capitalist enterprises?

What does the well-known professor of economics, the Englishman Marschall [sic] say on the subject?

> Experience has shown that creative ideas and experiments in the sphere
> of technology and business management and organization are quite
> rare in government enterprises and not very common in those private

enterprises that as a result of their long existence and large dimensions incline toward bureaucratic methods. Thus restriction of the sphere of industrial development, which is determined by the energetic initiative of smaller enterprises, is a new danger![6]

And thus cooperativism in making its goal the organization and support of small production forces is in accord with social economics and the national need.

A list of bankruptcies among private and cooperative enterprises would show the greater durability and vitality of the latter.

Furthermore, cooperatives, in removing the excess of organs mediating between the producer and the consumer, contribute to strengthening the forces of production and increasing the producer's revenues without raising prices.

We are a poor nation; the growth of our population is greater than the growth of our wealth; we are threatened by the lowering of our culture, by weakened energy and ability to develop better-organized enterprises.

In these conditions cooperativism acquires particular importance for us as the best means to strengthen the weak and create great things from small savings. If cooperativism did not exist, we would have to invent it to deal with our deficiencies.

Political independence is only the ability for the broad development of the nation's genius and work, the setting in motion, unhampered by anyone, of all the forces that previously slumbered in its depths.

Seeing the weight of responsibilities and work that have fallen to our generation, more than one Pole indulges in the previous passivity and apathy and expects everything from the welfare state.

Those who only live for the present day want instant improvement—they say "enough dedication and sacrifice, let the next generations work it out for themselves."

But is that how the good head of a farming family speaks, who with toil and hardship grubs the land, builds a house, denies himself for the sake of others, and whose joy is the conviction that he is establishing a new farm, from which his children will be the ones to benefit in full?

In Denmark forty years ago a plan was made to eliminate wasteland; this is done in part annually and by the year 1950 there will be no wasteland in Denmark.

The improvement of a nation can not be the work of brief heroic efforts, and cooperativism is not a miraculous cure whose application will instantly change everything for the better.

---

6 Translated from the Polish—Tr.

Cooperatives can gradually improve the conditions of our existence, increasing savings, production, credit, and inexpensive goods, but they can not replace the lack of inner goods—intellectual and moral—in their members.

If under the influence of a practical stimulus, in order to accommodate members at once, cooperatives cultivate the old bad habits, and above all the rift between heart and reason, then we won't get far.

There can be no effective cooperation in the long term if the members of a cooperative see only the good business aspect and managers only the idea. It is better thus for initiators to wait with the founding a cooperative until they understand well what the conditions will allow them to do at once and what in the future, and how to approach the matter, rather than to create something substandard—a bad example for others.

Cooperatives are acts of the enduring will of the associated members with the aim of managing material forces for the service of the nation. Enduring will can not be achieved without the accord of heart and reason and in this regard cooperatives are excellent means of national education through the development of noble characters.

A national program of social work can not be the work of a few individuals and can not be established temporarily.

I would simply like to draw attention to a great lacuna in our cooperative movement; we do not have cooperatives for piece-work craftsmen and laborers. Before the war we found a solution in central Europe and South America to the oversupply of working hands—now this no longer exists and France is approaching saturation with our emigration. Thus it is necessary, after the example of Italy, which has been effectively struggling with that national ill for a long time, to organize work cooperatives.

In Poland the field for the use of cooperativism to manage various national needs is unlimited. We have whole swathes of the country where nothing is heard about cooperativism. There is sufficient field for the activity of all the existing unions without the danger of overstepping one another.

The most important thing is the ideological unity of the movement, in the sense that every association in the sphere of its influence tries to provide the nation with the greatest possible number of centers for collective work, which is remunerative and ennobling.

Under the influence of cooperativism a nation draws together, becomes stronger, democratizes the possession of wealth, and drives out everything that is foreign to the nation, including inefficiency, waste, or parasitism in regard to economics.

The ideal of a good Pole and cooperativist is to know how to live nobly and to help coming generations in the present time.

CHAPTER 11

An Economic Program for Consumer Cooperativism[1]

Marian Rapacki

Before I proceed to my topic, I would like to offer a few words of explanation about what this report concerns.

In recent times, Poland has been in search of an economic program. Programmatic speeches are given on economic policy in official and unofficial spheres; economic conferences are convened and these economic conferences resolve one thing or another. An exit is sought from the situation in which the social economy finds itself, not only in Poland but in the whole world. In this search for a program of economic policy, the economic organizations of the mass of working people in the towns and countryside have not expressed themselves with sufficient clarity.

The programs that have been developed or announced are either programs of the official governing spheres or of the propertied spheres of industry, the Leviathan, large property—in a word, an entity of the possessing spheres. On the other hand, the economic organizations of the great working masses have not yet expressed their views about the economic policy of the state and country, nor—although they were invited as observers to the above-mentioned conferences—could they express themselves, due to the nature of such conferences, which gives tremendous predominance to the owners of large landed estates and industry.

This program, this plan, of which I will speak and which moreover is to this time solely my personal view, I will treat more broadly than if it were only a program for the activity of cooperative organizations. We have our economic program and will proceed with it, because that is our most important task— but independently of this, the masses composing our society require us to

---

1 Marian Rapacki, *"Program gospodarczy spółdzielczości spożywców: referat wygłoszony na Zjeździe delegatów„Społem" Zw. Spółdz. Spożywców Rz. Polskiej dnia 14 czerwca 1936,"* ["An Economic Program for Consumer Cooperativism: A Report Presented at the Społem Congress of Delegates of the Union of Consumer Cooperatives of the Republic of Poland on June 14, 1936"] Warsaw 1936, "Społem" Związek Spółdzielni Spożywców Rzeczpospolitej Polskiej ["Społem" Union of Consumer Cooperatives of the Republic of Poland].

declare how we view not only our own policy but—as an economic organization of the unpropertied masses—the social and state economic policy, and not only how we, the managers, regard it but how everyone should view it. On the other hand, in the whole garland of views and programs which are publicly announced here and there, the voice and opinion of cooperative organizations, the economic organization of the unpropertied classes, is lacking.

Wishing to fill this lack, I would like to present to you an outline of the program that would be the working classes' view of requirements for the state's economic and social policy. As I said in the introduction, what I am presenting to you is my personal view. In the hope that this view will be adopted, supplemented, or changed by the entire cooperative movement, I am treating my report and its theses, which have been distributed, solely as material for further discussion. The objection has been expressed by certain delegates that the theses on such important questions were distributed only today. What I have said and the conclusion I intend to draw will remove this objection. This is only the initiation of discussion. I have the impression that today we will not be debating the subject, because my proposal states the following:

> The conference, in acknowledging the theses of M. Rapacki's report "The Economic Program of Consumer Cooperatives," recommends the Union Board to submit these theses for exhaustive discussion at regional councils and the Supervisory Board of the Union and to summarize the results of this discussion and the theses of the report in the pages of the cooperative press or in a special publication.

As you can see, these theses have not even been discussed in the Council.

It is a matter here of the standpoint of that part of the citizenry who are affiliated in our Union in regard to the economic politics of the state. This has serious significance because a whole series of public and social institutions and organizations are looking at us, at our activists, asking "what are their views?" and sometimes our activists do not know what position to take in response to one or another action of a public or local-government body. Formulating this program would meet a need that our movement undoubtedly feels.

Now I come to the report itself.

Before it will be possible to establish guidelines for a program of economic policy, first of all the present state of affairs and its causes should be stated. Undoubtedly, as we all know and feel, we are in a period that I would not call a crisis, not a turning point, but a period of a certain socio-economic change. Undoubtedly this change exists. It is characterized by the fact of multi-millions being unemployed in the world, of growing unemployment in spite of all the manifestations of temporary improvement. Even in those countries where the improvement can be felt, unemployment is dropping to a small degree and only temporarily; it never falls back to the pre-crisis norms. *It is an incontrovertible fact that there is a sufficient quantity of working hands, a sufficient quantity of raw materials, a sufficient quantity of means of production, and simultaneously there are shortages, deficiencies in meeting the needs of the great social masses even in rich countries.* There are millions, tens of millions of people who are underfed and unable sufficiently to satisfy even their basic needs.

The inability, the incapacity, to find a way out of this situation on the part of the present forms of political system indicates that the error lies in the position itself, in the very basis of the present organization of the social economy. Socio-economic systems, whether the one we have presently or a system the population has experienced sometime in the past, are indubitably not eternal things. Human society is a living organization, developing in the direction of self-improvement and change. And depending on those changes, that development of society, humanity finds one or another form of existence, trying to find such that best suit their needs. From the moment when a given formation of the system ceases in the best manner to meet the needs of a given society—from that moment there arises a natural striving in every society to find a better form.

Undoubtedly we now find ourselves in this period. We must say to ourselves quite clearly that we have no reason to claim—we have not the least argument—that the system that exists today is the ultimate system, the perfect system, and that it only requires some slight correction or other to correspond to social needs. If these corrections could eliminate the major causes of society's economic impoverishment they would fulfill the needs of which we are speaking. But, as we shall see, these corrections to the presently prevailing system would mean a change in its basic principles and what follows—a change in the system itself.

The present economic situation is characterized, as I have already mentioned, by continually growing unemployment, and further, by insufficient exploitation of the production abilities of industrial facilities, a huge amount of unused raw materials, a drop in prices, and the unprofitability of agricultural facilities. All these are phenomena that we see continually. The general cause of these phenomena is above all, in so far as it is a matter of external phenomena, the disparity that exists between the production capacity of existing facilities in industry and in agriculture and the abilities and purchasing power of the broad masses of society. With the present amount of raw materials, labor, and even facilities and machines, the production capability of industry and agriculture could even be doubled and yet it can not happen because the purchasing power of the social masses does not correspond to their needs: it remains in disproportion with the production ability of industry and agriculture.

As far as numbers go, the statistical data shows us the underuse of the production capacity of workplaces even in the years with best conditions. Thus in 1928 in the United States only 130 of 343 existing ironworks were operating, in England 141 of 427. In Poland, in the year 1926, that is, in a period of sufficient conditions, we had the following numbers: mines were exploited at 56%, petroleum refineries at 65%, sugar factories at 70%, artificial fertilizer factories at 40%, tanneries at 55%, cement factories at 41%, fermentation facilities at 33%, shoe factories at 37%. This shows us that the possibility of increasing production with the present amount of labor and the present production facilities exists.

At the same time there is an impossibility of using raw materials, of which there is a sufficient quantity. Here I want to draw attention to the fact that even in the period of best conditions the result of a disproportion between the population's purchasing power and the production capacity of industry was not only that the facilities were not entirely exploited but that surpluses grew. And thus world surpluses in the years of good conditions (1926–1929) grew annually: grain 20%, coal 9%, oil 7.5%. The non-exploitation of production capacity in industrial facilities was also very strong in Germany. The number of unemployed in relation to employed before the war, from 1907 to 1913, was 2.4% in Germany, 11% in the years 1923–1929, and 12% in the years 1926–1929. Of course, in the crisis period these numbers concerning the ratio of unemployed to employed persons have become even worse.

And thus the causes should be sought not in an inability to increase production, not in the lack of raw materials and labor, but in something else. We must look at the other side of the question. It has to be said that the purchasing power of the population is too small.

And what is purchasing power? Consumption capacity is large. The population in almost all countries is growing more or less quickly and thus consumption capacity—if only on account of the growth in population—should grow. Then again, new needs could appear. Moreover, if that capacity ceases to grow, it is not because the population is decreasing or doesn't want to buy, eat, and dress itself, but because its purchasing power is decreasing. What is purchasing power; how is it expressed? Purchasing power is expressed in the share of social revenue. The greater the social income of the population, the greater is its consumption power. The social income of the masses is insufficient; the share of the masses in the social income is too small and in consequence they can not satisfy their needs, nor can they sufficiently develop their consumption capacity.

Someone could ask, though, why this phenomenon of the insufficiency of the masses' share in the social income has appeared precisely now. For very simple reasons. In terms of the division of the social income, the capitalist system bases production and trade on the principle of profit from the capital invested in that production and not on the principle of satisfying a need, which is only a means to obtain profit. If capital were equally distributed among the entire population of the country, then that principle of the division of profit could be maintained. But unfortunately capital, as far as the majority of industry is concerned, has a quite different tendency.

Capital has a tendency to concentrate. Large factories, which require large investments of capital, have the ability to introduce technical improvements, and can spread their costs over a great quantity of goods, drive out small or very small factories. There is thus a decrease in the circle of those possessing capital, in the sense of means enabling production—in the sense of enterprises aiming to acquire profit through satisfying social needs (with the exception of agriculture)—and a new phenomenon appears: the owners of industrial enterprises are not able to consume, and thus to put into circulation, that social income that becomes their share. They are not able to do this even given the most luxurious consumption they can manage. And what then happens with the capital they have collected? It does not return to the masses. It does not increase the social income, but is used for further production, trying to bring further profit. New investments are created, new industrial factories; the old ones are enlarged—the consequences of this quantity of products increases too, while at the same time consumption power, the purchasing power of the population, does not increase.

And this is the reason why capitalism in its development must eventually slow, why this disproportion must reach such a degree that it becomes increasingly unsustainable. This is also why the basic source of the crisis, of the current turning point, is the main principle of the capitalist system resulting from its essential organizational structure—the principle of the division of social income, the principle of production not to satisfy needs but production for profit from capital, in which the fulfillment of needs becomes a means and profit the goal. On the basis of this reasoning we can claim with entire certainty—even though it is still being disputed, unnecessarily in my opinion—that the crisis through which we are passing is not one of adverse conditions such as has often appeared before in the capitalist system, but a crisis of the very structure, the very principle, of the capitalist system.

Since these are our findings, it is entirely clear that only a change in the bases of the existing system, only the elimination of the cause, the elimination of the sources of evil, can bring about a change in relations, can produce the elimination of those shortcomings which in spite of temporary slight fluctuations must worsen from year to year, from one five-year period to the next. And thus also the basis idea of every economic program, based on real conditions, must be a change in the bases of the system, the reconstruction of the socio-economic system.

Ladies and gentlemen, I would like to draw your attention to one more important fact. Primitive systems were to small degree the conscious work of human will. They emerged more or less under the pressure of the forces of nature. Man adapted himself only to those forces of nature that were operating around him. He tried to find the best manner of using them to his advantage, but these searches were limited to minor, fragmentary forms. Man in those times was not aware of the whole shape of socio-economic or even natural phenomena. Gradually, however, human knowledge increases, the sphere of awareness reached by human society expands. An understanding of the situation arose, an understanding of the shape of phenomena; and on the basis of consciousness, will always awakes. So here the social will, the will of man organized in society, is able to play and does play an increasingly large role as there is more social development, and as science and culture develops. And thus this becoming aware of the whole shape of social phenomena and developing a program is important not only scientifically and abstractly, but in practical terms, because on the basis of consciousness the will to change conditions is awakened and when the will awakens, this process—which is a natural process, based on the inviolable laws of social development, on the law of humanity's selection of increasingly better forms for fulfilling its needs—can be hastened. This is important for grasping the matter.

I would also add that to these causes, which exist in the system itself, one other has occurred, which is connected with the development of culture and civilization, with the achievements of society—a great development of technology and production has happened, which alongside those other causes has meant that human hands are increasingly being replaced by machines. And this thing, which could be a blessing for humanity, allowing man, instead of being an addition to a machine, to become a full human being, not solely a physical force in his vocational work, a unit calculated by a measure of physical strength—this development of technology has become, with the existing principle of the division of social income, a curse for all mankind because it has thrown several tens of millions of people out of work. It is not indeed technology that is to blame. After all, the development of technology should allow the organization of society to be changed in such a manner that people would not need to be supplements to machines, would not need to work so hard, and could develop their creative work in another field, more appropriate to their general talents than the performance of a purely mechanical activity.

This is the state of affairs. What are the conclusions? Since we see that economics based on the principle of production and trade for profit is the cause of evil and that even what should be a blessing for humanity has become a curse and is the cause, continually growing, of the insufficient fulfillment of needs of the increasingly numerous social masses, with misery and poverty in city and countryside, that economy should be rebuilt on the proper basis. The proper principle is production and trade for the fulfillment of social needs; it is social production and trade.

How should this reconstruction be commenced? Here we are entering into the sphere of the individual prescription. Above all, basic questions appear— whether that conscious human will is capable of changing the existing state of affairs at once. Of course, there could be cases, but I am rather of the opinion that even if the whole of society, or at least the great majority of it, have achieved the consciousness necessary to change, such a sudden change in the existing relations—the turn around of the main principle from one day to the next— could not occur without extraordinarily serious social losses, without chaos, without cessations and shocks in production and trade which would be reflected, temporarily at least, in the satisfaction of needs of the masses, and would further, although perhaps only temporarily, worsen the situation. And although there may be opinions that such a surgical intervention, such an operation, has to be suffered by the patient, in such social therapy I am rather not the adherent of surgical treatment but of bringing about change gradually, intentionally, and deliberately, in complete consciousness, particularly in regard to the social interest. Especially—let us not deceive ourselves—as for such a program we would not quickly acquire the support of not merely a large majority of society but a majority at all. We are dealing not only with resistance, bias, incomprehension, and lack of awareness, not only with the resistance that arises naturally in every person who has to make up his mind to something new, but also with decided, conscious opposition from the side of the social classes concerned. The social classes concerned, or at least the economists of these classes, know that without the reconstruction of the present system there can be no basic change in the situation. But reconstruction will produce for these classes a social degradation: their share in the social income must decrease, perhaps even by fairly significant amounts; part of the social income they have collected must be transferred to broad social layers. It will be very difficult for people to relinquish what they consider to be their material goods, and following the train of thought of one of the pre-revolutionary French kings—*"après nous le deluge"*—they will try to defend the present form of system by all means, by influence in government spheres, and above all by obscuring the awareness of that great part of society in whose interests the reconstruction of the system lies. In these conditions let us not deceive ourselves that we could quickly acquire support for reconstruction even from those levels of society in whose interest that reconstruction would be.

Thus an economic program that has as its main aim the rebuilding of society must be an evolutionary program, a program of gradual development, taking into account primarily the necessity of social awareness and of that kind of economic procedure that makes it possible to visualize the benefits of reconstruction. The principle of reconstruction itself, however, must remain the creation of a system of social economy, based on the principle of satisfying needs and not profit from capital.

The development of a social economy in place of the private-capitalist one should proceed in four directions: *state enterprises* of a public-use nature with an element of social control (by delegates of the clients and employees of the enterprises).

I intentionally reject the discredited idea of statism. I do not want to defend that statism that deserved criticism, but *only a foolish craftsman would throw away a tool because he does not know how to use it.* It would be better to learn to use the tool instead of throwing it away. The idea of statism is deliberately discredited today. I admit there is ample material for doing so, particularly as those who have undertaken to use this tool do not know how to use it and thereby discredit the principle itself. At the outside I wish to point out that I am not thinking of a mechanized, bureaucratized statism. Statism, which has a tendency to bureaucratization, must be controlled by the workers and administrative officials themselves.

The second direction—*self-government enterprises*, with the same principles of social control.

The third direction—to this I do not need to motivate you—is the creation of *cooperative enterprises*. This is what we are doing; this is our program of action, the aim of our portion of economic life. As it develops, as its work is perfected, it will satisfy people's needs increasingly well. Cooperativism will become the basic form of the future social system.

Finally, the fourth direction—*mixed enterprises*, formed from the above three types of enterprises—likewise does not require justification. We must be aware that this type of reconstruction program, which aims to bring into existence and properly administrate enterprises having as their aim the satisfaction of social needs, must in the nature of things meet opposition and difficulties from the existing economic forms. There must be no retreat before these difficulties. These difficulties must be removed. And therefore a higher force, the force of the state, must enter here.

In the event that the plan is considered to move in the direction of making production and trade a priority public-use function, the state should interfere to remove obstacles in the path of this form of social development in the name of the social interest. In the public interest the state should have the right to:

(a) regulate the economic function of private-capitalist enterprises;
(b) expropriate, as needed, those enterprises on behalf of the social form of economy in exchange for compensation in the form of long-term, low-interest bonds amortized from the revenues of the expropriated enterprises. Here, I say, the state must have recourse to expropriation, as needed.

This could most offend our current sense of liberty, which extends as well to the idea of property. But after all we have grown accustomed to this expropriation and it does not offend anyone that one or another community expropriates the owner of a building when the line of a street must be widened. And is not the employment of millions of unemployed people more important than the widening of a city street? And thus there must be no withdrawing from what at the moment offends our feelings but is in accord with the basic social interest, which should be the main aim of the economic policy of the state and society. We have grown accustomed also to other things—to the expropriation that at the moment is unfortunately applied predominantly in the law on expropriation in regard to agricultural reform. It is no novelty. Thus what I am proposing is only an extension of phenomena, which from the necessity of things had or has to occur. The state can not allow this weapon to be taken from it. It can use it gradually, in order not to produce upheavals in economic life, but it must use it to the extent that it becomes necessary.

Further, if one starts from the principle that one of the causes of the crisis is excess accumulation of capital, or rather social income, in the hands of one social layer, which is unable to consume it, then we must establish the principle that for as long as that form of private-capitalist economics still exists, the collection of capital above the needs—even the most luxurious—of the individual must be restrained. Of course, it is a matter here of a physical individual. We must establish for ourselves a certain maximum social income that a physical individual has the right to acquire. Let this maximum be high, let it encompass the luxury consumption of a given individual—I do not look with envy at people who have their own villas and cars, on the contrary, I would like there to be as many of them as possible—but what the individual and his family is unable to consume should not constitute their property. Thus the state should say that if an individual's income exceeds the maximum the state will impose a one hundred percent income tax on the surplus of that income. If we introduce this type of principle for income then we must introduce it analogously in relation to assets. It must be established that income, at the normal rate of interest, can not exceed the maximum I mentioned earlier. Thus in this case as well there should be a hundred-percent tax on assets above a certain high maximum.

These are general questions, necessary for the proper management of re-building the system. In order to achieve this goal, longer and deeper changes are necessary. In order to make these changes possible, certain shifts, which cooperatives are now conducting in the division of social income and which above all create or increase the social income, must occur. Because the capital-ist economists are right about one thing—that at this moment there is nothing to fight over, because due to the present economic structure (obviously, they do not say this) it would lead to a catastrophic decrease in the social income. We know how many factories are not working, how high the unemployment rate is. As a result, per capita social income has decreased and if we were to go farther the growing poverty of the masses would lead to its further diminish-ment and that averaging down would lead to zero.

Thus the immediate task of economic policy in this sense has to involve—what is often discredited by the very name—priming the situation. What this means is that we have to make a start. How is this to occur? We have above all a large number of unemployed persons. We have to get rid of this unemploy-ment. We have the decreasing profitability of agricultural properties, which in our country feed 65–70% of the population. We have to eliminate this lack of profitability—or rather this insufficient remuneration of the work of the farmer on his farm.

How is this to be achieved? This question came and went at a recent eco-nomic meeting called by the government and was thrown like a ball from the large estate owners to the side of large industry. To this question we—cooperativists—must give an answer. From which side is the improvement to begin—from the side of the worker, or of the farmer?

We have to approach this matter without bias and consider it objectively. At the economic meeting, the Leviathan said that improvement must occur on the side of industry, and the large farm owners consider that it must occur on the side of agriculture. The Leviathan said that in order to improve the con-ditions of industry, the profitability of industrial facilities must be improved. The idea of profitability is a sacred idea, thrown about by the Leviathan as if it were something that would save the entire world. But how is the profit-ability of industrial facilities to be achieved in such conditions, when they are decreasing production because they have no one to sell to and when as a result the trade costs per unit are increasing? Obviously workers' wages must be lowered and the natural growth of prices—as it is called—must not hampered: that is, raise the price of industrial products and lower wages.

The senselessness of this type of prescription jumps to the eye. First, labor costs in industrial production are playing an ever smaller role. I have mentioned the wonderful development of modern production technology. This development means that the labor cost of production is continually diminishing. I will give you a few figures. Labor in production costs in Poland, that is, in a country whose technology is still fairly poorly developed, amounts to between 2 and 20%, depending on the production. In such sectors as glass, porcelain, bricks, or furniture, where human labor is an important factor, the cost of labor will be more than 20%. In coal, whose production often occurs only on the basis of human labor—40%—and this is the only sector of production in which the costs of labor are such a high percentage. What thus can be gained in relation to the price of goods if we lower that 20% by 10%. We gain 2%, which obviously will not be sufficient or satisfy entrepreneurs.

But there is another aspect. If we lower wages and raise prices, who will buy those products? The workers won't buy them, because their wages have been lowered, and the farmers won't buy them, because if we lower incomes in the cities, whose populations are 30% of the total population but are responsible for significantly more of the consumption, then there will be a fall in consumption of agricultural articles, which constitute 60% of the expenditures of even a well-situated worker here. And because a fall in consumption will occur, this will in turn cause lower prices for agricultural products and that will deepen the crisis in the countryside even more. Who then will buy industrial products? There will be another leveling downwards and an even greater impoverishment of the masses.

Large agriculture has put forward another idea: raising the profitability of agricultural facilities, increasing rural consumption, and as a result creating a larger demand for the countryside's products. This will animate industry and thus animate all of economic life. But in what ways? A rise in agricultural articles. Very proper. Those prices are too small; they do not fully reward even the labor involved. But how should prices be raised? There is talk of export premiums; there is talk of the state's strong push for the export of agricultural products. These things could be tried through supporting exports. But we know that other states which are passing through such a crisis as Poland are capable of closing themselves off, if not by means of high tariffs, then, like England, by means of quotas or even transport bans. What will come of it? No premiums, no support for export, which in the nature of things is increasingly closed now, will aid agriculture. Agriculture can and must count only on the domestic market. Growth in population and that population's growth in consumption will provide an entirely adequate increase in the demand for agricultural products; it will also provide the possibility of evolution in the prices of those articles. And thus agriculture, if it wants to find greater demand, must say to itself: the requirements of the cities—of the broad masses of the urban population—for agricultural items must first of all be increased. In order to do this, it is necessary to increase the income of the urban population—above all to increase the share of the masses in the social income. And this is a fact of prime importance.

In order not to be accused here of a lack of objectivity, I will read a couple lines from an article written specially for the Polish journal *Rolnictwo* [*Agriculture*], the organ of the Ministry of Agriculture, by a German professor, Fritz Bade, who speaks of relations in Poland thus:

> Raising the price of agricultural products by halting exports abroad is nearly or completely impossible in these countries, and there is nothing to halt in any case. Attempts to create advantageous, or at least bearable, conditions for the export of agricultural production abroad is a hopeless matter on account of the state of the world market presented above. A farmer's income amounts solely to what domestic consumers can expend for their sustenance.

The purchasing power of consumers is the deciding factor of the agricultural products market in all countries standing on the border of self-sufficiency. Reducing purchasing power is the main cause of a drop in the price of agricultural products. Only through a reconstruction of purchasing power can the profitability of agricultural production be returned. Only by setting in motion the considerable reserves amassed in the needs for food of the non-affluent mass of the population is there a possibility of setting out the path not only toward freeing the great reserves of Polish agricultural production but, in addition, to putting these reserves on the domestic market without producing heavy tremors through a further fall in prices.

For illustration, I will give a few interesting figures. If it is a matter of consumption then the matter looks as follows: In 1929 (according to Kalecki and Landau's book)[2] urban consumption amounted to 12.5 billion zlotys in the area of industrial products, while rural consumption was 2.8 billion. Food, in terms of the money market, is primarily consumed by cities—workers spend 60% of

---

2   M. Kalecki, L. Landau, *Szacunek dochodu społecznego w r. 1929* [*Estimates of Social Income in 1929*], Warszawa 1934, Instytut Badania Konjunktur Gospodarczych i Cen [Institute for the Study of Economic Prosperity and Prices].

their budgets on food. And now who is above all interested in the growth of earnings of the working masses? In researching the division of labor income, families were divided into four categories. It was determined that in good conditions in our country passage from the first, that is, lowest paid, category of workers (above 600 zlotys annually) to the highest (over 1,200 zlotys) produces an increase in that family's consumption of milk by 156% and of meat by 120%; we don't have data concerning eggs but probably the relation is the same. And thus consumption is increased by two and a half times, and in what items?! Those that are produced by small farmers, not by large properties, which after all primarily bring grain to the market. I have calculated that 80% of the grain brought to market comes from large properties, while for milk, meat, and eggs the share of small landowners is almost 80%. Therefore, if the purchase of agricultural articles increased, the prices must also increase. Thus improvement should begin from that side, in my opinion.

Therefore, in the propositions, I favor:

(a) raising the wages of state and local government workers
(b) establishing a minimum wage for manual and white-collar workers, higher than the present level.

In present conditions, the increase in wages for state and local government workers appears to be an unusually bold proposal, in complete opposition to what could be done. But if capitalism wishes to extend its lease of life, and be reasonably conducted, it would get all the entrepreneurs together and pass a resolution to raise workers' wages. Then consumption of agricultural items would increase, and the result would also be more consumption of industrial items.

The following methods should be used to decrease the unemployment rate of wage laborers:

(a) the statutory shortening of working hours to 36–40 hours a week (note that all figures given here are only approximations);
(b) obligatory retirement for manual workers after 50–55 years of age, and for white-collar workers after 55–60 years of age
(c) the strict prohibition of child labor and limitations on women's doing physical labor;
(d) public works.

I left public works to last place. They admittedly do not affect the prices of any goods, but investment alone will not increase the social income at once; it is not consumed and thus the costs expended could be liquefied after a longer period of time. Thus I consider that public works can not resolve the problem on account of the financial side of affairs.

They have actually the benefit that they do not increase the prices of products. If, however, we raise the incomes of the population, those increases, in spite of the small share of workers' wages in the price of a good, could produce higher prices. But I consider that after a certain time these things will absolutely not have an influence on prices, because in the present minor use of production facilities, the fixed costs per product unit are unusually high; and if we increase the production capacities of factories, then we simultaneously decrease those costs and in many cases entirely cover the increase in laborers' wages in this manner. We know this from practice because we have the same situation in our workshops. If we could strengthen production, we could give a 10%-15% raise to workers, without needing to raise the price of goods. Of course, these things vary in various branches of production, but nevertheless the principle is always correct.

This is how the question looks from the side of the workers. But our program should also take into account the interests of the farming population. In order to decrease hidden unemployment, the following measures should be taken:

(a)   rapid and radical introduction of agricultural reforms;
(b)   leaving the farms remaining after parcellation to the estate workers, organized in cooperative agricultural communities;
(c)   parcellation of suitable state land;
(d)   public works on rural land.

If we look at the figures, we will be convinced that in Poland we have incredibly overpopulated rural areas, and above all overpopulation in relation to possession of land.

In Poland, for 100 hectares of so-called arable land, we have 45.5 people with a harvest of 11 q.

In France, for 100 hectares of so-called arable land, we have 25 people with a harvest of 14 q.

In Italy, for 100 hectares of so-called arable land, we have 44 people with a harvest of 15 q.

In Germany, for 100 hectares of arable land, we have 34.2 people with a harvest of 19 q.

We can see from this that the mass of farming people working the land in the countryside is unbelievably large. We must reduce this population. What is necessary above all is the parcellation of larger state lands, which at the moment are often lying fallow, then agricultural reforms, which at this moment are predominantly only on paper. Nevertheless, in making agricultural reforms thought should be given to estate workers. I would like to point out that this postulate was one of the points in the program of Romuald Mielczarski, who even had a conference with members of parliament and the government during the debate on agricultural reform, to try to make it possible for special cooperatives formed of laborers on large properties to buy farms. Furthermore, one other thing is necessary in agriculture—that the surplus, which will come with the increase of prices after increased demand, should go in its entirety into the pockets of the farmers. Thus an important task is the proper organization of food and agricultural-trade cooperatives to decrease the costs of mediation.

For the protection and intentional reconstruction in this manner of the planned social economy, certain abnormal phenomena, which have appeared in our country and which would restrict the natural processes of economic improvement, should be counteracted. Thus we must postulate the dissolution of all existing cartels and a prohibition against creating new ones. Cartels artificially raise the price of goods, and thereby allow the further development of production, through which they decrease the social income and in this manner deepen the crisis. What has been introduced to this time by the government is an interesting illustration. We know from the reports of the Union that the consumption of sugar has increased from the time the price was lowered, although insufficiently, by about twenty-some percent. If prices were naturally lowered, by dissolving the cartel, consumption would reach such a level that it would entirely absorb the production of all our sugar factories with no loss to them. The same can be observed in regard to cement.

Further, it will be necessary to take account of foreign relations; it will be necessary to expect that foreign goods will come to us, in the form of dumping, with premiums, which in this manner lessen the sale of our articles. Similarly, in the export of our articles we will meet with difficulties that will continually be increasing. If we are to avoid this, we must control the entirety of import and export. And thus a monopoly of foreign trade in the hands of a mixed social enterprise under the supervision of the state should be introduced. This institution will be able to apply the principle of compensation goods completely and then illicit export will stop.

Finally, in the further course, public control of prices of the more important industrial articles should be applied. What is currently done in the sphere of coal, sugar, and petroleum should be expanded. Until we introduce the reconstruction of which I spoke in the first part of my report, we will have to regulate economic life in this manner in order for it not to spoil our reconstruction plan.

I am coming to the last part of my theory. Everyone who has listened to my speech can say: that's all good, but how is it to be done, with what are wages to be increased? The matter is fairly simple. Remember what I said at the beginning. If we have sufficient numbers of hands, a sufficient quantity of raw materials, a sufficient number of production facilities, what prevents us from creating as many products as we need? Let us forget that money exists. Let us imagine that everyone works for free, but also receives products for free. In the three conditions of which I spoke—seeing that we have sufficient workers, materials, and production facilities—we would satisfy the needs of the population until one of these factors was missing. At the moment it isn't missing. Thus why should money bother us? All that is necessary is the proper reorganization of money. It will be self-sufficing if we can manage to raise the social income. From practice we know that with certain pumps, if we want to set them in motion, we have to pour in water and then the pump works on its own. It is the same in economic life. There has to be an advance payment, a prepayment, of a certain part of the social income. This advance payment could take the form of issuing a suitable amount of banknotes; that is, the state itself would raise wages and force all the business owners to raise wages, granting an appropriate discount in the Bank of Poland for the time necessary. This would be equivalent to the introduction of banknote inflation. In the present conditions I would be against this, because it would have to lead to the devaluation of our money. A panic would occur—everyone would be afraid that the zloty would fall; they would flee from the zloty; prices would rise and there would be a devaluation of the currency.

For this reason, an auxiliary currency, which would be issued by a special institution under state supervision, should be temporarily introduced. This currency would be so-called commodity vouchers. They would not have the nature of a compulsory form of payment in all instances; perhaps it would only be possible to use them to acquire goods and pay for all personal services and debts. However, they could not be used for the cancellation of old debts, and it would also not be possible to buy foreign currency with them. Their sphere of use would thus be limited. Another condition to prevent their being discounted, that is, worth less than gold, would be their short-term nature. It should be said that after a brief period they could be exchanged for ordinary zlotys. The period could be three or six months from the date of printing. After this period, they would be exchanged in all banks for the zloty in circulation. Then everyone would be able to expect that after a few months they would be able to receive the equivalent of the vouchers in zlotys. Of course, having bought a certain quantity of vouchers, the state would be able to issue new ones. The third thing that would facilitate the exchange of these vouchers would be the condition that acceptances, issued in these vouchers only for the above-mentioned reasons, that is, for goods or payments, would have priority of execution ahead of obligations in ordinary zlotys. In other words, these vouchers would be exclusively circulatory in nature; they would be issued for current expenditures. This would mean above all that current obligations should be paid and only afterwards the zloty ones.

The state would have to draw credit in these vouchers—payable gradually in ordinary zlotys after three years of grace period—in the above-mentioned banks to raise the salaries of its civil servants and functionaries.

This is naturally connected with the entirety of the transformation plan. I expect that in executing it the social income of the masses will rise and thus the state's income will increase—the state will be able gradually to pay the first debt that was drawn for the expenditures of which I spoke. From the moment when these vouchers will have fulfilled their function, the bank would be dissolved—10 to 15 years after its introduction—and the auxiliary currency would be eliminated. It would only be a temporary assistance.

There is one condition for conducting the entirety of this plan—the enthusiasm of the population for the principle of rebuilding the system; an enthusiasm which could be stimulated only by two factors: first, the population must have full faith that this planned reconstruction will bring an improvement. Such faith should be produced before this or any other plan is introduced. Second, the people must have entire confidence in the agents who would conduct this plan. The whole arrangement of political relations would have to be of such a kind that the entire society would have confidence in the persons leading the reform.

I have now entirely exhausted the subject. I repeat that, in my opinion, it would be best not to begin discussion here today but rather in the provinces first.

I have to say that it is my deep belief that, both for the whole world and in particular for Poland, the reconstruction of the system is nothing less than a question of existence, not only because the welfare of a great number of individuals must be raised but also in order for our state to exist. A state that will tolerate the poverty of millions of its citizens will be weak and sapless and could fall into ruin, and that poverty and want can not be removed other than by the reconstruction of existing relations.

CHAPTER 12

The Concept of Cooperativism[1]
Cooperativism as the Organization of Relatively Weak Economic Elements

Edward Taylor

It is entirely possible to hold the view that cooperativism does not principally differ from other forms of enterprise, that the work of its economy is based on the same principles as all other forms of enterprise in today's capitalist system, and thus that its aim is to obtain the greatest capital gain through its economic activity and furthermore that it is an association to produce the greatest possible profit for the capital of the associated members. Only one trait is supposed to differentiate it from other associations: that it is adapted to the needs of the economically weak social strata and is thus conducted with small amounts of capital. Its social importance therefore lies precisely in enabling "little people," small capitalists, to make advantageous use of their capital, their talents, and their personal prowess. The legal form of cooperativism is supposed to signify that it is the social equivalent of, and identical with, a joint stock company, democratically established by legislation, as in England, for example. Basically, this view is sometimes, perhaps even unconsciously, the foundation of a range of German cooperativist authors, who in general base their view primarily on the legal characteristics of the concept of *eingetragene Genossenschaft* of German legislation. The contradiction though is too great with real conditions and with the social ideas of the cooperative movement and its activity—with the general ideas and spirit of the legislation—to make it maintainable in its entirety without certain at least minimal social correctives.

---

1 Edward Taylor, *"Współdzielczość jako organizacja elementów relatywnie słabych gospodarczo"* ["Cooperativism as the Organization of Relatively Weak Economic Elements"], in: idem, *Pojęcie współdzielczości* [*The Concept of Cooperativism*], Kraków 1916, Nakładem Akademii Umiejętności [Published by the Academy of Learning].

The closest is the view of Hugenberg,[2] who nevertheless does not claim any scientific precision but confines himself, in his valuable, concise work,[3] to introducing a range of political and economic ideas in relation primarily to German credit associations. In general he considers cooperative associations (*Genossenschaft*) to be a whole range of very diverse institutions: "an association is a uniform thing only as a legal form."[4] He considers municipal associations to be capitalist financial institutions furthering the economic progress of the middle urban strata: "this aim," he says, "is served, alongside other forms of equal value, by the legal form of the association, which is artificially adapted to the needs of the capitalist organization of credit."[5] On the other hand, Hugenberg recognizes fundamentally different characteristics in rural credit associations of the Raiffeisen system, which aim at eliminating the moment of profit from their activity, but he explains them by their application to the special needs and ideas of peasant life, which are based on the idea of the common interest of the village, the district, and its members.[6] Such an association is "an aim, adapted to capitalism, of protecting special agricultural interests and ideals, and not a contradiction of capitalism, on whose basis it rests much more."[7]

The above views confirm the variety of institutions that are called cooperatives and the existence of a category of capitalistically organized institutions that preclude capitalist profits, but they do not at all explain the economic essence of the latter. At most, they explain why certain forms have spread more easily in given conditions; they explain erroneously, however. As far as Polish farming people are concerned, it is rare to see anywhere else such a clear attraction and understanding for typically capitalist organizations. Every rural worker confirms it, and the history of the Galician Agricultural Clubs, or even the Raiffeisen Bank, is a continual struggle of anti-capitalist cooperative ideas with the opposing drives and aspirations of the people. Thus there is no speaking here of rural "ideals." But the "commonality of interests" and its understanding is a condition of all association work in general, all association in the broadest sense.

---

2 Alfred Hugenberg (1865–1951), German businessman, national-conservative politician and economist in the times of the Weimar Republic, later a member of Adolf Hitler's cabinet.

3 A. Hugenberg, *Bank- und Kreditwirtschaft des deutschen Mittelstandes*, Munich 1906, J.F. Lehmann.

4 Ibidem, p. 5.

5 Ibidem, p. 11.

6 Ibidem, pp. 35–42.

7 Ibidem, p. 599, p. 600.

Biliński's[8,9] and Głąbiński's[10,11] definitions of cooperative associations also seem to be close to the basic concept put forward at the beginning. But in the case of both authors this closeness consists only in the incompleteness of their definitions. According to Biliński, they are associations "of voluntary unions of non-capitalists created for joint enterprise."[12] Further, however, the author sees a "social difference" between companies and associations in regard to the second trait of the concept mentioned at the outset, that is, profit as the aim of the institution's activity:

> The aim of a Company is purely egoistical: it is profit…an Association, on the other hand, serves indeed in first order the egoistical interests of the associated persons, as a company serves its shareholders; but this tendency is not necessarily manifested in formal profit and is not the association's exclusive goal, in so far as it should, in accordance with its immediate task and composition, simultaneously serve the interests of all the relevant underclasses.[13]

8   Leon Biliński (1846–1923), outstanding Austro-Hungarian and Polish politician, econo-
     mist, professor of the University of Lwów, minister of the treasury of Austria and Po-
     land, more important works: *Studya nad podatkiem dochodowym* [*Study on Income Tax*]
     (1870), *Wykład ekonomii społecznej* [*Lecture on Social Economy*] (1873–1874), *System nauki
     skarbowej* [*System of Fiscal Science*] (1876), *O istocie, rozwoju i obecnym stanie socjalizmu*
     [*On the Essence, Development, and Present State of Socialism*] (1883).

9   L. Biliński, *System ekonomii społecznej* [*A System of Social Economy*], vol. 2, ed. S. Głąbiński,
     Lwów 1894, Gubrynowicz and Szmidt, pp. 488–493, 530–610.

10   Stanisław Głąbiński (1863-ca. 1943) was a politician, lawyer, and economist. He was one of
     the main leaders of the National Democratic Party in Galicia, professor of economics at
     the University of Lwów, deputy, senator, minister of foreign affairs in the government of
     J. Świeżyński in 1918, minister of religious faiths and public education. and vice minister
     in the government of W. Witos in 1923. He was arrested by the NKVD and perished in the
     USSR. More important works: *O systemie Fizjokratow* [*On the System of Physiocrats*] (1898),
     Wykład ekonomiki społecznej [*Lecture on Social Economics*] (1913), *Nauka skarbowości* [*The
     Science of Revenue Services*] (1925), *Historia ekonomii* [*History of the Economy*] (1939) (edi-
     tor's footnote).

11   S. Głąbiński, *Wykład ekonomiki społecznej* [*Lecture on Social Economics*], Lwów 1913, pub-
     lished by the Association of Teachers of Institutions of Higher Education, pp. 598–608,
     395–400.

12   Ibidem, p. 489.

13   Ibidem, pp. 490–491.

The author thus quite explicitly emphasizes the point of entrepreneurial prof-it; therefore we must postpone a consideration of his views until later.

Głąbiński's reservations are less explicit. According to him, cooperative as-sociations are "permanent unions of non-capitalists for certain definite eco-nomic aims, based on self-help."[14] In this form, the definition would correspond entirely to the concept expressed at the outset, as self-help is an outstanding trait of capitalist companies, and furthermore, as we will discover later, it does not constitute anything essential or even characteristic in the concept of co-operativism. Further though, the author specifies that "associations differ from companies by their social character, the sense of the solidarity of interests link-ing members" and states that although dividends are permissible in an asso-ciation, its aim is "not providing incomes, but support through its activity for the employment or households of its members."[15] These reservations shift the above views into the category of authors who see the essence of cooperativism in the preclusion of capital gains, but link it causally with certain limitations on the extent of activity. We will discuss these views later.

We can see that the view that considers cooperativism to be a form of en-trepreneurship, differing from others only by the special composition of the associated entity, does not appear anywhere in full. Nevertheless, this trait is considered by the above-mentioned authors and also by many others—who perhaps do not ascribe such fundamental importance to it and whose views we will consider in other places—to be the distinguishing, if not the sole, fea-ture of cooperativism. We must therefore consider this trait and its proper significance.

At first glance, such a view of the essence of cooperativism appears prob-lematic. It introduces such an unclear distinction as that between capitalist and non-capitalist. Who are we to consider this latter? Is the matter to be decided by the possession of a certain amount of the means of production or consumption, of capital? However we pose the question, we always come upon a quantity of ambiguities. As a logical consequence, finding several or a dozen capitalists in an association—which is not only frequently encoun-tered in life, but is sometimes a necessity—would deprive it of its cooperative character: this consequence is absurd. In addition, such a thesis is contrary to real conditions. With the exception of workers' food associations, the great majority of cooperative institutions are composed of members of the proper-tied classes and are intended in fact sometimes for small capitalists. In general,

---

14   S. Głąbiński, *Wykład ekonomiki społecznej* [*Lecture on Social Economics*], op. cit., p. 598.

15   Ibidem, p. 599, p. 600.

cooperativism as a method of conducting business has already conceived the need for a certain capital: both founding and operating capital. It is a matter of entire indifference and does not at all influence the essence of the matter whether that capital is larger or smaller, or is provided by members in the form of money or contributions in kind, or by property surety.

These difficulties have been resolved by Biliński,[16] the sole author to address them, in the following manner: He accepts the participation of capitalists but claims that the majority of members must be composed of non-capitalists, which he defines as "persons not possessing any larger amount of capital, supporting their households predominantly by their work."

The thesis thus posed does not accord with reality, though; it would exclude from the sphere of cooperativism the major part of agricultural, trade, and production cooperativism, basing itself primarily on "large farmers"—as in Poland the people are generally called who in Germany are described by the term *Grossbauer*—and also cooperative unions of larger property, and even a good part of food cooperativism, in which sometimes persons living from capital gains, householders, or wealthier civil servants play a large role.

In essence, the question is raised of whether there is any difference between that same economic activity when it is performed now by a wealthy person and now by a non-wealthy person? If it is a matter of the essence of that same activity then the answer must be negative. On the other hand, differences doubtless occur in regard to the ability to perform a range of activities, in how they are individually appraised due to the diversity of resources possessed, and finally their significance in society. This last aspect is the most meaningful for us. For instance, the ability of a worker or of a millionaire to acquire foodstuffs cheaply has a different importance for society. Society's favorable view of all organizations changing the arrangement of social revenues in favor of the underclasses or in general being to their benefit rests on the fact that these latter are a large part of society, even its larger part, and that there is not generally a causal relation between their material situation and their personal activity: they are not in a state to change their situation, except possibly by special efforts, exceeding the norm, in special conditions. Therefore society links both interest and feeling with the question of the underclasses, which do not receive sufficient benefit from the present division of social revenue.

The difference of position between the wealthy and the non-wealthy classes in the economic sphere can be reduced to the inability, or relative difficulty, of the latter to make use of such an important factor of the economy as capital

---

16   Ibidem, p. 488.

in all its forms. But the idea of the amount of capital that makes it possible to better participate in the social income is exceedingly relative. Entirely different criteria appear in every area of the economy, and in consequence they change in relation to the same person depending on what aspect of the person or the person's economic activity we consider, because an individual never exhausts his economic life through activity of one kind. At least, with minor exceptions, a person nearly always appears simultaneously as consumer and producer. When the ability to make use of a better division of the social income is thus primarily dependent, all things being equal, on the quantity of available capital—where the quantity of capital necessary for this purpose is variable, diverse, and dependent on the type of business—and when finally the same individual usually combines in himself various kinds of economic activity, there can be no absolute criterion to determine whether a given individual has sufficient capital to participate advantageously with the whole of his business in the division of the social income, or whether he is a capitalist or not. Such an appraisal can only be of the roughest sort, distinguishing solely peaks from valleys, in which the relativity of the concept already begins to be lost. In other words, the concept of a "capitalist," which is usually used to describe the relation of the individual in the sphere of production and trade, or a wealthy person, when used to signify the position of the individual in relation to consumption, is a relative concept, measuring the ratio of his assets. The second member of this proportion, the object of the comparison, is the property of those individuals with whom the said individual enters into an economic relation. If the difference is large, then in the present system of basically free competition, the first individual will succumb to the second in the economic struggle; the division of income from the relative economic activity will be disadvantageous for that first individual. And it is not only a matter here of the size of assets, but simultaneously, to a certain degree, also of resources of expert knowledge, the abilities of the two sides entering the economic relation, then, all other things being equal, their personal ability, ingenuity, etc., and generally all the factors that influence relative economic strength or weakness.

Nevertheless—omitting this last matter in order not to complicate the question—we have to conclude that the concept we are considering appears to be equivalent with the concept of a weaker and stronger side in the respective economic relation: a purely relative concept, dependent on a range of conditions and above all on the social and economic system of the society. Only on the basis of these individual differences is a more general idea formed of the capital necessary for advantageous participation in the division of the social income from certain types of economic activities, certain of their branches, and further, in increasingly broad areas of the economy, creating a concept of what we would normally call a capitalist, a wealthy person, and so forth. However, the wider the extent of the idea we encompass, the more it loses in precision, always remaining relative to a certain degree.

In other words, in using the concepts of capital and capitalists in the question before us, it is not possible to think of defining them in terms of knowledge of production factors, where capital appears as a certain reserve of goods, nor exclusively in terms of knowledge of the division of business revenue, where capital appears as a substrate of the phenomenon of interest, but rather in terms of that special concept of capital produced by considering its significance for the functioning and characteristics of the so-called capitalist system of social economics.

And if we are to understand the concept of "non-capitalist" thus, then we must indeed recognize that one of the most important traits of economic co-operativism is that it is a non-capitalists' organization. However, to avoid the misunderstandings linked with this idea, let us rather use a definition that more precisely reflects it, namely, that cooperativism is an economic organization for classes or individuals who are relatively weak economically. It is a matter here only of relative weakness in regard to the type of economic activity in which the institution is engaged.[17] The characteristic of cooperativism thus defined corresponds to the real situation, to the principles of cooperative associations, to the general sense in which they are understood, and to the tendencies and ideas being the source and cause of their establishment.

The above definition of cooperative institutions, of their composition, is a social, politico-economic limitation of the concept of cooperativism, both representing its economic substance (its essence) and indicating the role of capital in the cooperative relative to its special ability to specifically influence the division of income from economic activities connected with its use in our economic system. Accordingly, the essential meaning of the above definition is closely related to the type of economic work of the cooperative enterprise, shifting it entirely to the latter, being derived from it.

---

17   This idea was emphasized unusually aptly and clearly by the late Professor Czerkawski in his lecture "On the Essence and Aims of Cooperativism" given in February 1913 during a "Scholarly Course in Cooperativism" in Kraków arranged within the framework of the School of Political Science by the author of the present work and Mr A. Kolarz. Unfortunately, the lecture has not been printed.

PART 3

The Social Bases of Labor Cooperativism

..

CHAPTER 13

Consumer Cooperatives and Trade Unions[1]

Jan Hempel

1 What is the Use of a Trade Union?

To the question of what induced each of us to join a trade union, we usually answer "the desire to improve our lives by receiving better wages." Certain persons—those who are deep thinkers—will also answer that they joined the union because worker solidarity requires it; others say that in joining the union they wanted to stand in the ranks of the great workers' army fighting for a new social order. Undoubtedly, though, the largest number are those who join simply to improve their lives.

And indeed, thanks to the union, they acquire significantly better wages than they had previously.

And this occurs in a very simple manner that is obvious to every one. If every worker had to come to an agreement with the entrepreneur individually as to his conditions of work, then the entrepreneur could employ only those who would agree to work for the least. He could choose between workers and in this manner lower wages by producing competition among them. On the other hand, that entrepreneur finds himself in an entirely different situation when he must come to agreement not with each worker independently but with all together through their chosen representative. And this occurs when the Trade Union acts in regard to the entrepreneur in the name of all.

Where there is no Trade Union, the workers compete among themselves and the entrepreneur gains by it; thanks to the union, competition between the workers is eliminated and capitalists can now be opposed by a large and strong workers' organization. Trade unions have recently come to have great importance. Their power in certain countries has grown so that not infrequently the conditions of work are not dictated to them, but they themselves dictate the conditions to the entrepreneurs, who do not have the strength to resist.

---

1 Jan Hempel, *Spółdzielnie Spożywców (kooperatywy) a związki zawodowe* [*Consumer Cooperatives and Trade Unions*, Warsaw 1921, Związek Robotniczych Stowarzyszeń Spółdzielczych [Union of Labor Consumer Cooperatives].

2   **Can the Trade Union Alone Raise the Worker's Standard of Living?**

Since unions have achieved such power that entrepreneurs must pay the work-er as much as the worker asks—and that is already the way it is in a few oc-cupations in our country—then it seems possible that the whole affair should be already resolved and the worker should no longer be exploited. That would be the case if a worker's poverty came only from the fact that the entrepre-neur pays less for work than it is worth on the market; that is, if the poverty of the worker came only from the fact that the entrepreneur does not pay him enough.

I repeat: if that were true, then the matter of workers' welfare would today be nearly resolved.

Unfortunately, this is not the case; our welfare is dependent not only on how much money we receive but also on what we can buy with that money. What good will it do me if I receive even a heap of money if I am unable to purchase for that money a sufficient amount of food, clothing, books, household goods, etc., for my family? In a word, what will I get for the raise for which the Trade Union fought, if simultaneously prices rise even faster than my wages?

If we look at social life then we are apt to observe that wages rise with prices, and prices rise with wages, and in the end it looks as if the struggle conducted by the Trade Union was pointless.

However, such a judgment on the activity of the Trade Union would be entirely incorrect. The Trade Unions and their struggle over wages are neces-sary, but we must understand what Unions can do and also what they can not manage.

A worker is a producer, because he produces; he makes various things that people need. And as a producer selling his work, the worker joins the Trade Union in order to effectively counteract exploitation from the side of capital.

But at the same time, this worker must daily buy various objects of necessity to himself; in addition, he buys them not for resale to someone else, but for his own use. All these objects of daily necessity the worker uses, that is, consumes. It ensues that he is not only a producer but also a consumer.

In Trade Unions, the worker is organized solely as a producer, selling his work. But here we see that with the rise in prices the Trade Union won't help him much, because that same worker as a consumer—that is, buying objects of daily necessity—must at once give back to capital what he fought for through the Trade Union, as a wage-laborer and producer.

We see thus that the worker is exploited not only as a wage-laborer and producer but also as a consumer. When the worker organizes exclusively as a producer, capital at once recaptures its loss from the other side. "You will receive, worker, larger earnings, but you will give it back, because I will raise the price of everything you can't do without"—that is what capital says and, sure of itself, again rakes in the profit, while the worker goes hungry, in spite of significantly higher earnings.

Is there no help for it? Is there nothing the worker can do, in order to counteract the double exploitation? What if we tried to use, from the other side, the same method that turned out to be so successful when we undertook the struggle over earnings? In a word, shouldn't an effort be made to organize also as consumers, in order from this side to oppose capital in a compact group, as we did in the struggle over earnings?

3   Where Does the Worker Organize as a Consumer?

When each of us daily buys the various necessities of life in a shop, he is behaving as if he himself were daily acquiescing to the factory owner, simply by not coming to an agreement with his comrades. Thus he must pay such a price and take such goods as the shopkeeper gives him. The shopkeeper in such a case makes the decision and the worker who buys from him must, whether he wants to or not, accept that decision. When there is no particular scarcity of the basic necessities, a person can in truth go to another shop, but there we usually find the same shoddy merchandise at the same high price. If we make objections to the shopkeeper, he will tell us that even if he wanted he could not sell the products more cheaply because he must pay high prices for them himself. Our anger won't help here, particularly as the shopkeeper is not at all the main culprit.

This small shopkeeper, from whom we buy our daily necessities in the majority of cases, is himself only an agent of a large wholesaler. The wholesaler takes the fattest cream in the trade operation, leaving the shopkeeper only the remains. The goods in various shops most often come from one and the same wholesaler; thus we will gain nothing if we go to another shopkeeper in another street or even a third one. We will usually find there the same goods at the same price, because the wholesaler sells everything for the same price and all the shopkeepers have to count more or less the same percent as their own profit.

If we compare this to the relations of factories or landed estates, we would conclude that the shopkeeper is only the watchman, skilled worker, or steward, exploiting the worker on behalf of the lord or entrepreneur. Having to associate with him is in truth very regrettable and most often such a person is morally disreputable, but in the end we must remember that he is not an exploiter but only a tool in the hands of the capitalists. Just as the owner of great factories or the heir of landed estates does not himself deal with workers or farmhands but entrusts that unpleasant activity to his directors, agents, stewards, master-workers, and caretakers, so a large merchant-wholesaler remains hidden while larger and smaller shopkeepers act in his name.

Now we come to the question of how to oppose them? How to defend ourselves against exploitation? We can not here use that weapon that has shown itself to be effective in the struggle with factory owners and which is called there a "strike"; we can not hold back, even for one day, from making purchases in shops because our stomachs would decidedly protest. Another method of combat must be found.

The method has been found and consists in doing without the shopkeeper and later without the wholesaler as well.

Actually, the shopkeeper is necessary only because each of us, or each of our wives, makes purchases in a shop, alone, independently of his or her comrades and does not have enough funds in order to make reserves, in order to buy from a wholesaler in large amounts. However, if we all put a little money toward purchases and instead of each one making those purchases separately, we began to buy in common, it would doubtless be possible to circumvent the shopkeeper.

Such an organization of common purchases, for money provided by everyone—called here shares—such a shop that we establish ourselves and that is directed by people we ourselves have chosen is called a cooperative, a consumer association, or a *consumer cooperative*. We know well that both here in Poland and abroad there are numerous consumer cooperatives; we are not always sufficiently aware of their significance and often treat them as if they were only ordinary small shops. These cooperatives are like trade unions of consumers; in them, the workers, organized as consumers, successfully oppose capitalist exploitation. And this takes place, as I have already indicated, in the following manner:

> Instead of each person buying separately, we all put in a certain amount of money and for this money we open a common shop, whose management is not in the hands of a shopkeeper who thinks only about his own profit and who is forced to obey the wholesaler regardless, but in the hands of a management board chosen by ourselves. The management board of the cooperative does not have profit as its aim but to supply us with what we need, at the lowest possible price and best possible quality. Acting in this manner we can do without the shopkeeper; that is, we eliminate him.

After getting rid of the shopkeeper, we still have to deal with the wholesaler, from whom we must acquire the goods for our shop. There is a way to deal with him, though.

If many cooperatives are established in the country, they all unite in a cooperative union, constructed on the same principles as every separate cooperative. Namely, all the cooperatives put in a certain sum of money; they contribute shares, the same as members in every cooperative. With the money collected in this manner a large, nationwide wholesaler is established, to which all the cooperatives associated in that wholesaler turn for goods.

Such a common wholesaler for many cooperatives is called a Cooperative Union and takes the place of a merchant-wholesaler. Thanks to the Union, we have already eliminated not just the shopkeeper but also the large merchant-wholesaler, which previously dictated prices to us and forced us to take even the shoddiest goods.

In some countries, particularly in England, such cooperatives and their Union have acquired enormous size and brought large benefits to the working class. Here in Poland there are a thousand cooperatives and several Unions, but the movement still lacks entire unification; then too, profiteering is significantly more strongly developed here than elsewhere. The Unions that are operating in Poland are the following: the Union of Workers' Cooperative Associations, (2) the Union of Polish Consumer Associations, (3) the Central Union of Railway Cooperatives, (4) the Unity Union in Lwów, (5) the Proletariat Union in Krakow, and (6) The Union of Consumer Associations in Poznan.

Polish workers will only be able to undertake a successful battle against private trade, against shopkeepers and wholesalers, when they bring about the unification of the entire cooperative movement, homogenize their method of proceeding and, making large purchases for the entire country, entirely free the country of merchants. As we have already indicated, this liberation will occur thanks to workers' organizing themselves as consumers. We are relying here on the same principle as in the trade union, but we are adapting it to the conditions in which the worker-consumer finds himself in relation to merchant capital.

The Trade Union itself, in bringing the worker higher earnings, will not provide his welfare, if prices simultaneously rise. Similarly, the cooperative itself would not improve anything if the trade unions were not simultaneously operating. It is only when these two organizations together put capital in a crossfire that they will prevent it from exploiting the worker either through cutting his earnings or through raising the price of basic necessities.

The Trade Unions and Cooperatives are two fraternal organizations, going hand in hand toward the same goal, toward the liberation of the working class.

4   Other Forms of Labor Organizations

This brochure would not be complete if we did not call attention, at least briefly, to other forms of the labor movement. Whoever thinks that cooperatives and trade unions themselves are sufficient to overthrow capitalism and entirely liberate the workers would be mistaken. Why, we are sill living under the rule of certain state laws established primarily by exploiters and these laws could be of a kind that entirely prevents the development of trade unions and cooperatives. In bourgeois republics—and Poland is now such a bourgeois republic—Trade Unions and Cooperatives possess slightly better conditions of development while here, however, the law and government are concerned above all for the merchants and entrepreneurs, and labor organizations are scarcely allowed to exist.

Therefore, the worker class still needs to possess an organization that would constantly struggle for the most convenient legal regulations for workers and which would constantly defend cooperatives and trade unions against persecution from the side of the bourgeoisie. Such an organization is a workers' political party, without which no trade union or cooperative could develop as it should. A political party must obviously strive not only to defend labor organizations but also toward an entire victory over the bourgeoisie, meaning the bringing about, throughout the country, of a legal and economic order in accord with workers' requirements and ideals.

It ensues that every worker, in addition to belonging to a trade union and a cooperative, should also belong to a workers' political party. But this is not enough, because in striving for the entire reconstruction of the social system, in striving for a new workers' order, the worker must learn a great deal. He must read, think, and talk with his comrades about what and how things should be organized. For this purpose there is one other form of workers' organization, and that is the cultural-educational organization. Only all four forms of the workers' movement comprise its entirety and are capable together of leading to the desired goal, that is, to the socialist order of justice.

Once again, we will enumerate the four forms of workers' organization:

1.   the trade union
2.   the cooperative
3.   the political party
4.   the cultural-educational organization.

CHAPTER 14

Work Cooperatives[1]

Jan Wolski

We Must Unite

We have a large country. Rich soil. In the earth there are rich deposits of salt, coal, oil, and all kinds of ore necessary for industry. The Polish nation is characterized by health, strength, and cleverness. It is talented and industrious. The Polish farmer, the Polish laborer, the Polish white-collar worker are highly valued in other countries.

Why then is Polish society so poor? Why are we afflicted by the disaster of unemployment? Why do so many Poles, in the prime of life and full of health, not finding occupation in their fatherland, leave their native lands and seek uncertain and unrewarding work in foreign countries beyond the seas, among foreigners and for foreigners?

Why isn't it as good as it could be in our Poland?

*

It is because we do not like, and do not know how, to work together. It is because instead of combining our efforts, we prefer to look after ourselves singly. And it is obvious, after all, that without the support of others the strongest person is often weak and helpless. The weakest, however, when they appear in a uniform group are always strong and capable.

Why should we then be surprised that Polish society, although more generously blessed by nature than many other nations, is—in comparison to the majority of civilized societies—very poor.

*

Nevertheless, in Poland too it is beginning to be understood, increasingly well, that unity is power. That we must join and act together.

---

1 Jan Wolski, *Spółdzielnie pracy* [*Work Cooperatives*], Warsaw 1929, Wydawnictwo Sekcji Kooperacji Pracy Polskiego Towarzystwa Polityki Społecznej [Published by the Department of Labor Cooperation of the Polish Social Policy Association].

In the times of bondage that joining together and acting together was made difficult by the partitioning powers, and sometimes even quite impossible. In independent Poland there are no longer such obstacles. In our country the most varied kinds of voluntary economic, trade, educational, or other organizations in which the members are consciously united by common efforts for a common goal, can freely be established and are being established.

But in relation to the large and various needs of our society, the association movement in Poland is so far still very weak and insufficient. And for many needs, sometimes we are not at all aware that we can and should unite.

Associations for Gainful Employment in Common

For instance, we have over two million wage-laborers, maintaining themselves and their families from their own earnings. Each one of them, whether a factory worker, craftsman, farmhand, or white-collar worker, is weak and often helpless when he seeks work on his own. He does not always find occupation, even though he may be a highly skilled worker and has tried as hard as possible to find work. And when a worker does not have earnings, then poverty, hunger, disease, and other misfortunes follow. But even having work, is he always satisfied with it? Is he not sometimes exploited? Does he not often experience adversity? Does he not sometimes perform work that is unworthy of him? We know that his work conditions are not always as they should be.

*

In many countries, employees who maintain themselves from their earnings from either manual or white-collar labor and who understand that in a duel each of them is weak, helpless, and easily injured, voluntarily combine in an association in order jointly to acquire occupation for all and to work together fraternally. Such associations are called work cooperatives.

They exist in many different kinds of industries and occupations.

And thus masons' cooperatives build houses. Estate-workers' cooperatives do the farming on large estates. Earth-workers' cooperatives build roads and railroads, dig canals, dig tunnels through the mountains, and drain swamps. Miners' cooperatives independently conduct work in mines. Printers' cooperatives run printing presses. Metallurgical-workers' cooperatives build various machines, iron bridges, wagons, agricultural tools, steamboats, etc.

There are also cooperatives for various white-collar occupations: for accountants, teachers, engineers, doctors, etc.

I could enumerate various occupations without end in which there are, or could successfully be, workers' cooperatives.

They are joined together in unions. These unions are sometimes very powerful and undertake enormous endeavors, which they conduct with the aid of the cooperatives.

*

The member-employees have great and various material and moral benefits from these associations.

Thus above all they free themselves from dependence on entrepreneurs, because for them the entrepreneur has become the cooperative. Those profits that the entrepreneur had from the work of his laborers remains within the association as the common income of the members. In this manner, large social capital can emerge to be used for various goals that are positive for the members, their families, and the whole society.

In a cooperative the members work with each other as free men with the free and equals with their peers. They do not have outside overseers above themselves, because they oversee themselves mutually, not allowing anyone to be idle. They choose their directors from among themselves. And when greater knowledge and ability is required than the workers possess, the cooperative invites in bookkeepers, technicians, foremen, engineers, agronomists, etc., who, in directing the work of the laborers there, are not superiors imposed from above but freely recognized leaders.

*

The most beautiful and most rapidly expanding of such cooperatives have developed in Italy. In France, England, Belgium, and many other countries they are also well known. They have been in use in Russia for a long time and are called "*artel*." In tsarist times they were primarily small, impermanent associations of carpenters, earth diggers, porters, messengers, and other such non-workshop occupations and also various peasant occupations. In recent years this movement has gained in strength enormously in Russia, although there too it has not really gone beyond the limits of small crafts and piece work.

In Poland, however, there are practically no such cooperatives.

Those few that exist do not provide the best examples. Because we do not know how to organize them properly and run them appropriately. We do not have experience and knowledge in this area.

And yet such cooperatives would be very useful in Poland for workers, piece-workers, and white-collar workers and could grow rapidly here and be very beneficial for society. All that is necessary is to approach the matter with understanding.

This is why we are writing our booklet, which provides a number of the most important observations and organizational pointers.

Who Can and Cannot be a Member of a Work Cooperative

The most important thing in a cooperative, as with every association, is the selection of suitable people. When the members are poorly chosen, when each has a different goal, when one is striving for something that to someone else might be undesirable or even harmful, when various members push the cooperative in various directions, then it is out of the question that the cooperative will develop well. It must either fail or follow the wrong path. An improper selection of members—this is one of the most frequent shortcomings in our inexperienced Polish cooperatives.

*

Who then can be a member of a work cooperative?

Only someone who has interests in common with all the members belonging to it.

And the interest is, obviously, to have gainful work in one's occupation in the cooperative.

Why in the cooperative, though, and not elsewhere? Because working in a cooperative is more secure than working for outsiders. Because labor is not exploited by an employer in a cooperative. Because in a cooperative the worker does not feel himself to be the servant of an outside employer but is working for himself, as an equal among peers and a free man among the free.

Who might have such an interest in belonging to a cooperative? Only a person who can thus avoid the necessity of working for an outside employer. The member of a pavers' cooperative will be a paver. The member of a fishers' cooperative will be a fisher, of a teachers' cooperative, a teacher, etc.

*

But a building entrepreneur should not be a member of a masons' cooperative. The owner of a secondary school should not be a member of a teachers' cooperative. The owner of a landed estate should not be a member of an agricultural workers' cooperative, etc.

Because being themselves owners of employment places and enterprises, and thus earning from their own facilities and the work of their hired labor, they do not have the same interests as others in belonging to a cooperative.

Thus if it happens that entrepreneurs want to be members of a work cooperative, they must have some other interest than the rest of the members—their own, often contradictory or even directly inimical interests to those of the proper members and the association.

Russian cooperatives often accepted entrepreneurs as members. And it worked out as badly as could be. Because the entrepreneurs became members in order craftily to destroy the association from inside, seeing it as an undesirable competitor, or in order cleverly to use the cooperative for their own enterprise, sometimes with great harm to the main body of the members.

As the work cooperatives in Italy understood this danger well, they have for a long time not accepted any entrepreneur as a member, even though the person might be the best expert in a field. This caution protects the cooperatives against failure and dissolution.

*

In work cooperatives in Poland we sometimes see among the members people who not only have not the least intention of working there gainfully but who would not even be capable of such work.

Thus, shall we say, a charitable aristocratic lady is a member of the chimney-sweepers' cooperative; a priest is a member of a seamstresses' cooperative; a retired general, who has never in his life held a brick in his hands or had anything to do with building, is a member of a construction-work cooperative; a high civil servant is a member of a shoemakers' cooperative, although he has never sewn a shoe and has no least intention of entering the shoemakers' trade.

Members of this kind join cooperatives for two reasons: either to make use of them for some lateral aim or out of an honest desire to render them aid.

*

Friends in the first of these two categories, who eagerly hasten to be members in order to use the institution for auxiliary purposes, should be guarded against the most.

The aims of these friends could be most lofty, most noble, but if they are nonessential and foreign to the cooperative they should not be imposed on it.

The cooperative has its own goals and tasks, its only proper ones, and should serve only those. If it undergoes outside influences, it will always neglect the essence of its tasks; often it simply will not have the ability to fulfill them properly and will cease to be that for which it was established. It will disappoint its members, disappoint society, discourage the unaware generality of people from cooperative matters and in the end will fail, leaving behind only a sad memory.

*

The second category of friends who seek membership in a cooperative are disinterested persons who wish the cooperative well and desire to help it without consideration of any alternative goals.

Such friends—wise, experienced, and connected—can be very useful to a cooperative. Their advice, their expert guidance, their help in seeking work for the cooperative, is simply invaluable for a cooperative.

It does not at all ensue, however, that such useful friends must necessarily be members of the cooperative. On the contrary! As outsiders, unconnected with the organization, they can more freely provide support to the association. Their opinion—wise, experienced, respected, and influential—can weigh more when it comes from them as a non-member, and thus from a person on the outside and entirely impartial, than when it is the opinion of a member.

But there is an even more important consideration, which is a decided warning against accepting even the most useful friend as a member of said cooperatives. We will discuss it at once.

In an average cooperative, whether it unites manual or white-collar workers, the members are not (at least in the first years of the cooperative's existence) very strongly united with one another and in addition do not have much organizational ability. These qualities are produced gradually, precisely through the daily necessity of the members' participation in the organizational activities of the association. The necessity for this participation in a work cooperative has enormous significance.

But when there are well-meaning "patrons" in the group of members, the inexperienced and insufficiently socialized general membership eagerly places on their shoulders the main—or sometimes the entire—weight of the organizational work along with the entire responsibility for the cooperative's fate. The result is that the proper members do not at all take an interest in or get involved in organizational matters and do not feel responsibility for the fate of the cooperative. Counting on the foresight and resourcefulness of the patron-members, they consider their association to be a charitable institution and behave in regard to the cooperative the same as they would behave in regard to an outside employer—with the sole difference being that they require more from the cooperative and count on it less. In other words, briefly speaking, the association is deprived of internal cohesion and strength.

Even if in one or two cases such an institution does display effective activity under its patrons' efficient management, this does not at all prove the real strength and durability of the association. It's only a beautiful ice castle.

*

The members of the cooperative should know that no outsider, even the most well-meaning and disinterested friend, should rule there—that they must manage the cooperative themselves.

This matter should be set forward clearly and firmly from the very beginning.

In Italy, a whole series of legal-statutory regulations prevent, or at least hamper, participation in the management boards of work cooperatives of any person from outside the group of persons for whom the cooperative is primarily a workplace. Italian cooperatives undoubtedly owe their beautiful development to their cautious protective regulations.

A Circle of Friends

But, not being able to be members of the said cooperatives, disinterested friends have a means of rendering very multidimensional and effective assistance to the cooperatives: namely, alongside the cooperatives there can and should be Circles of Friends, established of precisely such persons who wish the association well. The Circle of Friends does not have any formal rights in the cooperative. However, when it is comprised of persons who might be useful to the association, it could fulfill an extremely important role. The Circle can act in various matters. Its members are disinterested advisers to the management board in economic-administrative and legal matters. The cooperative's review committee, which is almost always composed of people with insufficient knowledge to conduct review activities, could find the proper experts in the members of the Circle. Internal misunderstandings among the members of the cooperative or dissension between the members and the authorities of the cooperative could best be resolved by a neutral court, chosen from among persons belonging to the Circle of Friends. Finally, the members of the Circle could be very useful in finding employment for the cooperative. The Circle guards the proper functioning of the institution in accord with cooperative principles. By its care and moral authority the influence of the Circle could

effectively counteract all unconscious or conscious attempts to lead the cooperative astray.

Thus every work cooperative should seek support by organizing a Circle of
Friends, which, naturally, must be composed only of disinterested friends. Because those who have an interest, even if they are only members of the Circle,
can sometimes cause serious damage to the association through attempts to
impose outside goals and tasks on the Circle or even by only giving the appearance of an improper hue.

Only Physical Persons Can be Members of a Work Cooperative

It sometimes happens that said cooperatives accept as members not only
workers but also various institutions with which they desire contact for one
reason or another. Thus one institution could supply the cooperative with
money on convenient conditions, another could make mass purchases of
the cooperative's goods, a third could give the cooperative ideological support, and so on. In these cases, the cooperative has two kinds of members—
physical members, that is, the individual workers whose work is the essence
of the cooperative's activity, and legal persons, that is, various institutions,
each with its own goals, which are different from the cooperative's, and
conducting its own activities, which are different from the cooperative's.
Understandably, in these cases, the cooperative and the institutions that
are its members need to have contact with each other (each for different,
personal, reasons), and to maintain that connection the institution becomes
a member of the cooperative. Does this give the desired effect? Considerable
experience is against entering on that road, for two reasons, which we will discuss in turn.

*

The first reason is the same that forbids the admission to membership of all
patrons and protectors. If in addition to physical members, the cooperative
has legal persons in its membership (particularly if they are rich and influential institutions, and these are the ones in which cooperatives are most interested) then the general, proper membership, that is, those persons gainfully
employed in the work cooperative, begin to see the member-institutions as the
patrons of their association, and eagerly place on them all the burden of the
cooperative's financial-economic—and even administrative—cares and difficulties and make them the recipient of the most baseless requirements and

expectations. It is unnecessary to prove that the effects of such a state of affairs can be, because it has to be, most lamentable for both sides.

*

The second reason against admitting institutions to membership is that the proper general membership (physical persons) have other interests in the cooperative than the interests of the "institution-members" (legal persons). These interests in certain cases could even turn out to be contrary, particularly given the small social skills of either side, which in our conditions is very natural.

It is understandable that each kind of member looks after its own interests. Each tries to conduct its own business above all, counting less on the interests of members in the other category. On the other hand, this evokes vigilant distrust, dislike, and opposition. Sometimes in this context permanent discord prevails in a cooperative.

It often happens that the "member-institution" makes requirements that are unambiguously contrary to the body of "worker-members." But the latter, although they have the majority of votes and thus have a formal advantage and the right to decide, must sometimes give way to the will of the "member-institution" because that institution has contributed considerable capital to the cooperative or in general can exert a strong economic influence on it and thus has a factual advantage allowing it to exercise an autocratic rule even against the will of the whole of the real membership.

The predominance of the "institution-member" sometimes even impinges in the area of internal relations between the "worker-members" and penetrates all corners of the cooperative's life, depriving the general membership of the important ability to manage its own association.

Such a state of affairs deprives the cooperative of its essential cooperative nature.

It creates false relations, not in accord with the cooperative's statute and principles. In these conditions, the "worker-members" necessarily develop a dislike for their association and begin to consider (correctly or incorrectly is another question) the "institution-member" to be their employer, while the cooperative is a convenient form by which the employer exploits their labor.

*

But even if the "institution-member" does not have economic predominance in the cooperative, it always tries to achieve such aims or others there. They might not be contrary to the aims of the cooperative, but for it and for "person-members" they will always be either foreign or indifferent or less essential and important than for the "institution-member." In wanting to realize its goals by means of the cooperative, the "institution-member" either meets with the opposition of the real members, which produces undesirable and sometimes dangerous discord inside the association, or, in controlling the cooperative by its influence, it contributes inevitably to a greater or lesser skewing of its direction or even existence.

*

Thus the cooperatives of which we are speaking in our booklet should not accept as members any institutions, even the most friendly-seeming, even those with whom the cooperative desires and must establish and maintain close and lasting relations.

On the other hand, they can and should enter into various contracts with these institutions, depending on the kinds of relations they intend to have with them.

*

For instance, a printers' cooperative is established.

In order to ensure its success, it must enter into close and lasting relations with a host of institutions in order that they place orders with it. Such institutions should even, in their own interest, put together a significant amount of capital in order properly to equip the press that will, after all, be working for their needs. Because the better the printing press is equipped the less expensive will be the work performed in it. The printing press employees themselves, however, not being wealthy persons, will be unable to contribute the necessary capital. If these institutions were to join the printers' cooperative, all the above-mentioned disadvantages would inevitably occur.

However, these institutions, instead of applying for admission as members of the work cooperative, should in company with it establish another new association, a mixed enterprise, in which both the cooperative and those institutions are members. A serious sum of capital, necessary for the establishment of a properly equipped printing press, could be produced from member contributions (with the cooperative's contribution being naturally much smaller than the contributions of all the other members). The work of this press will be managed by the work cooperative, but according to the general guidelines and under the general supervision of the collective owner of the press, that is, all the institutions that are its shareholders. Work cooperatives would thus have only workers as members and solely and exclusively members would decide about the cooperative's internal affairs.

As we have seen from this example, the cooperatives of which we have been speaking could cooperate very closely and even join with institutions that are necessary for themselves without admitting them to membership but creating with them joint mixed enterprises. Such a manner of cooperating will be good for both sides.

Belonging Voluntarily and Member Awareness

Work cooperatives, like all cooperatives, are voluntary associations. Members belong of their own free and unforced will.

However, in order for someone to voluntary join an association he must—naturally—be convinced to do so.

And he should not be convinced by hazy promises. The future member should be made fully conscious—he should clearly understand what he can expect from the association and what obligations he must undertake. And only when he is thus informed should he be taken as a member.

In Poland they sometimes say that uninformed persons can be admitted as members of a work cooperative—that sometimes there is no harm in forcing some person or other to register as a member. And awareness, they say, will come later, when the member has spent some time in the association. Sad experience has proven irrefutably, though, that such a view is quite mistaken.

In a work cooperative, a member's connection with the association is very close. People work together with each other here. Here, through their daily toil they earn their livings. If a member does not understand his obligations in the association, if he is not well aware what the cooperative expects of him, then he will not always behave as he ought, and sometimes could be harmful or dangerous for the association. Not necessarily through ill will but only through lack of awareness. Thus experienced people correctly say that the greatest enemy and the most dangerous misfortune for a work cooperative are its own uninformed members.

*

This misfortune must be carefully avoided.

Before setting the work cooperative in motion, all its founding members without exception must first have a basic knowledge of cooperativism. They must also know the statutes and principles of internal regulations for associations. Only then can they set the cooperative going.

This matter must not be overlooked. Neither time nor efforts should be spared in working to raise the level of awareness. A cooperative should not be started up before every last member is thoroughly prepared. It is better to delay for a few weeks or even months than to begin activity with poorly prepared members. Because then already, at the beginning, which is never very easy, the cooperative will not be able to run well. And it is harder to repair the evil later than to prevent it in time.

*

However, people who are themselves able to conduct cooperative-awareness work among their own are not to be found everywhere, and the work must be managed skillfully in order to evoke interest and teach everything necessary.

Thus in these matters one should turn for help and advice to the Section of Work Cooperation of the Polish Society for Social Policy (Warsaw, 21 Nowogrodzka Street, telephone 257–230). This section exists for precisely such a purpose—to render organizational aid to such cooperatives. In case of need, the Section can even delegate on the spot its representative for organizational-preparatory work.

The Work of Non-members and the Preparation of New Members

A work cooperative exists for the purpose of giving employment to its members. Its purpose is not therefore to make use of the work of non-members.

For what reason would the cooperative employ them? In order to profit?

But should a cooperative, which exists precisely in order that outside entrepreneurs should not profit by its members, profit by others itself? Making use of the work of non-members in order to profit is contrary to the very essence of a work cooperative.

Experience in all countries has shown irrefutably that cooperatives that employ non-members for the sake of profit either fail or are transformed into private companies exploiting the work of others no less than other businesses.

*

Moreover, a work cooperative, which from the very beginning must be very careful to choose people who are suitable in every respect (that is, good skilled workers, who are industrious, reliable, harmonious and aware of cooperative matters), must in the future choose its new members carefully as well.

There are numerous instances where work cooperatives that for years were healthy and developing beautifully failed miserably. Inappropriate behavior and the harmful influence of new members brought the cooperatives to destruction.

But a work cooperative can not and should not box itself in with the small group of its original founders. On the contrary, it must strive to associate with itself the most workers in its trade as possible; in order even to unite and give employment to all without exception—as occurred in several Italian provinces in the building industry and earth work, where private entrepreneurs were left nothing to do because they no longer had anyone to hire.

Thus the work cooperative can give occupation to non-members as well. But not for the purpose of profiting by their work, but to try whether they are suitable to become members. And after a trial period and their ideological preparation, the non-members become members.

In the work cooperative statute the longest trial period of work (for instance, one year) should be clearly indicated. No extension to the trial period should be allowed for anyone. After the trial period, an unsuitable worker should be removed from the cooperative. But whoever has worked for this period in the cooperative (even with interruptions) must be accepted as a member, if he makes the application in writing and performs all the formalities required by statute. The cooperative authorities do not have the right to refuse admission to such a person. For well-known, reliable persons, who are properly informed about cooperative matters, the cooperative authorities could shorten the trial period or waive it entirely. They should do this with great caution, however.

*

The cooperative can not pay non-members, during their trial period, worse than members performing the same work. This must be contained in the statute as well, in order to prevent the exploitation of non-members for their work.

In general, members must not receive any material personal benefit from the work of non-members.

*

The conditions of the non-member work trial mentioned above do not concern—clearly—underage and unqualified apprentice-learners.

However, they should not be used in excessive number nor should their work be exploited by the cooperative. They too must be considered as future members of the association and correspondingly treated with the greatest goodwill.

Every cooperative should establish the number of apprentices and their work conditions, instruction, and pay through an understanding with the proper trade union or, respectively, labor inspector.

*

In Poland, a large portion of associations considered to be work cooperatives make broad use, for profit, of the work of non-members and unqualified apprentices, without thinking of admitting them to the group of members.

Such associations should not be called work cooperatives.

Work Cooperatives and Capital

To give gainful employment to its members—this, as we know, is the basic task of a work cooperative.

But for this, a certain capital is almost always necessary. For some cooperatives it could be very little, for others, it must be considerable.

Let us take, for example, a messengers' cooperative. The cooperative does not produce anything, does not use any raw materials, does not require machines or factory tools. Thus the matter of capital will not pose a major concern for such a cooperative. The same, more or less, can be said about cooperatives for porters, accountants, house servants, and many other types of work.

But in the significantly greater number of occupations, the question of capital is much more serious for the cooperative. For example, a metal workers' cooperative. In order to employ its members, it must have at its disposal appropriate factory premises supplied with the proper machines and equipment, which are sometimes very costly. In addition, the raw materials for working are also necessary and are not to be procured for free.

In general, serious capital is needed. How do work cooperatives resolve the matter of capital?

Cooperatives with High Member Shares

But not every worker and not every white-collar employee can pay a large sum to the cooperative for his member share.

We must remember that these cooperatives are intended to unite people who are not well-to-do, whose only source of income is their own work, which is not highly paid, and that these people with few exceptions have no savings, particularly here in Poland, where earnings are so very low.

Thus the cooperatives with high member shares are inaccessible for ordinary wage-laborers and piece-workers.

Such cooperatives can be founded by minor capitalists, who, in contributing a large sum for their share, then have for their aim not only and not so much the ensuring for themselves of gainful employment as—above all—ensuring themselves nice profits from the invested capital and (sooner or later) the profit from the work of apprentices and non-members. Moreover, such associations unwillingly accept new members or do not accept them at all, unless presumably the candidate invests a larger bit of capital. The work of non-members is naturally remunerated less well than members' work; the apprentices and unqualified help serve as broadly as possible here, if only it brings a profit.

So in Italy, for example, such associations are not even counted as real cooperatives. And that is correct.

We need not distract our attention with such companies, because neither the laborers nor the piece-workers nor the white-collar workers—that is, all those for whom we are concerned—could imitate them (even if they wanted to), not having their own capital.

*

A laborers' or white-collar workers' cooperative, in striving to bring together all those who are employed in its trade, should not set high shares or require the applicants for membership to pay such.

The height of the obligatory contribution must not be a barrier to anyone's becoming a member of the cooperative.

Thus the member contribution should not exceed the average monthly wage that members could receive by working in the cooperative. And as not everyone would be able to pay such a sum at once, the cooperative statute must allow members to pay their contribution gradually, in easy payments, preferably by docking their wages over an extended period of time.

Two Types of Labor Cooperatives: Production Cooperatives and Work Cooperatives

As we have indicated, the employment of reliable manual or white-collar workers predominantly requires capital.

Most often, members are unable to create the necessary capital from their small contributions. How then is this matter to be arranged?

The manner depends on the nature of the association: will it be a production cooperative or a work cooperative?

*

We call "production cooperatives" those enterprises that run entirely on their own account and risk—that is, the purchase of raw materials, the production of goods, and the sale of their products.

Work cooperatives, on the other hand, limit their activity to work for other persons or—predominantly—institutions, which when the work requires it, provide the cooperative with materials and tools, furnish the means, and take the finished work from the cooperative. Sometimes the employer does not provide such means and materials but rather a down payment is made to the association toward the work commissioned. The cooperative, although it is working for the employer, yet manages its work itself and is responsible for the work of the persons to whom it gives employment. The cooperative takes from the employer joint payment for the work of all, with the administrative costs. It then pays its member-workers itself, being for its part their own employer.

From the difference between the production cooperative and the work cooperative we can see that they differ in the matter of the capital necessary for their activities. The production cooperative must acquire that capital for itself; the work cooperative transfers the main worry about the capital onto the body for which it works.

The Financial Difficulties of Production Cooperatives

A production cooperative requires considerable financial means. And as the member contributions are generally insufficient, the cooperative must take credit.

It draws loans from credit institutions. It takes credit from its suppliers. It takes credit from its customers. It sometimes takes loans from private persons or friends, or sometimes from loan sharks. And it conducts its business with borrowed money, in the hope that with time it will manage to acquire its own capital.

*

But before that uncertain hope is realized, the production cooperative is not truly an independent enterprise, protecting its members from the exploitation of their labor.

It is a laborer working for the profit of its creditors.

Because those to whom the cooperative has become indebted want to have, and require, high returns from the money loaned or the raw materials.

*

Forced to work for the profit of the creditors, the cooperative does not have the wherewithal to increase its own capital and perfect the facilities of its labor. On the other hand, the largest part of the small shares contributed by members melts away in it. Due to paying the heavy exactions of their creditors, production cooperatives are often unable to pay those they employ. The earnings of members in such cooperatives are many times lower than in private enterprises in the same sector.

Production cooperatives, being unable to satisfy their creditors even by paying their own members the least wages possible, are frequently forced to make excessive use of the work of underage or unqualified workers, who are horribly exploited.

In such cooperatives it is often impossible even to dream that the length of the work day, established by law, or other benefits required by social legislation (vacations, health insurance, etc.) will be observed.

*

It happens sometimes that in actuality the creditors take over management of the production cooperative. And they "rule it like gray geese," egoistically imposing their will. For them, such cooperatives are very convenient. With their help the merchant-entrepreneur can exploit the labor of the workers to a considerably larger degree and with greater impunity then he could do in his own factory.

Until the poor members, suffering exploitation and humiliation in such a pseudo-cooperative, lose faith that they will succeed in setting the cooperative on its legs, relinquish their shares, and liquidate the cooperative—often as a bankrupt institution.

*

It rarely happens that a production cooperative, particularly one needing large capital sums, manages to free itself from its unbearable dependence on various creditors and to acquire sufficient sums of its own and thereby independence.

But then, almost without exception, these cooperatives lose their social nature and change into companies drawing profit from capital, from the work of non-members, and from trade speculations.

Why Production Cooperatives are Subject to Degeneration

In the middle of the last century, great hope was placed in production cooperatives.

The most outstanding thinkers and social activists believed that these associations would become one of the main, if not the main, centers for the improvement of economic life and the complete reconstruction of the social system. Particularly in France, there was great enthusiasm for them.

In order to facilitate their emergence and help the development of production cooperatives, the French treasury offered them large financial assistance on the most convenient terms. France expended millions on supporting production cooperatives.

And what were the consequences?

In spite of the financial aid, the vast majority of those associations ceased to exist after a very short time. A small number survived longer, but they were also gradually eliminated as a result of their lack of success. A certain number were finally transformed into ordinary companies with a few shareholders, who, not always working personally in the associations, receive returns for their shares and from the work of hired labor.

Why was there such a lack of success? Why did the cooperatives either fail or depart from the proper path?

*

The cause of the production cooperatives' lack of success was that there was a deep internal contradiction between the motives that induced the members to found the cooperative and the motives by which such an association must be guided in its daily practical activities.

*

The motive for founding a production cooperative, as in general all work cooperatives, is the desire of the employees to defend their work against exploitation, by their joint efforts.

This lofty fraternal idea of defense against exploitation links members of the production cooperative, ignites their enthusiasm, and stimulates them to united action. The deeper that idea remains in their minds and hearts, the stronger is the cooperative.

Where that idea does not exist, the members do not feel internally united with each other and stick together like potatoes in a bag with holes.

Thus the main motive for establishing a production cooperative and at the same time the idea that gives the cooperatives its solidarity and internal strength is that of effective protest against exploitation.

*

But a production cooperative, at its own risk and on its account, both buys raw materials and sells its own products. In other words—it has business interests. It is thus a business enterprise.

And in business—naturally—each entity is striving for gain. It wants to buy with profit. It wants to sell with profit.

But to buy or sell with profit means to receive more than give.

When is that possible? Who agrees to let another profit by him? Only someone who is in great need or is unresourceful or is unaware that he is allowing himself to be exploited.

The production cooperative, like every business enterprise, must also be guided by the same motives as business in general. That is, it must manage its business affairs with profit to itself—which is difficult and worthless. The old adage says: "you crawled up among crows, now caw like one."

That the production cooperative is usually weaker than those with whom it has business interests is a separate question. In reality it is rather exploited itself than exploiting others.

But whether the cooperative profits from its business activity is not the point in the given instance.

The point is that in conducting such activity it must inevitably strive for business profits.

*

Thus a production cooperative emerges to combat exploitation; but in its daily activity it must pursue profits, that is, the exploitation (in as far as it can) of others' needs, others' lack of resourcefulness or awareness.

Two opposing ideas are forced to nest in the same institution. They must find room in the minds and hearts of the same people.

A thick book could be written about how these two ideas clash with one another on the ground of the production cooperative. What fatal consequences result for the cooperative as a social center and as a business enterprise!

In these conditions hypocrisy is created—sometimes involuntarily and very often quite consciously—mendaciously reconciling the high ideal of the struggle against exploitation with the daily chase after business profits.

*

The said cooperatives are associations of exploited people and not exploiters. People who know how to work and produce and not do business.

Business was not their field of expertise. They do not have business abilities inherited from their forebears, or knowledge, or practice. And what is most important—they do not have the attitude for it in their hearts and minds.

How is it thus surprising that they turn out to be poor businesspeople? Particularly as the original idea of combating exploitation, which united them, does not incline them to business activity either.

It is thus understandable that the business activity of production cooperatives, if they are essentially (and not solely outwardly) cooperatives, is usually done ineptly, improperly, and sooner or later leads the cooperative to fail.

Sometimes it happens though that among the members there are one or more persons with a liking and aptitude for business.

For them, obviously, the real goal of the cooperative is not very important. The possibility of gain from a cleverly conducted business move amuses them more than the matter of ensuring the general membership proper remuneration for the work.

And if such members gain influence in the cooperative and take control of the management, then the cooperative will begin to stray from its proper path. Then all the principles of which there was talk at the beginning of our booklet will be inconvenient and cramping for the management of the cooperative. The cooperative with such management will either go completely to waste and fail, or, as sometimes happens, it will be transformed into a company of small capitalists and day laborers.

*

There are also cases where the main goal of the organizers of the cooperative from the beginning is not to ensure gainful employment for the body of future members in their proper trade but to create well-paid management positions for their small group.

And such organizers push the cooperative on an improper and risky path from the start. They are chasing above all after business in which they can achieve high returns and which will allow them to pay themselves high wages. They make use of the work of non-members, as it can be paid worse than the work of members, and often lead the cooperative into the disorderly wilderness of speculation. In Poland in recent years we have had a number of sad examples of this type, which ended in publicized scandals and the downfall of the institution.

This mainly—or, more correctly, always—happens in cooperatives that admit as members not only workers who desire to work in the cooperative in their proper trade, but also persons for whom belonging to a cooperative seems to be an easy way to acquire money.

*

In order to make it impossible or at least difficult for cooperatives to come apart in this manner, Italian work cooperatives, in appointing a person from outside the group of workers to be a technical or administrative director or to fulfill some other position (which in fact always happens if the cooperative is large and is involved in complex work), do not accept such a person as a member and do not transfer to him the rights and obligations of the management board.

The board must absolutely be composed only of worker-members. It does not have the right to transfer its basic privileges to the directors but must make decisions on its own responsibility in regard to the cooperative's most important moves.

It is clear that in all these decisions of the board, the directors and other engaged managers are its necessary and principle advisors. But only advisors. If such a director has tact and understands the nature of the institution, his role does not at all diminish his stature and authority in the cooperative.

As to members of the board, in fulfilling those activities, they simultaneously work as ordinary workers, in their own trade, and receive for that the normal workers' wages. For participation in the board they sometimes have a shorter work day in their trade or receive a small addition to their basic earnings as workers.

Opponents of such caution object that it cramps the expansion and development of a cooperative. However, experience clearly confirms that in the final analysis it is in the best interests of the cooperatives. That it protects them very often from risky enterprises, from the unreasonable and greedy pursuit of profits, from an incautious haste in undertaking too large and difficult work without proper preparation and a sufficient number of members.

This carefulness of the board, which is composed solely of workers, gives the said cooperatives exceptional solidity, which is very much prized by institutions giving cooperatives work to perform.

*

Such precautions ensure that the workers themselves have the main importance in managing the cooperative's affairs and prevent board members from
taking too high salaries, thus avoiding many dangerous temptations. Thanks to
this, production cooperatives, in convincing themselves that the production
path is not the proper one, sometimes quite deliberately take another path, of
which we will now speak.

The Proper Path of the Work Cooperative

Work cooperatives do not experience either those financial-economic difficulties, or those internal conflicts, or the unhealthy temptations we observed in
production cooperatives.

They leave concern for capital to those for whom they work. They do not
conduct business activities. They are not threatened by business risks. They are
not allured by business profits. The work cooperative has no other goals except
those by which every work cooperative should be guided.

It also does not have a task above its strengths. It undertakes to do that for
which it has the capability, namely, to perform skilled work in common. If it
is properly organized, with suitable people, it always manages to perform the
work it takes on as well as can be, to the satisfaction of its clients.

*

But there is a condition without which the work cooperative is not on stable
ground. Namely, it should be strongly based on permanent and mass customers of its work, who would give it work and (where the necessity arises) provide the capital necessary to finance the work. Without such solid customers
for a cooperative's work, the cooperative will not have firm bases, will easily
fail, and often from necessity stray onto the uncertain route of the production
cooperative.

*

A question arises: Can the cooperative always have such solid, certain, mass
customers for its work?

If the cooperative brings together good workers, belonging to a useful
occupation, that is, those whose work is necessary to society, then doubtless

customers for that work must be found. They only need to be sought, near or far.

Thus the organizers of the cooperative, before they set their cooperative in motion, should look around at the various social, local-administrative, or government institutions and find among them customers for the future work of the association.

And only after entering into an understanding with these institutions and after ensuring work for the cooperative from them, can the cooperative be set in motion without fear.

Thus pavers, for instance, should enter into an understanding with the magistrate or the local council; shoemakers with large consumer cooperatives, army suppliers, trade unions, or other purchasers of shoes in bulk; doctors with health insurance companies; construction workers with housing cooperatives building houses for themselves, or with government offices, magistrates, local councils, and various institutions in general that have building needs.

*

In seeking future customers for the work of their association, the organizers of the work cooperative should sometimes get involved themselves in organizing those customers.

I gave above, as an example, a cooperative of printing press workers, who, in desiring to work cooperatively, organized for themselves an appropriate commissioning institution for their work. For this purpose they convinced a range of social institutions about the benefits of founding a common printing press that would work for all of them as its shareholders, protecting them from the exploitation of private printers. And by this path they managed to create a large social graphics enterprise, whose management was entrusted to the work cooperative.

*

If in the locality there isn't—or even couldn't be—an appropriate institution that could give work to the cooperative, then the search must be made further afield. For example, a cooperative of workers producing bentwood furniture could perfectly well emerge in a suitable place in the provinces and find customers for its production in Warsaw, for instance, in the form of the Central Union of Consumer Cooperatives.

*

In a number of countries there are known cases where production cooperatives, not being able to manage the proper management of their enterprise on
their own risk and financing, have entered into an agreement with consumer
cooperatives or with other social consumers of their work, transferred to these
institutions the main burden of financing their work, and transformed themselves into a work cooperative—with visible benefit to their members.

*

Thus, in establishing a cooperative for laborers, piece-workers, or white-collar
workers, and aiming to provide employment for the members in their proper
vocation, it is necessary first of all to ensure for them the proper support in the
form of a mass customer of their goods or services. In other words, the association should be directed along the line of a work cooperative.

This is why, in desiring to mark the proper road as clearly as possible, we
gave our booklet the title "Work Cooperatives."

There are some occupations among craftsmen and piece-workers, though,
where work cooperatives will not always manage to rely on a mass customer
for their work (at least at the beginning). Such occupations include fashion
designers, embroiderers, hat-makers, etc.

These occupations are terribly exploited and a cooperative organization for
such workers is a burning need. In these areas, cooperatives can and must arise
that (at least initially) are partly similar to production cooperatives.

Nevertheless, both the nature of their activity (primarily commissioned
work), as well as the conditions of its execution, are similar to the type of
work-cooperative association discussed above and allows us to count them as
such.

*

We already know about the benefit that members receive from belonging to a
work cooperative (obviously, a properly run one).

Now I will say a few words about the benefit to clients and to the whole
society.

In giving work cooperatives or their union various kinds of work to do, the
customers rid themselves of the problems and difficulties—sometimes large
and costly—which they would have to incur in managing the work themselves
and engaging each of the workers separately. Here the work cooperative, if it is
properly set up, gives a full guarantee that everything will be done—and done
honestly, efficiently, and as it should be.

Relying on work cooperatives allows the state, local administration, and various social institutions to expand their economic activity in a manner based exclusively on general benefit, not profit, and to enter a field where previously the greed for profit of private business initiatives reigned indivisibly, extorting payment from the helplessness of society and the state.

The advantage to the country from work cooperatives could be and will be enormous.

PART 4

Universal Cooperativism or Labor Cooperativism

∴

CHAPTER 15

The Universal or Class Nature of Cooperativism[1]

Marian Rapacki

The question of the class nature or classlessness of the cooperative movement is purely theoretical and would be fairly idle if the adherents of the so-called class trend did not draw practical consequences from their position. These consequences consist in the organizational separation of labor cooperatives from the general consumer organization and in their open or silent subordination to one or another labor political party. And even though it may be a neutral matter for the development of the cooperativist movement whether a cooperative is a class institution or a classless one, the practical consequences that its adherents draw from their class position—though not all and not everywhere—are not a matter of indifference to it. Therefore, the theoretical issue acquires greater weight because its comprehensive clarification could have an influence on those practical consequences, which are of primary importance for the cooperativist movement.

***

Above all, there should be mutual understanding as to the meaning of the term "class nature." In regard to a given social institution it will mean that the institution unites members of one or another class; it is an organization of the given class and expresses its class interests.

From this viewpoint, very far-reaching consequences can be drawn. As all people belong to some social class, and as social institutions are composed of people, therefore, depending on a given institution's composition or the preponderance in it of one or another social class, institutions are organizations of a given class—are class organizations. Thus the state (with the exception of Russia) must be a class organization of the class of capitalists, who impose their dominance (which is not so much numerical as material, and a commune, or even a church of one faith or another, does the same). From this viewpoint, which does not see in social life any other phenomena than class struggle, there are obviously no classless institutions: every social or economic

---

1 Marian Rapacki, *"Powszechność czy klasowość kooperacji"* ["The Universal or Class Nature of Cooperativism"], *Rzeczpospolita Spółdzielcza* [*The Cooperative Republic*] 1923, no. 10.

institution must be an expression of the interests of one class or another—must be a class institution. Clearly, a cooperative must also, in the light of such views, be a class institution.

Such a view, however, precludes a strict scientific definition of a given institution's "class nature." On these terms, neither personal composition nor the numerical predominance of the members of a certain class in a given institution determines that nature; contrary to the claim of this view's adherents, a western European state would not then be a class institution of capitalism because it has only a negligible minority of capitalists. The deciding factor would thus be the position a given institution occupies in the class struggle. But appraisal of the role of an institution with a mixed social composition in class struggles is such a subjective matter, and the institution's relation to social struggles is so incredibly variable and complex, that constructing the scientific hallmarks of "class nature" on this basis is entirely out of the question.

Thus including an institution of a mixed social composition in the category of "class" institutions, in conditions in which their activity expresses the variable resultant clash of individual social classes desiring to make a given institution the exponent of their interests, can not be justified theoretically.

> Accordingly, we can consider as class institutions those that are exclusively or almost exclusively composed of a uniform social class, that are able to express solely the class interests of the given class, and that are consequently not an organizational form for supporting the interests of another class.

Laborers' trade unions and entrepreneurs' professional organization are undoubtedly class institutions. It is unthinkable that great landowners, to support their class interests, would make use of the organizational form of the trade union with its strike fund—an organizational system, but above all a fundamental aim. Contrarily, it is also impossible that workers should organize in the form of cartels or trusts to collude for the purpose of raising the prices of goods.

Production cooperatives of all types are indisputably class organizations. The production cooperatives of industrial workers express exclusively the interests of the factory or craft proletariat and can be used as an organizational form by no other class. Craft and agricultural cooperatives of all types constitute specific organizational forms for each class.

Consumer cooperatives are another matter. Consumers do not constitute a social class: they are recruited from all classes. Therefore, the organizational form expressing the interests of consumers is not a form proper to solely one social class, but must be—and in reality is—used by the members of all social classes separately, or even in combination.

It is clear that the interests of a given social group, as consumers and as entrepreneurs, play an entirely unequal role in various classes. The interests of entrepreneurs do not play any role in the working class. However, a rational organization of the interests of consumption is of primary importance for this class. A middle place in this respect is occupied by small farmers and small craftsmen, and a quite opposite position by the class of large landowners, industrialists, or financiers, that is, the upper bourgeoisie. Nevertheless, the interests of the members of all these classes *as consumers* are uniform and can be organized with the aid of one and the same organizational form—that is, consumer cooperatives.

Theoretically, therefore, on the basis of the above definition of the essence of the "class nature" of social institutions, consumer cooperatives are not class institutions. Furthermore, if this theoretically correct definition were to be adopted, we wouldn't find many institutions of a strictly class nature. Moreover, the essence of the dispute over the "class nature" of cooperativism does not at all lie in the theoretical plane. It is a matter of the role of cooperation and its practical position in regard to class struggle. It is a matter of whether consumer cooperativism is to remain "neutral" in this struggle or whether it is to take an "active part" in it. In addition, the question arises of how this active participation is to be expressed.

Let us first consider the very essence of class struggle. That struggle is a conflict between social classes—which have emerged in the context of the socio-economic relations of the capitalist system—over the largest possible share in the social income. From the viewpoint of the proletariat, the class struggle has a dual aim: an *immediate* one, consisting of obtaining better conditions of work and pay and in general better living conditions on the basis of the existing system; and a *fundamental* one, which is to overthrow the existing system and replace it with a different one, better corresponding to the interests of the proletariat.

In either case, class struggle is a *means* for the proletariat, not an *end*. This needs to be specially emphasized, because in the view of certain social theorists, and particularly certain journalists, class struggle has become a kind of goal toward which the working class must strive by all possible means and on the basis of all its organizations. Class struggle or social struggle as a striving to change the existing socio-economic system and to create a classless society is simultaneously a struggle for self-abolition. It is the result of the capitalist class system and should disappear along with the class system.

We must now consider the attitude of consumer labor cooperatives to these two types of aims of the class struggle: the immediate improvement of the existence of the working class on the basis of the existing system and the fundamental change of this system.

Let us note that in consumer cooperativism as well we can find these two purposes. On the one hand, consumer cooperativism gives its participants a whole range of immediate benefits, expressed in lowering the prices of market goods, in their good quality, conscientious weighing and measuring, savings on purchases, etc., and on the other hand, in developing and growing more powerful, it gradually replaces capitalist enterprises, putting collective, social enterprises in their place. Regardless of how we view the final result of the process, in either case it involves the displacement of the capitalist system and the creation of cells of the new, classless system.

Thus a labor consumer cooperative provides certain immediate benefits to the worker, leading to his improved well-being on the basis of the existing social relations, and this is its major aim. Removing the capitalist system and building new social forms occurs rather automatically—most often entirely unconsciously—through the very emergence and development of consumer cooperatives. In order to fulfill this task, consumer cooperatives do not need to create special organs or to direct their activities in some special direction. It is enough that the cooperative develops and goes about its normal activities with increasing intensity, *because it is itself a cell of the new system* and its development and growth is simultaneously the growth and development of the new system. Therefore, too, in achieving this goal, it is not necessary for a cooperative's members to be conscious of the final aim, although if such a consciousness is present it can be a powerful driver of the cooperative's development and thus of a faster achievement of its end purposes. However, the development of consumer cooperatives is in general based on awareness among the masses of those above-mentioned immediate benefits and for the generality of cooperative participants they are its essential and proper task.

There are other proletarian organizations involved in improving living conditions for the working class on the basis of the present social conditions: trade unions above all, and political organizations in part.

Nevertheless, we can at once spot a difference in the methods of the cooperative on the one hand and of trade unions or political organizations on the other. Trade unions and political organizations arrive at their achievements in the sphere of improved living conditions for the working class by means of struggle, whether it is for higher pay, a shorter working day, or better legal protection of employment, etc. For the proletariat these are *typical organs of class struggle*. Cooperatives, though, do not operate by means of direct struggle for one or another gain but by creating better economic conditions for their participants. Of course, the fact that a majority of consumers should create their own institutions in place of those run for profit by private entrepreneurs produces conflict between these institutions and the private enterprises that are directly affected, but this is a conflict similar to the one that once arose between carters and the first railways and does not have a *direct* class-struggle nature, as do the activities of trade unions and political organizations.

From the viewpoint of the proletariat, we are dealing here with a certain rational division of work between the organs of struggle and the economic organizations.

Let us now consider whether from the viewpoint of proletarian interests it is proper and justifiable to break this rational division and create *organs of direct class struggle* out of consumer cooperatives.

Above all, how might such an immediateness of the struggle be expressed? In two directions, presumably: (1) appropriate social, educational, and organizational activities; (2) material aid to the organs of direct struggle. The question of the proletariat's class awareness is naturally extremely important for the sake of class struggle. However, this awareness may arise by other means than social organizations; activities to promote such awareness are conducted by the proletariat's political organizations and cultural-educational organizations, and as they are specifically adapted to this aim, they do it better and more effectively than consumer cooperatives. Furthermore, given the other, opposing factors, this is not a question of such weight as to be decisive.

The other issue—material aid from the cooperative to organs of direct class struggle—is theoretically of greater importance. In the course of their development, cooperatives can acquire fairly significant funds. Pouring such funds into the organs of direct struggle—trade unions and political parties—could significantly strengthen their activities. In actuality, it is the political party that should be helped, because except in periods of unemployment, strikes, or lockouts, trade unions generally have enough funds for their activities and in normal conditions frequently loan their own funds to cooperatives. However, in practice, cooperatives are faced with a dilemma here: either to transfer their surplus in whole or in part to the party and not to develop, and in this case the material aid given to the party will be insignificant, or to use that surplus in accordance with its own aims and organizational principles.

This dilemma is closely connected with the whole practical aspect of the class-nature question. The principle of class nature leads to closing the consumer cooperative within the framework of a sole class, contrary to the principle of universality, which has been recognized to this time as one of the immovable bases of consumer cooperativism.

From the viewpoint of the working class, this issue leads to the question of which principle better answers the interests of the working class: the principle of *universality* or the principle of a *closed, class association*?

We have already seen that the benefits of direct engagement by consumer cooperatives in the sphere of class struggle are nugatory in fact. Let us now see what the benefits are of applying the opposite principle.

We have already spoken about how the direct and important task of a consumer cooperative—the task for which it is suited and equipped—is to improve the material well-being of its participants by creating better conditions for providing basic necessities. Thus the interest of the workers organized in cooperatives lies in the cooperative's *best fulfillment of this task.*

Additionally, in terms of the consumer cooperative's further tasks, which it fulfills automatically—that is, replacing capitalist enterprises—the efficient operation of consumer cooperatives, as the most important condition of this replacement, lies in the broadest interests of the working class.

Thus the development of the institution of consumer associations is primarily of importance for the working class and no other. No secondary aims and tasks can equal the fundamental importance of consumer cooperatives for the working class—either in its struggle to improve daily living conditions or in regard to the broadest social ideals.

The working class must thus seek conditions for consumer cooperatives that will enable their fullest and most comprehensive development in the direction of their immediate and essential purposes.

The most important condition of this development is *universality.*

No one, it seems, can contradict the claim that universality is a condition for the healthy and efficient management of an association. The logical placement of shops, large turnover, an advantageous ratio of administrative costs, capture of the local market, strength in organizing wholesale purchases—all this can be brought about only in applying the principle of universality: the principle of one association encompassing the entire population of a given territory. Because healthy and efficient management is a condition for cooperatives' development, and thus of their significance for the working class as well, consequently the creation of a *universal* and not *class-based* or closed consumer cooperative lies in the rational interests of that class.

The fears that if consumer cooperatives are universal in nature, the interests of the working class might be insufficiently regarded are doubly unjustified. First of all, the economic development of the cooperative sufficiently takes into account the interests of workers as consumers, and even if a consumer cooperative is universal there is no possibility of the hegemony in it of other social strata than the working class and small farmer strata, both on account of their numbers and because consumer cooperativism has the most importance for precisely these groups. This importance is greater for workers than for small farmers, particularly in regard to the increasing profitability of farms.

For this reason, even in countries that are largely agricultural in nature—such as Poland, for instance—laborers, in spite of their lesser numbers, achieve a numerical balance with the rural population and thanks to their greater social abilities and temperament, most often a moral advantage as well.

We encounter this moral advantage in all countries where there is one universal social organization, regardless of the social character of those countries. We can list agricultural France alongside industrial England, Switzerland, Sweden, and lastly Holland. Only Denmark could constitute an exception, but there the great advantage of well-organized and socialized farmers does not at all disturb the harmonious cooperation in consumer cooperatives of farmers and workers, just as the predominance of workers in the former countries does not affect their coexistence with farmers' consumer cooperatives.

This harmonious cooperation is not harmed in the least by either a difference of views on the *ultimate* aims of consumer cooperativism between farmers or workers or even within these last two groups. In these conditions, the disputed question between Marxists on one side, cooperativists on another, and liberal economists on a third, over whether consumer cooperatives are replacing—and are in a condition independently to replace—the capitalist system and substitute another is purely a theoretical one, which can be resolved according to a simple principle: "wait and see." This does not at all disturb the mutual cooperation of the adherents of various theoretical trends on the development of consumer organizations, in so far as they recognize them to be useful in general.

Finally, we should deal here with the legend, which—if it were true—could hamper cooperation between the adherents of a Marxist view of cooperativism and independent cooperativists. It incorrectly ascribes to cooperative activists so-called neutral tendencies, called solidarist, whose aim is to counter class struggle and to bring understanding between the classes on the basis of the existing social system. Cooperativists, even the School of Nîmes, head their program with the displacement of the capitalist system by consumer cooperativism and the construction of a new system in its place—a fact that is denied by class-nature proponents. If they speak about a solidary society—that is, a classless one—then it is about the kind that cooperativism will create as a *society of the future*. The cooperativists of this camp never oppose the class struggle conducted by the proletariat through organizations created for this purpose; on the contrary, they frequently work together with those organizations on an appropriate plane. They only oppose use of the cooperative as a tool in direct class struggle, because it is counterproductive and harmful for the working class itself. The firm and energetic statements of independent cooperativists against the capitalist system and their deep faith in the role of cooperativism in displacing this system places them in the same camp as the followers of class ideology, who consider the overthrow of the capitalist system to be their chief aim.

The creation, in these conditions, of a separate "class" organization of cooperativism is not justified either theoretically or practically, and from the viewpoint of the working class, as of social development in general, is very harmful.

CHAPTER 16

The Ideology of Labor Cooperativism[1]

Adam Próchnik

Cooperativism has a class foundation. However, not all cooperativists occupy the same position. Alongside the socialist cooperativists there are the "neutral" cooperativists; there is bourgeois cooperativism, which links cooperativism with a quite different worldview. We must thus remember the difference between these contrary methods of understanding cooperativism.

It should first of all be pointed out that the cooperativism, in its very cradle, was class cooperativism, labor cooperativism. The creators of cooperativism considered it to be a form of struggle against exploitation. Only later did a neutral, classless cooperativism, which departed from the natural substrate of the world of work, begin to be created and as a result to hang in suspension.

Neutral cooperativism differs first of all from labor cooperativism in that it rejects the principle of class struggle. Labor cooperativism leads a conscious struggle with capital; bourgeois cooperativism rejects that struggle. It desires to exist beside capital, parallel to it, and not against it. In this manner, however, cooperativism loses all its sense. Cooperativism is fundamentally contrary to the capitalist economic system. The basis for capitalist economics is the desire for profit; the basis of cooperativism is the desire to satisfy needs.

Can these two economic forms exist quietly beside one another, without blocking each other's paths? This is entirely impossible. One of the basic traits of capitalism is expansion; it is the striving to control the broadest possible markets. Capitalism, without its pursuit of markets and profit, would cease to be capitalism. Capitalism not only fights for external, foreign markets, it not only tries to engage the state in the politics of acquiring those markets, but it also fights for complete control of the domestic market. Cooperativism is struggling for that same market. The expansion of capitalism thus strikes directly at the very existence of cooperativism. This is something more than the competitive struggle of shops or enterprises; it is a struggle of two entirely different systems—a system of individual economics and a system of social economics. But cooperativism, if it is to have any sense, must not only defend itself against the possessiveness of capitalism, it must itself be characterized by expansion.

---

1   Adam Próchnik, *Ideologia spółdzielczości robotniczej* [*The Ideology of Labor Cooperativism*], Warsaw 1937, TUR.

Cooperativism is not an idea for selected groups; it is an idea whose aim is to spread, to encompass the whole world. Cooperativism can not depend only on the good management of its own home, but is a struggle to transform the economic forms of the whole society. Furthermore, even if cooperativism wanted to close itself within a narrow circle, cut itself off by a Great Wall of China from the rest of society and leave that society to the mercy of capitalist economics, it would not be able to do so without harming itself. As an institution of an economic nature, it lives in society; it is connected with that society by a thousand bonds; it perfectly feels that society's pains and suffering, its successes and good fortune. But cooperativism is primarily a new economic form and its striving must be to spread, to acquire the whole market for itself.

Two contrary economic systems which have undefined fields of activity, are striving to control the whole, and possess unlimited energy, must come into conflict with one another. The victory of cooperativism can only happen on the rubble of the capitalist system. Every strengthening and maintenance of this system is a blow that strikes directly at cooperativism. The neutrality of cooperativism equals its capitulation; it equals its relinquishment of expansion, its resignation from its own development. Therefore it can not preserve its neutrality in regard to the class struggle. It would be an error to suppose that this is a struggle that is occurring off to the side. Cooperativism can be neutral only in matters that do not interest it. Meanwhile, the idea of class struggle is embedded in the very idea of cooperativism; it is a matter of life and death for it.

What idea can neutral cooperativists oppose to the idea of socialism, which is based on the principle of class struggle? The idea of solidarism is often considered to be behind the idea of cooperativism. They don't argue for class struggle, but general solidarity.

The idea of general solidarity encompassing all of humanity is undoubtedly beautiful. There can be no discussion over whether it is desirable. There is only the question of whether it is possible and achievable given the prevailing social and systemic conditions. The point is whether solidarism can be achieved by maintaining these conditions or only by abolishing them, by removing them. Solidarity is treated in detachment from the conditions. In practice, this leads to cooperativism's loss of an important role. Instead of resting cooperativism on the idea of the solidarity of the world of labor in the fight against exploitation, it rests on an idea that simultaneously encompasses both the exploiter and the exploited. It is hard to imagine an idea more contrary to the basic principles of cooperativism. Whoever proposes solidarism in an era where the wolf still has fangs is not facilitating but hindering the advent of universal solidarity.

Proponents of basing cooperativism on the idea of solidarism usually refer to the idea of mutual aid, to the eternal idea of cooperation giving vitality to nature. In nature, both factors exist beside each other: on the one side there is the struggle for existence, on the other there is mutual aid. Both these factors exist in human society as well. Socialism, which is based on the idea of class struggle, does not at all thereby deny the idea of cooperation. On the contrary—after all it is based on the idea of group solidary, class solidary, the solidarity of the entire world of labor. No one holds the idea of solidarity as high as does socialism. It does not, however, mix fire with water. Cooperation must be based on the existence of common linking elements. In the capitalist system there are factors contributing to the disappearance of the idea of mutual aid, factors raising individual interest above the collective interest. Socialism, though, with its stance on the solidarity of the world of labor, strives for a system based on universal cooperation. It is a simplified manner of understanding socialism to think that its position of unending class struggle is eternally set or that it considers class struggle as an ideal.

Class struggle is a necessity and not some devilish invention of Marxism. But we do not consider this struggle to be a social necessity. The solidarists who base themselves on the natural law of mutual aid are doing a disservice to the very idea of solidarity. If the analogy of nature is recognized as an absolute law, then both mutual aid and class struggle will be natural phenomena, justified in the natural order of things and eternal, never ending. Analogies with nature are fortunately not laws though. In human life, class struggle and cooperation are social phenomena resulting from specific social conditions and changing as those conditions change. In the order of social relations, the abolition of class struggle is a definite possibility. Socialism is the sole ideological trend that consciously, consistently, and effectively strives for the abolition of class struggle. To close one's eyes, hide one's head in the sand, and say that class struggles don't exist, that they shouldn't exist, will not change real conditions one iota. To remove the source of class struggles, to create the basis for universal cooperation, is the sole political aim.

Between the principle of class struggle and the principle of mutual aid there is thus no contradiction. Class struggle is based on the principle of solidary cooperation in the world of labor, and at its end lies the principle of universal cooperation. Cooperativism thus, being a form of cooperation, is participating in the class struggle. The essence of cooperativism is replacement of the capitalist-individualist form of production and apportionment with social forms. Cooperativism thus abolishes the causes of class antagonisms in a certain area. The question thus arises of whether in consequence cooperativism should strive for the spread of its social form? If yes, then cooperativism will have to strive for the entire removal of the capitalist economy and the entire liquidation of the causes of class struggle. Thus cooperativism, being a form of cooperation, is simultaneously a form of struggle. The role of cooperativism depends on recreating society and therefore it is revolutionary.

All attempts to reconcile cooperativism with capitalism or to make it neutral in class struggles strikes at the principles of cooperativism, depriving cooperativism of its greatest importance. Class cooperativism must be conscious of its aims and strivings; it must remember that it is a form of struggle against exploitation; it must be convinced that it is not a simple supplement to the existing situation but a revolt against it. Cooperativism must occupy an active position in the process of social transformation that is under way. This process is after all a struggle and in this struggle nothing links cooperativism with the capitalist economy. There is no room here for solidarism or for any sort of alliance with the dying world.

This does not at all mean that we want to consider cooperativism as a tool in political playoffs. What we require from cooperativism is a clear ideological platform, a clear awareness of its place in the proceeding struggle but not participation in the current political struggle. It must only be imbued with the desire to transform all of life according to its main social principles.

The harmfulness of a delusion about cooperativism's neutrality is thus clear. There is another delusion, however, that should not be underestimated. This second stands at the opposite extreme. If some claim that cooperativism should take no part in the class struggle, others take the position that the whole work of transforming the social system can be achieved on the grounds of cooperativism itself. Since cooperativism introduces the principles of social economy to certain areas of life, and because it actualizes in them the rules of a new life, gradually the development of cooperativism, its control of ever more numerous areas and territories, becomes simultaneously the elimination of capitalism. The consequences of this theory are clear. The realization of socialism is achieved by the path of cooperativism's continual development. These are essentially two extremes. One says that socialism does not at all concern them; the others claim that the whole struggle for socialism, for the principles of a new social system, is playing out within the sphere of cooperativism. At the moment when the whole world recognizes the principles of cooperativism, the change of system will be automatically complete. Through cooperativism there is thus socialism.

Let us consider, for a moment, this path to socialism, which is extremely seductive and alluring. If the whole world and all its areas were to be taken over by cooperativism, if consumer cooperativism were to encompass the whole organization of the division of products, if all the factories and workshops were to become labor cooperatives, if credit cooperatives were to drive out capitalist banks, humanity would indeed enter on an era of cooperative socialism. Obviously, all this would have to be included within the framework of a planned economy, subordinated to the general plan and management. All this would happen without shocks, without great sacrifices, without revolution, without exhausting political struggle.

It is unfortunately too beautiful to be true. This delusion belongs to the category of the delusions of utopian socialism, which imagined that a parallel system could arise at the side of the capitalist system and slowly take over the whole world. Roads that are too easy rarely lead to their goals. Great social breakthroughs are not achieved without hard, fierce struggles and conflicts.

In first order, it should be noted that cooperativism, in the conditions of the capitalist system, does not have universal opportunities for development. At every step it meets with difficulties resulting from the entirety of the existing relations. Periods of crisis, which are increasingly long and reach ever deeper into social life, are extremely harmful for cooperativism. Capitalist exploitation, which reduces the consumer ability of the masses, directly limits the developmental capabilities of cooperativism. Given the level of wages in the capitalist system's world of work, housing cooperatives are not able to develop to the degree where they could control the whole housing market. For the same reasons, consumer cooperatives can not acquire sufficient capital of their own and can not get out of the vicious circle created by the economic weakening of consumers.

But consumer-housing cooperativism is still comparatively in the best position. It has a chance of acquiring at least a fairly major part of the market. Restricting consumption has its limits, and consumer cooperativism, which operates by rapid and frequent turnover, does not require large capital. The chances for production cooperativism or labor cooperativism are incomparably worse. It is usually limited to organizing work teams either without their own workshops or creating small common workshops. In the period of cartelization, in the period when small capitalists are being absorbed by large ones, in the period of monopoly capitalism, in the period when the development of technology requires ever greater and more frequent capital expenditures, in the period of great economic crises, labor cooperativism, which consists in the unification of economically weak, usually unemployed individuals, can not in its wildest dreams be considered a means, a method, of expropriating capitalists of their tools of work, by way of socializing production.

The weakest point in this plan of overcoming the capitalist system by cooperativism itself involves the control of financial capital. We have already confirmed financial capital's leading role in today's phase of the capitalist system. It exercises a sort of dictatorship over other forms of capital and over the entire society. Cooperativism is also to be found in its hands to a large degree. Credit cooperativism could play an important role in assisting other forms of cooperativism, but it does not begin to have the conditions to deal with financial capital, which is the result of large processes of accumulating capital, one of the bases of the capitalist system.

Independently of all these factors, capitalism should not be treated as a passive force, which quietly and indifferently looks on at the dangers gathering against it. The greater cooperativism's progress, the greater will be the resistance of the capitalist world, which, in addition to economic power, possesses a range of materials of a political nature for the defense of its position; firstly, it has influence on legislation and the state apparatus of contemporary countries. Just as the progress of democracy was not passively observed by capitalism but produced a reaction in the form of fascism, so the successes of cooperativism call forth counterattacks from capitalism when threatened. These things go together. In democratic countries, cooperativism has greater possibilities of development; in fascist countries, cooperativism is limited in its development (Germany, Italy, Austria—a prohibition against opening new cooperative shops). And in Poland, under the *Sanacja*[2] governments, conditions for the development of cooperativism worsened, and cooperativism can expect nothing good from the hundred-percent-fascist National Democrats. It might have seemed that passionate anti-Semites, in combating Jewish trade, would support cooperativism—if not to be consistent then at least for the sake of demagoguery. Nothing of the sort. National Democracy does not hide its dislike of cooperativism and its program consists in replacing Jewish intermediaries with Polish intermediaries. Cooperativism must thus expect to be attacked not only on economic grounds but also on political ones and that it could receive a fatal blow from that direction.

Thus the faith that an exclusively cooperative road could change the social system entirely is utopian and harmful like every utopia. Cooperativism ceases to be a utopia only when it gets down to the role that is proper to itself, that is, to the role of one of the branches of the liberation movement of the working class. The task of changing the system is a task that could be the result of a combined harmonization of the activities of all forms of the labor movement but not solely of one.

---

2   Sanation (Polish *Sanacja* – an act of moral healing), a Polish political movement created after the Józef Piłsudski's May 1926 Coup d'État. In 1928 politicians and activists gathered around Piłsudski formed the Nonpartisan Bloc of Cooperation with the Government (BBWR). The main reason for the creation of the movement was a critique of parliamentary democracy and willingness to govern the state by more radical and authoritarian rules.

Even the greatest development of cooperativism and of trade unions will not break the might of capitalism. A political revolution is needed to give power to the working class and a social revolution is needed to destroy the economic bases of capitalist might. We have written about the economic front that brings together the cooperative movement and the trade union movement. Beside it there is a second front, the political front, which attacks the main positions of the capitalist system. There is also a third front, the educational front, which is focused on the cultural-educational and sports movement of the working class, and has as its task to influence the feelings, understanding, and character of the masses for the purpose of raising fighters against the old world and builders of a new tomorrow.

Each of these forms has its tasks, which mutually complement each other. If cooperativism can not thus claim to be the factor that is to bring about the entire work of social reconstruction, it nevertheless has an important role to fill.

1) Cooperativism defends the economic interests of the working class and the entire world of labor in the present day.

2) It creates new economic forms, based on introducing the socialist principle of acting to satisfy needs and on rejecting the capitalist principle of acting for profit.

3) In this manner it forms the future socialist economy and leads it through the test by fire—experience.

4) It raises future economic activists, whose task will be to take in their hands the entire mechanism of a socialized economy.

This educational work is not fulfilled by any other form of the labor movement, because only in the workplace of active, positive economic activity, only in contact with specific questions, in overcoming difficulties, can those values be produced that are necessary to bring our creative abilities to the surface.

PART 5

The Agricultural Cooperative Movement and the Stefczyk Savings and Loan Fund

∴

CHAPTER 17

The Past and Future of the Farmers' Agricultural and Trade Cooperatives[1]

Fr. Stanisław Adamski

This brochure is a summary of a report given on 14 April 1924 at a congress of representatives of the Supervisory Council and Board of Management of the Agricultural and Trade Cooperatives belonging to the Union of Labor Cooperatives and Agricultural Labor Societies in Poznań.

Within the Poznań and Pomeranean voivodeships, the Polish part of Upper Silesia, and the vicinity of Włocławek, there are presently 89 associated agricultural, trade, or production cooperatives, including 81 Farmers' Cooperatives engaged particularly in the purchase and sale of grain, potatoes, fertilizers, feed, and coal. Changes in relations require the cooperatives' activities to be extended to the sale of other goods, which were previously supplied by private commerce.

The division of work between trade and educational-occupational organizations in agriculture, whose borders have become blurred by postwar relations, also require clarification. Given the necessity of making wider strata of farming society acquainted with the concerns, position, and plans of our Union of agricultural and trade cooperatives, we are printing a report by our patron, Fr. Adamski; its content and principles were enthusiastically and unanimously adopted.

—Union of Labor Cooperatives and Agricultural Labor Societies in Poznań

∴

---

1 Fr. Stanisław Adamski, *Przeszłość i przyszłość „Rolników" spółdzielni rolniczo-handlowych* [*The Past and Future of the Farmers' Agricultural and Trade Cooperatives*], Poznań 1924, Związek Spółdzielni Zarobkowych i Gospodarczych [Union of Occupational and Farming Cooperatives].

1   The Beginnings and Aims of Agricultural and Trade Cooperativism
       in Specific Areas of Poland

At the moment when the Bank of Poland has been established, on the eve of
a new era in Poland's economic life, which will be at the same time a new era
in social life, we should take a look back at what agricultural and trade cooperativism has managed to achieve and to consider whether the chosen road is
good, if something should be changed in the current work, and how to satisfy
new needs.

Belonging to all Poland, today we can no longer look at our cooperativism—
and particularly not the agricultural and trade cooperatives—from the
viewpoint of only one area. We have to be aware that agricultural and trade
cooperativism throughout Poland is unusually varied and try to understand
why it has developed in certain areas in one way and not another. The local
conditions have meant that agricultural and trade cooperatives have acquired
separate characters and spheres of activity.

Agricultural and trade cooperatives in Małopolska arose as a defense against
Jewish merchants, who, being established in the countryside and selling the
local people everything they might need, at the same time bought all their agricultural products from them. And because they tried to exploit the farmer,
they sold bad goods at a high price, and conversely, paid the farmer the lowest
possible price, while at the same time inclining the older locals to drink, and
the children to steal, so it is not strange that when the locals began to organize in agricultural clubs in Małopolska, the establishment of their small shops
was one of the first manifestations of self-help against the dishonest Jewish
merchants.

From the beginning the shops were modest and small. They sold all kinds of
goods, as in the shops they were combating. From these small shops emerged
the agricultural and trade cooperatives in Małopolska. Only later did they begin to grow and change into ever larger cooperatives. Predominantly they sold
all kinds of goods necessary to agriculture. The sale of grain did not come to
the fore, particularly in those areas where the land was divided into small parcels and where on this account a surplus of grain for export did not exist.

In the Russian partition, the situation was different. The customs and railway
policy of the Russian government was aimed at preventing, by all means, the
rise of Polish agriculture, while facilitating the export of Russian grain to the
Polish market. As a result, Russian grain in the Kingdom was cheaper than that
produced on the spot. Agriculture could not raise itself. The merchants providing agriculture with machines, iron products, agricultural tools, and so forth,
were predominantly Jews. Thus when the Kingdom's agricultural community

established its first cooperatives, the Agricultural Syndicates, they were engaged not in the grain trade, but in the buying and selling of machines, iron, coal, fertilizers, and all agricultural necessities. There was practically no grain commerce. The grain that was produced was consumed on the spot; there was no surplus of grain for export and thus the necessary conditions were lacking for the creation of grain commerce.

Under the former Prussian partition, matters developed quite differently. Bismarck's policy surrounded Germany, to which we belonged, with protective tariffs, which are extremely convenient for agriculture. The price of grain in the country was high, yet nevertheless the government rewarded the export of grain abroad. In this manner the Prussian government achieved two goals. First, it encouraged agriculture to increase production; it encouraged agriculture to become as intensive—costly but productive—as possible; on the other hand, in giving agriculture significant income, it caused agriculture to become ever wealthier, and thus capable of buying industrial goods and thereby contributing to the development of industry and trade. In enriching agriculture, Bismarck created willing purchasers for industrial and trade products; he invigorated German trade and industry, giving workers jobs and earnings.

Polish agriculture made complete use of these conditions, particularly as Germany, in removing us from the state administration and offices, caused the sons of landowning Poles to acquire thorough acquaintance with agriculture at universities and then to work their own land themselves. In raising the farming culture on their own lands, they increased production and simultaneously taught the local people how to farm progressively. In this manner they caused the average level of farming culture in Poznań and Pomerania to be significantly higher than the level of the German areas.

The Poznań area and Pomerania were always a country where grain was overproduced. The export of grain beyond the border of these areas was necessary. Long years of work by credit cooperatives ("people's banks") created there, with the passage of time, a healthy Polish state of commerce, which in increasingly encompassing more retail trade, even in small towns, provided agriculture with all kinds of good-quality products and at reasonable prices. On the other hand, the trade in grain and artificial fertilizers, which requires large amounts of capital and is a wholesale trade, was overwhelmingly in Jewish and German hands.

Thus the route for agricultural and trade cooperativism was indicated from the outset. We did not want to create unnecessary competition for our own merchants, but it was necessary to create competition for the Jewish and German grain trade, in order to snatch trade in the most important products and basic necessities of Polish agriculture out of foreign hands. When we lacked people for work, when we had to get the greatest results from work with the least number of people, we established agricultural and trade cooperatives mainly for the trade in grain and artificial fertilizers, and we established great, strong cooperatives that could deal with the enormous German and Jewish competition.

This is the context in which the Farmers' Cooperatives[2]—agricultural and trade cooperatives intended mainly for the sale and purchase of grain, potatoes, coal, artificial fertilizers, and feed—emerged among us. The Farmers' Cooperatives were not engaged in selling machines or other agricultural necessities, which were provided by private Polish merchants in a manner that did not produce dissatisfaction in agricultural circles.

After the world war, the economic bases of agriculture in Pomerania and the Poznań area changed fundamentally. Incorporated in an agricultural state, whose agricultural production had increased greatly during the war and afterwards, and which will always have a surplus of agricultural products, particularly as the neighboring state to the east is also engaged in agriculture, these areas seemed to have irretrievably lost the prewar conditions that allowed them to cultivate grain, mainly rye, intensively.

Given the competition from other areas of Poland, the agriculture of the western provinces of Poland is not going to be able to obtain prices that will allow it to maintain the previous, costly, intensive agriculture and ensure the previous profitability, if in the near future the direction of its production does not change and it does not itself begin to consume more rye for greater production of meat, dairy, eggs, etc. In addition, the agriculture of the western provinces will have to make a better search than previously in order to satisfy its needs more cheaply. As Polish commerce has been so weakened by the war and today for lack of capital is unable to supply agriculture as conveniently as in the past with all the minor articles necessary to farmers, it is not strange that farmers are turning to cooperatives with the request that the sphere of their activity be extended to the new needs.

The least changes to the general structure of society were produced by postwar relations in Małopolska. For this reason as well, there is less call there for a change in the direction of agricultural and trade cooperativism. Cooperativism

---

2   There is an extensive work on the Farmers' Cooperatives by Bronisław Załuski, entitled *Spółki zarobkowe i gospodarcze w Poznańskiem i Prusach Zachodnich ze szczególnym uwzględnieniem „Rolników"* [*Labour and Agricultural Companies in Poznań and Western Prussia, with Particular Attention to the Farmers' Cooperatives*] Warsaw, 1921, Spółka Wydawnictw Spółdzielczych [Cooperative Publishing Company], p. 238. The book can be purchased from the Cooperative Publishing Company in Poznań, Plac Wolności 18.

itself suffered vastly as a result of being based on minor cooperatives, which today are practically at a standstill.

On the other hand, postwar relations had a very strong effect in the Congress Kingdom and Eastern Borderlands. For a certain time, the high prices of agricultural products enabled and encouraged the agricultural community to more intensive farming and today the surplus of grain that has been created in these lands needs to be transported abroad or to areas with greater consumption. In this manner there has suddenly arisen a need to trade in grain and therefore in the Kingdom voices are calling ever more insistently for agricultural and trade cooperativism—which to this time has practically not dealt in grain—to take this route as soon as possible. This is also why special grain cooperatives, in the style of our Farmers' Cooperatives, have been received with such recognition in the Kingdom, particularly in those areas where good soil is abundant.

Given such a state of affairs, it should not be wondered at that in nearly all areas of Poland there is a demand that cooperatives—which before the war were entirely satisfactory for agriculture—should change direction. The situation is also influenced by the fact that a quantity of farming people and other citizens have migrated from other areas to our districts in particular. Being accustomed to another method of work in the cooperatives of those areas and not yet understanding sufficiently the cooperative trend that was of necessity created in our parts, they want to bring to our lands the type of cooperativism they knew in the place of their former residence.

The majority of our farmers are not aware how agricultural and trade cooperativism affects the general agricultural trade market; they do not know that under the impact of regulation our cooperatives are being used even by those who buy goods not in our cooperatives but from firms that are foreign to us and in competition with us. They do not understand that if they receive good prices and good products in these firms it is in large measure thanks to the cooperative movement. It is sufficient to remember the times when the Farmers' Cooperatives were first established. We founded a Farmers' Cooperative in Nakło. The large Baerwald firm was there. The farmers complained that being the sole merchant on the spot Baerwald paid much lower prices than others. Scarcely had the founding protocol for the Farmers' Cooperative been signed, and before it was registered, much less begun to operate, when Mr. Baerwald began to raise his prices and adapt them to the general market out of fear of future competition. In Wągrowiec and Gniezno, farmers complained that they had to pay rather too high prices in our Farmers' Cooperatives for artificial fertilizer, while the local merchant supplied fertilizer at a much lower price. Knowing the international price of the product, we knew that this was impossible. Thus we bought phosphorous fertilizer in Wągrowiec and saltpeter in Gniezno; we sent them for analysis and learned that phosphorous fertilizer was being sold at four percent instead of fourteen percent. The supposedly lower price, given such contents, was naturally extremely high. In Gniezno, the competitor of the Farmers' Cooperative, a Jew, sold saltpeter much more cheaply but added half kainite and in this manner made it up to himself.

We, however, observe strict honesty in our goods and do not allow any abuses. When, contrary to the prohibition, the director of one of the Farmers' Cooperatives brought in several tens of bags of four-percent phosphorous fertilizer, we removed him from the Cooperative, because we did not want the fact that such a low-value good was being brought in to ruin the good reputation of our cooperatives. In this manner, the activity of the Farmers' Cooperatives regulated the prices of agricultural products and protected agriculture against the purchase of low value—and thus always overpriced—goods. This matter is simultaneously closely connected with the cultural-educational work of our local clubs and other agricultural labor associations. Wherever a merchant has been on the prowl to sell expensive, worthless fertilizer to the local farmers, though, the agricultural club has been unable to boast of its results. It is not surprising, because after all, when a farmer has been repeatedly persuaded to use artificial fertilizer and buys lesser value fertilizer, he can expect to be disappointed in his crops; the work of the farmers' clubs has naturally been barren. Thus the cooperatives' activity must be combined with the educational activities of the agricultural societies.

2   The Current State of the Farmers' Cooperatives

Our Farmers' Cooperatives mostly began work during the year 1910 and 1911. Shortly thereafter the war came and destroyed all our organizational proceedings. After the war, devaluation destroyed the Farmers' Cooperatives' funds. Simultaneously, there was a need to provide farmers with shoes, clothing, iron, etc., and our commerce, deprived of funds and cut off from its former source of purchases, could not provide any goods at a reasonable price; our Farmers' Cooperatives, which had been intended for different tasks, were unable to satisfy the needs that suddenly arose. Their directors were after all predominantly in the army. When there was a lack of funds even for maintaining the grain trade, if was even less possible to think of beginning to trade in a new field.

The financial state of our Farmers' Cooperatives was as follows: July 1, 1916, operating capital amounted to 13 million marks, including shares and reserves, that is, the capital sums paid in by farmers, 2.8 million = 1/5 part; July 1, 1923, operating capital amounted to 3.1 billion, shares and reserves 415 million = 1/7 part; December 31, 1923, operating capital of 47 Farmers' Cooperatives (not all) amounted to 560 billion, including 15 billion shares and reserves = 1/35 part.

If we accept that on January 1 of the present year, the operating capital of all the Farmers' Cooperatives amounted to 900 billion, that is 500,000 zlotys, we can claim that in comparison to 13 million in 1916, we have today an operating capital of scarcely 1/32 part. The assets of the Farmers' Cooperatives and their commercial value are obviously many times higher than the present working capital. There is considerable real estate, transportation stock, and other equipment; an old and tested commercial organization partially makes up for the present lack of working capital.

We have become very much diminished. If in spite of such small operating capital we overtake the prewar turnover by a greater amount of goods bought and sold than before the war, this testifies solely to the enormous rapidity of the turnover and the extreme credit tension.[3] If the Farmers' Cooperatives lost part of their operating capital through such a great devaluation, where did the difference go? Who gained from that devaluation? Some blame the managers, claiming that royalties and pensions ate up the profits; others say that the Farmers' Cooperatives injured their members because the members paid for shares in zlotys and today they only have paper marks, etc.

In answer to these accusations we can claim on the basis of our books that the trade costs of our cooperatives did not at all exceed the permissible boundaries. On the other hand, if our capital decreased through devaluation, in that case, the devaluation could benefit only those of our members who were debtors of our Farmers' Cooperatives. Our debtors, who had credit or who had not paid their debt, gained what the Cooperatives lost through the devaluation. It does not at all result thereby that farmers enriched themselves from the Farmers' Cooperatives. Other conditions meant that the farmers incurred losses much greater than the comparatively small advantages from the devaluation of capital in the Farmers' Cooperatives. I am speaking here, though, about my claim that neither the administration of the Cooperatives or the Cooperatives themselves got rich at the cost of the agricultural community, but that they incurred losses and that this devaluation difference remained in the pockets of our debtor-clients.

There is no doubt that with an operating capital of a half million zlotys, agricultural and trade cooperatives can not engage in commerce to the degree

---

3   The balance of the above-mentioned 47 Farmers' Cooperatives on December 31, 1923 shows that the farmers' debts exceeded their credit in the Farmers' Cooperatives by 55 billion: more or less 80 billion in all the Farmers' Cooperatives.

they should in the interest of agriculture. There is no doubt that the Farmers' Cooperatives should as soon as possible expand their operating funds and create reliable foundations of the most abundant credit. Thus our cooperatives and their authorities must inevitably strive first to:

a) return shares, liabilities, and reserves to the height of the amount in prewar zlotys;

b) compel their clients, more vigorously than previously, to join as members in order thus to expand the guarantees of the Farmers' Cooperatives.

In the present conditions, the rule must inexorably be followed that only members may benefit from a Farmers' Cooperative; non-members may make use of the cooperative only when the needs of the members have been satisfied. On the other hand, as much effort as possible should be made to accustom farmers to giving trade bills in credit transactions. With the aid of such bills, it will be possible to obtain rediscount credit, which in Poland today is the most important source of credit in general. It will not be possible to speak of long-term or current-account credit until, through savings and productive work, new capital grows in the credit cooperatives and banks.

People should also get the idea out of their heads once and for all that the Farmers' Cooperatives might be liquidated and sold to the directors, because we have already many times declared in regards to the statement of the late Fr. Wawrzyniak ("that a time could come when the Farmers' Cooperatives are liquidated and sold to the directors") that these words spoken at the very beginning of agricultural cooperativism—when it was not possible to judge of its future—were admitted to be unjustified by that same late Fr. Wawrzyniak, seeing the development of the Farmers' Cooperatives. Today everyone knows that agricultural and trade cooperativism is an agricultural institution so indispensably necessary that it would be impossible to do without it.

Similarly, all ideas about changing the cooperatives into stock companies should be abandoned. Today these ideas, which were supported until recently even by members of the supervisory council, have ceased to be current, particularly when it has been determined that the stock form is inconvenient and that even cooperatives that adopted the stock form in their first fright, like the agricultural syndicates in the Kingdom, would gladly revert to the cooperative form. We have proofs of the usefulness of the cooperative form even in our own Union. The cooperative in Lubraniec, which was founded as a cooperative, later chose to be a stock company and even had permission for that from the Minister of the Treasury. Before the transformation could be conducted, however, it gave up the idea and returned to the cooperative form, being convinced that a stock company would not be able to replace an agricultural cooperative.

3   The Union of Cooperatives' Relations with Agricultural Organizations

Our relations with agriculture, organized either in local government organizations, private trade associations, or in so-called agricultural trade companies, have often been the subject of discussions and reflections. The government representative of agriculture, the Greater Poland Chamber of Agriculture in Poznań, which is by the nature of things neutral, is an organization that must maintain warm relations with all organizations operating in the farming sphere and try to be a center for them. Our relations with the Greater Poland Chamber of Agriculture are very friendly and supportive, as is proven by the fact that the Greater Poland Chamber of Agriculture delegated its representative to the Board of Management of an Agricultural and Trade Cooperative Branch. The Union in return delegated its representative to the economic committee of the Chamber of Agriculture.

Our relations with trading companies created with the participation of the agricultural community remain within the framework of friendly trade relations, which are created according to need and circumstance. The question of the agricultural nature of individual trading firms does not depend on the fact of whether and to what degree the actions of these enterprises are in the hands of the agricultural community and what their present relation is to agricultural labor organizations. Only later evolution will show how far the change in ownership of shares will simultaneously change the relation to the organized agricultural community.

Our relations with the professional agricultural organizations of Greater Poland and Pomerania have led to some interesting negotiations. Before the war there were two types of professional agricultural organizations in our lands: the farmers' clubs and the Central Farming Society. In 1918, fully appreciating the necessity of working together, we entered into an agreement with both the Union of Farmers' Clubs and the Central Farming Society for the purpose of providing mutual support to one another. A year later, we terminated this agreement by common consent, particularly because in the meantime a third agricultural labor organization, the Union of Agricultural Producers, had appeared in the area.

Originally founded to regulate the relations of employers to employees in agriculture, the Union of Agricultural Producers later was engaged, very beneficially, in the ad hoc organization of a supply of shoes, clothes, and agricultural articles, which were not provided or not sufficiently provided by Polish commerce in the postwar period. The commercial side was imagined initially as a temporary and transitional aid for farming; later it began to be maintained, adding ever more trade departments. Several times the Union of Agricultural Producers contacted us for the purpose of entering into an agreement with our Union. Our Union was ready to negotiate, particularly as it emerged that the UAP brought together all the agricultural labor organizations and would be the sole labor representative for the whole agricultural community in Greater Poland and Pomerania. Negotiations with the UAP went very far. As the UAP had a trade division and was acting nationwide in trade policy not only as the labor representative of the agricultural community but also as a trading company, which obviously wanted to obtain benefits for its trading division by its professional influences, what to do with the UAP's trade division was naturally one of the primary questions in discussing the conditions of the agreement.

It would have been impossible for two organizations to be mutually contracted in the area of trade and to maintain separate and competing representative bodies. In order to overcome this difficulty, the Union thought the best route would be to combine the trade representatives through the fusion of the UAP's Trade Division with the Farmers' Central.[4] Our Union submitted to the UAP a written proposal on the matter, in which, in our opinion, we went as far as the Union could go without devaluing its own organization. Namely, we proposed a fusion of the trade division with the Farmers' Central, and in exchange the Union of Agricultural Producers would receive damages in the form of shares in the Farmers' Central, becoming thus the largest shareholder in the Central after the Union of Cooperatives. At the same time, we proposed a contract between the Union and the UAP, by which the Union wanted to ensure itself, during the length of the contract, half the members of the supervisory council of the Farmers' Central, while giving the chairmanship of

---

4   The Farmers' Central, founded in 1919 as a stock company, presently has a share capital of 600 million marks, and real estate in Poznań, Gdańsk, Bydgoszcz and Katowice; in addition to the central in Poznań, there are branches in Bydgoszcz, Toruń, Włocławek, Gdańsk, and Katowice. 121 office workers are employed; the Central operates as a wholesaler for the Farmers' Cooperatives, buying and selling, through the Central, goods that are exclusively from cooperatives and trading companies. The shares are divided into privileged and ordinary shares. All the privileged shares are held by the Union of Cooperatives, giving it a decisive influence in general assemblies. A large part of the ordinary shares are held by the Union and the Cooperatives; part is in private hands. The statute ensures cooperatives a majority in the Supervisory Council; the Patron of the Union is at the same time the curator of the Central. Cooperative influence in the Farmers' Central is thus entirely secure.

the Supervisory Council to the UAP. In addition, the Union proposed that the agreement would ensure permanent payments from the revenues of the Farmers' Central for the purpose of the occupational organization of the UAP and for the management by mutual agreement of the general economic policy of the Farmers' Central and the cooperatives connected with it.

To our great surprise, however, the Supervisory Council of the UAP rejected our proposal, making the main condition of the agreement that the Union should give the UAP privileged shares in the Farmers' Central, which the Union of Cooperatives possesses and which undoubtedly give it a decisive influence in the Farmers' Central. The Union could absolutely not accept this request. It would mean, after all, tearing the Farmers' Central from the organization of our Union and placing the cooperative trade central under the decisive influence of an organization outside our Union. Obviously, everyone who understands the structure of the cooperative organization and centralization must see from the outset that the Union could not accept a proposition aimed at destroying its organization. In this manner, the arrangements with the UAP fell through—not, in our opinion, through the fault of the Union.

From that time, more than one thing has changed. The Central Farming Society did not agree to join the United Agricultural Producers, and the matter of combining producers with the farmers' clubs will only be decided in half a year. Therefore, it has turned out to be much better that the Union's proposal was not accepted. We would be in a very difficult situation if we had joined with one agricultural organization and overlooked another. We, as the Union of Cooperatives, naturally are concerned above all not to lose the close contact with the agricultural organizations that represent a wide range of small farming people, who can't get along without cooperatives at all. From this it does not follow, however, that we intended to exclude the gentry, which has for ages been hand in hand with the small farmers and contributed to the high agricultural culture of small farms in Greater Poland and Pomerania. On the contrary, we wish to maintain the cooperation between the gentry and the small farmers within the cooperatives.

Relations with the agricultural societies in Pomerania took shape differently. After liquidation of the Division of the Union of Agricultural Producers in Pomerania, an agricultural society was opened in Pomerania, which the farmers' clubs joined but the Central Farming Society in Pomerania did not. The Chamber of Agriculture was founded with state funds in Pomerania by a special grain firm, "Wholesale," which after a brief existence changed into the "Pomeranian Agricultural Syndicate," combining with the existing "Pomeranian Agricultural and Trade Association" cooperative in Toruń. Relations in Pomerania, which does not have a natural center accessible from all ends of

Pomerania, are different as a result of the influence of the idea of separation from Poznań—an idea whose application, it would seem, has not always been beneficial for Pomerania. We are in the midst of negotiations with administrative and private organizations in Pomerania. The negotiations are not yet finished, though.

In all negotiations with organizations outside of our Union, however much they may be our friends, we are guided by the following principles:

a)   We can not agree to any manner of violation of the independence of the cooperative organization and can not make that organization or its components fundamentally dependent on any other organizations.

b)   The cooperative organization is a separate, closed structure. On the basis of the local cooperatives spread around the country, we create financial and trade centrals, which are dependent on the Union (the cooperatives' overseer) and are the superstructure, wholesaler, and intermediary for the local cooperatives. These centrals, as cooperative organizations of the highest order, must be subordinate to the Union of Cooperatives and be directed by the principles that the cooperative movement, organized in its Union, produces itself.

c)   Cooperativism strives to combine with other cooperatives and to create within the country an enormous block of trade and credit enterprises serving cooperativism, united by cooperative thinking and organization, and directed by the desire not to achieve the greatest profit but to give the greatest benefit to its members. In this manner, the cooperative organization comes to regulate prices, as well as trade and financial conditions, throughout the country, and by its competition to cause all other trading companies to be satisfied with moderate profits and to provide full-value goods. There is no doubt that at some point in time cooperative organizations will be a control and competition even for those trade organizations that farmers have established in a non-cooperative form and that have, or will have, the form of capitalist enterprise, resting on the highest profit for their shareholders and not on the benefit of the farmers who buy or sell through them.

d)   We can not agree to the breaking off of individual branches from the cohesive cooperative organization, and their dependence on non-cooperative organizations and thereby their weakening of the substance and force of cooperative Unions.

e)   We will always be ready to come to agreement and cooperate with all agricultural organizations on the condition that they respect our separateness and independence and that mutual relations are arranged on the basis of equality, and not on the basis of dependence. A similar discussion on the question of whether cooperative agricultural organizations should have equality with, or be subordinate to, cooperative agricultural organizations and occupational organizations has occurred in Germany. All German cooperative unions have decided to retain their independence on the one hand and the cohesion of the cooperative movement on the other. The congresses of Polish cooperative directors have declared themselves in favor of proceeding along similar lines. The position occupied by our Union does not ensue from any special resistance of its directors but results from organizational needs recognized by the whole cooperative movement.

We have noticed that in this area the hardest for us is to convince those persons who have little contact with cooperativism and those who are unacquainted with either the ideological bases of cooperativism or the real activities of our Farmers' Cooperatives. They sometimes combat our Farmers' Cooperatives without knowing them, persuading themselves of incredible things and basing themselves on imprecise or entirely erroneous information. When the economic conditions become more normal, and when the currency reform has been completed, then the question of the cooperation of labor and trade organizations will mature to a resolution. Today, all we want is for those who do not understand or appreciate our cooperative movement to try to understand and instead of seeking new roads, to join their efforts with ours, in order to work more usefully on the perfection of our cooperative movement and its adaptation to the needs of the present day.

4   Program for the Near Future

We have to be aware that an economic transformation has occurred in Poland, with the result that the agriculture of the Poznań and Pomeranian voivodeships will be in more difficult financial and economic circumstances than previously. Therefore, the agriculture community will be attaching greater weight than previously to the advantageous cooperative purchase of necessities, including those that were previously purchased through private commerce. We are aware that by working in our own country, we are living in an atmosphere that is favorable to cooperativism and we can begin, without fear, to increase the network of cooperatives. We are aware that before long we should have more people for cooperative work. However, those persons who have recently arrived in our districts must not turn away from us but should try to get closer to our organizations and understand them, and on the other hand, the people who have been long settled here should not hamper the entry of the new citizens to our organization but on the contrary should make every effort to draw them in, come to agreement with them, and acquire them for joint labor.

In the area of the special range of work of our agriculture and trade cooperatives, we are not limiting ourselves any more exclusively to cooperatives intended for trading in grain, fertilizers, and feed, but will be founding and uniting agricultural cooperatives of all types in our Union. Today in our Union there is a whole range of dairy, sugar, and egg cooperatives, etc.

For the purpose of facilitating the export of eggs and milk products we have entered into close contacts with the Union of Milk and Egg Cooperatives for all Poland, which is our common trade headquarters in this sphere, while individual dairy and egg cooperatives belong to our Union for control purposes. When a greater number of dairy cooperatives have joined our Union we intend to seek specialists in this area, in order to provide them with expert assistance not only in the field of commerce but especially in the field of production. A separate report with detailed information on the subject will be given at today's meeting.

In accord with the needs of agriculture, we are beginning to supplement our agricultural cooperatives with machine departments or departments of other agricultural items. For this purpose we created the Union Machine Headquarters a few years ago. I will not dwell on this question, though, as we have dedicated a separate report to it.

Foreseeing that our agriculture will have to move toward meat production, our Union has taken a major part in creating a meat preserve factory in Mikołów in Upper Silesia (which will be able to produce 20,000 two-kilogram tins of preserved meat daily, not counting the transport of refrigerated or frozen meat and cold cuts). This factory has received a permit to transport the meat of 70,000 pigs and is in close contact with agricultural organizations that were engaged in the transport of swine and the provision of meat to other countries. This affair is developing in a major way. It may lead to the creation of a new area in the agricultural cooperative movement, namely to cooperatives established for the purpose of buying, butchering, and transporting cattle and swine.

Before long, a period of unrestricted grain export will arrive. The Farmers' Headquarters, which has been changed into a stock company from the former secretariat of the Farmers' Cooperatives, is making special preparations to become a place for concentrating grain surpluses and exporting them to foreign markets. We will hear a special report on the subject.

In the organizational field, our ideas are moving toward making every effort to draw the wide range of farmers' clubs into cooperative work as members, to increase the network of our Farmers' Cooperatives, and by narrowing the field of work to cause the Farmers' Cooperatives to work more deeply and go into the heart of agriculture, while simultaneously expanding the Farmers' Cooperatives' activities to machines, tools, and other farming necessities.

With the help of collective arrangements, and by allowing exclusively good firms to trade with the Farmers' Cooperatives, on terms we set forth from the outset, we will be able as before the war to eliminate abuse and speculation, to regulate prices, and to create and deepen a spirit of solidarity in our cooperatives, which is absolutely necessary for the cooperative movement to become a major force. By centralizing cooperative agricultural trade around our trade headquarters such as the Farmers' Headquarters and the Union Machine Headquarters we will combat all attempts by individual cooperatives to break away from trade solidarity. We know that such breakaways can sometimes bring individual units temporary benefits but they are always injurious to the whole and to the broader idea. Moreover, they are often proof of inadmissible interests in our cooperatives.

Special courses will serve to educate the people who are to work in the cooperative movement. The question will be facilitated for us by close contact with the Chamber of Agriculture and Farmers' Clubs, which in the nature of things must devote more attention than previously to the cooperative field. We will ask agricultural organizations to work together to increase education about the cooperative movement among farmers.

We can still expect to have the unpleasant work of removing from the boards of managements and supervisory councils those persons who are not qualified for that work or are not performing it as the importance of the matter requires.

5   Conclusions

For all this work we need the vigorous cooperation of present cooperative members and of new friends of cooperativism. We must not hang on spasmodically to what was once good and is presently outdated. We must go forward with the needs of the times. Given the lack of capital the work will be difficult and hard, while the development and expansion of work will require acquaintance with both cooperative work and agriculture. At this moment the Union is making a particularly urgent appeal to the chairmen of the supervisory councils. In every cooperative a more or less clear struggle is under way between local—naturally narrow and often personal—views, egoistic interests, and ambitions, and the desire to realize a broader, more progressive, inclusive idea, as represented by the Union of Cooperatives. By its management, its regulations, and the centralization of trade, the Union is changing local cooperatives into part of a great organization, a cog in a great cooperative machine, constituting power and force. In harmonizing methods of work and strictly defining work conditions, the Union, on the basis of painful past experiences, desires to spare other cooperatives those unfortunate experiences and sad losses.

The chairmen of the supervisory councils should become the Union's main helpers in this area—representatives of the broader idea. The council chairmen should consider themselves the Union's delegates, whose main purpose is to take special care that all the Union's decrees, even those that are unpleasant or sometimes cramp the board members' freedom, should be acted upon regardless, in the name of the wider and more general need.

The cooperative movement in Polish agriculture has not at all reached the end of its development yet. Polish agriculture, particularly farming in the western voivodeships, will find in the cooperative organization the help necessary to combat the economic difficulties of the near future. The change of direction in agricultural production from grain to another kind can only occur with the help of a universally developed cooperative movement and by the efforts of the Union of Cooperatives and the agricultural community's educational organizations.

CHAPTER 18

The Position of Cooperativism in Agriculture[1]

Franciszek Stefczyk

The abnormal relations that prevailed in our state under the impact of the destructions of war and the continual great fall in the value of the Polish mark vastly hampered the activity and entirely depreciated the funds of the cooperative movement, including in agriculture. On the other hand, they favored speculative enterprises and the development of capitalist share companies, which are multiplying at this time like mushrooms after a rain. But *"Fortuna variabilis, Deus mirabilis."*[2] Poland's currency had scarcely been established and the state treasury begun to improve through the beginnings of state and social savings, and more effective tax organs, when the situation of cooperativism and capitalism turned around. From its present defensible position, the cooperative movement looks with pity at the miserable price of shares, and with hope at the opening prospects of successfully expanding and creating local savings as well as using them for cooperative organization and work.

It is proper for me to mention this because it is important to be aware that the cooperative movement is not solely a fashionable form of passing, superficial attitudes and socio-economic acts, without lasting foundations in the nature of real relations, but on the contrary, it is a great and deep natural current in the development of economic and social relations in nations at the highest level of civilization. It has its source in the development and consequences of capitalism, which took shape over whole centuries and grew slowly before it managed at an ever faster tempo to control all areas of social and economic life. Only then, under the pressure of the negative effects of capitalism, but also in connection with the development of modern democracy, the idea of cooperativism was born and a new socio-economic current, called cooperativism, began to flow. In its more than eighty years' march and expansion, the cooperative movement has survived many war reverses, many changes in governmental systems, many upheavals in trade, financial, credit,

---

1 Franciszek Stefczyk, *Stanowisko spółdzielczości w rolnictwie* [*The Position of Cooperativism in Agriculture*], Warsaw 1927, Wydawnictwo Zjednoczenia Związków Spółdzielni Rolniczych Rzeczpospolitej Polskiej [Published by the League of Agricultural Cooperative Unions of the Republic of Poland].

2 Latin: *Fortune is variable, but God creates miracles.*

and employment relations. It felt these various crises and they were not without having a temporary effect on it, but in general the cooperative movement has not been arrested in its progress or come off its main tracks. Even in western societies cooperativism is far from being able to compare its forces with the might of capitalism, but it is striving in that direction with irresistible force and the future belongs to it. I do not imagine, however, the absolute rule of cooperativism, nor do I consider that desirable: in no sphere of human relations is a monopoly a factor of progress and healthy development. Alongside the cooperative movement, capitalist forms of organizing economic work will doubtless persist, as equally legitimate, because we can count on human nature, in which self-interest and self-love will remain a strong and even valuable driver of work and creativity. But no less legitimate is an organization and work in which there is the essence of the command to "love thy neighbor as thyself." All civilized nations are striving to raise their economic and social culture to the level of this commandment through the cooperative movement, and an understanding of the value and significance of the cooperative movement should penetrate the consciousness of our nation and stimulate it to earnest efforts toward realizing the great cooperative goals.

The whole cooperative movement is based on the same ideological bases; it has common general goals and the same main principles of acting, which I can not and need not dwell on here. But in this whole cooperative movement, which is unified in its foundations and general aims, we should distinguish the major group and trend of agricultural cooperativism—that is, the cooperativism that encompasses masses of agricultural producers—from the movement's other large group, which is consumer cooperativism. It would be a good thing for both these currents of cooperativism to remain in spiritual and practical connection and to preserve the unity of the cooperative movement. Nevertheless, agricultural cooperativism must be completely conscious of its separate qualities, special interests, and prerequisites for being active and developing— in the same way as the vigorous food cooperative movement is doing. This will protect it from going astray and facilitate finding good paths and methods of work; above all, it will maintain the necessary cooperation, connectedness, and internal cohesion within the agricultural cooperative movement.

Such a program, or, shall we say, small catechism of agricultural cooperativism obviously requires work, consideration, and thorough discussion before being established and acquiring general recognition. The first Polish Agricultural Congress can have neither the ambition nor the task of creating and imposing such a program. However, it would achieve a lofty aim by at least pointing out and confirming the need for such a program, while sketching its contours—which would not preclude changes and in any case would require knowledgeable supplementation and completion. Thus I have tried to comprise such a very general outline of a program in the following nine theses setting forth the cooperative movement's position in agriculture.

1   A General Description of the Cooperative Movement's Position in Agriculture

a)   Cooperativism in agriculture is a modern form of voluntary organization of the economic work of agricultural producers in all spheres.

b)   This organization rests on the democratic basis of individual equality of rights and obligations, the freedom to work and earn, and respect for the private right to ownership of land.

c)   In its activities, cooperativism in agriculture is directed by the general principles, tested methods, and guiding principles of the cooperative movement, applying them independently and in a manner appropriate to the working conditions of agricultural producers.

2   The Aims of Cooperativism in Agriculture

In agriculture, cooperativism aims especially to help small and medium-size farms:

1)   free themselves from dependence on capitalist intermediaries;

2)   improve their working methods, industrialize production, and increase their incomes;

3)   base all work, all economic relations, and interhuman relations in general, on principles of reliability, justice, mutual aid, and solidarity, both in terms of interests and the actions of individual entities.

3   Main Paths to the Goal

Cooperativism in agriculture obtains its aims by bringing together farms in their own voluntary, cooperative organizations of higher and lower degree and various types, which:

1)   in eliminating the trade intermediaries of outside entrepreneurs and striving for direct trade contacts with consumer cooperatives, take into

their own hands both the provision of household and farming articles and the sale of agricultural products;

2) create their own financial, credit, and banking management based on local savings and the cooperative's own share and reserve capital;

3) give small and medium-size farms access to all the achievements and progress of human knowledge, the best technical methods and equipment, and the best and most energetic, creative, and leading human resources;

4) propagate the cooperative spirit and virtues systematically and knowledgeably and spread cooperative education in practice.

4   The Social Ideal and the Limits of Cooperativism in Agriculture

However, the cooperative movement in agriculture does not at all aim for the gradual transformation of individual farms into one great collective farm, hiring the cooperative members to work on the common property as employees participating solely in the division of income from the common work. On the contrary, while retaining the idea of individual private property, cooperativism wants to increase the productive powers of individual farms as well as the social independence of their owners or holders.

5   Relation to Smaller Farmers and Farm Workers

a) On account of the division of farms into very small properties in the major part of Poland, the cooperative movement in Polish agriculture is called upon to organize the industrialized production and purchase not only of large crops such as grain, potatoes, beets, and large numbers of livestock, but also to deal particularly carefully and attentively with smaller types of farm produce, which are important to very small farms, such as fruit, berries, vegetables, fish, fur, wool, feathers, eggs, honey and wax, horn, and many other such items, as well as folk crafts.

b) In organizing small and medium-size farms on these bases, agricultural cooperativism is also simultaneously concerned, through its agricultural-consumer, trade, and financial cooperatives, for the interests of non-independent farms and farm workers, with the guiding idea and systematic aim of helping them—through work, savings, and cooperative self-help—to the gradual acquisition and enlargement of their own farms.

6   Relation to Larger Farmers

a)   Cooperativism in agriculture does not close itself to the participation in its organizations of larger farms, which within the framework of the co-operative organization can satisfy all or a large part of their basic farming needs and at the same time can contribute very effectively to strengthening and developing the activities of the cooperative organization, and also to their increased influence on the harmonious shaping of social relations in the field of agriculture;

b)   However, the participation of larger farms in cooperative organizations is in no case desirable at the price of any sort of statutory or capital privileges, or at the cost of those democratic values and arrangements that make agricultural cooperatives (and unions of such cooperatives) important self-help and mutual-aid organizations for small and medium-size farms and that are a necessary condition of mutual confidence, friendly feelings, and solidarity among members, and thus are necessary conditions of the economic and moral force and cohesion of cooperative organizations.

7   Position of Cooperativism in Agriculture

The development of agricultural cooperativism depends to a large degree on the effectiveness of agricultural organizations in spreading agricultural knowledge, creating and strengthening the occupational solidarity and connectedness of farmers in the sphere of economic matters, and defending and supporting agricultural interests. Thus permanent cooperation must be created between agricultural cooperative organizations and occupational organizations, without disturbing the complete independence of either of these organizations.

This cooperation should be based on mutual services and representation in the main organs of both organizations. A necessary condition of close cooperation between agricultural cooperative organizations and occupational organizations is the elimination of differences and the attainment of uniform organization and activity within the framework of these two types of collective work by associated farmers.

8   Relation to Political Parties

In spite of its outstandingly democratic nature and system, and, in no less degree, its democratic aims and purposes, agricultural cooperativism does not and should not serve the interests of any political party and should not lower itself to the position of being a tool of political-party aims and maneuvers. On the contrary, all political parties considering themselves the representatives and defenders of the interests of small and medium-size farmers should serve the great cultural, social, and economic ideals, principles, and aims represented by cooperativism. Therefore they should relinquish all activities that could hamper, weaken, or harm the healthy, proper, and cohesiveness cooperative movement in agriculture, while supporting the activity of important cooperative agricultural organizations in every direction, particularly through vigorous participation in skilful propagandizing of the organization and of cooperative work, always in close coordination and agreement with the leading institutions of the agricultural cooperative movement.

9   Relation to the State

a)   As to the position of agricultural cooperativism in relation to the state, it should first of all be stated that there is complete concordance and similarity between the basic conditions, development, and strengths of the modern state under the rule of law (recognizing the right of private property, including of the means of production), and agricultural cooperativism, which is based on the principles set forth above. Thus the natural and necessary cooperation of the state with the agricultural cooperative movement within the proper limits of their mutual interest ensues.

b)   Agricultural cooperativism does not require and in particular does not need any subsidies to give direct material benefits to cooperative members at the cost of the state, or to free them from all efforts to increase the founding or operating funds of cooperatives or their unions.

c)   Nevertheless, what agricultural cooperativism wants is at least equal treatment and support by the state in the sphere of education, propaganda, credit, and help in rebuilding after the destructions of the war, as for capitalist—particularly industrial—organizations and enterprises, which received from state institutions more than the 9/10ths of all loans and state credit guarantees and thus rebuilt and enriched themselves at the cost—particularly in the agricultural sphere—of individual and cooperative savings, which are being devalued at an increasing tempo. The state thus has the responsibility to help agricultural cooperativism in rebuilding rural savings and agricultural cooperative credit, (which has been ruined by the state's current tax and financial policy), by giving cooperative organizations access to sources of credit funded by the state

or by otherwise strengthening agricultural cooperatives' financial headquarters with operating funds so they can use that indispensable aid to
rebuild rural savings.

d)   Cooperative agricultural institutions should make their voice more heard
and should be more taken into consideration than previously in state
economic advisory and decision-making institutions.

On account of the time restrictions for giving this report, there can be no question of a precise commentary on these basic theses, but I would like to emphasis certain of the more important points.

A farmers' cooperative organization can not be treated solely as an enterprise bringing people together to ensure themselves the greatest and most immediate material benefits without regard for the manner and conditions in
which that is to occur. Agricultural cooperativism, like consumer cooperativism, also takes into consideration social and moral factors and aims to improve
the social and economic system, to support economic and social relations between people on the principles of reliability, correctness, economic solidarity,
mutual aid, and democracy.

At the same time, agricultural cooperativism firmly and clearly stands for
western culture's most valued achievements, which besides freedom and personal liberty in earning a livelihood include respect for individual rights, for
private property. This last point must be particularly emphasized because agricultural cooperativism is a union of small and medium-size farm owners, who
want to remain farm owners and for whom respect for the right to possess
the means of work is an attainment of western culture equal to the right to
individual freedom and freedom to make a living. The agricultural cooperative movement can not thus share the tendency that frequently emerges within consumer cooperativism—and is particularly likely to appear among the
proponents of workers' production cooperatives—to expand cooperativism's
aims to the conscious and deliberate transformation of individual workplaces
into collective workplaces, constituting a common property, cooperatively organized and operating. In my formulation of a program for agricultural cooperativism, I preclude such aims and consider them contrary to the proper aim
and purpose of agricultural cooperativism, which is not to deprive its members
of the right to individual ownership of a workplace, but on the contrary, only
to improve those workplaces, to increase their profitability, and to increase the
social standing of farm owners through cooperative organization and work.

We must further be aware that agricultural cooperativism is dealing with
members who are in large part small capitalists and that agricultural cooperativism, in wanting to facilitate and perfect the management of precisely such

private enterprises, must also deal with a whole range of specific tasks, the same or similar to those that are faced by large capitalism, and that sometimes it must thus use the practical methods and achievements of capitalist development in a much greater measure than is done, or needs to be done, by consumer cooperativism.

In particular then, agricultural cooperativism must create its own savings and loan financial system, such as large capital interests have, in consideration of the need for both operating capital and founding and investing capital. The system of cooperative finance and credit, both local and central, is of fundamental importance for the development of agricultural cooperativism—different from and incomparably wider and more important than in consumer cooperativism, where the question is treated as a side issue and is much more easily resolved. Financial credit for consumer cooperatives generally has a secondary importance in connection with the cooperative's relations with its members: as the members are purchasers of goods in the cooperative consumer shops, trade credit is basically out of the question. However, in agricultural cooperatives and their farm headquarters, which are associations of producers, financial and trade credit has and must have a broad and indispensable application. As cooperativism must take care of its own financial system (that is, of a system drawing its main working funds from those clubs of small and medium-size farmers for whom cooperativism is primarily intended), to operate it must have a financial organization devoted to it, adapted to its needs and work conditions but able to connect with the general state and world financial market and to maintain relations with the entire financial and banking system in the country and abroad. We had the serious foundations of such an agricultural credit system before the emergence of the Polish state; it already disposed of considerable funds collected from the savings of the local people and with its own considerable funds as well. However, these savings and funds fell victim to our state's self-construction in a period of unregulated, inflationary economics. Thus that cooperative savings and loan system must once again be rebuilt and further expanded—above all by our own efforts and measures but also with the necessary and well-deserved credit assistance from the state, in its own interest and obviously within the limits of its possibilities.

More than consumer cooperativism, agricultural cooperativism must also be certain to use the other great tools of the capitalist system, for instance, all the achievements in the field of technology and equipment, all progress in agricultural knowledge, as well as drawing on, acquiring, and shaping for itself the best and boldest ideas of people capable of the most successful management of farming enterprises. These are the main levers of capitalist production and trade organizations, and small and medium-size farmers can in no other manner than through the cooperative movement make use of these powerful levers and funds for direct action, without paying the capitalist tribute and without loss of economic independence and thus of social independence. This has greater significance because for those masses of farmers' clubs what is almost more important than the production of large farming goods such as grain, beets, and large livestock, are small agricultural products such as swine, poultry, eggs, honey, teasel root, fruit, vegetables, linen, flax, etc., and also often folk crafts. The production of these minor items is territorially dispersed and also divided between numerous small farms, and thus provides more fertile ground for exploitation by trade intermediaries and large capitalist enterprises; it can only be homogenized, regulated, improved, and capitalized with greatest benefit to the producers through their own—that is, cooperative—organization, which has their confidence and has proper influence on them on account of truly working in their interest.

Even though the small and medium-size farmers are the main body and foundation of agricultural cooperativism, it also gathers in the legions of non-independent farms and farm workers. These latter can satisfy their food needs in agricultural consumer cooperatives, which are full fledged members of the farming cooperative movement, because the masses of small agricultural producers are at the same time masses of consumers. Moreover, agricultural credit cooperatives are an excellent economic and social lever supporting the work and foresight of non-independent farmers and farm workers, both as a receptacle for their savings and as a favorably inclined provider of credit, by which the bolder non-independent elements can raise themselves to independent farming and gradually improve their position.

In this manner, agricultural cooperativism largely fosters economic and social connectedness between various layers of the farming population. This occurs in particular because cooperativism is also open to large farmers and can provide them with important services if they are willing to adapt themselves to the organizational conditions and manners of operating proper to cooperativism. Then they contribute to strengthening and hastening the economic development of that cooperativism and facilitate unification and solidarity between various social levels, replacing social struggle with economic and social cooperation in the sphere of agricultural relations, in accord with the guiding ideas of cooperative thinking.

For this purpose, the spread of good occupational education among the masses of farmers is necessary, particularly with the help of experiences, trials, making the effects of improved production visible, and by spreading the spirit of connectedness and an understanding of the importance of collective action for protecting and supporting the common interests of agriculture in the state. The need for farmers' occupational organizations to collaborate on the development of agricultural cooperativism—and its reciprocal support for the development and activities of those organizations—should be emphasized and should also find appropriate expression in mutual services and representations in the proper organs of both organizations, without limiting the independence of either in its own sphere of activity.

For the development of cooperativism thus understood, concerned in spite of toil and hardship with the real good and long-term economic and social rise of the masses of the farming population, there are two particularly dangerous threats. One is the creation—often under the umbrella of the cooperative movement—of private enterprises, which although founded by cooperative efforts have nothing in common with cooperativism but which therefore proclaim their supposedly popular nature the louder. These enterprises also lay claim to equal treatment by cooperative organizations and even to exceptional protection by government bodies and state institutions, but above all they seduce the masses and lead them away from the proper cooperative system. This danger can be stopped in its tracks only if public entities and the masses of the farming people are made aware of it by the cooperative organizations, and the farming-occupational organizations working with them.

The second danger for the development of the cooperative movement is produced by the transfer of party and political differences and struggles into cooperative work. This is a factor that disrupts the strength and cohesion of the cooperative movement, demoralizing it and weakening its growth, distorting its proper tasks and aims. Therefore cooperativism, in accord with its tasks, aims, and methods of acting, should stay far away from party struggles and slogans, and always remain a neutral terrain for the cooperation of people of goodwill, capable of rising above the level of party interests and striving toward the heights where partisan grappling quietens and ceases and the horizon of thoughts and feelings expands, so that they bring neighborly love to life in people's hearts and souls—the living desire for the public good and the will to act toward that end.

In agricultural cooperativism thus understood and defined, there are a lot of creative state elements. Under the rule of law our state will also find a very valuable source of strength and permanency in cooperativism, a faithful ally in fulfilling its tasks and improving its structure. It must also remember that the modern state is established to protect and support the interests of all spheres of the population but above all the interests of the economically weaker parts, in order to raise them and strengthen them in their own properly comprehended interest and in order for the state structure and power to rest on broad levels of conscious citizens, who are attached to their greatest cooperative, the state.

In thus defining its position in regard to the state, the agricultural cooperative movement remains above all under the standard of self-help and mutual aid, and may it stay faithful to that sign, because there it will be victorious. Thus let millions of scattered farmers come together in answer to this call; let them collect and organize in thousands of cooperatives of various kinds and purposes; let them combine in their own unions and headquarters in order to create together one strong army of work, an obedient army, motivated by a good spirit. Let that army struggle manfully with passivity and against helpless, depressive complaining and lamentation, against selfishness and exploitation, ignorance and ill will; let that cooperative army gather numerous brave volunteers, particularly those rich in knowledge and ability to act, so that under the guidance of outstanding leaders the whole of Polish agriculture and all farmers will be led along the path of progress to prosperity, and the whole nation—in the spirit of Mickiewicz's line "Everyone's aims are the happiness of all"—will be led to the fundamental rebirth of our state and to a Poland worthy of the name, fulfilling its aims and destiny in the family of great nations of this world.

CHAPTER 19

The Farming Cooperative and Its Development[1]

Zygmunt Chmielewski

In the two previous chapters we explained that for the increase and long-lasting improvement of production on individual farms, a farming cooperative should be founded and that the proper basis for requisite sales is a cooperative on the spot in the countryside. The question here arises of whether two cooperatives should be established in the countryside? No: the sole rational thing is to combine those tasks in one farming cooperative.

If the cooperative were only to encompass the planned organization of production, its development would proceed very slowly, given the rather far-reaching limitations in the cooperative on the prevailing manner of working—expressed by the proverbs "every man's a king in his own house" and "everyone suits himself"—would lead to serious fears and resistance, even if personal property remained unaffected. Therefore, the farming cooperative must also provide benefits whose clarity and obviousness make it easier for persons to jettison their excessive trust in their own judgment and agree to subordinate themselves within certain bounds—as we will see below—to a work plan set forth in their own collective organization.

Thanks to the fact that a farming cooperative engages in the sale of products, it is considerably easier for it to win over members.

The scope of activities of the farming cooperative can and should be extended wherever it is possible and desirable due to the actions being easy and not entailing risks for any members. It has to be ruled out, however, that a farming cooperative could simultaneously be a Stefczyk savings and loan society, because being based on liability limited only by relatively small shares, it can not provide sufficient guarantees for deposits and should entirely rule out giving loans and credit to anyone. Furthermore, it should be ruled out that a farming cooperative could be, at the same time, a consumer cooperative,

1 Zygmunt Chmielewski, *"Spółdzielnia gospodarska"* ["The Farming Cooperative"], in: idem: *Przyszły ustrój gospodarczy wsi w Rzeczypospolitej Polskiej* [*The Future Rural Agricultural System in the Republic of Poland*], Warsaw 1938, Książnica dla Roczników Centralnego Towarzystwa i Organizacji Kółek Rolniczych [Library for Farmers of the Central Society and Organization of Farmers' Clubs.

because the latter essentially serves housekeeping and not farming needs and has great tasks in this area—tasks that require particular preparation.

If a creamery division of the regional dairy cooperative is to be established in a given village, it is proper for it to be managed by the farming cooperative because it does not present either a risk or any particular difficulties, and could contribute in a high degree to uniting the members.

If the consumer cooperative in a given village runs a goods warehouse, a division of labor should be made with it, above all on the principle that bartered goods, that is, minor trade goods, (eggs, mushrooms, etc.) should belong to the consumer cooperative, and mass goods (grain, sugar beets, potatoes, fruit, vegetables, etc.) should belong to the farming cooperative. It is not important that the division should be the same everywhere, in all cooperatives, but that a given item should always end in the proper cooperative trade headquarters; we explained above what an important role the trade headquarters play in regard to managing the market.

If a consumer cooperative does not sell farming goods (machines, tools, artificial fertilizer, etc.) or there is no agricultural-consumer cooperative on the spot, the farming cooperative should engage in the matter, with the clear reservation that no risk or losses should result to it therefrom. In regard to the provision of goods necessary for agricultural production, the farming cooperative can only be the agent of the regional agricultural and trade cooperative, that is, it can stock the goods only at the latter's risk and can order goods previously ordered by its members, either collectively or individually. It should be emphasized as strongly as possible that ruling out the possibility of losses in the farming cooperative is one of the main bases for its healthy development and a great encouragement for an ever larger number of farms to join it.

The farming cooperative would lose the proper line of its development if it were to serve non-members in any of its divisions. Precautions should be taken, even in running a creamery branch of the regional dairy, to ensure that the suppliers are exclusively members. Only by such absoluteness will it be possible to cause all farms to become, even if slowly, members of the cooperative. This high achievement is extremely important because only after all farms have been included will it be possible to complete all the tasks; only then will the future rural system be entirely achieved. We are here at an unusually important point in our development. If after reading the whole of this work, we come to the conclusion that the system being proposed is in all degrees rational, we will be left facing the question of what roads we should take to reach it.

Many people might then think "there is so much ignorance in our country that the only path is coercion, that is, legislating that farms must by a given day join a farming cooperative in the countryside and those who resist will have very heavy fines imposed on them." As was proven in many countries in similar circumstances, such a method of direct force does not work and causes many negative consequences. In laying out the future rural system, we are mainly concerned to raise humanity higher, and direct force, with all its apparatus of punishment and oppression, does not raise but lower a human being. Thus co-operativism is against direct coercion and is building voluntary organizations. Nevertheless, we should be aware that in the vast majority of cases a person's voluntarily joining a cooperative is not at all equivalent to being conscious of the cooperative's major aims and occurs under the influence of secondary or even tertiary factors.

Let us take, for example, the dairy movement, which is developing with particular success in our country. Among the members who apply to join, it is rare to find someone who is aware that the dairy cooperative is striving to abolish intermediaries and to obtain better prices for milk products through-out the country, or that it is working on improving the product and encour-ages farms to change their methods of farming. People become aware of these aims very slowly and only on condition of belonging to a cooperative. Dairy cooperatives are on the wrong path in not requiring their suppliers to belong to the cooperative, because they are not undertaking the work of economic enlightenment, which is achievable solely through joint action and common responsibility.

Usually a new member joins a cooperative for low, practical reasons, for ex-ample, a dislike to processing the milk at home. And thus we say to him: "yes, we'll collect your milk, but register as a member." We thus place him in the situation of indirect coercion, which in many areas turns out to be unavoidable and effective.

The same occurs in savings and loan cooperatives, in which we say "yes, we will give you a loan, but register as a member."

We should use such indirect coercion—which has nothing in common, in spite of the partial similarity of names, with direct coercion—in managing farming cooperatives, and in such a manner that all its services are rendered exclusively to members. If that principle is not observed as closely as possible, the development of the cooperative will be uncertain. Those who argue that "conditions are different in our area" are taking the wrong path. In work it is not those methods that seem easiest that should be used, but those that truly lead to the goal.

We stated above that a farming cooperative obtains its full goal when it unites all the farms. Nevertheless, here or there it can happen that a certain farmer on account of his particularly overgrown selfishness, stubbornness, and quarrelsomeness is entirely unfit for collective work. But it is out of the question that the cooperative should be closed to—for example—the poorer farmers or should unite only those with the same views.

The question of the cooperative's territorial sphere is obviously important. We are not currently able to give here a complete, precise definition; we will only emphasize, strongly, that it should be a small territory, at most a parish, and not a large one. A large, fairly compact village (of above 100 farms) is the most convenient sphere in which to act. A very small village (30–40 farms) should combine with hamlets or even with neighboring villages with which it gets along well. It is better to begin with a small territory, and in case of necessity to extend it, than the contrary.

As we have said, the sphere of a cooperative's activity may be fairly extensive.

Planned production is its nucleus. We must consider this matter in as much detail as possible.

Let us take the simplest question—combating weeds. The first founders of a cooperative—and according to the provisions of the law on cooperatives there have to be at least ten of them—by reading and asking for advice from a member who is an expert (an agricultural instructor), plan the order of procedures in destroying specific weeds and how the work is to be performed, including whether it is to be done simultaneously. It is clear that the non-participation in this work of non-member farms will lessen the possibility of obtaining complete results, but the outcome will undoubtedly be better than if each of the members works on his own, without the necessary knowledge and at different times. An increasing number of farming cooperatives have managed to get rid of weeds entirely and thereby to increase crop yields.

Members have orchards, but the income from them is poor, as they are taken over by fungi and other pests. The orchards have to be sprayed; at common cost the cooperative brings in a sufficiently large and rapid sprayer and, following the instructions of the horticulturist, sprays members' orchards several times a year. This is work which requires knowledge and appropriate equipment to be effective.

Members who do not have orchards get expert advice on choosing the most appropriate fruit varieties for the local conditions, what time of year to plant, and how it should be done to avoid errors. Every member places an order, which the cooperative directs to the proper purchasing source.

The cooperative takes care to teach one of the local people to sort fruit and all the members possessing orchards are taught to pick the fruit from the tree rather than to shake it down; it buys the members boxes or material, at their cost, and makes sure the fruit is properly packed and finds sales, on the principle of payment after receipt of dues (payments to the Stefczyk Savings and Loan Society) and with consideration for the quality of the goods. Fruit can be sold either to be consumed raw or for processing in the cooperative processing plant. If it seems desirable, the cooperative can build a fruit storage unit or, for example, a drying facility for plums—always, however, after careful investigation of the matter and receiving expert advice. Finally, the cooperative teaches the members how to make domestic use of the fruit that is not suitable for selling.

In a word, thanks to its collective activities, the farming cooperative improves the production of fruit and makes orchardry increasingly profitable.

If the raising of vegetables for sale is widespread in a given village, the cooperative plays the same role, and it can also have greenhouses providing seedlings for all the members, in order to facilitate the production of uniform crops, which will be raised on individual farms from choice, homogenous seeds.

The uniformity of goods—in this case of fruits and vegetables—is one of the main conditions for obtaining a better price. Because larger amounts of a uniform good fetch better prices than small ones, the advantage of the cooperative is obvious.

We have discussed three examples of planned work, which in our opinion seem the most accessible and easiest to perform.

We will now turn to an example that involves the necessity of educating individuals among the local population so as to provide benefit for all. Vaccinations have to be given, animals in labor need to be skillfully helped, and advice is needed in emergencies, and even for less dangerous illnesses. The farming cooperative should help in this matter by sending one of the local inhabitants for suitable courses in the appropriate knowledge, either by a loan from the Stefczyk Savings and Loan Society or by a non-refundable payment. It is most fitting that the person should be the blacksmith, who can become a kind of cooperative employee not only in the above-mentioned field but also in maintaining the proper order and maintenance in the cooperative's machines and equipment, as we will discuss below.

The above example leads us to consider a very important task of the farming cooperative. Real progress will spread in the Polish countryside when more people are working there who have finished elementary school and a rural agricultural school, and in addition, there are those who have been on various courses and have thus become better acquainted with a given specialty. In this connection, the management organs (the management and supervisory board) of the cooperative can be particularly proud when in their report to the general assembly they can annually repeat such a paragraph as the following:

> We have ensured, in close cooperation with their parents, that not one child belonging to our members left elementary school before its full

completion; we have given prizes in the form of books for the best boy students and girl students finishing school in the present year; further, through services and even arranging credit from the Stefczyk Savings and Loan Society, we have facilitated for their parents the placement of 6 boys in agricultural schools and 7 girls in home economics schools; we have directed 23 farmers and 18 housewives to special courses in the *powiat*[2] Chamber of Agriculture; and finally, at the cooperative's expense, we have educated one young person in a special course as a future employee of our cooperative.

If we want our long-term plans to become reality, we have to prepare good executors.

Let us move now to those long-term plans.

The rural production plan, in both the plant and animal sphere, should be made for the long term in its main outlines. It is necessary to decide whether to go in the direction of grain or predominantly toward the raising of livestock, or livestock and orchardry, or vegetables, etc. This should be decided in close agreement with the *powiat* Chamber of Agriculture, which can draw up such a plan not only for a given village but also for the neighboring villages. When a series of neighboring agricultural cooperatives introduce a plan for an agreed goal, a great collective strength is created, which, thanks to the use of experts with higher educations from the *powiat* Chamber of Agriculture, is capable of more quickly pushing production to a higher level and throwing onto the market large amounts of a uniform good, thus obtaining a better price.

If a cooperative does not have very many members (10–15), such a plan could be drawn up with the participation of all of them, in the presence of the agricultural inspector. In cooperatives with larger numbers of members, this work will be done by the board of management and the supervisory council— always in the presence of the agricultural inspector and with members being permitted to state their desires. Members who are dissatisfied with the resolution have the right to demand a new review of the matter and then to appeal to the general assembly.

When the plan has been announced and within the course of a month none of the members has voiced an objection, it becomes obligatory for all members of the cooperative. The change in crops need not be the same for all farms, as the difference in soils in individual farms should be taken into account and individual preferences should be considered to the furthest degree. Although it

---

2 An administrative unit larger than a *gmina* (district or commune) but smaller than a voivodeship (province)—Tr.

is not at all easy, the greatest efforts should be made so that during the change in crops and the whole planning process in general each individual's spiritual values should be respected and utilized.

For instance, if in a given cooperative nearly all the members are engaged in dairy and orchard farming, there is no obstacle to several members engaging strictly in the cultivation of grain. The essence of planned production in a given instance would be that in all the orchards there would be a prescribed number of those same good varieties of fruits, and the grain should be of a uniform variety, established by the Chamber of Agriculture for the vicinity. None of those things a farm produces exclusively for its own use (vegetables, fruit, flowers, linen, flax, etc.) are subject to the management of the cooperative, but everything that is partially or entirely intended for collective sale enters into the sphere of the plan, that is, the cooperative's activities.

The following example may clarify the matter: if honey is produced exclusively for use in the farm household, or is sold privately, it's "everyone suits himself," but if there are several producers of honey in the village and the cooperative has undertaken to sell it, then the principle prevails of uniformity, as established by the cooperative in consultation with experts (efficient beekeeping, provision of sufficient plants for the honeybees, combating contagious diseases in hives, etc.).

This would obviously be nonsense if the cooperative required all or individual members to raise bees, poultry, rabbits, etc. Only a person who really wants to engage in such an activity should do so, and the cooperative has the responsibility to help him acquire the appropriate knowledge and to organize harmonized production and advantageous sales.

The raising of poultry and production of eggs should play a large role in raising rural prosperity, but the previous motley varieties must disappear, and proper feeding and protection must be introduced at once, and this is achievable only through collective action according to an established plan, foreseeing the continual improvement of that area of work through the members' strict application of the cooperative's guidelines.

The raising of rabbits can significantly improve a household's diet, but the sale of furs, or the sale of breeding bucks or does in particular, will only bring the desired results if the village has uniform material to sell. Rabbit skins, which are presently sold for nothing, can bring a good price when they are collected in larger quantity, properly preserved and tanned, and most importantly, are from animals of a suitable, uniform variety.

Respect for the preferences of individual farmers should be particularly far-reaching in regard to raising cattle, swine, horses, and sheep. It must be understood that the true treasure in the countryside is the farmer who raises a cow that gives a lot of milk, and from that cow, bull calves, because the village will have generations of good cows from them. A farming cooperative would take the wrong path if it copied kolkhozy and established a breeding barn; what is necessary for livestock husbandry to truly succeed, that is, for positive results, is the care and loving eye of the owner, who only needs help in acquiring knowledge and preventing livestock diseases.

It is worthy of notice and remembering that the best cattle breeds were bred not by great estates or experimental stations, but by small farmers with a love for husbandry: first of all, Dutch, Swiss, and Danish farmers. A farming cooperative should have an experimental plot, but it can not ensue therefrom that the members should be prohibited from conducting their own. On the contrary, the cooperative should encourage its members, because this is one of the best ways to learn. The high level of development of the cooperative is dependent primarily on the spiritual values of its members: education, conscientiousness in work, understanding of the importance of the group's efforts, and eagerness in fulfilling obligations to the cooperative. This work of members in the cooperative and for the cooperative will be achieved only when the cooperative accomplishes its hardest task—supporting and assisting individual talents and individual efforts to achieve larger—or even new—attainments in any field.

Where the kolkhozy stifle the development of an individual's spiritual development in adopting planning (and the Bolsheviks are not at all its inventors), the farming cooperative in Poland is simultaneously making efforts to respect and improve the individual person. A kolkhoz is a cooperative only in name, because in reality it applies direct force, and a farming cooperative should be one in the full sense of the word, meaning, it should raise the human being.

Having explained the goals and tasks of the cooperative in this very simplified manner in the most important area of its work—production—we come to outlining its organizational system. We are not appending the statutes, as our intention with this work is only to present certain ideas. Let the readers think about them. If the farmers of a village are persuaded, let them turn to the Union of Agricultural Cooperatives, the Farming Society, of the Chamber of Agriculture for the statutes. Let these organizations consider whether the introduction in the Republic of Poland of the kind of farming cooperatives proposed here corresponds to real needs and augurs successful development. My long years of sometimes painful experiences have entitled me to express here my view that that statute should be living: it should contain only those limitations that result from the law on cooperatives (which is not free of excessive restrictions) and should explain matters in a manner so accessible and even attractive that it will not remain solely in the archives of the board of management and will not repel members by its Mandarin legalese.

There is no need for the organizational system of the farming cooperative to differ fundamentally from other agricultural cooperatives. Here too, the general assembly should be the highest power, which establishes a council from among its members, with the council establishing a board of management. For the cooperative's development what is very important is not the number of board members in the statute (it could differ in individual villages) but rather the selection of appropriate persons.

One of the board members—never mind what title we give him—should be in charge of production. One of the most knowledgeable farmers in the village should be appointed to this position—a bold person, but at the same time one knowing how to get along with people and to influence them by his calm and expert treatment of affairs. The success of the cooperative is to a large degree dependent on his ability to act, that is, on an ability to combine real, sincere brotherly relations with the members with ensuring their exact fulfillment of their obligations toward the cooperative. Members who acknowledge his leadership will willingly consider him their "commander"—when he obtains their confidence and goodwill, when he is their "brother-commander."

The responsibilities and activities of the production manager throw the best light on the essence of planning and therefore we will consider them a little more extensively here.

In one of the following chapters ("Farming Self-Management") we show that planned agricultural production could be introduced, with the passage of time, throughout the entire country, and in the *powiat* it could be directed by the *powiat* Chamber of Agriculture, which has experts—persons with higher educations in agriculture and sufficient practical experience.

The production manager maintains close contact with the *powiat* Chamber of Agriculture and its employees. At the beginning of the cooperative's activities, when the type of production is supposed to be decided with the Chamber's advice, the manager makes sure that a Chamber representative takes part in the meeting in order to produce an agreement of views between the council and the Chamber. The same will be the case in regard to deciding on a change of crops or on varieties of plants and animals. We want to emphasize that there should be an agreement of views between the council and the Chamber. It is out of the question that the Chamber should impose anything or adopt any sort of coercion: representing knowledge, it can only attempt to persuade others which direction is the proper one.

In consequence of the general plan, plans must be made for individual members' farms. Every member has the right to submit the draft of a plan for himself. However, this is only a draft, which should be reviewed by the production manager and given by him for expert appraisal to the Chamber of Agriculture. In the case of a divergence of opinions, the matter is resolved by the cooperative's council.

The production manager ensures that the established economic plans, both general and individual, are appropriately preserved in the cooperative's archives, as indisputable proofs of a concluded agreement and for the resolution of disputes that could emerge later.

The plans are not made to lie in the archives but to be executed as closely and fully as possible. Only then will their value be sufficiently revealed. If we are to bring about in our country the wise "order in freedom" slogan of the Swiss farmers—it's worth thinking deeply about it!—then in making the individual plans we must take the distinctness of the individual into fullest account; but after the plan has been agreed upon, we should insist upon rigor in its execution, and that is precisely the hardest and most important obligation of the production manager.

He directs the battle with weeds and all types of pests and diseases, and requires his instructions to be properly observed, in accordance with the plan confirmed by the council; he takes care that each member, at the proper time, prepares good seed of the set variety, performs the sowing and harvest, sprays the orchard, has a cow covered by a bull approved by the council, etc.

The question arises here of what means can be used to incline the resistant to obedience; the subject of penalties arises. There can be only two penalties: an announcement in the cooperative premises until the guilty party reforms, or specification of the offense and in case of further intransigence, removal from the cooperative. The penalty can be assigned only by the council at the petition of the manager and after hearing the accused party. Only the penalty of removal from the cooperative can be appealed to the general assembly.

Increasing rigor in following plans will be the best reflection of the cooperative's development on a foundation of growing awareness among the members. Such consciousness can be hastened to a degree by the fact that all kinds of prizes and distinctions (from the cooperative, the Chamber of Agriculture, or the state) will be granted on the basis of the representations of the cooperative's council and board of management. A seemingly trivial proceeding of the following sort is not without significance: every general assembly, at the petition of the management and council, it should be resolved to enter into the protocol that, for instance, in the past year the following three members distinguished themselves by their eagerness in fulfilling their obligations to the cooperative. This type of resolution can become a very effective basis for awarding state distinctions and local self-government prizes.

Let us return, though, to discussing the manager's range of activities and to considering those of his activities in which strict observance does not play any role or is applied less often and to a much lesser degree.

The farming cooperative should step by step increase its use of agricultural machines and equipment. This action should be conducted with care and caution in accord with the plan, that is, the basic plan, established for the long term. The leading idea here should be to begin with the most simple, most urgent machines and equipment that the cooperative does not have and that can be bought for use by individual members.

In certain villages it will be necessary to convince individual farmers of the benefits of the use of efficient plows, harrows, and cultivators. The poorer farmers will be unable to buy cultivators, thus the cooperative should buy one and rent it to them for a fee.

Grain cleaning still leaves much to be desired. Thus a cooperative should have its own winnower, grinder, separator, and conveyor, that is, it should run a station for cleaning grain. As it is not profitable for every farm to possess such machines, and as they are not needed at the same time by all, their use in a station can be extended over a longer period of time; these machines will thus be well used and can easily be put under expert supervision, and therefore payment for their use will be low. Concentrating grain cleaning in the cooperative's station furthermore makes sense because it will allow oversight of the preparation of seeds for sowing and sale.

Field harrows and large sprayers for fruit trees (motorized with time!) are classic examples of equipment that should be the property of the cooperative and not of individual farms.

Since sowing can not be delayed, the cooperative should keep seeders only when it can have a sufficient quantity to serve all members on time—without wrangles and disputes, which poison the development of mutual labor. Before it gets to the point where the cooperative will be able to collect seeders, they should be either the individual or joint property of several farms. A well-run cooperative machine station should, with the passage of time, be able to have a motorized threshing machine and tractor. These machines will give great service and will show the benefit of collective efforts, however slow and arduous.

Nevertheless, we must emphasize that expanding the machine station should be treated with the utmost caution, as otherwise it would be easy to unsettle or unbalance the cooperative. Machines and equipment should be bought only on the basis of resolutions passed by the general assembly or on the basis of available means (reserve funds), or on the basis of a resolution to raise the price of shares. Moreover, it will not be easy to ask payment for use: too high a price will repel the members (only they can make use of the machines); too low a price will not cover in full the costs of repair, amortization of the purchase price, storage, supervision, etc. The hardest part is to avoid even the appearance of someone being given priority or special treatment in using the machine, that is, that absolute fairness is not observed.

We have not yet exhausted the duties and tasks of the production manager. He should be truly pleased with the results of his work only when agricultural knowledge increases among the members, because he will have put a lot of effort toward this goal, encouraging the members to educate themselves and facilitating their acquisition of knowledge. He himself should continually explain to the members why the planned work of the cooperative is taking one path and not another, and why a given activity should be performed in one way and not another. In order to further this work, he should persuade the members to belong to a farmers' club (a place for occupational training) and in his work he should take an active part in this club, making certain above all that the club has a well-stocked library on agriculture and a reading room with farm journals. He should further be aware what courses will be given in the near future in the *powiat* Chamber of Agriculture and the voivodeship Association of Farmers' Clubs, and consider which farmers, which housewives, and which youths should be directed to specific courses, and he should persuade the chosen ones to leave for education. He must also be concerned to seek out, among the rural youth, appropriate male candidates for agricultural schools and female candidates for home economics schools, to persuade their parents to let them study, and in case of need, to help them in acquiring loans from the Stefczyk Savings and Loan or even a stipend from the *gmina* or *powiat*. Achievements in this area of work will reward the manager a hundred fold for disappointments that will be nearly unavoidable in other areas.

Those who do not believe that there are an increasing number of persons capable of properly and fruitfully performing the responsibilities of a production manager should read *Życiorysy wiejskich działaczy społecznych* [*Biographies of Rural Social Workers*] and *Pamiętniki chłopow* [*Farmers' Memoirs*][3] and they will be convinced that we have a supply of real pioneers and that the effectiveness of their activities will be considerably increased by organizing help for them, as we will discuss in the following chapters. By now, many bright lights have emerged from the morass of our ignorance and all types of misery, and though some have occasionally led us astray they are certain to become much more numerous and real heralds of progress when they are set on the road of carefully considered, planned, far-reaching cooperative work.

---

3 *Farmers' Memoirs*, Warsaw 1935, 1936, Institute of Social Economics.

The production manager's colleague in the board of the farming cooperative is the sales director. We will not here discuss his activity in full, as the question of sales was presented in Chapter IV and in general is doubtless more or less familiar to readers from the descriptions of agricultural and trade cooperatives. A farming cooperative should be a member of the regional agricultural and trade cooperative and cooperative trade headquarters. The sales director maintains very close relations with them, and works with the production manager to ensure that the goods provided to the cooperative by members are of the best quality and especially that they are entirely homogenous.

Farming cooperatives can also engage in supplying their members with the items necessary for their farms only when there is no agricultural-consumer cooperative or food cooperative on the spot, or their activity is unsatisfactory or negative. In such cases, receipt of deliveries can occur, but on the basis of an agreement and not through dispute.

Long-term experience—ours as well as foreign—has indisputably shown what should definitely not be done in that commercial activity.

The following should be excluded: (1) extending anyone even the slightest credit; (2) serving non-members; (3) buying any sort of goods from members at a negotiated price; (4) treating members who make continual use of the cooperative's services as equal with those who are sometimes customers and sometimes not; (5) accepting goods without careful attention to their quality; (6) making goods available to any sort of intermediary, or acquiring goods through an intermediary; (7) not keeping the books conscientiously; (8) aside from the issue raised in point 4, the extension of any sort of privileges to relatives, influential persons, etc. These eight sins should be avoided like the plague.

Only the immaculate management of supplies will benefit the cooperative: it will encourage persons to join the cooperative and will give the cooperative income from modest commissions, which should cover the costs (of keeping paid employees, etc.) and even provide some small profits, which can be used according to the resolutions of the board or general assembly.

However, the chief commerce of a farming cooperative is sale of the members' main agricultural products. There can be no effective organization of sales if they do not bring together the major part of the producers or if they do not allow the small farmer to join in the collective action. This task can be fulfilled solely by a dense network of small local cooperatives, based on the regional agricultural and trade cooperative and cooperative trade headquarters. The local cooperative must operate effectively and full effectiveness can be achieved only when sales are combined, in one organization, with work to raise both the quality and quantity of production. This is the most important reason for us to introduce farming cooperatives.

The question appears here of whether a farming cooperative should be concerned with the sale of everything the small farmer produces. Above all, the principle is to head for the goal prudently, step by step, undertaking only what can be performed conscientiously and for which we are prepared. We should begin thus with the sale of products that are produced in greatest mass in a given village: in one area this will be rye, in another it will be onions or cucumbers, in another it will be fruit, and so forth. It is not enough to have an assured supply of a given item; it is necessary to train an employee (at the beginning this will be the sales director himself) to be an expert on the given article so he can properly evaluate the quality of the good. Here the regional cooperative or headquarters should be able to help us.

When we have implemented the sale of the current good or goods, we can proceed to learn about a new one.

The work schedule should take utmost account of time-saving measures and the necessity of introducing more expensive equipment. The receipt of goods should take place solely on the day that has been established or announced. Before receipt it will be necessary to obtain as exact information as possible as to the amount of goods to be received in order to be able to deliver them at once and not to store them (when no plans have been made to do so). At the beginning, a cooperative should be careful in undertaking construction (of granaries, fruit storing facilities, areas for keeping machines and equipment, etc.), while keeping in mind the slimness of the cooperative's fund and that a more expensive building will burden the expense account with the necessary amortizations.

Aside from the production manager and the sales director, the third member of the board of management is the chairman, who is in a manner the leader of the cooperative's work. Without sparing either time or energy, he spreads the spirit of cooperativism among the members, uniting the dilatory in the common effort, encouraging the bold to influence their milieus, the strong to support the weaker, and supporting all manifestations of mutual aid and friendship. He takes care that any conflict between members, or between members and the board, is quashed at the outset. He persuades the members that it will be beneficial for the cooperative to participate in the general cooperative movement and in particular to belong to a central association, a trade headquarters, and the regional agricultural and trade cooperative, as well as having relations with local cooperatives. Being conscious that there can be no question of the cooperative's healthy development without good bookkeeping, he makes sure the books are in proper order and often informs the council and general assembly about the precise state of the cooperative's interests.

The sphere of the council's activity is broader than in other kinds of cooperatives because it passes resolutions on important planning matters, based on drafts presented by the management. The council chairman should make every effort, particularly in the planning period, to have disputed issues harmoniously resolved by the council and not go for review and final decision to the general assembly, where, obviously, the strife is likely to spread and the voice of reason and purposefulness will not always prevail.

The general assembly fulfills obligations that are ordinarily listed in detail in the statute. A farming cooperative will strengthen that very important spirit of confidence among the members when, in addition to its statutory requirements, it calls an extraordinary quarterly meeting for the submission of an accounting report and to inform the members of the planned work for the coming quarter. It is also recommended that after an increase of any kind in the sale of products provided by members they should be called together and specifically informed about the results, so that each understands why he received such a payment and not another. The initial difficulties must be persistently overcome, because indubitably the members will come fairly rapidly to a just opinion of the transparency of the cooperative's activity and be convinced of the benefit of sales on commission.

The financial affairs of the farming cooperative have certain distinct characteristics. While in nearly every other cooperative the amount of the necessary participatory fund can be foreseen over a longer period and thus the amount of a single share, the farming cooperative begins with a very small amount and can proceed to a considerable expansion of its activities. The farming cooperative should also begin with small shares and increase them (which will require a change in the corresponding paragraph of the statute) in accord with the general membership's recognition of the need to do so and growing confidence that the money invested here will not be lost but will increase the benefits received. It should be clearly stated in the statute that a member is obliged to have a number of shares equal to the number of hectares of arable land possessed, just as in dairy cooperatives the shares equal the number of cows.

It would seem that setting individual shares at the sum of 5 zloty per hectare might be sufficient. Among other things, it should be foreseen that contributions are necessary for paying shares in the regional agricultural and trade cooperative and to the cooperative headquarters. When, for example, the question of equipping the cooperative with a machine station or expanding the storehouse arises, the contributions are increased (only by a resolution of the general assembly). Sales activity, which can be conducted only on a commission basis—as we have emphasized several times—does not require any serious operating funds and should bring profits, even if not large ones. If there are losses, then either the costs (particularly in terms of remunerating the staff) were too high or the commission was too low. The calculation should be made after every sale, and when everything is recorded there shouldn't be any unpleasant surprises.

The enterprise should be run so there are neither losses nor extravagant profits. The collection of a reserve fund is not proper, particularly at the beginning when the cooperative has only a few members, because consequently the new members would take advantage of arrangements created by that fund. Particularly at the beginning, members should be attracted through good payments, which naturally should not be done at the risk of ultimate losses.

The bookkeeping of a farming cooperative should be devised by the central association in the simplest manner. The most important part should be the balance sheet, in which the detailed calculation of every transaction is recorded.

PART 6

Housing Cooperativism

∵

CHAPTER 20

The Importance of Cooperative Housing[1]

Teodor Toeplitz

1   Social Housing

The subject encompassed by the above title is so broad that it covers almost all housing questions; these obviously can not be the topic of a brief report, which naturally elucidates only one side of the issue, in the narrowest possible manner.

Furthermore, I consider it unnecessary today to describe the failed state of Poland's housing situation. The data of the population census of 1921, the Warsaw housing census of 1919, a whole range of presentations and publications, and recently the report entitled *Budownictwo mieszkaniowe* [*Housing Construction*] of the survey commission studying the costs and conditions of production and trade, sufficiently clarify the matter.

If under the name of "housing affairs" we understand the question—which I consider to be the only proper one—of how to house the masses, then there can be no doubt after reading those materials that the term "housing crisis" is not in the least exaggerated in describing existing conditions. It should also be considered proven that mass housing, consisting of small apartments whose rent corresponds to the ability to pay of white-collar and physical workers, must be based on public funds. (First and second conclusion of the survey commission, p. 44). The commission's claim that "without improvement in housing conditions, without the possibility of a given family to ensure its housing, there can be no question of the healthy development of Poland's economic, moral, and political life" (p. 39) is entirely sufficient to demonstrate, by a simple syllogism, the significance of social housing. Since improvement in housing conditions is possible only by means of social housing, and improvement is necessary, then the importance of such housing is obvious.

The importance of social housing is not the subject of the present report, however. Its subject are those traits of social housing that differentiate it from for-profit housing and which produce its particular importance for the physical

---

1   Teodor Toeplitz, *Znaczenie spółdzielczego budownictwa mieszkaniowego* [*The Importance of Cooperative Housing*], Warsaw 1928, Komitet Polski Międzynarodowej Służby Społecznej [Polish Committee of the International Social Service].

and moral health of the population: an importance that would exist even if for-profit housing were capable, in quantitative terms, of entirely satisfying the population's needs. What I call social housing is all construction that is not intended to bring direct profit, that is, construction of homes for the sake of the inhabitants and not for the rent they will pay.

Social housing can belong to the state or the commune; it can be conducted by institutions specially established for the purpose (for instance, the French Offices Publiques d'Habitation à bon marché, the Italian Instituti Autonomi Case Popolare, etc.) or by foundations, as for example, the Warsaw foundation of Wawelberg and Rotwand; lastly, it can be cooperative housing or even housing provided by an employer. Housing provided by an employer, even though it may be intended to facilitate production by giving workers better apartments and thereby to increase the profit of enterprises, does not aim directly at profit from rent and therefore may retain many of the additional traits of other forms of social housing.

The late Professor Eberhardt (deceased last year), an outstanding expert on housing affairs, said that all progress in the housing sphere is the result of social housing. For-profit construction, the construction of rental units, has created only one form of housing, and that of the worst type—the large barracks-type building. The idea of such construction was always to divide a given piece of land into the greatest number of building parcels and to build up each parcel in such a manner as to locate the largest number of apartments on it, and finally to exploit those apartments so as to obtain from them the highest amount of rent.

From the moment when for-profit construction met with obstacles in its activity of this kind, it ceased production of small apartments, which were previously the most profitable in terms of rent. In a simplified manner it can be claimed that for-profit construction ceases to produce small apartments under pressure of the housing inspectorate.

It emerged in this instance, as in many others, that inspection activity, whose only weapon is prohibition, is barren. Housing inspection was supposed to be a factor contributing to a higher housing culture. The hopes placed in it were vain, however. Not being based on creative activity, it is unable to fulfill this task.

The decisive factor in raising housing culture has turned out to be social housing. It has simultaneously become the creator of a new form of human coexistence.

1.1   *Housing Culture*

Raising housing culture can occur by two paths: first of all, by making all conveniences that previously existed only for rich people accessible to the masses.

This means the introduction of electric lighting; the use of gas as fuel for cooking; arrangements facilitating the removal of garbage; providing access to a bath, either in each apartment or by facilities for a group of residents; cold running water in every apartment, and perhaps warm water as well; the use of warm water in appropriately equipped washing rooms; and finally central heating, which so significantly decreases the difficulties of heating apartments and simultaneously makes them easier to keep clean.

All these conveniences are not always or everywhere provided. There is no social housing, though, that does not provide some of them, and often many. Almost everywhere we find an absolute satisfactoriness in terms of the hygienic requirements of a separate water closet in every apartment. The introduction of the principle of bilateral ventilation of every apartment, even the smallest, is almost universal. The ability to open two opposite windows is the trait that most distinguishes construction adapted to the health requirements of the inhabitants from the lesser quality apartments of rental buildings, whose windows, opening onto a narrow courtyard, at most allow for an exchange of bad air between two apartments located across from one another.

Out of concern for making life and work easier for the inhabitants of the homes built for them, social housing has also been very intensively engaged in the question of making housework more efficient.

Aside from the above-mentioned central equipment, this has produced a range of very interesting building solutions and solutions for equipping the kitchen, as a place in which the main work of the house is concentrated. In many cities, headed by Frankfurt am Main, every apartment is supplied with all the kitchen equipment, which is adapted to the construction of the kitchen and thus permits significant savings in its dimensions.

In itself, making civilized appliances accessible to the masses will not raise the housing culture. It must be admitted that a considerable number of the persons who find themselves in new housing conditions that significantly depart from their accustomed ones must be suitably instructed and guided in order for the level of their housing culture to be truly raised. It is not enough to have the proper equipment; it is necessary to use it in the proper manner. Only social housing can teach this. For this purpose, detailed regulations and instructions, clear prohibitions, and real control over the manner of abiding by the regulations and observing the prohibitions are necessary, including, unfortunately, penalties in the case of glaring violations of the proper way of using an apartment.

Only a body that is an authority for the housing inhabitants can allow itself to be sufficiently categorical in the matter of maintenance; it must also be an authority to which the inhabitants submit willingly; the source of power and authority must either be the same, or they must consider the source to be completely legitimate. This kind of compliance is entirely impossible in relation to persons who in any way represent the pursuit of profit. It exists, though, wherever there is social housing, as is proven by the regulations issued by the administration of municipal homes: for instance, the *Hausordnung* issued by the city hall in Vienna, or those placed in lease agreements concluded by institutions letting affordable apartments, such as, for instance, the French Offices Publiques d'Habitation à bon marché. The numerous regulations issued by a housing cooperative are also an integral part of its lease agreement; they concern all the matters connected with use of the apartment and make the inhabitants' harmonious common use of a building or settlement possible. These regulations concern, for instance, the necessity of preserving the quiet during certain hours of the night and day. There are regulations so far-sighted as to require that sewing machines or typewriters used in the apartments be placed on soft surfaces to stifle the sound.

Particular attention is paid to keeping the apartments clean. The regulations contain purely technical guidelines concerning maintaining the cleanliness of the water closet, the manner of using the bath, of removing dust from the central heating radiators, etc.

Certain lease agreements even contain a direct requirement to bathe, which is applied in housing settlements where each apartment does not contain a bath but there is a bathing facility intended for common use. Every tenant is obliged in paying the rent to buy as many bathing tickets per month as there are persons living in the apartment. Of course, no one can force a person to use those tickets; however, practice shows (such coercion exists in Suresnes near Paris) that a person who has paid for a ticket ordinarily uses it.

In the range of regulations we find very severe rules concerning neglecting the apartment, and particularly about permitting insects to proliferate. The appropriate paragraph of the lease agreement with the Office Publique d'Habitation à bon marché reads as follows:

Confirmation of the presence of cockroaches in the apartment will result in the immediate dissolution of the lease agreement, while the cost of disinsectization, as well as all costs of renovating the premises, will be borne by the tenant.

Other regulations contain similar warnings.

There is a widespread prohibition against doing the laundry or drying it in an apartment if there is a space provided for the purpose in the building or settlement.

The battle with humidity in apartments and concern for good air leads to guidelines and decrees about ventilation being placed in the regulations.

In order for the tenants to understand the necessity of proper use of the apartment and its equipment, the cost of internal renovations is everywhere borne by the tenants; there are agreements formulated in such a manner that the tenant gains materially by proper maintenance of the apartment. In Belgium, the draft agreement established by the Société Nationale des Habitations et des Logements à bon marché provides for the lease of the apartment on the condition that the tenant bears the costs of all internal renovations; but the renovations are done solely by the Cooperative Management, which obtains funds by raising a set percentage of the rent. The sums acquired in this manner are recorded to the benefit of the individual tenant, who has the right to collect the remainder, that is, the sum that has not been used for the renovation of his apartment. For a tenant who has properly maintained his apartment this is a kind of compulsory savings.

Concern for the proper use of an apartment concerns not only the technical side, or matters of cleanliness, etc., it goes further: an apartment is an apartment for a family and it can not thus be changed into a workshop or a place of trade unless it was specially prepared and let for that purpose. In no case can it be a place for the sale of alcohol. Areas that are not living quarters (the basement, for instance) can not be used for dwelling purposes.

On principle, subletting is precluded in all the lease agreements and regulations concerning housing built by non-profit institutions known to me. The institutional authorities and cooperative might allow a temporary sublet only in exceptional, precisely defined circumstances, confirmed each time—although the conditions of that sublet must be entirely under their control.

Many regulations also involve matters of housing aesthetics, uniform garden design, the decoration of balconies, etc.

To prevent the conditions and limitations set forth in the regulations from being the dead letters of a paper contract, apartments are everywhere visited and sanctions—which are sometimes quite severe, as we have seen above—are applied.

In Vienna, such visitations take place regularly, at least once a month, by inspectors (municipal employees), who give the tenant a form with a grade for the condition of each individual element of the apartment (the floors, walls, ceilings, windows, doors, water pipe, stove, sink, kitchen, and water closet). If these grades (from 1 to 3) turn out to be insufficient (1) three times, the tenant will be forced to move from a new apartment to an old one. In addition to the thirty-some thousand new apartments that the labor council of Vienna has itself built, it also bought—as we know—a whole range of buildings with workers' apartments built before the war. Considering that it is not possible to deprive someone of a roof over their heads, the municipal government believes that a tenant who is unable to maintain an apartment built specially for him does not deserve such an apartment and should be moved to one of the narrow, unventilated holes that were built for profit; his apartment, on the other hand, will be occupied by someone who can better appreciate and adapt to civilized conditions. In France, the Office of Affordable Housing conducted visitations by female functionaries or social inspectors (literally, *infirmière sociale*—a social nurse). The purpose is not only to investigate the manner of housekeeping but also the life situations of the families residing in the Office's buildings. The inspectors' task is not only to investigate but also to provide the farthest reaching aid and assistance. We find here an attempt to combine the activities of housing assistance with social care.

In Belgian cooperatives, inspections are conducted by a committee established on the basis of the cooperative's council, as is the case with us in the Warsaw Housing Cooperative, where visitations are conducted by an overseer appointed by the Supervisory Council for each colony.

1.2   *Participation of the Residents*

A few such examples will be enough to understand how deeply social housing involves organizing the life of its inhabitants. But its influence does not stop there. Social housing residents are not solely the passive objects of institutional functionaries and authorities' activities. Social housing requires the active participation of all its inhabitants and thus necessarily produces new organizational forms. The requisite thrift in constructing the largest possible number of small apartments means that some of the activities that could previously be accomplished within a single apartment must be accomplished outside of it and that the most economic manner of satisfying the common needs of the inhabitants must be sought.

Regardless of whether these apartments are located in a large collective building or in a settlement of small single-family houses, the number of spaces for common needs is ever increasing. Meeting rooms or club rooms, reading rooms and libraries, nurseries for small children, preschools for the older ones, a whole range of the above-mentioned utilities of a technical nature (laundry rooms, bathing rooms, central heating, etc.)—all this requires planning for the satisfaction of these needs.

Planning is essential both in designing a settlement and in organizing its life.

The organization of life in new settlements requires, and contributes to, a radical change in the attitude of the residents to the real estate they inhabit.

The beginning of change in a tenant's attitude is his manner of maintaining the apartment. A characteristic of many social housing regulations concerns the allocation of apartments, which depends primarily on the housing conditions in which the candidate finds himself at the time of application.

All other conditions being equal, a new apartment is received by the candidate whose present apartment is the worst. Financial considerations do not play any part—or an entirely secondary one—in the decision. Above all, the family conditions of the tenants are taken into account.

The vast majority of the inhabitants of a new settlement feel, to the greatest degree, the difference between their previous manner of living and what they have received thanks to social housing. The sentiment of gratitude for having been provided with human living conditions facilitates their compliance with regulations which are sometimes quite strict.

Nevertheless, the administration of large concentrations of small apartments, with common facilities, is not easy. It can never be done successfully without the creation of a tenants' organization.

Therefore, the emergence of such organizations meets with the encouragement of the administrative authorities of the social housing, and not infrequently the authorities themselves even establish tenants' organizations.

In large Viennese apartment buildings, at the recommendation of city hall, the tenants choose one representative per stairwell. A representatives' meeting is called by the chief representative for each housing settlement.

The housing inspectors, who are the municipal authorities' organ of direct supervision, are obliged to maintain continual contact with the representatives. The institution of representatives does not at all limit the rights of the inhabitants to form committees, with which, if they exist, the inspectors or functionaries should cooperate.

The large German cooperatives (for instance, the Housing Cooperative in Duisburg) provide for the existence of administrative committees in each housing colony. Such a committee is composed of three members named by the cooperative's board of management after hearing the recommendations of the tenants. These three members co-opt two further tenants. If a given colony is composed of a large number of apartments, the number of members of the committee grows so that every one hundred apartments are represented by three members.

The administrative council is constituted by all the committees together.

The extent of both the committees' and the council's activities is very large. It encompasses both representation of the inhabitants' interests and support of the cooperative's board of management in all its directives aimed at preserving the rental conditions and regulations.

Among other matters, the administrative council gives its opinion on the submissions of the committees concerning lease terminations.

Individual committees also regulate the manner of utilizing the facilities that are in common or successive use by all the inhabitants.

The tasks of the tenants' organization are not easy, particularly in cooperatives where the aim should be to strengthen the significance and importance of the cooperative, defend its material and moral interests, and simultaneously satisfy the sometimes justified grievances of the inhabitants. To ameliorate the emerging oppositions and in no way increase them is the only path by which these institutions can operate.

Following such a path is significantly facilitated if the tenants' organization has further aims—if it fulfils additional useful functions for its members other than those arising from relations connected with the administration of homes.

Tenants' organizations that are involved in cultural, social, or philanthropic activities will have such a nature.

Examples of such are, above all, the Mutual Aid Societies (*Mutuelles*) which exist in France in housing settlements built by the Office of Affordable Apartments of the Department of the Seine. Belonging to these societies is not actually obligatory, but under the influence of the institution's board of management, nearly all the tenants participate in it.

Contributions to the Society are collected by the administration as a set percentage of the rent and paid into the Society's fund.

The Society provides material aid to the tenants in case of accidents of fate justifying such assistance.

If the tenant has not paid the rent and the council of the Society recognizes that he deserves assistance, it pays the rent to the administration, while in principle treating such aid as a loan.

When the reason for nonpayment is a temporary circumstance, the loan is returned and the Mutual Aid Fund is not decreased. In the contrary case, where the circumstances become even worse (in the case of death, severe illness, or long-term unemployment), the loan is changed into assistance.

In this manner, the tenants of a housing settlement, having precise knowledge of their neighbors' situations, provide mutual aid. The administration thus has an ensured rental income, without which no economic activity is sustainable. In cases where the neighbors/companions consider that offering help is not indicated, the administration is free to proceed with evicting a tenant who is behind on his rent for no justifiable reason.

At the end of the year, the administration investigates the losses the "*Mutuelle*" incurred through aid or unreturned loans and part of these losses (usually 1/3) are covered by a subsidy to the Society.

The certainty of regular receipt of rent has greater importance for a housing cooperative than for the Office of Affordable Housing.

Thus the Warsaw Housing Cooperative, whose aim is to supply the greatest possible number of workers and employees with apartments meeting all the norms of social housing, considered it necessary to establish an organization similar to that which exists in the Department of the Seine.

"Glass Houses," the mutual aid society of the tenants of the Warsaw Housing Cooperative, aims to create the foundations of neighborly coexistence for all the persons living in homes built by the Warsaw Housing Cooperative.

In order to fulfill its tasks, the Society is involved in all matters affecting the moral and material well-being of the cooperative's tenants, by organizing institutions facilitating child raising; organizing entertainment, lectures, concerts, competitions, etc.; establishing a tenants' representative body in regard to the administration and cooperative authorities; granting financial assistance or loans to members who find themselves in a difficult material situation due to accidents of fate (death, illness, lack of work); and finally, possibly, by administering buildings which the cooperative has given it to manage, or by other matters entrusted to it by the Cooperative's board of management.

The Society does not allow any political or religious discussions at its meetings.

Are we not witnesses to the emergence of a new form of human coexistence, which is entirely thanks to not-for-profit building, to a type of construction which, in aiming solely to satisfy the needs of tenants, could not manage without their participation and help?

And the mutual aid rendered in these new settlements—is it not the beginning of the Friendship Unions imagined by Edward Abramowski?

"Mutual aid, expanded to all areas of life and provided in small groups of people who know each other personally."[2] "The union in which there should be no bureaucracy ... the pure type of union between people of goodwill, doing good disinterestedly, not like the personnel of philanthropic societies but helping as friends do."[3]

Social housing is only at its beginnings, but today all its hidden possibilities are visible, as is the importance that it could have for shaping the living standards of the population in urban housing settlements.

---

2   E. Abramowski, "Czym mają być związki przyjaźni?" [*What Are Friendship Unions?*], in: idem, *Braterstwo, solidarność, współdziałanie. Pisma spółdzielcze i stowarzyszeniowe* [*Fraternity, Solidarity, Cooperation: Cooperative and Association Writings*], Łódź–Sopot–Warsaw 2009, Citizens to Citizens Society, National Cooperative Council, Institute of Citizen Affairs, Stefczyk Institute, p. 277.

3   Idem, "Związki przyjaźni" ["Friendship Unions"], in: ibidem, p. 221.

CHAPTER 21

"Glass Houses": An Experiment in Cooperative Life[1]

Adam Próchnik

On the grounds of the largest housing cooperative in Poland, the Warsaw Housing Cooperative, an experiment is under way that is worthy of attention. This experiment bears the name of "Glass Houses." What is this "Glass Houses," whose name was taken from Żeromski's fantasy?[2]

The Warsaw Housing Cooperative is a large entity. It lies in two districts at two ends of Warsaw (Żoliborz and Rakowiec); it has created two housing settlements, with a population of over 4,500. The emergence of this kind of entity is a social fact with unavoidable consequences. The entity is a phenomenon creating a terrain for the realization of a whole range of possibilities. Let us add that the entity is not at all the product of accidental selection. There could be between the inhabitants of these settlements the most varied differences in terms of occupation, politics, or ideologies, but they have one thing in common, which is that they all belong to the world of work. This social unity is a very strong bond. It involves the commonality of important interests, a unity of concerns, and common sources of existential reverses; it is a platform on which, without any basic obstacles or internal oppositions, a feeling of full solidarity can be created. Even within the world of work, though, the Warsaw Housing Cooperative does not admit members by chance but on the basis of close contact with the organized world of work, making its selection through trade unions. These are the factors that give the human group brought together within the walls of the WHC settlement its distinct social physiognomy.

---

1 Adam Próchnik, "*Szklane Domy: eksperyment z życia spółdzielczego*" ["'Glass Houses': An Experiment in Cooperative Life"], *Biuletyn Związku Spółdzielni i Zrzeszeń Pracowniczych Rzeczypospolitej Polskiej* [*Bulletin of the Union of Cooperatives and Labor Associations of the Republic of Poland*] 1937, no. 16.

2 Stefan Żeromski (1864–1925), a Polish novelist and dramatist, he was called the "conscience of Polish literature", four times nominated for the Nobel Prize in Literature. In 1905 he was a member and one of the founders of the Cooperativists' Society, also the author of the title *Społem!* – a journal edited by the Cooperativists' Society. Main works: *Przedwiośnie* (*Seedtime*), *Syzyfowe prace* (*The Labors of Sisyphus*), *Popioły* (*Ashes*), *Ludzie bezdomni* (*Homeless People*). In *Przedwiośnie* he created the vision of "Glass Houses" which has become the founding myth and symbol of the Warsaw Housing Cooperative and Polish modernity in general.

It is clear that this kind of human group, living within a common area, can not display the chill indifference to neighbors that is found in large-city apartment buildings. The shared desire to ensure oneself an inexpensive and comfortable apartment will not exhaust the common goals of such a grouping. Living in a cooperative settlement is not an end—not the final aim. On the contrary, it is a beginning, the entry point for broader activity. The entity that has arisen can not be a lifeless expanse; it must bustle with life and must develop that life abundantly.

Thus from the moment the Warsaw Housing Cooperative emerged—from the moment the group began to settle in the cooperative—the question of self-organization appeared: the question of creating a kind of cooperation. It was thus decided to establish a union of the cooperative's tenants, an association that would undertake the various tasks arising from that collective. This association was established nine years ago, shortly after the first homes constructed by the cooperative were inhabited, and took the name "Glass Houses—The Mutual Aid Society of the Tenants of the Warsaw Housing Cooperative."

Glass Houses has three main aims: (1) to defend the interests and needs of the cooperative tenants and to work with the cooperative authorities in this regard; (2) to organize care and material aid for its members; (3) to develop activities to satisfy the cultural-educational needs of the housing settlement and to realize social-cooperative educational aims. If treated seriously, each of these aims would open an enormous field of activity for the society. Permit us today, after nine years of accomplishment, to look at the institution's material and moral achievements and in their light to recognize the breadth of its activities. Before we proceed to draw this picture, we must not overlook the conditions in which the activities were organized.

We will only raise facts of major importance. Thus it should be remembered that those nine years fell perfectly, almost entirely, in years of severe economic crisis, which for a huge number of social institutions were necessarily years of stagnation and limited activities and efforts. For institutions of the Glass Houses type, these conditions were doubly heavy as they decreased the association's material possibilities, but at the same time, they increased its responsibilities. There had to be an expansion of aid and care, which were needed by the associated members in all areas. In the period when the association was able to do the least it had to be able to do the most, because that is what the situation required. Let us turn our attention next to the consequences of the social composition of the cooperative's membership. Ideologically, it was a desirable fact that they came exclusively from the world of work, but at the same time this meant limitations on their financial possibilities and thus on the possibility of contributing to the association's aims. But the other side of this question should not be forgotten. Perhaps if the cooperative were populated by rich entrepreneurs and representatives of the financial spheres, there would be people in this milieu capable of contributing significantly more to the aims of the institution, but it could also be said with a large degree of likelihood that they would not want to do so. The milieu that organized the Warsaw Housing Cooperative is indubitably poor, but it has one quite irreplaceable trait; it is comparatively very well socialized. It is only due to this factor that in a period when most such institutions experienced weakened activity and growth, Glass Houses was on the path of continual development.

One expression of the social value of this cooperative environment was the drive to organize. The numerical growth in the membership of Glass Houses clearly illustrates the phenomenon. The idea that all the tenants of the Warsaw Housing Cooperative would automatically belong to the tenants' association, which might have been desirable from certain angles, turned out not to be workable. The association is based on voluntary membership. In addition, the scope of membership enrollment is limited, as in nearly every association. Only a resident of the Warsaw Housing Cooperative can be a member of Glass Houses, and there are only 4,600 such residents. But it is only the adult residents who are eligible and of these there are not quite 3,200. While other associations operate among tens or hundreds of thousands of persons, Glass Houses is limited to 3,000 from which to enroll its members. Furthermore, in today's economic conditions, can it be expected that there will be a mass movement for all the adult members of a family to belong to the association? It is clear that this could happen only exceptionally. There are only around 1,300 independent tenants in the cooperative.

Table 21.1 presents the results of the organizational drive and of Glass Houses' organizational activities over the course of its existence:

Thus 44% of all the adult inhabitants of the settlement belong to the tenants' organization. If we discount family members from the total number of members of the association, and count only the main tenants, we will see that 63% of them are members of Glass Houses. The ideal is undoubtedly 100%, but there is an excuse for what has been achieved. It should not be forgotten that

TABLE 21.1   *The numbers of members*

Year	1928	1929	1930	1931	1932	1933	1934	1935	1936
Number of members	143	232	372	531	789	1078	1001	1152	1403

what comes into play here is a dual self-organization and that all are already united within the cooperative itself.

This is a quantitative achievement; let us thus delve into those figures. We want to call attention to a certain moment as being special. The cooperative, and Glass Houses with it, organizes the world of workers, both white-collar and physical ones. In this manner, workers in these two categories meet in the common sphere of social work. This is an enormously desirable phenomenon. Everything works toward dividing the world of work, of separating the white-collar worker from his colleague who works physically. The ideas of solidarity are beginning, though, to put down roots. But no declarations, no official resolutions of congresses, no ceremonious manifestations of solidarity, mean as much as the practical school of cooperation. And in this field Glass Houses has achieved noteworthy results. How the present-day practice of constructing special workers' settlements only for manual laborers departs from this activity! Glass Houses can claim that it has been possible to at least partially tear down that wall by which the workers' camp was divided into two parts, unacquainted and mutually distrusting each other, but bound together by the same misery.

Organizing a considerable number of people is only a positive social manifestation if it is a prelude to action. Thus among the guidelines by which Glass Houses operates—right beside the idea of organizing the largest possible percentage of the cooperative's residents (the ideal is 100%)—another was placed: to activate the largest possible number of members. To have passive members, even paying regular dues, would not have satisfied the association's ambitions. Work had to be organized in such a way that the largest possible number of members would volunteer to work and not solely a few compulsive social workers connected with the management. This requires skilful organization. The work of the members might be dual in nature: as active creators of the association's benefits and as consumers of those benefits. Participation in consumption, which is passive, through use of the association's arrangements, has reached various levels in various areas. The highest level is reached in the library, with up to 80% of members making use of its collections. Active participation is harder to achieve. But in this area as well the results are considerable. It has been possible to enlist several hundred persons to work in the management board, in a range of committees, in tenants' clubs, and in various musical and artistic groups; thus in all 25% of the members are continually and actively involved in directing the association's agendas. In this case, the hundred-percent ideal has to be the guiding light, but anyone who is familiar with the internal life of associations in Poland will admit that this level of activity is relatively high.

How does Glass Houses achieve its aims? We will discuss three of the above-mentioned areas. Defense of the interests and concern for the needs of the tenants occurs in quite special conditions. There is no question here of tenants' relations with the building owners; there is no social opposition, no opposition of interests. The relation of the tenants' association to the cooperative authorities consists in the division of work. There are things that the authorities, in the onslaught of tasks, might overlook or be unable to cope with. Finally, the cooperative authorities must represent a special viewpoint—the viewpoint of the whole, we could call it. The tenants' association must look at questions from the side of the tenants, their needs and possibilities. The cooperative authorities will naturally be guided by the tendency to build as much as possible, to pay the cooperative's debts as soon as possible. The tenants' association must balance these proper aims with the financial possibilities of its members. The proper policy of the cooperative can only emerge from this opposition. The task of the tenants' organization, acting within the cooperative to protect the interests of the tenants, must therefore consist of: (1) representing the body of tenants externally, in regard to the state authorities and local self-government bodies; (2) representing the tenants' internally, in regard to the cooperative authorities; (3) organizing cooperation with these authorities by creating a tenants' self-management group, to adopt part of the administrative tasks and take over the provision of relief in paying rent, based on an exact acquaintance with the precise situation of particular tenants.

This borders another of Glass Houses' fundamental tasks—organizing care and material aid for the members. This is an activity with a clear self-help rather than philanthropic nature because it must encompass all residents who find themselves in a situation requiring help, and must likewise burden all. The cooperative can not descend to the role of a landlord, who provides an apartment and is concerned with nothing beyond the receipt of rent and the state of the premises. The cooperative can not be indifferent to the fact that tragedies may be unfolding in certain apartments. It is a matter of creating an interest in the fate of other residents—not a gossip's interest but a social one. The cooperative is a society based on the principles of solidarity and cooperation. It must cooperate in the elimination of evil as well. It would be proof of a lack of all socialization if, as in private apartment buildings, the neighbors remained indifferent to the fact that beyond their walls someone might be dying from lack of funds for treatment or the neighbor's children are unable to attend school. Glass Houses organizes loans, and in certain cases nonrefundable financial aid, for everyone affected by misfortune. It organizes this aid out of its own funds or from funds provided for its disposition by the cooperative itself, either in the form of permanent participation in covering the association's budget or

TABLE 21.2   *Glass houses fund activity*

Year	From the associa- tion's own funds	Loans guaranteed by the association	From the tempo- rary aid fund	Total
1930	7,330			7,330
1931	15,524			15,524
1932	30,474		25,885	66,359
1933	24,394	18,064	63,918	106,376
1934	19,015	18,755	62,840	100,610
1935	21,028	10,571	61,737	93,336

through creation of a temporary aid fund at the disposal of Glass Houses. This fund emerged in the period when the crisis was most intense, that is, in 1932.

The dimensions of this activity are shown by the numbers in Table 21.2 below:

If we add the year 1936, it can be assumed that the financial aid granted by the association in various forms (99% in loans paid on easy terms) amounted to around half a million zlotys in the course of a few years. Most of these sums were provided to cover rent or as relief in paying rent for unemployed or poorly paid persons. On average 65% of loans from the association's own funds, all the guaranteed loans, and around 25% of the temporary aid fund, were provided for these purposes every year. Other than that, the temporary aid fund served to cover part of the costs of heating apartments for all tenants, to feed children, and to cover the school registration costs for the less well-to-do members. Around 11% of the loans from the association's own funds were designated for aid in cases of illness or death. It should not be forgotten that the majority of members of the association have access to aid from various kinds of health insurance. Before exhausting the subject of self-aid, it should still be noted that the association organizes employment mediation for its members. The development of cooperative life creates a range of employment opportunities (putting up new buildings, maintaining the institutions operating within the cooperative settlements). This does not eliminate the unemployment crisis within the cooperative circle, but at least it contributes to its amelioration.

Glass Houses' main activities, however, are in the sphere of culture and education. Due to the narrowness of this article, we must limit ourselves to a brief list of the association's departments in this kind of work. It should be mentioned that these departments have grown so much with the association's

TABLE 21.3   *The growth of libraries*

Year	1929	1930	1931	1932	1933	1934	1935	1936
Books	2,259	3,435	3,682	5,441	6,448	7,172	8,022	9,232
Readers	197	411	512	730	950	1,008	1,115	1,322

development that the association was obliged to rent a whole single-story house—which turned out to be insufficient—for these purposes, and in addition it has the use of a lecture hall and theatre room in the cooperative's buildings for larger events.

Three departments in the association are devoted to the organization of reading facilities: (1) two main libraries in both of the cooperative's settlements; (2) an academic library in premises in Żoliborz; (3) two reading rooms for journals in both settlements. The growth of the book collections and reading in libraries is illustrated by Table 21.3 below:

It can be calculated on the basis of library statistics that in the course of these years around 200,000 books were loaned to library users. The statistics show the gradual strong growth in the reading of scientific texts. It should be pointed out that these libraries are continually supplemented and added to and are at the level of the contemporary publishing movement. The academic library, which has textbooks and encyclopedias, provides an important service.

The next department of educational work involves lecturing. This occurs in three forms: (1) lectures; (2) discussion evenings combined with reading a report; (3) regular courses. Until 1930 these activities were occasional, but since 1931 they have become permanent features. With the exception of the summer months and the holiday weeks, every week there is either a lecture or a discussion evening. Thus every year thirty-some evenings are devoted to these purposes, with the participation of outstanding speakers. The discussions can be very lively, are at a good level, and sometimes draw attendance from the whole city. In total Glass Houses has organized to this time around 180 lectures, on a range of social and scientific topics and with the participation of over a dozen thousand audience members. The regular courses are various in nature. Glass Houses has so far organized: (1) general scientific courses; (2) courses in social education; (3) courses for social workers; (4) general education courses; (5) language courses; (6) vocational courses. Over the space of four years several tens of courses of this type have been conducted, with the participation of several hundred persons.

Another important department of the association's work concerns art and music. This is developing along several paths: (1) the creation of musical groups (in the course of recent years the association has provided for a wind orchestra, a symphonic orchestra, a mandolin orchestra, and a choir); (2) the organization of musical training for particular groups; (3) the giving of popular concerts; (4) the organization of chamber concerts (in the last several years thirty-some concerts were organized and over a dozen academies, combined with lectures and the participation of over a dozen thousand attendees); (5) the organization of exhibitions of fine arts; (6) the creation of art workshops; (7) the offering of courses in drawing and painting; (8) the organization of artistic and literary evenings.

All this activity is supplemented by a whole range of clubs, of which each has some tens of members. At various times, there have also been clubs for art, Esperanto, women, stamp collecting, tourism, and intellectual games. Some have organized lectures and talks from time to time. The women's club, for instance, organizes them every week.

Finally, we should mention a department which was the last to be organized but which has grown into one of the most important organizational units—the department of work among the youth. It consists in created youth groups and guiding them by means of self-learning, sports, culture and education, clubs, and workshops.

Given the existence of so many varied departments it is not surprising that every evening over a dozen association rooms and other social premises are packed with occupants. Here there is a lecture; there various courses are taking place; here a musical group is practicing; here again youth groups are gathering; over there are artists; here books are being loaned; there in the reading room several tens of persons are reading newspapers; and there in the club people are playing chess. If one notes the fact that the participants in these activities are people who are prevented by the difficult conditions of the present era from possessing very large personal apartments, we will understand that the club premises of the association are an important supplement to their own "corner." It not infrequently happens that a father is at a lecture or in the mental-games club, his wife is in the women's club, and their son or daughter is taking classes in the youth center.

Glass Houses' activity relies almost exclusively on funds provided by members, either directly or indirectly. And these are relatively large sums for a social organization of a labor nature. In 1930 the association expended 14,000 zlotys annually; presently the sum has grown to over 50,000. The sum the members pay directly as dues is fairly large. It amounted to over 6,000 annually in 1930; in 1936 it is over 17,000. If we add to this the sum of 8,000 from the cooperative's so-called social-education fund, which comes from the monthly contributions of all the tenants, paid together with the rent, we receive 25,000 zlotys from the residents of the housing settlement. Around 5,000 zlotys comes from library, lecture, course, or concert fees. The rest are mainly "operating" sums, which for various reasons the cooperative pays for loans; these are guaranteed by contributors' shares and thus also come indirectly from the tenants. The institution practically does not receive outside subsidies. The development of so much activity based on the association's own forces is a fact worthy of emphasizing today.

There is one more point worthy of attention. In the association, people of varying, often divergent, ideologies meet. How do they coexist? Does the association avoid the dual danger of: (1) falling under the sway of one ideology; (2) turning into a field for fierce political fighting? We can not conceal that Glass Houses passed through some difficult moments in this regard before matters were properly settled. And yet they were settled. After many conflicts, the principle was introduced that the association was a ground for the cooperation of people of differing views. If the members had not been linked by social bonds, it would perhaps have been impossible to accomplish. But the differences in worldview can not be so fundamental when all belong to the world of work and are on the same side of the social divide. The principle of cooperation does not in the least exclude the exchange of ideas and the comparison of varying views. But the principles of social life make it possible for this to occur in an atmosphere of well-meaning cooperation and mutual respect, in an atmosphere in which it is possible to be persuaded, to understand another position, and even to agree.

The additional results that have been achieved in this area are undoubtedly an indication that the cooperative environment is an ideal sphere for the development of far-reaching, planned, and vigorous cultural and educational activity. The cooperative effort has given birth to new efforts, which have changed the passive environment of the co-residents into a center for the growth of a new kind of life.

Bibliography

Edward Abramowski

The largest selection of Edward Abramowski's works can be found in *Pisma* [*Writings*]
K. Krzeczkowski (compilation and introduction), vol. 1–4, Warsaw 1924, 1927, 1928,
edition of the Związek Spółdzielni Spożywców Rzeczpospolitej Polskiej [Union of
Consumer Cooperatives of the Republic of Poland].

Selected Works

"Budowa domow mieszkalnych" ["Construction of Residential Buildings"], *Społem* 1907,
no. 14.

"Czym mają być Związki Przyjaźni" ["What Are Friendship Unions to Be?"], *Społem* 1912,
no. 6; reprinted in: idem, *Pisma* [*Writings*], vol. 1.

[Stanisława Motz-Abramowska], *"Dobra nowina robotnikom wiejskim"* ["Good News for
Rural Workers"], London-Paris 1892, reprinted in: idem, *Pisma* [*Writings*], vol. 4.

"Idee społeczne kooperatyzmu" ["The Social Idea of Cooperativism"], *Społem* [*Together*]
1907, no. 1–6; reprinted in: idem, *Pisma* [*Writings*], vol. 1.

"Kasy pomocy wzajemnej i ubezpieczenia" ["Mutual Aid and Insurance Funds"], *Społem*
[*Together*] 1907, no. 13.

"Kooperatywa jako sprawa wyzwolenia ludu pracującego" ["The Cooperative as a Matter
of Freeing the Working People"], Warsaw 1928, Wydawnictwo Związku Spółdzielni
Spożywów [Union of Consumer Cooperatives Publishers]; reprinted in: idem,
Pisma [*Writings*], vol. 1.

"Korzyści jakie daje kooperatywa spożywcza" ["The Advantages of a Food Cooperative"],
Społem [*Together*] 1907, no. 10–12.

"Kto jest właścicielem fabryk kooperatywnych" ["Who Owns Cooperative Factories?"],
Społem [*Together*] 1907, no. 26.

"Listy w sprawie zwołania pierwszych zjazdów spółdzielców" ["Letters in the Matter of
Convening the First Cooperative Congresses"], in: idem, *Pisma* [*Writings*], vol. 1.

"O znaczeniu stowarzyszeń" ["On the Meaning of Associations"], in: idem, *Pisma* [*Writings*], vol. 1.

"Odczyt o Związkach Przyjaźni" ["Lecture on Friendship Unions"], in: idem, *Pisma*,
vol. 1.

"Projekt ustawy Związków Przyjaźni" ["Draft Rule for Friendship Unions"], *Społem*
[*Together*] 1912, no. 7; reprinted in: idem, *Pisma* [*Writings*], vol. 1.

"Rzeczpospolita kooperatywna" ["The Cooperative Republic"], *Społem* [*Together*] 1912,
no. 4.

"Socjalizm i kooperatyzm" ["Socialism and Cooperativism"], *Społem* [*Together*] 1912, no. 3.

Statut Stowarzyszenia Komuna w Genewie [*Statute of the Association of Geneva Communes*], London 1900.

"Stowarzyszenia i ich rola" ["Cooperatives and their Role]", in: idem, *Pisma* [*Writings*], vol. 1.

[E.A.] *"Stowarzyszenia i państwo"* ["Associations and the State"], *Gazeta Wileńska* [*Vilnius Gazette*] 1906, no. 31.

"Stowarzyszenie wytwórcze robotników przemysłowych" ["Production Cooperatives of Industrial Workers"], *Społem* [*Together*] 1907, no. 17.

[Stanisława Motz–Abramowska], *"Ustawa kasy oporu wśród robotnic"* ["Rule for a Resistance Fund Among Workers"], *Przedświt* [*Daybreak*] 1895, nos. 1, 2, 3.

"Ustawa stowarzyszenia „Komuna'" ["Rule of the Association of Communes"], London 1900; reprinted in: idem, *Pisma* [*Writings*], vol. 1.

"Warunki pracy w zakładach kooperatywnych" ["Work Conditions in Cooperative Factories"], *Społem* [*Together*] 1907, no. 25.

"Warunki rozwoju produkcji kooperatywnej" ["Development Conditions of Cooperative Production"], *Społem* [*Together*] 1907, no. 24.

Zagadnienia socjalizmu [*Issues in Socialism*], Lwów 1899, B. Połoniecki.

"Zasada ekonomiczna kooperatywy spożywczej" ["Economic Principle of a Food Cooperative"], *Społem* 1907, no. 7, 8.

"Zasady republiki kooperatywnej" ["Principles of a Cooperative Republic"]; reprinted in: idem, *Pisma* [*Writings*], vol. 1.

"Znaczenie społeczne instytucji ludowych" ["The Significance of the People's Social Institution"], *Społem* [*Together*] 1907, no. 16.

"Znaczenie spółdzielczości dla demokracji" ["The Importance of Cooperativism for Democracy"], *Idee Współdzielczości* [*The Ideas of Cooperativism*] (daily), Biblioteka Kooperatysty [Cooperativists' Library] no. 1, Warsaw 1906, Towarzystwo Kooperatystów [Cooperativists' Society]; reprinted in: idem, *Pisma* [*Writings*], vol. 1.

"Związki Przyjaźni" ["Friendship Unions"], *Społem* [*Together*] 1912, no. 2; reprinted in: idem, *Pisma* [*Writings*], vol. 1.

"Związki zakupów hurtowych" ["Wholesale Purchase Unions"], *Społem* [*Together*] 1907, no. 22.

Selected Texts Published after 1945

Braterstwo, solidarność, współdziałanie: Pisma spółdzielcze i stowarzyszeniowe [*Fraternity, Solidarity, Joint Action: Cooperative and Association Writings*], Łódź–Sopot–Warsaw 2009, Stowarzyszenie „Obywatele Obywatelom," Krajowa Rada Spółdzielcza, Instytut Spraw Obywatelskich, Instytut Stefczyka [Citizens-to-Citizens Association, National Cooperative Council, Institute of Civil Affairs, Stefczyk Institute].

Filozofia społeczna. Wybór pism [*Social Philosophy: Selected Writings*], Warsaw 1965, PWN.

Kooperatywa: polskie korzenie przedsiębiorczości społecznej [*The Cooperative: The Polish Roots of Social Entrepreneurship*], Łódź 2010, Stowarzyszenie Obywatele Obywatelom [Citizens-to-Citizens Association].

Metafizyka doświadczalna i inne pisma [*Experiential Metaphysics and Other Writings*], Warsaw 1980, PWN.

Pisma filzoficzno-psychologiczne [Philosophical and Psychological Writings], Warsaw 2016, Fundacja Augusta Hrabiego Cieszkowskiego [Count August Cieszkowski Foundation].

Pisma popularnonaukowe i propagandowe [*Popular-Scientific and Promotional Writings*], Warsaw 1979, KiW.

Rzeczpospolita przyjaciół: wybór pism społecznych i politycznych [*A Republic of Friends: Selected Social and Political Writings*], Warsaw 1986, PAX.

Wybór pism estetycznych [*Selected Esthetic Writings*], Kraków 2011, Universitas.

Zagadnienia socjalizmu. Wybór pism [*Issues of Socialism: Selected Writings*], Kraków 2012, Ośrodek Myśli Politycznej, Wydział Studiów Międzynarodowych i Politycznych UJ [Center for Political Thought, Department of International and Political Studies, Jagiellonian University].

Selected Subject Bibliography

Augustyniak M., *Myśl społeczno-filozoficzna Edwarda Abramowskiego* [*Edward Abramowski's Social and Philosophical Thinking*], Olsztyn 2006, Wydawnictwo Uniwersytetu Warmińsko-Mazurskiego [University of Warmia and Masuria Publishers].

Biliński K., *Idea spółdzielczości w koncepcji ustrojowej Edwarda Abramowskiego* [*The Idea of Cooperativism in Edward Abramowski's Concept of a Political System*], Toruń 1994, s.n., Acta Universitatis Nicolai Copernici. Nauki Humanistyczno-Społeczne. Prawo XXXIV, z. 284 [Record of Copernicus University, Humanities and Social Sciences, Law XXXIV, no. 284].

Borzym S., *"Etyka społeczna Edwarda Abramowskiego"* ["The Social Ethics of Edward Ambramowski"], in: idem, *Panorama Polskiej Myśli Filozoficznej* [*Panorama of Polish Philosophical Thought*], Warsaw 1993, PWN; reprinted in: Poznań 2002, Oficyna Wydawnicza Bractwa Trójka [Trójka Brotherhood Publishers].

Borzym S., *"Edward Abramowski"* ["Edward Abramowski"], in: *Zarys dziejów filozofii polskiej 1815–1918* [*Outline of the History of Polish Philosophy, 1815–1918*], A. Walicki (ed.), Warsaw 1983, PWN.

Borzym S., *"Edward Abramowski—filozof epoki modernizmu"* ["Edward Abramowski— Philosopher of the Modern Era"], in: E. Abramowski, *Metafizyka doświadczalna i inne pisma* [*Experiential Metaphysics and Other Writings*], Warsaw 1980, PWN.

Borzym S., *W kręgu idei bergsonowskich w Polsce: Abramowski i Znaniecki* [*Bergsonian Ideas in Poland: Abramowski and Znaniecki*], *Archiwum Historii Filozofii i Myśli Społecznej* [*Archive of the History of Philosophy and Social Thought*] 1977, vol. 23.

Dąbrowska M., *Życie i dzieło Edwarda Abramowskiego* [*The Life and Work of Edward Abramowski*], Warsaw 1925, Wydawnictwo Związku Polskich Stowarzyszeń Spożywców [Publishing House of the Union of Polish Consumer Cooperatives].

Dobrzycka U., *Abramowski*, Warsaw 1990, Wiedza Powszechna.

Dziedzic A., *Antropologia filozoficzna Edwarda Abramowskiego* [*The Philosophical Anthropology of Edward Abramowski*], Wrocław 2010, Wydawnictwa UWr [University of Wrocław Press].

Chyra-Rolicz Z., *"Edward Abramowski—prekursor społeczeństwa obywatelskiego i społecznej gospodarki rynkowej (1869–1918)"* ["Edward Abramowski—A Forerunner of Civil Society and Social Market Economy (1869–1918)"], in: *Od Edwarda Abramowskiego do Jana Jozefa Lipskiego. Z dziejów niepodległościowego i demokratycznego nurtu w polskim ruchu socjalistycznym* [*From Edward Abramowski to Jan Józef Lipski: On the History of the Independence and Democracy Current in the Polish Socialist Movement*], M.M. Drozdowski (ed.), Warsaw 2002, Towarzystwo Miłośnikow Historii, Komisja badania Dziejów Warszawy IH PAN [Friends of History Society, Committee Studying the History of Warsaw, Institute of History of the Polish Academy of Sciences], letterpress.

Giełżyński W., *Edward Abramowski: zwiastun „Solidarności"* [*Edward Abramowski: Herald of Solidarity*], London 1986, Polonia.

Jezierski R., *Poglądy etyczne Edwarda Abramowskiego* [*Edward Abramowski's Ethical Views*], Poznań 1970, Wydawnictwa Poznańskie [Poznań Publishers].

Kaczyński J., *Studia z historii idei w Polsce. Edward Abramowski i Jan Karol Kochanowski* [*Studies in the History of Ideas in Poland: Edward Abramowski and Jan Karol Kochanowski*], Olsztyn 1989, Wydawnictwo WSP [WSP Publishers].

Krawczyk Z., *Socjologia Edwarda Abramowskiego* [*The Sociology of Edward Abramowski*], Warsaw 1965, KiW.

Krzeczkowski K., *Dzieje życia i twórczości Edwarda Abramowskiego* [*The Life and Work of Edward Abramowski*], Warsaw 1933.

Krzeczkowski K., *"Edward Abramowski (1879–1939)"* in: E. Abramowski, *Pisma* [*Writings*], vol. 1.

Lange O., *Socjologia i idee społeczne Edwarda Abramowskiego* [*The Sociology and Social Ideas of Edward Abramowski*], Kraków 1928, Krakowska Spółka Wydawnicza [Kraków Publishing Company].

Mencwel A., *"Edward Abramowski,"* in: *Kulturologia polska XX wieku* [*Polish Culturology of the 20th Century*], G. Godlewski et al. (ed.), A. Mencwel (introduction), vol. 1: A–K, Warsaw 2013, Wydawnictwa Uniwersytetu Warszawskiego [University of Warsaw Publishers].

Okraska R., *Posłowie. Braterstwo ponad wszystko* ["Deputies: Brotherhood Above All"], in: *Braterstwo, solidarność, współdziałanie: Pisma spółdzielcze i stowarzyszeniowe* [*Fraternity, Solidarity, Joint Action: Writings on Cooperatives and Associations*], Łódź–Sopot–Warsaw 2009, Stowarzyszenie „Obywatele Obywatelom," Krajowa Rada Spółdzielcza,

Instytut Spraw Obywatelskich, Instytut Stefczyka [Citizens-to-Citizens Association, National Cooperative Council, Institute of Civil Affairs, Stefczyk Institute].

Paradowski R., *Światopogląd Edwarda Abramowskiego* [*The Worldview of Edward Abramowski*], Warsaw 1990.

Salwiński J., *"Edward Abramowski. Poglądy na temat państwa i demokracji parlamentarnej"* ["Edward Abramowski: Views on the Subject of the State and Parliamentary Democracy"], *Rewolta* [*Revolt*] (an anarchistic publication) 1989, no. 3.

Samotyhowa N., *Edward Abramowski i jego poglądy na znaczenie dobra i piękna w przebudowie życia* [*Edward Abramowsi and his Views on the Meaning of the Good and the Beautiful in the Rebuilding of Life*], Warsaw 1931, Wydawnictwo Towarzystwa Kultury Etycznej im. Edwarda Abramowskiego [Edward Abramowski Ethical Culture Society Publishers].

Światło R., *Przedmowa* ["Foreword"], in: E. Abramowski, *Filozofia społeczna. Wybór pism* [*Social Philosophy: Selected Writings*], Warsaw 1965, PWN.

Fr. Stanisław Adamski

Selected Works

Dlaczego duchowieństwo zajmuje się pracą społeczną [*Why the Clergy Is Engaged in Social Work*], Poznań 1921, Księgarnia św. Wojciecha [St. Adalbert Bookstore].

Kasy oszczędnościowe w obrębie towarzystw [*Savings Banks Within Societies*], Poznań 1904, Drukarnia i Księgarnia św. Wojciecha [St. Adalbert Bookstore and Press].

Kilka słow o „Zakładzie Kornickim" ["A Few Words About the 'Kórnickie Facilities'"], *Wiadomości dla duchowieństwa* [*News for the Clergy*] 1921, no. 12.

Najbliższe zadania spółdzielczości zorganizowanej w Związku Spółdzielni Zarobkowych i Gospodarczych [*The Most Pressing Tasks of Cooperativism Organized in the Union of Labor and Farm Cooperatives*], Poznań 1924, Związek Spółdzielni Zarobkowych i Gospodarczych [Union of Labor and Farm Cooperatives].

Podstawy pracy stowarzyszeń Akcji Katolickiej [*Work Bases of the Catholic Action Association*], Poznań 1937, Naczelny Instytut Akcji Katolickiej [Main Institute of Catholic Action].

Przeszłość i przyszłość „Rolników" Spółdzielni rolniczo-handlowych [*The Past and Future of the Farmers' Agricultural and Trade Cooperatives*], Poznań 1924, Związek Spółdzielni Zarobkowych i Gospodarczych [Union of Labor and Farm Cooperatives].

Ruch spółdzielczy w Polsce oraz znaczenie i zadania unji związków spółdzielczych [*The Cooperative Movement in Poland and the Meaning and Tasks of the League of Cooperative Unions*], Poznań 1930, Unja Związków Spółdzielczych w Polsce [League of Cooperative Unions in Poland].

Spółdzielczość w Wielkopolsce i na Pomorzu ["Cooperativism in Greater Poland and Pomerania"], *Poradnik Spółdzielni* [*Guide for Cooperatives*] 1925, no. 7.

Sposób zakładania towarzystw robotników katolickich [*How to Found Catholic Workers' Societies*], Poznań 1907, Drukarnia i Księgarnia św. Wojciecha [St. Adalbert Bookstore and Press].

Stowarzyszenia Katolickich Towarzystw Robotników Polskich w obrębie archidiecezji gnieźnieńskiej i poznańskiej, ["Catholic Associations of Polish Workers' Societies Within the Gniezno and Poznań Archdioceses"], *Unitas*, 1910, vol. 3, no. 13–18.

Stowarzyszenia polskie wobec ustawy o stowarzyszeniach i zebraniach obowiązującej od 15-go maja 1908: praktyczne wskazówki dla zarządów i przewodniczących ze szczególnem uwzględnieniem sposobu zakładania nowych stowarzyszeń [*Polish Associations and the New Act on Associations and Assemblies in Force from May 15, 1908: Practical Guidelines for Management Boards and Leaders with Particular Consideration of the Establishment of New Associations*], Poznań 1909, s.n. *Unja Związków Spółdzielczych w Polsce* [*The League of Cooperative Unions in Poland*], Poznań 1929, Unja Związków Spółdzielczych w Polsce [League of Cooperative Unions in Poland].

Z dziejów rozwoju spółkowego w naszym związku ["On Company Development in Our Union"], *Poradnik dla Spółek* [*Guide for Companies*] 1915, no. 8.

Z dziejów rozwoju społecznego w naszym Związku ["On Social Development in Our Union"], *Poradnik dla Spółek* [*Guide for Companies*] 1917, no. 8.

Z ideologii spółdzielczości w ostatniej dobie [*On the Ideology of Cooperativism in the Recent Period*], *Poradnik Spółdzielni* [*Guide for Cooperatives*] 1925, no. 9.

Zapasy narodowościowe we „wschodnich dzielnicach" ["Resources of Nationalities in the 'Eastern Districts'"], *Ruch Chrześcijańsko-Społeczny* [*Christian Social Movement*] 1906, no. 7.

Zasadnicze kierunki katolickiej pracy społecznej [*Basic Trends in Catholic Social Work*], Poznań 1923, Księgarnia Społeczna [Social Bookstore].

Zasady pracy spółkowej: w świetle uchwał i doświadczeń Związku Spółek Zarobkowych i Gospodarczych na W.X. Poznańskie i Prusy Zachodnie [*Principles of Social Work: In the Light of the Resolutions and Experiences of the Union of Labor and Farm Companies in the Grand Duchy of Posen and Western Prussia*], Part 1: *Materyały* [*Materials*], Poznań 1918, Drukarnia i Księgarnia św. Wojciecha [St. Adalbert Bookstore and Press].

Zasady pracy społecznej [*Principles of Social Work*], Poznań 1918.

Selected Subject Bibliography

Michalski B., "*Działalność społeczno-polityczna księdza Stanisława Adamskiego w latach 1899–1930*" ["The Socio-Political Activities of Fr. Stanisław Adamski in the Years 1899–1930"], *Chrześcijanin w Świecie* [*The Christian in the World*] 1977, no. 59–60.

Szaraniec K., *Ks. Stanisław Adamski* [*Fr. Stanisław Adamski*], Part 1: *W kręgu społecznej działalności: 1904–1918* [*In the Sphere of Social Activity: 1904–1918*], Katowice 1990, Muzeum Śląskie [Museum of Silesia].

Szaraniec K., *Ksiądz Stanisław Adamski: duchowy przywódca Polaków pod zaborem pruskim, patron polskiej spółdzielczości, poseł, senator, biskup* [*Fr. Stanisław Adamski:*

Spritual Leader of Poles in the Prussian Partition, Patron of Polish Cooperativism, Deputy, Senator, Bishop], Katowice 2011, Wydawnictwo Unia Jerzy Skwara [Unia Publishers, Jerzy Skwara].

Z życia i publicznej działalności biskupa Stanisława Adamskiego [*On the Life and Public Activities of Bishop Stanisław Adamski*], A. Gulczyński (ed. and compilation), Poznań 2000, Drukarnia i Księgarnia Świętego Wojciecha [St. Adalbert Bookstore and Printers].

Leopold Caro

Selected Works

"Chrześcijańskie pojęcie własności prywatnej" ["The Christian Idea of Private Property"], *"Gazeta Kościelna"* [*Church Gazette*] 1907.

"Duchowieństwo a kwestja społeczna" ["The Priesthood and the Social Question"], *"Gazeta Kościelna"* [*Church Gazette*] 1907.

"Ekonomia społeczna Karola Gide'a" ["The Social Economics of Charles Gide"], 1893, no. 255.

"Idea spółdzielczości" ["The Idea of Cooperativism"], *Przegląd Powszechny* [*General Review*] 1922, July.

"Istota solidaryzmu" ["The Essence of Solidarism"], *Przegląd Powszechny* [*General Reivew*] 1930, May.

"Nowe poglądy na rolę altruizmu w gospodarstwie społecznem" ["New Views on the Role of Altruism in the Social Economy"], *Słowo Polskie* [*Polish Word*] 1930, May.

Pomoc dla rolników w Austrii ["Help for Farmers in Austria"], Lwów 1895, s.n.

"Przedmowa" ["Foreword"], in: W. Jenner, *Ekonomika ruchu spółdzielczego* [*Economics of the Cooperative Movement*], Lwów 1932, Dom „Książki Polskiej" [main supply, House of Polish Books].

"Przedmowa" ["Foreword"], in: H, Korowicz, *Polityka agrarna w zarysie* [*Agrarian Policy in Outline*], Part 1, Lwów 1933, Wyższa Szkoła Handlu Zagranicznego [Higher School of Foreign Trade].

"Przewrót agrarny w Rosji" ["Agrarian Upheaval in Russia"], *Rolnictwo* [*Agriculture*] 1928, no. 12.

"Przewrót w ekonomice społecznej" ["Upheaval in Social Economics"], Przegląd Powszechny [*General Review*] 1931, November.

"Przez spółdzielczość do solidaryzmu" ["Through Cooperativism to Solidarism"], *Biuletyn Naukowego Instytutu Spółdzielczego* [*Bulletin of the Cooperative Scientific Institute*] 1929.

"Przyszłe drogi naszej polityki gospodarczej i społecznej" ["The Future Paths of Our Economic and Social Policy"], *Przemysł i Handel* [*Industry and Trade*], December 1, 1928.

Reformy gospodarcze i społeczne faszyzmu [*The Economic and Social Reforms of Fascism*], Warsaw 1938.

"Solidaryzm a spółdzielczość" ["Solidarism and Cooperativism"], *Prąd* [*The Current*] 1926, no. 7–8.

Solidaryzm: jego zasady, dzieje i zastosowania [*Solidarism: Its Ideas, History, and Application*], Lwów 1931, on a grant from the Fundusz Kultury Narodowej [National Culture Foundation].

Studya społeczne [*A Social Study*], Kraków 1906, main supply in the Księgarnia S.A. Krzyżanowskiego [Bookstore of S.A. Krzyżanowski].

"Szkoła solidarystyczna i Kościół Katolicki o kwestii społecznej" ["The Solidarist School and the Catholic Church on the Social Question"], *Ateneum Kapłańskie* [*The Priestly Atheneum*] 1927, no. 27.

Własność prywatna, jej utrzymanie czy ograniczenie? [*Private Property: Its Maintenance or Limitation?*], Lwów 1933.

Współczesne prądy gospodarcze a spółdzielczość [*Contemporary Economic Currents and Cooperativism*], Lwów 1932, Związek Towarzystw Gospodarczych i Zarobkowych [Union of Farm and Labor Societies].

"Zadania katolicyzmu społecznego" ["The Tasks of Social Catholicism"], *Ateneum Kapłańskie* [*The Priestly Atheneum*] 1926, January.

"Zawodowe organizacje rolników" ["Farmers' Organizations"], *Przegląd Powszechny* [*General Review*] 1902.

Zasady nauki ekonomii społecznej [*The Principles of Social Economics*], Lwów 1926, K.S. Jakubowski.

Załęcki G., *„Zasady nauki ekonomii społecznej" dra Leopolda Caro w świetle polemiki* [*Dr. Leopold Caro's 'The Principles of Social Economics' in the Light of Polemics*], Warsaw 1927.

"Zmierzch kapitalizmu" ["The Decline of Capitalism"], Poznań 1934, *Dziennika Poznańskiego* [*Poznań Daily*] print.

Zmierzch kapitalizmu. Wybór pism [*The Decline of Capitalism: Selected Writings*], Kraków 2012, Ośrodek Myśli Politycznej, Wydział Studiów Międzynarodowych i Politycznych UJ [Center for Political Thought, Department of International and Political Studies, Jagiellonian University].

Selected Subject Bibliography

50 lat życia ekonomicznego i społecznego. Księga pamiątkowa ku czci śp. dra Leopolda Caro [*50 years of Economic and Social Life: Memorial Book in Honor of the Late Dr. Leopold Caro*], E. Hauswald (ed.), Lwów 1939, Polskie Towarzystwo Ekonomiczne we Lwowie [Polish Economic Society in Lwów].

Księga pamiątkowa ku czci Leopolda Caro [*Memorial Book in Honor of Leopold Caro*], K. Paygert (ed.), Lwów 1935, Książnica–Atlas [Atlas Library].

Bomanowski D., *"Poglądy solidarystyczne Leopolda Caro"* ["The Solidarist Views of Leopold Caro"], in: *Myśl ekonomiczna II Rzeczpospolitej. Materiały z konferencji* [*Economic Thought in the 2nd Republic: Materials from a Conference*], U. Zagora-Jonszta (ed.), Katowice 1997, Wydawnictwa Uczelniane Akademii Ekonomicznej im. Karola Adamieckiego w Katowicach [Academic Publishers of the Karol Adamiecki Academy of Economics in Katowice].

Lejman W., *"Ekonomia polityczna, idea solidaryzmu i polityka gospodarcza w pracach L. Caro: (1864–1939)"* ["Political Economics, the Idea of Solidarism, and Economic Policy in the Works of L. Caro (1864–1939)]," *Międzyuczelniane Zeszyty Naukowe* [*Intercollegiate Academic Papers*] 1972, no. 18.

Lityńska A., *"Poglądy ekonomiczne Leopolda Caro"* ["The Economic Views of Leopold Caro"], *Zeszyty Naukowe Akademii Ekonomicznej w Krakowie* [*Academic Papers of the Academy of Economics in Kraków*] 1993.

Luszniewicz J., *"Pokusa proroctwa absolutnego: wokół teorii solidaryzmu Leopolda Caro"* ["The Temptation of Absolute Prophecy: On Leopold Caro's Theory of Solidarism"], *Przegląd Powszechny* [*General Review*] 1988, no. 10.

Roszkowski W., *"Korporacjonizm Leopolda Caro"* ["Leopold Caro's Corporationism"], *Przegląd Powszechny* [*General Review*] 1983, no. 10.

Zygmunt Chmielewski

Selected Works

Czynniki psychiczne spółdzielczości [*Mental Factors in Cooperativism*], Warsaw 1925, Spółdzielczy Instytut Naukowy [Cooperative Scientific Institute].

"Energia społeczna" ["Social Energy"], *Biuletyn Spółdzielczego Instytutu Naukowego* [*Bulletin of the Cooperative Scientific Institute*] 1928, no. 3.

"Fryderyk Wilhelm Raiffeisen" ["Fryderyk Wilhelm Raiffeisen"], *Spółdzielczy Przegląd Naukowy* [*Cooperative Scientific Review*] 1938, no. 4.

"Horyzonty spółdzielczości" ["The Horizons of Cooperativism"], *Spółdzielczy Przegląd Naukowy* [*Cooperative Scientific Review*] 1935, nos. 2–3.

"Izby rolnicze" ["Chambers of Agriculture"], *Spółdzielczy Przegląd Naukowy* [*Cooperative Scientific Review*] 1933, no. 9.

Kartki z dziejów Centralnej Kasy Spółek Rolniczych [*Pages from the History of the Agricultural Companies' Central Bank*], Warsaw 1939, Spółdzielczy Instytut Naukowy [Cooperative Scientific Institute].

Kasy Stefczyka a banki ludowe [*Stefczyk Savings and Loan Banks and People's Banks*], Lwów 1926, Zjednoczenie Związków Spółdzielni Rolniczych Rzeczypospolitej Polskiej [The League of Agricultural Cooperative Unions of the Republic of Poland].

"*Kasy Stefczyka a kasy komunalne*" ["Stefczyk Savings and Loan Banks and Communal Banks"], *Biuletyn Spółdzielczego Instytutu Naukowego* [*Bulletin of the Cooperative Scientific Institute*] 1930, nos. 1, 2.

"*Kryzys a spółdzielczość rolnicza*" ["The Crisis and Agricultural Cooperativism"], *Czasopismo Spółdzielni Rolniczych* [*Agricultural Cooperatives' Journal*] 1930, no. 21.

"*Mleczarnia zbiorowa*" ["The Collective Dairy"], *Gazeta Mleczarska* [*The Dairy Gazette*] 1906, no. 6.

"*Moc ducha*" ["The Power of the Spirit"], *Społem* [*Together*] 1931, no. 16.

"*Najbliższe możliwości rozwoju u nas rolniczego ruchu spółdzielczego*" ["Upcoming Opportunities of Development Here for the Cooperative Agricultural Movement"], *Spółdzielczy Przegląd Naukowy* [*Cooperative Scientific Review*] 1931, no. 8.

"*Nowelizacja ustawy o spółdzielniach*" ["Amendment of the Law on Cooperatives"], "*Spółdzielczy Przegląd Naukowy*" [*Cooperative Scientific Review*] 1933, no. 10.

"*O korzyściach utworzenia w Krakowie spółkowej mleczarni producentów*" ["On the Benefits of Opening a Milk-Producers' Cooperative in Kraków"], *Gazeta Mleczarska* [*The Dairy Gazette*] 1906, no. 9.

"*O korzyściach z mleczarń spółkowych*" ["On the Benefits of Dairy Cooperatives"], Warsaw 1910, Wydawnictwo Wydziału Kółek Centralnego Towarzystwa Rolniczego w Królestwie Polskim [Publishing House of the Department of Clubs of the Central Agricultural Society in the Kingdom of Poland].

"*O korzyściach ze spółek mleczarskich*" ["On the Benefits of Dairy Cooperatives"], *Czasopismo dla Spółek Rolniczych* [*Journal for Agricultural Companies*] 1906, no. 1.

"*O właściwą literaturę spółdzielczą dla młodzieży*" ["On the Proper Cooperative Literature for Youth"], *Spółdzielczy Przegląd Naukowy* [*Cooperative Scientific Review*] 1936, no. 5.

"*Organizacja mleczarstwa w Austrii Górnej*" ["The Dairy Organization in Upper Austria"], *Czasopismo dla Spółek Rolniczych* [*Journal for Agricultural Companies*] 1904, no. 1.

"*Pogląd Stefczyka na Centralny Związek*" ["Stefczyk's Views of the Central Union"], Spółdzielczy Przegląd Naukowy [*Cooperative Scientific Review*] 1935, no. 1.

"*Poglądy Stefczyka na samorząd rolniczy*" ["Stefczyk's Views on Farmers' Self-Goverment"], *Spółdzielczy Przegląd Naukowy* [*Cooperative Scientific Review*] 1933, no. 10.

Podręcznik dla spółek mleczarskich [*Manual for Dairy Cooperatives*], Lwów 1907, Wydział Krajowy Królestwa Galicji i Lodomerji [National Department of the Kingdom of Galicia and Lodomeria].

Podręcznik spółdzielczości [*Manual of Cooperativism*], Warsaw 1936, Spółdzielczy Instytut Naukowy [Cooperative Scientific Institute].

"*Podstawy planowości pracy i zespolenia wsi*" ["Fundamentals of Planning Rural Work and Unification"], *Spółdzielczy Przegląd Naukowy* [*Cooperative Scientific Review*] 1938, no. 7–8.

"*Pomoc państwowa dla spółdzielczości rolniczej*" ["State Aid for Agricultural Cooperatives"], *Spółdzielczy Przegląd Naukowy* [*Cooperative Scientific Review*] 1932, no. 7.

"Postacie współdziałania" ["Forms of Joint Action"], *Spółdzielczy Przegląd Naukowy* [*Cooperative Scientific Review*] 1933, no. 1.

"Praca w kółku rolniczym" ["Work in Farmers' Clubs"], *Zaranie* [*Dawn*] 1911, no. 16.

Prowadzenie i zakładanie spółdzielni mleczarskich [*The Foundation and Management of Dairy Cooperatives*], Warsaw 1927, Wydawnictwo Zjednoczenia Związków Spółdzielni Rolniczych [Publishing House of the League of Agricultural Cooperative Unions].

Przyszły ustrój gospodarczy wsi w Rzeczypospolitej Polskiej [*The Future System of Rural Economics in the Republic of Poland*], Warsaw 1938, Książnica dla Roczników Centralnego Towarzystwa i Organizacji Kółek Rolniczych [Library for the Yearbooks of the Central Society and Organization of Farmers' Clubs].

"Rozważania" ["Reflections"], *Czasopismo Spółdzielni Rolniczych* [*The Agricultural Cooperative's Journal*] 1925, nos.19–21, 25, 26, 29, 31.

"Rozważania" ["Reflections"], *Czasopismo Spółdzielni Rolniczych* [*The Agricultural Cooperative's Journal*] 1926, nos. 15, 18, 21, 25.

Ruch spółdzielczy na Ziemiach Polskich [*The Cooperative Movement in Polish Lands*], collective work, Lwów 1916, Wydawnictwo Krajowego Biura Patronatu Spółek Oszczędnościowych i Pożyczkowych [Publishing House of the National Office of the Patronat Savings and Loan Company].

"Ruch spółdzielczy w Państwie Litewskim" ["The Cooperative Movement in the Lithuanian State"], *Spółdzielczy Przegląd Naukowy* [*Cooperative Scientific Review*] 1936, nos. 7–8.

"Samorząd rolniczy" ["Agricultural Self-Government"], *Biuletyn Spółdzielczego Instytutu Naukowego* [*Bulletin of the Cooperative Scientific Institute*] 1928, no. 2.

Spółdzielcze Związki Rewizyjne w Polsce [*Cooperative Central Unions in Poland*], Warsaw 1936, copied typsescript.

Spółdzielczość na konferencji w Genewie [*Cooperativism at the Conference in Geneva*], Lwów 1927, Union of Agricultural Cooperatives of the Republic of Poland.

Spółdzielczość rolnicza w rozmaitych krajach [*Agricultural Cooperativism in Various Countries*], Warsaw 1937, Spółdzielczy Instytut Naukowy [Cooperative Scientific Institute].

"Spółdzielnia rolnicza w Dużycach (Czechosłowacja)" ["Agricultural Cooperatives in Dużyce (Czechoslovakia)"], *Czasopismo Spółdzielni Rolniczych* [*Agricultural Cooperatives' Journal*] 1925, no. 30.

"Spółka mleczarska w Chmielniku" ["The Dairy Cooperative in Chmielik"], Czasopismo dla Spółek Rolniczych [*Journal for Agricultural Companies*] 1905, no. 3.

"Tworczość społeczna" ["Social Production"], *Spółdzielczy Przegląd Naukowy* [*Cooperative Scientific Review*] 1933, no. 3.

"Uspółdzielczenie rolników w Rzeczypospolitej Polskiej" ["The Cooperativization of Farmers in the Republic of Poland"], *Spółdzielczy Przegląd Naukowy* [*Cooperative Scientific Review*] 1938, no. 6.

"Ustroje zespolenia organizacyjnego (o federalizmie spółdzielczym)" ["Organizational Amalgamation Systems (On Cooperative Federalism)"], *Spółdzielczy Przegląd Naukowy* [*Cooperative Scientific Review*] 1938, no. 9.

"Uwagi o kasach Stefczyka" ["Remarks on the Stefczyk Savings and Loan Banks"], *Spółdzielczy Przegląd Naukowy* [*Cooperative Scientific Review*] 1931, nos. 3–4.

"Uwagi w sprawie programu gospodarczego M. Rapackiego" ["Remarks on M. Rapacki's Economic Program"], *Spółdzielczy Przegląd Naukowy* [*Cooperative Scientific Review*] 1936, no. 10.

"Wychowanie spółdzielcy" ["Raising Cooperativists"], *Spółdzielczy Przegląd Naukowy* [*Cooperative Scientific Review*] 1932, no. 3.

"Wyszkolenie spółdzielcze" ["Cooperative Training"], *Czasopismo dla Spółek Rolniczych* [*Journal for Agricultural Companies*], January 20, 1926.

"Wzorowy spółdzielca (o Mielczarskim)" ["The Model (Dairy) Cooperativist"], *Spółdzielczy Przegląd Naukowy* [*Cooperative Scientific Review*] 1936, no. 3.

Zakładanie i prowadzenie spółdzielni mleczarskich: praca zbiorowa [*Founding and Running Dairy Cooperatives*] collective work, Warsaw 1927, Wydawnictwo Zjednoczenia Związków Spółdzielni Rolniczych Rzeczypospolitej Polskiej [Publishing House of the League of Agricultural Cooperative Unions of the Republic of Poland].

"Związek ruskich kółek mleczarskich" ["The Union of Russian Dairy Clubs"], *Gazeta Mleczarska* [*Dairy Gazette*] 1906, no. 16.

Selected Subject Bibliography

Chmielewski K., Gojski J., *Zygmunt Chmielewski, teoretyk i działacz spółdzielczości wiejskiej* [*Zygmunt Chmielewski, Theoretician and Cooperative Activist*] Warsaw 1961, Zakład Wydawnictw Centrali Rolniczych Spółdzielni [Publishing House of the Agricultural Cooperatives' Headquarters].

Uziembło A., *Zygmunt Chmielewski. Życie, praca, myśli* [*Zygmunt Chmielewski: Life, Work, and Thought*], Warsaw 1939, Spółdzielczy Instytut Naukowy [Cooperative Scientific Institute].

Zofia Daszyńska-Golińska

Selected Works

Ekonomia społeczna [*Social Economics*], part. 1: Warsaw 1906; Part 2: Warsaw 1907, B. Wychowańcy Szkoły Handlowej im. Leopolda Kronenberga [Alumni of the Leopold Kronenberg School of Commerce].

Krawczynie i szwaczki chrześcijańskie w Warszawie 1911 ["Christian Tailors and Seamstresses in Warsaw, 1911"], *Bluszcz* [*Ivy*] 1922, no. 2–13.

Miasta i cechy w dawnej Polsce [*Towns and Guilds in Poland in the Past*], Warsaw 1906.

Miasta rolników. Jako dopełnienie reformy rolnej [*A Town of Farmers: As a Fulfillment of Agricultural Reform*], Warsaw 1922.

Najnowsze badania w kwestyi cechów ["The Most Recent Research in the Question of Guilds"], *Przegląd Tygodniowy* [*Weekly Review*] 1890, no. 6.

Podstawy teoretyczne polityki społecznej w zarysie [*Theoretical Bases of Social Policy in Outline*], Warsaw 1932, Sekcja Wydawnicza Towarzystwa Bratniej Pomocy Studentów Wolnej Wszechnicy Polskiej [Publishing Section of the Fraternal Student Aid Society of the Free Polish University].

Polityka społeczna [*Social Policy*], Warsaw 1933, Towarzystwo Bratniej Pomocy Studentów Wolnej Wszechnicy Polskiej [Fraternal Student Aid Society of the Free Polish University].

Przełom w socyalizmie [*A Turning Point in Socialism*], Lwów 1900, Towarzystwo Wydawnicze Almae Matri Iagellonicae 1400–1900 [Publishing Society Almae Matri Iagellonicae].

Przez kooperatywy do przyszłego ustroju [*Through Cooperatives to the Future Order*], Warsaw 1921, Wydział Propagandy Związku Polskich Stowarzyszeń Spożywców [Propaganda Division of the Union of Polish Consumer Associations].

Przez spółki spożywcze do przyszłego ustroju [*Through Food Cooperatives to the Future Order*], Kraków 1909, Wydawnictwo Latarnia [Latarnia Publishers].

Spółki rolnicze i handlowe [*Farming and Trade Companies*], Warsaw 1904, K. Kowalewski.

Teoretyczne podstawy polityki społecznej w XIX stuleciu [*Theoretical Bases of Social Policy in the 19th Century*], Warsaw 1906, Księgarnia Naukowa [Academic Bookstore].

Uście Solne. Przyczynki historyczno-statystyczne do dziejów nadwiślańskiego miasteczka [*Uście Solne: Historical and Statistical Contributions to the History of a Small Town by the Vistula*], Kraków 1906, Akademia Umiejętności [Academy of Learning].

Zarys ekonomii społecznej [*Outline of the Social Economy*], Lwów 1898, Księgarnia Polska [Polish Bookstore].

Selected Subject Bibliography

Owadowska R., *Zofia Daszyńska-Golińska—o nurt reformistyczny w polityce społecznej* [*Zofia Daszyńska-Golińska: On the Reformist Current in Social Policy*], Poznań 2004, Zakład Badań Narodowościowych PAN [Nationalities Research Division of the Polish Academy of Sciences].

Maria Dąbrowska

Selected Works

Codzienna praca [*Daily Work*], Warsaw 1924, Wydział Propagandy Związku Polskich Stowarzyszeń Spożywców [Propaganda Division of the Union of Polish Consumer Associations].

Cudowny okręt. Opowieść o braterstwie robotników ["A Marvelous Ship: A Tale of Workers' Fraternity"], *Społem* [*Together*] 1913, no. 21.

[M.D.], *Czy spółdzielnia jest przedsiębiorstwem handlowym?* ["Is a Cooperative a Commercial Enterprise"], *Spólnota* [*Community*] 1923, no. 26.

Czystość ideału a mądrość życia ["The Purity of the Ideal and the Wisdom of Life"], *Spólnota* [*Community*] 1924, no. 1946.

Dawne „Społem" ["The Former 'Społem'"], *Społem* [*Together*] 1956, no. 20.

[Maria Nowa], *Dla ludu* ["For the People"], *Kurier Kaliski* [*The Kalisz Courier*] 1911.

"Edward Abramowski jako socjolog" ["Edward Abramowski as a Sociologist"], *Wiadomości Literackie* [*Literary News*] 1924, no. 16.

Finlandia, wzorowy kraj kooperacji [*Finland: A Model Cooperativist Country*], Warsaw 1913, Towarzystwo Kooperatystów [Cooperativists' Society].

[M.], *"Kobieta w ruchu spółdzielczym"* ["Women in the Cooperative Movement"], *Społem. Kalendarz Spółdzielcy* [*Together: Cooperative Calendar*] 1919.

"Kooperacja spożywcza i zagadnienie pracy" ["Food Cooperatives and Labor Issues"], *Społem* [*Together*] 1914, no. 10.

"Kooperatyści a wydajność pracy" ["Cooperativists and Labor Productivity"], *Społem* [*Together*] 1920, no. 33.

"Kooperatywa czyni człowieka użytecznym i twórczym" ["The Cooperative Makes a Person Useful and Creative"], *Społem* [*Together*] 1913, no. 24.

[Jan Stęk], *"Kooperatywa rolnicza we Francji"* ["The Agricultural Cooperative in France"], *Zaranie* [*Dawn*] 1912, no. 8.

[Jan Stęk], *"Kooperatywy rolniczo-gospodarcze za granicą. W Finlandii"* ["Farming Cooperatives Abroad: In Finland"], *Zaranie* [*Dawn*] 1913, no. 18, 19.

[Jan Stęk], *Kooperatyzm we wsi belgijskiej* [*Cooperativism in the Belgian Countryside*], Warsaw 1913, Towarzystwo Kooperatystow [Cooperativists' Society].

[Jan Stęk], *"Listy z Belgii. O stowarzyszeniach współdzielczych, czyli kooperatywach"* ["Letters from Belgium: On Cooperative Associations"], *Zaranie* [*Dawn*] 1910, nos. 42, 44.

"Listy z Londynu. Moja wycieczka do londyńskiej hurtowni" ["Letters from London: My Vist to a London Wholesale Enterprise"], *Społem* [*Together*] (single-day issue), January 15, 1914.

"Myśli kooperatysty" ["Thoughts of a Cooperativist"], *Społem* [*Together*] (single-day issue), March 24, 1914.

Nieporozumienia w pracy współdzielczej [*Misunderstandings in Cooperative Work*], Rocznik Centrali Współdzielczych Stowarzyszeń Rolniczo-Handlowych [Annual of the Headquarters of the Cooperative Farming and Trade Associations] 1921.

[Jan Stęk], *"O człowieku pracowitym i człowieku społecznym"* ["On the Industrious Person and the Social Person"], *Zaranie* [*Dawn*] 1913, no. 17.

[Jan Stęk], *"O dzierżawach zbiorowych"* ["On Collective Leases"], *Zaranie* [*Dawn*] 1913, no. 9.

"O kilku pionierach polskiej spółdzielczości" ["On Several Pioneers of Polish Cooperativism"], *Młody spółdzielca* [*The Young Cooperativist*] 1946, no. 5.

[Jan Stęk], *"O nauce zakładania spółek"* ["On the Science of Founding a Company"], *Zaranie* [*Dawn*] 1912, no. 11.

[Jan Stęk], *"O odpowiedzialności społecznej"* ["On Social Responsibility"], *Zaranie* [*Dawn*] 1913, no. 13.

[M.D.], *"O podwalinę pracy"* ["On the Foundations of Labor"], *Społem. Kalendarz Spółdzielcy* [*Together: Cooperative Calendar*] 1919.

"O wychowaniu człowieka społecznego i obywatela w Polsce" ["On Shaping the Social Person and Citizen in Poland"], *Zaranie* [*Dawn*] 1913, nos. 24, 25, 27, 28.

"O zjednoczonej Polsce i jej mieszkańcach i gospodarstwie" ["On United Poland and its Inhabitants and Economy"], Warsaw–Kraków 1919, Towarzystwo Wydawnicze w Warszawie [Publishing Society in Warsaw].

"O zrzeszenia kobiet" ["On Women's Associations"], *Społem* [*Together*] 1914, no. 13.

[M.], *"Odpowiedzialność spożywcy"* ["Consumer Responsibility"], in: *Społem. Kalendarz Spółdzielcy* [*Together: Cooperative Calendar*] 1919.

"Pionierzy nowego życia. Kooperatywa w Pabianicach" ["Pioneers of a New Life: The Cooperative in Pabianice"], *Tygodnik Polski* [*Polish Weekly*] 1913, no. 20.

"Popierajmy wiedzę" ["Let's Support Knowledge"], *Spólnota* [*Community*] 1925, no. 24.

"Postępy polskiej współdzielczości" ["The Progress of Polish Cooperativism"], *Bluszcz* [*Ivy*] 1913, nos. 37, 38.

"Pralnia współdzielcza" ["The Cooperative Laundry"], *Społem* [*Together*] (single-day issue), March 24, 1914.

"Przyjaźń społeczna a kooperacja" ["Social Friendship and Cooperativism"], *Społem* [*Together*] 1918, no. 6.

"Przyszłość kooperacji" ["The Future of Cooperativism"], *Społem* [*Together*] 1913, no. 11.

"Ręce w uścisku: rzecz o spółdzielczości" ["Clasped Hands: On the Cooperative Movement"], Warsaw 1938, J. Mortkowicz, Towarzystwo Wydawnicze [Publishing Society].

"Rola kobiety w kooperatyzmie" ["The Role of Women in the Cooperative Movement"], *Bluszcz* [*Ivy*] 1913, nos. 39, 40.

[M.D.], *Sklepy spółdzielcze* [*Cooperative Shops*], Kalendarz Spółdzielcy [Cooperative Calendar], Warsaw 1925.

"Spółdzielczość w Warszawie" ["Cooperativism in Warsaw"], in: *Jesteśmy w Warszawie* [*We're in Warsaw*], collective work, Warsaw 1938, by the efforts of ZZLP.

Spółdzielczość zwyciężająca: dzieje angielskiej Hurtowni Stowarzyszeń Spożywców [*The Cooperative Movement Triumphing: The History of the English Consumer*

Associations' Wholesale Enterprise], Warsaw 1920, Związek Polskich Stowarzyszeń Spożywców [Union of Polish Consumer Associations].

"Sprawa mieszkaniowa a kooperacja" ["The Housing Issue and the Cooperative Movement"], *Spólnota* [*Community*] 1921, nos. 20–28, 30–33.

Śląsk spółdzielczy ["The Cooperative Movement in Silesia"], *Wiadomości Literackie* [*Literary News*] 1936, nos. 48.

"Tradycja polskiej kooperacji kredytowej" ["The Tradition of the Polish Credit Cooperative"], *Społem* [*Together*] 1914, no. 12.

"Uniwersytety ludowe jako grunt dla kooperacji" ["People's Universities as the Foundation of the Cooperative Movement]," *Społem* [*Together*] 1917, nos. 14, 15.

"Wielki kooperatysta—uczony samouk Jan Shillito" ["A Great Cooperativist: The Self-Educated Scholar Jan Shillito"], *Społem* [*Together*] 1917, no. 7.

"Wychowujmy pokolenia kooperatystow" ["Let Us Shape a Generation of Cooperativists"], *Społem* [*Together*] 1913, no. 9.

"Wycieczka. Z życia kooperatywnego w Anglii" ["An Excursion: From Cooperative Life in England"], *Społem* [*Together*] 1913, no. 26.

"Wyższość kooperatyw nad innymi typami stowarzyszeń" ["The Superiority of Cooperatives over Other Types of Associations"], *Społem* [*Together*] 1913, no. 9.

"Znaczenie kobiety w ruchu spółdzielczym" ["The Importance of Women in the Cooperative Movement"], *Zaranie* [*Dawn*]1913, no. 22.

[Jan Stęk], *"Z ruchu kooperatywnego w krajach skandynawskich"* ["On the Cooperative Movement in the Scandinavian Countries"], *Zaranie* [*Dawn*]1912, no. 31.

"Życie i dzieło Edwarda Abramowskiego" ["The Life and Works of Edward Abramowski"], Warsaw 1925, Wydawnictwo Związku Polskich Stowarzyszeń Spożywców [Publishing House of the Union of Polish Consumer Associations].

Selected Subject Bibliography

Wojciechowska J., *Maria Dąbrowska—jej związki ze spółdzielczością* [*Maria Dąbrowska: Her Connection with the Cooperative Movement*] Warsaw 1984, Wydawnictwo Spółdzielcze [Cooperative Publishing].

Franciszek Dąbrowski

Selected Works

"Dzień spółdzielczości: (jak zorganizować i obchodzić)" ["Cooperative Day (How to Organize and Celebrate It)"], F. Dąbrowski (compilation), Warsaw 1926, Wydaw. Centralnego Komitetu Dnia Spółdzielczości w Polsce [Publishing House of the Central Committee of Cooperativism Day in Poland].

Historia Towarzystwa Kooperatystów [*History of the Cooperativists' Society*], Warsaw 1931, Cooperativists' Society.

Die Konsumgenossenschafts-Bewegung in Polen [*The Consumer-Cooperative Movement in Poland*], Warsaw 1927, Verlag des Verbandes der Konsumvereine Polens [Publishing House of the Union of Polish Consumer Associations].

"Organizacja i stan ruchu spółdzielczego: 4 wykłady" ["Organization and the State of the Cooperative Movement: 4 Lectures"], 1943, *Społem* [*Together*].

Polska bibljografja spółdzielcza ["The Polish Cooperative Bibliography"], in: *Kalendarz Spółdzielczy* [*Cooperative Calendar*], Warsaw 1921.

Spółdzielcze szkolnictwo zawodowe w Polsce [*Cooperative Occupational Training in Poland*], Warsaw 1939, Spółdzielczy Instytut Naukowy [Cooperative Scientific Institute].

Spółdzielnie uczniowskie: podręcznik praktyczny z il. i wzorami [*Students' Cooperatives: A Practical Manual with Illustrations and Models*], Warsaw 1925, Wydawnictwo Związku Polskich Stowarzyszeń Spożywców [Publishing House of the Union of Polish Consumer Associations].

"Szkolnictwo spółdzielcze" ["Cooperative Schooling"], in: *Informator Spółdzielczy* [*Cooperative News*], Warsaw 1937, Wydawnictwo Spółdzielczego Instytutu Naukowego [Publishing House of the Cooperative Scientific Institute].

Średnia Koedukacyjna Szkoła Spółdzielczości im. Romualda Mielczarskiego [*The Romuald Mielczarski Co-Educational Cooperative Secondary School*], Warsaw 1933, Stowarzyszenie Szkoły Spółdzielczej [Cooperative School Association].

Wychowanie spółdzielcze w wojsku [*Cooperative Training in the Army*], Warsaw 1933, Wydawnictwo Związek Rewizyjny Spółdzielni Wojskowych [Publishing House of the Central Union of Army Cooperatives].

Karol Haubold

Selected Works

Elementy społeczne i gospodarcze księgarstwa spółdzielczego [*Social and Economic Elements of Cooperative Bookselling*], Warsaw 1939, Samorządowy Instytut Wydawniczy [Self-Government Publishing Institute].

Młodzież wiejska w ruchu spółdzielczym [*Rural Youth in the Cooperative Movement*], Warsaw 1937, Towarzystwo Kooperatystów [Cooperativists' Society].

Spółdzielcze koła oświatowe przy spółdzielniach spożywców [*The Cooperative Educational Club in Consumer Coooperatives*], Warsaw 1933, Spółdzielnia Wydawnicza Związku Młodzieży Spółdzielczej „Zew" [Publishing Cooperative of the "Call" Youth Cooperative Union].

Spółdzielcze organizacje młodzieży: młodzież a spółdzielczość [*Cooperative Youth Organizations: Youth and Cooperativism*], Warsaw 1931, Spółdzielnia Wydawnicza Młodzieży „Zew" [Publishing Cooperative of the "Call" Youth].

Spółdzielczość w drukarstwie, przemyśle wydawniczym i księgarstwie [*Cooperativism in Printing, the Publishing Industry, and Bookselling*], Warsaw 1934, F. Wyszyński.

Urządzanie wystaw okiennych w sklepie Spółdzielni Spożywców: (wzory i tekst) [*The Arrangement of Window Displays in the Consumer Cooperative Shop (Patterns and Text)*], 1934.

Program samokształcenia spółdzielczego: materiały dla kółka społecznego [*A Program of Cooperative Self-Formation: Materials for a Social Club*], co-author O. Haubold, Warsaw 1934, Związek Młodzieży Spółdzielczej „Zew" ["Call" Youth Cooperative Union].

Jan Hempel

Selected Works

(ed. and co-author), *Burzymy tworząc* ["We Destroy by Creating"] (single-day issue), Warsaw, August 25, 1920.

Co to jest spółdzielnia? Jeszcze jedna próba określenia [*What is a Cooperative? Another Attempt at Definition*], Warsaw 1921, Związek Robotniczych Stowarzyszeń Spółdzielczych [Union of Labor Cooperative Associations].

Czem są spółdzielnie? Dla działaczy wiejskich [*What Are Cooperatives? For Rural Activists*], Warsaw 1921, Zakład Graficzno-Wydawniczy „Książka" [The "Book" Graphics and Publishing House].

"Czy stowarzyszenia spożywcze są organizacjami klasowymi" ["Are Food Associations Class Organizations?"], *Nowy Kurier Łodzki* [*New Łódź Courier*] 1914, no. 69.

"Idea spółdzielcza" ["The Cooperative Idea"], *Kurier* [*The Courier*] 1913, no. 16.

"Idea spółdzielcza" ["The Cooperative Idea"], *Przegląd Wileński* [*Vilnius Review*] 1913, no. 4.

Jak powstał i czym jest Związek Robotniczych Stowarzyszeń Spółdzielczych [*What the Union of Labor Cooperative Associations Is and How It Arose*], Warsaw 1919, Związek Spółdzielni Spożywców Rzeczypospolitej Polskiej „Społem" [Społem Union of Consumer Cooperatives of the Republic of Poland].

Jak założyć robotnicze stowarzyszenie spożywców [*How to Found a Workers' Consumer Association*], Warsaw 1920, Związek Robotniczych Stowarzyszeń Spółdzielczych [Union of Labor Cooperative Associations].

Jedyny środek na paskarstwo [*The Sole Remedy Against Profiteering*], Warsaw 1921, Związek Robotniczych Stowarzyszeń Spółdzielczych [Union of Labor Cooperative Associations].

[Jan Wiślak], *Komuny rolne w ZSRR* [*Agricultural Communes in the USSR*], Warsaw 1926, Zakład Graficzno-Wydawniczy „Książka" [The "Book" Graphics and Publishing House]

Próchnik A., *Pan Hempel w zachwycie* ["A Delighted Mr. Hempel"], *Robotnik* [*The Worker*] 1926, no. 128.

(ed. and co-author), *Kooperatysta* [*The Cooperativist*] (single-day issue), Warsaw August 14, 1920.

Narodziny robotniczego ruchu spółdzielczego w Polsce [*The Birth of the Labor Cooperative Movement in Poland*], Warsaw 1921, Związek Robotniczych Stowarzyszeń Spółdzielczych [Union of Labor Cooperative Associations].

O niezależną spółdzielczość robotniczą: (ku rozwadze delegatow II-go Zjazdu ZRSS) [*On Independent Labor Cooperativism: (For Deliberation by the Delegates of the 2nd Congress of the ULCA)*], [unauthorized brochure], Warsaw 1921, published by a group of independent class cooperatives.

PPS w ruchu spółdzielczym [*The Polish Socialist Party in the Cooperative Movement*], Warsaw 1925, Zakład Graficzno-Wydawniczy „Książka" [The "Book" Graphics and Publishing House].

Społeczne znaczenie robotniczych instytucji gospodarczych [*The Social Significance of Labor Economic Institutions*], Warsaw 1920, Związek Robotniczych Stowarzyszeń Spółdzielczych [Union of Labor Cooperative Associations].

Spółdzielczość „neutralna" a klasowa [*Neutral and Class Cooperativism*], Warsaw 1921, Związek Robotniczych Stowarzyszeń Spółdzielczych [Union of Labor Cooperative Associations].

Spółdzielczość robotnicza w Polsce. Rzut oka na sytuację obecną [*Labor Cooperativism in Poland: A Glance at the Present Situation*], Warsaw–Sosnowiec 1922, Robotnicze Stowarzyszenie Spożywców Zagłębia Dąbrowskiego [Labor Consumer Associations of the Dąbrowskie Basin].

Spółdzielnie Spożywców (kooperatywy) a związki zawodowe [*Consumer Cooperatives and Trade Unions*], Warsaw 1921, Związek Robotniczych Stowarzyszeń Spółdzielczych [Union of Labor Cooperative Associations].

[H. Janowicz], *Spółdzielczość robotnicza w Polsce: rzut oka na sytuacje obecną* [*Labor Cooperativism in Poland: A Glance at the Present Situation*], Warsaw 1922, Robotnicze Stowarzyszenie Spożywców Zagłębia Dąbrowskiego [Labor Consumer Associations of the Dąbrowskie Basin].

[Jan Wiślak], *Spólne gospodarstwa chłopskie* [*Communal Peasant Farms*], Moscow 1926.

[H. Janowicz], *Utopia kooperatystyczna i jej apostołowie w Polsce* [*Cooperativist Utopia and its Apostles in Poland*], Warsaw 1931, Robotnicza Spółdzielnia Spożywców Zagłębia Dąbrowskiego i innych spółdzielni klasowych [Labor Consumer Associations of the Dąbrowskie Basin and other class cooperatives].

Selected Subject Bibliography

Dominko J., *Jan Hempel. Teoretyk i działacz spółdzielczości robotniczej* [*Jan Hempel: Theoretician and Labor Cooperative Activist*], Warsaw 1960, Zakład Wydawnictw Spółdzielczych [Cooperative Publishing House].

Papiewska W., *Jan Hempel: wspomnienia siostry* [*Jan Hempel: A Sister's Reminiscences*], Warsaw 1958, KiW.

Szmyd J., *Jan Hempel. Idee i wartości* [*Jan Hempel: Ideas and Values*], Warsaw 1975, KiW.

Tadeusz Kłapkowski

Selected Works

Istota społeczeństwa [*The Essence of Society*], Kraków 1939, Drukarnia „Krakowska" [Krakowska Printers].

Patronackie spółdzielnie rolnicze w Małopolsce [*Patronat Agricultural Cooperatives in Lesser Poland*], Kraków 1927, Spółdzielczy Instytut Naukowy [Cooperative Scientific Institute].

Polskie spółdzielnie rolnicze w dobie kryzysu [*Polish Agricultural Cooperatives in the Time of Crisis*], Warsaw 1931, Towarzystwo Oświaty Rolniczej Księgarnia Rolnicza [Agricultural Education Society of the Agricultural Bookstore].

Problem przebudowy ruchu spółdzielczego [*The Question of Transforming the Cooperative Movement*], Warsaw 1935, Ministerstwo Rolnictwa [Ministry of Agriculture].

Społeczeństwo w rozwoju historycznym [*Society in its Historical Development*], Warsaw 1935, edition of the Spółdzielnia Wydawnicza „Spólnota Pracy" ["Community of Work" Publishing Cooperative].

Spółdzielcze związki rewizyjne w Polsce według stanu z 1933 [*Cooperative Central Unions in Poland as of 1933*], Warsaw 1935, Spólnota Pracy [Community of Work].

Spółdzielczość w rolnictwie polskim [*Cooperativism in Polish Agriculture*], Warsaw 1929, Państwowy Instytut Naukowy Gospodarstwa Wiejskiego w Puławach [The National Scientific Institute of Rural Economy in Puławy].

Spółdzielnie rolnicze w wojewodztwach centralnych i wschodnich [*Agricultural Cooperatives in the Central and Eastern Voivodeships*], Warsaw 1928, Zjednoczenie Spółdzielni Rolniczych Rzeczypospolitej [League of Agricultural Cooperatives of the Republic].

Współpraca spółdzielczych organizacji rolniczych z zawodowymi organizacjami rolniczymi i reprezentacją interesów rolnictwa polskiego [*The Collaboration of Agricultural Cooperative Organizations and Farmers' Occupational Organizations and Representation of the Interests of Polish Agriculture*], Warsaw 1929, Spółdzielczy Instytut Naukowy [Cooperative Scientific Institute].

Wspołpraca spółdzielni rolniczych ze spółdzielniami spożywców [*The Collaboration of Farming Cooperatives and Consumer Cooperatives*], Warsaw 1929, Spółdzielczy Instytut Naukowy [Cooperative Scientific Institute].

Zrzeszenia rolnicze w Szwajcarii [*Farm Associations in Switzerland*], Warsaw 1930, Spółdzielczy Instytut Naukowy [Cooperative Scientific Institute].

Konstanty Krzeczkowski

Selected Works

Byt i warunki pracy robotników w przemyśle cukrowniczym Królestwa Polskiego: dane ankiety Związku Zawodowego Robotników Cukrowni Królestwa Polskiego [*The Life and Work Conditions of Workers in the Sugar Industry in the Kingdom of Poland*], Warsaw 1911, Związek Zawodowy Robotników Cukrowni Królestwa Polskiego [Trade Union of Sugar Workers in the Kingdom of Poland].

"Czy istnieją nauki komunalne?" ["Do Communal Sciences Exist?"], *Samorząd terytorialny* [*Territorial Self-Government*] 1932, no. 2.

Dzieje życia i twórczości Edwarda Abramowskiego [*The Life and Works of Edward Abramowski*], Warsaw 1933, Spółdzielczy Instytut Naukowy [Cooperative Scientific Institute].

"Edward Abramowski (1879–1939)" ["Edward Abramowski (1879–1939)"], in: E. Abramowski, *Pisma* [*Writings*], vol. 1, Warsaw 1924, Związek Spółdzielni Spożywców Rzeczypospolitej Polskiej [Union of Consumer Cooperatives of the Republic of Poland].

"Gmina jako podmiot polityki komunalnej" ["The District as an Entity of Communal Policy"], *Samorząd terytorialny* [*Territorial Self-Government*] 1938, no. 3.

Kwestia mieszkaniowa w miastach polskich [*The Housing Issue in Polish Towns*], Warsaw 1939, edition of the Związek Miast Polskich [Union of Polish Towns].

"O reformę ubezpieczeń społecznych" ["On the Reform of Social Insurances"], *Wiadomości Aktuarialne* [*Actuarial News*] 1922, no. 1.

"O własnym i niewłasnym zakresie działalności gminnej" ["On a District's Own Activity and Outside Help"], *Samorząd Terytorialny* [*Territorial Self-Government*] 1934.

"Polityka społeczna" ["Social Policy"], in: *Encyklopedia Nauk Politycznych* [*Encyclopedia of Political Sciences*], vol. 4, no. 2.

Polityka społeczna: wybór pism z życiorysem i charakterystyką tworczości [*Social Policy: A Selection of Writings with Biographies and Descriptions of Works*], Łódź 1947, Polski Instytut Służby Społecznej [Polish Institute of Social Services].

"Problemat polityki społecznej" ["Questions of Social Policy"], *Ekonomista* [*The Economist*] 1930, vol. 3.

Rozwój ubezpieczeń publicznych w Polsce [*The Development of Social Security in Poland*], Warsaw 1931, Powszechny Zakład Ubezpieczeń Wzajemnych [General Mutual Insturance Institution].

"Ubezpieczenia społeczne w polityce związków komunalnych" ["Social Security in the Policy of Communal Unions"], *Samorząd Terytorialny [Territorial Self-Government]* 1933, no. 2.

"Uwagi nad drogami opieki społecznej" ["Remarks on Paths of Social Welfare"], *Samorząd Terytorialny [Territorial Self-Government]* 1936, nos. 1–2.

[B. Waśniewski], *"Walka ekonomiczna robotników Królestwa Polskiego w roku 1912"* ["The Economic Struggle of the Workers in the Kingdom of Poland in the Year 1912"], *Z walki i pracy [On the Struggle and Work]* (a single-day issue devoted to the occupational affairs of workers in the Kingdom of Poland), 1913.

"Z zagadnień polityki gruntowej" ["On Questions of Land Policy"], *Samorząd Terytorialny [Territorial Self-Government]* 1935, nos. 1, 2.

"Zagadnienia mieszkaniowe Warszawy" ["Housing Issues of Warsaw"], *Kronika Warszawy [Warsaw Chronicle]* 1926, no. 4.

"Zagadnienia przedsiębiorczości komunalnej" ["Issues of Communal Enterprise"], *Samorząd terytorialny [Territorial Self-Government]*1933.

Zarys życia i pracy Ludwika Krzywickiego [An Outline of the Life and Work of Ludwik Krzywicki], Warsaw 1938, Instytut Gospodarstwa Społecznego [Institute of Social Economy].

Selected Subject Bibliography

Balicka-Kozłowska H., *Konstanty Krzeczkowski, badacz życia społecznego [Konstanty Krzeczkowsi, Researcher of Social Life]*, Warsaw 1966, KiW.

Jerzy Kurnatowski

Selected Works

Doktryny ekonomiczne [Economic Works], Warsaw 1909, Drukarnia Noskowskiego.

Esquisse d'évolution solidariste [Sketch of a Solidarist Evolution], Paris 1907, Libraire des Sciences Politiques et Sociales [Library of Political and Social Sciences].

Francuskie idee społeczne [French Social Ideas], Warsaw 1933, Federacja Stowarzyszeń Polsko-Francuskich w Polsce [Federation of Polish-French Associations in Poland].

Historja doktryn ekonomicznych [History of Economic Doctrines], Warsaw 1927, Sekcja Wydawnicza T-wa Bratnia Pomoc Stud. Szkoły Nauk Politycznych [Publishing Section of the Fraternal Society of Student Aid of the Political Sciences School].

Kooperatywa i kooperatyzm [The Cooperative and Cooperativism], Warsaw 1911, Towarzystwo Wzajemnej Pomocy Pracowniczej Handlu i Przemysłu [The Society for Mutual Aid for Workers in Trade and Industry].

Kooperatywa spożywcza: praktyka i teorja [The Food Cooperative: Practice and Theory], Warsaw 1912, Noskowski.

Le mouvement coopératif en Pologne [*The Cooperative Movement in Poland*], Paris 1929, Les Presses universitaires de France.

"Nowa ekonomia" ["A New Economy"], *Rzeczpospolita Spółdzielcza* [*The Cooperative Republic*] 1923, nos. 7–8.

O solidaryzmie [*On Solidarism*], Warsaw 1908, Bibljoteka Społeczno-Polityczna [Social and Political Library].

Polityka gminna: notatki z wykładów [*District Policy: Notes from Lectures*], 1910.

Pomoc wzajemna [*Mutual Aid*], Warsaw 1910, St. Sadowski.

Robotnicze związki zawodowe: praktyka i teorja [*Labor Trade Unions: Practice and Theory*], Warsaw 1911, Noskowski.

Rozejm pomiędzy pracodawcami a pracownikami [*A Truce Between Employers and Employees*], Warsaw 1909, E. Wende i Spółka [E. Wende and Co.].

"Solidaryzm" ["Solidarism"], *Prawo i Ekonomia* [*Law and Economics*] 1928, no. 9.

Solidaryzm jako doktryna demokracji [*Solidarism as a Doctrine of Democracy*], Warsaw 1922, edition of the Polskie Zjednoczenie Mieszczańskie Narodowo-Postępowe [Polish National-Progressive Townspeople's Union].

Współczesne idee społeczne [*Contemporary Social Ideas*], Warsaw 1933, Fundacja Wieczysta im. H.J. Chankowskiego [H.J. Chankowski Perpetual Foundation].

Zarys solidarności politycznej [*Outline of Political Solidarity*], Paris 1905, Heymann and Guelis.

Selected Subject Bibliography

Wise A., "Jerzy Kurnatowski and Polish Solidarism", *The Polish Review*, 2001, vol. 46, no. 3.

Romuald Mielczarski

The largest selection of Romuald Mielczarski's works can be found in: *Pisma* [*Writings*], K. Krzeczkowski (compilation), vol. 1–2, Warsaw 1936, „Społem" Związek Spółdzielni Spożywców Rzeczpospolitej Polskiej [Społem Union of Consumer Cooperatives of the Republic of Poland].

Selected Works

"Cel i zadania Stowarzyszenia Spożywców" ["The Aim and Tasks of Consumer Cooperatives"], *Społem* [*Together*] 1917, nos. 5–6; reprinted in: idem, *Pisma* [*Writings*], vol. 2.

"Działalność Biura Informacyjnego" ["Activities of the Information Office"], *Społem* [*Together*] 1910, no. 11; reprinted in: idem, *Pisma* [*Writings*], vol. 2.

"Dziennik—główna" ["Main Ledger"], *Społem* [*Together*] 1907, no. 32; reprinted in: idem, *Pisma* [*Writings*], vol. 2.

"*Dziennik kasowy w mniejszych sklepach spółkowych*" ["The Ledger in Smaller Cooperative Shops"], *Społem* [*Together*] 1907, no. 16; reprinted: idem, *Pisma*, vol. 2.

"*Jadłodajnie spółdzielcze*" ["Cooperative Eateries"], *Społem* [*Together*]1906, no. 5; reprinted in: idem, *Pisma* [*Writings*], vol. 2.

"*Jak prostuje się niedokładność dziennika—głownej*" ["How to Fix Inaccuracies in the Main Ledger"], *Społem* [*Together*] 1909, no. 19; reprinted in: idem, *Pisma* [*Writings*], vol. 2.

"*Kiedy będziemy mieli swoją hurtownię*" ["When We Have Our Own Wholesale Enterprise"], *Społem* [*Together*] 1910, no. 6; reprinted in: idem, *Pisma* [*Writings*], vol. 2.

"*Kontrola sklepowego*" ["Shop Monitoring"], *Społem* [*Together*] 1907, no. 33; reprinted in: idem, *Pisma*, vol. 2.

"*Kontrola zakupów członków*" ["Monitoring Members' Purchases"], *Społem* [*Together*] 1907, no. 36; reprinted in: idem, *Pisma* [*Writings*], vol. 2.

"*Kooperacja spożywców w Królestwie Polskiem i jej dezyderaty*" ["Consumer Cooperativism in the Kingdom of Poland and its Desiderata"], in: *Prace pierwszej konferencji przewodników polskiej kooperacji, odbytej w Lublinie w dn. 7, 8 i 9 lutego 1918 r.* [*The Work of the First Conference of Leaders of Polish Cooperativism, Held in Lublin on July 7, 8, and 9, 1918*], Kraków 1918; reprinted in: idem, *Pisma* [*Writings*], vol. 2.

"*List nasz do Międzynarodowego Związku Spółdzielczego w Londynie*" ["Our Letter to the International Cooperative Alliance in London"], *Społem* [*Together*] 1919, no. 10; reprinted in: idem, *Pisma* [*Writings*], vol. 1.

"*Najbliższe zadania spółdzielczości spożywców w Polsce*" ["The Next Tasks of Consumer Cooperatives in Poland"], *Społem* [*Together*] 1925, no. 8; reprinted in: idem, *Pisma*, vol. 2.

"*Najprostsza rachunkowość w stowarzyszeniach spożywczych*" ["The Simplest Bookkeeping in a Food Cooperative"], *Społem* [*Together*] 1907, no. 29; reprinted in: idem, *Pisma* [*Writings*], vol. 2.

"*Od redakcji "Społem!""* ["From the Editors of *Together!*"] *Społem* [*Together*] advertising brochure 1906; reprinted in: idem, *Pisma* [*Writings*], vol. 2.

"*O polityce handlowej stowarzyszeń spożywczych*" ["On the Trade Policy of Food Cooperatives"], *Społem* [*Together*] 1907, nos. 30–31; reprinted: idem, *Pisma* [*Writings*], vol. 2.

"*O zamknięciu rachunków i bilansie w stowarzyszeniu spożywczem*" ["On Closing Accounts and the Balance in a Food Cooperative"], *Społem* [*Together*] 1907, no. 38; reprinted in: idem, *Pisma* [*Writings*], vol. 2.

"*O zjednoczeniu ruchu*" ["On Unifying the Movement"], in: idem, *Pisma* [*Writings*], vol. 2.

"*Odezwa Biura Informacyjnego stowarzyszeń spożywczych przy Towarzystwie Kooperatystów*" ["Appeal of the Information Office of the Food Associations of the Cooperativists' Society"], *Społem* [*Writings*] 1909, no. 1; reprinted in: idem, *Pisma* [*Writings*], vol. 2.

"Organizacja pośrednictwa pracy sklepowych i buchalterów" ["The Organization of Mediation in Shop and Bookkeeping Work"], Społem [*Together*] 1910, no. 12; reprinted in: idem, *Pisma* [*Writings*], vol. 2.

"Organizacja wielkich stowarzyszeń" ["The Organization of Large Associations"], Społem [*Together*] 1918, no. 6; reprinted: idem, *Pisma* [*Writings*], vol. 2.

"Przed zjazdem" ["Before the Congress"], Społem [*Together*] 1917, no. 3; reprinted in: idem, *Pisma* [*Writings*], vol. 2.

"Rachunek towarów w mniejszych sklepach spółkowych" ["The Bill of Goods in Small Cooperative Stores"], Społem [*Together*] 1907, no. 18; reprinted: idem, *Pisma* [*Writings*], vol. 2.

"Rachunkowość spółdzielni spożywców" ["Accounting in Consumer Cooperatives"], Warsaw 1933, Społem [*Together*], Związek Spółdzielni Spożywców Rzeczpospolitej Polskiej [Union of Consumer Cooperatives of the Republic of Poland].

Razem! Czyli Społem. Wybór pism spółdzielczych [*Together! That is Społem: A Selection of Cooperative Writings*], Łódź–Sopot–Warsaw 2010, Stowarzyszenie „Obywatele Obywatelom" [Citizens-to-Citizens Association], Instytut Stefczyka [Stefczyk Institute], Krajowa Rada Spółdzielcza [National Cooperative Council].

"Rozwój hurtowni związkowej" ["The Development of Union Wholesale Enterprises"], Społem [*Together*] 1913, no. 17; reprinted in: idem, *Pisma* [*Writings*], vol. 2.

"Sprawozdanie roczne stowarzyszenia spożywczego" ["Annual Report of the Food Association"], Społem [*Together*] 1913, no. 1; reprinted in: idem, *Pisma* [*Writings*], vol. 2.

"Sprawozdanie Warszawskiego Związku Stowarzyszeń Spożywczych. Od 1-go stycznia do 31-go grudnia 1916 r." ["Report of the Warsaw Union of Food Associations: From January 1 to December 31, 1916"], Społem [*Together*] 1917, no. 1; reprinted in: idem, *Pisma*, vol. 2.

"Trzeba tylko chcieć" ["It's Enough to Want It"], Społem [*Together*] 1918, no. 1; reprinted in: idem, *Pisma* [*Writings*], vol. 2.

"Uwagi spowodu bilansów" ["Remarks on Balances"], Społem [*Together*] 1908, no. 8; reprinted in: idem, *Pisma* [*Writings*], vol. 2.

"W górę serca" ["Take Heart"], Społem [*Together*] 1917, no. 1; reprinted in: idem, *Pisma*, vol. 2.

"W sprawie hurtowni centralnej" ["On the Question of Wholesale Headquarters"], Społem [*Together*] 1908, no. 20; reprinted in: idem, *Pisma*, vol. 2.

"W sprawie pomnożenia środków obrotowych związku" ["On the Question of Increasing a Union's Operational Funds"], Społem [*Together*] 1917, no. 5–6; reprinted in: idem, *Pisma*, vol. 2.

"W sprawie soli" ["On the Question of Salt"], Społem [*Together*] 1913, no. 3, 7; reprinted in: idem, *Pisma* [*Writings*], vol. 2.

"Wspólne zakupy" ["Common Purchases"], Społem [*Together*] 1910, no. 12; reprinted in: idem, *Pisma* [*Writings*], vol. 2.

"*Ze sprawozdania dyrekcji Warsz. Zw. Stow. Spożywców za rok 1917*" ["From the Report of the Direction of the Warsaw Union of Consumer Associations for 1917"], *Społem* [*Together*] 1918, no. 3; reprinted in: idem, *Pisma* [*Writings*], vol. 2.

"*Ze sprawozdania Związku Polskich Stowarzyszeń Spożywców za rok 1918*" ["From the Report of the Union of Polish Consumer Associations for 1918"], in: *Sprawozdanie Dyrekcji Warsz. Zw. Stow. Sp. za r. 1918* [*Report of the Direction of the Warsaw Union of Polish Consumer Associations for 1918*], Warsaw 1919; reprinted in: idem, *Pisma* [*Writings*], vol. 2.

"*Ze sprawozdania Związku Polskich Stowarzyszeń Spożywców za rok 1919*" ["From the Report of the Union of Polish Consumer Associations for 1919"], in: *Sprawozdanie Zw. Pol. Stow. Spoż. za r. 1918* [*Report of the Union of Polish Consumer Associations for 1919*], Warsaw 1920; reprinted in: idem, *Pisma* [*Writings*], vol. 2.

"*Ze sprawozdania Związku Polskich Stowarzyszeń Spożywców za rok 1920*" ["From the Report of the Union of Polish Consumer Associations for 1920"], in: *Sprawozdanie Związku Polskich Stowarzyszeń Spożywców* [*Report of the Union of Polish Consumer Associations for 1920*], Warsaw 1921; reprinted in: idem, *Pisma* [*Writings*], vol. 2.

"*Ze sprawozdania Związku Polskich Stowarzyszeń Spożywców za rok 1921*" ["From the Report of the Union of Polish Consumer Associations for 1921"], in: *Sprawozdanie Zw. Pol. Stow. Spoż. za r. 1921* [*Report of the Union of Polish Consumer Associations for 1921*], Warsaw 1922; reprinted in: idem, *Pisma* [*Writings*], vol. 2.

"*Ze sprawozdania Związku Polskich Stowarzyszeń Spożywców za rok 1922*" ["From the Report of the Union of Polish Consumer Associations"], in: *Sprawozdanie Zw. Pol. Stow. Spoż. za r. 1922* [*Report of the Union of Polish Consumer Associations*], Warsaw 1923; reprinted in: idem, *Pisma* [*Writings*], vol. 2.

"*Ze sprawozdania Związku Polskich Stowarzyszeń Spożywców za rok 1923*" ["From the Report of the Union of Polish Consumer Associations for 1923"], in: *Sprawozdanie Zw. Pol. Stow. Spoż. za r. 1923* [*Report of the Union of Polish Consumer Associations for 1923*], Warsaw 1924; reprinted in: idem, *Pisma* [*Writings*], vol. 2.

"*Ze sprawozdania Związku Polskich Stowarzyszeń Spożywców za rok 1924*" ["From the Report of the Union of Polish Consumer Associations for 1924"], in: *Sprawozdanie Zw. Pol. Stow. Spoż. za r. 1924* [*Report of the Union of Polish Consumer Associations*], Warsaw 1925; reprinted in: idem, *Pisma* [*Writings*],vol. 2.

"*Źrodła nabywania towarów*" ["Sources for Acquiring Goods"], *Społem* [*Together*] 1907, no. 13; reprinted in: idem, *Pisma* [*Writings*], vol. 2.

Selected Bibliography

Dąbrowski S., *Program spółdzielczy Romualda Mielczarskiego* [*The Cooperative Program of Romuald Mielczarski*], Warsaw 1927, Związek Spółdzielni Spożywców [Union of Consumer Cooperatives].

Dziewulski S., *Romuald Mielczarski i jego praca 1871–1926* [*Romuald Mielczarski and His Work, 1871–1926*], Warsaw 1926.

Romuald Mielczarski: materiały dotyczące życia i działalności [*Romuald Mielczarski: Materials Concerning His Life and Activities*], Z. Chyra–Rolicz (compilation), Warsaw 1977, Zakład Wydawnictw CZSR [CZSR Publishing].

Okraska R., *"Marzyciel i realista. Romuald Mielczarski i spółdzielczość spożywców w Polsce"* ["Dreamer and Realist: Romuald Mielczarski and the Consumer Cooperative Movement in Poland"], in: R. Mielczarski, *Razem! Czyli Społem. Wybor pism spółdzielczych* [*Together! That is, Społem: Selected Cooperative Writings*], Łodź–Sopot–Warsaw 2010, Stowarzyszenie „Obywatele Obywatelom" [Citizens-to-Citizens Association], Instytut Stefczyka [Stefczyk Institute], Krajowa Rada Spółdzielcza [National Cooperative Council].

Selerowicz W., *Romuald Mielczarski 1871–1926—pionier spółdzielczości polskiej* [*Romuald Mielczarski, 1871–1926: A Pioneer of Polish Cooperativism*], Warsaw 2011.

Thugutt S., *Romuald Mielczarski: spółdzielca, patrjota, człowiek* [*Romuald Mielczarsi: Cooperativist, Patriot, Human Being*], Warsaw 1936, Związek Spółdzielni Spożywców Rzeczypospolitej Polskiej [Union of Consumer Cooperatives of the Republic of Poland].

Edward Milewski

Selected Works

Kooperacja i jej znaczenie w Polsce [*Cooperativism and Its Importance in Poland*], Kraków 1915, Centralne Biuro Wydawnictw N.K.N. [Central Office of N.K.N. Publishers]

Kooperatyzm a kwestya robotnicza [*Cooperativism and the Labor Question*], Lwów 1912, Księgarnia Polska B. Połonieckiego.

Sklepy społeczne [*Social Shops*], Lwów 1910, edition of the Związek Stowarzyszeń Zarobkowych i Gospodarczych [Union of Occupational and Farming Associations].

Sklepy społeczne (Rzecz o kooperacji spożywców) [*Social Shops (On Consumer Cooperativism)*], M. Orsetti (ed.), Warsaw 1930, Związek Spółdzielni Spożywców Rzeczypospolitej Polskiej [Union of Consumer Cooperatives of the Republic of Poland].

W sprawie samokształcenia spółdzielczego [*On Cooperative Self-Education*], Warsaw 1930, Spółdzielnia Wydawnicza Młodzieży „Zew" [Publishing Cooperative of the "Call" Youth].

Selected Subject Bibliography

W pierwszą rocznicę: pamięci Edwarda Milewskiego [*On the First Anniversary: In Memory of Edward Milewski*], M. Orsetti (compilation), Lublin 1916, Wydział Społeczno-Wychowawczy Lubelskiego Stowarzyszenia Spożywczego [Social-Educational Division of the Lublin Food Association].

Maria Orsetti

[Edmund Godwin], *Co zdziałały duńskie stowarzyszenia spółdzielcze?* [*What Helped the Danish Cooperative Associations?*], Warsaw 1921, Zakład Graficzno-Wydawniczy „Książka" [The "Book" Graphics and Publishing House].

"Czy kobieta jest równouprawniona w ruchu spółdzielczym?" ["Does a Woman Have Equal Rights in the Cooperative Movement?"], *Społem* [*Together*] 1928, no. 11.

Działalność Międzynarodowej Ligi Kooperatystek w latach 1930–1932 ["The Activities of the International Cooperative Guild Women in the Years 1930–1932"], *Spółdzielczy Przegląd Naukowy* [*Cooperative Scientific Review*] 1933, no. 12.

[Edward Godwin], *"Działalność Międzynarodowej Ligi Kooperatystek w latach 1934–1937"* ["Activities of the International Cooperative Guild Women in the Years 1934–1937"], *Społem* [*Together*] 1937, no. 13, 14.

Karol Fourier—apostoł pracy radosnej [*Charles Fourier: The Apostle of Joyous Work*], Warsaw 1927, Związek Spółdzielni Spożywców [Union of Consumer Cooperatives].

Kobieta, której na imię miljony. Rzecz o zadaniach kobiet w ruchu spółdzielczym [*Woman, Whose Name is Millions: On the Tasks of Women in the Cooperative Movement*], Kraków 1933, Wydawnictwo Stowarzyszenia „Służba Obywatelska" [Publishing House of the "Civil Service" Association].

"Księgarstwo a spółdzielczość" ["Bookselling and Cooperativism"], *Rzeczpospolita Spółdzielcza* [*The Cooperative Republic*] 1921, nos. 3–5.

Liga kooperatystek w krajach skandynawskich ["The League of Women Cooperativists in Scandinavian Countries"], *Społem* [*Together*] 1937, no. 10.

Osiągnięcia spółdzielczości brytyjskiej w detalicznym obrocie towarowym w oświetleniu krytycznym [*The Achievements of the British Cooperative Movement in Retail Trade in a Critical Light*], Warsaw 1950, Spółdzielczy Instytut Naukowy [Cooperative Scientific Institute].

Piotr Kropotkin (1842–1921), Warsaw 1928, Związek Spółdzielni Spożywców [Union of Consumer Cooperatives].

"Polemika w sprawie spółdzielczości we Włoszech faszystowskich" ["Polemic in the Matter of Cooperativism in Fascist Italy"], *Społem* [*Together*] 1935, no. 5.

"Poprzez Anglię kooperatystyczną" ["Across Cooperativist England"], *Odrodzenie* [*Rebirth*] 1913.

"Projekt reformy systemu kontroli zakupow członkowskich" ["Plan for the Reform of the System for Monitoring Members' Purchases"], *Społem* [*Together*] 1957, no. 11.

[Edward Godwin], *"Przedmowa"* ["Foreword"], in: P. Kropotkin, *Zdobycie chleba* [*The Conquest of Bread*], Kraków–Warsaw 1925, in the bookstore of J. Czernecki.

[Edward Godwin] Orsetti M., *"Przedmowa"* ["Foreword"], in: P. Kropotkin, *Spólnictwo a socjalizm wolnościowy* [*Community and Libertarian Socialism*], Warsaw 1930, main supply in the Księgarnia Robotnicza [Workers' Bookstore].

"Przedmowa" ["Foreword"], in: Tugan-Baranowskij, M.I. (ed.), Stowarzyszenia Wytworców i Stowarzyszenia Pracy [Producers' Associations and Labor Associations], trans. M. Orsetti, Warsaw 1919, Warszawski Związek Stowarzyszeń Spożywczych [Warsaw Union of Food Associations].

Przedwojenne obrazki z belgijskiego życia spółdzielczego [*Prewar Pictures of Belgian Cooperative Life*], print from the journal *Społem* [*Together*], Warsaw 1918.

Referat na Zjeździe Założycielskim Ligi Kooperatystek w Polsce ["Report on the Congress of the Founders of the Cooperativist Women's League in Poland"], *Społem* [*Together*] 1935, nos. 21, 22.

Robert Owen—wielki przyjaciel ludzkości (1771–1858) [*Robert Owen: A Great Friend of Humanity (1771–1858)*)], Warsaw 1926, Związek Spółdzielni Spożywców [Union of Consumer Cooperatives].

"Socjalistyczne kooperatywy belgijskie" ["Belgian Socialist Cooperatives"], Warsaw 1921, Związek Robotniczych Stowarzyszeń Spółdzielczych [Union of Labor Cooperative Associations].

"Sprawa kobieca w spółdzielczości—ongiś i dziś" ["The Issue of Women in the Cooperative Movement—In the Past and at Present"], *Społem* [*Together*] 1931, no. 20.

"Spółdzielczość we Włoszech" ["The Cooperative Movement in Italy"], Spółdzielczy Przegląd Naukowy [*Cooperative Scientific Review*] 1934, no. 7–8.

"Spółdzielnie uczniowskie w świetle ankiety GUS w roku szkolnym 1929/30" ["Student Cooperatives in Light of Central Statistical Office Surveys in the School Year 1929/1930"], Spółdzielczy Przegląd Naukowy [*Cooperative Scientific Review*] 1934.

Szkice z teorii kooperacji ["Outline of the Theory of Cooperativism"], Rzeczpospolita Spółdzielcza [*The Cooperative Republic*] 1922, nos. 1–4.

Tajemnice tkaczy roczdalskich. Szkice z dziejów kooperacji spożywczej [*The Secret Rochdale Weavers: Sketches from the History of the Food Cooperative Movement*], Warsaw 1914.

"W jaki sposob kooperatyści belgijscy zyskują nowe zastępy zwolenników" ["How Belgian Cooperativists Acquire New Followers"], *Społem* [*Together*] 1913, no. 2.

Selected Subject Bibliography

Wojciechowska J., *Maria Orsetti, niestrudzona reformatorka* [*Maria Orsetti, a Tireless Reformer*], Warsaw 1985, Wydawnictwa Spółdzielcze [Cooperative Publishers].

Adam Próchnik

The largest selection of Adam Próchnik's work can be found in: *Wybór publicystyki* [*Selection of Journalism*], M. Drozdowski (collection and preparaton), Warsaw 1971, KiW.

Selected Works

"*Dlaczego spółdzielczość mieszkaniowa?*" ["Why Housing Cooperativism?"], Robotnik [*The Worker*] 1937, no. 373; reprinted in: idem, *Wybór publicystyki* [*Selection of Journalism*].

"*Gł. w dysk. na XXVI Zjeździe Pracownikow „Społem," obradującym w Gdyni w dn. 28–29 kwietnia 1938*" ["A Voice in Discussions at the 26th Congress of *Społem* Employees, Meeting in Gdynia on April 28–29, 1938"], *Społem* [*Together*] 1938, no. 11.

Ideologia spółdzielczości robotniczej [*The Ideology of Labor Cooperativism*], Warsaw 1937, TUR.

"*Istota, zadania i cel spółdzielczości*" ["The Essence, Tasks, and Aims of the Cooperative Movement"], *Kolejarz Związkowiec* [*The Union Railway Worker*] 1937, nos. 19–24.

"*Kobieta w ruchu spółdzielczym*" ["Women in the Cooperative Movement"], Robotnik [*The Worker*] 1935, no. 364; reprinted in: idem, *Wybór publicystyki* [*Selection of Journalism*].

"*Kongres Międzynarodowego Związku Spółdzielczego*" ["The Congress of the International Cooperative Alliance"], *Życie WSM* [*WHC Life*] 1937, no. 9; reprinted in: idem, *Wybór publicystyki* [*Selection of Journalism*].

"*Osiągnięcia*" ["Achievements"], *Życie WSM* [*WHC Life*] 1935, no. 12; reprinted in: idem, *Wybór publicystyki* [*Selection of Journalism*].

Pisma: studia i szkice. 1864–1918 [*Writings: Studies and Sketches, 1864–1918*], Warsaw 1963, KiW.

"*Problemy samorządu stołecznego*" ["Problems of Municipal Government in the Capital"], *Życie WSM* [*WHC Life*] 1938, November; reprinted in: idem, *Wybór publicystyki* [*Selection of Journalism*].

"*Przed walnym zebraniem budżetowym „Szklanych Domow": u wstępu nowego roku pracy*" ["Before the General Budget Assembly of Glass Houses: At the Start of a New Year of Work"], *Życie WSM* [*WHC Life*] 1939, no. 2.

"*Przed zjazdem spółdzielczym*" ["Before the Cooperative Congress"], *Robotnik* [*The Worker*]1939, no. 153; reprinted in: idem, *Wybór publicystyki* [*Selection of Journalism*].

"*Ruch robotniczy a spółdzielczość*" ["The Labor Movement and the Cooperative Movement"], *Kolejarz Związkowiec* [*The Union Railway Worker*] 1938, no. 17.

"*Ruch robotniczy a spółdzielczość*" ["The Labor Movement and the Cooperative Movement"], Robotnik [*The Worker*] 1938, no. 161.

Socjalizm a ruch spółdzielczy: zjazd „Społem" w Gdyni 28–29 maja 1938 ["Socialism and the Cooperative Movement: The *Społem* Congress in Gdynia, May 28–29, 1938"], Robotnik [*The Worker*] 1938, no. 154; reprinted in: idem, *Wybór publicystyki* [*Selection of Journalism*].

"*Socjalizm a spółdzielczość*" ["Socialism and Cooperativism"], *Robotnik* [*The Worker*] 1937, no. 172; reprinted in: idem, *Wybór publicystyki* [*Selection of Journalism*].

"*Socjalizm a spółdzielczość*" ["Socialism and Cooperativism"], *Życie WSM* [*WHC Life*], no. 6.

"Spółdzielczość a własność" ["Cooperativism and Property"], *Głos Spółdzielczy [The Co-operative Voice]* 1937, no. 1.

"Spółdzielnia czy społeczność" ["The Cooperative or the Community"], *Życie WSM [WHC Life]* 1934, September; reprinted in: idem, *Wybór publicystyki [Selection of Journalism]*.

"„Szklane Domy": eksperyment z życia spółdzielczego" ["Glass Houses: An Experiment in Cooperative Life"], *Biuletyn Związku Spółdzielni i Zrzeszeń Pracowniczych Rzeczypospolitej Polskiej [Bulletin of the Union of Cooperatives and Worker Associations of the Republic of Poland]* 1937, no. 16.

"W sprawie zmiany ustroju organizacyjnego" ["In the Matter of Changing the Organizational System"], *Życie WSM [WHC Life]* 1934, no. 10; reprinted in: idem, *Wybór publicystyki [Selection of Journalism]*.

"Zjazdy spółdzielcze: spółdzielczość spożywców" ["Cooperative Congresses: Consumer Cooperativism"], *Życie WSM [WHC Life]* 1938, no. 6.

"Zmarnowane wysiłki" ["Wasted Efforts"], *Robotnik [The Worker]* 1939, no. 12; reprinted in: idem, *Wybór publicystyki [Selection of Journalism]*.

Selected Subject Bibliography

Adam Próchnik: człowiek, myśliciel, polityk [Adam Próchnik: Human Being, Thinker, and Politician], J. Mulak (compilation), Warsaw 1947, Wiedza. Wydział Polityczno-Propagandowy CKW PPS [Knowledge. Political and Propaganda Division of the Central Executive Committee of the Polish Socialist Party].

Nicieja S., *Adam Próchnik: historyk, polityk, publicysta [Adam Próchnik: Historian, Politician, Journalist]*, Warsaw 1986, PWN.

Radwański J., *"Ideowe podstawy spółdzielczości"* ["The Ideological Foundations of Cooperativism"], *Głos Spółdzielczy [The Cooperative Voice]* 1937, no. 2.

Marian Rapacki

Selected Works

Co to jest spółdzielczość? (materjały do odczytów i referatów) [What is Cooperativism? (Materials for Lectures and Reports)], Warsaw 1935, Społem Związek Spółdzielni Spożywców Rzeczpospolitej Polskiej [Społem Union of Consumer Cooperatives of the Republic of Poland].

"Dwa programy" ["Two Programs"], in: J. Jasiński, *Marian Rapacki*, Warsaw 1958, Ludowa Spółdzielnia Wydawnicza [People's Publishing Cooperative].

Jakie są spółdzielnie [What Cooperatives Are Like], s.l. 1937, Społem.

Korzyści stowarzyszeń spożywczych ["The Benefits of Food Asssociations"], *Odrodzenie [Rebirth]* 1912, r. 4.

O współdziałaniu [On Acting Together], s.l. 1937, Społem.

Organizacja i struktura Związku „Społem" [*The Organization and Structure of the Społem Union*], s.l. 1940, Społem.

Położenie spożywcy [*The Consumer's Situation*], Warsaw 1923, Związek Polskiego Stowarzyszenia Spożywców [Union of Polish Consumer Associations].

"*Powszechność czy klasowość kooperacji*" ["The Universal or Class Nature of Cooperativism"], *Rzeczpospolita Spółdzielcza* [*The Cooperative Republic*] 1923, no. 10.

Program gospodarczy spółdzielczości spożywców: referat wygłoszony na Zjeździe delegatów „Społem" Zw. Spółdz. Spożywców Rz. Polskiej dnia 14 czerwca 1936 [*The Economic Program of the Consumer Cooperative Movement: A Report Given at the Congress of the Delegates of the Społem Union of Consumer Cooperatives of the Republic of Poland*], Warsaw 1936, „Społem" Związek Spółdzielni Spożywców Rzeczpospolitej Polskiej [Społem Union of Consumer Cooperatives of the Republic of Poland].

"*Program gospodarczy Związku. Według referatu wygłoszony na Zjeździe kierowników oddziałów w dniu 8 listopada 1930 r.*" ["The Economic Program of the Union: According to a Report Given at a Conference of Division Directors on November 8, 1930"], *Społem* [*Together*] 1931, nos. 1, 2.

"*Przedmowa*" ["Foreword"], in: Tugan-Baranovskij M.I., *Społeczne zasady kooperacji* [*The Social Principles of Cooperativism*], trans. J. Hempel i M. Orsetti, Warsaw 1923, Zakład Graficzno-Wydawniczy „Książka" [The "Book" Graphics and Publishing House].

Robotnicze spółdzielnie wytwórcze [*Workers' Production Cooperatives*], s.l. 1937, Społem.

Rola i zadania spółdzielczości w obronie państwa: referat wygłoszony na Zjeździe delegatów „Społem" Związku Spółdz. Spożywców R.P. dn. 4 czerwca 1939 r. [*The Role and Tasks of the Cooperative Movement in Defense of the State: A Report Given at the Congress of Delegates of the Społem Union of Consumer Cooperatives of the Republic of Poland on June 4, 1939*], Warsaw 1939, „Społem" Związek Spółdzielni Spożywców Rzeczpospolitej Polskiej [Społem Union of Consumer Cooperatives of the Republic of Poland].

Ruch spółdzielczy a polityka gospodarcza: 2 referaty wygłoszone na XIV Zjeździe Pełnomocników Związku Spółdzielni Spożywców Rzeczypospolitej Polskiej, w dniu 30 maja 1926 r. [*The Cooperative Movement and Economic Policy: 2 Reports Given at the 14th Congress of Envoys of the Union of Consumer Cooperatives of the Republic of Poland on May 30, 1926*], Warsaw 1926, Związek Spółdzielni Spożywców Rzeczypospolitej Polskiej [Union of Consumer Cooperatives of the Republic of Poland].

Spółdzielczość spożywców na wsi [*The Consumer Cooperative Movement in the Countryside*], Warsaw 1938, „Społem" Związek Spółdzielni Spożywców Rzeczypospolitej Polskiej [Społem Union of Consumer Cooperatives of the Republic of Poland].

Spółdzielnie konsumentów [*Consumer Cooperatives*], s.l. 1937, Społem.

Spółdzielnie pracy [*Labor Cooperatives*], s.l. 1937, Społem.

Spółdzielnie rolników [*Farmers' Cooperatives*], s.l. 1937, Społem.

Spółdzielnie rzemieślników [*Craftsmen's Cooperatives*], s.l. 1937, Społem.

Spółdzielnie w dziedzinie obrotu pieniężnego [*Cooperatives in the Field of Cash Transactions*], s.l. 1937, Społem.

"*Stosunek państwa do kooperacji*" ["The State's Attitude to Cooperation"], in: J. Jasiński, *Marian Rapacki*, Warsaw 1958, Ludowa Spółdzielnia Wydawnicza [People's Publishing Cooperative].

Tezy do referatu „Program gospodarczy spółdzielczości spożywców" [*Theses for the Report "The Economic Program of Consumer Cooperativism"*], Warsaw 1936, F. Wyszyński i S-ka [F. Wyszyński and Co.].

"*W sprawie nowelizacji ustawy o spółdzielniach*" ["On the Question of Amending the Law on Cooperatives"], *Społem* [*Together*] 1933, no. 19.

Zasady i podstawy spółdzielczego systemu gospodarczego: 3 wykłady [*The Principles and Foundations of the Cooperative Economic System: 3 Lectures*], s. l. 1940, „Społem" Związek Spółdzielni Spożywców [Społem Union of Consumer Cooperatives].

Selected Subject Bibliography

Jasiński J., *Marian Rapacki*, Warsaw 1948, Związek Gospodarczy Spółdzielni [Union of Cooperatives].

Świtalski Z., *Marian Rapacki—prezes „Społem" (1926–1944)* ["Marian Rapacki—Chairman of Społem, (1926–1944)"], *Spółdzielczy Kwartalnik Naukowy* [*Cooperative Scientific Quarterly*] 1984, no. 3.

Stanisław Rychliński

Selected Works

"*Czas pracy w przemyśle polskim w świetle ankiety Związku Stowarzyszeń Zawodowych*" ["Length of Work in Polish Industry in the Light of the Survey of the Union of Trade Associations"], *Sprawy Robotnicze* [*Labor Issues*] 1929, no. 5.

"*Gildie budowlane w Wielkiej Brytanii*" ["Construction Guilds in Great Britain"], *Ekonomista* [*The Economist*] 1925, vol. 2.

"*Na marginesie struktury podziału dochodu społecznego w Anglii*" [*On the Margins of the Structure of the Division of the Social Income in England*], Warsaw 1938.

"*Niemiecki ruch zawodowy*" ["The German Trade Movement"], *Robotniczy Przegląd Gospodarczy* [*The Workers' Economic Review*] 1925, no. 12.

Repetytorium dla spółdzielców z zasadniczych pojęć ekonomicznych: rok szkolny 1938/1939 [*Review Course for Cooperativists in the Basic Economic Concepts: The School Year*

1938/1939], 1939, „Społem" Związek Spółdzielcow Spożywców [Społem Union of Consumer Cooperatives].

Robotniczy ruch zawodowy w Polsce w 1926 r. ["The Workers' Trade Movement in Poland in 1926"], co-author Z. Szempliński, *Praca i Opieka Społeczna* [*Work and Social Care*] 1927, no. 3.

Ruch Zawodowy w niepodległej Polsce [*The Trade Movement in Independent Poland*], Poznań 1928, Wydawnictwo Powszechnej Wystawy Krajowej [General National Exhibition Publishers].

"*Społeczne przedsiębiorstwa budowlane w Niemczech*" ["Social Construction Enterprises in Germany"], *Rzeczpospolita Spółdzielcza* [*The Cooperative Republic*] 1926, no. 1, 2.

Spółdzielczość i chałupnictwo w socjalizmie [*The Cooperative Movement and Cottage Industries in Socialism*], co-author S. Miłkowski, Warsaw 1943, the material disappeared during the Warsaw Uprising.

"*Spółdzielczość pracy w Palestynie*" ["Labor Cooperativism in Palestine"], *Rzeczpospolita Spółdzielcza* [*The Cooperative Republic*] 1926, no. 9.

Zagadnienia pracownicze w spółdzielczym zakładzie wytwórczym [*Labor Issues in a Cooperative Production Facility*], s.l. around 1941, Związek Spółdzielni Spożywców „Społem" [Społem Union of Consumer Cooperatives].

"*Zagadnienie podstawy ustroju związkow zawodowych w Niemczech*" ["Questions of the Foundations of the System of Trade Unions in Germany"], *Robotniczy Przegląd Gospodarczy* [*The Workers' Economic Review*] 1926, no. 10, 12.

"*Zasadnicze kierunki robotniczego ruchu zawodowego w Polsce*" ["Basic Trends of the Labor Trade Movement in Poland"], *Rocznik WSH* [*Yearbook of the Warsaw School of Economics*] 1929.

Selected Subject Bibliography

Wójcik P., *Z rodowodu socjalistycznej polityki społecznej: koncepcje i poglądy Stanisława Rychlińskiego* [*On the Lineage of Socialist Social Policy: The Ideas and Views of Stanisław Rychliński*], Warsaw 1976, KiW.

Franciszek Stefczyk

Selected Works

Handlowa działalność kółek rolniczych w Galicji [*The Trade Activity of Farmers' Clubs in Galicia*], Lwów 1894.

Jakie korzyści przynieść może gminie lub parafii założenie spółki oszczędności i pożyczek [*The Benefits That Founding a Savings and Loan Company Can Bring a District or Parish*], Lwów 1899.

O rządowym projekcie założenia centralnej kasy dla stowarzyszeń [*On the Government Plan to Found a Central Bank for Associations*], Kraków 1906 (review of this work: Bujak F., *Ekonomista* [*The Economist*] 1907, vol. 1, no. 2).

O spółkach kredytowych systemu F.W. Reiffeisena [*On Credit Companies in the F.W. Reiffeisen System*], Kraków 1890.

O spółkach oszczędności i pożyczek (systemu Reiffeisena) pod patronatem Wydziału Krajowego we Lwowie [*On Savings and Loan Companies (of the Raiffeisen System) under the Patronage of the National Division in Lwów*], Lwów 1914, Wydawnictwo Biura Patronatu dla Spółek Rolniczych we Lwowie [Publishing House of Patronat's Office for Farmers' Clubs in Lwów].

O zakładaniu spółek mleczarskich pod patronatem Wydziału Krajowego [*On the Foundation of Dairy Companies under the Patronage of the National Division*], Lwów 1905.

Początki i ogólne warunki rozwoju spółdzielczości w Polsce [*The Beginnings and General Development Conditions of the Cooperative Movement in Poland*], Warsaw 1925, Wydawnictwo Spółdzielczego Instytutu Naukowego [Publishing House of the Cooperative Scientific Institute].

Podręcznik dla kas Stefczyka [*Manual for Stefczyk Savings and Loan Banks*], Lwów 1927, Patronat Spółdzielni Rolniczych [Patronat Agricultural Cooperatives].

Podręcznik dla spółek oszczędności i pożyczek systemu F.W. Raiffeisena [*Manual for Savings and Loan Companies of the F.W. Raiffeisen System*], Lwów 1914, edition of the Wydział Krajowego Królestwa Galicji i Lodomeryi [National Division of the Kingdom of Galicia and Lodomeria].

Projekt statusu Centralnej Kasy Spółek Rolniczych [*Status Draft of the Central Bank of Farmers' Clubs*], Lwów 1905.

Przesilenie ludowe a sprawa ludowa w Galicji [*The People's Crisis and the People's Issue in Galicia*], Lwów 1907.

"*Rola spółdzielczości w uprzemysłowieniu rolnictwa*" ["The Role of Cooperativism in the Industrialization of Agriculture"], Czasopismo dla Spółek Rolniczych [*The Journal for Farmers' Clubs*] 1923, no. 8, 9.

Rolnicze spółki magazynowe [*Agricultural Storehouse Companies*], Lwów 1909.

Rolnicze stowarzyszenia pożyczkowe [*Farmers' Savings and Loan Associations*], Warsaw 1914.

Spółki systemu Reiffeisena ["Companies of the Raiffeisen System"], in: *Statystyka stowarzyszeń zarobkowych i gospodarczych za rok 1895* [*Statistics for Occupational and Farming Associations for the Year 1895*], Lwów 1896.

Sprawozdanie w sprawie organizacji pomocy Wydziału Krajowego dla rękodzieł i drobnego przemysłu [*Report on the Organization of Aid by the National Division for Handwork and Minor Industry*], Lwów 1910.

Stanowisko spółdzielczości w rolnictwie [*The Position of the Cooperative Movement in Agriculture*], Warsaw 1927, Wydawnictwo Zjednoczenia Związku Spółdzielni Rolniczych Rzeczpospolitej Polskiej [Publishing House of the League of Agricultural Cooperative Unions of the Republic of Poland].

W sprawie organizacji krajowego rolnictwa [*On the National Organization in Agriculture*], Lwów 1909.

Wskazówki o zakładaniu i prowadzeniu włościańskich spółek mleczarskich [*Guidelines for Founding and Managing Rural Dairy Companies*], Lwów 1897.

Współdzielczy Instytut Naukowy jako doniosła potrzeba ludu i narodu polskiego [*The Cooperative Scientific Institute as an Important Need of the People and the Polish Nation*], Kraków 1918.

Zadania spółdzielczości rolniczej w dobie obecnej [*The Tasks of Agricultural Cooperativism in the Present Day*], Warsaw 1921.

Zasady i reguły dobrego zarządzania spółdzielnią oszczędnościowo-pożyczkową [*The Principles and Rules of Good Management for a Savings and Loan Cooperative*], Warsaw 1947, Biuro Wydawnicze Związku Rewizyjnego Spółdzielni Rzeczpospolitej Polskiej [Publishing Office of the Central Union of Cooperatives of the Republic of Poland].

Znamiona i zadania kas Stefczyka [*Characteristics and Tasks of Stefczyk Savings and Loan Banks*], Warsaw 1927, Wydawnictwo Związku Rewizyjnego Polskich Spółdzielni Rolniczych [Publishing House of the Central Union of Polish Agricultural Cooperatives].

Selected Subject Bibliography

Bielecki J., *Dr Franciszek Stefczyk—pionier spółdzielczości rolniczej w Polsce* [*Dr. Franciszek Stefczyk—A Pioneer of Agricultural Cooperativism in Poland*], Warsaw 1927, Wydawnictwo Związku Rewizyjnego Polskich Spółdzielni Rolniczych [Publishing House of the Central Union of Polish Agricultural Cooperatives].

Cywiński B., *Idzie o dobro wspólne: opowieść o Franciszku Stefczyku* [*A Matter of the Common Good: The Story of Franciszek Stefczyk*], Sopot 2004, Fundacja na rzecz Polskich Związków Kredytowych przy współpracy Wyższej Szkoły Finansów i Administracji [The Foundation for Polish Credit Unions with the cooperation of the Higher School of Finance and Administration].

Doskocz M., *Raiffeisen, Stefczyk, Kampelik*, Gdynia 2006, Stowarzyszenie Krzewienia Edukacji Finansowej [The Association for Promulgating Financial Education]

Gurnicz A., *Franciszek Stefczyk: życie, poglądy, działalność* [*Franciszek Stefczyk: Life, Views, Activity*], Warsaw 1976, Zakład Wydawnictw CRS [CRS Publishing House].

Skodlarski J., *Franciszek Stefczyk (1861–1924): pionier spółdzielczości kredytowej w Polsce* [*Franciszek Stefczyk (1861–1924): A Pioneer of Credit Cooperativism in Poland*], Łódź 2010, Wydawnictwo Uniwersytetu Łódzkiego [University of Łódź Publishers].

Weydlich K., *Działalność pisarska Franciszka Stefczyka* [*The Writings of Franciszek Stefczyk*], Warsaw 1934, *Spółdzielczy Przegląd Naukowy* [*Cooperative Scientific Review*].

Weydlich K., *Franciszek Stefczyk, pionier polskiej spółdzielczości rolniczej* [*Franciszek Stefczyk, Pioneer of Polish Agricultural Cooperativism*], Warsaw 1936, Spółdzielczy Instytut Naukowy [Cooperative Scientific Institute].

Weydlich K., *Wspomnienia o dr Stefczyku w dziesiątą rocznicę śmierci* [*Reminiscences of Dr. Stefczyk on the 10th Anniversary of His Death*], Lwów 1934, Patronat Spółdzielni Rolniczych [Patronat Agricultural Cooperatives].

Edward Taylor

Selected Works

"*Katolicyzm a ekonomika wobec kwestji robotniczej*" ["Catholicism and Economics in Regard to the Labor Question"], *Przegląd Katolicki* [*Catholic Review*] 1931, nos. 42, 43.

O istocie spółdzielczości [*On the Essence of Cooperativism*], Lwów 1916, B. Połoniecki.

"*O zmierzchu kapitalizmu i nowym ustroju słów kilka*" ["A Few Words on the New Order and the Decline of Capitalism"], *Myśl Narodowa* [*National Thought*] 1932, nos. 46, 47.

"*Organizacja kredytu rękodzielniczego: Akcja kraju*" ["The Organization of Credit for Handicrafts: Action within the Country"], in: *Kredyt rękodzielniczy* [*Handicraft Credit*], Lwów 1911.

Pojęcie spółdzielczości [*Concepts of Cooperativism*], Kraków 1916, Akademia Umiejętności [Academy of Learning].

"*Ruskie stowarzyszenia zarobkowo-gospodarcze w Galicji*" ["Ruthenian Labor and Farm Associations in Galicia"], in: *Ruch spółdzielczy na ziemiach polskich* [*The Cooperative Movement in Polish Lands*], Lwów 1916.

Sprawa robotnicza w oświetleniu idei chrześcijańskiej [*The Labor Question in Light of the Christian Idea*], Poznań 1921, Św. Wojciech [St. Adalbert].

Zasady spółdzielczości handlowo-rolniczej w świetle doświadczeń Galicji [*The Principles of Agricultural and Trade Cooperativism in the Light of the Experience of Galicia*], Kraków 1918, Gebethner.

Selected Subject Bibliography

Borkowska-Bagieńska E., *Edward Taylor—czy wartości niedoceniane?* [*Edward Taylor—Underappreciated Values?*], Poznań 2004, Wydawnictwo Poznańskie [Poznań Publishers].

Edward Taylor 1884–1964—wartości niedoceniane a nieprzemijające [*Edward Taylor 1884–1964—Underappreciated and Abiding Values*], W. Wilczyński (ed.), Warsaw—Poznań 1988, PWN.

Skowroński A., *Poglądy gospodarcze Edwarda Taylora* [*The Economic Views of Edward Taylor*], Poznań 1934, Drukarnia Katolicka [Catholic Press].

Stanisław Thugutt

Selected Works

XXV lat w pracy i walce. Krotka historia Związku Społem [*25 Years of Work and Struggle: A Short History of the Społem Union*], Warsaw 1936, Dział Wydawniczy Związku Spółdzielni Spożywców Rzeczpospolitej Polskiej [Publishing Division of the Union of Consumer Cooperatives of the Republic of Poland].

Co to jest spółdzielnia spożywców [*What is a Consumer Cooperative?*], Warsaw 1932, Związek Spółdzielni Spożywców Rzeczypospolitej Polskiej [Union of Consumer Cooperatives of the Republic of Poland].

"Czas próby" ["Time of Trial"], *Społem* [*Together*] 1932, no. 11.

Informator spółdzielczy Towarzystwa Kooperatystow [*Cooperative Bulletin of the Cooperativists' Society*], idem (ed.), Warsaw 1932, Spółdzielczy Instytut Naukowy [Cooperative Scientific Institute].

"Jakich Polsce rządow potrzeba" ["What Kind of Governments Does Poland Need?"], Warsaw 1920, *Siew* [*Sowing*].

"Konkretne poczynania na terenie spółdzielczości" ["Specific Actions Within Cooperatives"], *Młoda Myśl Ludowa* [*Young Popular Thought*]1938, no. 1.

"Kooperatyzm" ["Cooperativism"], *Spółdzielczy Przegląd Naukowy* [*Cooperative Scientific Review*] 1935, no. 3.

"Kooperatyzm Gide'a" ["Gide's Cooperativism"], *Spółdzielczy Przegląd Naukowy* [*Cooperative Scientific Review*] 1937, no. 3.

Kredyt zły przyjaciel [*Credit is a Bad Friend*], Warsaw 1931, Związek Spółdzielni Spożywców Rzeczpospolitej Polskiej [Union of Consumer Cooperatives of the Republic of Poland].

Ku lepszemu życiu. Rzecz o spółdzielczości [*Toward a Better Life: On Cooperativism*], Warsaw 1931, Związek Spółdzielni Spożywców Rzeczypospolitej Polskiej [Union of Consumer Cooperatives of the Republic of Poland].

Listy do młodego przyjaciela [*Letters to a Young Friend*], Kraków 1939, Czytelnik.

"Młodzież a spółdzielczość" ["Youth and Cooperativism"], *Młoda Myśl Ludowa* [*Young Popular Thought*] 1937, no. 6.

"Nowe prawo o stowarzyszeniach" ["The New Law on Associations"], *Społem* [*Together*] 1932, no. 24.

Pionierzy [*Pioneers*], Warsaw 1931, Związek Spółdzielni Spożywców Rzeczypospolitej Polskiej [Union of Consumer Cooperatives of the Republic of Poland].

Porównawcze ustawodawstwo spółdzielcze [*Comparative Cooperative Legislation*], Warsaw 1931, Spółdzielczy Instytut Naukowy [Cooperative Scientific Institute].

"Przedmowa" ["Foreword"], in: K. Haubold, *Młodzież wiejska w ruchu spółdzielczym* [*Rural Youth and the Cooperative Movement*], Warsaw 1937, Towarzystwo Kooperatystów [Cooperativists' Society].

Przewrót czy droga rozwoju [*Reversal or the Path of Development*], Warsaw 1938, author's edition.

Romuald Mielczarski: spółdzielca, patriota, człowiek [*Romuald Mielczarski: Cooperativist, Patriot, Human Being*], Warsaw 1936, Związek Spółdzielni Spożywców Rzeczpospolitej Polskiej [Union of Consumer Cooperatives of the Republic of Poland].

"Społeczne cele spółdzielczości" ["The Social Aims of Cooperativism"], *Spółdzielczy Przegląd Naukowy* [*Cooperative Scientific Review*] 1931, no. 7.

"Spółdzielczość a przyszły rozwój wsi" ["Cooperativism and the Future Development of the Countryside"], *Młoda Myśl Ludowa* [*Young Popular Thought*] 1937, no. 12.

Spółdzielczość w szkole [*Cooperativism in Schools*], Warsaw 1939, Nasza Księgarnia [Our Library].

"Spółdzielczość wychowawczynią" ["Cooperativism as a Preceptor"], *Społem* [*Together*] 1931, no. 20.

"Spółdzielczość sowiecka" ["Soviet Cooperativism"], *Społem* [*Together*] 1931, no. 9.

"Stosunek między spółdzielczością a państwem" ["The Relation Between Cooperativism and the State"], *Spółdzielczy Przegląd Naukowy* [*Cooperative Scientific Review*] 1932, no. 4.

"Warunki rozwoju" ["Conditions of Development"], *Społem* [*Together*] 1938, nos. 21, 22.

"Wrogowie reformy rolnej" ["The Enemies of Agricultural Reform"], Warsaw 1920, Polskie Stronnictwo Ludowe [Polish People's Party].

Współzawodnictwo czy współdziałanie [*Competition or Cooperation*], Warsaw 1937, „Społem" Związek Spółdzielni Spożywców Rzeczypospolitej Polskiej [Społem Union of Consumer Cooperatives of the Republic of Poland].

Wybór pism i autobiografia [*Selected Writings and Autobiography*], Warsaw 1939, Wydawnictwo Towarzystwa Kooperatystów [Publishing House of the Cooperativists' Society].

Wykłady o spółdzielczości [*Lectures on Cooperativism*], Warsaw 1939, „Społem" Związek Spółdzielni Spożywców Rzeczpospolitej Polskiej [Społem Union of Consumer Cooperatives of the Republic of Poland].

Wytwórca czy spożywca ["Producer or Consumer"], Warsaw 1938, „Społem" Związek Spółdzielni Spożywców Rzeczypospolitej Polskiej [Społem Union of Consumer Cooperatives of the Republic of Poland].

Selected Subject Bibliography
Wójcik A., *Myśl polityczna Stanisława Augusta Thugutta* [*The Political Thought of Stanisław August Thugutt*], Lublin 1992, UMCS Publishing.

Teodor Toeplitz

Selected Works
Anglia jako przykład rozwoju polityki mieszkaniowej [*England as an Example of the Development of Housing Policy*], Warsaw 1937, Wydawnictwo Polskiego Towarzystwa Reformy Mieszkaniowej [Publishing House of the Polish Housing Reform Society].
"Błędy i winy spółdzielczości mieszkaniowej" ["Errors and Faults of the Housing Cooperative Movement"], *Dom Osiedle Mieszkanie* [*House, Settlement, Apartment*] 1936, nos. 5–6.
"Budownictwo mieszkań robotniczych" ["Construction of Workers' Housing"], S. Tołwiński (ed.), Warsaw 1927, publication of the *Robotniczego Przeglądu Gospodarczego* [*Workers' Economic Review*].
Do społeczeństwa—przez samorząd ["To Community—Through Self-Government"], *Samorząd Miejski* [*Municipal Self-Government*] 1936, no. 1.
Istota spółdzielczości mieszkaniowej ["The Essence of the Housing Cooperative Movement"], *Robotnik* [*The Worker*] 1925, no. 245.
Klęska mieszkaniowa i proba jej usunięcia [*The Housing Failure and Attempts to Overcome It*], Warsaw 1920, Wydawnictwo Urzędu Mieszkaniowego [Housing Administration Publishers].
Komisja do spraw faworów. Z materiałów do historii publicznej własności nieruchomej w Warszawie [*Commission on Favors: From Material on the History of Public Real Estate Property in Warsaw*], Warsaw 1922.
"Mieszkanie „na własność'" ["Living in a Home One Owns"], *Biuletyn Związku Rewizyjnego Spółdzielni Mieszkaniowych i Budowlano-Mieszkaniowych w Polsce (dodatek do „Spólnoty Pracy")* [*Bulletin of the Central Union of Housing and Housing-Construction Cooperatives in Poland* (supplement to *Community of Work*] 1933, nos. 10–12.
"Nowy okres rozwoju W.S.M." ["A New Period in the Development of the WHC"], *Życie W.S.M.* [*WHC Life*] 1934, no. 9.
O zasady podziału kosztów administracji ["On the Principles of the Division of Administrative Costs"], *Biuletyn Związku Rewizyjnego Spółdzielni Mieszkaniowych i Budowlano-Mieszkaniowych w Polsce (dodatek do „Spólnoty Pracy")* [*Bulletin of the Central Union of Housing and Housing-Construction Cooperatives in Poland* (supplement to *Community of Work*)] 1934, nos. 4–7.
Produkcja mieszkań a gminy [*Housing Production and the District*], Warsaw 1922, Ignis.
"Robotnicza spółdzielczość mieszkaniowa" ["The Workers' Housing Cooperative Movement"], *Robotnik* [*The Worker*] 1928, no. 10.

Robotnicze spółki budowlane [*Workers' Construction Companies*], Warsaw 1923, Księgarnia Robotnicza [Labor Bookstore].

"*Społeczne budownictwo mieszkalne*" ["Social Housing Construction"], *Dom Osiedle Mieszkanie* [*House, Settlement, Apartment*] 1929, no. 1.

"*Spółdzielnie pracownicze w ramach jednolitego Związku*" ["Labor Cooperatives Within a Uniform Union"], *Biuletyn Związku Rewizyjnego Spółdzielni Mieszkaniowych i Budowlano-Mieszkaniowych w Polsce (dodatek do „Spólnoty Pracy")* [*Bulletin of the Central Union of the Housing and Housing-Construction Cooperative in Poland* (supplement to *Community of Work*)] 1935, no. 1.

"*Święto*" ["Holiday"], *Robotnik* [*The Worker*] 1927, no. 8.

"*Walka z bezrobociem przez budownictwo mieszkaniowe*" ["The Struggle Against Unemployment Through Housing Construction"], Robotniczy Przegląd Gospodarczy [*The Workers' Economic Review*] 1926, no. 3.

"*Własność lokali*" ["Ownership of Locales"], *Biuletyn Związku Rewizyjnego Spółdzielni Mieszkaniowych i Budowlano-Mieszkaniowych w Polsce (dodatek do „Spólnoty Pracy")* [*Bulletin of the Central Union of the Housing and Housing-Construction Cooperative in Poland* (supplement to *Community of Work*)] 1934, no. 8.

Znaczenie społecznego budownictwa mieszkaniowego [*The Importance of Social Housing Construction*], Warsaw 1928, Komitet Polski Międzynarodowej Służby Społecznej [Polish Committee of the International Conference of Social Service].

Zrzeszenie społecznego budownictwa mieszkaniowego [*The Association of Social Housing Construction*], Warsaw 1928, Komitet Polski Międzynarodowej Konferencji Służby Społecznej [Polish Committee of the International Conference of Social Service].

"*Związki międzykomunalne*" ["Inter-communal Unions"], *Robotniczy Przegląd Gospodarczy* [*The Workers' Economic Review*] 1928, no. 4.

Selected Subject Bibliography

Tołwiński S., *Program Teodora Toeplitza. Przemówienia na Akademii ku czci Teodora Toeplitza, urządzonej w Dzień Spółdzielczości 13 czerwca 1937 r. przez Warszawską Spółdzielnię Mieszkaniową* [*Teodor Toeplitz's Program: Speech at the Academy in Honor of Teodor Toeplitz, Organized on Cooperativism Day, June 13, 1937, by the Warsaw Housing Cooperative*], Warsaw 1937, WHC.

Stanisław Wojciechowski

Selected Works

Historia spółdzielczości polskiej do r. 1914 [*The History of the Polish Cooperative Movement to the Year 1914*], Warsaw 1914, Spółdzielczy Instytut Naukowy [Cooperative Scientific Institute].

Jak założyć Stowarzyszenia Spożywcze? [*How to Found a Food Association*], Warsaw 1911, s.n. (2nd edition: Warsaw 1912, Związek Stowarzyszeń Spożywczych) [Union of Food Associations].

Kooperacja w rozwoju historycznym [*The Cooperative Movement in Historical Perspective*], Warsaw 1923, Wydział Propagandy Związku Polskich Stowarzyszeń Spożywczych [Propaganda Division of the Union of Polish Food Associations].

Moje wspomnienia [*My Reminiscences*], Lwów—Warsaw 1939, Książnica–Atlas [Atlas Library].

Narodowa ideologja spółdzielczości [*The National Ideology of Cooperativism*], Lwów 1928, Nakładem Związku Stowarzyszeń Zarobkowych i Gospodarczych [edition of the Union of Occupational and Farming Associations].

"*O zgodności teorii z praktyką*" ["On the Agreement of Theory and Practice"], *Społem* [*Together*] 1932, no. 6.

Organizacja zbytu i produktów rolniczych. Podręcznik dla szkół rolniczych [*Agricultural Products and the Organization of the Sales: A Manual for Agricultural Schools*], Warsaw 1931, Spółdzielczy Instytut Naukowy [Cooperative Scientific Institute].

Prawodawstwo o kooperatywach [*Legislation and Cooperatives*], Warsaw 1912.

Romuald Mielczarski—pionier spółdzielczości w Polsce [*Romuald Mielczarski—A Pioneer of Cooperativism in Poland*], Warsaw 1927, Wydawnictwo Związku Spółdzielni Spożywców Rzeczpospolitej Polskiej [Publishing House of the Union of Consumer Cooperatives of the Republic of Poland].

Ruch spółdzielczy [*The Cooperative Movement*], Warsaw 1930, Spółdzielczy Instytut Naukowy [Cooperative Scientific Institute].

Ruch spółdzielczy i rozwój jego w Anglii [*The Cooperative Movement and its Development in England*], Warsaw 1907, Rubieszewski i Wrotnowski [Rubieszewski and Wrotnowski].

Spółdzielnie rolnicze: jakie być mogą i powinny w Polsce według wzorów zagranicznych [*Agricultural Cooperatives: How They Can and Should Be in Poland, According to Foreign Models*], Poznań 1936, Księgarnia Św. Wojciecha [St. Adalbert Bookstore].

"*Stan obecny Stowarzyszeń Spożywczych w Królestwie Polskim i znaczenie ich dla podniesienia dobrobytu i kultury*" ["The Present State of Food Associations i the Kingdom of Poland and their Importance for Raising Prosperity and Culture"], *Społem* [*Together*] 1908, no. 21.

Statystyka Stowarzyszeń Spożywczych należących do Warszawskiego Związku Stowarzyszeń Spożywczych na 1912 [*Statistics of Food Associations Belonging to the Warsaw Union of Food Associations for 1912*], Warsaw 1913, Związek Stowarzyszeń Spożywczych [Union of Food Associations].

"*Uchwały XXVII Zjazdu „Społem" w sprawie zadania spółdzielczości w obronie Państwa*" ["Resolutions of the Społem's 23rd Congress in the Matter of Cooperativism in Defense of the State"], *Społem* [*Together*] 1939, no. 13/14.

W ruchu spółdzielczym 1906–1918 (Moje wspomnienia) [*In the Cooperative Movement, 1906–1918 (My Reminiscences)*], Lwów 1939.

Wspomnienia, orędzia, artykuły [*Reminiscences, Addresses, Articles*], M. Groń-Drozdowska, M. Drozdowski (compilation), Warsaw 1995, Wydawnictwo Bellona [Bellona Publishers].

Zadania wychowawcze spółdzielni. Referat prof. wygłoszony na 50 Walnym Zgromadzeniu Związku Stowarzyszeń Zarobkowych i Gospodarczych we Lwowie [*The Educational Tasks of a Cooperative: A Speech Given at the 50th General Assembly of the Union of Occupational and Farming Associations in Lwów*], Lwów 1931, edition of the Związek Stowarzyszeń Zarobkowych i Gospodarczych [Union of Occupational and Farming Associations].

Selected Subject Bibliography

Brudkowski J., *Stanisław Wojciechowski—jego słowa i dzieła* [*Stanisław Wojciechowski—His Words and Works*], Warsaw 1926, P. Laskauer.

Dąbrowska M., "*O kilku pionierach polskiej spółdzielczości*" ["On Several Pioneers of Polish Cooperativism"], *Młody Spółdzielca* [*The Young Cooperativist*] 1946, no. 5.

Grabski W., "*Stanisław Wojciechowski na tle 40 lat pracy dla społeczeństwa*" ["Stanisław Wojciechowski in the Context of 40 Years of Work for Society"], *Społem* [*Together*]1931, no. 11.

Rapacki M., "*Ideologia spółdzielcza prof. Stanisława Wojciechowskiego*" ["The Cooperative Ideology of Prof. Stanisław Wojciechowski"], *Społem* [*Together*] 1931, no. 11.

Jan Wolski

Selected Works

20 obrazków z życia spółdzielczego [*20 Pictures of Cooperative Life*], Warsaw 1921, Wydział Propagandy Związku Polskich Stowarzyszeń Spożywców [Propaganda Division of the Union of Polish Consumer Cooperatives].

Czy to bajka czy nie bajka [*Is It a Fairy-Tale or Not a Fairy-Tale?*], Warsaw 1925, Wydawnictwa Związku Spółdzielni Spożywców Rzeczypospolitej Polskiej [Publishing House of the Union of Consumer Cooperatives of the Republic of Poland].

"*Dla przyszłości. Piętnastolecie akcji pionierskiej na rzecz spółdzielczości pracy w Polsce 1924–1939*" ["For the Future: 15 Years of Pioneer Action on Behalf of Labor Cooperativism in Poland, 1924–1939"], Warsaw 1939, Towarzystwo Popierania Kooperacji Pracy [Society for the Support of Labor Cooperativism].

Do młodzieży o spółdzielczości. (Odczyt na dzień spółdzielczości) [*To Youth, About Cooperativism (Lecture on Cooperativism Day)*], Warsaw 1938, Centralny Komitet Dnia Spółdzielczości w Polsce [Central Committee of Cooperativism Day in Poland].

Dwa odczyty o spółdzielczości. (Dla miasta i wsi) [*Two Lectures on Cooperativism*], Warsaw 1926, Centralny Komitet Dnia Spółdzielczości [Central Committee of Cooperativism Day].

"Dwie wypowiedzi na krajowym zjeździe przedstawicieli centralnych organizacji spółdzielczych" ["Two Statements on the National Congress of Representatives of Central Cooperative Organizations"], in: *W sprawie ustawy o spółdzielniach* [*On the Question of the Law on Cooperatives*], Warsaw 1957, Zakład Wydawnictw Spółdzielczych [Cooperative Publishing House].

Dziatwie i młodzieży o spółdzielczości [*To Children and Youth, About Cooperativism*], Warsaw 1926, Centralny Komitet Dnia Spółdzielczości [Central Committee of Cooperativism Day].

Głos w dyskusji o schemacie organizacyjnym spółdzielni pracy [*A Voice in the Discussion on the Organizational Plan of a Work Cooperative*], Warsaw 1956, Drukarnia „Gryf" [Gryf Printers].

Istota spółdzielczości i jej cechy. Rodzaje spółdzielni [*The Essence of Cooperativism and its Traits: Types of Cooperatives*], Warsaw 1936, copied typescript.

Na dzień spółdzielczości. Pogadanka żołnierska [*On Cooperativism Day: Soldier Chat*], Warsaw 1927, H. Nowak.

Niezależność gospodarcza armii a spółdzielczość pracy [*The Economic Independence of the Army and Work Cooperativism*], Warsaw 1928, Zakład Graficzny Pracowników Drukarskich [Printing Employees' Graphics Works].

O rewizję kompetencji w spółdzielniach klijenckich opartych na pracy najemnej [*On Reviewing Competences in Client Cooperatives Based on Wage Labor*], Warsaw 1932, Związek Zawodowy Pracownikow Spółdzielczych Rzeczypospolitej Polskiej [Trade Union of Cooperative Employees of the Republic of Poland].

O zjednoczenie ruchu spółdzielczego w Polsce [*On Unifying the Cooperative Movement in Poland*], Warsaw 1923, Wydział Propagandy Związku Polskich Stowarzyszeń Spożywców [Propaganda Division of the Union of Polish Consumer Associations].

Podajmy sobie ręce. Spółdzielnie pomocy domowej [*Let's Give Each Other a Hand: Household Help Cooperatives*], Warsaw 1929, published through the efforts of the Ministry of Labor and Social Welfare.

"Polska kooperacja szkolna" ["Polish School Cooperativism"], *Praca i Opieka Społeczna* [*Work and Social Welfare*] 1928, no. 4, r. VII.

Problem samorządu spółdzielczego [*The Problem of Cooperative Self-Government*], Warsaw 1937, s.n.

"Program upowszechnienia spółdzielczości i uspółdzielczenia ustroju publicznego" ["A Program of Spreading Cooperativism and Cooperativizing the Public Order"], *Więź* [*Ties*] 1972, no. 2.

Projekt założeń organizacyjnych spółdzielni pracy [*Draft of Organizational Guidelines for a Labor Cooperative*], Warsaw 1937, s.n.

Przesłanki i wytyczne ustrojowe [*Political Rationale and Guidelines*], Warsaw 1937, s.n.

Spółdzielczy samorząd pracy [*Cooperative Labor Self-Government*], Warsaw 1957, Biuro Wydawnicze Centralnego Związku Spółdzielczości Pracy [Publishing Office of the Central Union of Labor Cooperativism].

Spółdzielnie pracy [*Labor Cooperatives*], Warsaw 1929, J. Gornicki.

Sprawa kooperacji pracy w Polsce [*The Issue of Labor Cooperativism in Poland*], Warsaw 1937, Wydawnictwo Towarzystwa Popierania Kooperacji Pracy [Publishing House of the Society for the Support of Labor Cooperativism].

Sprawa spółdzielczości w Polsce [*The Issue of Cooperativism in Poland*], Warsaw 1937, Towarzystwo Popierania Kooperacji Pracy [Society for the Support of Labor Cooperativism].

Swój do swego [*From One of Your Own*], Warsaw 1928, Związek Spółdzielni Spożywców Rzeczypospolitej Polskiej [Union of Consumer Cooperatives of the Republic of Poland].

W sprawie kooperacji pracy i ułatwienia jej rozwoju w Polsce [*On the Question of Labor Cooperativism and Facilitating its Development in Poland*], Warsaw 1927, Office of the Council of Ministers.

Warunki organizacyjno-gospodarcze pomyślnego rozwoju spółdzielni pracy i wytwórczych [*The Organizational and Economic Prerequisites for the Successful Development of Labor and Production Cooperatives*], parts I and II, Warsaw 1936, Wydawnictwo Kursy Korespondencyjne przy Szkole Przemysłowej Żeńskiej, maszynopis [Publishers of the Correspondance Courses of the Women's Industrial School].

Wyzwolenie. Wybór pism spółdzielczych z lat 1923–1956 [*Liberation. The Choice of Cooperative Writings from the Years 1923–1956*], Łódź 2015, Stowarzyszenie "Obywatele Obywatelom" [„Citizens-to-Citizens"Association].

Zasady i wytyczne spółdzielczości pracy: podręcznik instruktażowy [*Principles and Guidelines of Labor Cooperativism: An Instruction Manual*], Warsaw 1936, Wydawnictwo Towarzystwa Popierania Kooperacji Pracy [Publishing House of the Society for the Support of Labor Cooperativism].

Zbiór materiałów do nauki o spółdzielczości pracy [*Collection of Material for the Study of Labor Cooperativism*], Kraków 1948, Sekcja Wydawnicza Koła Studium Spółdzielczego UJ [Publishing Section of the Cooperative Studies Club of Jagiellonian University].

Z dziejów i doświadczeń włoskiej kooperacji pracy [*From the History and Experience of Italian Labor Cooperativism*], Warsaw 1927, Związek Spółdzielni Spożywców Rzeczypospolitej Polskiej [Union of Consumer Cooperatives of the Republic of Poland].

Selected Bibliography
Duszyk A., *"Anarchistyczny rodowód filozoficzno-etycznych koncepcji spółdzielczości pracy i użytkowników Jana Wolskiego"* ["The Anarchist Pedigree of Jan Wolski's

Philosophical and Ethical Concept of Labor Cooperativism and its Members"], in: *Szkice z dziejów polskiego ruchu spółdzielczego* [*Sketches on the History of the Polish Cooperative Movement*], A. Duszyk, D. Kupisz (ed.), Radom 2004, Wyższa Szkoła Handlowa w Radomiu [Radom Academy of Economics].

Duszyk A., *Ostatni niepokorny: Jan Wolski 1888–1975* [*The Last Rebel: Jan Wolski 1888–1975*], Radom 2008, Radomskie Towarzystwo Naukowe [Radom Scientific Society].

Matejko A., *"Jan Wolski—obrońca demokracji gospodarczej"* ["Jan Wolski: Defender of Economic Democracy"], *Związkowiec* [*The Union Member*] (Toronto) 1974, no. 39.

Matejko A., "Marxists Against a Polish Anarchosyndicalist: The Case of Jan Wolski," in: *A Critique of Marxist and Non-Marxist Thought*, A. Jain, A. Matejko (ed.), New York–Philadelphia–Eastbourne–Toronto–Hong Kong–Tokyo–Sydney 1986, Praeger.

Matejko A., *"Wolszczyzna"* ["Wolskiana"] *Kultura* (Paris) 1971, no. 1.

Selected Works by Other Authors Connected with the Pre-war Cooperative Movement

Amberg W., *"Spółdzielczość mleczarska w Plissie"* ["The Dairy Cooperative Movement in Plissa"], Vilnius 1936 (review: Bargiel J., *Ruch Prawniczy, Ekonomiczny i Socjologiczny* [*The Legal, Economic, and Sociological Movement*] 1936, nos. 3, 4; Hermaszewski Z., *Roczniki Socjologii Wsi* [Annuals of the Sociology of the Countryside] 1937).

Badura W., *O zasady spółdzielcze* [*On the Principles of Cooperativism*], Warsaw 1929, s.n.

Badura W., *Włościańskie spółki mleczarskie* [*Rural Dairy Companies*], Lwów 1910, s.n.

Bagiński B., *Spółdzielczość na Wołyniu* [*The Cooperative Movement in Volhynia*], Łuck 1927, Sejmik Łucki [Łuck Regional Assembly].

Beck J., *Kooperatywy spożywcze* [*Food Cooperatives*], Lwów 1916, Księgarnia Polska B. Połoniecki [B. Połoniecki Polish Bookstore].

Beck J., *Współdzielczość jako program życiowy* [*Cooperativism as a Life Program*], Kraków 1907, G. Gebethner.

Biedrzycki S., *Spółki maszynowe w gospodarstwie rolnem* [*Machine Companies and the Farm*], Warsaw 1921, Księgarnia Rolnicza [Agricultural Library].

Bielecki J., *Związek Spółdzielni Rolniczych i Zarobkowo-Gospodarczych RP* [*The Union of Agricultural and Farm-Labor Cooperatives*], Warsaw 1937.

Bielecki J., *Kasy gminne wobec spółdzielni rolniczych* [*Municipal Banks and Farm Cooperatives*], Warsaw 1930.

Bliziński W., *Działalność spółdzielni i organizacji rolniczych w Liskowie* [*The Activities of Cooperatives and Agricultural Organizations in Lisków*], Warsaw 1928, Związek Rewizyjny Polskich Spółdzielni Rolniczych [Central Union of Polish Agricultural Cooperatives].

Bońkowski S., *Szkolna kasa oszczędności* [*School Savings Banks*], Warsaw 1926, Wydawnictwo Czasopism „Oszczędność" [The *Savings* Journal Publishers].

Borkiewicz S., *Historia organizacji społeczno-rolniczych w woj. kieleckim (1898–1933)* [*History of Social and Agricultural Organizations in the Kielce Voivodeship*], Kielce 1934, Kielecka Izba Rolnicza [Kielce Chamber of Agriculture].

Bujak F., *Franciszek Stefczyk: z powodu 10-letniej rocznicy założenia Patronatu dla Spółek oszczędności i pożyczek przy Wydziale Krajowym we Lwowie* ["Franciszek Stefczyk: On the 10th Anniversary of Founding 'Patronat' for Savings and Loan Companies in the National Division in Lwów"], *Ekonomista* [*The Economist*] 1909, vol. 2, no. 4.

Bujak F., *Fundacja Hrubieszowska Staszica: obecny stan ludności wsi należących do Towarzystwa rolniczego w Hrubieszowie fundacji St. Staszica* ["The Hrubieszów Staszic Foundation: The Present State of the Population of Villages Belonging to the Agricultural Society of the Hrubieszów Foundation of Stanisław Staszic"], *Ekonomista* [*The Economist*] 1920, vol. 3.

Bulsa J., *Zrzeszenie rolników* [*The Farmers' Association*], Warsaw 1938, Państwowy Bank Rolny [National Agricultural Bank].

Bzowski W., *Co to jest spółdzielczość rolnicza?* [*What is Farm Cooperativism?*], Warsaw 1930, Centralne Towarzystwo Organ. i Kółek Rolniczych [Central Society of Farmers' Organizations and Clubs].

Charszewska Z., *Spółdzielnie młodzieży* [*Youth Cooperatives*], Warsaw 1938, Związek Spółdzielni Rolniczych i Zarobkowo-Gospodarczych RP [Union of Agricultural and Farm-Labor Cooperatives of the Republic of Poland].

Chmielińska A., *Wieś polska Lisków w ziemi kaliskiej* [*A Polish Village, Lisków in the Kalisz Region*], Lisków 1925, Komitet Wystawy w Liskowie [Exhibition Committee in Lisków].

Czerwniński B., "*Polityka finansowa spółdzielni spożywców w różnych krajach*" [*Financial Policy of Consumer Cooperatives in Various Countries*], Warsaw 1938, „Społem" Związek Spółdzielni Spożywców [Społem Union of Consumer Cooperatives].

Dania, kraj uniwersytetów ludowych i spółdzielczości [*Denmark, A Country of People's Universities and Cooperatives*], F. Wisti (ed.), Warsaw 1938, Spółdzielnia Turystyczno-Wypoczynkowa „Gromada" [Gromada Tourist and Leisure Cooperative].

Dąbrowski S., *Co czynią spółdzielnie spożywców dla przebudowy ustroju społecznego?* [*What Do Consumer Cooperatives Do to Transform the Social Order?*], Warsaw 1928, Wydawnictwo Związku Spółdzielni Spożywców [Publishing House of the Union of Consumer Cooperatives].

Dąbrowski S., *Gospodarka finansowa stowarzyszenia spożywców* [*Financial Management of Consumer Associations*], Warsaw 1928, Związek Spółdzielni Spożywców [Union of Consumer Cooperatives].

Dąbrowski S., *Przez spółdzielczość odbudujemy Polskę* [*Through Cooperatives We Are Rebuilding Poland*], Warsaw 1929.

Dąbrowski S., *Regulaminy i instrukcje dla spółdzielni spożywców* [*Regulations and Instructions for Consumer Cooperatives*], Warsaw 1926, Wydawnictwo Związku

Spółdzielni Spożywców Rzeczpospolitej Polskiej [Publishing House of the Union of Consumer Cooperatives of the Republic of Poland].

Dąbrowski S., *Zagadnienia praktyki spółdzielni spożywców* [*Issues of Consumer Cooperative Practices*], Warsaw 1928, Wydawnictwo Związku Spółdzielni Spożywców Rzeczpospolitej Polskiej [Publishing House of the Union of Consumer Cooperatives of the Republic of Poland].

Dębski J., *O konsolidację ruchu spółdzielczego w Małopolsce* [*On the Consolidation of the Cooperative Movement in Lesser Poland*], Lwów 1928, Związek Rewizyjny Spółdzielni Kółek Rolniczych [Central Union of Farmers' Club Cooperatives].

Dmochowski J., *O kółkach i spółkach rolniczych* [*On Farmers' Clubs and Companies*], Warsaw 1907, s.n.

Dmochowski J., *Rozwój instytucyi społecznych w XIX stuleciu* [*The Development of Social Institutions in the 19th Century*], Warsaw 1908, s.n.

Dobrzyński W., *Kooperatywy mieszkaniowe. Wskazówki praktyczne z polecenia Ministerstwa Zdrowia Publicznego* [*Housing Cooperatives: Practical Guidelines Recommended by the Ministry of Public Health*], Warsaw 1921, Instytut Wydawniczy „Biblioteka Polska" [Polish Library Publishing Institute].

Doskocz M., *Raiffeisen—Stefczyk—Kampelik*, Warszaw 1929, Związek Rewizyjny Spółdzielni Rolniczych [Central Union of Agricultural Cooperatives].

Drożniak E., *Centralna Kasa Spółek Rolniczych* [*The Farming Companies' Central Bank*], Kraków 1927, Centralna Kasa Spółek Rolniczych [Farming Companies' Central Bank].

Dutlinger E., *Stowarzyszenia spożywcze. Szkic ekonomiczny* [*Food Associations: An Economic Outline*], Warsaw 1901, Redakcja „Gońca Handlowego" [Editorial board of the *Commercial Courier*].

Dzień Spółdzielczy [*Cooperativism Day*] (single-day issue), S. Jasiński (ed.), Opoczno, June 21, 1931, edition of the Piotrkowsko-Opoczyński Związek Spółdzielni Spożywców [Piotrków-Opoczno Union of Consumer Cooperatives].

Dziewulski S., *Stowarzyszenia spożywcze w Królestwie Polskim* [*Food Associations in the Kingdom of Poland*], Warsaw 1909, published by the efforts of the editorial board of *Ekonomista* [*The Economist*].

Gargas Z., *Stowarzyszenia spożywcze w Galicji* [*Food Associations in Galicia*], Kraków 1907, Księgarnia Spółki Wydawniczej Polskiej [Bookstore of the Polish Publishing Company].

Gandecki A., *Spółdzielczość a reforma mieszkaniowa* [*Cooperativism and Housing Reform*], Warsaw 1934, s.n.

Gąsiorowski M., *Położenie i zadania stowarzyszeń spółdzielczych w dobie powojennej* [*The Situation and Tasks of Consumer Associations in the Post-War Period*], Warsaw 1922, Uniwersytet Warszawski [University of Warsaw].

Gątkiewicz J., *Robotnicze spółdzielnie wytwórcze w Polsce w r.1920* [*Workers' Production Cooperatives in Poland in 1920*], Warsaw 1928, Główny Urząd Statystyczny [Central Statistical Office].

Gątkiewicz J., *Spółdzielnie mleczarskie w Polsce w 1929 r.* [*Dairy Cooperatives in Poland in 1929*], Warsaw 1931, Główny Urząd Statystyczny [Central Statistical Office].

Gątkiewicz J., *Spółdzielnie w Polsce w latach 1926–1928* [*Cooperatives in Poland in the Years 1926–1928*], Warsaw 1929, Główny Urząd Statystyczny [Central Statistical Office].

Goebel K., *"Kilka słów w sprawie syndykatów rolniczych"* ["A Few Words on Agricultural Syndicates"], *Gazeta Rolnicza* [*Farm Gazette*] 1921, no. 7.

Grabski S., *Spółki włościańskie* [*Rural Cooperative Companies*], Kraków 1905, Towarzystwo Rolnicze Krakowskie [Kraków Agricultural Society].

Grunwald J., *Rady fabryczne i związki zawodowe* [*Factory Councils and Trade Unions*], Lwów 1920, s.n.

Hajkowski F., *Spółdzielczość mleczarska w powiecie krasnostawskim* [*Dairy Cooperatives in the Krasnostaw Powiat*], Warsaw 1927, Wydawnictwo Związku Rewizyjnego Polskich Spółdzielni Rolniczych [Publishing House of the Central Union of Polish Agricultural Cooperatives].

Hajkowski F., *Spółdzielczość mleczarska w powiacie rypińskim* [*The Dairy Cooperative Movement in the Rypiń Powiat*], Warsaw 1929, Związek Rewizyjny Spółdzielni Rolniczych [Central Union of Agricultural Cooperatives].

Heczko K., Inleder H., *Spółdzielnie mieszkaniowe i budowlane* [*Housing and Construction Cooperatives*], Warsaw 1931, Związek Rewizyjny Spółdzielni Wojskowych [Central Union of Army Cooperatives].

Hoszowska W., *Idea spółdzielczości w gospodarczo-społecznym wychowaniu młodzieży w Polsce* [*The Idea of Cooperativism in the Socio-Economic Education of Youth in Poland*], Warsaw 1932, Spółdzielczy Instytut Naukowy [Cooperative Scientific Institute].

Hulewicz W., *Rolnicza spółdzielczość niemiecka i polska na Pomorzu* [*German and Polish Agricultural Cooperativism in Pomerania*], Toruń 1934, s.n.

Hulewicz W., *Stanowisko zorganizowanego rolnictwa pomorskiego wobec aktualnych zagadnień ruchu spółdzielczego* [*The Position of Organized Pomeranian Farmers and Current Issues in the Cooperative Movement*], Toruń 1934, Związek Rewizyjny Spółdzielni Rolniczych [Central Union of Agricultural Cooperatives].

Hupka J., *Zawodowe stowarzyszenia rolnicze* [*Farmers' Associations*], Kraków 1902, Krakowskie Towarzystwo Rolnicze [Kraków Farmers' Society].

Ihnatowicz Z., *Myśli programowe polskiej spółdzielczości rolniczej* [*The Guiding Ideas of Polish Agricultural Cooperativism*], Warsaw 1933, Drukarnia Rolnicza [Agricultural Press].

Ihnatowicz Z., *Związek Rolników z Wyższym Wykształceniem i jego rola w kształtowaniu polskiej myśli rolniczej* ["The Union of Farmers with a Higher Education and its Role in Shaping Polish Agricultural Thought"], in: *Księga pamiątkowa na 75-lecie „Gazety Rolniczej"* [*Commemorative Book on the 75th Anniversary of the "Farm Gazette"*], Warsaw 1937, Księgarnia Rolnicza [Farmers' Library].

Jasiński J., *Rola spółdzielczości w rozbudowie gospodarstwa narodowego w Polsce* [*The Role of the Cooperative Movement in Rebuilding the National Economy in Poland*], Warsaw 1937, Społem.

Jenner W., *Aktualia ruchu spółdzielczego w Polsce ze szczegolnym uwzględnieniem stosunków Małopolski* [*Updates on the Present Cooperative Movement in Poland with Particular Consideration of the Relations of Lesser Poland*], Lwów 1934, Związek Stowarzyszeń Zarobkowych i Gospodarczych [Union of Occupational and Farming Associations].

Jenner W., *Ekonomika ruchu spółdzielczego* [*Economics of the Cooperative Movement*], Lwów 1932, main supply in the Dom Książki Polskiej [Polish Book House].

Jenner W., *Kodeks spółdzielczy* [*The Cooperative Code*], Lwów 1926, Kodeks.

Jenner W., *"Nowe platformy rozwoju ruchu spółdzielczego w Polsce"* ["A New Platform for the Development of the Cooperative Movement in Poland"], in: *Księga pamiątkowa ku czci Ludwika Caro* [*A Memorial Book in Honor of Ludwik Caro*], K. Paygert (ed.), Lwów 1935, Książnica–Atlas [Atlas Library].

Jenner W., *Spółdzielczość kredytowa w Polsce* [*Credit Cooperatives in Poland*], s.l. 1929, s.n.

Kaczocha A., *"Spółdzielnia uczniowska w środowisku wiejskim"* ["Student Cooperatives in the Rural Environment"], *Spółdzielczy Przegląd Naukowy* [*Cooperative Scientific Review*] 1939, no. 1–2.

Kamiński L., *Robotnicze sklepy spożywcze* [*Workers' Food Shops*], Lwów 1908, edition of the journal *Sztandar* [*The Standard*].

Kania J., *Problem spółdzielczości rolniczej w Małopolsce* [*The Question of Farm Cooperatives in Lesser Poland*], Kraków 1928, s.n. (review: [A.C.], *Ruch Prawniczy, Ekonomiczny i Socjologiczny* [*The Legal, Economic, and Sociological Movement*] 1929, no. 4).

Kański E., *Znaczenie spółdzielczości kredytowej dla rolnictwa* [*The Importance of the Credit Cooperative Movement for Agriculture*], Warsaw 1938, s.n.

Karczewski W., *Liskow, wieś spółdzielcza* [*Liskow, A Cooperative Village*], Warsaw 1939, s.n.

Kielan F., *Cele i zadania wiejskich spółdzielni handlowych* [*The Aims and Tasks of Rural Trade Cooperatives*], Warsaw 1938, Kolumna.

Kojder W., *"Spółdzielczość w pracy Lwowskiego ZMW"* ["Cooperativism in the Work of the Lwów Union of Rural Youth"], *Znicz* [*Vigil Light*] 1938, no. 4.

Kojder W., *"Walka z chłopami w spółdzielczości rolniczej"* ["The Struggle with Peasants in the Farm Cooperative Movement"], *Znicz* [*Vigil Light*] 1938, no. 8.

Kojder W., *Po zjeździe spółdzielczym* ["After the Cooperative Conference"], *Zielony Sztandar* [*The Green Standard*], December 12, 1937.

Korporacjonizm [*Corporationism*], collective work, vol. 1, 2, Lublin 1939, Towarzystwo Wiedzy Chrześcijańskiej [Christian Knowledge Society].

Kozicki S., *Syndykaty rolnicze we Francji* [*Agricultural Syndicates in France*], Warsaw 1909, skład główny Księgarnia E. Wende [main supply in E. Wende Bookstore].

Koźlik R., *Spółdzielczość polska i niemiecka w wojewodztwach zachodnich* [*Polish and German Cooperativism in the Western Voivodeships*], Poznań 1933, Związek Obrony Kresów Zachodnich [Union of Western Borderland Defenses].

Krawczyński S., *Rolnik a organizacja* [*The Farmer and Organization*], Poznań 1928 (review: Kryński W., *Ruch Prawniczy, Ekonomiczny i Socjologiczny* [*The Legal, Economic, and Sociological Movement*] 1928, no. 4).

Krzywicki L., [pseud: J. Wojewodzki], *O stowarzyszeniach spożywczych* ["On Food Associations"], *Wiedza* [*Knowledge*] 1907,vol. 1.

Krzywicki L., *Stowarzyszenia spożywcze. Ustęp z dziejów kooperacji* [*Food Associations: A Passage in the History of the Cooperative Movement*], Warsaw 1903.

Krzyżanowski A., *Towarzystwa i stowarzyszenia rolnicze* [*Agricultural Societies and Associations*], Kraków 1911, Krakówskie Towarzystwo Rolnicze [Kraków Agricultural Society].

Krzyżanowski A., "*Związki rolników*" ["Farmers' Unions"], *Roczniki Nauk Rolniczych* [*Agricultural Science Annuals*] 1905.

Kształcenie i wychowanie spółdzielcze w Polsce [*Cooperative Formation and Education in Poland*], Warsaw 1932, Spółdzielczy Instytut Naukowy [Cooperative Scientific Institute].

Kudelka T., *Nasze kółka rolnicze. Rzut oka na stan obecny, zadania i potrzeby kółek rolniczych w Galicji* [*Our Farmers' Clubs: A Glance at the Present State, Tasks, and Needs of Farmers' Clubs in Galicia*], Kraków 1899, s.n.

Kustroń J., *Ruch spółdzielczy w wojsku* [*The Cooperative Movement in the Army*], Warsaw 1922, s.n.

Kusztelan J., *Kilka uwag o organizacji i rozwoju spółek polskich pod panowaniem pruskim* [*Several Remarks on the Organization and Development of Polish Companies under Prussian Rule*], Poznań 1901.

Kusztelan R., *Rodowód spółek ludowych* [*The Lineage of People's Companies*], Poznań 1926.

Kwieciński J., *Spółdzielnia rolno-wytworcza źródłem powszechnego dobrobytu* [*Farm and Production Cooperatives as a Source of General Prosperity*], Warsaw 1928.

Lisak J., *Wady organizacyjne naszej spółdzielczości* [*The Organizational Faults of Our Cooperative Movement*], Kraków 1935, Instytut Administracyjno-Gospodarczy [Institute of Administration and Economics].

Łagiewski C., "*Polskie piśmiennictwo współdzielcze*" ["Polish Writing on Cooperatives"], *Ekonomista* [*The Economist*] 1916, vol. 3, 4.

Łagiewski C., *Ruch spółdzielczy* ["The Cooperative Movement"], in: *Dzieje gospodarcze Polski porozbiorowej w zarysie* [*The Economic History of Post-Partition Poland in Outline*], S. Kempner (ed.), vol. 2, Warsaw 1922.

Makowiecki A., *Spółki spożywcze* [*Food Cooperatives*], Warsaw 1868.

Marszałek J., *Spółdzielnie mleczarskie i ich centrale na terenie województw Lwowskiego, stanisławowskiego i tarnopolskiego w 1925–1932 r.* [*Dairy Cooperatives and their Central Institutions within the Lwów, Stanisławów, and Tarnopol Voivodeships*], Warsaw 1936, Związek Spółdzielni Rolniczych i Zarobkowo-Gospodarczych Rzeczypospolitej Polskiej [Union of Agricultural and Farm-Labor Cooperatives of the Republic of Poland].

Marszałek J., *Spółdzielnie rolniczo-handlowe i spożywców w latach 1924–1925 r.* [*Farm-Trade and Food Cooperatives in the Years 1924–1925*], Kraków 1928, Związek Rewizyjny Spółdzielni Kółek Rolniczych w Krakówie [Central Union of Farmers' Club Cooperatives in Kraków].

Marszałek J., *Spółdzielnie uczniowskie i ich centrale na terenie województw Lwowskiego, stanisławowskiego i tarnopolskiego w 1925–1932 r.* [*Students' Cooperatives and their Central Institutions within the Lwów, Stanisławów, and Tarnopol Voivodeships*], Warsaw 1936.

Miklaszewski S., *Izby rolnicze* [*Chambers of Agricultural*], Warsaw 1934, Związek Izb i Organizacji Rolniczych R.P [Union of Chambers and Organizations of Agriculture of the Republic of Poland].

Miklaszewski S., *Sieć ognisk kultury rolniczej na ziemiach polskich: stacyj i pól doświadczalnych, gospodarstw hodowli roślinnej i zwierzęcej, gospodarstw reprodukcji roślinnej i zwierzęcej czyli t.zw. ferm, niższych szkół rolniczych męskich i żeńskich i.t.p.* [*The Network of Farming-Culture Institutions in Polish Lands: Stations and Experimental Fields, Nurseries and Livestock Farms, Plant and Animal Breeding Farms, Lower Men's and Women's Agricultural Schools, etc.*], Warsaw 1921, M. Ostaszewska.

Miłkowski S., *Przebudowa ustroju rolnego a spółdzielczość* [*Cooperativism and the Transformation of the Agricultural System*], Warsaw 1938, s.n.

Miłkowski S., "*Spółdzielczość ogrodnicza w Polsce*" ["Gardening Cooperatives in Poland"], Spółdzielczy Przegląd Naukowy [*Cooperative Scientific Review*] 1939, no. 1–2.

Miłkowski S., *Spółdzielczość przemysłowa wiejska* [*Rural Industrial Cooperativism*], Warsaw 1938, Związek Spółdzielni Rolniczych i Zarobkowo-Gospodarczych R.P. [Union of Agricultural and Farm-Labor Cooperatives of the Republic of Poland].

Narbutt T., *Rozwoj spółdzielczości rolnej* [*The Development of Agricultural Cooperativism*], Warsaw 1928, s.n.

Obrzut F., *U wrot rewolucji gospodarczej w Polsce. Spółdzielnie pracy jako podstawowy czynnik w przebudowie ustroju gospodarczego w Polski* [*On the Threshold of the*

Economic Revolution in Poland: Labor Cooperatives as the Basic Factor in Transforming the Economic Order in Poland], Bielsko 1934, Główny Komitet Organizacyjny Spółdzielni Pracy [Main Organizational Committee of the Labor Cooperative].

Oksza S., *Przez spółdzielczość do gospodarczej niezależności Polski pracującej* [*Through Cooperativism to Financial Independence for Working Poland*], Warsaw 1938.

Patkowski A., *Wychowanie pokolenia w duchu demokratycznej idei spółdziałania* [*Educating the Generation in the Spirit of the Democratic Idea of Cooperation*], Warsaw–Łódź 1922, Nasza Księgarnia [Our Library].

Piątkowski A., *Spółdzielczość socjalistów i chłopów* [*The Cooperativism of Socialists and Peasants*], Warsaw 1938, s.n.

Pierwszy Kongres Centralnego Związku Młodej Wsi (19–20 czerwca 1937 r.) [*The First Congress of the Central Union of Rural Youth*], Warsaw 1937, s.n.

Pisarek E., *Od obszcziny do kołchozu. Z form pospolnego użytkowania ziemi na wschodzie Europy* [*From the Obshchina to the Kolkhoz: Forms of Communal Land Use in Eastern Europe*], Kraków 1936, author's edition.

Prace I Konferencji Przodownikow Polskiej Kooperacji odbytej w Lublinie w dniach 7, 8, 9. II. 1918 r. [*Works of the 1st Conference of Leaders of the Polish Cooperative Movement, Held in Lublin on February 7–9,1918*], Kraków 1918.

Prowalski A., "*Spółdzielczość żydowska w Polsce*" ["Jewish Cooperativism in Poland"], *Sprawy Narodowościowe* [*Minority Affairs*] R. 6, no. 2–5.

Romanowicz T., *O stowarzyszeniach* [*On Associations*], Lwów 1867, edition of the Wydawnictwo Dziennika Literackiego [*Literary Daily* Publishers].

Rozwój i działalność samorządowych instytucji kredytowych oraz spółdzielczości na terenie woj. Lubelskiego [*Development and Activity of Self-Government Credit Institutions and Cooperatives in the Lublin Voivodeship*], Lublin 1929.

Rząd A., *Spółdzielczość w praktyce, w teorii i prawodawstwie* [*Cooperativism in Practice, Theory, and Legislation*], Warsaw 1930, Bank Towarzystw Spółdzielczych [Cooperative Society Bank].

Ruch współdzielczy na ziemiach polskich [*The Cooperative Movement in Polish Lands*], Lwów 1916.

Sadlicki J., *Spółdzielcza organizacja zbytu produktów rolnych* [*The Cooperative Organization of the Sale of Agricultural Products*], Warsaw 1938.

Sadlicki J., *Spółdzielnie handlowe w środowiskach wiejskich: zadania i organizacja* [*Trade Cooperatives in Rural Environments: Tasks and Organization*], Warsaw 1938.

Sarwińska A., *Wiejscy działacze społeczni w ruchu spółdzielczym* [*Rural Social Activists in the Cooperative Movement*], *Spółdzielczy Przegląd Naukowy* [*Cooperative Scientific Review*] 1938, no. 4.

Schedlin-Czarliński L., *Rola i zadania towarzystw rolniczych w stosunku do izb rolniczych, samorządu terytorialnego i specjalnych zrzeszeń rolniczych* [*The Role and Tasks of Agricultural Societies Relative to Chambers of Agriculture, Territorial Governments, and Special Agricultural Associations*], Warsaw 1934, Związek Izb i Organizacyj Rolniczych R.P. [Union of Agricultural Chambers and Organizations]

Seydlitz W., *"Spółdzielczość w Polsce"* ["The Cooperative Movement in Poland"], in: *Bilans Gospodarczy Dziesięciolecia Polski Odrodzonej* [*The Economic Balance of Ten Years of Reborn Poland*], vol. 2, Poznań 1929, s.n.

Sikorski W., Żerkowski J., *Historia Warszawskiego Stowarzyszenia Spożywców w Warszawie* [*History of the Warsaw Consumer Association in Warsaw*], Warsaw 1923, s.n.

Sokołowski K., *"Spółdzielczość na ziemiach polskich w latach 1922–1924"* ["The Cooperative Movement in Polish Lands in the Years 1922–1924"], *Ekonomista* [*The Economist*] 1925,vol. 2.

Sokołowski K., *"Spółdzielnie w Polsce w latach 1925 i 1926"* ["Cooperatives in Poland in the Years 1925 and 1926"], *Kwartalnik Statystyczny* [*Statistical Quarterly*] 1928, vol. 5, no. 2.

Sokołowski K., *Uwagi o polskiej spółdzielczości spożywców* [*Remarks on Polish Consumer Cooperatives*], Warsaw 1933.

Sokołowski K., *Związki rewizyjne spółdzielni w Polsce* [*Central Unions of Cooperatives in Poland*], Warsaw 1923.

Sondel J., *Zagadnienie agrokooperatywy jako nowej formy spółdzielczości* [*Issues of Agro-Cooperatives as a New Form of Cooperativism*], Kraków 1935.

Spissvol., *Raz trzeba powiedzieć prawdę. Upadek spółdzielni rzeszowskich w rzeczywistym świetle* [*The Truth Must Be Told: The Failure of Rzeszów Cooperatives in a Factual Light*], Warsaw 1938.

Spółdzielczość mieszkaniowa w Polsce [*The Housing Cooperative Movement in Poland*], parts 1–2, Warsaw 1938, Wydawnictwo Związku Spółdzielni i Zrzeszeń Pracowniczych Rzeczypospolitej Polskiej [Publishing House of the Union of Labor Cooperatives and Associations of the Republic of Poland].

Spółdzielczy przemysł mleczarski w Polsce. Referaty wygłoszone na konferencji w Ministerstwie Rolnictwa [*The Cooperative Dairy Industry in Poland: Reports Given at a Conference in the Ministry of Agriculture*], Warsaw 1931, s.n.

Stokłosa J., *Organizacja popierania przemysłu ludowego* [*An Organization Supporting Cottage Industries*], Warsaw 1925, s.n.

Strasburger E., *Kooperacja spożywcza i jej rozwój w Kr. Polskim* [*Food Cooperatives and their Development in the Kingdom of Poland*], Warsaw 1909, Gebethner i Wolff.

Surzycki S., *Oddłużenie spółdzielni rolniczych* [*Discharging the Debts of Agricultural Cooperatives*], Warsaw 1936, Wydawnictwo „Spólnota Pracy" [Community of Work Publishers].

Surzycki S., *Spółdzielczy Instytut Naukowy. Dziesięciolecie istnienia 1919–1929* [*The Cooperative Scientific Institute: Ten Years of Existence, 1919–1929*], Warsaw 1929, Wydawnictwo Spółdzielczego Instytutu Naukowego [Publishing House of the Cooperative Scientific Institute].

Surzycki S., *Studia ekonomiczno-spółdzielcze w Uniwersytecie Jagiellońskim* [*Studies in Economics and Cooperativism at Jagiellonian University*], Kraków 1936, s.n.

Szapiro B., *Związki zawodowe robotnicze. Związki zawodowe bezpartyjne* [*Labor Trade Unions; Non-Partisan Trade Unions*], Warsaw 1906, Towarzystwo Wydawnictw Ludowych [People's Publishing Society].

Szymkiewicz Cz., *Spółdzielczość rolna* [*Agricultural Cooperativism*], Warsaw 1932, s.n.

Śledziński L., *Jak to było w latach 1905–1908: wspomnienie o powstaniu Organizacji Związku Zawodowego Robotników Cukrowni b. Królestwa Polskiego* [*How It Was in the Years 1905–1908: Remembrances of the Founding of the Organization of the Sugar Workers' Trade Union in the Former Kingdom of Poland*], Warsaw 1931, Zarząd Główny Związku Zawodowego Robotników Cukrowni Rzeczpospolitej Polskiej [Main Board of the Sugar Workers' Trade Union of the Republic of Poland].

Świeżyński W., *Organizacje ogólnorolnicze, ich cele, zadania i metody pracy* [*General Agricultural Organizations, Their Aims, Tasks, and Work Methods*], Warsaw 1935, author's edition.

Targowski Z., *Rada Spółdzielcza 1921–1936* [*The Cooperative Council, 1921–1936*], Warsaw 1936, Spolnota Pracy [Community of Work].

Tołwiński S., *Planowanie i rozbudowa mieszkań robotniczych* [*Planning and Expansion of Housing for Workers*], Warsaw 1936, SARP.

Tołwiński S., *Wspomnienia 1895–1939* [*Reminiscences 1895–1939*], Warsaw 1971, PWN.

Tomaszewski W., *Pół wieku polskich spółek zarobkowych i gospodarczych w W. Ks. Poznańskim, Prusach Zachodnich i na Gornym Śląsku* [*Half a Century of Polish Labor and Farm Companies in the Grand Duchy of Posen, Western Prussia, and Upper Silesia*], Poznań 1906, author's edition.

Truszyński A., *Organizacja i zadania okręgowej spółdzielni mleczarskiej* [*The Organization and Aims of a Regional Dairy Cooperative*], Warsaw 1937, s.n.

Twarecki L., *Rola Kas Stefczyka w walce z lichwą na wsi* [*The Role of Stefczyk Savings and Loan Banks in Combatting Usury in the Countryside*], Warsaw 1928, Zjednoczony Związek Spółdzielni Rolniczych Rzeczypospolitej Polskiej [Association of Agricultural Cooperative Unions of the Republic of Poland] (review of this work: Całkosiński A., *Ruch Prawniczy, Ekonomiczny i Socjologiczny* [*The Legal, Economic, and Sociological Movement*] 1928, no. 4).

Twarecki L., *Zadania i cele rolniczej spółdzielczości kredytowej* [*The Tasks and Aims of Agricultural Credit Cooperatives*], Lwów 1930.

Tymiński E., *Obecna wojna o stowarzyszenia spółdzielcze w Królestwie Polskim* [*The Current War over Cooperative Associations in the Kingdom of Poland*], Warsaw 1914, s.n.

U kolebki polskiej spółdzielczości rolniczej [*At the Cradle of Polish Agricultural Cooperativism*], [collective work], Lwów 1929, Zjednoczenie Związków Spółdzielni Rolniczych Rzeczypospolitej Polskiej [Association of Agricultural Cooperative Unions of the Republic of Poland].

Weydlich K., *Franciszek Stefczyk—pionier polskiej spółdzielczości rolniczej* [*Franciszek Stefczyk: A Pioneer of Polish Agricultural Cooperativism*], Warsaw 1936, Spółdzielczy Instytut Naukowy [Cooperative Scientific Institute] (review of this work: Bargiel J., *Ruch Prawniczy, Ekonomiczny i Socjologiczny* [*The Legal, Economic, and Sociological Movement*] 1937, no. 1, 2; Kącki F., *Roczniki Dziejów Społecznych i Gospodarczych* [*Annals of Social and Economic History*]1937).

Weydlich K., *Ruch spółdzielczy w Polsce w latach 1914–1926. Zagadnienia dotyczące współdziałania grup i typów spółdzielni oraz zmiany zaszłe w ustroju ruchu* [*The Cooperative Movement in Poland in the Years 1914–1926: Questions Concerning the Collaboration of Groups and Types of Cooperatives and Changes Occurring in the Movement's Order*], Kraków 1927, Biblioteka Spółdzielcza [Cooperative Library].

Weydlich K., *Tęczowy sztandar spółdzielczy* [*The Rainbow Cooperative Standard*], Poznań 1939, Księgarnia św. Wojciecha [St. Adalbert Bookstore].

Zacharski A., *Jajczarstwo spółdzielcze* [*Egg Cooperatives*], Warsaw 1932, Zjednoczenie Związków Spółdzielni Rolniczych Rzeczypospolitej Polskiej [Association of the Agricultural Cooperative Unions of the Republic of Poland].

Zakrzewski T., *Dwadzieścia pięć lat pracy spółdzielczo-rolniczej w woj. centralnych i wschodnich* [*25 Years of Agricultural and Cooperative Work in the Central and Eastern Voivodeships*], Warsaw 1934, Związek Rewizyjny Spółdzielni Rolniczych [Central Union of Agricultural Cooperatives].

Zakrzewski T., *Spółdzielnie niezwiązkowe i walka z nimi* [*Unaffiliated Cooperatives and the Struggle with Them*], Warsaw 1938, Spółdzielczy Instytut Naukowy [Cooperative Scientific Institute].

Zakrzewski T., *Zjednoczenie Związków Spółdzielni Rolniczych RP* [*The Association of Agricultural Cooperative Unions of the Republic of Poland*], Lwów 1927, s.n.

Zalewski S., *W służbie spółdzielczej* [*In the Cooperative Service*], Warsaw 1923, Społem.

Załuski P., *Jak mogą współpracować ze sobą spółdzielnie rolnicze* [*How Agricultural Cooperatives Can Work with Each Other*], Warsaw 1938, s.n.

Zdanowska A., *Koła Gospodyń Wiejskich* [*Rural Housewives' Clubs*], Warsaw 1928, Wydawnictwo Gazety Gospodarskiej [*Farm Gazette* Publishers].

Zębalska S., *Jakie są spółdzielnie w Polsce* [*What Cooperatives in Poland Are Like*], Warsaw 1938, s.n.

Zjazd Delegatów Polskiego Związku Zawodowego Robotników Cukrowni w Królestwie Polskim [*Conference of Delegates of the Polish Sugar Workers' Union in the Kingdom of Poland*], Drukarnia „Gazety Rolniczej" [*Agricultural Gazette* Printers].

Zjednoczona spółdzielczość rolnicza [*United Agricultural Cooperativism*], Warsaw 1937, Związek Spółdzielni Rolniczych i Zarobkowo-Gospodarczych RP [Union of Agricultural and Farm-Labor Cooperatives of the Republic of Poland].

Żelechowski A., *Rozprawa o spółdzielczości kredytowej w Polsce* [*Essay on Credit Cooperativism in Poland*], Tarnów 1932, s.n.

Żerkowski J., *PPS a ruch spółdzielczy w Polsce* ["The Polish Socialist Party and the Cooperative Movement in Poland"], in: *Księga Jubileuszowa Polskiej Partii Socjalistycznej (1892–1932) [Jubilee Book of the Polish Socialist Party (1892–1932)]*, A. Strug (introduction), Warsaw 1933, Robotnik [The Worker].

Życie i praca pisarza polskiego na podstawie ankiety Związku Zawodowego Literatów Polskich w Warszawie [The Life and Work of a Polish Writer on the Basis of a Survey by the Polish Writers' Trade Union in Warsaw], Warsaw 1932, Instytut Gospodarstwa Społecznego [Institute of Social Economics].

Selected Compilations

Chyra-Rolicz Z., *Baza źródłowa i stan badań nad dziejami spółdzielczości w Polsce* ["Database of Sources and the State of Research into the History of the Cooperative Movement in Poland"], *Spółdzielczy Kwartalnik Naukowy [Cooperative Scientific Quarterly]* 1976, no. 1.

Chyra-Rolicz Z., *Burzymy—tworząc: spółdzielczość robotnicza na ziemiach polskich do 1939 r. [We Destroy—in Building: Labor Cooperativism in Polish Lands to 1939]*, Warsaw 1991, Wydawnictwo Spółdzielcze [Cooperative Publishing].

Chyra-Rolicz Z., *Kobiety w organizacjach spółdzielczych Wielkopolski w XIX i XX wieku* ["Women in the Cooperative Orgaizations of Greater Poland in the 19th and 20th Century"], w: *Aktywność kobiet w organizacjach zawodowych i gospodarczych w XIX i XX wieku [The Activeness of Women in Labor and Farm Organizations of Greater Poland in the 19th and 20th Centuries]*, K. Makowski (ed.), Poznań 2007, Instytut Historii Uniwersytetu im. Adama Mickiewicza [History Institute of Adam Mickiewicz University].

Chyra-Rolicz Z., *"O związkach ruchu emancypacji kobiet ze spółdzielczością przed odzyskaniem niepodległości"* ["On the Relations of the Women's Emancipation Movement with Cooperativism before Indepedence"], Spółdzielczy Kwartalnik Naukowy [Cooperative Scientific Quarterly] 1983, no. 3.

Chyra-Rolicz Z., *Pamięci Mariana Rapackiego* ["In Memory of Marian Rapacki"], *Spółdzielczy Kwartalnik Naukowy [Cooperative Scientific Quarterly]*1984, no. 2.

Chyra-Rolicz Z., *Pod spółdzielczym sztandarem: z dziejów spółdzielczości polskiej do 1982 r. [Under the Cooperative Standard: On the History of Polish Cooperativism to 1982]*, Warsaw 1985, Wydawnictwo Spółdzielcze [Cooperative Publishing].

Chyra-Rolicz Z., *Stanisław Staszic—prekursor spółdzielczości rolniczej [Stanisław Staszic—Precursor of Agricultural Cooperativism]*, Siedlce 2004, Instytut Historii, Akademia Podlaska [History Institute, University of Podlasie Siedlce].

Chyra-Rolicz Z., *"Towarzystwo Kooperatystow a rozwoj polskiego ruchu spółdzielczego"* ["The Cooperativists' Society and the Development of the Polish Cooperative Movement"], *Spółdzielczy Kwartalnik Naukowy [Cooperative Scientific Quarterly]* 1989, no. 4.

Chyra-Rolicz Z., *Z tradycji polskiej spółdzielczości II Rzeczpospolitej. Idee, fakty, doko-nania* [*The Tradition of Polish Cooperativism in the 2nd Republic: Ideas, Facts, and Achievements*], Warsaw–Poznań 1992, Ławica.

Chyra-Rolicz Z., *Związki ruchu emancypacji kobiet ze spółdzielczością na ziemiach pols-kich przed 1939 r.* [*The Relations of the Women's Emancipation Movement with Coop-erativism in Polish Lands Before 1939*], Warsaw 1993, Spółdzielczy Instytut Badawczy [Cooperative Research Institute].

Dominko J., "*Z dziejów Lubelskiej Spółdzielni Spożywców (1919–1925)*" ["On the History of the Lublin Consumer Cooperatives"], *Spółdzielczy Kwartalnik Naukowy* [*Coopera-tive Scientific Quarterly*] 1968, no. 2.

Dominko J., *Z minionych lat: wspomnienia działacza spółdzielcy z okresu pracy na tere-nie Lublina* [*From Past Years: A Cooperative Activist's Reminiscences of a Period of Working in the Lublin Region*], 1945, Czytelnik.

Duszyk A. (ed.), *Między ideą a polityką. Ruch spółdzielczy centralnych ziem polskich w XX wieku* [*Between the Idea and the Policy: The Cooperative Movement of the Central Polish Lands in the 20th Century*], Radom 2004, Wyższa Szkoła Handlowa w Radomiu [Higher School of Economics in Radom].

Duszyk A. (ed.), *Szkice z dziejów polskiego ruchu spółdzielczego* [*Sketches on the His-tory of the Polish Cooperative Movement*], Warsaw 2007, Krajowa Rada Spółdzielcza [National Cooperative Council].

Duszyk A., Kołodziej E., "*Historia radomskiej kooperacji 1869–1939*" ["History of the Radom Cooperative Movement, 1869–1939"], *Biuletyn Kwartalny Radomskiego Towarzystwa Naukowego* [*Quarterly Bulletin of the Radom Scientific Society*] 2009, vol. XLIII, no. 3.

Goebel W., *Spółdzielczość rolniczo-handlowa w Poznańskiem i na Pomorzu w latach 1918–1939* [*The Agricultural-Commercial Cooperative Movement in the Poznań Region and Pomerania in 1918–1939*], Warsaw 1964, Zakład Wydawnictw CRS [CRS Publishers].

Hoszowska W., *Rola nauczycielstwa w rozwoju ruchu spółdzielczego w Polsce w latach 1918–1958* [*The Role of Teaching in the Development of the Cooperative Movement in Poland in the Years 1918–1958*], Warsaw 1965, Zakład Wydawnictw CRS [CRS Publishers].

Jarzyński A., *Trzydzieści lat Spółdzielni Kółek Rolniczych. Wspomnienia—cyfry—wydarzenia* [*Thirty Years of Farmers' Club Cooperatives: Reminiscences, Figures, and Events*], Rzeszów 1947, own edition.

Kędziorek F., *Nurty społeczno-gospodarcze w polskim ruchu spółdzielczym w latach 1918–1939* [*Socio-Economic Currents in the Polish Cooperative Movement in the Years 1918–1939*], Warsaw 1969, Zakład Wydawnictw CRS [CRS Publishers].

Kowalak T., *Spółdzielczość niemiecka na Pomorzu 1920–1938* [*German Cooperativism in Pomerania 1920–1938*], Warsaw 1965, KiW.

Mariański W., „Społem" wczoraj i dziś [Społem: Yesterday and Today], Łódź 1946, Komisja Jubileuszowa Obchodu 35-lecia „Społem" [Jubilee Committee for Celebrating Społem's 35th Anniversary].

Niemiec J., Geneza i rozwój spółdzielczości (przyczynki i materiały) [The Genesis and Development of Cooperativism (Contributions and Materials)], Warsaw 1957, Wydawnictwo Przemysłu Lekkiego i Spożywczego [Publishing House of Light Industry and the Food Industry].

Orłowski, Banki Ludowe na Śląsku Opolskim w latach 1895–1939 [People's Banks in Silesia Opole in the Years 1895–1939], Opole 1962.

Pawluczuk Z., Spółdzielczość rolniczo-spożywcza w Polsce w latach 1918–1939 [Agricultural and Food Cooperativism in Poland in the Years 1918–1939], Warsaw 1970, Zakład Wydawnictw CRS [CRS Publishers].

Pawluczuk Z., Spółdzielczość w myśli programowej i działalności polskiego ruchu robotniczego w latach 1892–1939 [Cooperativism in the Ideas and Activities of the Polish Workers' Movement in the Years 1892–1939], Toruń 1977, Uniwersytet Mikołaja Kopernika [Copernicus University].

Piechowicz S., Związek Robotniczych Stowarzyszeń Spółdzielczych [Union of Labor Cooperative Associations], Warsaw 1963, Zakład Wydawnictw CRS [CRS Publishers].

Piechowski A., 120 lat spółdzielczości mieszkaniowej w Polsce [120 Years of Housing Cooperativism in Poland], Bydgoszcz 2010, Agencja Reklamowo-Wydawnicza „Promocja Polska" [Poland Promotion' Advertising and Publishing Agency].

Piechowski A., Księga polskiej spółdzielczości [The Book of Polish Cooperativism], Bydgoszcz 2006, Agencja Reklamowo-Wydawnicza „Promocja Polska" ["Polish Promotion" Advertising and Publishing Agency].

Piechowski A., Spółdzielczość polska. Monografia [Polish Cooperativism: A Monograph], Bydgoszcz 2012, Agencja Reklamowo-Wydawnicza „Promocja Polska" ["Polish Promotion" Advertising and Publishing Agency].

Pietrzak-Pawłowski K., Spółdzielczość polska na ziemiach zachodnich i północnych. 1918–1939 [Polish Cooperativism in the Western and Northern Territories, 1918–1939], Warsaw 1967, KiW.

Rainer J., Spółdzielczość pracy w Polsce do roku 1939 [Labor Cooperativism in Poland to the Year 1939], Warsaw 1965.

Romanowski, "Przemiany organizacyjne polskiej spółdzielczości rolniczej w latach 1918–1924" ["Organizational Changes of Polish Agricultural Cooperativism in the Years 1918–1924"], Roczniki Dziejów Społecznych i Gospodarczych [Annals of Social and Economic History] 1962, vol. XXIV.

Romanowski, Z dziejów spółdzielczości rolniczej w latach wielkiego kryzysu 1929–1934 [On the History of the Agricultural Cooperative Movement in the Years of the Great Crisis, 1920–1934], Warsaw 1964, KiW.

Światło A., *Poglądy społeczne przedstawicieli neutralnej myśli spółdzielczej do roku 1939* [*Social Views of the Representatives of Neutral Cooperative Thought to the Year 1939*], Warsaw 1963, Zakład Wydawnictw CRS [CRS Publishers].

Światło A., *Polska spółdzielczość spożywców w latach 1869–1925* [*Polish Consumer Cooperatives in the Years 1869–1925*], Warsaw 1972, Zakład Wydawnictw CRS [CRS Publishers].

Światło A., *Spółdzielczy Instytut Naukowy 1919–1939* [*The Cooperative Scientific Institute, 1919–1939*], Warsaw 1973, Zakład Wydawnictw CRS [CRS Publishers].

Tomiczek H., *"Rozwój organizacyjny ruchu spółdzielczego na Gornym Śląsku do 1939 r."* ["The Organizational Development of the Cooperative Movement in Upper Silesia to 1939"], *Sobotka* 1970, z. 4.

Tomiczek H., *Spółdzielczość na Gornym Śląsku do 1922 roku. Przyczynek do historii spółdzielczości gornośląskiej* [*The Cooperative Movement in Upper Silesia to 1922: A Contribution to the History of Upper Silesian Cooperativism*], Opole 1965, Instytut Śląski [Silesian Institute].

Tomiczek H., *Spółdzielczość pracy na Gornym Śląsku w dwudziestoleciu międzywojennym. Przyczynek do historii spółdzielczości gornośląskiej* [*The Labor Cooperative Movement in Upper Silesia in the Two Inter-War Decades: A Contribution to the History of Upper Silesian Cooperativism*], Warsaw 1965, Zakład Wydawnictw CRS [CRS Publishers].

Tomiczek H., *Spółdzielczość spożywców w województwie opolskim do 1969 r.* [*The Consumer Cooperative Movement in the Opole Voivodeship to 1969*], Opole 1972, Instytut Śląski [Silesian Institute].

Tomiczek H., *Spółdzielczość w Zawadzkiem do 1939 roku* [*The Cooperative Movement in Zawadzkie to 1939*], Opole 1969, Zakład Nauk Społeczno-Ekonomicznych Instytutu Śląskiego w Opolu [Department of Social and Economic Sciences of the Silesian Institute in Opole].

Tomiczek H., *Z historii spółdzielczości na Górnym Śląsku do 1939 r.* [*On the History of the Cooperative Movement in Upper Silesia to the Year 1939*], Warsaw 1965, CRS.

Trocka H., Rainer J., *Polskie czasopiśmiennictwo spółdzielcze* [*Polish Cooperative Journals*], Warsaw 1962, Zakład Wydawnictw CRS [CRS Publishers].

Wojcik J., *Bibliografia wydawnictw spółdzielczych* [*Bibliography of Cooperative Publishing*], parts 1–3, Warsaw 1962, Zakład Wydawnictw CRS [CRS Publishers].

Wrzosek S., *Z historii spółdzielczości mleczarskiej w Polsce do r. 1939.* [*On the History of the Dairy Cooperative Movement in Poland to the Year 1939*], Warsaw 1965, Zakład Wydawnictw CRS [CRS Publishers].

Wspomnienia działaczy spółdzielczych [*Reminiscences of Activists in the Cooperative Movement*], vol. 1: B. Krauze (ed.), Warsaw 1963; vol. 2: Z. Kossut (ed.), Warsaw 1965, Zakład Wydawnictw CRS [CRS Publishers].

Zarys historii polskiego ruchu spółdzielczego [*An Outline of the History of the Polish Cooperative Movement*], pt. 1, to 1918, S. Inglot (ed.), Warsaw 1966, Zakład Wydawniczy CRS [CRS Publishers].

Zarys historii polskiego ruchu spółdzielczego [*An Outline of the History of the Polish Cooperative Movement*], pt. 2, 1918–1939, W. Rusiński (ed.), Warsaw 1967, Zakład Wydawniczy CRS [CRS Publishers].

Zbiór statutów spółdzielni górnośląskich 1871–1939 [*Collection of Statutes of Upper Silesian Cooperatives*], H. Tomiczek (collection and complilation), Warsaw 1964, Zakład Wydawnictw CRS [CRS Publishers].

Żerkowski J., *100-lecie warszawskiej spółdzielczości spożywców 1869–1969* [*The 100th Anniversary of the Warsaw Consumer Cooperative Movement, 1869–1969*], Warsaw 1969, Zakład Wydawnictw CRS [CRS Publishers].

Żerkowski J., *Najstarsze spółdzielnie spożywców w Polsce, wraz z zarysem 95-lecia spółdzielczości spożywców* [*The Oldest Consumer Cooperatives in Poland, with a Description of the 95 Years of the Consumer Cooperative Movement*], Warsaw 1964, Zakład Wydawnictw Centrali Rolniczej Spółdzielni [Publishing House of the Agricultural Cooperative Headquarters].

Żerkowski J., *Spółdzielczość spożywców w Polsce: 1918–1939* [*Consumer Cooperatives in Poland: 1918–1939*], Warsaw 1961, Zakład Wydawnictw CRS [CRS Publishers].

Żerkowski J., *Zarys historii spółdzielczości spożywców w Polsce jako ruchu społeczno-gospodarczego* [*An Outline of the History of the Consumer Cooperative Movement in Poland as a Socio-Economic Movement*], Warsaw 1959, Zakład Wydawnictw Spółdzielczych [Cooperative Publishers].

Selected Cooperativist Journals from the Interwar Period

Biuletyn Informacyjny [*Information Bulletin*] for the regional councils of the Społem Union, Warsaw 1938–1942.

Biuletyn Prasowy [*Press Bulletin*], Warsaw 1934–1936.

Biuletyn Prasowy [*Press Bulletin*], a monthly publication of the Fr. Piotr Wawrzyniak Union of Labor and Farm Cooperatives, Poznań.

Biuletyn Rady Spółdzielczej [*Cooperative Councils' Bulletin*], a quarterly of the Rada Spółdzielcza [Cooperative Council], Warsaw.

Biuletyn Spółdzielczego Instytutu Naukowego [*Bulletin of the Cooperative Scientific Institute*], Warsaw 1928–1931.

Biuletyn Związku Spółdzielni i Zrzeszeń Pracowniczych R.P. [*Bulletin of the Union of Labor Cooperatives and Associations of the Republic of Poland*], Warsaw.

Cielarka Standardo (*Tęczowy Sztandar*) [*The Rainbow Standard*]—a monthly in Esperanto (*Internacia kooperativa gazeto*), Warsaw 1936–1937.

Czasopismo Spółdzielni Rolniczych [*Agricultural Cooperatives' Journal*], a bimonthly of the Związek Spółdzielni Rolniczych i Zarobkowo-Gospodarczych R.P. [Union of Agricultural and Farm-Labor Cooperatives of the Republic of Poland], Warsaw.

Di jidisze Wirklichkajt [*Jewish Reality*], organ of the Związek Żydowskich Towarzystw Spółdzielczych w Polsce [Union of Jewish Cooperative Societies in Poland], 1921, only one issue appeared.

Dom Osiedla Mieszkanie [*House, Settlement, Apartment*], organ of the Polskie Towarzystwo Reformy Mieszkaniowej [Polish Housing-Reform Society].

Głos Spółdzielczy [*Cooperative Voice*], organ of the Centralny Związek Spółdzielni Samopomocowej w Polsce [organ of the Central Union of Mutual-Aid Cooperatives in Poland], Lwów.

Głos Spółdzielczy [*Cooperative Voice*], organ of the Związek Spółdzielni i Zrzeszeń Pracowniczych R.P. [Union of Cooperatives and Labor Associations of the Republic of Poland], Warsaw 1937–1938.

Kultura Polska [*Polish Culture*], organ of the Towarzystwo Kultury Polskiej [Polish Culture Society].

Młody Spółdzielca [*The Young Cooperativist*], monthly, a guide for student cooperatives, Społem, Warsaw.

Poradnik Mleczarski i Jajczarski [*The Dairy and Egg Guide*], bimonthly of the Związek Spółdzielni Rolniczych i Zarobkowo-Gospodarczych [Union of Agricultural and Farm-Labor Cooperatives], Warsaw.

Poradnik Spółdzielni [*Cooperative Guide*], bimonthly of the Unia Związków Spółdzielczych w Polsce [Union of Cooperative Associations in Poland], Poznań 1926–1927.

Praca i opieka społeczna [*Work and Social Welfare*], 1923–1932.

Praca i oszczędność [*Work and Savings*], monthly of the Spółdzielnia Wydawnicza *Spólnota Pracy* [Publishing Cooperative of the Community of Work], Warsaw.

Pracownik Polski [*The Polish Employee*], organ of the Stowarzyszenia Robotników Chrześcijańskich [Association of Christian Workers].

Pracownik Spółdzielczy [*The Cooperative Employee*], a quarterly, organ of the Związek Pracowników Spółdzielczych R.P. [Union of Cooperative Employees of the Republic of Poland], 1926–1927.

Ruch Spółdzielczy [*The Cooperative Movement*] (*Di Kooperatywe Bawegung*), organ of the Związek Żydowskich Towarzystw Spółdzielczych w Polsce [Union of Jewish Cooperative Societies in Poland], 1923–1939.

Rynek Rolniczy [*The Agricultural Market*], appeared twice a week, Związek Spółdzielni Rolniczych i Zarobkowo-Gospodarczych [Union of Agricultural and Farm-Labor Cooperatives], Warsaw.

Rzeczpospolita Spółdzielcza [*The Cooperative Republic*], a monthly of the Związek Spółdzielni Spożywców R.P. [Union of Consumer Cooperatives of the Republic of Poland], Warsaw.

Społem, the organ of cooperative societies.

Spólnota, the organ of the Społem Związku Spółdzielni Spożywców R.P. [Społem Union of Consumer Cooperatives of the Republic of Poland], Warsaw.

Spółdzielczość Pracy [*Work Cooperativism*], a quarterly of the Towarzystwo Popierania Kooperacji i Pracy [Society for the Support of Cooperativism and Work], Warsaw.

Spółdzielczy Przegląd Naukowy [*Cooperative Scientific Review*], a quarterly of the Spółdzielczy Instytut Naukowy [Cooperative Scientific Institute], Warsaw.

Sprzedawca Spółdzielczy [*The Cooperative Salesman*], monthly of the Społem Związek Spółdzielni Spożywców R.P. [Społem Union of Consumer Cooperatives of the Republic of Poland], Warsaw.

Wiadomości Międzynarodowej Spółdzielni Powierniczej [*The International Trust Cooperative News*], organ of the Związek Spółdzielni Rolniczych i Zarobkowo-Gospodarczych [Union of Agricultural and Farm-Labor Cooperatives], Warsaw 1937–1941.

Wiedza [*Knowledge*], from 1907 the unofficial organ of the Polish Socialist Party-Leftists.

Wojskowy Przegląd Spółdzielczy [*Army Cooperative Review*], quarterly of the Związek Spółdzielni Wojskowych [Union of Army Cooperatives], Warsaw.

Wspolna Praca [*Common Work*], quarterly of the Wołyński Związek Spółdzielczy „Hurt" ["Wholesale" Volhynia Cooperative Union], Równe–Łuck.

ZEW [*The Call*], organ of the Związek Młodzieży Spółdzielczej [Youth Cooperative Union], Warsaw.

Związkowiec [*The Union Member*], organ of the Bezpartyjnych Klasowych Związków Zawodowych [Nonpartisan Class Trade Union] and its continuation *Promień* [*Ray*].

Życie Robotnicze [*Workers' Life*], organ of the Polskich Związków Zawodowych [Polish Trade Unions].

Życie W.S.M. [*WHC Life*], monthly of the Warszawska Spółdzielnia Mieszkaniowa [Warsaw Housing Cooperative], Warsaw.

Życie Spółdzielcze [*Cooperative Life*].

Personal Index

www.ingramcontent.com/pod-product-compliance
Lightning Source LLC
Chambersburg PA
CBHW062106040426

42336CB00042B/2254

* 9 7 8 1 6 0 8 4 6 0 9 0 8 *